S0-BTD-829

THE ENCYCLOPEDIA OF THE AMERICAN REVOLUTIONARY WAR

A Political, Social, and Military History

THE ENCYCLOPEDIA OF THE AMERICAN REVOLUTIONARY WAR

A Political, Social, and Military History

VOLUME I: A–D

Gregory Fremont-Barnes
Richard Alan Ryerson
Volume Editors

James Arnold and
Roberta Wiener
Editors, Documents Volume

FOREWORD BY
Jack P. Greene

ABC CLIO

Santa Barbara, California Denver, Colorado Oxford, England

Cataloging-in-Publication Data is on file with the Library of Congress

ISBN 1-85109-408-3 ebook: 1-85109-413-X
ISBN-13: 978-1-85109-408-0 ebook: 978-1-85109-413-4

10 09 08 07 06 05 10 9 8 7 6 5 4 3 2 1

This book is also available on the World Wide Web as an ebook.
Visit abc-clio.com for details.

ABC-CLIO, Inc.
130 Cremona Drive, P.O. Box 1911
Santa Barbara, California 93116–1911

This book is printed on acid-free paper ♾.
Manufactured in the United States of America

Gregory Fremont-Barnes

To my wife, Judith, and our sons, William and Monty,
for their love and support.

Richard Alan Ryerson

To my wife, Marla Eby, and to my daughter, Anna Ryerson,
two of my strongest supporters.

About the Editors

Gregory Fremont-Barnes holds a doctorate in Modern History from the University of Oxford, where he studied under the distinguished military historians Sir Michael Howard, Regius Professor of Modern History, and Robert O'Neill, Chichele Professor of the History of War. After leaving Oxford he lived briefly in London before moving to Japan, where he spent eight years as a university lecturer in European and American history. He is the author of numerous books, including *The French Revolutionary Wars; The Peninsular War, 1807–1814; The Fall of the French Empire, 1813–1815; The Boer War, 1899–1902; Trafalgar 1805: Nelson's Crowing Victory; Nelson's Sailors;* and *The Wars of the Barbary Pirates: To the Shores of Tripoli, the Rise of the U.S. Navy and Marines.* He is also the editor of the three-volume *Encyclopedia of the French Revolutionary and Napoleonic Wars.* Dr. Fremont-Barnes's next book will be *The Indian Mutiny, 1857–1858.* He lives near Oxford with his wife and two sons.

Richard Alan Ryerson earned his doctorate degree in early American history at Johns Hopkins University. He held postdoctoral fellowships at the University of Pennsylvania (1975–1976) and at Harvard's Charles Warren Center (1978–1979). He was associate editor of the *Papers of William Penn* at the Historical Society of Pennsylvania (1979–1983) and editor in chief of *The Adams Papers* at the Massachusetts Historical Society (1983–2001). He is currently Academic Director of The David Library of the American Revolution, at Washington Crossing, Pennsylvania. His major publications are, as author, *The Revolution Is Now Begun: The Radical Committees of Philadelphia, 1765–1776,* and, as editor, *Adams Family Correspondence,* vols. 5 and 6 (1782–1785), and *John Adams and the Founding of the Republic.* In 1995, the American Historical Association awarded the *Adams Family Correspondence* volumes its J. Franklin Jameson Prize as the best edited volumes of historical documents published during the previous five years. Dr. Ryerson also contributed to the editing of three other volumes of *Penn Papers* and seven other *Adams Papers* volumes. His next project, for which he was awarded an NEH grant that he took up in 2004, is a study of John Adams's political and constitutional thought, to be titled *John Adams's Republican Monarchy.*

Editorial Advisory Board Members

Cartographer

International Mapping

Contents

List of Entries

Schoharie Valley, New York, Raid on (16–18 October 1780)
Schuyler, Philip (1733–1804)
Scott, Charles (1739–1813)
Seabury, Samuel (1729–1796)
Sears, Isaac (1730?–1786)
Secondat, Charles-Louis de, Baron de Montesquieu (1689–1755)
Secret Committee of the Continental Congress (September 1775–July 1777)
Secret Correspondence, Committee of (1775–1777)
Sevier, John (1745–1815)
Sharon Springs Swamp, New York, Action at (10 July 1781)
Shays's Rebellion (August 1786–February 1787)
Shelby, Isaac (1750–1826)
Shell's Bush, New York, Raid on (6 August 1781)
Shepard, William (1737–1817)
Sherman, Roger (1721–1793)
Shippen, William (1712–1808)
Siege Warfare (1775–1781)
Simcoe, John Graves (1752–1806)
Skene, Philip (1725–1810)
Skenesborough, New York, Action at (6 July 1777)
Slaves and Free Blacks
Smallpox
Smallwood, William (1732–1792)
Smith, Adam (1723–1790)
Smith, Francis (1723–1791)
Smith, Joshua Hett (1749–1818)
Smith, William (1727–1803)
Smith, William, II (1728–1793)
Society of the Cincinnati
Solemn League and Covenant
Somerset Courthouse, New Jersey, Actions at (20 January, 14 June, and 17 June 1777; 17 October 1779)
Sons of Liberty (1765–1774)
South Carolina
Southern Campaigns
Sowers, Christopher, III (1754–1799)
Spain
Spencer's Tavern, Virginia, Action at (June 26, 1781)
Springfield, New York, Raid on (May 1778)
Springfield and Connecticut Farms, New Jersey, Raids on (7 and 23 June 1780)
St. Clair, Arthur (1734–1818)
St. Eustatius, Operations against (1776 and 1780–1781)
St. John's, Actions against (17–18 May 1775 and 12 September–2 November 1775)
St. Kitts, Battle of (25–26 January 1782)
St. Leger Expedition (23 June–23 August 1777)
St. Lucia, Naval and Military Operations against (December 1778)
Stamp Act (22 March 1765–18 March 1766)
Stamp Act Congress (October 1765)
Stark, John (1728–1822)
Staten Island, New York, Actions at (22 August 1777 and 15 January 1780)
Stephen, Adam (1721?–1791)
Steuben, Friedrich von (1730–1794)
Stewart, Alexander (1737–1794)
Stewart, Walter (1756–1796)
Stockton, Richard (1730–1781)
Stono Ferry, South Carolina, Action at (20 June 1779)
Stony Point, New York, Capture of (15–16 July 1779)
Stuart, Gilbert (1755–1828)
Stuart, John (1718–1779)
Stuart, John, 3rd Earl of Bute (1713–1792)
Suffolk Resolves (9 September 1774)
Suffren, Pierre-André de (1729–1788)
Sugar Act (1764)
Sullivan, John (1740–1795)
Sullivan Expedition (May–November 1779)
Sullivan's Island, Battle of (28 June 1776)
Sumner, Jethro (1733–1785)
Sumter, Thomas (1734–1832)
Sunbury, Georgia, Attacks on and Capture of (April 1776, November 1778, and January 1779)

Tallmadge, Benjamin (1754–1835)
Tappan, New Jersey, Action at (28 September 1778)
Tappan Zee, New York, Action at (16 August 1776)
Tarleton, Banastre (1754–1833)
Tarrant's Tavern, North Carolina, Action at (1 February 1781)
Tea Act (10 May 1773)
Tearcoat Swamp, South Carolina, Action at (25 October 1780)
Teissèdre de Fleury, François-Louis (1749–?)
Ternay, Charles Henri Louis (1723–1780)
Thomas, John (1724–1776)
Thompson, Benjamin, Count Rumford (1753–1814)
Thompson, William (1736–1781)
Thomson, Charles (1729–1824)
Throgs Neck, New York, Action at (12 October 1776)
Tories
Toussaint, Jean-Guillaume, Comte de La Motte-Picquet de La Vinoyère (1720–1791)
Townshend, Charles (1725–1767)
Townshend Acts (1767)
Trade
Trade, Board of
Treadwell's Neck, New York, Raid on (11 October 1781)
Treaty of Amity and Commerce with the Netherlands (8 October 1782)
Trenton, Battle of (26 December 1776)

List of Maps

Preface

Putting the American Revolution in Perspective

As the founding event in the history of the United States of America, the American Revolution has always enjoyed a special place in American historiography. For most of the past two centuries, most historians, like the broader public, have looked upon it principally as the first step in the creation of the earliest independent modern state in the western hemisphere. They have stressed the process of nation building epitomized by the creation of a republican political regime in each state followed by the formation of a federal system for the distribution of authority between the states and the nation. They have emphasized the centrality of the drive for national self-realization that, beginning during the revolutionary era, provided the foundation for an American national identity. From the national-state perspective that has largely shaped the writing of United States history, such an emphasis makes considerable sense.

For developing an understanding of why a revolution occurred in North America and what kind of revolution it was, however, the national-state perspective is inadequate. The American Revolution can be more fully comprehended when it is viewed as the first step in the still-incomplete process of dismantling the imperial structures created by the emerging states of Europe during the early modern era. Like other revolutions, the American Revolution had its own peculiar sources, character, and trajectory. Like them, it was profoundly shaped by the natures of the social polities in which it occurred and their historical experiences. And, like all revolutions, it moved in unanticipated directions. Yet the American Revolution was also different from other revolutions. Its particularity can best be understood by exploring three large subjects: the nature of the British imperial polity in which the revolution occurred; the character of the political societies that participated in it; and the nature of the republican polities that were created during it.

With regard to the first subject, the early modern English or, after 1707, British Empire was not held together by force. England may have been one of the most centralized and efficient of the nation-states to emerge in Europe during the early modern era, but, like all such states, it was a composite state characterized by indirect governance, fragmented authority, an inchoate theory of national sovereignty, and limited fiscal, administrative, and coercive resources. These conditions dictated that the extended transatlantic polity we now call the British Empire would be a negotiated empire held together largely by bonds of interest and affection. Far from being an authoritative entity from which power flowed outward from the center, the British Empire involved the construction of authority inward from the peripheries in two phases. The first involved the creation in America, through the activities of participants in the colonizing impulse, of new arenas of local and family power. The second involved the actual creation of authority negotiations between these new arenas and metropolitan representatives of the center that aspired to bring them under its jurisdiction and to which they desired to be attached.

Most of the agency in this process rested in the hands of the settlers. They took possession of the land, turned aboriginal landscapes into European ones, and created towns, parishes, counties, or other political units. They built farms, estates, and businesses. At the provincial level, their agents—in the form of representatives and magistrates—largely fashioned the system of laws and governance that enabled them to regulate social relations and govern the acquisition and circulation of property. Responding to local circumstances, each colony reproduced a variant of the English common law culture, which gave settlers enormous flexibility in adapting the law to local conditions while at the same time marking them as resolutely, even militantly, English.

Once these centers of local power had been established, agents of metropolitan centralization found it difficult to bring them under regulation, and royal officials found themselves having to govern large populations of independent property holders who insisted on living under political arrangements that provided them with extraordinary local autonomy and with the fundamental guarantees of Englishness, including especially government by consent, rule by law, and the sanctity of private property. Combined with the scarcity of fiscal and coercive resources for imperial management in Britain, settler expectations inevitably meant that authority in the early modern British Empire would be distributed between the center and the peripheries, that central direction of the empire would be minimal, that metropolitan authority in the colonies would be consensual and heavily dependent on provincial opinion, and that effective power in distant colonial polities would be firmly situated in provincial and local governments, which were widely participatory and solidly under the control of large, broadly based, and resident property-owning classes. The early modern British Empire was thus a loose association of largely self-governing polities. The self-made, possessing settler classes of these polities acknowledged metropolitan authority not because it was imposed upon them, but because it incorporated them into a larger system of national identity that guaranteed their Englishness, their inheritance in the form of English legal and constitutional traditions, and their continuing control over the polities they had helped to create and maintain over several generations.

What was legal, what was constitutional, in the large extended polity that was the British Empire, was determined not by fiat from the center but by negotiation. These negotiations led slowly during the generations after 1607 to the creation of what Edmund Burke referred to in the 1770s as an imperial constitution that governed political workings within the empire. The central principle of this customary constitution was a division of authority within the empire into external and internal spheres, with the metropolitan government exercising jurisdiction over external affairs such as war and trade and the several colonies having almost total control over their internal polities. It is important to note that this division of power made the British Empire, in essence, a federal empire.

If the British Empire was a consensual empire composed of a loose association of essentially self-governing polities, the settler societies that emerged in colonial British America were, both socially and politically, certainly the most radical in the contemporary western world. Colonial enterprisers and many of the earliest settlers hoped to establish hierarchical social orders and authoritative institutions of state and church of the kind they had known in England. From the beginning, however, social and economic conditions in America operated to prevent them from realizing their aspirations. The wide availability of land and the scarcity of labor incited individual settlers to activity and schemes of improvement, and they built societies that were radically different from most societies in the Old World. These new settler societies had, among the free segments of the population, significantly higher proportions of property holders, higher rates of family formation, broader opportunities for achieving economic competence, less poverty, fewer and less rigid social distinctions, and far less powerful political and religious establishments.

In the expanding world of colonial British America, characterized, especially during the six decades just before the American Revolution, by extraordinary territorial, demographic, and economic growth, social hierarchies were always open to infiltration or challenge from below: elite authority was tenuous, deference was weak, social relations exhibited a deeply egalitarian cast, gentility coexisted uneasily with commonality, and the combination of older and newer gentlemen who presided over public life on the eve of the Revolution did so at the sufferance of their less wealthy neighbors. In contrast to the complex and highly stratified world of early modern Europe, these settler societies were essentially *rankless* societies in the sense that all free people occupied the same status before the law.

If these settler societies were exceptional in terms of their abundant life chances for free individuals and their social elasticity, they were also latently republican. With economic competence and political empowerment so widely distributed, government rested on a broad popular base. Political leaders, increasingly drawn from the narrow band of those ambitious to shine in the public realm, could retain office only by catering to the wider interests they shared with this larger settler citizenry. In the remarkably popular polities they created, settlers dominated both the legislatures that enacted the laws and the courts and civil offices that enforced them, and laws principally expressed settler concerns to preserve the property they were creating through their individual pursuits of happiness.

Throughout the colonial period and beyond, however, the radical character of these social polities always existed in tension with another, perhaps even deeper social impulse, the impulse to transform American cultural spaces into ones that were recognizably English. By the late colonial era, settlers everywhere took pride in the degree to which they had managed to realize this goal. Along with their ancient bonds of consanguinity, culture, traditions, law, and language, their close ties of economic interest, their continuing need for metropolitan military and naval protection, and their enjoyment of the laws and liberties of Britons, the obvious achievements represented by this ongoing transformation powerfully reinforced, throughout the late colonial era, settler attachment to Britain. Simultaneously, however, the continuing gap between those achievements and the standards of the metropolitan center, between the relatively undifferentiated and simple agricultural societies settlers had created in America, many with the extensive use of African slavery, and the increasingly refined and cultivated world of metropolitan Britain rendered settler claims to Britishness problematic and stimulated in them a profound yearning for metropolitan recognition of the validity of those claims.

From the perspective of later modernizing political revolutions, the revolution that occurred in this particular empire on the part of these particular societies was unlike any other. It was not the result of internal tensions, social, religious, or political. Although the southern and middle colonies were wealthier than New England, and although high military expenditures during the Seven Years War had produced short-term economic problems, all of the colonies were broadly prosperous on the eve of the American Revolution. Throughout the 1760s and 1770s, the colonies continued to exhibit the territorial expansion, the economic and demographic growth, and the social elaboration that had long characterized them. What makes the American Revolution different is that its origins lay not in America but in Britain. As metropolitan officials began to appreciate the growing economic and strategic importance of the colonies to British prosperity and national power in the 1740s and 1750s, they also began to worry lest the weakness of metropolitan authority and the extensive autonomy enjoyed by the colonies might somehow lead to their loss.

Moved by such fears and developing a new sense of imperial order that would only reach full flower in the nineteenth century, they undertook a series of measures intended to change the British Empire from the loose federal polity it had long been into a more unitary polity with authority fixed more clearly at the center. Not only did such measures directly challenge the autonomy of colonies over their local affairs, but by subjecting the colonies to legislation and other directives to which the settler populations had not given their consent, they called into question settler claims to a British identity and their right, as Britons, to enjoy a Briton's traditional liberties. Unsurprisingly, these measures, interpreted by the vast majority of the broadly empowered settler populations in the colonies as an effort to subject them to a far more intrusive imperial order, elicited a powerful defense of the local corporate rights of the colonies and a rising demand for explicit metropolitan recognition of settler entitlement to the British liberties and the British identity settlers associated with those local rights.

The intense settler resistance to these new measures combined with the stridency of settler demands wounded metropolitan pride and provoked highly condescending counter assertions of metropolitan superiority that suggested that colonists, far from being true Britons, were a kind of Others whose low characters, rude surroundings, and barbarous cruelty to their African slaves rendered them, on the scale of civilization only slightly above the Amerindians they had displaced or the Africans among whom they lived. The metropolitan measures that elicited the broad-based and extensive settler resentment and resistance of 1774–1775 and the decision for independence in 1776 were powerfully informed by such attitudes. The American Revolution can thus best be understood as a settler revolt, a direct response to metropolitan measures that seemed both to challenge settler control over local affairs and to deny settler claims to a British identity.

In rejecting monarchy and the British connection and adopting republicanism, the leaders of these settler revolts did not have to preside over a wholesale, much less a violent, transformation of the radical political societies that colonial British Americans had constructed between 1607 and 1776. In every state, peculiar social, religious, economic, and political tensions shaped the course of revolutionary development. Indeed, these local tensions primarily account for the substantial differences in the revolutionary experiences from one state to another. Wherever during the late colonial era there had been abuses of executive authority, judicial or civil corruption, unequal representation, opposition to a state church, or other political problems, the new republican state constitutions or later legislation endeavored to address those problems. Against the background of the deepening political consciousness generated by the extensive political debates over the nature of the British imperial constitution after1764, the creators of state constitutions also experimented, in limited ways, with improvements to their existing political systems. The widespread political mobilization that occurred after 1764 and especially in 1775–1776 also resulted, in many states, in an expansion of legislative seats and public offices and a downward shift in political leadership that brought somewhat more setters having somewhat less property, into active roles in the public realm. With astonishingly few exceptions, however, leaders of late colonial regimes retained authority through the transition to republicanism, and the republican regimes they created in 1776 and after bore a striking resemblance to the social polities that they replaced.

Everywhere, political authority remained in the hands of the predominant group among the existing settler population. As during the colonial period, the central government, an unintended consequence of the union of the colonies that had come together to resist metropolitan aggression, was weak. In contrast to the French Revolution, the American Revolution did not produce a unitary national state, or reorganize existing polities, or standardize law. Effective power remained in the states, even after the strengthening of the national government with the Federal Constitution in the late 1780s. An American identity began to develop only during the 1760s and 1770s, and for another century, at least among the original states, provincial or state identities remained more powerful than a continental one.

The pattern of dispersed authority initially set during the long colonial era meant that during the Revolution and for long thereafter, government at the state and local levels remained an instrument of settler desires. Although somewhat more broadly participatory than before, it continued to rest for many decades on a conception of civic competence limited to independent males, and an idea of equality, meaning usually only civil or religious equality, that did not reach beyond them. During the Revolution, the exigencies of war stimulated an extraordinary expansion of the public realm, and, at least during the earliest decades, republican government turned out to be far more intrusive and expensive than colonial government had ever been. Yet settler leaders continued to prefer inexpensive and small government. As during the colonial era, they kept bureaucracies small, refused to pay for permanent peacetime military and naval establishments, and were cautious in supporting public works. Like their colonial counterparts, these republican polities everywhere continued to be instruments of the predominant settler classes, principally concerned with the maintenance of orderly social relations, the dispensing of justice, and, most important of all, the protection of private property.

Nor did the new republican regimes preside over a large-scale social reconstruction. The pursuit of individual domestic happiness in the private realm remained the central cultural imperative. The social order continued to be open; social relations within the free population continued to be fundamentally egalitarian; wealth remained the primary criterion for social standing; and aspiring elites continued to decry the absence of deference from those of less wealth. With few restraints on the accumulation of private wealth, social differentiation continued unabated. Despite their own frequent, albeit often unintentional, transgressions against private property, republican state settler regimes continued to affirm the sanctity of private property. Except for some of the loyalists who opposed the revolution, some of whose land was confiscated and sold to pay public expenses, land titles remained secure. Next to land, slaves were the most valuable form of property in the states as a whole, and notwithstanding the emergence of a powerful antislavery movement after 1760, the institution of slavery persisted in every state in which it retained its economic viability and represented a substantial investment. In effect, the decision to retain or abolish slavery was, like so much else in the new American republic, a matter of local option.

Indeed, the driving concern within the colonies that participated in the resistance movement we know as the American Revolution was to preserve the principle of consent in relation to all matters involving taxation and internal governance. The adoption of a republican form of government and the formation of a national union were unintended consequences of their efforts to achieve this objective. Once they had declared independence from the monarchy of Great Britain, formal republican government was simply their only viable option, and a union was an obvious necessity if they were to have any chance of success against the most powerful military and naval establishment in the western world at that time. As they transformed themselves from colonies to states, however, their integrity as separate polities with full authority over their internal affairs was never in doubt.

In this situation, it is scarcely surprising that the union—one cannot yet call it a country—founded during the Revolution was little more than a league of states, that the Congress had such enormous difficulties in mobilizing an effective war effort, that the states resisted efforts to extend the taxing power to the national government, that the centrifugal tendencies within the United States would emerge so strongly after the immediate objective of the war—independence of the several states—had been established, or even that the state governments, bowing, as their colonial predecessors had always done, to the demands of their constituents, would behave in ways calculated to put the interests of the states and their free inhabitants above those of the nation as a whole.

The architects of the constitutional settlement of 1787–88, which represented a logical culmination of the American Revolution, were principally nationalizers who feared that the fissiparous tendencies within the existing union under the Articles of Confederation would lead to disunion and the evaporation of the military and diplomatic achievements of the long and expensive War for Independence. They intended the Constitution they framed in 1787 and then implemented over the next decade to give vastly more energy to the national government. Yet, their success was always predicated upon an overwhelming consensus about the importance of keeping authority over internal matters—that is, in the conditions operative at the end of the eighteenth century and for long thereafter, *most* matters—in the hands of the state governments. Not even the most radical nationalizers among the Framers wanted to dispense with the states or saw the Constitution as an instrument to do so. They virtually all saw the states as the proper venue for most governance that would occur in the United States. They made no effort to deprive the states of the taxing power or to prevent them from exercising virtually total authority over their internal affairs, albeit the states now had to operate within new guidelines with respect to money emissions and contractual obligations. This division of authority into external and internal spheres was precisely the distribution they had in 1776 revolted to maintain.

Notwithstanding the Framers' decision to bypass the states and go directly to the people in the adoption of the Constitution, the state legislatures were intimately involved in the entire process. They selected the delegates who went to Philadelphia in 1787; the Convention sent its work to Congress, certainly a creature of the states, which in turn sent it on to the state legislatures, which authorized the calling of a state convention to ratify it. It is important that the sovereign people in these state conventions gave their consent to the new Constitution and signified their approval of vesting some powers in a national government as citizens of particular *states* acting in *state* ratifying conventions. There was no national ratifying convention to adopt the new Constitution.

Once the new national government was up and running, moreover, it rarely transgressed or showed any inclination to set further limits upon the power of the states. The Senate continued to represent the states. The national government used its taxing power in limited ways, raising money principally by imposts and excises of the sort imposed by the metropolitan government during the long years of empire. What one of the writers of *The Federalist Papers* called "feudal baronies" in the states remained intact, and state courts continued to hand down the overwhelming majority of judicial decisions issued in the United States. The national government made no effort to interfere with the integrity of the states nor to adopt a uniform code of laws. Every state continued to operate within its own peculiar legal and judicial system. Surely, the important point about the tenth amendment is that it left the line between national and state authority to be negotiated—and re-negotiated.

How much energy the national government was able to muster during the 1790s is also open to question. Whenever the legislature endeavored to expand national power or the executive displayed too much pretentiousness, they encountered enormous opposition, even when, as with Hamilton's financial program, they were successful. Some of this opposition was on republican grounds but some of it also reflected the widespread preference for a system of governance in which most authority lay within the individual states. The national government, even at the height of its power in the early 1790s, remained distant, small, and unobtrusive, and the experience of most United States residents with governance continued to be at the state and local levels. Jefferson's election in 1800 with its emphasis on limiting the scope of national authority provides powerful testimony to the contention that the constitutional settlement worked out in the late 1780s and 1790s was less a *national* than a *federal* settlement in which both national and state governments, each operating within its respective sphere, would be powerful. If there was a broadly shared "original intent" in this era it was an intent to create for the United States a federal polity that was neither completely state-centered nor national. As for the national judiciary, it did little for a century and a half.

This reading of the history of the American Revolution stresses the powerful continuities between the colonial and the national eras. In some important ways, however, the Revolution saw significant departures from the colonial era. Like the British constitution, colonial constitutions and the British imperial constitution had been customary, unwritten constitutions, but the constitutions adopted by the new republican state regimes and at the national level were all written down in short formal documents. Unprecedented in the British constitutional system, the development of the important principle, first torturously worked out in Massachusetts in 1779–80, that constitutions—fundamental law—could not be made by legislatures elected for the ordinary purposes of making legislation, but only by conventions of delegates chosen specifically for that purpose, was a genuine innovation that became an enduring part of the process of constitution making, not only in the United States but elsewhere in the world. The theoretical device of locating sovereignty, not at either level of government, but in the people themselves, resolved the classic question of how to divide authority without dividing sovereignty, a question that had obsessed metropolitan analysts during the debate leading up to the imperial breakup, and thereby represented an important intellectual breakthrough. Finally, while they did not bespeak a very expansive concept of equality during the American Revolution, the egalitarian principles expressed in public documents such as the Declaration of Independence and many of the declarations of rights associated with the state constitutions provided the foundations for a steady and substantial reconception of social and political relations over the subsequent half century and for the later appeals for full equality by those categories of people, such as women and the enslaved, whom the end of the Revolution had left unequal.

Users of this Encyclopedia will find more than nine hundred articles that together reveal the full richness of this complex event. All written by experts, these articles examine in detail the lives and contributions of the most prominent actors, the critical events and measures that led to resistance and revolution, the instruments of resistance, the process by which the public was mobilized for revolution, the campaigns and battles of the war that followed, the transformations of the colonies into republican states, the creation of a political union among them, and a wide assortment of other topics related to the context, causes, and results of the Revolution. Together, they provide the reader with a sure guide to the state of knowledge of all these subjects. The volume is a remarkable achievement, and its editors and authors are to be congratulated.

Jack P. Greene

General Maps

Central Theater of Operations, 1776 – 1778

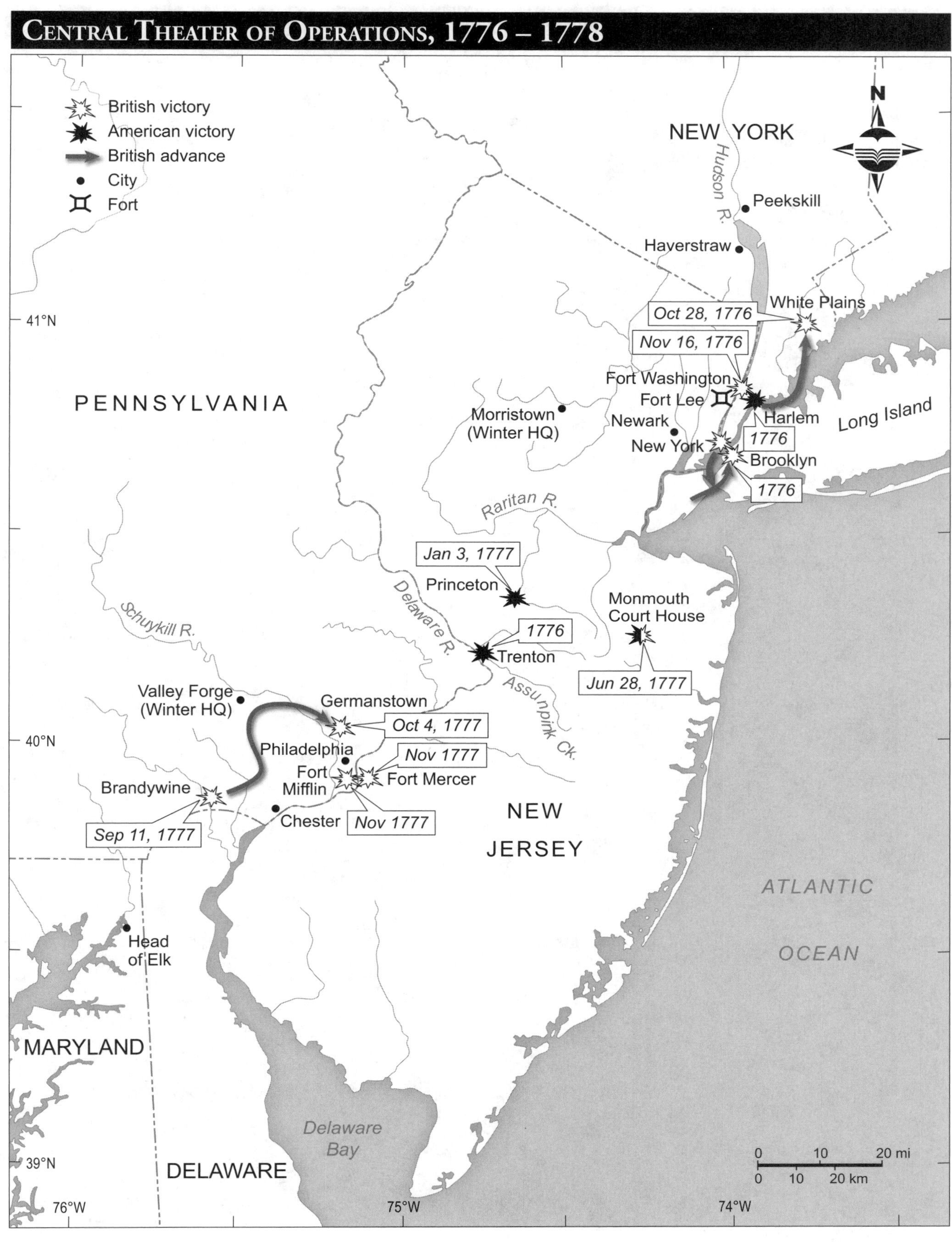

British victory
American victory
British advance
City
Fort
NEW YORK
N
Hudson R.
Peekskill
Haverstraw
White Plains
Oct 28, 1776
Nov 16, 1776
Fort Washington
Fort Lee
Harlem
Long Island
Morristown
(Winter HQ)
Newark
New York
1776
Brooklyn
1776
41°N
PENNSYLVANIA
Raritan R.
Jan 3, 1777
Princeton
Delaware R.
Monmouth
Court House
Schuylkill R.
1776
Trenton
Assunpink Ck.
Jun 28, 1777
Valley Forge
(Winter HQ)
Germanstown
Oct 4, 1777
40°N
Philadelphia
Nov 1777
Fort
Mifflin
Fort Mercer
Brandywine
Chester
Nov 1777
Sep 11, 1777
NEW
JERSEY
ATLANTIC
OCEAN
Head
of Elk
MARYLAND
Delaware
Bay
0 10 20 mi
0 10 20 km
39°N
DELAWARE
76°W
75°W
74°W

North America, 1783

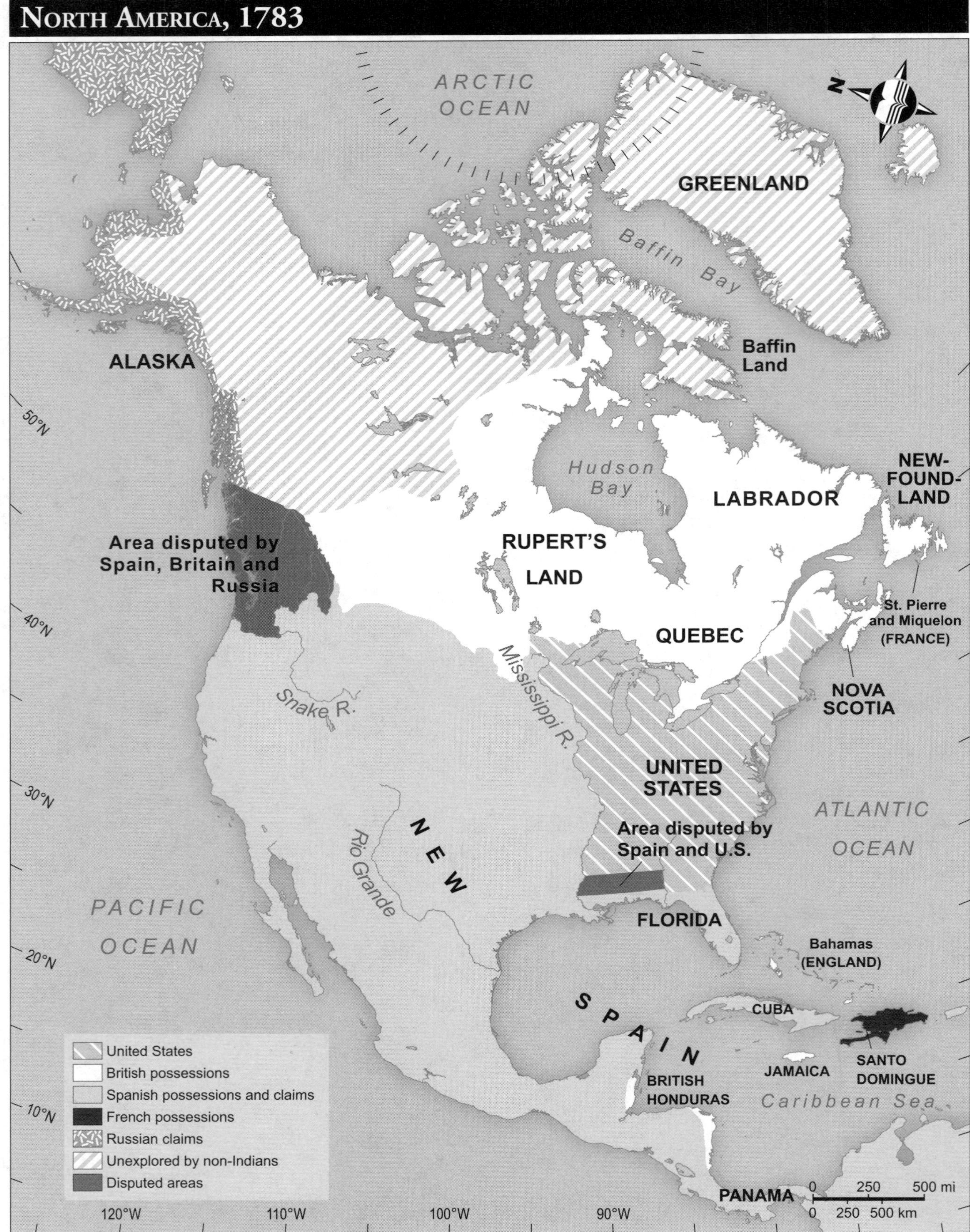

ARCTIC OCEAN
GREENLAND
Baffin Bay
Baffin Land
ALASKA
Hudson Bay
LABRADOR
NEW-FOUND-LAND
RUPERT'S LAND
Area disputed by Spain, Britain and Russia
St. Pierre and Miquelon (FRANCE)
QUEBEC
Mississippi R.
Snake R.
NOVA SCOTIA
UNITED STATES
ATLANTIC OCEAN
Area disputed by Spain and U.S.
Rio Grande
NEW SPAIN
PACIFIC OCEAN
FLORIDA
Bahamas (ENGLAND)
CUBA
SANTO DOMINGUE
JAMAICA
BRITISH HONDURAS
Caribbean Sea
PANAMA
United States
British possessions
Spanish possessions and claims
French possessions
Russian claims
Unexplored by non-Indians
Disputed areas
0 250 500 mi
0 250 500 km
50°N
40°N
30°N
20°N
10°N
120°W
110°W
100°W
90°W

NORTHERN THEATER OF OPERATIONS, 1775 – 1776

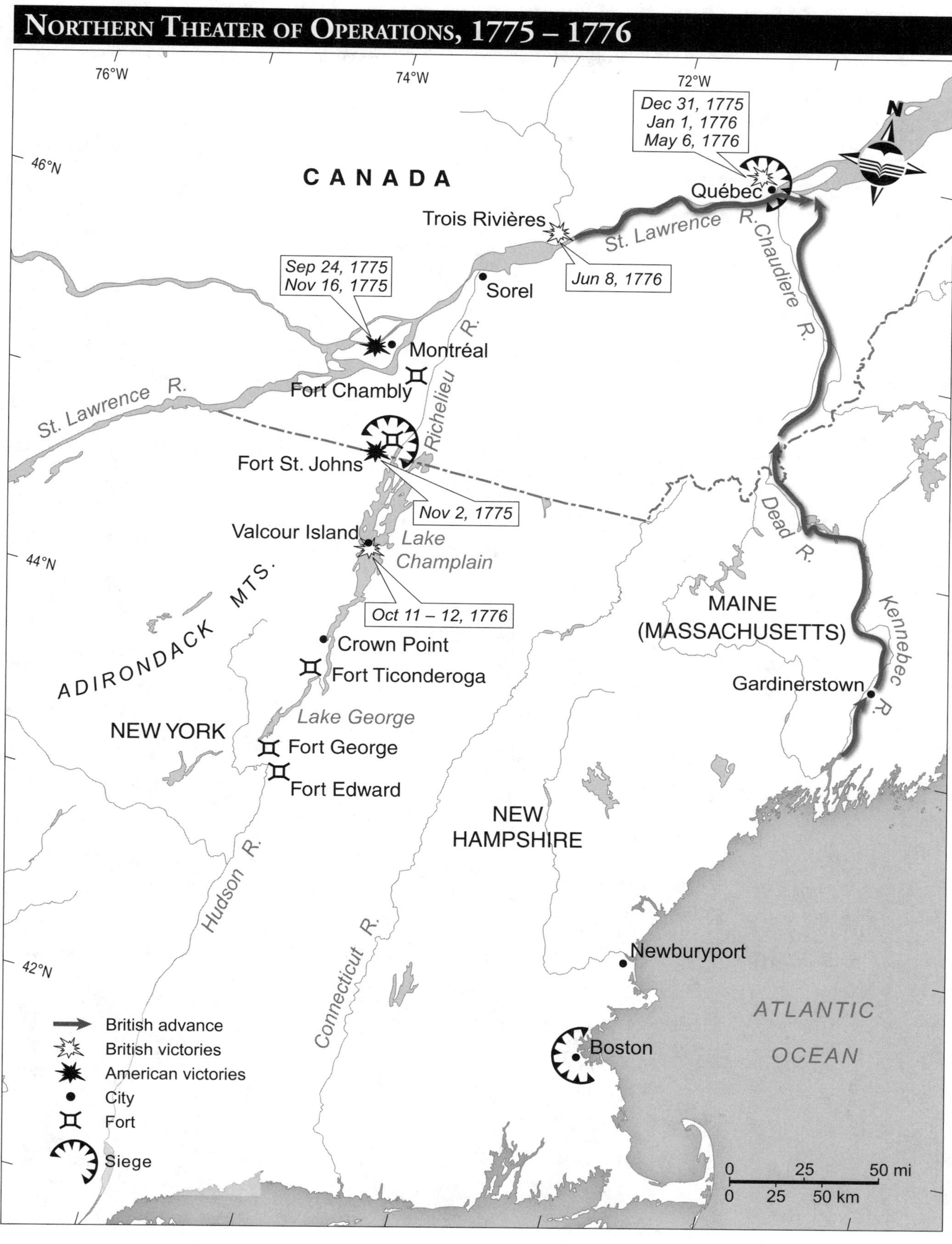
76°W
74°W
72°W
46°N
44°N
42°N
N
CANADA
Dec 31, 1775
Jan 1, 1776
May 6, 1776
Québec
Trois Rivières
St. Lawrence R.
Chaudiere R.
Jun 8, 1776
Sep 24, 1775
Nov 16, 1775
Sorel
Montréal
Richelieu R.
Fort Chambly
St. Lawrence R.
Fort St. Johns
Nov 2, 1775
Valcour Island
Lake Champlain
Oct 11 – 12, 1776
Dead R.
Kennebec R.
MAINE
(MASSACHUSETTS)
Gardinerstown
ADIRONDACK MTS.
Crown Point
Fort Ticonderoga
Lake George
NEW YORK
Fort George
Fort Edward
NEW
HAMPSHIRE
Hudson R.
Connecticut R.
Newburyport
ATLANTIC
OCEAN
Boston
British advance
British victories
American victories
City
Fort
Siege
0 25 50 mi
0 25 50 km

Southern Theater of Operations, 1778 – 1781

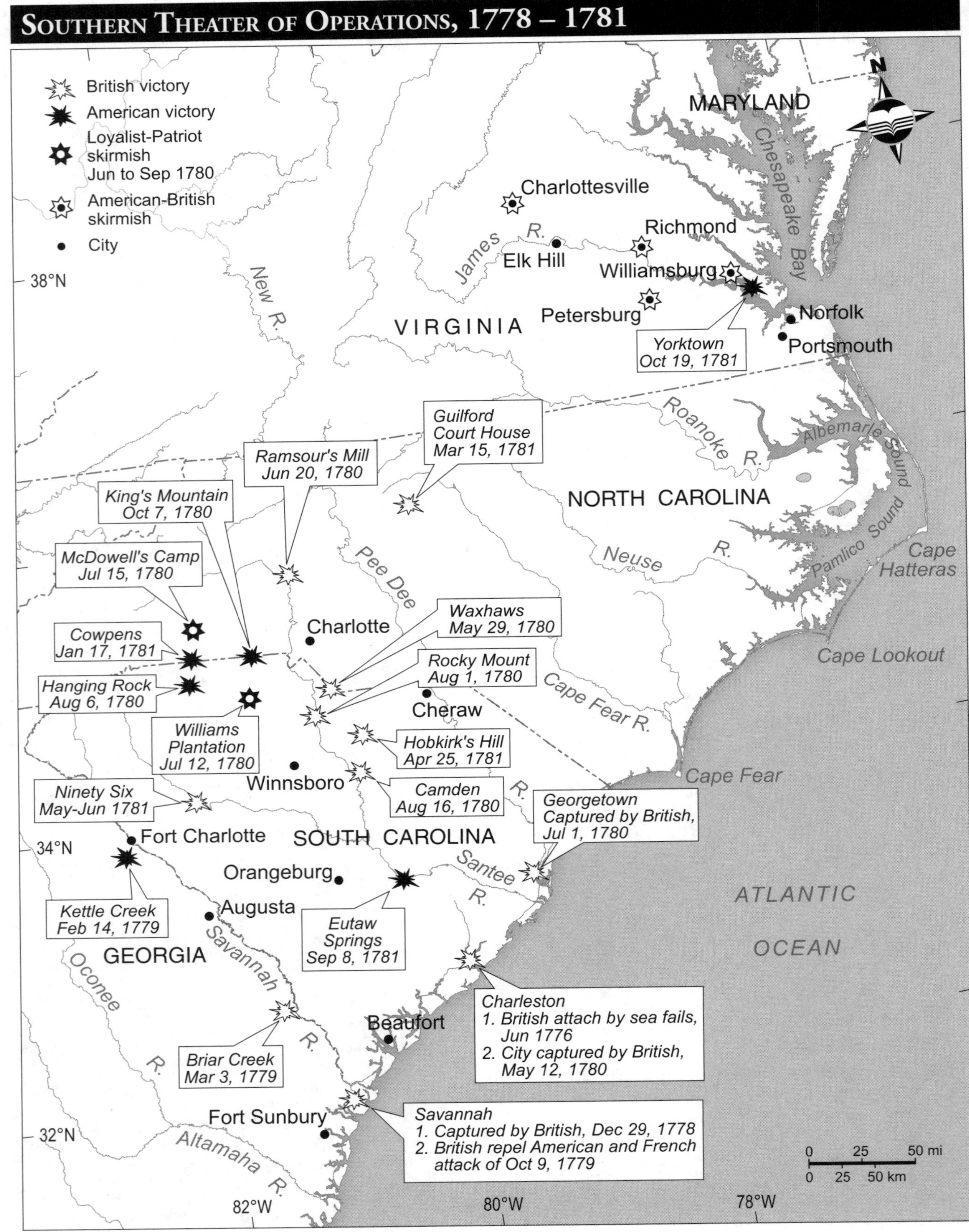

The American Revolution, 1775 – 1783

90°W
85°W
80°W
75°W
70°W
65°W
60°W
45°N
40°N
35°N
30°N
25°N
N
Lake Superior
Lake Michigan
Lake Huron
L. Ontario
Lake Erie
Quebec
Montreal
Caughnawaga
Crown Point
Saratoga
Bennington
Concord
Ticonderoga
Ft. Stanwix
Ft. Oswego
Lexington
Boston
Ft. Niagara
Cherry Valley
Albany
Ft. Johnson
Newport
Tioga
Onoquaga
Detroit
Forty Fort
Gnaddenhutten
Ft. McIntosh
Easton
New York
Ft. Miami
Valley Forge
Philadelphia
Ruddle's Station
Piqua
Ft. Pitt
Ft. Henry
Washington
Chillicothe
St. Louis
Vincennes
Ft. Randolph
Martin's Station
Richmond
Bryant's Station
Yorktown
Cahokta
Kaskaskia
Boonesborough
Harrodsburg
Ft. Massac
Ft. Jefferson
Nashville
Watanga
ATLANTIC OCEAN
Wilmington
Charleston
Savannah
Mobile
St. Augustine
Pensacola
New Orleans
Gulf of Mexico
Extent of settlement (1760)
Proclamation Line of 1763
Town
Fort
Indian settlement
0 125 250 mi
0 125 250 km

French and Indian War, 1754 – 1763

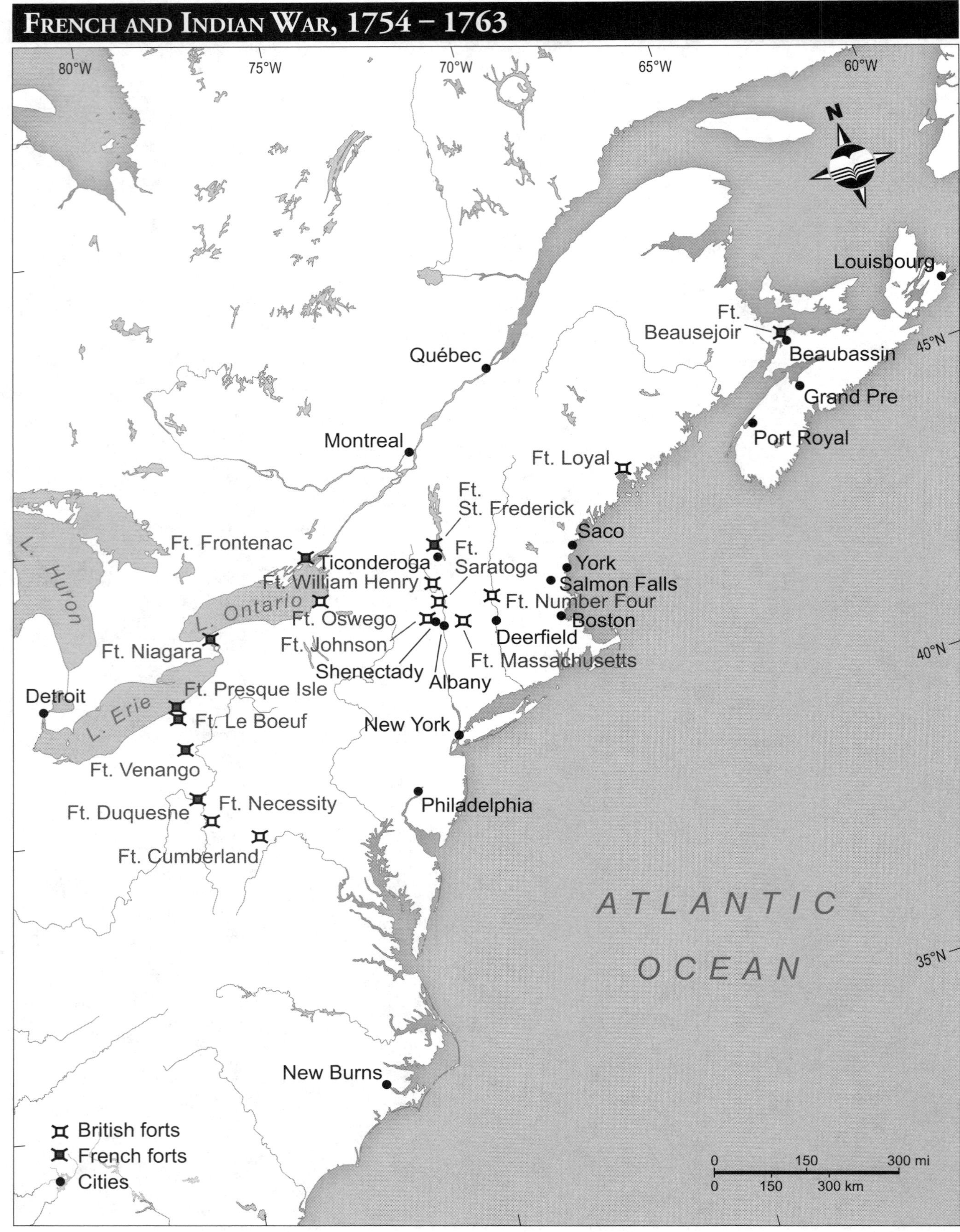

Treaty of Paris, 1783

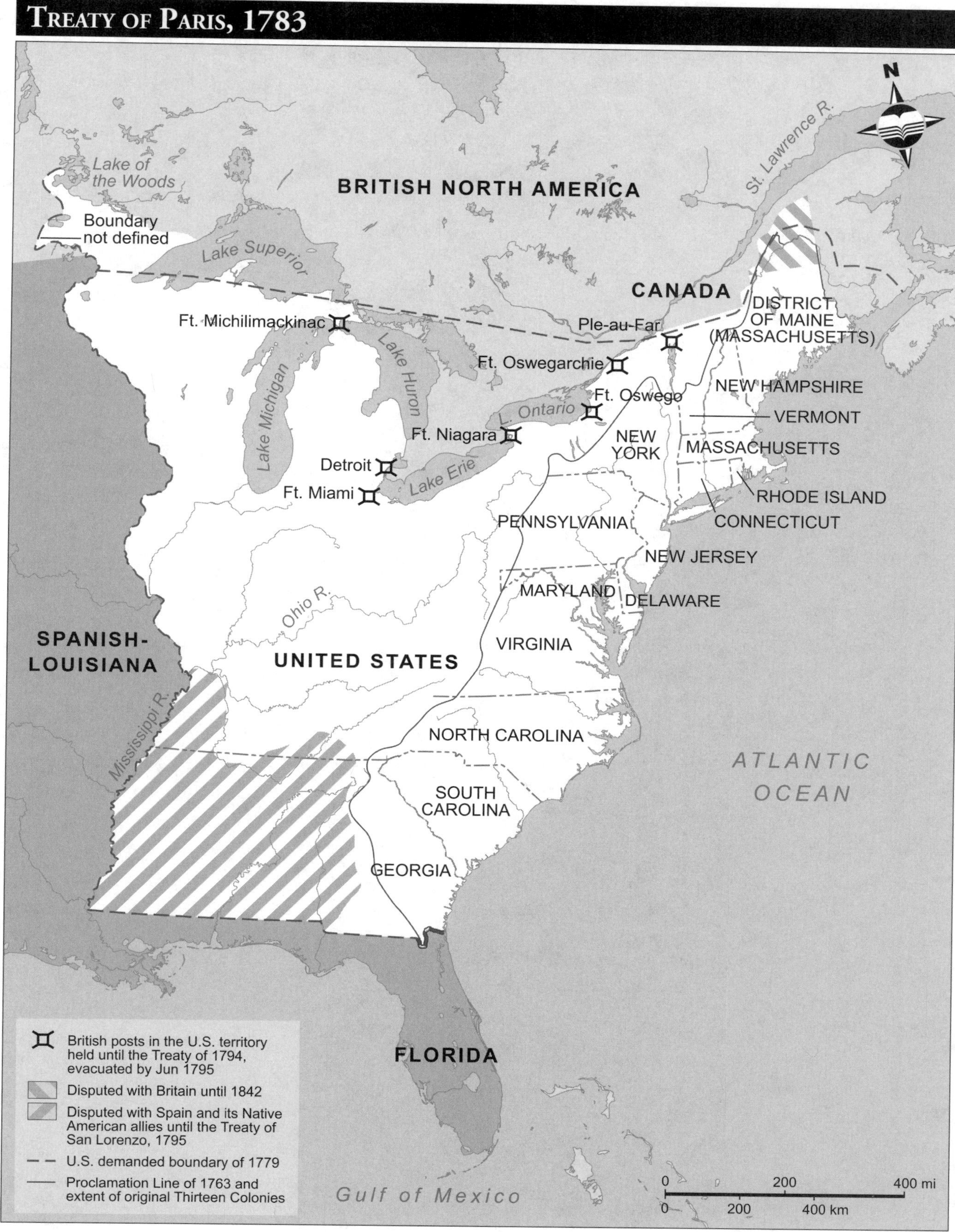
N
St. Lawrence R.
Lake of the Woods
BRITISH NORTH AMERICA
Boundary not defined
Lake Superior
CANADA
DISTRICT OF MAINE (MASSACHUSETTS)
Ft. Michilimackinac
Ple-au-Far
Lake Huron
Ft. Oswegarchie
Lake Michigan
Ft. Oswego
NEW HAMPSHIRE
L. Ontario
VERMONT
Ft. Niagara
NEW YORK
MASSACHUSETTS
Detroit
Lake Erie
Ft. Miami
RHODE ISLAND
PENNSYLVANIA
CONNECTICUT
NEW JERSEY
MARYLAND
DELAWARE
Ohio R.
SPANISH-LOUISIANA
VIRGINIA
UNITED STATES
Mississippi R.
NORTH CAROLINA
ATLANTIC OCEAN
SOUTH CAROLINA
GEORGIA
FLORIDA
British posts in the U.S. territory held until the Treaty of 1794, evacuated by Jun 1795
Disputed with Britain until 1842
Disputed with Spain and its Native American allies until the Treaty of San Lorenzo, 1795
U.S. demanded boundary of 1779
Proclamation Line of 1763 and extent of original Thirteen Colonies
Gulf of Mexico
0 200 400 mi
0 200 400 km

General Essays

Origins of the American Revolution

To identify and explain the causes of any large and complex historical event is difficult, and the character of the American Revolution presents additional difficulties to understanding its origins. The American Revolution was the world's first modern revolution, that is to say, the first revolution to claim, successfully, a universal right of revolution by any people who believe that their government, by its arbitrary and tyrannical behavior, has forfeited its right to rule over them. As a novel event, the Revolution was thoroughly unexpected, both by Americans and by their British opponents. For anyone attempting to understand the Revolution from something approaching the perspectives held by Americans or Britons before the Declaration of Independence, this historical surprise can seem most puzzling.

One way to resolve the problem is to begin by asking how Americans were able to stage a successful revolution. This may seem an unusual way to begin; we might more naturally first want to ask what made Americans angry enough to turn to revolution. But for centuries there have been rebellions on nearly every continent, many of which might have become successful revolutions had they not been crushed by powerful governments. There have also been several full-scale revolutions, notably those in France, Russia, and China, that ended by replacing one autocratic government with another. Because the American Revolution began as a highly successful rebellion under the direction of the First and Second Continental Congresses, then became a revolution that created a new independent nation, and finally reformed and strengthened its national government while retaining the liberties of a republic, we can best understand its origins by first assessing its capacity to assert its political independence.

This approach brings us to the heart of the surprise of the American Revolution. In the 1760s and early 1770s, the inhabitants of British North America had one of the lowest rates of taxation in the world, far lower than the rate in Britain. They enjoyed one of the world's higher per capita incomes and, in those colonies that had relatively few slaves, one of the most nearly equal distributions of wealth and economic opportunity of any people anywhere. A higher proportion of their adult males could vote for public officials and legislators than in any large established nation. Their own local governments had in practice, although not in official British legal theory, an exclusive right to levy internal taxes. Their economy was among the most prosperous of any part of the globe, and their population growth, by both immigration and natural increase, was correspondingly high. Thus, we might well ask, what could such a people have to rebel about?

Colonial America's many strengths, however, suggest the answer to that question. If Americans saw their relatively satisfactory levels of taxation and standard of living, their strong local governments, and their expanding economy and population seriously threatened by their own legitimate sovereign, King George III, and his government and Parliament, they might well react not with the desperation of those who had nothing to lose by rebelling—a position of weakness that generally does not create effective revolutionary power—but with the determination of those who knew they had very much to lose by not rebelling.

Americans also enjoyed a geographic advantage that, while not giving them an immediate motive to rebel, greatly increased their ability to do so. If they could effectively unify against any outside forces—which America's leaders recognized as the biggest challenge facing their rebellion from the outset—they could not easily be defeated by any European power because of their defensive wall, the Atlantic Ocean. After 1760 this wall became even more effective, as Britain's conquest of French Canada in that year meant that in the 1770s rebelling Americans would face only one enemy, Great Britain, and had a fair prospect of gaining one ally, a resentful France. If America remained unified, Britain could not

George III, king of Great Britain during the American Revolution. A staunch advocate of the parliamentary measures respecting the American colonies introduced before the war and a firm opponent of independence, he was unyielding in the prosecution of the war until General Charles Cornwallis's surrender at Yorktown in 1781 obliged him to begin negotiations with the Americans and their European allies. (Library of Congress)

easily gain control of enough territory to mount an effective campaign that moved far from its powerful base of warships and supply vessels, and in fact the British Army ultimately failed in every attempt to invade deep into the interior.

On the North American continent, a unified British North America had important military advantages over Britain. If the rebel leadership could retain the loyalty of the majority of the civilian population—which it generally did in most colonies/states, most of the time—and if it could keep open several ports to receive arms and war material from Europe (which it did), it could supply its forces anywhere on the continent. British North America's free population, although much smaller than that of Britain, was at least 2 million by 1775, large enough to field sizable armies in a few locations and smaller units everywhere and to replenish their battle losses (if they had enough money to support their armies, which was nearly always a difficulty). And America's population was growing so rapidly that it continued to increase right through the Revolutionary War; it was perhaps 50 percent larger in 1790 than it had been in 1775.

Therefore, despite Britain's great financial, technological, and naval capacity, British Americans could rebel successfully, and they did so. Yet simply to rebel in 1774 and 1775 took determination and sacrifice. To declare independence from the world's greatest imperial power and win that independence from 1776 to 1783 demanded years of physical and economic suffering, political and constitutional innovation, and diplomatic initiative. What could have motivated such bold, if not slightly reckless, actions by so many people?

The simple answer is that by 1774 the majority of politically active Americans in twelve British colonies (with Georgia joining in 1775) believed that their traditional political autonomy, their economic prosperity, and their very identity as freeborn men who enjoyed the rights of Englishmen (whether they were English or not) were immediately threatened by the official policies of King George III's ministers and the Parliament of Great Britain. This conviction was new. In 1763, these same Americans had gloried in being British, as the Peace of Paris, granting Britain sovereignty over French Canada, promised to open up all of eastern North America to aggressive English-speaking colonists. Eleven years of mounting conflict between Britain and her North American colonies changed everything, but the origins of this change began much earlier.

Traditions of Autonomy, 1607–1763

The conditions shaping English settlement in North America were not conducive to creating a tightly controlled empire. Unlike Spanish and French settlement of the Americas, English colonization began just as Englishmen at home were claiming new powers of self-government through their Parliament, which, some forty years after the first English settlement at Jamestown, became powerful enough to behead England's Charles I. Moreover, again in contrast to Spanish and French colonies, native populations in eastern North America, while quite sizable, were neither large enough, or willing, to become a permanently valuable labor source for the English colonists nor strong enough to resist gradual dispossession by the settlers, who pushed them west without assistance from the English (British from 1707) Crown. Finally, as a reflection both of its small size and limited treasury and of the nation's rapidly growing merchant class, England's government never initiated settlements in North America but instead encouraged private companies and individuals to do so.

At their initial settlement, no English colonies in North America were directly controlled by the English monarch or

Parliament, and nearly every colony enjoyed some rights of local government under a corporate or proprietary charter. Well over a century later, on the eve of the Revolution, six of the thirteen colonies that eventually rebelled—including Massachusetts, which had long since become a royal colony—still enjoyed such charter rights. The seven other colonies that had been royalized without receiving formal charters all had strong local governments. In all thirteen colonies, the central institution of local autonomy was an elected assembly. These bodies became stronger throughout the eighteenth century, often through contentious battles with the governors appointed by the British Crown or, in Maryland, Pennsylvania, and Delaware, by the proprietary Calvert and Penn families, and the legislatures were still claiming new powers when Britain began its major imperial reforms in 1763. Even the principal official British institution that supervised the governors and their colonies, the Board of Trade, was unable to arrest the thirteen assemblies' quest for power.

The effect of this long history of growing colonial autonomy on British North Americans in the 1760s and 1770s was enormous. Virtually every free white male, whether of English, Scottish, Irish, French, Dutch, or German origin, saw himself as possessing the fundamental rights of Englishmen. Chief among these were the right to elect members of a colonial legislature that would make most if not all laws governing the internal affairs of the colony and the right not to be taxed by any institution except that legislature. The colonists also shared a more general feeling, built up during more than a century of living in North America, that they knew and understood the land, its resources, and its proper development better than anyone who lived in Britain. This feeling, well developed everywhere, could be particularly intense along the Western frontier.

Imperial Reform, 1763–1773

For the first four decades of the eighteenth century, Britain's governing officials—the handful of ministers who enjoyed the confidence of Queen Anne, and then of King George I and King George II, and who could command majorities in Parliament, along with the civil servants who ran the major government departments—had governed their American colonies in a relatively casual manner. Both their preoccupation with matters closer to home and, on the part of some officials, a conviction that the colonies could best develop under an easy rule, which has come to be characterized as a "salutary neglect," shaped this policy. In the 1740s, however, several key officials began paying increasing attention to the independent political and commercial behavior of the American colonies. The officials first became concerned that whenever Britain went to war with France—which it did repeatedly in the eighteenth century—several colonial legislatures were slow to vote for support, by providing men and supplies, for campaigns against the French on the Western frontier and in Canada, while several merchants and sea captains flouted the Navigation Acts, which were designed to keep all profitable trade centered on Britain. Both behaviors, the British government believed, tended to deny Britain the resources it needed to win its wars.

Before the Seven Years' War (commonly called the French and Indian War in America)—which began in America's Ohio Valley in 1754, spread to Europe, Africa, and Asia in 1756, and ended in a total British victory over France in 1763—the attention of British officials to the colonies was sporadic, with just a few individuals, such as the Earl of Halifax on the Board of Trade, pushing hard to bring colonial behavior into line with British objectives. In 1763, however, Britain faced both an enormous national debt from its victorious war and increased military and administrative costs needed to run conquered French Canada and control the Native American tribes in the Mississippi Valley. The expanded, expensive British Empire called for a redefinition of the imperial relationship.

In 1763, a new government, led by George Grenville (the First Lord of the Treasury and, in effect, Britain's prime minister), began to introduce a major reform program. Grenville and his allies in Parliament, with the full support of the new monarch, George III, had several objectives. The first was to contain American settlers east of the crest of the Appalachian Mountains so that Britain's new subjects, the Native Americans of the Ohio and Mississippi valleys, could continue their pursuit of the valuable fur trade undisturbed and Britain's troops could avoid policing white-Indian conflicts. The second was to bring the colonies into a close observance of the Navigation Acts so that all colonial trade would move in channels that enriched Great Britain rather than Dutch smugglers, continental European merchants, French West Indian planters, or anyone else outside the British Empire. The third was to force the colonists to contribute directly to the military and administrative costs of expanded British rule in North America through both increased trade duties collected in American ports and direct, internal taxes, which Britain had never before levied in America. All three objectives had a common goal: to make British North America a more loyal, supportive part of the new British Empire.

In every year between 1763 and 1770, the British government either introduced a new reform or made a renewed effort to enforce a recent reform. The government first tackled territorial control with its Proclamation of 1763. This official order by King George III in his Privy Council forbade all new settlement by white colonists west of the Appalachian Mountains. The proclamation, which had the force of law, was both widely resented in America and ultimately not very effective. Settlers, especially in Pennsylvania, Virginia, and the Carolinas, widely ignored it. And many British officials did not exert themselves to meet its objectives. In the Northwest, the proclamation may have helped calm the Native American tribes involved in Pontiac's Rebellion (1763–1766). But many Indians continued to resent the behavior of British military officers who, under the leadership of General Jeffrey Amherst and his successor, General Thomas Gage, were far less generous in giving chiefs gifts than the French had been. In New York, Sir William Johnson, Britain's superintendent of Indian affairs for the Northern Department, ably defended his Iroquois neighbors at the Treaty of Fort Stanwix (1768) but at the expense of other tribes in the upper Ohio Valley whose borderlands were opened up to white settlement. And in 1774, Virginia's governor, John Murray, the Earl of Dunmore, went so far as to start a war against the Shawnee Indians on Virginia's frontier.

Britain's control of colonial trade under the Navigation Acts had always been more successful than its control of American land, but the new attempt to strengthen that control in the 1760s also ran into serious difficulty. Parliament's first major reform statute, the Revenue Act of 1764, popularly called the Sugar Act, reduced the import duty of the old Molasses Act (1733) levied in American ports, but it was so vigorously collected that the statute's true intent, to collect a tax rather than to discourage New England trade with the French West Indies, was apparent to everyone. In 1766, when the duty was reduced yet again but coupled with even more vigorous collection, colonial resentment focused not only on the tax but on the customs agents who collected it. And in 1767, the Townshend Revenue Act brought new import duties that did not even pretend to be commercial regulations, while companion legislation created a greatly strengthened Board of Customs in America and another Order in Council expanded the number and scope of the vice-admiralty courts used to enforce the Navigation Acts.

Popular resistance to the new trade laws, and to other taxes that had no commercial objective, soon showed Britain the need to exert its authority in America in yet another way: by directly controlling crowds with armed soldiers. Britain's new Quartering Act (1765), which empowered British commanders, when necessary, to quarter troops in inns, taverns, and vacant buildings anywhere in America and directed provincial assemblies to provide certain supplies for any troops quartered within their borders, quickly became an incitement to hostile crowds in New York City, the only major American port that had hosted a sizable number of British troops on a long-term basis, both in war and peace. But the act was soon used to expedite the relocation of British troops from the frontier to the coast and from New York to Boston, where in 1768 armed soldiers were placed directly in the crowded, hostile city to protect the unpopular customs collectors.

The most direct and universal new imperial obligation in America, however, was the levying of new taxes. Here Grenville stepped over a clear but unstated line: Britain would not tax its colonies directly. The Stamp Act of 1765 permanently changed the character of Britain's relationship with America. The tax, in the form of stamped paper required for virtually all legal and commercial documents as well as stamps affixed to newspapers, pamphlets, and even playing cards, could not easily be avoided, especially by the most articulate and influential Americans: lawyers, merchants, newspaper editors, and the urban educated elite. But the statute, which was dependent for its operation on a handful of appointed stamp agents in each major city and the cooperation of colonial judges, quickly proved unenforceable. When urban crowds in each major port forced the agents to either resign their offices or pledge not to exercise their authority, most judges eventually agreed to open the courts without stamped paper to avoid political and economic paralysis.

George Grenville himself fell from power on an unrelated issue before the Stamp Act could even go into effect, but Britain's rulers, in conceding the necessity of repeal to restore trade with America, were determined to maintain their full rights to control their colonies. In March 1766, on the same day it approved repeal, Parliament passed the Declaratory Act, stating its right "to make laws and statutes of sufficient force and validity to bind the colonies and people of America, subjects of the crown of Great Britain, in all cases whatsoever." Taxation was not mentioned but did not need to be; Parliament had asserted its right both to legislate and to tax when, where, and how it wished to do so.

In practice, however, Parliament began taxing the colonies more cautiously. Many members felt some sympathy with the colonists' principled opposition to any taxes levied by a legislature in which they had no voice. Others saw no value in trying to collect taxes in America. But in 1767, enough members of Parliament thought that both the principle of taxing America and the likely gain in revenue justified revisiting the issue. Noting that in opposing the Stamp Act some Americans seemed to make a distinction between direct and indirect or internal and external taxes, Charles Townshend, Britain's chancellor of the Exchequer, persuaded Parliament to pass the Townshend Revenue Act, which levied new duties on certain goods imported into America from Britain, primarily manufactured products and tea.

The colonists' reaction to the new taxes was less explosive than it had been to the Stamp Act. But at both the intellectual level (as in John Dickinson's *Letters of a Pennsylvania Farmer*) and on the waterfront through nonimportation agreements in all the major port cities, they made it clear that they objected to all taxes levied without their consent. The Townshend Revenue Act was intended solely to raise a revenue; it did not pretend to regulate the channels of trade. In 1770, after a long commercial battle, the new ministry of Frederick, Lord North, repealed all the Townshend taxes except that on tea, and colonial resistance to this one tax soon

The TIMES are Dreadful, Dismal Doleful Dolorous, and DOLLAR-LESS.

An Emblem of the Effects of the STAMP

O! the fatal Stamp

Thursday, October 31, 1765. THE NUMB. 1195.

PENNSYLVANIA JOURNAL; AND WEEKLY ADVERTISER.

EXPIRING: In Hopes of a Resurrection to LIFE again.

I AM sorry to be obliged to acquaint my Readers, that as The STAMP-ACT, is fear'd to be obligatory upon us after the First of November ensuing, (the fatal To-morrow) the Publisher of this Paper unable to bear the Burthen, has thought it expedient TO STOP awhile, in order to deliberate, whether any Methods can be found to elude the Chains forged for us, and escape the insupportable Slavery, which it is hoped, from the last Representations now made against that Act, may be effected. Mean while, I must earnestly Request every Individual of my Subscribers, many of whom have been long behind Hand, that they would immediately Discharge their respective Arrears, that I may be able, not only to support myself during the Interval, but be better prepared to proceed again with this Paper, whenever an opening for that Purpose appears, which I hope will be soon. WILLIAM BRADFORD

Masthead from the 31 October 1765 issue of *The Pennsylvania Journal and Weekly Advertiser,* depicting a skull and crossbones representation of the official stamp required by the Stamp Act of 1765. (Library of Congress)

collapsed. Most colonists who insisted on drinking tea but hated the tax turned to Dutch smugglers for their supply.

At this point, between the summer of 1770 and the summer of 1773, relations between Britain and America entered what has sometimes been called the Quiet Period. The British Parliament passed no new imperial legislation, and Americans staged no new massive protests. But in fact this period was not quiet, and it showed no signs of good feeling between the metropolis and its colonies. In part this was because the general deterioration of relations in the wake of the Stamp Act and the Townshend Act had begun to involve several colonial legislatures in angry battles with their royal governors, while many colonial merchants and mariners continued their bitter feuds with British customs agents. In Boston, popular discontent with British authority had erupted in a full-scale riot between angry civilians and British troops on 5 March 1770, soon known as the Boston Massacre.

In half a dozen colonies, the imperial relationship had, by 1770, become one of fear and resentment. New York's assembly and people were still bitter at being forced to support and accommodate British troops in 1769 under the Quartering Act. South Carolina's assembly began a long feud with the royal governor over its right to spend public money in support of the radical British Whig John Wilkes. In 1772, several Rhode Islanders became so incensed at the British revenue vessel the *Gaspée* that they seized and burned it. In 1773, Virginia became so alarmed at the threat to colonial liberties posed by Britain's aggressive inquiry into the *Gaspée* incident that it urged every colonial legislature to appoint committees of correspondence to begin intercolonial discussions of British policy. And in Massachusetts in 1772, the British Crown's new policy of paying the provincial governor and judges led to Boston's creation of the local committee of correspondence, a resistance institution that quickly spread across the province. By early 1773, Governor Thomas Hutchinson had become so alarmed at these developments that he decided to lecture his legislature, which had already been feuding with the British Crown for five years, on the unlimited nature of parliamentary sovereignty over the colonies. But, to his dismay, the legislature soon replied that Parliament simply had no sovereignty over America.

Into this troubled setting Parliament suddenly interjected a new statute that in short order brought on a full crisis in the imperil relationship. The Tea Act of 1773 might seem like an improbable catalyst for a crisis. It levied no new tax and was primarily designed to rescue the floundering East India Company by allowing it to sell its tea so cheaply in America that it would undercut smuggled Dutch tea. For many colonists, however, the new act was yet another attempt to force their behavior into channels designed by British rulers. As a tax, it seemed a particularly devious plan to collect revenue that the colonists had avoided paying even while continuing to drink tea. And it awarded the lucrative position of tea agent to just a few well-connected merchants in each port city, merchants who were already resented for their support of British policy. For Americans, the Tea Act was not really about revenue but about control, and this is what made its enforcement explosive.

Most executive officers in America sensed the danger in the new import and, after going through the motions of enforcing the trade laws, allowed the colonists to reject the tea and send it back to Britain. Governor Hutchinson, however, insisted on making the importation of the tea a test of his, and Britain's, legal control over Americans. On 16 December 1773, Boston's radical leaders and their supporters responded by destroying the entire cargo in an act known as the Boston Tea Party. The period of imperial reform now abruptly ended, to be replaced by punitive British measures and massive colonial resistance leading directly to rebellion. And the reform measures recounted above might well be adequate to explain a rebellion. What they cannot explain is a revolution. For that, we must look at the developing colonial response to Britain's reforms.

Colonial Protest, 1763–1773

As soon as the British Parliament began passing statutes to tax America, American orators and penmen began opposing its right to do so. The Boston lawyer James Otis Jr., who in 1761 had denounced the granting of writs of assistance to aid customs agents in their searches for smuggled goods, wrote a tract that rejected Parliament's right to raise revenue through the Sugar Act of 1764. The following year, Daniel Dulany, a well-connected Maryland lawyer who eventually became a Loyalist, wrote a powerful pamphlet against the Stamp Act. And in May 1765, the young legislator Patrick Henry persuaded Virginia's House of Burgesses to condemn all taxes levied on its people without their consent, citing as the basis of this right two charters granted to Virginia by King James I more than 140 years earlier.

The colonists' most creative opposition, however, was the gathering of delegates from nine colonies to the Stamp Act Congress in New York City in October 1765. This body, the first intercolonial gathering since the Albany Congress of 1754, and the last before the First Continental Congress in 1774, issued a Declaration of Rights and Grievances, drafted by the rising Philadelphia lawyer John Dickinson, asserting that only representatives elected by the colonists could legitimately tax them. The declaration did not concede any legitimacy to indirect or external taxation of the colonies by Parliament, but it did state that while the Stamp Act was flatly unconstitutional, duties such as those raised by the Sugar Act were burdensome and harmful to trade. Such a distinction, and the willingness of Benjamin Franklin to concede in testimony before Parliament that Americans might accept it, encouraged Charles Townshend to bring in his revenue bill based on import duties in 1767.

This forced Dickinson, in *The Letters of a Pennsylvania Farmer* (1767) (probably the most widely read American pamphlet before Thomas Paine's *Common Sense*), to refine the American position. Reviewing both direct, internal taxes such as the Stamp Act and duties attached to imports such as those levied by the Townshend Act, Dickinson argued that any measure that was designed to raise a revenue, even if it were expressed as an import duty, was a tax and therefore was unconstitutional unless it was approved by representatives of those who were to pay it. Parliament could only claim a right to levy duties that were truly intended as trade regulations, such as the 1733 Molasses Act's prohibitively steep tax on French West Indian sugar.

For British North Americans, at least, *The Letters of a Pennsylvania Farmer* settled the issue of taxes. From 1767 onward, the majority of the inhabitants in every colony believed that all parliamentary taxation in America was unconstitutional, and they adhered to this conviction in every public document until they declared their independence. Their immediate task was to force Parliament to repeal the offending Townshend Revenue Act. The extended nonimportation movements run by the merchants in all the major ports largely achieved this goal; in 1770 Parliament repealed all the Townshend duties except that on tea.

By this date, however, a few American leaders had begun thinking about the imperial relationship in a new way. Although parliamentary taxation had been the primary offense to most colonists from 1764 to 1770, they began to sense how unhappy they were about other issues as well and to understand that their problem was not just with Parliament but with the whole structure of imperial rule. Three major colonial legislatures, in Massachusetts, New York, and South Carolina, had recently been or were engaged in protracted battles over other issues with their royal governors and with their governors' superiors in Britain: the Board of Trade, the secretary of state for the Southern Department, and, after 1770, the new secretary of state for America. Moreover, certain important imperial controls, such as the Proclamation of 1763 and the strengthening of the vice-admiralty courts in 1768, were not expressed as parliamentary statutes but as the formal orders of King George III in his Privy Council. And in all their struggles over trade, the colonists had to deal with hostile customs collectors, admiralty court judges, and British Army officers.

Until armed rebellion actually began, however, colonial leaders continued to think of Parliament as the central core of their problem. All important government ministers and Privy Council members, including the secretaries of state, were members, usually leading members, of Parliament. Perhaps even more important, it was an article of faith in the colonies that George III himself was not personally guilty of any malevolence toward America. It was only his corrupt ministers, those same leaders of Parliament, who were advising him to curtail American liberties and persuading him that Americans were not loyal subjects. This conviction and a growing sense of their early, more autonomous history as English colonies prompted a few colonial thinkers to propose the first broad intellectual solution to their problem: not "no taxation without representation" but "no parliamentary authority over America."

One of the first men to hold this view was the Scottish-born Pennsylvania lawyer James Wilson. In 1768 he proved to his own satisfaction that the history of Britain and its colonies made it clear that no line could be found separating legislation that Parliament could legitimately pass for America from legislation (such as taxation) that Parliament could not legitimately pass. Therefore, he concluded, Britain's Parliament had no lawful authority in America. But in 1770, with the repeal of most of the Townshend duties and the end of America's nonimportation movements, Wilson chose not to publish his *Considerations on the Nature and Extent of the Legislative Authority of the British Parliament,* and he withheld this tract until August 1774, the same month in which Thomas Jefferson, in his *Summary View of the Rights of British-America,* reached the same conclusion.

Massachusetts, however, did not need the lash of Britain's Coercive Acts (March–June 1774) or even the crisis brought on by the Tea Act (July–December 1773) to decide that Britain was engaged in an all-inclusive, unrelenting conspiracy against American liberties and to reach even more radical conclusions about British authority in America. In November 1772, Samuel Adams persuaded the Town of Boston to bring in a sweeping indictment of British oppressions, from restraints on colonial trade and manufactures early in the century to the latest outrage, the announcement that henceforth the Crown would directly pay the salaries of Massachusetts's governor and all superior court judges, thereby robbing the inhabitants of an important means of controlling their officials. This "List of Violations of Rights" accompanied the creation of a committee of correspondence, a novel institution that Boston recommended to every Massachusetts town.

In January 1773, the Massachusetts House of Representatives went further. Governor Thomas Hutchinson, alarmed at the province's enthusiastic reception of Boston's "List of Violations of Rights" and its call for committees of correspondence, called the legislature into session to explain that there could not be two separate, coequal legislatures in one political state and that Parliament must be supreme. The Massachusetts House recruited the lawyer John Adams to help draft its reply.

On 26 January 1773, the House stated its agreement with Hutchinson that no clear line could be drawn "between the supreme authority of Parliament and the total independence of the colonies." But exactly because this was so, they continued, it was evident that the American colonies, on the basis of their initial charters and the conditions of their settlement, were distinct states from Great Britain, sharing only a common sovereign. This official declaration of a colonial assembly essentially argued that neither Parliament nor the British Crown—the whole apparatus of ministers, the Privy Council, the Board of Trade, customs commissioners, and other officers—had any legitimate authority in Massachusetts beyond what was granted in the Massachusetts Charter of 1692 and that their only legitimate sovereign across the Atlantic was the person of King George III. The legislators closed with a remark that foreshadowed the beginning of unified colonial resistance to British rule in Philadelphia some nineteen months later. If the governor, they wrote, expected them to draw any line between the supreme authority of Parliament and the independence of the American colonies, they would not presume to propose such a line, even if they could discern it, "without [the] Consent [of all the other colonies] in Congress."

By early 1773 in Massachusetts, the imperial problem had been recast. The critical issue was no longer a matter of taxes or of parliamentary statutes but of ultimate sovereignty. There were still, even in Massachusetts, adequate foundation materials for maintaining the British Empire: ancient colonial statutes and rights, the need for a central authority to structure the empire's trade, and a still-revered king. But if Britain did not use these materials soon, the issue of sovereignty would spread south and become more critical in every colony. At this point, however, Parliament passed the Tea Act, and the colonists resisted the tea cargoes as fatal challenges to their control of their own affairs. And in December 1773 in Boston, Governor Thomas Hutchinson tried to win by naked authority the battle for control that he could not win in debate with his legislature the previous January. In the Boston Tea Party, colonial leaders more than matched his escalation of the contest by turning from protest to defiance. The imperial relationship, deeply strained since the Stamp Act, now moved into crisis.

The Imperial Crisis, 1774

When the British government learned of the Boston Tea Party in February 1774, it faced a difficult choice. It could have downplayed the seriousness of the event, but at the expense of looking weak, and ignoring Boston's defiance would likely not have made it disappear. The British government could have recognized that its reforms were a failure, that it simply did not understand the colonial position and needed to listen more carefully to what colonial leaders were saying. This approach, however, would have been even more difficult than denying the gravity of the situation. Few members of Parliament, even among the Whig friends of America, quite knew where or how to begin afresh. What the government did, of course, was to choose even tighter control, backed by the full authority of the British Parliament, the army and navy, and King George III himself.

Most of Britain's new measures of control, which the colonists called the Coercive or Intolerable Acts, were aimed at Massachusetts, and the government apparently believed that it could discipline one colony without alarming the others. The means chosen to do this, however, had unintended effects. The Boston Port Act, passed in March, closed Boston Harbor to all trade until Bostonians, in some manner, paid for the destroyed tea. To other colonies, this collective punishment looked mean-spirited, and everyone understood that Boston, perhaps more than any other port city, was absolutely dependent upon trade and could not even be easily supplied with emergency relief except by water.

Three other measures also created difficulties. A new Quartering Act (May 1774) made it easier than ever for British officers to quarter their troops wherever they wished. The Administration of Justice Act (called by colonists the Murder Act) allowed all British civil and military personnel who were charged by local officials with felonies in the course of exercising their proper authority over colonial civilians to be sent to Britain for trial whenever it was determined that they could not get a fair trial in America. Although Massachusetts was the target of this act, its principle was chilling in every colony. And the Quebec Act (June 1774), although an enlightened piece of statesmanship from the French Canadian point of view, was condemned by many British colonists for denying the residents of a colony their own legislature—even if they did not want one—and placing the Northwest Territory within the borders of this somewhat foreign entity.

Britain's most extreme measure, however, was the Massachusetts Government Act (May 1774). This statute unilaterally altered important clauses of Massachusetts's Charter of 1692 in order to make the provincial council a complete instrument of Crown policy and curtail the independence of local government. To administer this newly designed colony, Britain appointed as governor General Thomas Gage, commander of the British Army in North America. It would be hard to imagine a more impolitic piece of legislation. The Massachusetts Government Act, technically in force from 1 August 1774, was never effective beyond the borders of Boston, and by the fall Massachusetts was divided between a royal government in Boston, with some 3,000 troops controlling little more than a square mile of land and 15,000 civilians, and a rebel government centered in the country west of Boston with more than 20,000 militiamen, nearly every acre of Massachusetts (and Maine), and some 300,000 civilians. Britain never regained more than a mile of this territory, and after Lexington-Concord, its army was trapped in Boston until it evacuated in March 1776.

The greater problem with the Massachusetts Government Act, however, was its impact outside Massachusetts. Nearly every American colony either had an operative charter that it regarded as an almost sacred repository of its rights or once had a charter that it still regarded with respect. In 1765, Virginia's House of Burgesses cited the colony's early charters as foundations of the rights of its inhabitants even though the colony had operated strictly under the commissions issued to its royal governors for more than 140 years. The Boston Port Act created a sense of crisis in colonial America that could have, and probably would have, led to a Continental Congress. But the Massachusetts Government Act settled any doubt on this matter. By July 1774, every colony in America north of Georgia was convinced that Britain could attack their rights next and that their only salvation was a congress.

By the summer of 1774, any possible reconciliation between Great Britain and America faced two obstacles that had not existed just one year before. First, the constitutional position of each side had hardened. The British Parliament and the king, through the Coercive Acts, were determined to establish Parliament's authority over America "in all cases whatsoever," as they had expressed in the Declaratory Act of 1766. In America, Pennsylvania's James Wilson as well as Thomas Jefferson, writing officially for Virginia, joined John Adams and the Massachusetts legislature in utterly rejecting parliamentary authority. So complete was this transformation in America that the First Continental Congress, in October 1774, refused to acknowledge the smallest amount of parliamentary authority in its several declarations and addresses and put all its hopes in the British public and King George III.

Second, by July 1774 Americans had begun to fear Britain in a way they never had before. Their response, however, was not to despair but rather to take immediate and decisive action. They formed committees of correspondence everywhere—in cities, counties, and towns—so that they could exchange information with other communities and alert everyone to all dangers to "the common cause" (an expression that now came into widespread use). They began increasing the size of their militias, supplying them more effectively, and training them more frequently. In Massachusetts this soon

Cartoon shows Lord North, with the "Boston Port Bill" extending from a pocket, forcing tea (the Intolerable Acts of 1774) down the throat of a partially draped Native American female figure, representing "America," whose arms are restrained by Lord Mansfield, while Lord Sandwich, a notorious womanizer, restrains her feet and peeks up her skirt. "Britannia," standing behind "America," turns away and shields her face with her left hand. At the left, two figures, representing France and Spain, look on with keen interest. (Library of Congress)

created a sizable army. And they began persecuting Loyalists, at first verbally but, beginning in 1775, legally and physically. We sometimes think of America's rebellion as beginning with Lexington and Concord in April 1775, but that event only marks the beginning of armed rebellion. Massive, coordinated resistance to British authority began in the summer of 1774 and had become the colonies' official stance by October under the leadership of the First Continental Congress.

From Rebellion to Revolution, 1774–1776

If Wilson, Hutchinson, Adams, and Jefferson, between 1768 and 1774, could see no clear line dividing the supreme authority of Parliament from the total independence of the colonies, it is equally difficult to see clear divisions marking the escalating stages of America's rebellion from Britain between the convening of Congress in September 1774 and the first public advocacy of independence in January 1776. Every decision taken by both Britain and America during those sixteen months pointed in the same direction: a full-scale, protracted, bitter colonial rebellion that could only end either in independence or political repression.

The First Continental Congress began the process. After considering and rejecting Joseph Galloway's proposal of a new Plan of Union that would restructure the colonies' relationship with both Parliament and the Crown, the Congress ignored both institutions and appealed directly to King George III to grant them relief from the many grievances—carefully listed in their Declaration and Resolves of 14 October 1774—that they had against his government. To get his undivided attention, they also appealed directly to the British public and passed the Continental Association, a total trade embargo with Britain. The Continental Association not only controlled all colonial trade but also gave an official role to the widespread committee movement, thereby connecting every American community with Congress.

George III, however, refused to receive Congress's petition, and Lord North's government proceeded with plans to have Britain's armed forces repress the rebellion in New England. The British Army's march through the Massachusetts countryside on 19 April 1775 was a crucial part of this plan, and the militia's resistance at Lexington and Concord was equally a part of Massachusetts's plan to defend its rebellion.

This event, brilliantly exploited by Massachusetts propagandists in Britain as well as America, sparked a call to arms in every colony. The Second Continental Congress, convening in May 1775, immediately began planning for armed resistance, and in June it created the Continental Army and appointed George Washington its commander in chief.

On 3 July 1775 when Washington assumed command of the army in Massachusetts, America was still in rebellion, not yet in revolution. On 6 July, Congress issued its Declaration of the Causes and Necessities of Taking Up Arms, which again dispensed with any role for Parliament in America and went so far as to threaten that America might seek foreign—that is, French—assistance in its cause. Again, however, Congress asserted that America was loyal to George III himself and, at the insistence of its moderate members, authorized John Dickinson to prepare one last petition to the king, Congress's Olive Branch Petition.

Neither George III nor Lord North heeded this plea. Spurred on by Massachusetts's resistance to the British Army at Bunker Hill (17 June 1775), the bloodiest conflict of the entire Revolutionary War, George III formally declared the American colonies in rebellion on 23 August, and Britain began preparing for a protracted war. Because enthusiasm for the conflict was not high in Britain, the government took one final step that alienated America: the hiring of thousands of German mercenary soldiers to augment their armies. Americans learned of this as the winter of 1775–1776 began and also heard that the British had attempted to hire several thousand more Russian mercenaries, which Empress Catherine II ("Catherine the Great") refused to supply. The German forces, eventually numbering some 30,000 and drawn heavily from Hesse-Kassel (hence their common name, Hessians), became a vital element in Britain's invading armies in the middle states and greatly increased both the power of British arms and the depth of American resentment.

By the fall of 1775, many Americans could see no way of protecting their liberty short of declaring independence and seeking vital foreign aid. But so strong was the traditional allegiance to their king and so uncertain were the prospects of success as an independent nation that all suggestions for independence were confined for several months to private conversations and personal correspondence. What was needed to break the inhibition of public opinion was a clear public voice that would say that George III had forfeited his right to rule America, that America deserved to be independent, that America could win its independence, and that both independence and a republican form of government, with no king, was America's natural destiny. On 10 January 1776, Thomas Paine, a recent immigrant to Philadelphia from Britain, said all of this and more in a pamphlet entitled *Common Sense.* This remarkable tract, written in a direct style that every reader—and listener—could easily comprehend, became America's first best-seller, and within a few months more than 100,000 copies were printed. This amounted to one copy for every twenty-five inhabitants of the colonies, or one for every five adult white males.

Independence and Revolution, 1776

Paine's *Common Sense* and the plain facts that Britain had hired Hessian mercenaries and was mobilizing for a full-scale war gradually persuaded most Americans in most colonies that they must declare independence if only to secure French support in firearms and money, and possibly in armed men and warships, that they desperately needed to win. But America's war would not have progressed beyond a rebellion, even a successful rebellion, if independence had been only a tactic to preserve liberty. It quickly became more than that, as Americans used independence to shape a political identity for themselves that was distinct from their old British identity, distinct even from that of the venerable Englishmen whose rights they had claimed just a few years before. To do this, Americans asserted their independence in legal terms that justified a decision that made them distinct from all other peoples, but they enclosed that justification within a grander assertion that claimed their brotherhood with all peoples.

The first thing they needed in the spring of 1776 was to sever all ties, emotional as well as legal, with their king. Since 1773 in Massachusetts, and 1774 in every colony, American leaders had been able to reject Parliament and Crown authority by claiming allegiance only to George III. To be independent, however, they had to reject the king. Paine's *Common Sense* helped them by arguing that hereditary monarchy was an inferior form of government that existed, from the Jewish kingdoms of the Old Testament to their own day, only because most peoples had been too unruly for self-government. The American colonists, Paine argued, did not need this harsh means of control; they could successfully govern themselves. In May, Congress urged every colony to form new governments that suppressed every form of royal authority. Only in June, however, did Virginia become the first colony to formally and fully repudiate King George III.

To have the best chance of winning foreign support and, more important, to believe in the rightness of their own cause, Americans had to justify rejecting their king. To do this emotionally was not too difficult for many colonists. Raised in an eighteenth-century Anglo-American political world where liberty was taught as being eternally locked in a struggle with tyranny and in which conspiracies against liberty were a widely accepted explanation for political difficulties, in Britain as well as America, they finally had to conclude that a king who would ignore their repeated cries for justice must himself have become corrupted by his corrupt ministers. But Americans still needed to make their case to the world, and to themselves.

America's Revolutionary leaders did this in two ways, both of which found full expression in the Declaration of Independence. The greater part of that document is taken up with a detailed indictment of George III in which he is charged with every grievance that Americans had suffered since 1763. Not only had he supported his Parliament—referred to only as "others," "they," and "them" in the actual document—but he was personally responsible for every act of repression devised by every one of his ministers. Americans here abandoned the traditional doctrine that "the king can do no wrong," to which they had clung tenaciously as recently as 1775, to charge that King George III had done everything wrong and that he did so out of personal malice and lust for power. This rejection of their lawful monarch separated Americans from all other peoples; no large nation had utterly repudiated monarchy since the rise of the Roman Empire some 1,800 years earlier.

Americans began their Declaration of Independence, however, in a quite different manner. To revolt against a king, they declared, was not simply their right against a ruler who had proved to be a tyrant but the right of all men, who were "endowed by their Creator with certain unalienable Rights, that among these are Life, Liberty and the pursuit of Happiness. That to secure these rights, Governments are instituted among Men, deriving their just powers from the consent of the governed. That whenever any Form of Government becomes destructive of these ends, it is the Right of the People to alter or to abolish it, and to institute new Government."

In universalizing their right to revolt against their sovereign, Americans had moved beyond appeals to their autonomous early settlements; their ancient charters, whether still operative or merely remembered; and their rights as Englishmen to seize new ground. In July 1776, by declaring that they had a right to rebel simply because they were men and that all men had the sole right to determine whether they were governed well or ill, accept or reject their government, and make new governments more to their liking, Americans finally became revolutionaries. Their claim did not come out of a vacuum; they constructed it from their reading of secular history, their several religious faiths, and the political writings of Europeans, Englishmen, and Americans over centuries. But in 1776, Americans turned centuries of political theory and colonial experience into the beginning of a new nation.

Summary

The American Revolution had complex origins and many causes, as any full narrative of the event makes clear. Ultimately, however, the Revolution grew out of well over a century of colonial self-government that collided with the centralizing forces of a global empire. By the eighteenth century, Britain had fused all political power in a tight alliance of king and Parliament and could not allow its monarch to exercise separate powers that were dependent upon any legislature or body of men outside Britain. Nor could they imagine their empire surviving if individual colonies were not totally subject to the will of the central government. Creative solutions to this problem within the British Empire would have to wait until the nineteenth century.

Americans, however, could not wait. Most of the new imperial taxes of 1764–1773 were not a crushing burden, perhaps not even the Stamp Act. And the colonists might have been able to work out a practical compromise with Britain over competing interests on the Western frontier. But the issue of control over their own political destinies, which was so closely tied up with their right to control their own taxation and with all their rights as "Englishmen," and finally as free men, could not be resolved. What made the American Revolution possible was that British North Americans, unlike settlers in other parts of the British Empire, had a choice. They could defend their rights by arms and have a reasonable chance of winning against the full might of the British Empire. This they did, between 1775 and 1783.

And, in the phrasing of the Declaration of Independence, Americans could "institute new Government, laying its foundations on such principles and organizing its powers in such form, as to them shall seem most likely to effect their Safety and Happiness." This they also did in their several state governments with new constitutions, in their Articles of Confederation, and finally in the U.S. Constitution.

Richard Alan Ryerson

Military Operations of the American Revolutionary War, 1775–1781

Opening Moves

The first military encounter between British and colonial forces took place in Massachusetts, as revolutionary agitation was strongest in Boston. It did not follow a formal declaration of hostilities or come as a consequence of deliberate planning by either side; rather, it was almost accidental, though if fighting had not commenced in the spring of 1775 it would certainly have broken out at some point later in the year.

Lieutenant-General Thomas Gage, commander-in-chief of British forces in North America with headquarters in Boston, received word that colonists had stockpiled arms and ammunition at the small town of Concord. Therefore, on the night of 18 April, he dispatched a column of 1,800 troops to destroy these stores, expecting that the mission would be carried out without opposition. The rebels, however, were warned of the British advance, and when the column reached Lexington at daybreak on the following morning, it discovered a company of militia assembled on the village green waiting to oppose its progress. The British commanding officer, Colonel Francis Smith, ordered the colonists to disperse, but when a shot was fired (by whom is not known) a general exchange followed. The militia fled, leaving behind 8 men dead and 10 wounded. The British proceeded on their march to Concord and destroyed what remained of the stores that the rebels had not yet removed.

The Americans were not prepared to allow the British to return to Boston unpunished. On its return march, Smith's command was attacked by swarms of militia, making the affair more of a retreat and causing 273 British casualties, all of whom had to be left on the road. Having run this gauntlet but reaching the safety of Boston, the British were then penned into the city, while militia from throughout the colonies of New England arrived to answer the call for resistance issued by Massachusetts authorities. Militia numbers grew so rapidly as to enable the rebels to place Boston under virtual siege, with little chance for the garrison to break out, though Gage continued to have unhindered communication by water. Since the rebels did not possess artillery in sufficient numbers to bombard the city or aid in its assault, the two forces sat opposite one another while Gage waited for reinforcements and supplies to arrive by sea.

Reinforcements arrived the following month, increasing Gage's force to 6,500, including Major-Generals Sir William Howe and Henry Clinton and Brigadier-General John Burgoyne, all of whom would play substantial parts in the remainder of the war. The generals developed a plan to free themselves of their confinement, stressing in particular the occupation of the Charlestown peninsula immediately across the harbor. When news of this reached the Americans, they immediately occupied this position with 1,200 men on the night of 16 June. There they constructed a redoubt on an eminence called Breed's Hill (rather than on Bunker Hill, as was the original intention) and, with additional cover provided by lesser obstacles, awaited a British attack.

They did not have long to wait. On the following day, Howe was dispatched across the water with 2,200 troops with orders to seize the peninsula and drive off the rebels. Contemptuous of his adversaries' martial abilities, Howe decided upon a simple frontal attack—a blunder that was to cost him dearly. As the close-packed red-coated ranks advanced slowly up the hill, the Americans held their fire until they were certain of striking their targets. The first two attacks were repulsed with heavy losses, providing time for the rebels to reload. Resolved on a third attack, the British managed to turn the American left and storm the redoubt, their success owing to a shortage of rebel ammunition. The Americans retreated, leaving behind about 400 casualties; the British declined to pursue, having suffered more than 1,000 killed—a staggering 40 percent of their force.

Although the battle changed nothing strategically, as both sides remained in place, psychologically the Battle of Bunker

General Richard Montgomery and his troops at Crown Point, New York, in September 1775, en route to Canada. Despite the capture of Montreal, the subsequent assault on Quebec failed disastrously, leaving Montgomery dead and the invaders obliged to remain in winter quarters. (Library of Congress)

Hill emboldened the rebels, encouraged them to continue resistance, and demolished any fixed ideas they may have entertained of British invincibility. To the British it demonstrated in shocking terms that their opponents constituted a serious force with which to be reckoned and a painful warning that a possibly long campaign lay ahead. In short, the rebels, though poorly armed and undisciplined, were more than mere rabble.

General George Washington assumed command of the American forces, now known as the Continental Army, around Boston, shortly after the battle. He quickly began to organize the army but required heavy artillery. He hoped that he would not have to fight for the city, which was not, as Howe understood, a useful base from which to launch offensive operations.

The Invasion of Canada

While operations came to a stalemate around Boston, Congress developed a plan for the invasion of Canada, using the traditional route through New York via the lake and river chain that connected the Hudson with the St. Lawrence River. By occupying Canada, the Americans reckoned that they would be able to deprive the British of a base for an invasion of the American colonies from the north, as any enemy force advancing up the Hudson from the south could, in conjunction with one from Canada, cut the colonies in two. The French Canadians were thought to be well disposed to the American cause, and even if that sentiment did not manifest itself in the form of active cooperation, the Quebecois' supposed resentment of British rule suggested that they would welcome the liberators from the south. Operations looked more promising when, in May 1775, American militia had captured Fort Ticonderoga that, being situated between Lake George and Lake Champlain, could serve as a base for offensive operations northwards. The American commander there, General Philip Schuyler, led a force of 2,000 men, and in June Congress ordered him to proceed against Montreal and Quebec, taking the St. Lawrence Valley in the process.

A column left Ticonderoga in September under General Richard Montgomery, proceeding mainly by water and seizing Montreal from its small garrison on 13 November. At the same time a second column, under Colonel Benedict Arnold, advanced slowly through difficult Maine country where the rebels were beset by natural obstacles and shortages of food and supplies. Several hundred men turned back, but Arnold resolutely pushed on with the remainder, eventually reaching the outskirts of Quebec on 8 November with fewer than 700 men and after an exhausting march that took twice as long as expected.

The British withdrew into the fortress and waited. Unable to storm the place, Arnold waited for Montgomery to appear and for the help expected from the Canadians. Montgomery arrived soon enough but, having left some of his men to garrison Montreal, had only 300 troops with him. To make matters worse, the Canadians did not flock to the American banner as predicted. Yet in spite of the small number of troops at their disposal, Montgomery and Arnold decided to storm the city, aware that in a few days' time the enlistments of half their troops would expire and the militia would be free to return home. The assault, launched in a snowstorm on the night of 31 December, was badly defeated, with Montgomery shot dead and Arnold wounded. The latter nevertheless remained with his troops outside the city, hoping for reinforcements. These did arrive, but not in numbers sufficient to render Arnold confident enough to risk another attack. The Americans therefore sat out the winter, harsh though it was certain to be.

Far to the south, meanwhile, the siege of Boston continued until March 1776, when Washington rendered the British presence there untenable by deploying on Dorchester Heights, a rise to the south of the city, a quantity of heavy artillery taken from Ticonderoga. Howe, realizing that he could not maintain a garrison in a built-up area under bombardment, evacuated Boston by water and conveyed his troops to Halifax, Nova Scotia, with the result that the British had, at least for the moment, no base from which to conduct military operations within the thirteen colonies.

The Americans could be justly pleased with the first year of operations, for they had managed to raise an army from nothing, had begun to build a small navy, had forced the British from Boston and elsewhere, and had reached the walls of Quebec. Such successes, however, were illusory, for the full resources of Britain and her empire had yet to be deployed.

Operations in the South and in Canada, 1776

In 1776 the British dramatically intensified the war effort. A large expeditionary force was dispatched across the Atlantic, the Royal Navy appeared in American waters in large numbers, and the British had conceived a strategy involving three coordinated offensives meant to occupy important points and eventually to break rebel morale and resistance. Supreme command in Canada was placed in the hands of its governor, General Sir Guy Carleton, while Gage, having been recalled the previous September, was replaced by Sir William Howe as commander of forces in the American colonies. British grand strategy involved two major offensives and one smaller operation. With reinforcements from Britain, Howe was to sail to New York City, take it, and then proceed up the Hudson and into New England. Meanwhile Carleton, after expelling the Americans from Canada, was to move south, retake Fort Ticonderoga, and advance into New England. Once the two armies combined forces, they would recapture Boston and defeat the rebels in the surrounding area. Finally, a small expedition under Major-General Clinton was to be dispatched by sea to the southern colonies in the belief that the inhabitants were largely loyal to the Crown and would support British troops on the ground. Clinton was to reestablish British authority before proceeding to New York, where presumably he would find Howe.

When Clinton appeared off Cape Fear, North Carolina, in mid-March he found no evidence of a Loyalist uprising—indeed, a Tory force had been decisively defeated at Moore's Creek Bridge—and no fleet as promised by his superiors. When the fleet and troops finally arrived in late May, there was no Tory force with which to coordinate operations, though Commodore Sir Peter Parker resolved to attack Charleston, South Carolina, the principal port and city in the South. Clinton and Parker launched the attack in late June, by which time the city had prepared itself. The Americans could only deploy a small force of Continentals (regulars) and militia to defend the approach to the city by land, but this, together with natural obstacles and batteries mounted in a fort commanding the harbor entrance, was enough at the Battle of Sullivan's Island on 28 June 1776 both to prevent Parker from disembarking his troops and to bar Clinton's advance on foot. After three weeks spent refitting the fleet Clinton sailed for New York, where he arrived on 1 August; he found that Howe had arrived a month earlier and was now encamped, awaiting a favorable time to assault the city.

Meanwhile, far to the north, with the initiative lost by the Americans, the British offensive from Canada still could not proceed until the arrival of reinforcements, for without them Carleton could not drive out the rebels still encamped outside Quebec, much less retake Montreal. With the ice melted, the promised relief expedition arrived at the St. Lawrence in May, bringing a squadron of ships and 10,000 troops. Facing overwhelming force, the Americans could not remain, and a sortie by Carleton from Quebec with some of the reinforcements forced the Americans to retreat upriver beyond even Montreal, with the British in pursuit. The rebels, their forces now shattered and too small to be called an army, eventually halted in July at Ticonderoga. The invasion of Canada had ended in abject failure.

Carleton, with a respectable force of 13,000, stopped south of Montreal and made plans for an attack on Ticonderoga. In order to do so he required a secure line of communication back to Canada by water and hence gave orders for the construction of a flotilla to operate on Lake Champlain. Arnold, meanwhile, appreciating that halting the further progress of the enemy obliged him to contest command of the lake, began work on his own squadron of boats, in this case shallow-draft vessels propelled by sail and oar and armed with light cannon. Both sides made strenuous efforts, but Arnold's boats, though fewer in number, were ready first, and he sailed up Lake Champlain in mid-October to confront Carleton off Valcour Island. There Arnold's force was practically annihilated, giving the British command of the lakes and free passage to Ticonderoga. Carleton, however, declined to carry on and went into winter quarters at St. John's, giving as his excuse the strength of the fort and the lateness of the year, for sieges could not easily be conducted in winter. He reasoned on resuming operations in the spring. With the onset of winter Carleton understood that he could not have cooperated with Howe even if he had taken Ticonderoga. Still, by declining to take this strategic point Carleton failed to provide the British with an advance base from which to open the campaign of 1777. The consequent delay in assuming the offensive southward was to have a profound effect on the subsequent operations conducted by now Major-General John Burgoyne.

Operations in New York and New Jersey, 1776

Howe did not sit idle for long in Nova Scotia. Indeed, his offensive fared much better than those of his colleagues and nearly succeeded in ending rebel resistance. After receiving reinforcements and a naval force in Halifax, Howe sailed for New York with a formidable army of 32,000 regulars, which he landed on Staten Island, opposite Manhattan. The fleet, under his brother Vice-Admiral Richard, Lord Howe, consisted of ten ships of the line, twenty frigates, hundreds of transports, and thousands of seamen. By the time Howe had assembled his force to reach its peak strength in late August, he judged it too late in the year to move up the Hudson and into New England. All eighteenth-century campaigns were dictated by the weather, and with little time left for campaigning, Howe decided instead to capture New York and Newport, Rhode Island, with its harbor ideally suited as a naval anchorage, thus establishing for himself bases from which to open an offensive in 1777.

All that faced the British in New York was George Washington, who had arrived from Boston in April with a much smaller army than his opponent and no naval vessels. Washington had at his disposal about 20,000 regulars and militia, but most of these had little in the way of training or discipline. The strategic importance of New York had not escaped the notice of the American commander in chief, and Washington had seen fit to garrison it, as Congress directed, but it was not so advantageous a position if garrisoned in insufficient force. The British, in command of the water, could land their troops practically anywhere on Manhattan. Indeed, not only was New York difficult to defend, it could trap any force attempting to hold it, for being situated at the southern tip of the island it was bounded by the Hudson River to the west, the East River to the east, and the Harlem River to the north. The British could easily cut off the Americans' line of retreat by disembarking troops and preventing a crossing at the only point available to Washington: to the north. Washington's position was rendered all the more difficult to defend because of Brooklyn Heights, which overlooked the city from across the river on Long Island and on which artillery could be positioned. With little choice but to occupy Brooklyn Heights, Washington had to divide his numerically inferior force, separating the two elements by water. The British might easily defeat each contingent in turn or perhaps even capture them both at the same time.

Washington proceeded to entrench 10,000 men in field fortifications along the Heights of Guan, some 2 miles south of Brooklyn Heights, despite the fact that no lateral communication by road existed between the various positions. Howe, when finally prepared to open his offensive in late August, sought to dislodge his opponents. Shifting, unopposed, 20,000 troops from Staten Island to Long Island on 28 August, Howe outnumbered the Americans by a factor of two to one. Pushing against the rebel front and left at the same time and discovering an undefended road leading to the American rear, Howe inflicted 2,000 casualties and routed the rebels, who fled to the safety of Brooklyn Heights. The British victory might have been overwhelming had Howe persisted in his attack, but he halted and began to construct trenches with the intention of laying siege to the fortifications on the heights.

Washington could see that the only sensible decision was to withdraw his troops from Long Island, which he did by boat on 29 August. No British vessels appeared to intercept this operation on the East River, whether because of poor weather or Howe's ignorance of Washington's plan.

Washington now began a deployment whereby the bulk of his troops were left in New York City and the remainder were stretched along Manhattan up to the Harlem River to observe any landings the British might make as well as to cover his escape route. Yet by choosing to extend his troops thus, he left himself vulnerable. Howe took advantage of the fact and on 15 September sent troops by boat up the East River to Kips Bay, from where on 18 September he sought to turn Washington's left and force his troops against the Hudson. Washington had no choice but to abandon New York in haste and assemble all his forces at Harlem Heights, where he not only occupied a strong defensive position but provided himself with a line of retreat across the Harlem River.

In October, Howe landed more troops at Pell's Point, farther up the East River. With enemy forces now behind his main position, Washington had to withdraw to avoid being trapped. He crossed the Harlem River, abandoned Manhattan altogether, and marched to White Plains, where he held a position strong enough to withstand Howe's attack on 28 October. In undertaking this withdrawal, however, Washington had left forces behind at two forts constructed on the Hudson meant to block the British from passing upriver. Fort Washington stood on the east bank and Fort Lee on the west. These points need not have been retained after the loss of New York City, nor did their isolation make them particularly advantageous to hold. Nevertheless, Washington declined to withdraw the garrisons, each numbering around 3,000 men.

Hessian troops surrender to George Washington at Trenton, December 1776. The Americans quietly crossed the Delaware before dawn on 26 December, achieving complete surprise over the enemy. (Library of Congress)

Howe, determined to take the forts, quickly reached Dobbs Ferry on the Hudson, placing himself between Washington and his objectives. Despite imminent danger, Washington still refused to order the evacuation of the forts, and after detaching 8,000 men to defend the New York highlands, he crossed the Hudson at two points and entered New Jersey. Howe, supported by ships of the Royal Navy sailing up the Hudson, seized Fort Washington on 16 November, in the process taking 3,000 prisoners and large quantities of weapons and provisions. Realizing that Fort Lee would inevitably fall, Washington ordered it evacuated and, together with its garrison and his much-reduced army, retreated through New Jersey with Major-General Lord Cornwallis in pursuit.

Operations in Pennsylvania and New Jersey

When Washington crossed the Delaware into Pennsylvania in early December, Cornwallis halted his advance. The Americans now possessed only a scratch force of 2,000 men—one-tenth the size the army had been in Manhattan only months before. Many men had been killed or captured in the actions around New York, many others had deserted, and finally more were lost in the surrender of Fort Washington. Only 2,000 of the 8,000 men left to defend the highlands eventually reached the main American force. The Patriot cause was at its lowest ebb, and the Revolution might have been lost had Howe persevered and taken Philadelphia, the rebel capital and seat of the Continental Congress. Further pursuit might have led to the dissolution of Washington's little army, bringing a certain end to the rebellion. The capture of Philadelphia could wait until the spring of 1777, Howe decided, for the winter was now upon him and the tenets of eighteenth-century warfare dictated retirement to winter quarters rather than a strategy of headlong pursuit and destruction of an opponent, as later advocated by Napoleon and confirmed by Clausewitz.

Conscious that with his army having been driven from New York the rebels might now have doubts about the outcome of the war or the soundness of continuing to fight it, Washington decided to strike at the British, in spite of the winter and even if such a move failed to prove decisive. Morale had to be restored and an opportunity seized to show the enemy that they could not lower their guard. At the end of December 1776, after having received reinforcements of both regulars and militia, Washington had an army of a mere 6,000 men. His principal object was the Hessian garrison at

General William Howe was commander in chief of the British Army in the American colonies between 1776 and 1778. He led the campaigns in New York and Pennsylvania but rarely demonstrated any instinct for rapid advance or for delivering a decisive blow against the Americans. (Library of Congress)

Trenton, New Jersey, against which he planned a surprise attack on the morning after Christmas day using 2,400 regulars led by himself. Washington would cross the Delaware above Trenton with the main force, while a contingent of militia would cross near Trenton itself and prevent the Hessians from escaping once the alarm was raised. Finally, another force of militia would cross at Bordentown and create a feint there so as to pin the Hessians in place. Having collected from the Pennsylvania side of the Delaware whatever craft were found available, the army crossed at night amid freezing and windy conditions using boats propelled by poles and sails. In all, the journey took ten hours. The two militia contingents failed to reach their appointed posts, but Washington's own force arrived in Trenton early on the morning of the 26th, achieving complete surprise over the Hessian garrison of 1,000 men, which surrendered after a brief skirmish in the streets. With his prisoners, Washington withdrew back across the river to Pennsylvania. His raid had perturbed the British, whose detachments in the area retired to the town of Princeton. Now confident of further successes, Washington crossed the Delaware again, on the night of 30 December, and established his forces near Trenton.

Meanwhile, General (now Sir) Howe, headquartered in New York and irritated by Washington's boldness, ordered General Cornwallis to pursue him. As he advanced, Cornwallis increased his forces by absorbing troops stationed in New Jersey. He arrived in Trenton on the evening of 2 January 1777, with the American camp in sight. Cornwallis decided to postpone his attack until morning in order to allow his troops to rest and fight in the clear light of day. It apparently did not occur to him that Washington's men might not be there the next morning, and they were not. That night, Washington ordered the campfires to remain burning as a ruse and proceeded to Princeton, in Cornwallis's rear. When morning broke, Washington surprised and dispersed a body of troops advancing to join Cornwallis who, hearing the sound of gunfire in the distance and seeing the abandoned American camp, marched back to Princeton in a fury. On learning of the British approach, Washington withdrew into the New Jersey highlands near Morristown, where the rough terrain, in combination with winter conditions, rendered his position safe from attack. His new position also enabled him to harass British lines of communication.

Finding himself unable to bring the main American army to battle, Howe ordered most of his troops to leave New Jersey and concentrate outside New York City. Despite a good deal of hard campaigning in 1776, Howe had little to show for it, holding only New York, Newport, and a small area of New Jersey. The Americans had declared their independence on 4 July, and their army remained in being. Washington had recovered much of central New Jersey and some of the Hudson Valley, and, above all, he had shown that the war was not over and that resistance could and would continue.

The Philadelphia and Saratoga Campaigns, 1777

The British developed a hopelessly unrealistic strategic plan for 1777. Conceived by Colonial Secretary Lord George Germain, and by Generals Howe and Burgoyne, it would require the convergence of two British armies at the same point, one to proceed largely through heavily forested territory and the other by water.

Howe proposed a plan whereby he would require reinforcements to increase his strength to 35,000 men. After leaving behind garrisons in New York, New Jersey, and Newport, he would move up the Hudson and rendezvous with another British force, under Burgoyne, moving down the lake-river route from Canada to Albany, New York. With the junction of the two main British forces and the subsequent occupation of New England, Howe could then concentrate on defeating the rebels in the southern colonies at the close of the year. The plan was terribly flawed, not least because it was never Howe's strict intention to make the junction along the Hudson, or at least not with a sizable force. In the end, Howe decided to march against the rebel capital, Philadelphia, leaving 9,000 men on the lower Hudson to link up with those under Burgoyne moving south from Canada.

In June, the armies under Howe and Burgoyne began their respective campaigns. Howe maneuvered around New York for two months in an attempt to deceive Washington as to his intentions. He chose a long and circuitous route to reach

Philadelphia, deviating from his original plan to march by land across New Jersey, which was only 100 miles. He would move by sea through Chesapeake Bay and disembark his forces at Philadelphia—a route three times longer than the alternative.

Howe took his time and did not leave New York until late July, by which time he had already learned that Burgoyne had taken Fort Ticonderoga and was on his way from Canada. When anticipated supplies from England arrived, Howe set off, though without the reinforcements he had requested. In the end, his force consisted of only 15,000 troops, with 8,500 other troops left behind on the lower Hudson under (now Sir) Henry Clinton.

Washington, determined to defend the capital, maintained his army of 11,000 troops in a position to oppose Howe. He encountered the enemy first at the mouth of the Delaware and then at the head of Chesapeake Bay. Howe's decision to try to deceive Washington proved a mistake, for it took him thirty-five days to go by water from New York to Head of Elk, in Maryland, approximately 50 miles south of Philadelphia. Putting his troops ashore in early September, he proceeded north to discover Washington attempting to block his advance at Chadds Ford on Brandywine Creek. Howe took the initiative, moving part of his force upstream to threaten the American flank, which he surprised at the Battle of Brandywine on 11 September. After the rebels fled, Howe moved on Philadelphia, which he entered on 26 September. He then left 9,000 men at Germantown to the north of the city and the rest in New Jersey on the opposite side of the Delaware. Washington saw his opportunity and decided to strike the force that Howe had left isolated at Germantown. Using separate roads, four columns were to converge on the British position at daylight on 4 October. Poor training and the presence of fog prevented the columns from arriving at the same time. After two hours' fighting, during which the militia had difficulty in distinguishing their own troops from those of the enemy, the Americans withdrew with losses of 1,000 men, while the British lost only half that number. Washington proceeded to establish winter quarters at Valley Forge. Howe remained active, operating against the forts at the mouth of the Delaware.

Howe had Philadelphia, but it was too late in the year to do much else, and Washington's army, though recently defeated, had not been destroyed. Loyalists did not appear in large numbers to assist the British as Howe had hoped. Operations would therefore resume in the spring.

In the meantime Burgoyne, with about 9,000 men, mostly regulars but also French Canadian militia, Tories, and Indians, was moving down from St. John's, Canada, by water toward Albany. He had the advantage of transport and supply by boat, but he failed to give adequate consideration to the fact that once he had advanced beyond the lakes, he would have to move not only his troops but also his supplies on foot. He had very little in terms of animal transport, was largely ignorant of the (hostile) territory into which he was to advance, and proved to be unaware of how little the land could provide in terms of forage for the horses and food for his men. To create a diversion, Burgoyne detached a force under Colonel Barry St. Leger consisting of 900 regulars and about 1,000 Indians at Oswego, on Lake Ontario, ordering it to proceed down the Mohawk Valley and link up with Burgoyne's main force near Albany.

Burgoyne's army sailed down Lake Champlain and reached Fort Ticonderoga on 1 July. Opposing this force was General Arthur St. Clair, who commanded about 3,000 Americans. After offering little resistance at Ticonderoga, Schuyler retired to Fort Edward on the Hudson. Burgoyne now chose to carry on, moving from Skenesborough at the southern end of Lake Champlain toward Fort Edward (on the Hudson River, north of Saratoga), a long and arduous route to the Hudson—for he chose a path through dense forest crisscrossed by ravines, creeks, and streams—that required his advance guard to clear obstacles and create a path as it went. Schuyler's men cut down trees in the enemy's path and destroyed bridges, seriously delaying British progress. Although Burgoyne was merely delayed rather than stopped, he did not reach Fort Edward until 29 July.

Burgoyne remained at the fort for over a month, aware that his supply line, which now extended almost 200 miles north to Montreal, was failing to provide enough food for his dwindling forces. He had a choice: to either retrace his steps and return to Canada with nothing to show for his efforts or carry on to Albany. Burgoyne chose the latter. Hoping to secure a supply of horses near Bennington, Vermont, he dispatched a column of 800 Hessians, Tories, and regulars to capture them, together with supplies. He underestimated the force of militia present in the area, which outnumbered him by nearly two to one. The Americans launched a frontal and flank attack on 16 August, inflicting enormous casualties before Burgoyne sent a relief force, which itself was pushed back by another American attack. Burgoyne could not afford such heavy losses, and what men he still had were beginning to go hungry.

As for St. Leger, he and his mixed force of regulars, Indians, and Tories had arrived before Fort Stanwix and laid siege. New York militia under Colonel Nicholas Herkimer marched to its relief, but at Oriskany on 6 August they were ambushed by St. Leger's Indians and forced away after a seesaw action that resulted in heavy losses on both sides. Schuyler, on receiving an urgent request for assistance, sent a force of 900 regulars under General Benedict Arnold. Near Fort Stanwix he tricked the Indians into believing that the American force was much larger than it was, whereupon they abandoned the campaign, forcing St. Leger to withdraw to

Oswego and eventually into Canada. Burgoyne now lost the chance of bolstering his army with St. Leger's troops.

Notwithstanding this setback, Burgoyne decided in mid-September to press on to Albany, even though he was aware that Clinton would offer him nothing substantial in the way of reinforcements or direct assistance from New York. Clinton had no order from Howe to assist Burgoyne. Burgoyne refused to declare the campaign a failure, cut his losses, and return to Canada, nor could he wait out the winter in the midst of hostile territory with no suitable accommodation for his troops and a long and vulnerable supply line. Moving to the west side of the Hudson, he decided to advance against Bemis Heights, where the Americans had established themselves behind entrenchments.

Schuyler had meanwhile been replaced by General Horatio Gates, who now commanded an expanded force of 11,000 regulars and militia, compared to only the 6,000–7,000 men remaining to the British. Burgoyne duly assaulted the American position on 19 September in the Battle of Freeman's Farm, where he was repulsed with serious losses. For the next three weeks, he dared not make another attempt on the American position. He was later heartened to learn that Clinton had begun an advance up the Hudson, but despair began to set in when he subsequently learned that Clinton had established himself above Stony Point, from which position he would not go farther. Things were going from bad to worse for Burgoyne: his men were seriously short of food, enemy detachments constantly threatened his communications and supply, and his foragers could not bring in food except under heavy guard. At Bemis Heights on 7 October, Burgoyne tried once more to push through American lines only to be repulsed again with terrible losses. Retreating to an entrenched position at Saratoga and realizing that his situation was hopeless, Burgoyne surrendered to Gates on 17 October, turning over command of about 6,000 men and a large quantity of artillery and ammunition. By the terms of the surrender, the captives were to be released on parole and allowed to return to Britain on condition that they agreed not to fight in North America for the duration of the war. The Continental Congress, however, later reneged on the agreement, and the prisoners remained in American hands until the end of hostilities.

Saratoga marked the turning point of the war, for it struck a decisive blow for the rebel cause. Seeing a chance to seek revenge against their traditional foe and possibly to recover some of the territory lost in 1763, France joined the war on the American side as a direct result of Saratoga.

The Northern Theater, 1778

Washington and his troops spent the winter of 1777–1778 in winter quarters at Valley Forge, 20 miles northwest of Philadelphia. He had 6,000 Continentals, the militia having returned to their homes after their terms of enlistment had expired. Although the cold, combined with poor accommodation and lack of food, clothing, and blankets, caused severe suffering, the army survived to emerge from its ordeal more hardened and better trained than before. Notwithstanding difficult conditions, Friedrich Wilhelm von Steuben, a former officer in the Prussian army, had spent the season drilling the men and fashioning them into an efficient fighting force. By the spring of 1778 the American army was thus familiar with European-style tactics and had acquired a degree of professionalism hitherto unseen. Prospects rose with the addition of America's new ally France, which formally joined the American cause by a treaty of alliance concluded in February 1778. Louis XVI sent troops and naval vessels but also much-needed weapons, ammunition, and other supplies to the rebels.

Meanwhile, the British government replaced Howe with Lieutenant-General Sir Henry Clinton, who received orders to evacuate Philadelphia and assume the defensive in New York as well as to keep possession of Newport. In the intense June heat Clinton marched from Philadelphia through New Jersey en route to New York. Washington, with approximately 12,000 men, followed Clinton, who had about 10,000 troops. On 28 June, Washington's forces engaged the British at Monmouth. The fighting continued for several hours, and although the Americans demonstrated their ability to stand as equals in the field with their opponents, they were unable to prevent Clinton from reaching New York. Washington wanted another chance to strike, and with the arrival in Boston of a French fleet and 4,000 troops under the comte d'Estaing, the Americans and French tried to attack Newport in August 1778. However, when a British naval force arrived to lend aid at a critical point, the offensive was abandoned, the British and French fleets were scattered by a gale, and d'Estaing had to return to Boston for repairs. He then set sail to the West Indies to pursue attacks on British colonial possessions.

Without further French aid, Washington could not alone make an assault on New York, but he was able to ring the city with troops and keep Clinton bottled up. In fact, no further major operations were to take place in the north for the rest of the war. There were minor clashes with the British and with the Indians who conducted raids in New York and Pennsylvania as a result of attacks ordered by Washington against the Indians in the same states, but these did not affect the overall course of the war in the northern theater. In September 1780 Benedict Arnold nearly succeeded in handing over the fortified position at West Point to the British, but his plot was discovered. Arnold himself managed to elude capture and would thereafter fight on the British side. A small force under George Rogers Clark conducted an extraordinary campaign against British posts as far west as Indiana and Illinois, denying the Indians support and supplies. Moreover, in 1780, 5,000 French troops under the comte de Rochambeau landed at Newport, which the British had abandoned in order to

Jean-Baptiste Vimeur, the comte de Rochambeau, directs General Charles O'Hara to surrender his sword to George Washington at Yorktown. Contrary to popular belief, Charles Cornwallis was not present to deliver over his force of more than 5,000 troops. Instead, pleading ill health, he assigned his second in command this odious task. (Library of Congress)

strengthen their forces in other areas. But before the Americans and French could combine forces to attack New York, a British fleet arrived and blockaded the French at Newport. These events constituted the course of the war in the North. Hereafter, the focus of attention would shift to the South.

Operations in the South, 1778–1781

In the early months of 1778 the British decided that Clinton should remain in his defensive posture in New York, detaching limited numbers of troops to operate in the South in conjunction with others to be sent from the West Indies. This army would be supported, it was hoped, by the not insubstantial numbers of Loyalists then operating in Georgia and the Carolinas. Once the South was subdued, colony by colony, the North could then finally be brought to heel and the rebellion ultimately crushed. But by opting for this strategy the British were separating their two main armies by 1,000 miles, and if the French could achieve even temporary naval superiority they could cut supplies and reinforcements to British forces in the South and possibly defeat them without interference from Clinton in New York. In December 1778 the British captured Savannah—a promising start to their operations in the South.

Since 1776, when the Americans had repulsed Parker's attack on Charleston, the British had posed no major threat to the South. In 1778, however, General Benjamin Lincoln, commanding 3,500 American troops, mostly militia, foiled another British attempt against Charleston. But Lincoln's offensive against Savannah in 1779, in which he received a substantial number of French troops from d'Estaing, failed disastrously when, instead of opening a conventional siege with parallels and trenches, they assaulted the fortified position on 9 October and lost 20 percent of their force. D'Estaing withdrew to the West Indies and Lincoln to Charleston.

Charleston itself was to be the next British objective. Once in their hands, they would use it as a base for further operations in the South. In order to capture the city, Clinton had to reduce his garrison in New York to supply enough troops for the campaign, thus obliging him to evacuate Newport for the sake of defending New York against Washington. In late

December 1779, Clinton took 8,000 men and went by sea to South Carolina, arriving off the coast on 1 February 1780 after a delay caused by stormy weather. Once ashore, he increased his strength to 14,000 by calling on troops from Savannah, while inside the city Lincoln had only 5,000 regulars and militia. Charleston was well fortified, obliging Clinton to dig approach trenches in traditional siege fashion while his fleet stood at anchor in the harbor. Once the siege artillery was in place and ready to bombard the city as a prelude to an assault, Lincoln realized that resistance was foolhardy and capitulated on 12 May. The fall of Charleston constituted the greatest British victory of the war.

Clinton returned to New York, leaving two-thirds of his troops behind with Lord Cornwallis, whose command numbered more than 8,000 men, including Tories who served with the British as they advanced through the Carolinas establishing posts at places such as Camden and Ninety-Six. After the fall of Charleston, the British had no American army with which to contend, but they were harassed on a regular basis by partisans under men such as Thomas Sumter, Francis Marion, and Andrew Pickens.

The Continental Congress dispatched General Horatio Gates, as the new commander in the South, to Hillsborough, North Carolina, where he found a force of only 1,500 Continentals. Notwithstanding this paltry force he decided to attack the British encampment at Camden, South Carolina. By the time he approached the enemy position Gates had collected 4,000 troops, which Cornwallis confronted with 2,000 men on 16 August 1780. Despite his numerical inferiority, Cornwallis attacked, easily driving off the militia and defeating the Continentals, who put up respectable resistance. British losses were light; the Americans, however, lost 1,000 killed and wounded and an approximately equal number taken prisoner. By the time Gates reached Hillsborough, he found that he had fewer than 1,000 men left after desertions and losses in the field. The Americans were again left without a substantial fighting force in the South. Congress removed Gates, the erstwhile hero of Saratoga, from command.

Cornwallis saw the conquest of North Carolina as essential to success in the South. In the fall of 1780 he moved toward Charlotte but in doing so extended his supply line, which ran to Charleston on the coast. During his march, Cornwallis detached 1,000 Loyalists under Major Patrick Ferguson, a British regular army officer, who moved through the North Carolina interior recruiting men to the British cause. Patriot militia groups grew rapidly in size to meet the threat, and on 7 October, 900 rebels confronted Ferguson at Kings Mountain on the border of North and South Carolina. The Tories found themselves surrounded, and after about 400 were killed the remainder surrendered; many of these were murdered by the enraged backwoodsmen who opposed them, offering yet another example of the brutality of the war in the South, where murder and the destruction of property had become common practice. Doubtless the victors at Kings Mountain sought to avenge Colonel Banastre Tarleton's massacre of 350 Patriot militia at the Waxhaws on 29 May.

Although most of the militia disbanded after Kings Mountain and returned to their homes, their operations persuaded many Tories to stay clear of the fighting and at the same time encouraged the growth of Patriot militia units. Kings Mountain also disrupted Cornwallis's campaign plans, for being ignorant of the size of militia forces in the interior, he withdrew to Winnsboro, South Carolina.

At the same time, the new American commander in the South, Nathanael Greene, arrived in Charlotte in early December. He had only 1,500 men, of which half were militia, but he appreciated that he could not hope to attract more without achieving at least a limited success against Cornwallis. Greene detached part of his force under Daniel Morgan to proceed around Cornwallis's left. Cornwallis also divided his force, sending Tarleton with 1,100 men to pursue Morgan, while himself advancing into North Carolina. Tarleton and Morgan faced one another at Cowpens on 17 January 1781. Morgan employed innovative tactics, first ordering his militia to fire and then withdraw to the rear to allow the Continentals to hold the line, then employing concealed cavalry to assault the enemy right while the militia, once reformed, attacked the British left. Tarleton walked into the trap and lost 900 men—most of his force—though Tarleton himself and a handful of cavalry escaped. Nor did Cornwallis catch up with Morgan, who managed to join Greene in early February. Cornwallis pursued, but the Americans crossed into Virginia, whereupon the British ceased to follow. Greene returned to North Carolina, where he gathered more men and, by March, had 1,500 Continentals and 3,000 militia with which he confronted Cornwallis at Guilford Courthouse on 15 March. Greene was defeated after severe fighting, but the British lost a quarter of their fighting force—a proportion they could not afford to sacrifice.

Cornwallis was also isolated. Partisans prevented him from receiving supplies from Charleston, and his foraging parties were not safe in the countryside. He therefore marched his exhausted force of 1,500 to Wilmington—a 200-mile journey to the coast. He had almost 8,000 more men in the South, but these were widely dispersed throughout South Carolina and Georgia. By concentrating them he would have to abandon various posts, and, in any event, these disparate forces could not have obtained food in the course of marching. Thus, Cornwallis actually possessed a negligible force. In April he decided to march to Petersburg, Virginia, and link up with troops sent there by Clinton. As Cornwallis proceeded north, Greene, en route to South Carolina, was moving south to try to seize the various British posts in turn. The local commander,

Lieutenant-Colonel Alexander Stewart, gathered the garrisons of some of these posts and fought Greene at Hobkirk's Hill on 25 April and again at Eutaw Springs on 8 September. On both occasions the British drove the Americans from the field but lost heavily. Greene on the other hand received reinforcements of militia, backed by partisans, and with these by the end of the year he managed to take all British posts in the South Carolina interior, leaving the enemy in control of only three cities, all of them fortified and enjoying naval protection: Charleston, Savannah, and Wilmington.

Meanwhile Cornwallis, on reaching Petersburg, assumed command of British troops in Virginia, which now numbered 7,000. In contrast, the Americans possessed only 2,000 Continentals, commanded by the Marquis de Lafayette, who had been dispatched there by Washington. Clinton had never authorized Cornwallis to leave the Carolinas for Virginia, but now that it was done, Cornwallis was told to establish himself at Yorktown or some other place on the coast where he could have access to seaborne communication and supply. From such a place he could also be embarked by the Royal Navy if necessary, as his position was vulnerable: the French, however, had fleets both in the West Indies and at Newport, from which places they could rendezvous, appear off the Virginia coast, and isolate Cornwallis if they could drive the British fleet away from the Chesapeake. Cornwallis chose Yorktown, where he began to fortify his position.

Washington proposed a combined Franco-American attack on New York, but when he learned in mid-August that the French fleet in the West Indies was bound for the Chesapeake, he realized that he had an opportunity to isolate and destroy Cornwallis. Washington reasoned that if he could establish a large force outside Yorktown on the land side, working in conjunction with a French fleet operating a blockade offshore, Cornwallis would be trapped. On 19 August, therefore, Washington and Rochambeau began the long march to Virginia while the French squadron in Newport sailed to join the West Indies fleet bound for the Chesapeake.

It was crucial that Clinton, in New York, not become aware of allied intentions. Leaving a force of 2,000 men to make feints against the city, the French and Americans moved into New Jersey to deceive Clinton into expecting an attack on Staten Island. In fact, their combined forces proceeded first to Philadelphia and then farther south by boat down the Chesapeake. At the same time, the French fleet in the West Indies arrived in the Chesapeake and disembarked 3,000 troops to reinforce Lafayette's men in Virginia. Once Clinton realized that the allies were headed for the South, he sent Admiral Thomas Graves, the British commander in American waters, to the Chesapeake in order to intercept the French and evacuate Cornwallis. On 5 September, Graves and Admiral de Grasse, commander of the French fleet, fought an action off the Virginia Capes that came to an indecisive finish when Graves withdrew to New York at the sight of the arrival of the French squadron from Newport. Graves intended to return with additional ships, but in the meantime the French had the all-important control of the bay. Crucially, Cornwallis's access to the sea was now severed.

Franco-American troops, armed with heavy guns and other requisite equipment, appeared before Yorktown on 26 September and began constructing siege works. After several sorties made by the garrison and limited assaults conducted by the besiegers, Cornwallis, running short of supplies and unable to withstand the bombardment before the arrival of Clinton's relief force, surrendered his army of 7,000 men on 19 October.

Yorktown was the last major action of the war in America, for although Clinton remained in possession of New York, the British had to abandon Wilmington and Savannah and concentrate all their southern forces in Charleston—their sole remaining possession in the region. The British no longer had sufficient forces with which to mount any sort of meaningful offensive, and there was fighting to be done in the West Indies with the French. The war did not actually end for another two years, but Yorktown marked the effective conclusion of hostilities with the American rebels. The government of Lord North in London left office as a result of Cornwallis's defeat, and the new government opened negotiations in Paris with the Americans and French, ultimately resulting in a treaty in September 1783 that formally recognized the independence of the United States. The new republic would stretch from the eastern seaboard north to Canada, south to Spanish Florida, and west as far as the Mississippi.

Gregory Fremont-Barnes

See also

Arnold, Benedict; Bennington, Battle of; Brandywine, Battle of; Bunker Hill, Battle of; Burgoyne, John; Camden Campaign; Canada, Operations in; Carleton, Guy; Charleston, South Carolina, Expedition against (1776); Charleston, South Carolina, Expedition against (1780); Chesapeake, Second Battle of the; Clark, George Rogers; Clinton, Henry; Cornwallis, Charles; Cowpens, Battle of; Eutaw Springs, Battle of; Fort Ticonderoga, New York; Gage, Thomas; Gates, Horatio; Germantown, Battle of; Greene, Nathanael; Guilford Courthouse, Battle of; Harlem Heights, Battle of; Hobkirk's Hill, Battle of; Howe, William; Kings Mountain, Battle of; Lafayette, Marquis de; Lexington and Concord; Long Island, Battle of; Marion, Francis; Monmouth, Battle of; Morgan, Daniel; New Jersey, Operations in; New York, Operations in; Northwest Territory; Oriskany, Battle of; Pickens, Andrew; Princeton, Battle of; Rawdon, Francis; Saratoga Campaign; Savannah, Georgia, Allied Operations against; Schuyler, Philip; Southern Campaigns; Steuben, Friedrich von; Sumter, Thomas; Tarleton, Banastre; Trenton, Battle of; Valcour Island, Battle of; Valley Forge, Pennsylvania; Vimeur, Jean-Baptiste, Comte de Rochambeau; Washington, George; Waxhaws, South Carolina, Action at; White Plains, Battle of; Yorktown, Virginia, Siege of; Yorktown Campaign

References

Barnes, Ian. *The Historical Atlas of the American Revolution.* New York: Routledge, 2000.

Bicheno, Hugh. *Rebels and Redcoats: The American Revolutionary War.* London: HarperCollins, 2003.

Black, Jeremy. *War for America, 1775–1783.* Cambridge: Harvard University Press, 1964.

Buchanan, John. *The Road to Guilford Courthouse: The American Revolution in the Carolinas.* New York: Wiley, 1997.

Carrington, Henry B. *Battles of the American Revolution, 1775–1781.* 1876. Reprint, New York: Promontory, 1974.

Chadwick, Bruce. *George Washington's War: The Forging of a Man, a Presidency and a Nation.* Naperville, IL: Sourcebooks, 2004.

Coakley, Robert W. *The War of the American Revolution: Narrative, Chronology, and Bibliography.* Washington, DC: Center for Military History, U.S. Army, 2004.

Conway, Stephen. *The War of American Independence, 1775–1783.* London: Arnold, 1995.

Countryman, Edward. *The American Revolution.* New York: Hill and Wang, 2003.

Diamant, Lincoln. *Chaining the Hudson: The Fight for the River in the American Revolution.* Secaucus, NJ: Lyle Stuart, 1989.

Fischer, David Hackett. *Washington's Crossing.* Oxford and New York: Oxford University Press, 2004.

Griffith, Samuel B. *The War for American Independence: From 1760 to the Surrender at Yorktown in 1781.* 1976. Reprint, Champaign: University of Illinois Press, 2002.

Ketchum, Richard. *Saratoga: Turning Point of America's Revolutionary War.* New York: Henry Holt, 1997.

———. *Victory at Yorktown: The Campaign That Won the Revolution.* New York: Henry Holt, 2004.

Ketchum, Richard M. *The Winter Soldiers.* Garden City, NY: Doubleday, 1973.

Konstam, Angus. *Guilford Courthouse, 1781: Lord Cornwallis's Ruinous Victory.* Oxford, UK: Osprey, 2002.

Lancaster, Bruce. *The American Revolution.* Boston: Houghton Mifflin, 2001.

Marston, Daniel. *The American Revolution, 1774–1783.* Oxford, UK: Osprey, 2002.

McCullough, David. *1776: America and Britain at War.* London: Allen Lane, 2005.

Middlekauf, Robert. *The Glorious Cause: The American Revolution, 1763–1789.* 1981. Reprint, Oxford: Oxford University Press, 2005.

Morrissey, Brendan. *The American Revolution: The Global Struggle for National Independence.* San Diego, CA: Thunder Bay, 2001.

———. *Boston 1775: The Shot Heard Around the World.* Oxford, UK: Osprey, 1995.

———. *Monmouth Courthouse 1778: The Largest Battle in the North.* Oxford, UK: Osprey, 2004.

———. *Quebec 1775: The American Invasion of Canada.* Oxford, UK: Osprey, 2003.

———. *Saratoga 1777: Turning Point of a Revolution.* Oxford, UK: Osprey, 2000.

———. *Yorktown 1781: The World Turned Upside Down.* London: Osprey, 1997.

Morton, Joseph C. *The American Revolution.* Westport, CT: Greenwood, 2003.

Nester, William R. *Frontier War for American Independence.* Mechanicsburg, PA: Stackpole, 2004.

Patterson, Benton Rain. *Washington and Cornwallis: The Battle for America, 1775–1783.* New York: Taylor Trade Publishing, 2004.

Russell, David Lee. *The American Revolution in the Southern Colonies.* Jefferson, NC: McFarland, 2000.

Seymour, William. *The Price of Folly: British Blunders in the War of American Independence.* London: Brassey's, 1995.

Shelton, Hal T. *General Richard Montgomery and the American Revolution: From Redcoat to Rebel.* New York: New York University Press, 1994.

Symonds, Craig L. *A Battlefield Atlas of the American Revolution.* Mount Pleasant, SC: Nautical and Aviation Publishing Company of America, 1986.

Ward, Christopher. *War of the Revolution.* 2 vols. New York: Macmillan, 1952.

Ward, Harry M. *The War of Independence and the Transformation of American Society.* London: University College London Press, 1999.

Weintraub, Stanley. *Iron Tears: America's Battle for Freedom, Britain's Quagmire, 1775–1783.* New York: Free Press, 2005.

Wilson, David K. *The Southern Strategy: Britain's Conquest of South Carolina and Georgia, 1775–1780.* Columbia: University of South Carolina Press, 2005.

Wood, W. J. *Battles of the Revolutionary War, 1775–1781.* Chapel Hill, NC: Algonquin, 1990.

AMERICAN REVOLUTION

A

Abercromby, Sir Robert (1740–1827)

Born in Scotland, the younger brother of the distinguished soldier Sir Ralph Abercromby of later Napoleonic fame, Robert Abercromby served with distinction in the French and Indian War (1756–1763) at the assault on Fort Ticonderoga, at Niagara, and at the capture of Montreal. In the American Revolutionary War Abercromby again distinguished himself in numerous battles, including Harlem Heights, where his brother James was killed, and at Brandywine, Germantown, and the occupation of Charleston. He served as a lieutenant-colonel at the siege of Yorktown, where at 4 A.M. on 16 October 1781 he made a partially successful sortie against American batteries positioned extremely close to British lines. In 1782 he became a colonel and aide-de-camp to King George III and in 1788 went to India in command of the 75th Foot.

Abercromby's reputation was to be chiefly established in India. He was promoted to the rank of major-general in 1790 and appointed governor and commander in chief at Bombay. Under Lord Cornwallis, the governor-general of India, Abercromby served in the Third Mysore War (1789–1792). On 14 December 1790, leading a force from Bombay, Abercromby appeared before the town of Cannamore, whose resistance he broke within a day, before capitalizing on this achievement to occupy the whole of the Malabar coast. While Cornwallis was engaging Tipu Sultan, the Mysorean leader, at the Battle of Arikera (14 May 1791), Abercromby had advanced with nine battalions from Bombay as far as Periapatam, only 40 miles west of Tipu Sultan's formidable island stronghold at Seringapatam. Cornwallis proceeded to drive his adversary back into his fortress, but the lateness of the season prevented major siege efforts. Abercromby was ordered to return to Bombay while plans were drawn up for the decisive stage of the campaign to open the following year. When the campaign resumed in 1792, Abercromby, leading 9,000 British troops and sepoys and a train of siege artillery, arrived outside Seringapatam on 16 February, thus completing the investment of the town then being conducted by Cornwallis's mixed British and Indian force of 52,000. Tipu Sultan sued for peace on 16 March, granting British suzerainty over all of Malabar and direct control over other regions. For these services Abercromby was knighted and succeeded Cornwallis as commander in chief in India in October 1793.

The principal events during his period in office were the Second Rohilla War and the mutiny among various officers of the East India Company. When a Rohilla chieftain approved by Sir John Shore, the governor-general, as legitimate claimant to the district of Rampur was murdered, Abercromby was sent on a punitive expedition against the culprit. With a small force he defeated Gholan Mahommed at Battina, and though Abercromby's conduct was greatly praised, Shore nevertheless strongly criticized him for granting terms to his adversary. When mutiny arose among disaffected officers of the East India Company over the slow pace of promotions and the attitudes of superiority shown by officers in the British Army, Abercromby managed affairs deftly enough to diffuse the tension and prevent a general rebellion. The situation was ultimately settled when new regulations arrived from Britain, granting East India Company officers better terms of service. Acute loss of vision through an eye disease obliged Abercromby to return home in 1797, by which time he had earned the great respect and admiration of Shore. Abercromby held numerous military appointments in Britain and died at age eighty-seven in 1827, the oldest general in the army at that time.

Gregory Fremont-Barnes

See also

Brandywine, Battle of; Cornwallis, Charles; Germantown, Battle of; Harlem Heights, Battle of; Yorktown, Virginia, Siege of

References

Fortescue, John. *The War of Independence: The British Army in North America, 1775–1783.* London: Greenhill, 2001.

Wickwire, Franklin, and Mary Wickwire. *Cornwallis: The Imperial Years.* Chapel Hill: University of North Carolina Press, 1980.

Achard de Bonvouloir, Julien-Alexandre (1749?–1783)

Achard (sometimes Archard) de Bonvouloir provided the French government with information about the military state of the American colonies in 1775. This was instrumental in gaining clandestine military supplies for the Revolutionary War and led eventually to America's formal alliance with France.

Bonvouloir was born into a noble family in Normandy. He served in the French army as a volunteer until 1774, when, having lost a major part of his inheritance, he sought an opportunity to redeem his fortunes. He first traveled to Santo Domingo, and in July 1775 he decided to return home by way of British North America. He quickly assessed the state of America's rebellion, and on returning to France he reported his findings to the government. Bonvouloir had the ear of the comte de Guines, the French ambassador in London, who suggested to the comte de Vergennes, the French foreign minister, that Bonvouloir should be sent back to America to find out more about the situation in the colonies. Vergennes agreed, and Bonvouloir was given a commission and the small sum of 200 livres. He was warned, however, that if his mission failed the French state would deny any involvement with him.

Bonvouloir traveled to America disguised as a Belgian merchant. He arrived in Philadelphia late in 1775 and stayed in the home of Francis Daymon, who was teaching French to Benjamin Franklin. Daymon introduced Bonvouloir to Franklin, and three nocturnal meetings were held in Carpenter's Hall during December between Bonvouloir and members of Congress's Committee of Secret Correspondence, the forerunner of America's State Department. During these conversations Bonvouloir informed Franklin that the French state was prepared to offer America clandestine support. Although some Americans feared that Bonvouloir was a double agent, the committee decided to trust him. Bonvouloir produced a report on the condition of the American forces and their chances of success and sent it to France on 28 December 1775. His observations confirmed the encouraging information that had been collected by Caron de Beaumarchais, the French actor and playwright then operating as an agent in London.

The reports that Bonvouloir sent back to Paris prompted Vergennes to write two documents—"Reflections" and "Considerations"—about America's prospects and the opportunity for Franco-American relations. These he presented to Louis XVI and his council at Versailles. There was opposition to Bonvouloir's opinion that the French government should support the rebelling American colonists. Many Frenchmen were concerned that their navy would not be able to guarantee the delivery of supplies and troops, and many had doubts that the French economy could support the proposed financial help. But Louis XVI ultimately approved the decision to support the colonies, and Beaumarchais set up a false trading company—Rodrigue, Hortalez et Cie—to channel resources to America.

Bonvouloir, however, was soon abandoned by the French government. His patron, the comte de Guines, lost his post as ambassador to Britain, and Bonvouloir received no further instructions, despite writing many letters. He left America and died in India in 1783.

Ralph Baker

See also

Beaumarchais, Pierre-Augustin Caron de; Diplomacy, French; Franco-American Alliance; Franklin, Benjamin; Gravier, Charles, Comte de Vergennes; Secret Correspondence, Committee of

References

Dull, Jonathan R. *A Diplomatic History of the American Revolution.* New Haven, CT: Yale University Press, 1985.

Thompson, Edmund R., ed. *Secret New England: Spies of the American Revolution.* Portland, ME: Provincial, 1991.

Acland, John Dyke (1746–1778)

British politician and soldier, commander of the British grenadiers during Burgoyne's campaign, and husband of Lady Harriet Acland.

John Dyke Acland was born on 18 February 1746 in Tetton, Somerset, the eldest son of a baronet whose lineage went back to the twelfth century. As a member of Parliament for Callington, Cornwall, Acland was a vociferous opponent of the colonists' cause and of Lord North's attempts at reconciliation. So strong were Acland's feelings that on 23 March 1774 he purchased a commission as an ensign in the 33rd Foot and, exactly one year later, became a captain in that regiment. On 16 December 1775, he purchased a majority in the 20th Foot and later sailed to Canada, where he served in the relief of

Quebec and later at Trois-Rivières in command of the converged battalion of grenadier companies. Acland's lack of active service led to this appointment being criticized in some quarters, including by Major Alexander Lyndsay (the Earl of Balcarres) who commanded the converged battalion of light companies. However, Acland was not entirely ignorant of command. He had previously been a colonel in the Devonshire militia and acquitted himself well in the 1776 campaign and Burgoyne's expedition.

Acland was clearly a man who led from the front. At Hubbardton on 7 July 1777, his outnumbered grenadiers outflanked the American left, during which he was wounded in the thigh. He then fought at Freeman's Farm before commanding the British left during the second action on 7 October. Assaulted by Enoch Poor's veteran New Hampshire Continentals, Acland led a desperate counterattack, during which he was shot through both legs. Another officer tried to carry him to safety but had to abandon him beside a rail fence, where he narrowly escaped death by a youth through the intercession of the later notorious James Wilkinson. (Interestingly, after being wounded at Hubbardton, Acland was supposedly helped back to camp by another dubious character, the diarist Thomas Anburey.)

Acland was paroled and, when well enough to travel, returned to England and resumed his career in politics. He was now, by all accounts, more respectful of Americans, amongst whom he had made many friends during his captivity. However, just a few months later he died at Pixton, Somerset, on 31 October 1778, four days after having a fit at breakfast. (The date usually quoted for his burial, 22 November, is incorrect; he was buried on 28 November at Broad Clyst in Devon, according to the local parish records.) His death has variously been ascribed to either a stroke or a cold contracted during a duel earlier that morning. While there is evidence that this duel—possibly involving a fellow officer—did occur, there is no confirmation that Acland was defending either the honor of his newfound American friends or the British Army's failure to defeat them. (If a cold sounds an unlikely cause of death to modern readers, it is worth remembering that Washington also died from one.)

In 1770, Acland married Lady Christian Harriet Caroline Fox (1750–1815), daughter of the Earl of Ilchester. Lady Acland joined her husband in Canada in 1777, arriving in time to nurse him through a bout of fever at Chambly and then his wound from Hubbardton. Later, both had a narrow escape from a burning tent when their dog knocked over a candle. After his capture, Lady Harriet obtained Burgoyne's permission to enter the American lines to find Acland. Accompanied only by her husband's valet, her own maid, and a chaplain, she was rowed down the Hudson River through a fierce storm, arriving at Gates's headquarters on 10 October, where she was reunited with her husband. There is, however, no truth to the stories that she went mad after Acland's death or that she married the chaplain.

Brendan D. Morrissey

See also

Hubbardton, Battle of; Saratoga Campaign; Wilkinson, James

Reference

Digby, William. *The British Invasion from the North: The Campaigns of Generals Carleton and Burgoyne from Canada, 1776–1777.* Edited by James Baxter. Era of the American Revolution Series. New York: Da Capo, 1970.

Adams, Abigail (1744–1818)

Abigail Adams has become probably the most widely and intimately known woman of the Revolutionary era for three reasons. The first foundation of her fame is her visibility as the wife of John Adams, who was both a leader of the Revolution and second president of the United States. This has placed her in a select group of early presidential wives (not yet called First Ladies), along with Martha Washington and Dolley Madison. Abigail's position as John Adams's wife gave her access to several prominent persons, particularly Thomas Jefferson, who recorded their favorable impressions of her. Second, nearly sixty-five years after the Declaration of Independence, the correspondence that she exchanged with her husband as well as letters written to her sisters and to a few close friends, notably Mercy Otis Warren and Jefferson, began to appear in print. These intimate letters, never intended for publication, portray her as a lively and intelligent woman who made her own sacrifices to achieve her country's freedom. Finally, with the gradual development of feminism in American life, Adams has been anointed, on the basis of a few of her letters, as a powerful voice for women's rights in an age that afforded women little independence of thought and action.

Abigail Smith was born on 22 November 1744 in Weymouth, Massachusetts. She was the second child of the Reverend William Smith, pastor of the town's first parish church, and Elizabeth Quincy, a member of the most prominent family in neighboring Braintree (now Quincy). Adams was somewhat sickly as a child and, like nearly all women of her day, was educated entirely at home. In her case, however, home was full of books containing history, theology, and literature in English and several works in French, Latin, and Greek. She did not study the ancient classics, but she read European history of every period from the ancients to her own day, plus copious amounts of Shakespeare and the English poets, especially Alexander Pope and James Thompson, whom she quoted frequently in her letters. At some point, perhaps shortly before her marriage, her brother-in-law, Richard Cranch, also taught her some French.

Abigail Adams, the wife of President John Adams and mother of President John Quincy Adams. While John was serving the Revolutionary cause, Abigail raised their children and struggled to maintain their farm amid inflation and shortages of labor. After the Revolution, she accompanied her husband to London as ambassadress and ably served as First Lady during his presidency in the capital, Philadelphia. (Library of Congress)

On 25 October 1764, Abigail Smith married John Adams of neighboring Braintree after a three-year courtship that is charmingly described in a handful of surviving letters exchanged between the two. Her parents may have disapproved their daughter's marriage to a lawyer, a profession that was still struggling for full respectability in post-Puritan New England, but she was determined in her choice of a husband. She continued her self-education in her new husband's growing library and raised four children, Abigail (b. 1765), John Quincy (b. 1767, later sixth president of the United States), Charles (b. 1770), and Thomas Boylston (b. 1772).

The Adamses lived alternately in Braintree and Boston until the Revolution. In the next decade (1774–1784), Adams stayed in Braintree with her daughter and younger sons while John spent most of his time first in Congress and, after 1778, in France and Holland, to which he took John Quincy. Adams joined her husband in Europe in 1784, returned with him to America in 1788, and lived mostly in Braintree (renamed Quincy in 1792) for the rest of her life, with extensive stays in New York and Philadelphia and one brief visit to the new executive mansion in Washington, D.C., while John served as vice president and president. Even in the 1790s, however, Adams often remained in Quincy in rather poor health while her husband was in the nation's capital.

These long separations were emotionally hard on both Adamses and especially on Abigail, who during the Revolutionary War had to run both her household and small farm for years with little assistance, tasks she performed with dedication and skill, while also educating her children. This experience was one she shared with tens of thousands of other women, a few richer but most poorer than herself, while their husbands, fathers, brothers, and sons were off at war. And at age thirty-nine Adams, who had never left Massachusetts, crossed the ocean, of which she was terrified, to join her husband and manage two substantial houses in Paris and London. Used to having just one or two servant girls, she now supervised staffs of eight to ten, considered the minimum that anyone in John Adams's diplomatic posts could keep in a respectable home.

These same long, painful separations made Abigail's reputation. Between their first courtship letter in 1762 and President Adams's last letter home to Quincy in 1800, Abigail and John Adams exchanged more than 1,000 letters, one of the largest, and incomparably the finest, correspondences of any presidential couple in American history. The quality of this exchange owes much to the exciting times and places in which they lived and much to John's lively pen, but it owes most to Abigail, who was as fine a letter writer as any American of her century. Her range of interests was broad, her reporting on America's home front—the farms and villages away from the congresses and battles—was superb, and she had a talent for expressing, in a few short passages, the vital truths of Revolutionary politics that no writer has ever exceeded.

Adams's claim to fame as an early American feminist—a label and concept that would have astonished her—are solid but must be seen in context. When in her most famous letter (30 March 1776) she urged her husband in Congress to "remember the ladies" as he and his colleagues framed laws for the new nation just taking shape, she was not, as some have imagined, advocating suffrage for women. Instead, she had her eye on the central legal and cultural problem for most women of her day: the nearly absolute power that husbands had over their wives' persons, time, and property. It was, in short, equality within marriage that concerned Adams. Her husband, however, while probably genuinely sympathetic to her view, was embarrassed by her exhortation. Congress had no power to give women any rights within marriage, and if they had enjoyed such power, John Adams would not have had the courage, or foolhardiness, to propose such rights in 1776. The simple legal justice within marriage that Abigail sought—let alone the right to vote—lay far in the future for most American women.

And Abigail herself played a fairly traditional role within marriage. She and John did discuss such matters as land purchases, a matter that most wives would have thought beyond their sphere, but John probably listened to her advice on this matter because she had proven herself to be so sensible in household management and so generally intelligent. In raising her children, Adams was the classic "republican mother," exhorting her three boys to virtue, self-sacrifice, and public service and urging her daughter to prepare for becoming a mother who could raise virtuous and achieving sons. And she was a spirited advocate for the full recognition of John Adams's political and intellectual achievements, whether in Massachusetts or Philadelphia.

Adams's long life was not without bitter disappointments. Her alcoholic son Charles died in 1800, thoroughly estranged from his father. Beginning in the 1790s, she became even more deeply estranged by partisan politics from her old friend Thomas Jefferson than was her husband, who was eventually reconciled to Jefferson and resumed a rich correspondence with him. And her daughter Abigail, after playing the dutiful wife to an unworthy husband for more than two decades, came home to Quincy to die of cancer in 1813. Adams's own health was often poor from the 1790s onward, but she lived until shortly before her seventy-fourth birthday, dying on 28 October 1818, survived by her eighty-three-year-old husband and two sons, including John Quincy Adams, then America's secretary of state.

Richard Alan Ryerson

See also

Adams, John; Jefferson, Thomas; Warren, Mercy Otis; Women

References

Akers, Charles W. *Abigail Adams: An American Woman.* Boston: Little, Brown, 1980.

Butterfield, L. H., and others, eds. *The Book of Abigail and John: Selected Letters of the Adams Family, 1762–1784.* Cambridge: Harvard University Press, 1975.

Gelles, Edith B. *Portia: The World of Abigail Adams.* Bloomington: Indiana University Press, 1992.

Levin, Phyllis Lee. *Abigail Adams.* New York: St. Martin's, 1987.

Adams, John (1735–1826)

The colonial lawyer, Patriot pamphleteer, and political theorist John Adams first achieved local fame in defending the British soldiers in the Boston Massacre. National prominence came in 1776 in the debates over separation from Britain when his congressional colleagues saluted the short, stout Adams as the "Atlas of Independence." Immediately thereafter, he began his diplomatic career in France and Holland, culminating in his heading the American delegation that negotiated the Treaty of Paris with Britain in 1783. Adams finished his public career as first vice president and second president of the United States, followed by a long retirement as one of the oldest surviving signers of the Declaration of Independence.

Portrait of John Adams, president of the United States (1797–1801). (Library of Congress)

Birth, education, and the law. Born in Braintree (later Quincy), Massachusetts, on 19 October 1735, Adams was the eldest child of "Deacon" John Adams, a Braintree farmer, shoemaker, and local officeholder, and Susanna Boylston, whose family was prominent in medicine and trade in Boston. Samuel Adams was the younger John's second cousin. John's father hoped that he would become a minister and placed him with a series of Braintree schoolmasters. Adams entered Harvard College in 1751, excelling in mathematics, natural philosophy (astronomy and physics), and debating, and graduated in 1755. But while he was still in college, a rancorous dispute between Braintree's minister and his parishioners confirmed Adams's growing conviction that the pulpit was not for him, and several of his classmates suggested that he had the talents for a legal career. Upon graduation, he briefly taught school in Worcester and began reading law with a prominent local attorney. In 1758 Adams returned to Braintree, sought the support of the eminent Boston lawyer Jeremiah Gridley, and was admitted to the Suffolk County bar. After a faltering beginning, Adams made rapid progress and was admitted as a barrister before Massachusetts's Superior Court in 1762.

Buoyed by his growing success and the inheritance of a house from his father, Adams wed Abigail Smith in 1764.

Marriage to this bright and spirited daughter of the Reverend William Smith of Weymouth and Elizabeth Quincy, a member of Braintree's leading family, enhanced Adams's local standing, but Abigail's great contributions to John's career were her willingness to endure long separations, her unshaken belief in his abilities, and her perceptive advice on people and events. The Adamses raised four children: Abigail, who later married one of General Washington's aides, Colonel William Stephens Smith; John Quincy, who would become America's leading diplomat and sixth president; Charles; and Thomas Boylston.

Like most enterprising eighteenth-century New England lawyers, Adams practiced every kind of law that came his way and regularly rode circuit to county courts from Cape Cod to the Maine frontier. Unlike most lawyers, he soon became a widely read and profound legal scholar. At first his progress was slow and painful. He began his career with only modest family and professional connections, and in 1758 he confided to his diary that "it is my destiny to dig treasures with my own fingers. No body will lend me or sell me a pick axe." Within a dozen years, however, he was regarded as the most learned and successful attorney in Massachusetts.

Amid a welter of cases large and small, Adams handled two of particular importance to the growing resistance to British authority in Boston. In 1768 he defended John Hancock, whose ship *Liberty* had been seized by British customs agents for violating the Navigation Acts. Adams lost the case but enhanced his standing in Boston, where the customs officers had become so unpopular that British soldiers were sent to the port to ensure order. That troop deployment set the stage for Adams's most celebrated legal triumph. In 1770, following the Boston Massacre, Adams risked his reputation with Boston's Patriots but did them a valuable service by defending both the commanding British officer and the soldiers charged with murdering Boston civilians. Their acquittal greatly contributed to the reputation for the fairness and integrity of Boston, the resistance movement, and John Adams.

From his early twenties Adams felt a keen hunger for fame. Unlike many colonial lawyers, however, Adams sought renown largely within his profession and seems not to have regarded the law as an avenue to public office, particularly elective office. He served for only two years (1766–1768) as a Braintree selectman and for just a single year (1770–1771) representing Boston in the Massachusetts legislature. Yet the young attorney was intensely involved in public life, from his drafting of Braintree's protest of the Stamp Act in 1765 to his legal defense of Hancock in the *Liberty* case, of the British soldiers in the Boston Massacre trials, and of the constitutional position of the Massachusetts House in its controversy with Governor Thomas Hutchinson in 1773.

Adams also became one of America's most prolific political pamphleteers in the decade preceding independence. His earliest pseudonymous newspaper essays attacked the spirit of political faction in Massachusetts. Later works, most of which also appeared under pseudonyms, sought to keep the province independent of the control of what he saw as a succession of corrupt British ministries. Some of these pieces, notably his "Dissertation on the Canon and Feudal Law" and "On the Independence of the Judges," made a rather limited case for colonial autonomy within the British Empire. But the logic of his argument eventually drove Adams, as the principal but unnamed author of the Massachusetts House of Representatives' replies to addresses by Governor Hutchinson in 1773, to declare well in advance of most other colonial spokesmen that the British Parliament had no absolute authority over Massachusetts (or, by extension, over other North American colonies).

Convinced now of the gravity of the imperial crisis, the heretofore politically cautious Adams welcomed the Boston Tea Party as a bold and daring act that would alter history. Britain's Parliament apparently agreed and promptly closed the port of Boston to all trade and passed the Coercive Acts. The most important of these statutes, for Adams and his neighbors, was the Massachusetts Government Act, which unilaterally altered their cherished Charter of 1692 to effect British control of the rebellious province. To meet the crisis, the Massachusetts House, in its last official act before being prorogued by the new royal governor, General Thomas Gage, in June 1774, named Hancock, Samuel and John Adams, and Robert Treat Paine to confer with leaders from Britain's other colonies in the First Continental Congress in Philadelphia.

After the Boston Tea Party, Adams never admitted any doubts about joining the resistance movement or later in working for American independence, even in his intimate diary. But his decision was not without costs, both professional and personal. The legal profession in Massachusetts was deeply split over resistance to Britain. Many of the lawyers who had taught and inspired Adams and most of the province's superior court judges were Tories, and many became Loyalist exiles. Adams felt most keenly the loss of some of his closest professional friends, especially Daniel Leonard (with whom he would soon cross swords in print without knowing his identity) and Jonathan Sewall. His final parting with Sewall in June 1774, as they rode circuit together in Maine, is one of the most poignant scenes in his diary.

Congress and independence. Adams's earlier career as a lawyer, pamphleteer, and political theorist was already quite distinguished, but from the time he entered Congress in September 1774 to his final departure from that body in 1777 he displayed a level of energy, creativity, and political sensitivity that he had never shown before. Congress's task was difficult: to persuade or force the British Parliament to rescind its Boston Port Act, Massachusetts Government Act, and the other Intolerable Acts and reach a new accommodation with all the colonies over imperial taxation. Adams was mildly disappointed that Congress even bothered to petition both George III and the British public for a redress of America's grievances, but he was pleased with the measures in which he had a hand: a bold Declaration of Rights and its coercive companion, the nonimportation Continental Association (October 1774). No member of Congress took its work more seriously, as evidenced by the fact that Adams's personal diary and correspondence are the only contemporary record of many of that body's important deliberations.

Upon his return to Massachusetts in November, Adams found a vigorous Patriot government, headed by a provincial congress that exercised nearly all of the powers of the old legislature, controlling every town except Boston, home to General Gage's army. But Massachusetts's Loyalists were beginning to speak out, and when Daniel Leonard, as "Massachusettensis," assaulted the work of Congress, Adams, as "Novanglus" (January–April 1775), replied in a series of learned essays that justified congressional resistance to a tyrannical ministry. Only a "republican" government, he declared, could protect the people's liberties. And in an argument that was unique among America's Patriot leaders, he explained that a republic could take the form of either a scrupulously constitutional hereditary monarchy—as he believed Great Britain's government had been before 1763—or a state dependent entirely upon the authority of the people.

In April 1775 open warfare broke out between British regulars and Massachusetts militiamen at Lexington and Concord. Adams immediately returned to Philadelphia to attend the Second Continental Congress, and in June he led Massachusetts's delegates to propose that their province's forces, then besieging General Gage in Boston, become a "Continental Army" under Congress's control, with George Washington as its commander in chief. In Congress's fall session, Adams threw himself into incessant committee work to supply the new army and take the first steps toward establishing the Continental Navy, a venture to which he would return nearly a quarter century later when, as president, he initiated the establishment of the Department of the Navy (1798). By the spring of 1776 Adams, always a key member of Congress, had become its single most important, and overworked, member.

His first challenge in this remarkable new year, however, came from outside Congress. Thomas Paine's *Common Sense,* appearing in January, swept the colonies with its enthusiasm for independence, which Adams admired, and its call for new governments with single-house legislatures and weak or nonexistent executives, which he deplored. Several congressmen whose provinces were restructuring their governments turned to Adams for advice, and he responded with the most influential pamphlet of his career, *Thoughts on Government* (April 1776). In just ten pages, Adams considered the role of the people, lower legislative houses, councils,

THOUGHTS

ON

GOVERNMENT:

APPLICABLE TO

THE PRESENT STATE

OF THE

AMERICAN COLONIES.

In a LETTER from a GENTLEMAN
To his FRIEND.

PHILADELPHIA:
PRINTED BY JOHN DUNLAP.

M,DCC,LXXVI.

Title page of *Thoughts on Government,* John Adams's 1776 treatise on American liberty, prepared as suggestions for new governments in several colonies on the eve of independence. (Library of Congress)

and executives as well as qualifications for voting and office holding. Explicitly allowing for considerable variation from one province to another, he recommended a balance between two legislative chambers and a strong executive, a formula that would soon characterize most of America's new state governments. He then wrote Congress's recommendation that every province establish a government under which "every kind of authority under the [British Crown] should be totally suppressed, and all the powers of government exerted, under the authority of the people."

Adams now took on the central role in each of Congress's major decisions. Appointed in June to the committee to draft the Declaration of Independence, he assisted Thomas Jefferson in that endeavor and on 1–2 July led the debate on the floor of Congress to approve independence itself. From June to September, Adams labored to produce Congress's Plan of Treaties,

America's first blueprint for its foreign policy. He also assumed the presidency of the Board of War, the most demanding post in Congress, and held this position from June 1776 until his final departure from Congress in November 1777.

In September 1776, in a most unexpected event, Adams joined Benjamin Franklin and Edward Rutledge in a conference with Britain's Admiral Richard Howe on Staten Island. Lord Howe, fresh from the British victory over Washington at the Battle of Long Island, had requested the meeting in the hope that he could begin a reconciliation with America, as his instructions had directed him to do. Congress agreed to the conference to mollify its more timid members and supporters, and Adams reluctantly agreed to take part in a meeting that he regarded as pointless. But when Lord Howe told the three emissaries that he could not consider them as congressmen, but only as influential private persons and British subjects, Adams neatly summed up the meaning of 1776 to the Patriot cause. "Your Lordship may consider me in what light you please," he said, "and indeed I should be willing to consider myself, for a few moments, in any character which would be agreeable to your Lordship, except that of a British subject."

Republican diplomacy. Upon his return to Braintree at the end of 1777, Adams believed that his national career, sustained at considerable financial and emotional cost to his family and himself, was well over, and he immediately resumed his law practice. Congress had others ideas. In November, immediately after his departure for home, Congress appointed Adams to join its envoys Franklin and Arthur Lee in Paris. Recognizing both Congress's urgent need to bring order to its factious diplomatic commission and the signal honor it had given him, he accepted the appointment as soon as he received it, and in February 1778 he set sail for France with his young son John Quincy Adams.

Landing at Bordeaux in April, Adams learned that the American commissioners had secured their grand objective, a Treaty of Alliance with France, on 6 February, a week before he had left Boston. But there was still much to do, and over the next ten months he organized the commission's business, tried in vain to persuade his colleagues to seek more French naval aid, and tried to steer a neutral course between the feuding Franklin and Lee. As a friend and ally of Virginia Congressman Richard Henry Lee, Adams was widely expected to side with Lee's brother, and several historians to this day blithely assume that Adams did so. But Adams soon concluded that Lee was no diplomat and that Franklin was the only envoy America needed in Paris. Adams discreetly suggested this measure to friends in Congress, but the full body had already reached the same conclusion and, without bothering to dissolve the commission and recall Adams and Lee, named Franklin its sole minister to Versailles.

Receiving the news in February 1779, Adams felt humiliated at this cavalier treatment but was delighted to return home and resume his private career. This time it was his Braintree neighbors who had other plans. In August they elected him to Massachusetts's constitutional convention. That body's drafting committee chose Adams to compose the constitution, and in the early fall he crafted an intricate, detailed, and remarkably clear organic law. In a happy innovation, Adams organized his complex materials in hierarchically labeled articles and sections, a feature adopted by the Framers at Philadelphia for the U.S. Constitution. With modest changes by the full convention, the draft became the Massachusetts Constitution of 1780. This work, Adams's finest constitutional achievement, is the world's oldest written constitution still in operation.

But Adams had no time to admire his creation. In September, Congress named him its sole minister plenipotentiary to negotiate peace with Great Britain. Even Adams thought the appointment premature; Lord North's ministry was in no mood to concede American independence. Moreover, Adams was posted to Paris, where Congress directed him to coordinate his initiatives with America's only European ally. By early summer 1780, having been forbidden by the French minister, the comte de Vergennes, from publicly announcing his mission, Adams was drawn into quarrels with Vergennes over American currency devaluation, the level of French commitment to the naval war in North America, and of course, the status of his own appointment.

Adams was too enterprising to endure this confinement for long. His first initiative was to write several anonymous essays espousing peace with America, including *A Translation of the Memorial to the Sovereigns of Europe upon the Present State of Affairs between the Old and New World into Common Sense and Intelligible English* (based on a pamphlet by Thomas Pownall), published in 1781, and *Letters from a Distinguished American,* published in 1782, both in London. These works, while making at best a modest contribution to concluding peace with Great Britain, powerfully explain Adams's distinctive view of international relations.

In July 1780 Adams took more direct action by moving to Holland even before he received his congressional commission to the Netherlands. There, in two years of lobbying, propaganda, and negotiation, he secured recognition of the United States (April 1782), America's first Dutch loan (June), and a Treaty of Amity and Commerce (October). Meanwhile Congress, under pressure from France, had revoked his appointment as sole peace negotiator in favor of his heading a five-man commission, which it directed to consult with France in all its negotiations. But Adams promptly followed his triumph in Holland by returning to Paris and allying with commissioner John Jay to convince fellow commissioner Franklin to ignore Vergennes and conclude the preliminary treaty with Britain (November 1782) that became the definitive Treaty of Paris (September 1783).

Adams's remaining years abroad were anticlimactic but did have their rewards. In October 1783 he first visited England with his son John Quincy, and in 1784 his wife and daughter joined him in Europe. His appointment as America's first minister to the Court of St. James (Great Britain), from 1785 to 1788, proved less fruitful than his joint commission of 1784–1785, with Franklin and Jefferson in Paris, to negotiate commercial treaties with several foreign powers. Their collaboration, however, yielded only one treaty, with Prussia in 1785. (A second treaty, negotiated with Morocco by Thomas Barclay in 1786 under Jefferson's and Adams's supervision, followed Franklin's return to America.)

Adams's frustrating years in London, where the ministry of William Pitt the Younger proved uninterested in establishing friendly relations with the United States, was relieved by a visit with Abigail to Holland, where the couple witnessed the brief triumph of Adams's old friends in the republican Patriot Party over the Prince of Orange (August–September 1786). This event inspired Adams to begin his longest work, *A Defence of the Constitutions of the United States* (London, 1787–1788), a three-volume historical treatise that defended America's *state* constitutions, particularly Adams's Massachusetts Constitution of 1780, by showing the superiority of governments that distributed and balanced political power among a two-house legislature, a powerful executive, and an independent judiciary. Although *A Defence of the Constitutions of the United States* was of no help to the Dutch Patriots, who were overwhelmed by the invading Prussian army before its completion, its first volume may have afforded some inspiration to the delegates then gathering in Philadelphia to draft the U.S. Constitution. As he was completing his magnum opus, Adams, who could never persuade the Pitt ministry to negotiate a commercial treaty with America or even to resolve differences that remained outstanding under the Treaty of Paris, resigned his commissions to Britain and the Netherlands and returned to Massachusetts in the spring of 1788.

Federal executive. Again Adams thought that his public career might be at an end, but he was now less eager to resume his legal practice, and he did covet the political potential in one new office, vice president in the new federal government. This appeared to be the logical post from which to succeed the president-apparent, George Washington. In the first federal elections, held in 1788, Adams's countrymen ratified his ambition, but hardly with the unanimity they bestowed on Washington for president.

Adams's two-term vice presidency (April 1789–March 1797) keenly disappointed him. His only duty was to preside over the U.S. Senate without speaking his opinion on any issue. His occasional inability to observe this rule drew instant criticism from several senators, and his advocacy of quasi-monarchical titles for the office of president embarrassed Washington. Adams was able to assist the president by casting the greatest number of tie-breaking votes in the Senate by any vice president, but his unpopularity in the southern states and a distant relationship with Washington effectively locked him out of the president's informal counsels. Adams compounded his isolation by writing a series of newspaper essays, the *Discourses on Davila* (1790–1791), that attacked the principles of the French Revolution while praising the virtues of powerful executives, and even of monarchs.

When Washington issued his farewell address (September 1796), however, Adams was still the logical if not the inspiring choice for the general's Federalist supporters. In a close election Adams defeated his old friend and new rival, Jefferson, leader of the opposition Republicans. Adams's one-term presidency (March 1797–March 1801) was almost completely occupied with concerns over America's deteriorating relations with France and the attendant division of most Americans into fiercely anti-French (Federalist) and pro-French (Republican) factions. His great achievement as president was to prevent full-scale war and conclude his term with a lasting peace with France.

The Quasi-War with France began with the French Directory's decision to attack American neutral shipping that it saw as aiding its archenemy, Great Britain. Adams sent a peace mission to Paris, but the Directory and its foreign minister, Charles Talleyrand-Périgord, demanded humiliating terms and a secret bribe to agents labeled X, Y, and Z before negotiations could begin. In 1798, Adams revealed the bribe offer and called for raising an army and creating a permanent navy. Congress concurred and, in measures that later generations of Americans would find the most unfortunate of Adams's presidency, enacted an Alien Act to expel recent French and French-sympathizing immigrants and a Sedition Act to silence Republican newspaper editors who libeled the president and his war policy. In July, at the height of his popularity, Adams signed both measures.

Almost immediately France signaled a reassessment of its policy, and in December 1798 Adams named new peace commissioners, to be dispatched when the time was ripe. When that time came, in October 1799, Adams faced fierce criticism both from Congress and his own cabinet. By May 1800 the opposition of the Anglophilic, Francophobic High Federalists had become intolerable, and Adams forced Secretary of War James McHenry and Secretary of State Timothy Pickering from office. America's negotiators concluded a lasting peace with France with the Convention of Mortefontaine in October, but the widening split in Federalist ranks had become irreparable with the appearance of Alexander Hamilton's savage attack in his *Letter . . . Concerning the Public Conduct and Character of John Adams* (September 1800). That fall, Adams lost his bid for reelection to Jefferson.

Adams's last months in office were dismal. His second son, Charles, whose profligacy had alienated Adams, died of acute alcoholism in November 1800, just as the president occupied the still uncompleted executive mansion in Washington. He did exert a continuing Federalist influence on the government through his appointment of several new judges, notably John Marshall as chief justice of the Supreme Court. But Adams's estrangement from Jefferson prompted him to leave Washington early on inauguration day (4 March 1801) without seeing his successor take the oath of office.

Retirement and retrospective. Upon his retirement Adams felt rejected and misunderstood, especially by those who had once been close friends and allies. He crossed swords with his onetime friend and now Republican critic Mercy Otis Warren and sought to justify his career privately in his incomplete autobiography and publicly in his letters published in the *Boston Patriot* (1809–1812). Then in 1812, at the urging of his friend Benjamin Rush, Adams renewed his correspondence with Jefferson. This remarkably charitable and even-tempered exchange of views on a wide range of subjects, continuing until the eve of their deaths in 1826, characterized Adams's last years. He still faced two severe blows, the deaths of his daughter in 1813 and his wife in 1818. But the growing pride that Americans felt in their national union following the War of 1812 and the course of John Quincy Adams's brilliant career gave Adams real pleasure and assured him that the nation's grand experiment in republican government was not disintegrating quite so rapidly as he had once feared. The end came, fittingly, in Quincy on 4 July 1826, the fiftieth anniversary of the Declaration of Independence. Adams's last recorded words were: "Thomas Jefferson survives." But in fact Jefferson had died several hours before Adams, on this same bright day.

Adams was a remarkable public figure from several perspectives. He was probably the most learned of America's Founding Fathers in the fields of history, political theory, and the law, and his was an eminently practical learning. The "Atlas of Independence" in Congress was America's foremost civilian leader, its master constitutional architect in the 1770s, and its most effective diplomatic negotiator in the 1780s. Yet Adams was only rarely a popular leader, even in New England. He could work effectively with others, but his natural style was to think, write, and act on his own, often in isolation, not only in Europe but as chief executive. His presidency effectively defended America's national interests, but it was the least popular and perhaps the least important of his major contributions to his nation.

The man behind this exceptional career was equally distinctive. Socially and constitutionally conservative and viewed by his opponents as nearly a monarchist, Adams was always a moderate in his politics and a committed Revolutionary leader. In his cultural and scientific interests he was a progressive son of the Enlightenment, despite his dislike of the French philosophes. His liberal religious convictions placed him somewhere between orthodox Christianity and the deism of Franklin and Jefferson.

Adams was never close to most of his colleagues on the national stage, but in a long and often contentious public career he seems to have taken deep personal offense to just two men, Franklin during the peace negotiations in 1782–1783 and Hamilton during Adams's presidency.

Richard Alan Ryerson

See also

Adams, Abigail; Adams, Samuel; Boston, Massachusetts; Boston Massacre; Boston Tea Party; Coercive Acts; Congress, First Continental; Congress, Second Continental and Confederation; Constitutions, State; Continental Army; Continental Navy; Declaration of Independence; Franklin, Benjamin; Gravier, Charles, Comte de Vergennes; Hamilton, Alexander; Hancock, John; Howe, Richard; Hutchinson, Thomas; Jay, John; Jefferson, Thomas; Lee, Arthur; Lee, Richard Henry; *Liberty* Incident; Loyalist Exiles; Massachusetts; Netherlands; Paine, Thomas; Stamp Act; Treaty of Amity and Commerce with the Netherlands; War, Board of; Washington, George

References

Adams, John. *Diary and Autobiography of John Adams.* Edited by L. H. Butterfield. 4 vols. Cambridge: Harvard University Press, 1961.

———. *Legal Papers of John Adams.* 3 vols. Edited by L. K. Wroth and H. B. Zobel. Cambridge: Harvard University Press, 1965.

———. *Papers of John Adams.* 12 vols. to date. Edited by R. J. Taylor, G. L. Lint, and others. Cambridge: Harvard University Press, 1977–.

Adams, John, and others. *Adams Family Correspondence.* Edited by L. H. Butterfield, M. Friedlaender, R. A. Ryerson, and others. 6 vols. to date. Cambridge: Harvard University Press, 1963–.

DeConde, Alexander. *The Quasi-War: The Politics and Diplomacy of the Undeclared War with France.* New York: Scribner, 1966.

Ellis, Joseph J. *Passionate Sage: The Character and Personality of John Adams.* New York: Norton, 1993.

Ferling, John. *John Adams: A Life.* Knoxville: University of Tennessee Press, 1992.

Haraszti, Zoltan. *John Adams and the Prophets of Progress.* Cambridge: Harvard University Press, 1952.

Howe, John R., Jr. *The Changing Political Thought of John Adams.* Princeton, NJ: Princeton University Press, 1966.

Hutson, James. *John Adams and the Diplomacy of the American Revolution.* Lexington: University of Kentucky Press, 1980.

McCullough, David. *John Adams.* New York: Simon and Schuster, 2001.

Morris, Richard B. *The Peacemakers: The Great Powers and American Independence.* New York: Harper and Row, 1965.

Ryerson, Richard Alan, ed. *John Adams and the Founding of the Republic.* Boston: Massachusetts Historical Society, 2001.

Schulte Nordholt, Jan Willem. *The Dutch Republic and American Independence.* Translated by Herbert H. Rowen. Chapel Hill: University of North Carolina Press, 1982.

Shaw, Peter. *The Character of John Adams.* Chapel Hill: University of North Carolina Press, 1976.

Smith, Page. *John Adams.* 2 vols. Garden City, NY: Doubleday, 1962.

Thompson, C. Bradley. *John Adams and the Spirit of Liberty.* Lawrence: University of Kansas Press, 1998.

Wood, Gordon S. *The Creation of the American Republic, 1776–1787.* Chapel Hill: University of North Carolina Press, 1969.

Adams, Samuel (1722–1803)

Samuel Adams emerged as one of the leading figures in the American resistance to British policy after 1763. Most contemporaries, hostile and friendly alike, agreed on his significance. Thomas Hutchinson, the royal governor of Massachusetts, argued that there was no more important leader in the Revolutionary movement than Adams. When General Thomas Gage, who was both the commander of the British Army in North America and the last royal governor of Massachusetts, offered an amnesty in 1774 to all colonists who would submit to British authority, he exempted only two men: John Hancock and Samuel Adams. And when Samuel's cousin John Adams arrived in France on a diplomatic mission in 1778, he reported that everyone was disappointed to learn that he was not the "famous" Adams. Samuel Adams was probably Revolutionary America's greatest political organizer and one of its greatest propagandists.

Born on 16 September 1722, Adams was one of twelve children of Samuel Adams and Mary Fifield. His merchant father prospered through a variety of investments in Boston, including a wharf and a malt house. Young Samuel's parents sent him to Boston Latin School and to Harvard College, where they hoped he would train for the ministry. Yet although he received a bachelor's degree in 1740 and a master's degree three years later and was a deeply religious man throughout his life, Adams had no interest in becoming a clergyman. After a brief study, he also dismissed law as a career. His father found him work in a countinghouse, but its owner quickly determined that the young man had little business sense. Samuel Sr. extended his son a substantial loan, but Samuel Jr. soon lost that money. Adams did help his father in the family malt house, and he took over the family's business interests upon his father's death in 1748, but he never had any commercial success.

In 1749, Adams married Elizabeth Checkley, the daughter of the Reverend Samuel Checkley, pastor of the New South Church in Boston. The couple had six children, but only two survived to adulthood. Seven years after Elizabeth's death in 1757, Adams married Elizabeth Wells, the daughter of Boston merchant Francis Wells. The couple had no children.

In the late 1740s, Adams began his career of public service in minor municipal posts, including market clerk and town scavenger. In 1756, he became one of Boston's tax collectors, a position he held for nearly a decade. A combination of negligence and sympathy for hard-pressed taxpayers eventually left him more than £8,000 in arrears to the town. Despite this dismal record, town leaders soon recognized Adams's talents as a writer and assigned him the task of drafting the town meeting's instructions to its representatives in the provincial legislature. Adams also rapidly became a leader in the town caucus, an organization of merchants, shopkeepers, and artisans that set town meeting agendas and determined who would serve in town offices.

Samuel Adams, one of the Revolution's most famous agitators, advocated full independence from Britain, helped found the Sons of Liberty, and opposed parliamentary legislation that imposed a range of taxes on the American colonies. He served in both the First and Second Continental Congresses and was a signatory of the Declaration of Independence. (National Archives and Records Administration)

In his political activity, Adams closely followed in the footsteps of his father. Samuel Adams Sr. had been a leader in the Boston caucus for years and had served as a justice of the peace, Boston selectman, and representative in the provincial assembly. At the provincial level, Adams Sr. had been a key supporter of Elisha Cook Jr.'s Country Party that opposed the hard money policies of Boston's great merchants, led by Thomas Hutchinson, and the royal governors who supported them in the 1730s and 1740s.

Like his father, Adams was thoroughly at home in the complex political milieu of Boston. He belonged to several political clubs, both those of merchants and of artisans. He was never intimidated by the town's powerful merchants and eventually struck up an important political relationship with Hancock, one of the wealthiest and most influential citizens of Boston. While Adams disliked mobs and the violent extralegal political activity associated with them, he was always comfortable associating with Boston's artisans and often frequented their favorite taverns. Indeed, the always plainly dressed and rather rumpled Adams came to see himself as a defender of these working men.

In assuming an ever greater role in town government, Adams revealed the political thought that drove his commitment to public service. There were many sources of his beliefs, but they all began with his faith. A deeply pious man who regularly attended church all his life, Adams believed that God required more from his followers than mere avoidance of sin. He shared with the Puritans of the previous century an assurance that Americans had a mission to create a virtuous society, one in which the people were temperate, hardworking, and frugal but above all were willing to subordinate self-interest to the needs of the community. By embracing piety and virtue, Adams hoped that America could become a Christian Sparta.

In college, Adams read widely in political theory, but the works of John Locke particularly attracted him. Persuaded by Locke's argument that civil society rested on a contract, or, in Puritan language, a covenant, between the government and the people, Adams, like Locke, saw government's chief obligation as the protection of man's natural rights to life, liberty, and property. Should rulers fail to offer this protection, the people had not just a right but an obligation to rebel. As an undergraduate, Adams organized a debate on liberty, and for his master's thesis he defended the right of citizens to resist a repressive government. He developed these ideas further in the late 1740s in debates with friends in a club dedicated to the discussion of public issues and in his contributions to a newspaper called the *Independent Advertiser.* Ultimately, Adams concluded that liberty was always threatened by power, and, as a consequence, government could be entrusted only to virtuous men.

From his introduction into town politics and his father's considerable experience, Adams concluded that local government was most important in preserving the rights of citizens. He had learned the perils of being controlled by a distant government at a young age. His father had helped lead the province's Country Party to create a land bank that issued paper money to borrowers who secured their loans with their real estate. In 1741, in response to heavy lobbying efforts by Massachusetts merchants who favored a harder currency backed only by gold or silver, Parliament dissolved the land bank, leaving the directors, including Adams's father, liable for the institution's debts. A decade after his father's death in 1748, Adams was still struggling against the county sheriff's attempts to seize his father's estate to pay those debts.

Pious, well read, politically active, well connected, and committed to a defense of his deeply held principles, Adams was thoroughly prepared to play a key role in the American resistance to Britain's new imperial policies after 1763. Following its victory that year over France in the Seven Years' War, the British government had sought ways to fund the escalating costs of maintaining its expanded North American empire. Faced with growing resistance to heavier taxation in Britain, George Grenville, first lord of the Treasury, concluded that he must run the empire more efficiently and raise revenue in the colonies. He began in 1764 by gaining parliamentary approval of a Sugar Act that reduced the tax on foreign molasses imported into colonies. A thirty-year-old Molasses Act had imposed a prohibitively high tax that had led to widespread smuggling. The new law cut the tax in half but with stricter enforcement that was intended to produce revenue for imperial coffers. The following year Parliament passed the Stamp Act, which required revenue stamps on a whole range of paper products from legal documents to playing cards. When the inhabitants of several colonies defied the act, Parliament repealed it but in 1767 imposed the Townshend Acts, new duties on lead, paper, paint, and tea imported into the colonies. The British government also dispatched two regiments to Boston in 1768 to impose order and support its customs officers following the *Liberty* riot.

In 1764, when Adams drafted the town meeting's instructions to Boston's delegates in the House of Representatives, he denounced Parliament's efforts to raise revenue in the colonies through the Sugar Act. Colonists were not represented in the House of Commons, and Adams asserted that the Massachusetts Charter gave them the right to govern themselves. His strong statement and growing visibility led to his election to the House of Representatives in 1765, where he served for nearly a decade and swiftly emerged as Massachusetts's leading voice against changes in British imperial policies. The House quickly selected Adams as its clerk, which allowed him to craft petitions, resolutions, and letters denouncing the Stamp Act.

Adams also continued his informal agitation in Boston's clubs and taverns and along the docks, mobilizing popular opposition to British policy. Although he was not a member of Boston's Loyal Nine, an organization that became the town's Sons of Liberty, he supported the public demonstrations they organized to intimidate stamp distributor Andrew Oliver into resigning his post. When a mob subsequently destroyed the home of Lieutenant Governor Thomas Hutchinson, however, Adams joined other town leaders in condemning the violence. This instance and others reveal his reluctance to sanction violence in seeking the redress of grievances. He consistently saw it as a last resort when all other approaches had failed. Yet violent protests did force stamp distributors throughout the colonies to resign their commissions and, along with a series of protests contesting the constitutionality of the tax, led Parliament to repeal the Stamp Act in 1766.

In the three years following passage of the Townshend duties, Adams, in newspaper articles and town meeting debates, called upon citizens to join in and maintain a boycott of British imports. He urged them to embrace the virtuous path of sacrifice and simplicity and to forgo luxury and extravagance. In 1768, as clerk of the Massachusetts House, Adams drafted the first circular letter to other colonial assemblies; it denounced Parliament's taxes on the colonies as unconstitutional. As Adams agitated for an effective boycott, he learned of the British decision to dispatch troops to Boston, news that aroused his worst fears. Political opposition writers in England, such as the early-eighteenth-century essayists John Trenchard and Thomas Gordon, had argued that a standing army was the most ominous threat to liberty; Adams agreed with them. In dozens of newspaper articles written under a host of pen names and in frequent visits to taverns and political clubs, he condemned the decision to place troops in Boston and urged Bostonians to resist, at first to no avail.

After British soldiers fired into a threatening Boston crowd, killing five people, in March 1770, Adams headed a delegation to Lieutenant Governor Thomas Hutchinson to demand the removal of the troops from the town. After the governor acquiesced, Adams spent weeks spreading the word throughout the colonies of the "massacre" in Boston. Yet he fully supported giving the soldiers arrested for firing into the crowd a fair trial (where they were ably defended by Samuel's cousin, John Adams) to demonstrate the virtue of Bostonians, even in the face of such barbarity. With the conviction of two of the soldiers for manslaughter (resulting in branding, not execution) and the acquittal of the others, and with Parliament's repeal of all the Townshend duties except the one on tea, Adams's fellow citizens cooled in their enthusiasm for continued resistance to British rule.

Adams nonetheless continued to warn of the British threat to liberty in newspaper articles, and he promoted an annual oratorical commemoration of the Boston Massacre as a vivid reminder of the dangers that governmental power posed to citizens' rights. It was in this brief "quiet period" in the tumultuous decade before the Boston Tea Party, from 1771 to mid-1773, that Adams did some of his most creative work. In 1772 he persuaded Boston's town meeting to create a committee of correspondence to unite the province in defying the British. The following year, Adams began extending this network of committees of correspondence into neighboring colonies.

For some time, Adams had been persuaded that there was a conspiracy in the British government to destroy liberty in the colonies. He regarded the principal officeholders in Lord North's ministry as the antithesis of the virtuous men who should be in power: a cabal of British ministers and their minions in the colonies who were deliberately subordinating the natural rights of the colonists to the interests of a corrupted British Empire. In 1773, Adams came into possession of what he considered proof of a conspiracy against liberty. Benjamin Franklin, the Massachusetts House's agent in London, sent Adams some alarming letters that he had obtained. The letters, written to British officials by Massachusetts's former governor, Francis Bernard, and current governor, Thomas Hutchinson, called for limitations on the colonists' liberties.

Samuel Adams, a delegate from Massachusetts to the First Continental Congress, played a leading part in the anti-British agitation that preceded the Revolution and helped organize the Boston Tea Party. (National Archives and Records Administration)

After seeing to the publication of several of these letters in the Boston press and calling upon the king to recall Hutchinson, Adams turned his attention to a new piece of British legislation, the Tea Act. Intended as a way to raise revenue in the colonies while helping the nearly bankrupt East India Company, the law allowed the company to ship tea directly to the colonies. This permitted the company to avoid paying a large import tax normally levied in England and to sell its tea in the colonies exclusively through merchants, or consignees, that it selected rather than through public auctions. These provisions would lower the cost of tea to colonial consumers. Vigilant revolutionaries such as Adams saw the act as a ploy to get colonists to accept Parliament's taxing power through their purchase of cheap tea. Mass opposition meetings forced the resignation of tea consignees in Philadelphia, New York, and Charleston, but in Boston Governor Hutchinson refused to grant the tea ships a clearance to return to London until they had unloaded their cargoes and paid the duty. When a packed meeting received Hutchinson's final refusal, on 16 December 1773, Adams announced that nothing more could be done to save the country, an apparent signal for several dozen men, dressed as Indians, to board the tea ships and toss their cargoes overboard.

The British response to the Boston Tea Party triggered a chain of events that led to the American Revolution. Parliament passed a series of acts that the colonists labeled "Coercive" or "Intolerable," including closing the port of Boston until the town had paid for the destroyed tea and unilaterally altering the Massachusetts Charter to limit town meetings to one session per year. To Adams, these punitive measures directed at Massachusetts were a warning to all colonists of the vulnerability of liberty. In September 1774, he joined delegates from twelve colonies at the First Continental Congress in Philadelphia to plan their opposition to British policy. Adams ardently supported Congress's boycott of all British imports and helped draft its Declaration of Rights.

When Congress adjourned Adams returned to Massachusetts, where he won election in February 1775 to an extralegal provincial congress that met first in Cambridge and then in Concord and immediately became the de facto government of the province. Adams was staying at nearby Lexington with Hancock on the morning of 19 April 1775 when Paul Revere gave them sufficient warning to escape the approaching British troops who had been directed to arrest them and seize military supplies in Concord. Adams, however, did not leave the area but remained nearby to shape the sensational broadsides that announced the battles at Lexington and Concord to the world.

In May 1775, Adams was back in Philadelphia to attend the Second Continental Congress, where he served until 1780. Beyond working diligently for independence, Adams faithfully served on several congressional committees. He also continued to serve the citizens of Massachusetts, most notably in helping write and secure passage of a new state constitution (1780), one based firmly on the principle that all power came from the people. In all these political arenas, Adams proved to be a masterful politician. Although not an effective speaker, he was a superb organizer who tirelessly worked to build coalitions to support the war effort.

As he watched the struggles of the Continental Army and dealt with the frustrations in his work both as a state senator and as a congressman, Adams remained confident in the ultimate success of the new American republic. Ironically, this man who had promoted so much extralegal political activity prior to American independence judged such actions after the Revolutionary War as threats to America's new republican governments, both at the federal and state levels. He believed that America's republics provided peaceful means for redressing the grievances of all citizens. Indeed, he reasoned, since popular elections were available, aggrieved groups no longer needed to resort to popular protests. In 1787 he supported the suppression of the uprising of Massachusetts farmers in Shays's Rebellion. Enduring a postwar depression and lacking sufficient currency to pay their mounting debts, farmers petitioned the state government for relief. When legislative leaders refused, armed men, led by Revolutionary War veteran Daniel Shays, closed some courts in western Massachusetts to stop the legal proceedings against indebted farmers. The state militia, with Adams's blessing, quickly put down the rebellion.

Adams also worried that too many Americans failed to resist extravagance and immorality and too often placed self-interest above the general good. When he saw these very traits displayed by Hancock in the latter's unrelenting quest for high office and an ever more opulent lifestyle, he almost ended his friendship with his longtime Revolutionary ally. Most importantly, Adams remained persuaded that power always threatened liberty and that power concentrated in a distant national government was a grave danger to America's local republics. He supported the weak national government created by the Articles of Confederation in 1777 and viewed the 1787 Constitution with great skepticism, fearing that the government it created would undermine liberty. Nonetheless, when he was elected to the Massachusetts ratification convention, Adams listened carefully to the debate and ultimately supported the document, but only when persuaded that it would be amended to protect basic liberties.

Through all the tribulations of the Revolutionary era, Adams never lost his faith in the people. He knew that they might not always act correctly and that they might often stray from the virtuous life. Yet Adams remained confident that all property-owning citizens shared an essential commitment to a republican form of government. Once the Revolution ended, Adams promoted a number of reforms to ensure a republican future. Believing that an educated citizenry was critical in preserving rights and liberties, Adams worked to ensure that the Town of Boston educated its children, both boys and girls, of all social classes. He also felt it essential that Massachusetts promote morality as a key to the preservation of republican government. He supported the state constitution's requirement that the governor be a Christian and that the established Congregational Church, along with other churches that enjoyed significant local support, continue to receive revenue from public taxation. Indeed, Adams may have been the author of this establishment clause, which the constitution's principal author, his cousin John Adams, declined to write.

Rarely out of office, Adams continued to hold a succession of political posts after the American Revolution. In the 1780s and 1790s, he served as a state senator, lieutenant governor, and finally governor, from which post he retired in 1797. In national politics Adams became a Jeffersonian republican and in presidential contests supported Jefferson against his admiring younger cousin, John Adams. Adams died in Boston on 2 October 1803.

Larry Gragg

See also

Boston, Massachusetts; Boston Massacre; Boston Tea Party; Coercive Acts; Congress, Second Continental and Confederation; Constitutions, State; Correspondence, Committees of; Customs Commissioners, Board of; Hancock, John; Hutchinson, Thomas; Lexington and Concord; *Liberty* Incident; Massachusetts; Nonimportation Agreements; Sons of Liberty; Stamp Act; Suffolk Resolves; Tea Act; Townshend Acts

References

Alexander, John K. *Samuel Adams: America's Revolutionary Politician.* Lanham, MD: Rowman and Littlefield, 2002.

Ammerman, David. *In the Common Cause: American Response to the Coercive Acts of 1774.* New York: Norton, 1975.

Brown, Richard D. *Revolutionary Politics in Massachusetts: The Boston Committee of Correspondence and the Towns, 1772–1774.* Cambridge: Harvard University Press, 1970.

Brown, Robert Eldon. *Middle-Class Democracy and the Revolution in Massachusetts, 1691–1780.* Ithaca, NY: Cornell University Press, 1955.

Canfield, Cass. *Samuel Adams's Revolution, 1775–1776.* New York: Harper and Row, 1976.

Fowler, William M. *Samuel Adams: Radical Puritan.* New York: Longman, 1997.

Labaree, Benjamin Woods. *The Boston Tea Party.* New York: Oxford University Press, 1964.

Maier, Pauline. *From Resistance to Revolution: Colonial Radicals and the Development of American Opposition to Britain, 1765–1776.* New York: Knopf, 1972.

———. *The Old Revolutionaries: Political Lives in the Age of Samuel Adams.* New York: Knopf, 1980.

Miller, John Chester. *Sam Adams: Pioneer in Propaganda.* Stanford, CA: Stanford University Press, 1936.

Nash, Gary B. *The Urban Crucible: Social Change, Political Consciousness and the Origins of the American Revolution.* Cambridge: Harvard University Press, 1979.

Administration of Justice Act (1774)

Presented in Parliament by Lord North's ministry on 15 April 1774 in response to the Boston Tea Party, the Administration of Justice Act was one of the five statutes approved in the spring of 1774 that became known as the "Coercive Acts" or "Intolerable Acts" in America. This statute was specifically referred to in rebellious Massachusetts as the "Murderers' Act" or "Murder Act." It provided that royal officials such as customs officers, soldiers, and magistrates who were charged with capital offenses committed in the line of duty in Massachusetts could be sent by the governor to another colony for trial or to Great Britain for trial in the Court of King's Bench in London.

Supporters argued that the bill simply gave the province's royal governor discretion to grant a change of venue for officials charged with serious offenses committed while suppressing riots and other lawlessness when a fair trial was determined to be unobtainable before prejudiced local juries, especially Boston juries. Furthermore, the bill itself expressed the reasoning that the mere existence of the law would "remove every such discouragement from the minds of his Majesty's subjects, and . . . induce them, upon all proper occasions, to exert themselves in support of the public peace of the province, and of the authority of the King and parliament of Great Britain over the same." Opponents felt that it was an ill-timed and inflammatory proposal more concerned with punishing and insulting Massachusetts than with the impartial administration of justice. Many colonists saw it as the usurpation of another fundamental right of local governance and the thwarting of justice altogether.

The bill met with considerable debate in the House of Commons. Colonel Isaac Barré argued to the House that the bill was "full of evil." On 15 April, during the initial consideration of the bill and of its companion legislation, the Massachusetts Government Act, Parliament member Rose Fuller, believing that no coercive steps in the colonies could succeed while the Townshend duty on tea remained, announced to the House that he would move to repeal the duty and did so on 19 April. Fuller swiftly received the support of Edmund Burke during a speech on the taxation of America. Despite the small yet vocal opposition, the bill eventually passed on 6 May by a vote of 127–24. After approval by the House of Lords on 20 May, the king signed the bill on the same day.

In America, John Hancock declared that the law protected "bloodsuckers." One agitator asserted: "[any evildoer] who ravishes our wives [and] deflowers our daughters can evade punishment by being tried in Britain, where no evidence can pursue him." This measure, along with the other Coercive Acts, was declared unconstitutional in Massachusetts's Suffolk Resolves, in the Declaration and Resolves of the First Continental Congress, and in the Declaration of Independence.

Russell Fowler

See also

Barré, Isaac; Boston, Massachusetts; Boston Tea Party; British Parliament; Burke, Edmund; Coercive Acts; Congress, First Continental; George III, King of England; Hancock, John; Massachusetts; Massachusetts Government Act; North, Lord Frederick; Suffolk Resolves; Townshend Acts

References

Greene, Jack P., ed. *Colonies to Nation, 1763–1789: A Documentary History of the American Revolution.* New York: Norton, 1975.

Hawke, David. *The Colonial Experience.* Indianapolis: Bobbs-Merrill, 1966.

African Americans

See Slaves and Free Blacks

Albany Congress (19 June–10 July 1754)

The Albany Congress of 1754 was the British Crown's most ambitious attempt to bring order to Indian affairs in British North America by enlisting the aid and counsel of both colonial and Indian leaders. Although the congress failed to achieve this objective, it did produce the first major proposal for a governmental organization in America that would unite all of Britain's North American colonies.

The British Crown felt obligated to summon the congress because the Mohawk Indians had symbolically severed the Anglo-Iroquois alliance in 1753. This alliance, known as the Covenant Chain, had been a linchpin of British military strategy in North America. It was one reason the British were able to avoid quartering troops in the colonies in peacetime. Hoping to repair the situation, the British government called for colonial and Iroquois leaders to meet at Albany, New York, in June 1754 to resolve the issues, specifically land complaints, that had led the Mohawks to renounce the Covenant Chain. Seven colonies—New York, Pennsylvania, Maryland, and all of the New England colonies—sent delegates.

The Albany Congress occurred against the backdrop of George Washington's first armed conflict with the French and their Indian allies in the forests of western Pennsylvania. By the time the congress ended in early July, Washington had surrendered his small force at the Great Meadow (Fort Necessity) to the French. Although the British officials, colonial delegates, and Iroquois chieftains who met at Albany did not know it, the final struggle between Britain and France for control of North America had just begun. It was in preparing for possible conflict with France that the British government had taken note of the deteriorating relations between her colonists and those Indian nations traditionally allied with Great Britain.

Traditional interpretations of the Albany Congress emphasized the delegates' attempt to create the first extraconstitutional government for all the colonies and noted the similarity of the Albany Plan of Union's proposed grand council to the Continental Congress that came into existence just over twenty years later. More recent scholarship has placed less

Bearing the inscription "Join, or Die," this engraving of 1754 by Benjamin Franklin urges the British North American colonies to establish a loose union. The plan would empower a council to raise taxes, monitor the western frontier, and work together with British officials on matters of Indian affairs and defense. While it never came to pass, the plan represented an early example of some colonists' ideas on establishing a union among otherwise disparate territories. (Library of Congress)

emphasis on America's nation-building process and more on the effort to set the limits of both local and centralized power in the British Empire. These limits were intended to define not only imperial-colonial relations but also relations between Euro-Americans and Native Americans.

In an effort to address Mohawk complaints about the colonists' aggressive pursuit of new land, colonial delegates began to debate Pennsylvania delegate Benjamin Franklin's "short hints towards a scheme for uniting the Northern Colonies." Massachusetts delegate Thomas Hutchinson brought his own draft of a proposal for placing Indian affairs beyond the control of individual colonies by creating some kind of intercolonial organization. A full debate over these preliminary plans led to the Albany Plan of Union, for which the Albany Congress is most famous. The proposal that emerged at Albany would create a new colonial-wide government, consisting of a governor-general appointed and paid by the British Crown and a grand council composed of delegates chosen by the several British North American colonies. Colonial delegations would vary in size according to the contribution to the common defense made by each colony. This government would have control over treaty making, the Indian trade, and any declaration of war that involved the Indians and would also oversee the settlement of western lands.

Fearing the considerable powers of such a government, not a single colony accepted the Albany Plan of Union brought back to them by their delegates. Seven colonial legislatures officially voted the plan down, while the others let the events of the Seven Years' War overtake any concern about the Albany proposal. Britain's Board of Trade, for its own reasons, chose to reject the plan as well, and the failure of the colonial delegates to resolve Indian land complaints at Albany led the Board of Trade to reconsider Indian affairs in general. When it dispatched General Edward Braddock to Virginia in the spring of 1755, he carried with him instructions naming William Johnson Britain's Indian agent for the northern colonies, thereby initiating a struggle with several colonies over who was to control Indian affairs in the future—the Crown or the colonial governments. This struggle was not resolved until the American War for Independence.

Michael Mullin

See also

Franklin, Benjamin; Hutchinson, Thomas; Johnson, Sir William; Native Americans; Trade, Board of; Washington, George

References

Richter, Daniel K. *The Ordeal of the Longhouse: The Peoples of the Iroquois League in the Era of European Colonization.* Chapel Hill: University of North Carolina Press, 1992.

Richter, Daniel K., and James H. Merrell, eds. *Beyond the Covenant Chain: The Iroquois and Their Neighbors in Indian North America, 1600–1800.* Syracuse, NY: Syracuse University Press, 1987.

Shannon, Timothy J. *Indians and Colonists at the Crossroads of Empire: The Albany Congress of 1754.* Ithaca, NY: Cornell University Press, 2000.

Alexander, William (1726–1783)

William Alexander, a Continental Army officer who claimed to be the 6th Earl of Stirling, was a ruddy, heavyset, trustworthy soldier and a likable, decent man whose outgoing personality expressed his optimistic nature. He grew up in considerable opulence in New York City, the son of James Alexander, an eminent lawyer and politician, and Mary Spratt Provoost, daughter of a rich, successful merchant. In 1748 he married Sarah Livingston, the daughter of Philip Livingston, heir to the wealth, social position, and political power of the Livingstons of New Jersey. In 1752 Alexander became a member of the Whig Club, a group of young men who espoused principles of liberty and composed manifestos. He joined Governor William Shirley of Massachusetts in 1754 as private secretary and aide and during the Niagara

William Alexander, also known as Lord Stirling. In command of Continental Army forces in New York City, he oversaw the construction of Forts Washington and Lee. He fought in many battles and was captured at Long Island, though later exchanged. He is thought to have exposed the so-called Conway Cabal against George Washington. Alexander played a prominent role in the court-martial of General Charles Lee in 1778. (Library of Congress)

Campaign of 1755–1756, which Shirley commanded, and was in charge of the army's commissariat. In 1756 Alexander went to England seeking payment of bills accrued during the previous campaign and to defend Shirley, who was under attack for his conduct as commander. Alexander succeeded with his financial claims but not in his defense of Shirley, who lost his governorship and army command.

Alexander lived in Britain for the next five years, luxuriating in the lifestyle of landed aristocrats and befriending many highly placed Scotsmen. Early in his stay he determined to seek title to the lapsed Scots earldom of Stirling by becoming the sixth earl. Vanity played a part in his quest, but Alexander also wanted to lay claim to a huge tract of land in Canada and New York given to the first earl and an undischarged debt of £7,000, plus interest, owed by James II to earlier Alexanders. After spending prodigious sums pursuing the title, Alexander finally had to rely on the memories of two old men to affirm his descent from John Alexander, uncle of the first earl. A Scottish jury in Edinburgh was willing to accept this tenuous claim, but when it went to the House of Lords for final confirmation, the committee on privileges rejected it. Nevertheless, Alexander continued to claim and use the title of 6th Earl of Stirling to the end of his days and was so recognized in America.

In 1756 Alexander's father died, and he inherited social prestige, various offices, and an estate valued at £100,000. He became surveyor-general of New York and New Jersey and was appointed to the councils of both colonies. Having supported King's College (Columbia University) for years, he was appointed a governor of that institution. Emulating his British friends, he lived as a country gentleman and invested in various schemes such as iron smelting and grape cultivation. He was interested in science and was a contributing member of the American Philosophical Society and the Royal Society of Arts. A poor money manager, he wasted his entire fortune in less than twenty years. By 1772 he was destitute and was unsuccessfully attempting to recoup his losses with a lottery. He also developed a drinking problem. During the 1760s he supported British attempts to control the colonies and even urged the Board of Trade to be more forceful. However, when the Revolution began, he declared his support for the American rebels and in September 1775 was appointed colonel and given command of a New Jersey militia regiment. On 7 November he was promoted to colonel of the New Jersey Continentals and on 22 January 1776 captured a British armed transport.

In February 1776 Alexander was ordered to join General Charles Lee at New York. When Lee was sent south to Charleston in March, Alexander assumed command of New York and worked diligently to improve the city's defenses. On 1 March he was promoted to brigadier general. When General George Washington arrived in April, Alexander was relieved of this duty. At the Battle of Long Island on 27 August he was in command of the American right wing and reserves. Taken captive by the British, he was exchanged on 6 October and rejoined Washington's army. He was present at the Battle of White Plains on 28 October but took no direct part in the fighting. He participated in the retreat of the American army across New Jersey in November and December. On 26 December he commanded a brigade in the Battle of Trenton in which the Hessians were routed. He took charge of American troops at Basking Ridge, New Jersey, in early February and on the 19th was promoted to major general. On 26 June 1777 he was roughly handled by the British in the action at Metuchen and was compelled to retreat in haste. He commanded the reserves in the Battle of Brandywine on 11 September and committed them at a strategic time during the fight to avert a disaster. He also conducted himself well in the Battle of Germantown on 4 October. After spending the winter at Valley Forge, he fought in the Battle of Monmouth, 28 June 1778, placing his division's artillery with great effect to retard a British advance and later repulsing an assault on his flank. He chaired the court-martial of Charles Lee in July and in 1779 assisted Major Henry Lee in an attack on Paulus Hook, New Jersey. In January 1780, Alexander organized and led a raid on Staten Island. He was given an independent command at Albany, New York, in 1781 with instructions to defend Fort Ticonderoga from a potential British attack. No attack materialized, and his duties were not onerous. Alexander died on duty of a virulent and painful attack of the gout.

Paul David Nelson

See also

Brandywine, Battle of; Germantown, Battle of; Long Island, Battle of; Monmouth, Battle of; Paulus Hook, New Jersey, Action at; Trenton, Battle of

References

Duer, William Alexander. *The Life of William Alexander, Earl of Stirling: Major General in the Army of the United States, during the Revolution.* New York: Wiley and Putnam, 1847.

Nelson, Paul David. *William Alexander, Lord Stirling.* University: University of Alabama Press, 1987.

Schumacher, Ludwig. *Major-General the Earl of Stirling: An Essay in Biography.* New York: New Amsterdam, 1897.

Valentine, Alan. *Lord Stirling.* New York: Oxford University Press, 1969.

Allen, Ethan (1738–1789)

Land speculator, soldier, frontier rebel, backwoods Deist philosopher, Ethan Allen of Vermont was one of the most colorful and interesting individuals of the Revolutionary generation. Other leaders such as George Washington and Philip Schuyler admired him while at the same time mistrusting him as being unpredictable and radical. Allen was a frontiersman with practically no formal education, referring to himself as a clodhopper philosopher, but he was a self-taught writer and thinker. He learned primarily by talking with other

Ethan Allen. Commander of the Green Mountain Boys, he captured Fort Ticonderoga in 1775 but was taken prisoner during the march to Montreal. After being exchanged, he returned to duty, ultimately rising to the rank of general in the Vermont militia. (Library of Congress)

men, particularly Thomas Young, a physician in Albany, New York, who introduced him to the ideas of John Locke and the Deists. Born in Connecticut, Allen served in the French and Indian War for two weeks in 1757 at Fort William Henry. He began operating an iron forge in Salisbury, Connecticut, in 1762 but was driven off in 1765 because of his Deism. He settled in Northampton, Massachusetts, but in 1767 was forced to leave there as well.

In 1770, Allen moved to the Green Mountains in the New Hampshire Grants, controlled by New York and later to become Vermont. He began speculating in land and soon was leading local opposition to New York's authority over the Grants. In 1771, he organized the Green Mountain Boys, a sort of vigilante group with himself as colonel commandant, to defy New York's claims to their land. Governor William Tryon of New York offered a reward of £100 for Allen's capture. In numerous publications Allen evinced a flair as a propagandist, arguing that land possession should accrue to those who settled and tilled it, not to holders of vague titles. He and his followers were seen as heroes by their neighbors but as a mob of abandoned wretches by New York and British authorities. In April 1775, he was appointed with others to petition the king for a separate government for the Grants; a month later, the British government began planning a military expedition to suppress the Green Mountain Boys.

News of the fighting at Lexington and Concord brought an abrupt halt to altercations between Allen and the New Yorkers. He was willing to unite with his former enemies against a common enemy, Britain. Taking up the mantle of military leadership, he and the Green Mountain Boys cooperated with Colonel Benedict Arnold of Connecticut in capturing Fort Ticonderoga on 10 May 1775. Suddenly a war hero, he was appointed by Congress commander of the Green Mountain Regiment of the Continental Army. But his own men refused to accept the appointment, voting instead to give the command to Seth Warner. Allen recruited another small force with which he attempted to capture Montreal on 25 September, operating independently and ahead of General Richard Montgomery's army. Taken prisoner, Allen was sent to England and thrown into Pendennis Castle. Over the next two years, he endured harsh captivity aboard prison hulks and in a New York City jail, under threat of being hanged as a traitor. But the British government, fearing reprisals, finally exchanged him on 6 May 1778. Although a debilitated man, he reported to General George Washington at Valley Forge and on 14 May was breveted a colonel in the Continental Army. Quickly Allen returned to the Green Mountains, where he wrote *Narrative of Colonel Ethan Allen's Captivity* (1779), a best-selling work that excoriated the British and urged the Americans not to falter in their fight for independence. It went through eight editions.

While Allen was in captivity, Vermont declared itself an independent state. New York continued to resist the idea. Twice between 1778 and 1781 Allen unsuccessfully urged Congress to accept Vermont's claims. He commanded the Vermont militia from 1778 to 1784 with the rank of major general, intermittently conducting harassing operations against New York settlers. Disgusted with both New York and Congress, Allen and his brothers, Ira and Levi, opened a correspondence with General Frederick Haldimand, commander of British forces in Canada, even though that officer represented a country at war with America. The subject of discussion was a treaty that would make Vermont an autonomous province of the British Empire. It is unclear whether the Allens were seriously considering this option or whether they simply were putting pressure on Congress and New York to allow Vermont to become a state. In any case, they had broken off negotiations by 1784, and a few years later New York finally abandoned attempts to claim Vermont. It was not until 1791, after Allen had died, that Vermont finally achieved admission to the Union as a state.

In his later years, Allen lived peacefully with his family as a prosperous landowner, devoting his time to composing a book, *Reason the Only Oracle of Man; Or, A Compendious System of Natural Religion,* which was published in Bennington in 1784. Partly directed to pointing out what he maintained to be the illogic of the Christian religion, partly to arguing for a Deistic religion of nature, the book was a scandal. Many Americans were disgusted with Allen's arguments, considering them to be atheistic, and his previous high standing as a Revolutionary Patriot was weakened. Many copies of the book were destroyed in a fire at the printer's, generally believed to have been deliberately set by Allen's opponents. Most of the rest were burned by the printer himself because of their controversial content. Allen's only disappointment over the book not being more widely read was that it did not create even more controversy. In 1786, he helped squatters in the Wyoming Valley of Pennsylvania gain ownership of their land. When he died in 1789, despite his controversiality, he was given a stirring military funeral by his neighbors.

Paul David Nelson

See also

Fort Ticonderoga, New York; Green Mountain Boys; Haldimand, Frederick; Locke, John; Prisoners of War; Tryon, William; Vermont

References

Bellesiles, Michael A. *Revolutionary Outlaws: Ethan Allen and the Struggle for Independence on the Early American Frontier.* Charlottesville: University of Virginia Press, 1993.

Holbrook, Stewart H. *Ethan Allen.* New York: Macmillan, 1940.

Jellison, Charles. *Ethan Allen: Frontier Rebel.* Syracuse, NY: Syracuse University Press, 1969.

Pell, John. *Ethan Allen.* Boston: Houghton Mifflin, 1929.

Alligator Creek, East Florida, Action at (30 June 1778)

The skirmish at Alligator Creek, also known as Alligator Swamp, occurred on 30 June 1778, during a Patriot offensive in British-held East Florida. A Patriot force under Continental Army General Robert Howe moved southward through Georgia in the summer of 1778. The force, consisting of nearly 3,000 men, included Continental soldiers, militia from Georgia and South Carolina, and a naval flotilla. Howe's troops moved south toward Florida as the summer weather became very oppressive. The heat, lack of available food, and malaria took their toll on Howe's men, but they continued to move slowly toward the South.

The British troops withdrew before the Patriot invasion while a Loyalist force known as Brown's Rangers, led by Colonel Thomas Brown, watched for a Patriot attempt to cross St. Mary's River. Following Howe's successful crossing of the river, the British abandoned Fort Tonyn, a small fortification along the river. However, Brown's Rangers, numbering approximately 150 men, remained behind Patriot lines to harass their advance. Meanwhile, British Major Mark Prevost, the brother of General Augustine Prevost, erected a small redoubt at the Alligator Creek bridge to help slow the Patriots under Howe.

On 30 June 1778, a 300-man Patriot force under militia Colonel Elijah Clarke of Georgia spotted Brown's Rangers and gave chase. The outnumbered Loyalists headed for the relative safety of the British redoubt at Alligator Creek with Clarke's men in hot pursuit. Upon reaching the British redoubt, Brown's men dashed through the post with the Georgian Patriots on their heels. Both Loyalists and Patriots wore civilian clothes rather than military uniforms, leading the British soldiers defending the redoubt to assume that Clarke's men were the last element of Brown's Rangers, whose vanguard had just rode past their position. To add to the confusion, Clarke did not realize that he had ridden into a British post.

Chaos erupted when the two forces realized they had mistaken the identity of their opposition. The British soldiers opened fire, forcing Clarke's men to halt their pursuit of Brown, who in turn wheeled his force and struck the Patriot flank. Clarke, who received a wound in the engagement, managed to organize his men and flee the scene, leaving approximately thirteen dead. Two British regulars and two members of Brown's Rangers also died in the engagement.

Howe's 1778 offensive into Florida also met defeat as sickness and disease continued to decimate the Patriot ranks. Howe ordered his men to reverse their course and withdraw back toward South Carolina. Many Patriots died during the retreat, and stragglers were captured by Brown's Rangers and Native Americans supporting the British cause. Howe's offensive was the last Patriot attempt to invade Florida and was followed by a British counteroffensive in the fall that eventually led to the capture of Savannah in December 1778.

Terry M. Mays

See also

Clarke, Elijah; Florida, East and West; Savannah, Georgia, British Capture of

References

Lumpkin, Henry. *From Savannah to Yorktown: The American Revolution in the South.* New York: Paragon, 1981.

Wright, J. Leitch. *Florida in the American Revolution.* Gainesville: University Press of Florida, 1975.

Alsop, John (1724–1794)

A prosperous New York City merchant and prominent representative in the colonial legislature, John Alsop served in the Continental Congress from 1774 to 1776.

Alsop began his involvement in the Revolution by leading protests against the Townshend duties of 1767 and served in 1770 as a member of the Committee of Inspection to enforce New York City's nonimportation agreement against those taxes. In 1774 he was chosen as a member of the Committee of Fifty-One, which sought to unite the colony in resisting

Great Britain. He was elected deputy chairman of the committee at its first meeting on 23 May 1774.

In that same year, taxpayers elected Alsop, along with Philip Livingston, Isaac Low, James Duane, and John Jay, as a delegate from the City and County of New York to the First Continental Congress. Alsop was one of the fifty-two delegates who signed the Articles of Association on 20 October 1774, and in May 1775 he was appointed to New York's Committee of One Hundred, which enforced the Continental Association. Reelected to the Second Continental Congress, he was present at its first session on 10 May 1775. Alsop became an active member of Congress's Secret Committee and, drawing on his merchant connections, played an important role in procuring and distributing gunpowder, clothing, food, horses, and other supplies to the troops. Much of his work was directed toward ensuring continued supplies by processing and paying invoices received from merchants.

Although Alsop supported much of the Revolutionary agenda, he also retained a loyalty to the Crown. When the Second Continental Congress adopted the Declaration of Independence in 1776, Alsop declined to sign and resigned his seat. In his resignation letter to the New York Provincial Congress, dated 16 July 1776, he explained that independence was against his "judgment and inclination" and that he was willing to serve as a delegate only "as long as a door was left open for a reconciliation with Great Britain, upon honorable and just terms." The New York Provincial Congress accepted Alsop's resignation and conveyed the news to Philadelphia.

After British forces occupied New York City in September, Alsop withdrew with his family to Middletown, Connecticut, to await peace. Following the war, Alsop returned to New York and became a Federalist. He served as the president of the New York Chamber of Commerce in 1784 and 1785. Alsop died in 1794 and is interred in Trinity Church Cemetery in New York City.

Jason Mazzone

See also

Congress, First Continental; Congress, Second Continental and Confederation; Continental Association; New York City; Nonimportation Agreements

References

Ketchum, Richard M. *Divided Loyalties: How the American Revolution Came to New York.* New York: Holt, 2002.

Mason, Bernard. *The Road to Independence: The Revolutionary Movement in New York, 1773–1777.* Lexington: University of Kentucky Press, 1966.

Amherst, Jeffrey (1717–1797)

Jeffrey (sometimes Jeffery) Amherst was a British Army officer who became commander of the British Army in North America during the Seven Years' War and in Great Britain during the American Revolution.

Amherst was born in Kent, England, the son and grandson of barristers. With family connections to the neighboring Duke of Dorset, Amherst became a page for that family and then joined the British Army, serving during the War of the Austrian Succession in the 1740s. His military career advanced under the tutelage of Sir John Ligonier and the Duke of Cumberland, for whom he was an aide-de-camp. That connection served him well until, during the Seven Years' War, Cumberland suffered a disastrous 1757 defeat at Hanover. Amherst's career was not adversely affected, however, thanks to Ligonier, who by this time was the commander in chief of the British Army and a key advisor to William Pitt. In early 1758, Ligonier sent Amherst, now a major-general, to North America to lead an expedition against the French fortress at Louisbourg, Nova Scotia. This assignment began Amherst's long association with the American colonies.

Amherst's army forced the surrender of Louisbourg on 27 July 1758, giving Britain its first major victory in the war. That triumph won the respect of the American colonists, who named towns in Amherst's honor, and of Pitt, who made Amherst commander of British forces in North America. Amherst was a reserved, cautious, and deliberate individual who demonstrated himself to be a steady officer and an able administrator, even if he lacked the bold imagination of a great field commander. In 1759 he mounted a multipronged attack on Canada. Forces under his direct command captured Fort Ticonderoga, other forces took Fort Niagara, and a third expedition under Brigadier-General James Wolfe defeated General Louis-Joseph de Montcalm-Gozon at Quebec. Amid these triumphs, Amherst's critics have claimed that his decision to build a fort at Crown Point, rather than move quickly to reinforce the Quebec attack, delayed Britain's victory there. But in 1760, three columns converged on Montreal and finally wrested control of Canada from the French.

Amherst continued to serve in the American colonies after the final victory over France in North America. The war still raged elsewhere, and so the British commander continued to cajole the provincials to raise troops and supplies. If Amherst was generally reserved, he was not always able to suppress his contempt for the colonists, whom he resented for their limited martial skills, lackluster support, and ongoing trade with the enemy. He had even less respect for American Indians, who contributed to his decision to resign his command when they launched widespread attacks along the frontier in 1763. With family problems mounting and support in government declining, Amherst returned to England.

Amherst's subsequent career was mixed. He declined to serve again in America but was made a baron in 1776, named commander in chief of the army in Britain in 1778, and appointed field marshal in 1796. On the other hand, while Amherst had little influence on military policy in America during the American Revolutionary War, some critics held him responsible for Britain's defeat there and for the British Army's gradual decay in this period.

Mark Thompson

See also

Campbell, John, 4th Earl of Loudoun; Pitt, William, the Elder

References

Long, J. C. *Lord Jeffery Amherst: A Soldier of the King.* New York: Macmillan, 1933.

Nester, William R. *"Haughty Conquerors": Amherst and the Great Indian Uprising of 1763.* Westport, CT: Praeger, 2000.

André, John (1750–1780)

A British officer hanged by the Americans as a spy during the Revolution, John André was remembered on both sides of the Atlantic as an ideal soldier. In his youth, he studied mathematics and military drawing at the University of Geneva. Although he dreamed of a military career, his father called him home to join the family business before he completed his studies. After his father died in 1769, André inherited £5,000, thus securing his financial independence, but from a sense of obligation he continued in the family business. A year later a young woman named Honora Sneyd rejected his proposal of marriage. Disappointed, he revived his ambition to join the British Army and on 25 January 1771 was commissioned a lieutenant in the 23rd Foot (Royal Welch Fusiliers). A few months later, he purchased a second lieutenant's commission in the 7th Foot (Royal Fusiliers). Eight months later he bought a lieutenant's commission in the same regiment. In 1772 he traveled to Göttingen with George Rodney, son of the admiral. There André studied mathematics and joined the Hain, a literary society. In the summer of 1774 he was ordered to join his regiment at Quebec.

In September 1774, after a leisurely journey, André arrived in Philadelphia and then visited New York and Boston. He finally reached Quebec just before the harsh winter made travel extremely difficult. In the spring of 1775 he was ordered to St. John's on the Sorel River, where the British were preparing defensive works in preparation for an impending American invasion of Canada. When the rebels captured the city on 3 November, André was taken prisoner. Paroled, he lived in Lancaster and Carlisle, Pennsylvania, until 28 November, then was exchanged. Living in New York during the winter, he was promoted to captain of the 26th Foot and began keeping a journal. In June, on the recommendation of Sir William Howe, commander in chief of the British Army in America, André was appointed aide-de-camp to the newly arrived General Charles Grey. André found in Grey a congenial officer who agreed with him that the British should prosecute the war with harshness and vigor.

John André, a major in the British Army, held a clandestine meeting with Benedict Arnold to secure information on the fortifications of West Point. Captured out of uniform, André was tried as a spy and executed by the Americans. (Library of Congress)

In June 1777 André campaigned with Grey in New Jersey and a month later accompanied Grey as the British Army sailed toward Chesapeake Bay. André kept a journal in which he recorded his experiences of the numerous battles in which he participated during the campaign in Pennsylvania and of the capture of Philadelphia. He also was present at the battles of Germantown on 4 October and Whitemarsh on 4 December. In Philadelphia during the winter of 1777–1778 André staged theatricals, attended balls, and paid court to young ladies, especially Margaret (Peggy) Shippen. He designed the scenery and costumes for the *Meschianza,* a play given on 18 May 1778 in honor of Howe, who was resigning his command. On 18 June André accompanied Grey and Sir Henry Clinton, the new commander in chief, as the British Army evacuated Philadelphia. Ten days later André fought in the Battle of Monmouth. He was with Grey during the raids on New Bedford and Fairhaven, Massachusetts, on 5–7 September and in the attack on George Baylor's 3rd Continental Light Dragoons at Old Tappan, New Jersey, on 28 October.

After Grey returned to England in November 1778, he praised André to Clinton in the highest terms, and Clinton chose André as an aide. Soon the two men were close friends. While serving under Clinton, André became captain of the 44th Foot and later the 54th Foot. In the winter of 1778–1779, at New York, André wrote and staged plays and read poetry at gatherings of officers and at parties. The state of his finances suffered in July 1779 when the French captured the West Indian island of Grenada and seized his estates. He was appointed deputy adjutant-general of the army on October 23, with the rank of major, and in early 1780 accompanied Clinton to Charleston, South Carolina. After Charleston fell on 12 May, André returned with Clinton to New York. In the summer of 1780 he wrote "Cow Chase," a poem satirizing Anthony Wayne, William Alexander (Lord Stirling), and Henry Lee as drunkards and cowards.

As part of his staff duties André was in charge of Clinton's intelligence network and in May 1780 became enmeshed in the treasonous correspondence between Benedict Arnold and Clinton by which the former plotted to betray the rebel cause. On 20 September, as a part of his dealings with Arnold involving the surrendering of West Point, André sailed up the Hudson River aboard the sloop *Vulture* to negotiate with Arnold at Haverstraw, New York. He met with Arnold on the night of 21 September but was unable to return to the *Vulture* because it had been fired on and had sailed southward. Bearing a pass from Arnold, André spent the night with a friendly farmer, then changed into civilian clothes to make his way by land to British lines at Tarrytown. He concealed military documents that Arnold had given him in his boots. On the morning of 23 September, as André neared his destination, he was halted by three militiamen whom he thought to be Loyalists. Instead of producing his pass, he identified himself as a British officer and was searched. When the documents were found in his boots he was detained, notwithstanding an attempt to bribe his captors. Taken to a nearby command post, he and his American guards waited while the papers were sent to General George Washington. While there, André almost persuaded his captors to turn him over to Arnold. But Major Benjamin Tallmadge became suspicious and decided to await word from the commander in chief. Arnold, meanwhile, learned of André's capture and fled to British lines on 25 September.

André was taken to army headquarters at Tappan, New York, on 28 September. The following day, Washington convened a military tribunal of fourteen general officers to try André as a spy. He was found guilty on 29 September and sentenced to hang, with his conviction confirmed by Washington the following day. André asked Washington to allow him to be shot as a soldier, but the commander could not consent. The American commander was afraid that such a gesture would be interpreted by the British as an admission that André was somehow on a legitimate mission and had been unjustly condemned. On 1 October Clinton tried desperately to save his protégé, offering to exchange him for an American officer. Washington was willing to make an exchange, but for only one man: Benedict Arnold. To those terms Clinton could not accede. Hence, André was hanged on 2 October, dressed in the uniform of the 54th Foot. He died calmly and with dignity and was mourned not only by his colleagues but also by the Americans, who had grown to respect him during his brief period of captivity. He was buried on the hilltop where he was hanged. In Britain, André was honored with a monument in Westminster Abbey, and his remains were removed to that venerable site in 1821. André was a young man of many sterling qualities, among which were military ability, noble character, and fine manners as well as his various talents as a satirical poet, actor, playwright, stage and costume designer, and sketch artist.

Paul David Nelson

See also

Alexander, William; Arnold, Benedict; Charleston, South Carolina, Expedition against (1780); Clinton, Henry; Germantown, Battle of; Grey, Charles; Lee, Henry; Monmouth, Battle of; St. John's, Actions against; Tallmadge, Benjamin; West Point, New York; Whitemarsh, Pennsylvania, Action at

References

André, John. *Major André's Journal: Operations of the British Army under Lieut. Generals Sir William Howe and Sir Henry Clinton.* Tarrytown, NY: New York Times, 1968.

Flexner, James Thomas. *The Traitor and the Spy: Benedict Arnold and John André.* 1953. Reprint, Syracuse, NY: Syracuse University Press, 1992.

Hatch, Robert M. *Major John André: A Gallant in Spy's Clothing.* Boston: Houghton Mifflin, 1986.

Nelson, Paul David. *Sir Charles Grey, First Earl Grey: Royal Soldier, Family Patriarch.* Madison, NJ: Fairleigh Dickinson University Press, 1996.

Sargent, Winthrop. *The Life and Career of Major John André, Adjutant-General of the British Army in America.* New York: Abbatt, 1902.

Tillotson, Harry S. *The Beloved Spy: The Life and Loves of Major John André.* Caldwell, ID: Caxton Printers, 1948.

Armand-Tuffin, Charles, Marquis de la Rouerie (1750–1793)

Charles Armand-Tuffin, the Marquis de la Rouerie, one of the ablest foreign officers in the Continental Army, commanded cavalry units in both the northern and southern theaters of the Revolutionary War.

Born on 13 April 1750 near Saint Ouen, just north of Paris, Armand inherited the title of marquis at an early age and was educated by tutors. At seventeen he was commissioned an officer in the Corps de Gards Françaises, serving the French king at Versailles. Scorned in a love affair with an opera singer, Armand briefly sought refuge at a Trappist monastery. Not long after leaving the cloistered life, he quarreled with a cousin of the king. The two met in a duel, and Armand's opponent was gravely injured. Fearing the king's wrath, Armand fled to Switzerland. Eventually tempers cooled, and he received royal permission to volunteer for the American army.

Arriving in America at the end of 1776, Armand dropped the title of nobility from his name, becoming simply Charles Armand in deference to the republican cause, and applied to Congress for a position with the army. On 10 May 1777 he was commissioned a colonel, and on 11 June 1777 he succeeded Major Baron Dietrick Ottendorf as commander of an independent company. Technically, Armand's unit formed the 3rd Cavalry in Casimir Pulaski's legion. Armand and his troops fought a fierce battle at Short Hills, New Jersey, on 26 June 1777 and subsequently were engaged with the enemy at Red Bank, Brandywine, Whitemarsh, Gloucester (New Jersey), and Monmouth. On 25 June 1778, Congress reorganized Armand's unit as the Free and Independent Chasseurs, and in August the group became known as Armand's Partisan Corps.

Armand's corps was essentially a foreign legion. He recruited mainly German Americans and—permitted by Congress but disapproved of by George Washington—Hessian deserters and prisoners of war. Although Congress authorized a strength of 452 men, Armand could never enlist more than 300 troops, and usually the number in actual service was much less. From late 1778 through 1779, Armand's troops were active in the partisan war in the so-called Neutral Ground between the two major armies, chiefly in Westchester County, New York. He made two daring raids behind British lines at Morrisania (now in the Bronx), capturing important British military figures. After the death of Pulaski on 11 October 1779 at the siege of Savannah, the several dozen remnants of the Polish commander's legion were incorporated into Armand's Partisan Corps. In July 1780, with only 120 troops (60 mounted and 60 foot), Armand joined General Horatio Gates's Southern Army. Gates employed Armand's troops as an advance guard (but neglected to send out distant patrols) as the American army headed toward the British post at Camden. Armand's men were forced to retreat and did not play a significant role in the subsequent Battle of Camden (16 August 1780).

Armand continued to have difficulty enlisting men for his corps. Like several other independent units, his troops were considered outside all state lines and hence were not entitled to support by any state government. Pay and supplies were often inadequate. Armand took a six-month leave from the army to return to France in February 1781. While he was away his corps was attached to Lafayette's command in Virginia and suffered heavy casualties at the Battle of Green Spring on 6 July 1781. While abroad, Armand was made a Chevalier de Saint-Louis. He collected supplies at his own expense that he brought back with him for his troops. He arrived in America in August 1781, just in time to participate in the siege of Yorktown. Taking charge of his cavalry unit, which now numbered only one hundred men, he led the right column in Alexander Hamilton's daring and successful night attack of 14 October against the British Number 10 redoubt.

In February 1782 Armand joined forces with General Nathanael Greene's army in South Carolina. On 25 December of that year Armand and his troops arrived at York, Pennsylvania, where they remained until their discharge on 25 November 1783. At Washington's urging, Congress voted on 26 March 1783 to commission Armand a brigadier general and chief of Continental Cavalry. On 18 March 1784, Armand embarked for France. In 1786, he married the wealthy Marquise de Saint Bryce, who died six months later of tuberculosis. Armand carried on a substantial correspondence with Washington, frequently reminding the American leader that he had not been reimbursed for his personal contribution to the upkeep of his partisan corps. Washington always had a high regard for Armand, once stating that the Frenchman had "the address and bravery of a complete Partisan officer."

In 1791 Armand became the head of a secret royalist organization in northwestern France. To escape detection by agents of the Convention, he hid for a time in the woods and for six months disguised himself as a crippled beggar. He led a conspiracy for a general uprising by royalists that was scheduled for March 1793. But suffering from a nervous disorder and greatly saddened by the execution of Louis XVI, Armand died on 30 January 1793 at the Chateau de Guyemarais.

Harry M. Ward

See also

Brandywine, Battle of; Camden Campaign; German Mercenaries; Pulaski, Casimir; Yorktown, Virginia, Siege of

References

Lasseray, André. *Les Français sous les treize étoiles, 1775–1783.* 2 vols. Paris: Protat, 1935.

"Letters of Col. Armand (Marquis de la Rouerie), 1777–1791." *New York Historical Society Collections* 11 (1879): 287–396.

Stutesman, John H., Jr. "Colonel Armand and Washington's Cavalry." *New York Historical Society Quarterly* 4–5 (1961): 5–42.

Whiteridge, Arnold. "The Marquis de la Rouerie, Brigadier General in the Continental Army." *Proceedings of the Massachusetts Historical Society* 79 (1967): 47–63.

Armstrong, James (1748–1828)

James Armstrong was born in Carlisle, Pennsylvania, on 29 August 1748, the eldest son of John Armstrong Sr. (the hero of Kittanning in the French and Indian War) and brother of John Armstrong Jr. (author of the Newburgh Addresses and later secretary of war). James attended the Philadelphia Academy and the College of New Jersey (now Princeton University) and the School of Medicine at the College of Philadelphia (now the University of Pennsylvania). He graduated in 1769 and began the practice of medicine in Frederick County, Virginia. During the Revolution he served as a medical officer and surgeon and after the war practiced medicine and was active in public affairs. After several years he traveled to London to study medicine and then returned to Carlisle, Pennsylvania, in 1788. Upon arriving in the newly formed United States, he married May Stevenson in 1789 and moved to the Kishacoquillas Valley in Pennsylvania. He was elected to Congress from the 3rd District of Pennsylvania in 1793 but only served one term, through 1795. Armstrong was elected as a trustee of Dickinson College in 1796 and was chosen as president of the Board of Trustees in 1808, a position he held until 1824. He was appointed an associate judge in Cumberland County and served from September 1808 until his death on 6 May 1828.

Katie Simonton

See also

Congress, Second Continental and Confederation; Newburgh Addresses

Reference

Purcell, L. Edward. *Who Was Who in the American Revolution.* New York: Facts on File, 1993.

Arnold, Benedict (1741–1801)

A celebrated general who came to prominence at the siege of Quebec and emerged as a national hero during the Saratoga Campaign, Arnold became the most notorious traitor in American history through his attempt to turn the course of the war by betraying West Point to the British.

Born on 14 January 1741 in Norwich, Connecticut, Arnold was forced to leave school and begin an apprenticeship as an apothecary when his alcoholic father lost the family fortune in 1755. While still in his teens, Arnold volunteered in three campaigns during the French and Indian War but did not make any notable mark. Upon the completion of his apprenticeship, he opened a shop to sell drugs and books in New Haven in 1762. Arnold married Margaret Mansfield in 1767, a marriage that lasted until her death in 1775. He also captained ships that traded goods with Canada and the West Indies. The experiences that he gained as a trader in Canada gave Arnold a familiarity with the territory and its inhabitants that he would later put to use in wartime.

While in New Haven, Arnold began to display the qualities that would later bring him to ruin. Quick to take offense and especially skilled at making determined enemies, he demonstrated impulsiveness and aggressiveness in equal measures. The trading restrictions imposed by the British Empire upon the American colonies threatened Arnold's livelihood and bred an anger that ultimately led him to join the revolutionaries. In 1766 he emerged in local politics, leading the New Haven Sons of Liberty in a violent attack against a vengeful former crewman who had informed against him for smuggling. In 1774, as the imperial crisis intensified, Arnold joined a New Haven militia company, the Governor's Second Company of Foot Guards, which soon elected him captain. Following the bloodshed at Lexington and Concord, Arnold resolved to march his unit to Boston to reinforce the Massachusetts militia. The New Haven Board of Selectmen refused to furnish the troops with gunpowder and advised Arnold that he should not raise arms against the king without first seeking proper authority to do so. Arnold, in a confrontation that is commemorated annually in New Haven as Powder House Day on 22 April, demanded the keys to the ammunition depot and received them. He and his men then proceeded to Massachusetts to await orders.

Benedict Arnold, though infamous in American history as a traitor and spy, initially served the Revolutionary cause with considerable skill, especially during the American invasion of Canada in 1775–1776. His subsequent plot to betray West Point to the British failed, whereupon he escaped to their lines and served thereafter against his country in raids against Virginia and Connecticut. (Library of Congress)

On an earlier visit to Canada, Arnold had noticed that Fort Ticonderoga on Lake Champlain had a small garrison and much artillery. He now persuaded the Massachusetts Committee of Safety to order him, with the new rank of colonel, to capture the British fort and its guns, which could be employed in the siege of Boston. Empowered to lead 400 men, Arnold nevertheless rode ahead of his troops and en route met two rival parties—including a large contingent of Green Mountain Boys led by Ethan Allen—who had heard Arnold bragging of his observations and decided to seize Ticonderoga themselves. An infuriated Arnold forced an uncomfortable collaboration, and the rebel forces managed to take the fort in a brief dawn attack on 10 May 1775. Never a diplomatic man in the best of circumstances, Arnold proved unable to prevent the rowdy victors from pillaging long enough to attack other nearby British forces that would undoubtedly attempt to retake Ticonderoga. But when his own recruits finally arrived, Arnold used them to seize a schooner at the south end of the lake, renamed it *Liberty,* armed it with cannon from the fort, and sailed north to attack the British post at St. Jean, where he captured the small garrison and a sloop of war without a single shot fired. Back at Ticonderoga, he began to build a navy to hold the lake and to prepare for an invasion of Canada. Unsupported by Massachusetts, however, which had agreed to let Connecticut direct the campaign against Canada, Arnold resigned his command in late June and returned to New Haven.

Arnold's success at Ticonderoga proved him to be a resourceful, intelligent, and effective officer though also a complainer. Despite divisions of opinion about him, Congress appointed Arnold in September 1775 as the commander of the Continental Army's Kennebec expedition to take Quebec. His assignment involved conducting more than 1,000 green troops with provisions and equipment nearly 400 miles through poorly mapped and nearly impassable terrain, up the Kennebec River, down the Chaudière River, and into the Canadian city. It was one of the great marches of military history and one of the most brutal. Made miserable by freezing temperatures and reduced to eating their shoe leather, many of the men died and the remainder would never have made it to Quebec except for Arnold's inspiration.

The march made Arnold a hero, but the 31 December 1775 attack on the city failed. Arnold joined with another force under General Richard Montgomery that had invaded Canada from Lake Champlain to lead a night assault against the fortified city. Without the support of the citizenry, the effort was doomed; Montgomery was killed, and Arnold suffered a shot through the calf. Despite this setback, he wanted to make a second attempt to take the city. Congress ignored his entreaties for more men, instead demanding that he immediately provide a detailed accounting of all his expenditures in Canada to date. The heavily aggrieved Arnold also subsequently lost command of his army to Brigadier General David Wooster. When the ice melted in May and British reinforcements sailed up the St. Lawrence River to Quebec, the Americans, ravaged by smallpox, retreated from Quebec to Trois-Rivières, then to Montreal, and finally south up Lake Champlain to Crown Point.

Under General Philip Schuyler's command in 1776, Arnold began building a navy on Lake Champlain to resist the expected British advance from Canada toward Ticonderoga and the upper Hudson Valley. Even as he worked to assemble a fleet of galleys and sailing gondolas around the nucleus of ships captured on the lake in 1775, he was caught in the middle of a growing conflict between Generals Schuyler and Horatio Gates, whom Congress had sent to take command at Ticonderoga. Arnold also faced a court-martial for charges lodged by Captain Moses Hazen for defamation of character and by Captain John Brown for thirteen misdemeanors that allegedly took place in Canada, including spreading smallpox among the army, plundering enemy property, and making an attempt at Ticonderoga in 1775 to escape to the enemy. Congress would eventually exonerate Arnold of all these charges.

With his fleet complete, Arnold sailed north with ten ships in August 1776 to block a British advance. The far stronger British fleet bested the Continental forces on 11 October 1776 in the Battle of Valcour Island, but Arnold managed to set fire to his vessel and stay with the ship until the flames made it impossible for the enemy to strike its colors on their arrival. He fought his way to Fort Ticonderoga and fired on two ships that approached, thereby forcing a British withdrawal. In these engagements Arnold lost all but four of his ships as well as a few hundred men, but he delayed the British advance, making their move farther southward impossible as winter arrived.

Despite Arnold's heroics, Congress denied him promotion from brigadier general in early 1777, while elevating to major general five men who had been brigadiers a shorter time than he. Arnold planned to protest in person to Congress, but on his way to the capital at Philadelphia he led a 400-man militia force against a 2,000-man British contingent that had landed in Connecticut in April with the aim of destroying the Continental supply depot at Danbury. Too late to save the depot, Arnold attempted to prevent the British troops from returning to their ships. In the ensuing Battle of Ridgefield, Arnold inflicted heavy casualties. His skill and bravery won him promotion to major general but without the restoration of seniority over the men who had been promoted in February.

When the British invaded up Lake Champlain in June 1777, George Washington requested that Arnold, one of his favorite generals, head the militia reinforcements supporting the Continental Army. When Arnold arrived, Fort Ticonderoga had already fallen, and Generals Schuyler and Gates were vying for chief command. Both men had supported Arnold in the past, but Arnold sided with Schuyler, perhaps

Oct 20/1780

By.
Brigadier General Arnold
A Proclamation.

To the Officers and Soldiers of the Continental Army who have the real Interest of their Country at Heart, and who are determined to be no longer the Tools and Dupes of Congress, or of France. . .

Having Reason to believe that the Principles I have avowed, in my Address to ye Public of the 7th instant, animated ye greatest Part of this Continent, I rejoyce in the Opportunity I have of inviting You to joyn his Majesty's Arms.

His Excellency Sir Henry Clinton has authorized me to raise a Corps of Cavalry and Infantry, who are to be clothed, subsisted, and paid as the other Corps are in the british Service, & those who bring in Horses, Arms, or Accoutrements, are to be paid their Value, or have Liberty to sell them: to every non Commissioned Officer and Private a Bounty of three Guineas will be given, and as the Commander in Chief is pleased to allow me to nominate the officers, I shall with infinite Satisfaction embrace this Opportunity of advancing Men whose Valor I have witnessed, and whose Principles are favorable to an Union with Britain, & true American Liberty.

The Rank they obtain in the King's Service will bear a Proportion to their former Rank, and ye Number of Men they bring with them.

It is expected that a Lieutenant Colonel of Cavalry will bring with him, or recruit in a reasonable Time,

75 Men . Major of Horse 50 Men . Lieut. Col. of Infantry 75 Men

Captain of ditto 30	Major of ditto - - 50
Lieut.t of ditto - 15	Captain of ditto - - 30
Cornet of ditto - 12	Lieutenant of ditto - 15
Serjeant of ditto 6	Ensign of ditto - - 12
	Serjeant of ditto - - 6

N. B. Each Field Officer will have a Company.

Proclamation of 20 October 1780 by Benedict Arnold, inviting those Americans who felt they had been "fools and dupes of Congress or of France" to join His Majesty's army. Few men were attracted to changing sides because of the proclamation, and Arnold became the focus of considerable hatred in America. (Library of Congress)

dazzled by the New York patrician's background. Schuyler sent him into the Mohawk Valley in August to block a secondary British advance under Colonel Barry St. Leger. Arnold succeeded in doing so, but when he returned to the main army, a now unfriendly Gates commanded the forces. As the British engaged the Continental forces in the two battles at Saratoga that would turn the tide of war, Arnold commanded part of the left wing of attacking Americans at the Battle of Bemis Heights in October. Gates rejected Arnold's pleas for additional troops, ordered him back to headquarters, and relieved him of command. An apoplectic Arnold remained in camp and led troops against the second British advance. In the heat of battle, Arnold's horse fell and pinned him to the ground. His men rushed to his aid and extricated his leg, now crushed and torn by musket fire. Arnold withdrew to a field hospital. The injury, to the same leg wounded at Quebec, proved very slow to heal. It left the general too crippled to ride for many months and caused a permanent limp.

Unable to take a posting in the field for several months and still in considerable pain, Arnold reported to Washington at Valley Forge in May 1778, when the occupying British Army was clearly preparing to evacuate Philadelphia. Washington assigned Arnold to stay in Philadelphia as military commandant after the withdrawal. One of Washington's worst decisions, this move left a city with one of the largest Loyalist populations in the country in the hands of a man not known for his tact, patience, or sound judgment. Arnold immediately set gossips whispering by embarking on a conspicuously extravagant lifestyle. To finance his expenditures, he helped a ship captain evade an embargo in exchange for part ownership of the vessel's cargo, signed a secret compact to buy goods at low army prices and sell high on the private market, and used his position to offer protection to smuggled goods. None of these deals violated the law, but all involved a degree of influence peddling that was not entirely proper. Arnold raised additional eyebrows by courting Margaret (Peggy) Shippen, the daughter of a family rumored to be strongly Loyalist.

Arnold's pursuit of the high life attracted the notice of both the radical state government, which regarded all such indulgence as evidence of secret Tory sympathies, and a Congress that was still deeply suspicious of him. In February 1779, Pennsylvania authorities charged Arnold with eight counts of corruption and abuse of power. In March a congressional committee exonerated him of some charges but sent two others to Washington for court-martial: appropriating army wagons to transport private goods and imposing menial services upon the sons of freemen of Pennsylvania. The latter charge involved an officer who ordered a subordinate to procure a barber and clearly originated as part of a personal grievance against the general. In April, Congress added two more charges to the list of Arnold's alleged offenses: improperly issuing a pass to a merchant vessel and purchasing goods when the Philadelphia shops were officially closed. In the face of these charges and angered by his nation's ingratitude, Arnold resigned his Philadelphia command. In May 1779 he married Shippen and began the process of switching sides.

Through his new wife's family and friends, especially Captain John André, personal aide to the British Commander in Chief Sir Henry Clinton, Arnold had ready channels of communication to British headquarters in New York City. In May 1779, he first employed these channels to determine that the British intended to hold on to the colonies despite the entry of France into the conflict. He then informed Clinton that his services were available to the Crown. Arnold claimed political and ideological motives, explaining that he had lost faith in the Revolutionary cause when the United States allied itself with France. No evidence before May 1779 supports this claim, and Arnold's repeated efforts to obtain status and money from the British suggest less noble motives.

The British cautiously accepted Arnold's offer of information, and that same month Arnold sent his first report, couched according to André's instructions in the terms of an ordinary business communication with certain passages in cipher. Arnold informed the British that Congress would abandon Charleston, South Carolina, if challenged (which Congress did in May 1780, allowing the British to easily capture it); that only 3,000 to 4,000 militia could be mustered to fight any emergency; that the Continental forces lacked arms, ammunition, and soldiers; that no measures had been taken by Congress to prevent depreciation of the currency; that no foreign loan had been obtained; and, in a stab at one of the men who had loyally supported him, that Washington and the army would move to the area of the Hudson River as soon as forage could be obtained. In August, André requested an accurate plan of West Point with an account of the various vessels floating on the nearby Hudson River. The American post at West Point had been designed to block enemy access to the upper Hudson Valley. Its loss would deliver a staggering blow to American morale and strategy. Unfortunately for Arnold, West Point was undergoing extensive alterations according to a plan that Washington kept secret.

As the campaigning season ended, Arnold's postponed court-martial resumed. In January 1780, after listening to his spirited defense, the court acquitted him of fraud but convicted him of improper conduct in the matter of the illegal pass and sentenced him to an official public reprimand, which Washington duly issued several months later with a personal rebuke for Arnold's "peculiarly reprehensible" actions. At this point, Arnold extended an offer to the British to arrange the capture of a major Continental prize, identity unspecified, in exchange for £10,000 and command of a battalion in the British Army. He also notified the British of a planned invasion of Canada as well as the details of the summer 1780 campaign after a conference with Washington at his Morristown headquarters. Arnold also began campaigning hard to get command of West Point, which he received in August. The British remained noncommittal about the money he sought, instead advising Arnold to wait in an unspecified remote outpost for further orders.

Arnold would serve as commander of West Point for only fifty-two days. Within hours of his 5 August 1780 arrival at the fort, he obtained inventories of manpower, armaments, and supplies that he transmitted to British headquarters. Clinton made a firm commitment to pay £10,000 for Arnold's defection and £20,000 for the delivery of West Point and its 3,000 rebel troops. At Arnold's behest, André (now a major) made direct contact with him, and at this point the plan began to sour. While attempting to return to New York City, André was caught in civilian dress with a pass from General Arnold and the plans for West Point in his boots. Colonel John Jameson, the plodding commander of the men who had captured André, sent a dispatch to Arnold informing him that a man with a hidden parcel of dangerous papers and a pass with his signature had just been arrested. Not surprisingly, Arnold took this opportunity to flee. As Washington arrived at the front door to confront Arnold, the traitor rushed out the back, leaped on his horse, and hurried to a barge on the river that took him to a British ship. He left his pregnant wife to Washington's mercy. The bargemen, unaware of Arnold's intent, became prisoners of war of the British, and Major André was hanged as a spy.

Arnold's welcome as a failed traitor who had contributed to the execution of the popular André was not an especially warm one. The British made him a brigadier-general and gave him a Loyalist regiment and £6,000 for his troubles, but they never trusted him. Still, they sought to take advantage of his fighting skills. Clinton sent Arnold to seize Portsmouth, Virginia, in December 1780. Arnold's troops routed the Virginia militia; burned ships, munitions, and tobacco; and, moving far inland, forced Governor Thomas Jefferson into flight. In 1781 Arnold led a raiding party up the Connecticut coast, sacking and burning New London. Though blamed by both British and Americans for butchering the garrison at nearby Fort Griswold, Arnold was not at the fort during the fighting and may not have realized that a massacre was under way. In 1782, Arnold went to England in an effort to reinvigorate the war effort by persuading the government to commit more money, ships, and manpower, but the surrender of the British Army at Yorktown the previous fall had effectively ended the British war effort. Arnold would spend his remaining days in exile.

Snubbed by other Loyalist exiles as well as the British for being a traitor, Arnold never established a solid foothold in the peacetime world. In 1785 he sailed alone from England to St. John, New Brunswick, to open a store in a Loyalist exile community. The business prospered enough for his family to join him, but a 1788 fire wiped him out. Returning to England in 1791, Arnold struggled to make a living. He died on 14 June 1801, mourned only by his family. All of his sons by Shippen became high officers in the British Army or Royal Navy.

Caryn E. Neumann

See also

Allen, Ethan; André, John; Clinton, Henry; Fort Ticonderoga, New York; Gates, Horatio; Green Mountain Boys; Hazen, Moses; Hudson River and the Hudson Highlands; Lake Champlain, Operations on; Loyalist Exiles; Loyalist Units; Loyalists; Militia, Patriot and Loyalist; Montreal, Operations against; New York, Operations in; Quebec, Siege of; Saratoga Campaign; Valcour Island, Battle of; Washington, George; West Point, New York

References

Boylan, Brian Richard. *Benedict Arnold: The Dark Eagle.* New York: Norton, 1973.

Brandt, Clare. *The Man in the Mirror: A Life of Benedict Arnold.* New York: Random House, 1994.

Codman, John. *Arnold Expedition to Quebec.* New York: Macmillan, 1901.

Flexner, James Thomas. *The Traitor and the Spy: Benedict Arnold and John André.* 1953. Reprint, Syracuse, NY: Syracuse University Press, 1992.

Luzader, John F. "The Arnold-Gates Controversy." *West Virginia History* 27(2) (1966): 75–84.

Martin, James Kirby. *Benedict Arnold, Revolutionary Hero: An American Warrior Reconsidered.* New York: New York University Press, 1997.

Randall, Willard Sterne. *Benedict Arnold: Patriot and Traitor.* New York: Morrow, 1990.

Roberts, Kenneth Lewis. *Arundel.* Rockport, ME: Down East Books, 1995.

———. *March to Quebec: Journal of the Members of Arnold Expedition.* 1945. Reprint, Rockport, ME: Down East Books, 1967.

———. *Rabble in Arms.* Rockport, ME: Down East Books, 1996.

Thompson, Ray. *Benedict Arnold in Philadelphia.* Fort Washington, PA: Bicentennial Press, 1975.

Van Doren, Carl. *Secret History of the American Revolution: An Account of the Conspiracies of Benedict Arnold and Numerous Others from the Secret Service Papers of the British Headquarters in North America.* New York: Viking, 1941.

Wilson, Barry. *Benedict Arnold: A Traitor in Our Midst.* Montreal: McGill-Queen University Press, 2001.

Art

American art has developed to become as diverse as the American population, but this future was far from evident in the colonial period. The early European settlers brought their artistic traditions from their homelands, and their American descendants were slow to develop new artistic styles. The American Revolution, however, gave American artists something new to try to capture in their work: a uniquely American event, with implications for a distinctive American future. Although the Revolution affected all kinds of art, including architecture, furniture, and even domestic samplers and embroidery, it was in painting that a handful of American artists first tried to capture the character of their age.

The training of both painters and artisans in eighteenth-century America was based upon English artistic traditions. Silversmiths and furniture makers learned their crafts through traditional apprenticeship systems, and an artisan's training was firmly established within colonial society. Members of all trades frequently learned their craft from their fathers or were apprenticed to a successful local member of the profession. Many of these artisans did quietly become fine artists. Paul Revere's contemporary fame and posthumous reputation as a master silversmith and a talented engraver have been somewhat eclipsed in the popular mind by the legacy of his patriotic ride to Lexington, but his artistic merit remains as well known to historians of politics, because of his patriotic engravings (such as "The Boston Massacre"), as it is to historians of art and culture.

Because America had no art schools, however, aspiring American painters either contented themselves with looking at prints of paintings by Old Masters, journeying hundreds of miles to apprentice with the occasional established painter, or, if they could afford it, sailing to England to study at the Royal Academy in London. Several of America's best painters of the Revolutionary era took this journey, including Benjamin West and John Singleton Copley, who remained in England; Charles Willson Peale, who stayed only briefly; John Trumbull, who tarried a little longer; and Gilbert Stuart, who spent years in London but finally returned to America.

West (1738–1820), a Pennsylvania Quaker who went to London in the 1760s, was the father of American painting during the Revolutionary era. There he quickly became an established English painter and ultimately a court painter, and he never returned to America or painted any subject from the Revolution. Yet in his role as an established member of the Royal Academy, West taught, encouraged, and influenced talented American painters such as Peale, Copley, Trumbull, and Stuart. West largely worked in the eighteenth-century's dominant classical style but also fell under the influence of the emerging Romantic movement, which gradually affected all of the arts. He became best known as a history painter, an artist who could create large canvases filled with carefully selected historical figures at a particularly dramatic event.

West's greatest achievement, and the painting that had the greatest impact upon the art of the American Revolution, was his *Death of General Wolfe,* which commemorated Britain's great victory over France at Quebec in 1759. This work showed that the classical tradition of history painting could be equally effective when used to celebrate recent events, with every figure on the canvas in correct period dress rather than clothed in anachronistic classical tunics and togas and with fragments of classical architecture showing in the wings. West was equally innovative in portraying a heroic moment in the early history of America, whose grand events could rival those of Europe. Only five years after the painting was exhibited in London, the Declaration of Independence was signed in Philadelphia, and America soon created a grand opportunity for its own history artists.

Both in England and America, however, portraiture remained a painter's only constant source of income. American painters could also study portrait painting with West, and they did. But eighteenth-century British artists, notably

Death of General Wolfe, painted by Benjamin West. The image portrays Britain's victory over France at the Battle of the Heights of Abraham, outside Quebec, in 1759. West is known as a painter who created great scenes with an accuracy to period that was not commonly practiced at the time. His work, and this painting in particular, greatly influenced American painters John Singleton Copley and John Trumbull. (Library of Congress)

Thomas Gainsborough and Sir Joshua Reynolds, president of the Royal Academy from its founding in 1768, had already developed a distinctive portrait style that differed from the continental traditions that had dominated this field. Several American painters were greatly influenced by these artists.

The first great American painter to achieve fame was Copley (1738–1815) of Boston, New England's outstanding portrait painter. His work falls into two sharply contrasting periods. From about 1760 to 1775 he did his finest portrait work, almost entirely in Boston, where he extensively recorded the Patriot leaders of that city, notably Samuel Adams, John Hancock, and Paul Revere, as well as several Loyalist figures. After moving to England in 1775 with his Loyalist in-laws, Copley continued portraiture but also turned to history painting in the manner of West and finally created innovative dramatic canvases, notably *Watson and the Shark,* that brought the history painting style to events that had little historical significance. Following West's example, Copley made every detail as authentic as possible in both his American and English periods. Copley was also distinctive in that he produced nearly all his American paintings before ever visiting England.

The Maryland-born Peale (1741–1827) began his career shortly after Copley but traveled early to study with West before returning to Philadelphia, where he had a long career as an artist, Revolutionary politician, and pioneering museum curator. Peale was primarily a portrait painter and has the distinction of being the first artist to capture George Washington (1772) as a Virginia planter and militia colonel. Peale returned to paint Washington several times, notably in 1780 when he showed the now General Washington full-length, dressed in full uniform. To his left are gathered Hessian spoils and soldiers of the Continental Army under his command; to the right lie the fields of Trenton where his surprise attack on 26 December 1776 first turned the tide of war in America's favor. Peale also produced many other fine images of the Revolution's leaders, including the remarkable double portrait of Robert and Gouverneur Morris (1783).

With its background rich in historical details, Peale's portrait of Washington at Trenton was a kind of history painting, but this genre came to full flower in America only in the mid-1780s. A development of the Renaissance, history painting was not initially limited to the painting of real historical events. Canvases could depict events that may or may not have happened, drawn from classical mythology or the Bible. The genre could more accurately be called narrative painting, in contrast to other types of painting that do not attempt to tell a story.

Once West and then Copley expanded this form to include a kind of reportage of nearly current events in the 1760s and 1770s, the Connecticut-born Trumbull (1756–1843), one of West's students, set out to record America's recent political and military birth in great detail. Trumbull began with *The Death of General Warren at the Battle of Bunker's Hill* (1786)—an obvious tribute to West's *Death of General Wolfe*—that has the rare distinction of depicting a historical event at which the artist was actually present. Trumbull went on to salute the surrenders at Trenton, Saratoga, and Yorktown. His most famous work, *The Declaration of Independence,* shows Thomas Jefferson and his colleagues presenting the draft document to the full Congress. Trumbull's artistic—and financial—ambition was not simply to memorialize the Revolution but to produce iconic images of its critical events that could be readily engraved and produced for the edification of millions, both in America and Europe.

The American Revolution as a subject of American history painting did not end with Trumbull. John Vanderlyn (1775–1852), in the painting *The Murder of Jane McCrea* (1804), the first American history painting to be exhibited at a Paris salon, told a highly embellished story from General Burgoyne's 1777 invasion of northern New York in which the colonist Jane McCrea was murdered by two Indians who took her scalp to the British for a reward. Vanderlyn recast this tale in a dramatic reconstruction that based its large-scale figures on late classical sculpture.

The last great artist of the Revolutionary era, the Rhode Island–born Stuart (1755–1828), by portraying virtually all the notable men and women of Federal America, became the court portraitist to the young Republic. He was known to have painted more than 1,100 pictures over five decades in England, Ireland, and the United States, but his major career began with his return to America in the spring of 1793. His immediate intention was to paint President Washington's portrait. The shrewd artist knew that pictures of the celebrated hero would bring him further international recognition, and when he first painted Washington from life in 1795, the president's image was in great demand.

During many tiring sittings, Washington maintained a stricter formality with Stuart than he had earlier with Peale, with whom he had a much friendlier relationship. Despite

Drawing of the U.S. Capitol by architect Benjamin Henry Latrobe, circa 1806. The illustration differs slightly both from the original design and the capitol as it was built. (Library of Congress)

this stiffness, however, Stuart's first portrait of Washington was an immediate success, and he went on to capture America's hero in several other large portraits. Stuart was a charming conversationalist who kept his sitters entertained and thereby maintained the fresh spontaneity of their expressions during the hours of posing. To emphasize facial characterization, he eliminated unnecessary accessories and preferred dark, neutral backgrounds and simple bust or half-length formats. Though he commanded high prices, Stuart lived on the verge of bankruptcy because of his extravagant lifestyle. Yet in a ubiquitous memorial of the Revolutionary era, a time when the new nation was hungry for iconic images of its heroic birth, Stuart achieved a unique distinction: one of his many portraits of Washington found its way onto the face of the nation's one-dollar bill.

As America grew in prosperity, so did the demand by less famous but quite prosperous Americans to record their achievements. Portraits filled this desire by preserving likenesses for posterity. Individual and family portraits were equally popular. Cost varied according to the size of a painting and the sitter's pose. Notable portrait painters of the early national period were Connecticut's Ralph Earl and Baltimore's Joshua Johnston. Johnston, one of America's first black painters, lived as a freeman around the turn of the nineteenth century. Earl, Johnston, and many other local painters worked in a more colloquial American style, far removed from the Neoclassical and Romantic refinements of Peale and Stuart.

In architecture and sculpture, eighteenth-century Europe was stirred by two developments that eventually reached America: the rediscovery of Greek art as the original source of the classical style and the excavations of two buried Roman cities, Pompeii and Herculaneum. For the first time Europeans could see much of the daily lives of the ancients and the range of their arts and crafts. This brought about a reappraisal of ancient art and architecture as an inspiration for the late eighteenth and early nineteenth centuries.

At the same time, the English discovered the work of the Renaissance architect Andrea Palladio, a discovery eagerly embraced by Jefferson, whose home, Monticello, is America's most widely known example of the Palladian style. In America a fusion of late Georgian and Palladian architecture soon evolved into the classicalism of the Federal period, most closely associated with the Anglo-American architect Benjamin Latrobe (1764–1820), who left his mark on public buildings both in Philadelphia and America's new federal capital on the Potomac. The new classical style proved equally appealing for private homes, as Americans came to believe that it was the most effective way of expressing the new values of a new nation.

America's fascination with the classical style also extended to sculpture. Soon founders of the United States were depicted as figures from the ancient world. Both Benjamin Franklin and Washington were represented wearing togas like those of Roman senators. The statue of Washington, sculpted by the Frenchman Jean-Antoine Houdon (1741–1828) and located in the Virginia state capitol, became only slightly less well known than the portraits of Peale and Stuart. But America also retained a sense that its heroes were men of their own age, and Houdon carved two versions of Washington: one in classical garb, the other in modern costume. Sculptural patronage grew toward the end of the eighteenth century as Americans began adopting the English custom of creating statues in public places to honor political and cultural heroes, who appeared in contemporary dress.

By the end of the American Revolution, a new national public art and architecture had emerged that was both imitative of England and Europe and distinctive in some of its styles and themes. This high art developed alongside more distinctively American designs and decorations that found their way into local portraiture and architecture, and especially into domestic furniture, fabrics, and other local crafts. Both formal and vernacular art developed distinctive American features in the era of the American Revolution.

Linda Miller

See also

Copley, John Singleton; Jefferson, Thomas; Peale, Charles Willson; Revere, Paul; Stuart, Gilbert; Trumbull, John

References

Abrams, Ann Uhry. *The Valiant Hero: Benjamin West and Grand-Style History Painting.* Washington, DC: Smithsonian Institution Press, 1985.

Evans, Dorinda. *The Genius of Gilbert Stuart.* Princeton, NJ: Princeton University Press, 1999.

Jaffe, Irma B. *John Trumbull: Patriot Artist of the American Revolution.* Boston: New York Graphic Society, 1975.

Meany, Edmond S. *Washington from Life.* Seattle: Dogwood, 1931.

Nye, Russel B. *The Cultural Life of the New Nation, 1776–1830.* New York: Harper and Row, 1960.

Sellers, Charles C. *Charles Willson Peale.* 1947. Reprint, New York: Scribner, 1969.

Silverman, Kenneth. *A Cultural History of the American Revolution: Painting, Music, Literature, and the Theatre in the Colonies and the United States from the Treaty of Paris to the Inauguration of George Washington, 1763–1789.* New York: Crowell, 1976.

Articles of Confederation

The Articles of Confederation were the first national framework of government. A charter that established the United States of America, the Articles formally and explicitly bound the thirteen states into a perpetual union. Drafted in July 1776 and amended sporadically in 1777, the Articles did not go into effect until 1 March 1781, when they were finally agreed upon by all thirteen states. The kind of government enacted by the Articles reflected the assumptions of Revolutionary leaders: as they fought a war brought on by the ill effects of ministers and kings, America's first formal constitution limited the power of the central government, allowing the Continental Congress to act only in areas "expressly delegated" to it. Yet even though they would be held in high esteem by supporters of states' rights until the Civil War, the Articles were not a universal endorsement of state sovereignty. Although Congress proved increasingly ineffective in executing the Articles, it still retained powers of prosecuting and financing the war and retained jurisdiction over foreign relations, military affairs, and interstate disputes. Dissatisfaction with the Articles began almost immediately upon ratification, and attempts to reform the framework culminated in 1787 with the U.S. Constitution. Ratification of the Constitution in 1788 permanently discontinued the Articles of Confederation.

At other times of crisis in the eighteenth century, American colonial leaders tried to create a confederated union of equals. In 1754, Benjamin Franklin attempted to convince the mainland colonies to establish a defensive alliance. While his war-induced Albany Plan of Union—which called for the creation of a Grand Council to supervise Indian affairs, organize western settlement, and defend the continent—did not gain acceptance in either colonial legislatures or Parliament, it did highlight America's initial thoughts about union, thoughts that would crop up in the wake of another war in 1774.

In 1765, the colonies again tried to act in concert. After news of the Stamp Act reached the colonies, Massachusetts radical James Otis called for an intercolonial congress to coordinate America's reaction to the unpopular act. Leaders from nine colonies responded, sending twenty-seven delegates to New York. The main task taken up by the Stamp Act Congress, which convened for two weeks in October 1765, was to define the constitutional position of the colonies in the British Empire. Primarily concerned with political theory—the 1765 Congress left specific resistance methods to the colonial assemblies—the delegates attempted to persuade Britain that its method of internal taxation (placing a duty on consumption rather than trade) was illegitimate. Gathering to resist one single act, the Stamp Act, also served to make the Stamp Act Congress obsolete.

With the Coercive Acts (1774), however, the threat was greater than one odious piece of legislation. Britain's closing of the port of Boston, abolition of Massachusetts's seventeenth-century charter, and legalization of Catholicism and French civil law in Canada and the Ohio Valley initiated a general call for a continental congress. The First Continental Congress met in September 1774 and drafted the Continental Association, a binding pact that organized a national economic boycott. The Continental Association established local committees to supervise nonimportation and, in so doing, both created local structures of government and legitimated the national body. It did not provide for a permanent union of the thirteen colonies.

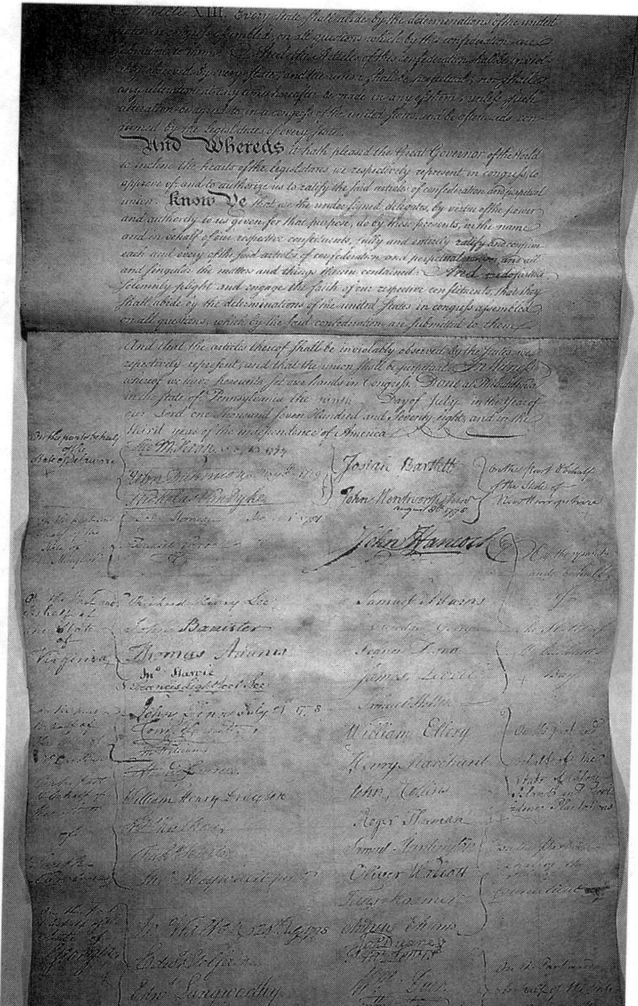

The Articles of Confederation, approved by the Second Continental Congress in November 1777, were ratified by all thirteen states by March 1781, thus establishing a confederal government for the independent United States. (Library of Congress)

The Second Continental Congress, scheduled to check on the progress of the Continental Association, was to meet in May 1775. Because war had already broken out in Massachusetts by that time, this second iteration of Congress became a permanent body, serving continuously as the national government for the duration. While its power had been granted by the separate legislatures (or in some cases by the people meeting in local conventions) and was reinforced by the provisions of the Continental Association, it was soon deemed necessary to define formally the role and proper activities of the Continental Congress. Work quickly began on drafting what would become the Articles of Confederation.

Of the six drafts of Articles attempted in 1775 and 1776, three are extant. The first known endeavor is Franklin's, written in May and presented to Congress in August 1775. Reminiscent of his twenty-year-old plan for union, Franklin's proposed framework reflected the insecurity of the summer of 1775. With war just beginning in Massachusetts, the Franklin draft called for a temporary union until reconciliation with Britain could be accomplished. In the meantime, his design for confederation, informed by the exigencies of war, relegated extensive executive powers to the Congress. As in the 1754 plan, Franklin saw western settlement and the potential instigation of Indians as principal concerns that warranted congressional supervision. Congress would also have jurisdiction over currency, diplomacy, and the military. Franklin also broached the prickly problem of representation and voting in the Congress by providing that delegates would be elected to Congress based on liberal apportionment (at a ratio of 1 delegate for every 5,000 voters) and that each would have their own vote. The looming question of sovereignty—who had ultimate authority in America—was opaque in the Franklin draft. Despite granting broad executive powers to Congress, Franklin insisted that each colony should retain "as much as it may think fit" of its own laws, institutions, and customs.

Another set of early plans came from Connecticut. One, from delegate Silas Deane, was written in the summer of 1775 and became a blueprint for a second Connecticut offering, drafted by Roger Sherman in March 1776. Both plans called for strict apportionment (1 delegate for every 25,000 "Souls" in the Deane iteration) and votes in Congress based on entire delegations (one state, one vote). As in the Franklin plan, congressional power was vaguely drawn, allowing for the necessities of war; again, the question of sovereignty was left unanswered. The Connecticut plans did suggest that Congress would assume a kind of external, executive sovereignty while the states would retain an internal, legislative jurisdiction. Domestic issues of commerce and western settlement—a crucial congressional function for Franklin—were relegated to the states under the Connecticut system.

On 12 June 1776, Congress appointed twelve delegates to a drafting committee in order to draw up the Articles of Confederation. Pennsylvania moderate John Dickinson took the lead and wrote a draft that became the Articles. The Dickinson draft as first conceived constituted a powerful theory of union. Dickinson sought to limit the ability of states to undermine national power. In direct opposition to Franklin's admission that each state retain control of its own laws and customs, Dickinson prevented the states from limiting the free exercise of religion. Congress would also have full jurisdiction over western lands and intercolonial disputes over boundaries in the Dickinson plan. In confronting the deepest sources of internal discord, Dickinson sought to enact a strong, healthy union through constitutional construction. Congress would control most duties of an executive: conducting foreign policy, prosecuting war, and negotiating treaties. The drafting committee revised Dickinson's draft throughout late June 1776, excising in full the provision on religious toleration but leaving the remainder largely intact.

The revised Dickinson draft was sent to Congress on 12 July 1776, albeit without its author. Dickinson, who dissented on the issue of American independence, resigned his position after Congress approved the Declaration of Independence and was not present to defend his theory of union. Congress debated Dickinson's plan from mid-July through August. On 20 August, a final report was printed that reflected the previous month's revisions. While much of Dickinson's work survived, Congress's amendments brought the Articles of Confederation closer to the form put forth the previous spring by the Connecticut plan, which differentiated between external responsibilities (diplomacy and war-making controlled by Congress) and internal ones (commercial and tax regulation supervised by the states). The question of sovereignty, still an informal division of powers, did not weigh heavily in the debates. As it had throughout previous iterations of the Articles, the central question of where ultimate authority would be located in the confederacy was left unexamined and unresolved.

The revised Dickinson draft reflected a general consensus in Congress, but that agreement was not broad enough to enact the Articles. Three divisive issues prevented passage: representation and voting, the apportioning of taxes, and what to do with western lands. The thorny problem over representation and voting arose over a natural conflict between "big" and "little" states. Bigger states argued that the number of delegates should be determined by the size of the franchised population. Moreover, the bigger states argued, each of these delegates should have his own vote in Congress. States with fewer citizens disagreed, contending that every state should elect a fixed number of representatives and that each delegation should cast one vote. Unequal population raised a second divisive issue: the apportionment of taxes. On this matter, consensus broke down over how to tax the slave population. Southerners rejected including slaves in tax calculations, arguing that only free people should be taxable. The question of western lands, however, was a most intractable problem. Colonial charters granted certain states—most importantly, Virginia—rights to enormous territories theoretically extending to the "South seas." Those states without western rights, including Maryland and Pennsylvania, demanded that the "landed" states forfeit their claims and establish a national domain, thus ensuring that profits from land sales would go to the union's benefit. Reluctance to cede charter rights on the part of "landed" states destroyed any agreement on the Articles. An inability to solve these three issues forced Congress to lay Dickinson's Articles to the side for several months.

When debate resumed in April 1777, North Carolina delegate Thomas Burke proposed a new article that changed the tenor of the Articles. Significantly changing the nationalistic tendency of the Dickinson draft, Burke's amendment (Article Two) declared that each state "retains its sovereignty, freedom, and independence" and every "power, jurisdiction, and right" not "expressly delegated" to the Congress. Here was born the idea that the Articles endorsed state sovereignty. "Expressly delegated" was indeed a powerful clause—one that Madison would purposely avoid in the Tenth Amendment to the Constitution—but Burke's revision did not fully ensure that states would hold ultimate sovereignty over Congress. Even with Article Two, executive powers, especially those that dealt with other nations, were still the responsibility of Congress. But after Burke's revision passed and entered the amended Articles, the problems of representation, apportionment, and the West again blocked passage.

In October 1777, motivated by spiraling inflation, the increasing need for French assistance, and military reversals that forced the rebels' evacuation of Philadelphia, Congress began a third push for confederation. The same problems remained, but by this time the need for union trumped disagreements over technical issues. Having reached critical mass, the Congress completed the final episode of the Articles with remarkable dispatch. Over a few weeks in October and November 1777, compromises were reached on the prickliest issues—solving the western problem and voting questions in just one day each—and the final version of the approved Articles of Confederation was sent to the states for ratification on 15 November 1777. No real breakthroughs enabled this success; only exigencies of the deepening crisis finally convinced Congress that its impotence might undermine the war and the Revolution.

In its official form, the Articles of Confederation authorized the smaller states' position of one state, one vote. In the matter of representation, delegations were capped at seven members, and state legislatures were to determine the method of their election (Article Five). The western problem was dealt with by leaving it unresolved: boundary disputes were left to the states, with Congress reserving the right of last appeal—a process, though, encumbered with very complicated rules and prerequisites (Article Nine).

With the addition of Burke's Article Two, the Articles of Confederation started as a statement of state sovereignty. Article One gave the nation its name, the United States of America, and Article Three declared the states' entrance into a "firm league of friendship" for the purpose of protecting and encouraging one another. Beginning with Article Four, however, ideas that the Articles were a compact between sovereign states began to blur—a fuzziness that marks the entire document. Offering "full faith and credit" to citizens of each state, allowing citizens to move freely and conduct business across state lines, and calling for rules of criminal extradition to be automatic and uniform reinforced notions of national sovereignty. Furthermore, Article Six served to curtail state jurisdiction, especially in the realm of foreign relations. Article Eight, on the other hand, took the power of raising funds out of the national government's hands, allowing each state to decide the method by which it would provide taxes to Congress. But Article Nine was perhaps most significant. Delegating executive powers to Congress, including complete sovereignty over diplomacy, treaty making, military affairs, coinage, and borrowing on credit, Article Nine refutes arguments that the Articles prevented the possibility of *any* effective central government.

The final four articles tied loose ends, including the establishment (and restriction) of an executive "Committee of the States" to conduct business when Congress recessed, an invitation for Canada to join the union, a stipulation that credit borrowed by the United States would be paid by the United States, and, most importantly, a declaration that the union was perpetual and the Articles binding. Although delegates had reached a written settlement on the union, hopes that it would quickly become law were soon dashed: unanimous approval was needed to initiate the Articles. By June 1778, ten legislatures had either granted or promised approval. The three remaining—Maryland, New Jersey, and Delaware—still nursed dissent about the failure of the Articles to establish a national domain and dragged their feet. In 1779, Delaware and New Jersey reluctantly ratified the Articles, leaving only Maryland. But Maryland adamantly stood alone and refused to assent to the Articles until Virginia ceded its rights to the West in 1780.

Congress assumed that the Articles would be approved eventually, and since 1778 it had been operating as if the frame were legally binding. The image of a legitimate, obligatory union, though, was nearly as essential to Congress as the provisions of the Articles themselves. This authority was withheld. Maryland's intransigence prevented the Articles from taking legal effect until 1 March 1781. By this time dissatisfaction with the Articles of Confederation had already begun. Already limited by the Revolutionary prejudice against centralized power—a suspicion manifested in the limitations of Article Two—Congress further suffered from an inability to curtail rocketing inflation, from diplomatic missteps, and from setbacks in provisioning and paying for the army. In a marked change from the loyalty Congress commanded during 1774–1775, by the war's end it was unable to induce the states into providing critical tax monies. Confidence dipped so low that elected delegates even began to sporadically attend Congress, further limiting its ability to conduct business effectively. In the interim—while Maryland kept the union in limbo—states drafted constitutions that legitimized their own sovereignty and made their national responsibilities secondary. It was the ascendant authority of state legislatures in the 1770s that partly influenced interpretations that the Articles were a coherent expression of state sovereignty. Proponents of states' rights constitutional theory, however, could equally point to the language of the Articles as evidence that American politics were indeed founded on the principles of local, decentralized government and a compact between corporate states. Advocates of states' rights, no aberrant strand of political theory, up through the Civil War contended that their ideas could be traced back to the first American constitution.

Peace only exacerbated Congress's problems. Virginia's cession and Maryland's ratification of the Articles did not wipe away the experience of the past four years. States had been more effective governors than Congress in the later years of the war. Already fuzzy on the issue of sovereignty due to a near total lack of substantive discussion on the matter, the limitations of the Articles on Congress became chains in the 1780s. Efforts to amend the Articles began as early as 1782 when Congress's inability to collect any revenue nearly brought about mutiny in the army. Congress tried to raise money by revising the tax on imports and adjusting the formula for apportioning taxes, but both efforts were rejected by the states. In the intervening years between passage and ratification of the Articles, any balance between internal and external sovereignty tipped decisively to the states. But this arrangement, with states fending for themselves, was also unsatisfactory. Left with no effective national body to conduct diplomacy, collect taxes, or ensure internal security—as was evident when Congress was unable to convince anyone to come to the aid of Massachusetts during Shays's Rebellion (1786)—many American leaders decided that a new constitutional framework was needed. Too many reforms to the Articles of Confederation were necessary, these nationalist leaders concluded; the whole agreement needed to be scrapped and recast. The Constitution of 1787—with its deliberate discussion of federalism and the precise location of sovereignty—was the result.

Robert G. Parkinson

See also

Albany Congress; Burke, Thomas; Coercive Acts; Congress, First Continental; Congress, Second Continental and Confederation; Constitution, United States; Constitutions, State; Continental Association; Deane, Silas; Declaration of Independence; Dickinson, John; Franklin, Benjamin; Northwest Territory; Otis, James, Jr.; Shays's Rebellion; Sherman, Roger; Stamp Act; Stamp Act Congress

References

Beeman, Richard, Stephen Botein, and Edward C. Carter II, eds. *Beyond Confederation: Origins of the Constitution and American National Identity.* Chapel Hill: University of North Carolina Press, 1987.

Greene, Jack P. *Peripheries and Center: Constitutional Development in the Extended Polities of the British Empire and the United States, 1607–1788.* Athens: University of Georgia Press, 1986.

———. "The Problematic Character of the American Union: The Background of the Articles of Confederation." Pp. 128–163 in *Understanding the American Revolution: Issues and Actors.* Charlottesville: University of Virginia Press, 1995.

Hoffman, Ronald, and Peter J. Albert, eds. *Sovereign States in an Age of Uncertainty.* Charlottesville: University of Virginia Press, 1981.

Jensen, Merrill. *The Articles of Confederation: An Interpretation of the Social-Constitutional History of the American Revolution, 1774–1781.* Madison: University of Wisconsin Press, 1940.

———. *The New Nation: A History of the United States during the Confederation, 1781–1789.* 1950. Reprint, New York: Knopf, 1965.

Matson, Cathy, and Peter S. Onuf. *A Union of Interests: Political and Economic Thought in Revolutionary America.* Lawrence: University Press of Kansas, 1990.

McDonald, Forrest. *E Pluribus Unum: The Formation of the American Republic, 1776–1790.* Boston: Houghton Mifflin, 1965.

Morris, Richard B. *The Forging of the Union, 1781–1789.* New York: Harper and Row, 1987.

Onuf, Peter S. *The Origins of the Federal Republic: Jurisdictional Controversies in the United States, 1775–1787.* Philadelphia: University of Pennsylvania Press, 1983.

———. "Reflections on the Founding: Constitutional Historiography in Bicentennial Perspective." *William and Mary Quarterly,* 3rd series, 46 (1989): 341–375.

Rakove, Jack. *The Beginnings of National Politics: An Interpretive History of the Continental Congress.* New York: Knopf, 1979.

Wood, Gordon S. *The Creation of the American Republic, 1776–1787.* Chapel Hill: University of North Carolina Press, 1969.

Ash Swamp, New Jersey, Action at (26 June 1777)

British and American troops fought at Ash Swamp, New Jersey, on 26 June 1777 as part of General William Howe's strategy to engage the American army of George Washington in a major battle. Howe had spent several weeks pursuing Washington's force through New Jersey and, a few days after the beginning of summer, spotted an opportunity to attack one of Washington's key corps, led by William Alexander, also known as Lord Stirling.

Howe's plan of attack involved a forced march under the cover of darkness. Disembarking from boats that had left from Staten Island at 2:00 A.M. on 26 June, two columns of Howe's men, led by Lord Cornwallis, quietly slipped along a chain of small hills toward Alexander's detachment, hoping to surprise the Americans in their sleep. Some of Alexander's pickets discovered the British approach and raised the alarm. Firing commenced in the darkness well before dawn and continued with hot exchanges of musket volleys until nearly noon. Under pressure from Howe's attack, Alexander retreated steadily until reaching the foot of the Waschung Mountains. Washington ordered units to harass the flanks of the attacking enemy. Knowing that further attacks in hilly terrain would put his men at risk, Howe ceased firing and retraced the morning's long march back toward Staten Island. During the action at Ash Swamp the Americans lost 63 soldiers killed, 180 wounded or captured, and 3 pieces of artillery, while the British suffered 35 casualties.

The action at Ash Swamp proved one of the few occasions when Howe pressed aggressively against American forces and pointed to his growing belief in 1777 that he must engage Washington's army in a major pitched battle. For the Americans, the encounter revealed Washington's Fabian strategy of resisting British advances while avoiding large-scale battles. As Alexander Hamilton noted after the battle in a letter to a friend, "We should not play a desperate game for it or put it upon the issue of a single cast of the die."

Daniel T. Miller

See also

Alexander, William; Cornwallis, Charles

References

Kwasny, Mark V. *Washington's Partisan War, 1775–1783.* Kent, OH: Kent State University Press, 1996.

Lundin, Leonard. *Cockpit of the Revolution: The War for Independence in New Jersey.* 1940. Reprint, New York: Octagon, 1972.

Nelson, Paul David. *William Alexander, Lord Stirling.* University, AL: University of Alabama Press, 1987.

Ryan, Dennis P., ed. *A Salute to Courage.* New York: Columbia University Press, 1979.

Valentine, Alan. *Lord Stirling.* New York: Oxford University Press, 1969.

Ashe, John (1720?–1781)

The North Carolina militia officer and Revolutionary political leader John Ashe helped win an important victory over North Carolina's Loyalists in 1776 and commanded American troops in the southern campaign until his defeat by the British at the Battle of Briar Creek in Georgia in 1779.

Born in Grovely, North Carolina, Ashe was the son of John Baptista Ashe, a prominent lawyer and member of the provincial council. Ashe attended Harvard College briefly in the 1740s but rebelled against college discipline and returned to North Carolina, where he held various minor civil offices and served as a militia officer. In 1747 he commanded a militia company that participated in repelling a Spanish attack on Brunswick during the War of the Austrian Succession.

Ashe was elected to the North Carolina assembly in 1752, where he was an ardent advocate of free public education. His leadership in the legislature resulted in his being chosen Speaker of the assembly, a position he held from 1762 to 1765, and he sat in the legislature until 1775. While he was Speaker he played an important role in local resistance to the Stamp Act, but when the Regulator revolt broke out in the backcountry in 1768, Ashe cooperated with Governor William Tryon to suppress the movement. He helped to finance the military campaign that defeated the Regulators and was promoted to the rank of major-general in the provincial militia.

Despite his cooperation with Governor Tryon, however, Ashe remained active in the Revolutionary movement, and at the outbreak of war he led the attempt to capture Tryon's successor, Governor Josiah Martin. Although Ashe's men captured Fort Johnston at the mouth of the Cape Fear River on 12 July 1775, Martin managed to escape to a British warship. On 9 February 1776, Ashe commanded a regiment of militia at the Battle of Moore's Creek Bridge, in which the Patriots defeated a numerically superior force of Loyalists who were attempting to reach the coast and join the British.

When British troops captured Savannah, Georgia, at the end of 1778, Ashe led a force of about 900 North Carolinians to reinforce South Carolina. Major General Benjamin Lincoln, commanding the American army, ordered Ashe to take a position on the north side of the Savannah River opposite Augusta, Georgia, to check the British detachment there. When the British withdrew from Augusta in mid-February 1779, Ashe crossed the river into Georgia but moved too slowly to impede the British retreat. He advanced his force southward, halting at Briar Creek where the British had destroyed a bridge. On 3 March 1779, British forces under Lieutenant-Colonel James Mark (Jacques Marcus) Prevost conducted a skillful flanking march that caught Ashe and his detachment by surprise and routed them in just a few minutes. The Americans suffered nearly 400 casualties, and Ashe was sharply criticized by other officers for negligence.

Ashe demanded a court-martial to clear himself of these accusations. The court acquitted him of misconduct but found that he had not taken adequate steps to guard against an attack. The stigma of the Briar Creek disaster ended Ashe's military career. Captured by the British Army as it occupied Wilmington, North Carolina, in the spring of 1781, he was later released but died in October of smallpox contracted during his imprisonment.

Jim Piecuch

See also

Briar Creek, Battle of; Moore's Creek Bridge, North Carolina, Action at; Regulator Movement

References

Davis, Robert Scott. "Ashe, John." Pp. 80–81 in *The American Revolution, 1775–1783: An Encyclopedia,* Vol. 1. Edited by Richard L. Blanco. New York. Garland, 1993.

Hooper, Archibald Maclaine. "John Ashe." Unpublished manuscript. Chapel Hill: Southern Historical Collection, Library of the University of North Carolina, n.d.

Associated Loyalists

During the American Revolution, persons who remained loyal to Great Britain had a number of options to choose from if they wished to join in organized resistance against their rebel neighbors. They could enroll in a Loyalist regiment, such as the Queen's Rangers, British Legion, Volunteers of Ireland, or some other less effective unit. Or they could join a Loyalist militia company if they were willing to settle for duty that involved only menial tasks such as guarding prisoners and constructing fortifications. A number of Loyalists, disliking the discipline of a soldier's life and looking down on militiamen as poor specimens, opted to participate in irregular warfare by joining various guerrilla units or more organized groups, usually designated by the generic name of associated Loyalists. These associated Loyalists, operating under a loose, almost guerrilla form of organization, operated at night in small bands on Long Island, in the Hudson River Valley, and around New York's Upper Bay. They attacked isolated American outposts, farmhouses, and villages; killed or captured prisoners; burned property; seized livestock; and gathered intelligence.

The more formal name of "Associated Loyalists" was applied to two groups during the war. During the British occupation of Rhode Island, Colonel Edward Winslow Jr. organized the Associated Loyalists of New England, also called the Loyal Association of Refugees. The purpose of this unit was to avenge what Colonel Winslow and his Loyalist friends saw as outrages perpetrated against them by rebels. This group conducted a number of raids on Long Island towns, killing or capturing foes, appropriating cattle and property, and seizing ships. The better-known organization came into existence in 1780, focusing on New Jersey, New York, and Connecticut. At that time, several prominent Loyalists, including William Franklin, the royal governor of New Jersey, proposed to organize an association for refugees who were not in a provincial regiment or the militia. Its purpose was to raid along the coasts near New York City and destroy the trade of the "revolted colonies." General Sir Henry Clinton, British commander in America, disliked the idea, for the association was to be an independent military unit, financed from army funds. But Sir William Pepperrell and Joseph Galloway in London prevailed upon King George III and Lord George Germain, secretary of state for the colonies, to approve the scheme. Thus Clinton was ordered to create the organization.

On 20 November 1780 Clinton wrote to Franklin and six other Loyalists in New York City, authorizing them to embody themselves as the Honorable Board of Associated Loyalists, to be headquartered in the city. Because Clinton continued to look askance at the organization, he gave it only the bare minimum of powers mandated by the authorities in London. He appointed Franklin its first director, with instructions to frame articles for the board and to recommend officers who would then receive their commissions from Clinton. Also, Clinton specifically admonished Franklin not to order any operations for the board without his consent and stipulated that its members were to obey Clinton's commands. As the board members would receive no pay for their services, save 200 acres of land to be given them when the rebellion was suppressed, they were given warrant to collect booty on their raids, which they were to distribute equally among themselves. Because of this clause, according to the Tory historian Thomas Jones, the Honorable Board of Associated Loyalists tended to plan and engage in operations designed more for the purpose of garnering plunder than for serving the larger strategic considerations of the British commander in chief. Moreover, the penalties that could be imposed against them did little to impose constraints. Any member who violated the rules of the organization could be tried by a board of officers and fined or expelled, but no harsher penalty could be imposed.

Despite Clinton's lack of enthusiasm for the Associated Loyalists, the unit seemed to be a reasonable way for the British to exert minimal discipline over Loyalist refugees who otherwise would be completely outside the ambit of military authority. The new organization, in theory at least, would help Clinton maintain control of the coasts of New Jersey and Connecticut and would discourage rebel privateering against British shipping. More importantly, the associators would gather supplies of forage, wood, food, and horses for the British Army in New York City. But the problem remained that the disgruntled Loyalists continued to engage in predatory warfare against the rebels and often perpetrated outright plunder, thievery, and murder. Franklin had no difficulty in recruiting men, for many Loyalists saw the Honorable Board of Associated Loyalists as an easy, and legal, way to punish rebels while lining their own pockets with wealth. By February 1781 Franklin had enlisted 500–600 men in New York and expected to enroll many hundreds more from Connecticut and New Jersey as soon as the Associated Loyalists could take up posts that were nearer to them.

In the next few months, Franklin and his board unleashed the Associated Loyalists to raid upon the coasts of nearby colonies, encouraging them to continue an already gruesome civil war with renewed enthusiasm and ruthlessness. The associators struck hard at the rebels, sparing little of property or life in any town that they assaulted. The American Patriots retaliated in kind, with both sides suffering great damage. It was only a matter of time before even greater atrocities would occur, with both sides committing acts of brutality against prisoners, up to and including executions. Germain,

Oliver De Lancey, a New York Loyalist, raised three battalions of Loyalist troops during the war, two of which fought with the British during the campaigns of 1780–1781 in the South. (Library of Congress)

Clinton, and Franklin should have anticipated the tragic consequences that would occur unless the associators were curbed. General George Washington was to some degree culpable on the Patriot side, but clearly the greater fault lay with the British, who were taking the initiative in these matters.

The situation reached crisis proportions in November 1781 when news of the surrender of General Lord Charles Cornwallis at Yorktown reached New York. Many Loyalists, feeling betrayed by their British friends, were alarmed for their future safety, and they vowed never to submit to what they saw as a royalist sellout of their interests. Although the tenth article of the capitulation stated that Loyalists in Cornwallis's army were not to be punished for joining the British Army, Washington refused to honor this part of the agreement. Declaring that it was a civil matter, he turned the question of treatment of Loyalist prisoners over to civilian governments. The New York Loyalists feared that they would be left to the mercies of Americans should Clinton's army suffer a similar fate. Their fears were not unreasonable, for the rebel legislatures of New York, New Jersey, and Connecticut had enacted laws to punish Loyalists. The associated Loyalists, thoroughly alarmed that if captured they might suffer civil penalties for what they considered to be bona fide military operations, declared that they would wreak vengeance on rebel Americans if they were not treated as military prisoners. They also pressed Clinton to issue a proclamation threatening rebels with retaliation for such unjust treatment, but Clinton refused to do so with so many of his soldiers in American captivity.

Governor Franklin bitterly resented the refusal of Clinton and other British officials to extend protection to the Loyalists. Therefore, he decided to act on his own and in defiance of Clinton's authority. In taking this action, he provoked an international incident and brought disgrace upon himself and the associated Loyalists. On 12 April 1782 Captain Richard Lippincott, a citizen of New Jersey and an associated Loyalist, hanged a rebel prisoner, Captain Joshua Huddy, in northern New Jersey. Lippincott and his fellow associators claimed that Huddy had murdered a Loyalist named Philip White, and they left on his body a paper that read, "Up Goes Huddy for Philip White." Adding to the horror of this act, Franklin, without any authorization from Clinton, condoned the murder and promised his followers that he would allow further retaliatory executions if necessary. When Washington learned of Huddy's death, he wrote to Clinton demanding that Lippincott be surrendered to him, implying that if his demand was not met, he would retaliate. Clinton responded that he was investigating the matter but refused to comply with Washington's peremptory edict.

Washington consulted his general and field officers to determine whether he would be justified in retaliating against a British prisoner for this crime. Receiving unanimous approval for this line of action, he ordered on 3 May that a prisoner be chosen by lot to die in Lippincott's stead. The unfortunate victim was Captain Charles Asgill, son of a rich banker who was former lord mayor of London and a baronet. That same day, Clinton, who was furious at Franklin for his actions, began court-martial proceedings against Lippincott. On 5 May, Clinton turned over command of the army to the newly arrived Lieutenant-General Sir Guy Carleton, who was informed by Franklin that Huddy's death was not murder and therefore not subject to trial by a court-martial. Chief Justice William Smith confirmed the validity of Franklin's position. Carleton learned, however, that there were no civil courts in New York to try the case, so he was at a loss as to what to do.

Playing for time, Carleton wrote to Washington on 7 May in an attempt to soothe the American commander's angry feelings and reach an understanding whereby both sides would end atrocities. Carleton told Washington (in an implied criticism of Clinton's handling of the matter) that private and unauthorized persons on the British side had been allowed to get out of control. At the same time, however, he condemned Washington's threatened act of reprisal as dishonorable and calamitous to all parties. He promised to embrace all measures to halt excesses in his own camp and, as a gesture of good faith, released Henry B. Livingston, son of the governor of New Jersey, from captivity. Washington bluntly retorted on 10 May that he would not change his mind about executing Asgill and strongly suggested that most of the atrocities throughout the war were the fault of the British. Meanwhile, Carleton remained perplexed as to how he should deal with Lippincott's court-martial. Maneuvering for time, he allowed Franklin and the Honorable Board of Associated Loyalists to get the trial adjourned to allow Lippincott more time to organize a defense. Chief Justice Smith believed that Carleton intended to get rid of the Lippincott affair by procrastination and then disband the board at the first opportunity.

In early June 1782 Carleton's difficulties mounted, for the news of Asgill's plight, which Carleton had attempted to keep secret, became public knowledge in New York. Immediately, it became clear that British soldiers and the populace favored saving Asgill's life, even if it meant that Lippincott must be court-martialed. Carleton reluctantly agreed, after consulting prominent civilian leaders, and so on 13 June Lippincott's military trial reconvened. Nine days later, the court acquitted him of the charge of murder, ruling that when he hanged Huddy he had been following the legal orders of the Honorable Board of Associated Loyalists. Carleton approved the court's verdict, but he also determined that those responsible for Huddy's death must be brought to justice. He ordered Deputy Judge Advocate Stephen Payne Adye to conduct an investigation. On 13 August, Carleton communicated these matters to Washington, making clear that he found Lippincott's actions reprehensible. Again, he urged Washington to overcome all barbarous impulses against Asgill and work within the law. Governor Franklin, whom many in New York now believed the guilty party in this sordid affair, was a thoroughly disillusioned man. Departing for England, he declared that Carleton was a "spirited General" but "bound Neck and Heels" by the House of Commons.

Washington's initial response to the news of Lippincott's acquittal was furious anger. He threatened to proceed with Asgill's execution, insisting that if Lippincott was innocent, then his superiors in the Honorable Board of Associated Loyalists were guilty. Although Washington did not mention Governor Franklin by name, clearly that was whom he had in mind. He did not respond directly to Carleton's letter, but he did send Congress the latest information about Lippincott on 19 August. By then his temper had cooled, and he made clear to the legislators that he had no desire to pursue the matter any further. Carleton's obvious disgust with the Honorable Board of Associated Loyalists, he said, had altered things considerably, and he did not wish to offend the British when news of a peace treaty might come at any time. Also, he was having moral qualms. A majority in Congress did not agree with these sentiments and still would have been willing to have Asgill executed. But they were in no great hurry to do so. Taking the matter under advisement, they procrastinated for the next two months.

In the meantime, events in Europe were leading to a resolution of this embarrassing dilemma for Carleton, Washington, Congress, and all other parties. When Lady Asgill, Captain Asgill's mother, learned of her son's plight, she intervened with Thomas Townshend, secretary of state for home affairs; King George III; King Louis XVI and Queen Marie Antoinette; and the comte de Vergennes, the French foreign minister. Townshend could do nothing more than urge Carleton to take every possible step to save Asgill's life. But the French king instructed Vergennes to intercede directly with Washington on behalf of Captain Asgill. Vergennes wrote to Washington, informing him that the king and queen of France were interested in the case and reminding Washington of America's obligations to them. When Washington received this letter, he rushed it off to Congress, for he was continuing to have doubts about the justice of his action against Asgill. Congress then voted unanimously to release the young man. Captain Asgill returned to his unit in New York City on 20 November and sailed for home on the next available ship. At the same time, Congress instructed Washington to remind Carleton in the most pointed terms of Carleton's promise to bring the murderers of Huddy to the bar of justice. Washington complied on 20 November, at the same time expressing his full confidence that Carleton was doing all within his power to fulfill this obligation.

Carleton certainly was desirous to put the entire matter of the Honorable Board of Associated Loyalists behind him, for he was thoroughly sick of it. He instructed Deputy Judge Advocate Adye to give him a report on where the investigation of Huddy's murder stood. Adye replied on 30 November that he had been unable to find enough evidence to indict anyone for the crime. Carleton so informed Washington on 11 December, reiterating his promise to bring the guilty parties to justice. He also declared that he would try to prevent any further outrages and that he had taken the custody of prisoners away from the Honorable Board of Associated Loyalists. Upon the counsel of his closest advisors, he contemplated dissolving the board entirely. But he knew that such an action was risky, for it might alienate Loyalists from British authority and trust even more than was already the case. Finally, he settled for depriving the Associated Loyalists of all their remaining powers, thus leaving the board a hollow shell.

There the matter of the Honorable Board of Associated Loyalists came to an end, much to the relief of Carleton, Washington, Congress, and Captain Asgill. The two commanders and Congress were happy to extricate themselves from a situation that could have been more damaging to their reputations than was already the case. Washington's and Congress's reputations had suffered more, for in their heedless vindictiveness in punishing Asgill, a completely innocent man, for another's crime, they had made a bad situation worse. Even as it was, they had compelled Asgill to undergo six months of close confinement and mental torture before they suffered qualms about their hasty actions and acted more humanely. Even then, their motivation seemed as much politics as simple decency.

Despite Loyalists' fears that they would be abandoned by Britain at the end of the war, such was not entirely the case. Carleton, with the approval of the government in London, refused American demands in 1782 and 1783 for an immediate evacuation, which would have meant leaving the Loyalists in the lurch. During that time, he dispatched some 35,000 Loyalists from New York to Nova Scotia, Quebec, the Bahamas, and Britain. The British government provided these refugees with land and provisions as well as courts to adjudicate claims for property losses. In the summer of 1783, at the urging of the British government, Carleton pleaded with Congress to rescind its discriminatory laws against Loyalists, but to no avail. On three separate occasions, he also asked Governor George Clinton of New York to do the same for his state. Clinton, who despised Loyalists, ignored all of Carleton's requests. Because of Carleton's many kindnesses to Loyalists, he was viewed by them during his later years as governor of Canada as a near-mythical figure. Thousands of other Loyalists, both white and black, also fled America from mid-Atlantic and southern seaports. Probably between 80,000 and 100,000 Loyalists finally departed America in one of the great diasporas of history. The British government disbursed thousands of acres of free land to the Loyalists and spent the modern equivalent of at least £30 million on transportation, provisions, and compensation. Governor Franklin and his Honorable Board of Associated Loyalists had underestimated the fidelity of the mother country to her loyal sons in America.

Paul David Nelson

See also

Carleton, Guy; Clinton, Henry; Huddy-Asgill Incident; Loyalist Exiles; Loyalists

References

Bowman, Larry. "The Court-Martial of Captain Richard Lippincott." *New Jersey History* 89 (1971): 123–136.

Brown, Wallace. *The Good Americans: The Loyalists in the American Revolution.* New York: Morrow, 1969.

Calhoon, Robert M. *The Loyalists in Revolutionary America, 1760–1781.* New York: Harcourt Brace Jovanovich, 1973.

Clinton, Henry. *The American Rebellion: Sir Henry Clinton's Narrative of His Campaigns, 1775–1782, with an Appendix of Original Documents.* Edited by William B. Willcox. New Haven, CT: Yale University Press, 1954.

Damon, Allan L. "The Melancholy Case of Captain Asgill." *American Heritage* 21 (1976): 19, 72–96.

Hoffman, Gerald O. "Captain Charles Asgill: An Anglo-American Incident, 1781." *History Today* 7 (1975): 325–334.

Jones, Eldon Lewis. "Sir Guy Carleton and the Close of the American War of Independence, 1782–1783." PhD diss., Duke University, 1968.

Nelson, Paul David. *General Sir Guy Carleton, Lord Dorchester: Soldier-Statesman of Early British Canada.* Madison, NJ: Fairleigh Dickinson University Press, 2000.

Skemp, Sheila L. "The Loyal American Tories in the Revolution." *American History Illustrated* 7 (1972): 36–43.

———. *William Franklin: Son of a Patriot, Servant of a King.* New York: Oxford University Press, 1990.

Tebbenhoff, Edward H. "The Associated Loyalists." *New York Historical Quarterly* 63 (1979): 115–144.

Van Tyne, Claude H. *The Loyalists in the American Revolution.* New York: Macmillan, 1902.

Ward, Harry M. *Between the Lines: Banditti of the American Revolution.* Westport, CT: Praeger, 2002.

Associators

The term "associators" was occasionally used before the outbreak of the Revolutionary War, in various locations, to describe civilians who subscribed to boycotts against British goods to protest British policy. Prominent examples of such agreements were Virginia's Nonimportation Association of 1769 and a similar agreement in Maryland that followed Virginia's lead. Boycotts and nonimportation agreements north of Maryland were seldom called by this name, and in Calvinist New England they tended to be thought of, and sometimes called, covenants. The most important of these acts, of course, was the First Continental Congress's Continental Association of October 1774 (modeled on a more recent Virginia plan), and the subscribers to this association numbered in the thousands, from Maine to Georgia. In addition, "associators" was occasionally used by or in reference to local groups, Loyalist as well as Patriot, who formed a political—as opposed to an economic—association in support of or opposition to British authority.

Once the war began, most uses of the term referred to Loyalist or Patriot military associations. The most important use of "associators" was as the official and preferred label for Pennsylvanians who associated in armed units for their common defense, beginning in May 1775. The term was rarely used for Patriot militiamen elsewhere in America, but Pennsylvania was unique among the rebelling colonies in having had no regular militia or militia law since its founding by English Quakers in the 1680s. The first appearance of the term in Pennsylvania was in response to a fear of attack by French or Native American forces during King George's War (1744–1748). When Pennsylvania's Quaker-dominated assembly refused to pass a militia law or appropriate funds for defense, Benjamin Franklin and others organized the Associated Regiment of Foot of Philadelphia in 1747. In the French and Indian (Seven Years') War in the 1750s, many Pennsylvanians again associated under arms.

In May 1775, upon hearing the news of Lexington and Concord, thousands of civilians rushed to take up arms as the

Associators of the City and Liberties of Philadelphia. The association movement quickly spread to every county in Pennsylvania, and within two months the associators were pressing the assembly to pass their province's first militia law. The assembly did pass a law in the fall and, after renewed and increased pressure, framed a statute in the spring of 1776 that paid the associators more generously for their training and service. Pennsylvania's associators were among the most ardent supporters of Pennsylvania's most radical leaders, the men who framed the unicameral Pennsylvania Constitution of 1776, which granted the franchise to every free Pennsylvania man who took up arms in defense of the new state.

In the war itself, Pennsylvania's associators engaged the British Army in New York and Pennsylvania from August to December 1776. Under Colonel John Cadwalader, they attempted to support General Washington's attack on Trenton in late December but were turned back by the difficult conditions of crossing the Delaware River. Thousands of Pennsylvania associators joined the Continental Army, often in entire regimental units. Many others formed the Philadelphia Brigade of Militia under Cadwalader's command in 1777. Yet others remained associators, in effect local militiamen, throughout the conflict.

Richard Alan Ryerson

See also
Cadwalader, John; Militia, Patriot and Loyalist; Pennsylvania; Philadelphia

References

Boatner, Mark. *Encyclopedia of the American Revolution.* Mechanicsburg, PA: Stackpole, 1994.

Rosswurm, Steven. *Arms, Country, and Class: The Philadelphia Militia and the "Lower Sort" during the American Revolution.* New Brunswick, NJ: Rutgers University Press, 1987.

Ryerson, Richard Alan. *The Revolution Is Now Begun: The Radical Committees of Philadelphia, 1765–1776.* Philadelphia: University of Pennsylvania Press, 1978.

Assunpink Creek, New Jersey, Action at (2–3 January 1777)

Assunpink Creek flows into the Delaware River just below Trenton, New Jersey. The engagement at this site, sometimes called the Second Battle of Trenton, between the American and British armies was a major part of George Washington's Trenton-Princeton Campaign.

Between August and early December 1776, George Washington's army suffered a series of humiliating defeats at the hands of the British. His forces were driven out of New York, through New Jersey, and across the Delaware River into Pennsylvania. Not content to cede New Jersey to the British and settle into winter quarters in Pennsylvania, Washington planned a three-pronged assault on the Hessian garrison at Trenton. The troops directly under his command crossed the Delaware in the midst of a sleet storm and marched 9 miles to surprise the unsuspecting enemy on the morning of 26 December. Colonel Henry Knox's artillery swept the streets and scattered the desperate Hessians. Many of them sought to escape the impending disaster by crossing the bridge over Assunpink Creek. General James Ewing's soldiers had been assigned to block that escape, but the storm prevented their arrival. Continentals managed to close the opening, but not before several hundred enemy troops had reached safety. Washington nevertheless won a lopsided victory and returned to safer ground in Pennsylvania.

The Continental commander was still not through for the season. On 30 December, his army crossed the Delaware again and reoccupied Trenton. Washington, Knox, and Thomas Mifflin averted one disaster by convincing their troops not to disband the following day when their enlistments expired. On 2 January, they faced another crisis when Lord Charles Cornwallis approached Trenton from Princeton with 5,000 redcoats. Colonel Edward Hand's Pennsylvanians slowed the British juggernaut, while Washington's army crossed the bridge over Assunpink Creek, spread out along the south bank, and slowed the enemy with fire from Knox's artillery. The British Army suffered heavy casualties while trying to cross the bridge under fire, and as darkness fell, Cornwallis decided to rest his army and then annihilate his foes the following morning.

During the night, Washington held a war council to discuss his options. The Continentals lacked the force to prevent the greatly superior Cornwallis from crossing Assunpink Creek at daybreak and pinning them against the Delaware, where he could destroy them. Washington therefore planned a bold move: to leave campfires burning, slip his men out of camp under cover of darkness, march east and north 12 miles, and attack the lightly defended British post at Princeton. Secrecy was imperative to keep Cornwallis at bay. The bulk of the Continental Army marched silently out of camp at 1:00 A.M. on 3 January 1777, with the wheels of Knox's guns wrapped in cloth to silence them. Five hundred men and two artillery pieces remained behind for several hours. These men built big fires, marched about, and swung picks and shovels to create the impression of an encamped and entrenching army.

The ruse worked. The American army at Princeton won another surprise victory and then evaded the oncoming troops under an angry Cornwallis and marched to safe winter quarters at Morristown. The action along Assunpink Creek was another bold maneuver by Washington that salvaged an otherwise disastrous campaign.

Mark Thompson

See also
Cornwallis, Charles; Knox, Henry; Princeton, Battle of; Trenton, Battle of; Washington, George

References

Dwyer, William M. *The Day Is Ours! An Inside View of the Battles of Trenton and Princeton, November 1776–January 1777.* New Brunswick, NJ: Rutgers University Press, 1998.

Fischer, David Hackett. *Washington's Crossing.* Oxford and New York: Oxford University Press, 2004.

Ketchum, Richard M. *The Winter Soldiers.* Garden City, NY: Doubleday, 1973.

Atrocities

In a military context, an atrocity commonly refers to any action falling outside the boundaries of what is considered acceptable violence in war. Thus, the term "atrocity" encompasses a wide variety of activities, from killing wounded enemy troops to raping civilians. These behaviors usually occur in the aftermath of battle. But what is considered improper military conduct was often conditioned by numerous other factors, such as the perceptions enemies held of one another and ethnic or cultural differences between them. Finally, if one group oversteps the boundaries of legitimate military conduct or is perceived to have done so, this can lead to retaliatory acts by the enemy, thus generating a spiral of violence and atrocity.

In the Revolutionary era, atrocities included such acts as the wanton killing of wounded soldiers after they had surrendered to their foe. This charge was leveled against British Colonel Banastre Tarleton after the Battle of Waxhaws in South Carolina. Atrocities also included the denial of proper military etiquette, such as the mutilation of the body of Major Patrick Ferguson by the victorious Patriot militia after the Battle of Kings Mountain. While most of the actions considered atrocities occurred during or immediately after combat, the term sometimes included the mistreatment of prisoners.

Atrocities also encompassed the actions of armies toward noncombatants. The abuse of civilians accompanied the march of the British Army across New Jersey in pursuit of General George Washington during the fall of 1776. In that campaign, numerous civilians, regardless of their political affiliation, had their property looted by British and Hessian troops, and they reported several acts of rape allegedly perpetrated by the king's troops on the women of the state regardless of their political affiliation. The abuses were so widespread that some Americans called Britain's march the Rape of the Jerseys.

The manner in which each side perceived the other during the American War for Independence strongly affected the treatment they accorded one another and may help explain both the charges of atrocity and the reality of that behavior. In the minds of many British officers, the officers and men of the Continental Army and various militia groups were simply rebels and therefore did not deserve the same respectful treatment often—but not always—accorded to soldiers in the army of another legitimate European state. Early in the war, Americans captured by the British did not know how they would be treated, and they were often treated harshly. But General Washington's threat to begin a retaliatory harsh treatment of British soldiers held captive by the Americans if American prisoners were not treated well soon pressured Sir William Howe to order a more humane treatment of his army's prisoners.

By the same token, when one side employed methods of fighting that differed substantially from those used by their opponents or came as something unexpected, this could be perceived as atrocious behavior as well. The British attack on General Anthony Wayne's command at Paoli, Pennsylvania, on 21 September 1777, often referred to as the Paoli Massacre, was viewed by Americans as beyond acceptable boundaries in combat because the British attacked at night and because the British troops had been ordered to remove the flints from their muskets and use their bayonets as their primary weapon. From the British perspective, of course, the American employment of expert riflemen to deliberately target British officers, especially during the Saratoga Campaign, was seen as barbaric. Yet neither practice would strike most students of warfare as unusually outrageous.

While the perceptions of opposing sides could have a significant bearing on the treatment they received if captured, clashes between militias and irregular forces generated significantly more violent behavior than did the engagement of regular armies. In this partisan warfare, less regard was shown for any idea of limitations on what could be done. Nowhere was this more so the case than in the South during the latter stages of the war. The conflict there degenerated into a barbarous civil war, with many communities rent from within by various members' differences of political allegiance. It should come as no surprise that incidents of atrocity, such as those recorded at the Battle of Kings Mountain, occurred with greater frequency in the southern theater.

Race and ethnicity could also influence the treatment enemies accorded one another. It is often stated that in the War of Independence, the usual practices of European warfare were not observed on the frontier, especially in confrontations between whites and Native Americans. In this arena of conflict, both sides practiced brutal methods, and violent acts were often perpetrated in order to send messages to the opposing side. Both sides took scalps and engaged in massacres. Loyalists and Native Americans launched a particularly harsh attack on civilians at Cherry Valley, New York, while Pennsylvania's Patriots slaughtered the peaceful Native American residents of Gnadenhutten in the Ohio Country. On the frontier, atrocities committed by both sides quickly degenerated into the spiral of retaliatory violence.

Yet atrocities and even single incidents of barbaric behavior, even when largely exaggerated, could harm perpetrators by stiffening their enemy's resolve to fight. A celebrated example of this effect was the incident known as the "massacre" of Jane McCrea during General John Burgoyne's Saratoga Campaign in 1777. Exaggerated and inaccurate reports of the Loyalist woman's fate—she was killed by a few Native American auxiliaries, acting without any orders, who were serving with Burgoyne's army—disseminated through the rural communities in the upper Hudson River Valley, galvanizing the formerly apathetic locals into putting up a stout defense.

Considered as a whole, especially in comparison to later warfare, the American Revolutionary War saw relatively few atrocities. Most brutal behavior by combatants and most attacks on civilians occurred in Loyalist-Patriot clashes in New Jersey, in the southern campaigns, and on the New York and Northwest frontier. General Washington's insistence on a high level of humane military conduct played a major role in keeping the principal engagements between the Continental and British armies, and the treatment of prisoners by those armies, relatively free of atrocities.

James R. McIntyre

See also

Cherry Valley Massacre; Ferguson, Patrick; Gnadenhutten Massacre; Kings Mountain, Battle of; Native Americans; New Jersey, Operations in; Paoli, Battle of; Prisoners of War; Saratoga Campaign; Tarleton, Banastre; Waxhaws, South Carolina, Action at; Wayne, Anthony

References

Knouff, Gregory T. *The Soldier's Revolution: Pennsylvanians in Arms and the Forging of Early American Identity.* University Park, PA: Penn State University Press, 2004.

Lee, Wayne E. *Crowds and Soldiers in Revolutionary North Carolina: The Culture of Violence in Riot and War.* Gainesville: University Press of Florida, 2001.

McGuire, Thomas J. *Battle of Paoli.* Mechanicsburg, PA: Stackpole, 2000.

Nestor, William R. *The Frontier War for American Independence.* Mechanicsburg, PA: Stackpole, 2004.

Augusta, Georgia, Operations at (1775–1781)

Many Augustans regarded the American Revolution, at its outset, as little more than a war against local Indians with land as a prize. Over the next six years, however, the conflict spread throughout Georgia and into Florida as well and involved local Patriots and Loyalists; Continental, British and French armies; and many Native Americans allied with the British.

Georgia's Indian country began at the Ogeechee River, less than 50 miles west of Augusta. British policy, since the Proclamation of 1763, opposed further encroachments upon Indian territory. Violence began in August 1775 when Augusta's Sons of Liberty, led by George Wells, tortured and nearly killed the Loyalist leader Thomas Brown for rejecting their notion of liberty. After recuperating, Brown rallied Loyalists in the South Carolina up-country who would declare for the king if British redcoats could offer protection. To avoid arrest by the South Carolina Council of Safety, Brown next fled to Florida. There he convinced Governor Patrick Tonyn that Augusta lay open to an Indian attack and volunteered to recruit and lead the Indians with a corps of loyal rangers. Tonyn commissioned Brown a lieutenant-colonel, and Brown's rangers and Indian allies were soon raiding the Georgia frontier.

When British warships first threatened Savannah in January 1776, the provisional government moved to Augusta and drew up Georgia's first constitution, called "Rules and Regulations." News of the Declaration of Independence in July required elections to a convention to draft a new constitution. More conservative Georgians abstained from voting, with the result that radicals such as Button Gwinnett and George Wells dominated the proceedings and produced a radically democratic document. As president of the convention, Gwinnett insisted on leading the Georgia militia in an invasion of Florida but refused to cooperate with the Continental brigade under General Lachlan McIntosh. Gwinnett and McIntosh blamed each other for the failure of the expedition, and in 1777 the two fought a duel in which both were wounded; Gwinnett died and McIntosh recovered. In the state legislature Wells railed against the McIntosh faction and called for the extermination of neighboring Indians.

In 1778 Georgians again attempted to invade Florida, skirmished with Brown's rangers, and accomplished little. But with the larger war at a stalemate in the North, the British turned their attention to the South, where thousands of Loyalists were supposed to be waiting to welcome British troops. A small British force under Lieutenant-Colonel Archibald Campbell quickly overwhelmed Savannah on 29 December and marched to Augusta, occupying that town on 31 January 1779. Although a few hundred men came in from the countryside to swear allegiance to the Crown, the Patriot militia of Georgia and South Carolina, under Elijah Clarke and Andrew Pickens, defeated a body of Loyalists at Kettle Creek, just upriver from Augusta. The Indian allies the British expected were late in arriving, and the approach of an army of North Carolina militia caused Campbell to retreat from Augusta on 14 February 1779. In early March the retreating British turned upon and defeated their pursuers at Briar Creek, 45 miles below Augusta, but made no attempt to march back inland. For some time thereafter, all of Georgia below Briar Creek remained in British hands, and the last royal governor, James Wright, returned from exile to restore the royal government.

In 1779 the Franco-American siege of Savannah failed disastrously, and "independent" Georgia continued to comprise just the backcountry around Augusta. A group of moderate supporters of independence, led by Savannah's John Wereat, organized an ad hoc government and claimed authority. The fiery Wells charged these conservatives with attempting to subvert the state's democratic constitution and called for elections. The voters elected a radical-dominated assembly that chose George Walton as governor. Because Wereat's council refused to recognize Walton, however, Georgia briefly presented the ludicrous picture of two rebel governments in Augusta and one royal government in Savannah.

When Congress recognized the radical government as constitutionally elected, the Wereat council gave up its pretense of government. On 23 January 1780, the legislature passed a comprehensive development program with generous land grants for settlers and still more generous grants for builders of sawmills, gristmills, and iron foundries. The legislation established a commission form of government for Augusta, with authority to lay out streets, sell land, build a courthouse, start a school, and do anything else that might be needed to build up the ad hoc capital. If nothing else, the act illustrated that Georgians valued land as a prize of war.

Before the law could take effect, Charleston, South Carolina, fell to the British in May 1780, and that summer Patriot resistance collapsed deep into the backcountry of both Georgia and South Carolina. Lieutenant-Colonel Brown returned to Augusta with his rangers and the new title of superintendent of Indian affairs. He invited Indian leaders to Augusta and opened a vast communication network that connected Augusta with points as far away as Fort Detroit and Pensacola.

Under Clarke, Georgia militiamen who had fled to the North Carolina mountains staged a raid on Augusta in late summer, with Indian supplies as their object. They besieged Brown's rangers and Indians in his storehouse and waged a four-day battle before British reinforcements arrived to rescue Brown's force. Major Patrick Ferguson then led a Loyalist force north to intercept Clarke's band as they retreated to North Carolina. Instead, on 7 October 1780, North Carolina's Over the Mountain Men, in company with Virginia and South Carolina militia, surrounded Ferguson's Loyalists at Kings Mountain, South Carolina, where they defeated and captured his force and killed Ferguson.

Kings Mountain proved to be a turning point in the southern campaign. Major General Nathanael Greene took charge of Patriot forces in the South in December 1780 and sent troops under Daniel Morgan west to encourage resistance in the backcountry. Morgan gained a smashing victory at Cowpens, South Carolina, in January 1781. Greene fought Cornwallis to a standstill at Guilford Courthouse, North Carolina, in March, and instead of following Cornwallis into Virginia, he moved into South Carolina to pick off isolated British garrisons. And he dispatched Lieutenant Colonel Henry "Light-Horse Harry" Lee to deal with Brown in Augusta. With South Carolina and Georgia militia under Pickens and Clarke, Lee's Continentals waged a fierce two-week attack on Brown's Fort Cornwallis, which fell on 5 June 1781.

General Greene continued to act as Georgia's godfather. With his eye to Georgia's future, he called for the immediate restoration of an independent government. Greene had learned that Russia and Austria were proposing to mediate a peace among Britain, France, and America in the summer of 1781, and, like General Washington and Congress, he feared there was a danger that the British could claim all territory they held at the time of the proposed negotiations. As Governor Wright still controlled Savannah and the low country, Britain might try to win the whole province at the peace table. Writing to an influential Georgian, he argued that a sitting independent legislature was necessary for Georgia's political existence, in Europe even more so than in America. The point was taken, and the scattered members of the general assembly gathered in Augusta on 17 August 1781 and elected Nathan Brownson governor.

Fortunately for the United States, the proposed mediation never materialized, and the great Franco-American victory at Yorktown in October immediately changed both the military and the political equations in America. General Greene dispatched General Anthony Wayne to Georgia to direct the final campaign against Savannah, which the British evacuated in 1782. For the last two years of the war, Georgia's militia, under Clarke and John Twiggs, conducted raids into the Indian country. With the formal conclusion of the war in 1783, Augusta became Georgia's postwar capital and the great market for the rapidly expanding backcountry.

Edward J. Cashin

See also

Briar Creek, Battle of; Brown, Thomas; Campbell, Archibald; Clarke, Elijah; Ferguson, Patrick; Georgia; Greene, Nathanael; Kettle Creek, Battle of; Kings Mountain, Battle of; Lee, Henry; McIntosh, Lachlan; Pickens, Andrew; Savannah, Georgia, British Capture of; Savannah, Georgia, Allied Operations against

References

Cashin, Edward. *The King's Ranger: Thomas Brown and the American Revolution on the Southern Frontier.* Athens: University of Georgia Press, 1989.

Cashin, Edward J., and Heard Robertson. *Augusta and the American Revolution: Events in the Georgia Backcountry, 1773–1783.* Darien, GA: Ashantilly, 1975.

Hall, Leslie. *Land and Allegiance in Revolutionary Georgia.* Athens: University of Georgia Press, 2001.

B

Backus, Isaac (1724–1806)

Isaac Backus was a Baptist minister who advocated the elimination of compulsory religious taxes by provincial and state governments. Born on 9 January 1724 in Norwich, Connecticut, Backus was one of eleven children of Samuel Backus and Elizabeth Tracy. Deeply affected by one of the many revivals collectively known as the Great Awakening, Backus became a member of the Norwich Congregational Church in 1742 and soon joined with those in the congregation who contended that church membership required a convincing testimony of a conversion experience. In 1746 this faction split from the main congregation to form a Separatist congregation. After a year as an itinerant minister, Backus became the pastor of the Separatist congregation in Middleborough, Massachusetts. In 1749 he married Susanna Mason, and the couple had nine children.

In 1756, after much study of the Bible, personal reflection, and debate within his congregation, Backus rejected infant baptism and persuaded his followers to join the Baptist movement. Through his extensive itinerant ministry, writings, and lobbying activity for the denomination, Backus rapidly became one of the most prominent Baptists of the eighteenth century. Between 1747 and 1806, he made more than 900 journeys, traveling nearly 68,000 miles, and delivering more than 9,000 sermons to promote the Separatist and then the Baptist movements. His sustained efforts contributed to a rapid growth of the Baptists in New England. In 1740 there had been only about 1,500 Baptists in the region, but by 1800 there were more than 20,000. Backus helped to establish the Warren Baptist Association, which worked to resolve doctrinal conflicts, and he served on the board of trustees of the College of Rhode Island (later Brown University), an institution established in the 1760s to develop a learned Baptist ministry.

Among Backus's many publications was a four-volume history of the New England Baptists. He lobbied on behalf of Baptists on the local, state, and federal levels and served as a delegate to the ratification convention in Massachusetts, convened to consider approval of the federal Constitution. The focus of his lobbying efforts was the elimination of compulsory religious taxes. His 1773 tract, *An Appeal to the Public for Religious Liberty against the Oppression of the Present Day*, was his clearest statement on the issue. Yet he was not in favor of a complete separation of church and state. Backus believed that America should be a Christian nation, and he fully supported the Massachusetts Constitution's requirement of a religious oath for all officeholders. He also advocated religious training in public schools and wholeheartedly endorsed the state's blue laws. While he could not persuade Massachusetts to abandon its commitment to compulsory religious taxes (which ended only in 1833), Backus remained optimistic. Before his death in 1806, he happily noted a growing wave of revivals around the nation, a development that he trusted would herald the millennium.

Larry Gragg

See also

Constitutions, State; Religion

References

McLoughlin, William G. *Isaac Backus and the American Pietistic Tradition.* Boston: Little, Brown, 1967.

———. "Isaac Backus and the Separation of Church and State in America." *American Historical Review* 73(5) (June 1968): 1392–1413.

Bahamas

In the seventeenth century, the Bahamas were not controlled by any European power, and the island of New Providence with its town of Nassau was a favorite base for pirates. They were finally expelled in 1718 by a British expedition, which took over the islands and installed a royal governor with a small garrison. In 1773, the colony had some 4,000 people, most of them on New Providence, which had some 1,000 white and 1,800 black inhabitants. Harbour Island, Eleuthera, and the Turks and Caicos islands (then part of the Bahamas) also had small populations. The Bahamas were not very prosperous and had no great plantations, but their settlers seemed content with their lovely, small islands.

On 3 March 1776, a fleet of two full-rigged ships, two brigs, a sloop, and a schooner appeared off Nassau. They landed an estimated 250 marines and sailors east of the town. These were American rebels led by Captain Esek Hopkins. Governor Montfort Browne had no garrison, and the militia was armed mostly with fowling guns. The island surrendered with no resistance, and, indeed, the settlers greeted the Americans warmly. The invaders took what guns and ammunition suited their purposes from Forts Nassau and Montague and, after a few weeks, sailed away. In early 1778 another American raiding flotilla, this time led by Captain John Peck Rathburne, repeated the bloodless feat, taking Fort Nassau by surprise on 27 January.

Britain finally sent troops to Nassau from New York in December 1778: four companies of the Garrison Battalion, a unit of invalid veteran American Loyalist soldiers suitable for garrison duty in a small colony. On 6 May 1782, Governor John Maxwell could see a Spanish fleet approaching Nassau. It was led by Juan Manuel de Cagigal, captain general of Cuba, and carried 2,000 regular troops. Maxwell had about 1,400 men, mostly sailors, with only about 170 regular soldiers. Bahamian militiamen felt that resistance was hopeless, and Nassau capitulated two days later.

The Spanish left a 450-man garrison in Nassau. Andrew Deveaux Jr., a Loyalist refugee who had been a lieutenant colonel in the South Carolina militia and was in exile in St. Augustine, decided to recapture the Bahamas. With a band of about 300 men, including some 170 Bahamians recruited at Harbour Island and Eleuthera, Lieutenant Colonel Deveaux and his men landed on New Providence east of Fort Montague on 13 April 1783 and captured the fort. Deveaux's men used various tricks to make the Spaniards believe that they were outnumbered; some dressed as Indians, whom the Spaniards particularly dreaded. The surprised Spaniards retreated to Fort Nassau. On 18 April, the Spanish garrison surrendered on condition of being repatriated to Cuba, to the great joy of the Bahamians, and the Bahamas remained under British sovereignty into the twentieth century.

René Chartrand

See also

Hopkins, Esek

References

Albury, Paul. *The Story of the Bahamas.* London: Macmillan Caribbean, 1975.

Cash, Philip, with Shirley Gordon and Gail Saunders. *Sources of Bahamian History.* London: Macmillan Caribbean, 1991.

Lewis, James A. *The Final Campaign of the American Revolution: Rise and Fall of the Spanish Bahamas.* Columbia: University of South Carolina Press, 1991.

Baldwin, Loammi (1745?–1807)

Loammi Baldwin was born in Woburn, Massachusetts, into a family of limited means. He attended the local grammar school and trained as a craftsman but also took advantage of his proximity to Harvard College, where he studied pumps, pneumatics, hydrostatics, and hydraulics and attended classes in natural science under Professor John Winthrop.

At the beginning of the American Revolution, Baldwin participated in the Middlesex County convention of 1774, but his military experience began even earlier, with his enlistment in the Horse Guards in 1768. At the Battle of Lexington in 1775 he was a major in the Woburn militia, which included 180 men. Although his force arrived after the initial skirmish at Lexington Green, he pressed on to Concord, taking a prisoner and coming under British fire. His most noteworthy accomplishment, on 19 April 1775, was ambushing a retreating British force at Bloody Angle, between Concord and Lexington. The road to Boston took two sharp turns at that point, providing natural ambush positions. Baldwin's troops took advantage of the cover to catch the British in a deadly crossfire, killing 8 soldiers and, far more important, wounding 9 of 10 officers in the advance guard, thereby weakening the British command structure.

In the siege of Boston in 1775 and 1776, Baldwin's unit primarily performed guard duty in Chelsea. In 1776, Baldwin was promoted to colonel and commanded the 26th Continental Regiment at the Battle of Trenton in December of that year. In 1777, however, ill health forced his retirement from the military.

Baldwin served in various political offices during and after the war. He became sheriff of Middlesex County in 1780 and was a state legislator in 1778, 1780, and 1800–1804. He also ran for Congress in 1794 and 1796 and variously for state senator, lieutenant governor, and presidential elector. He was willing to take the unpopular position, as in 1787 when he supported the state government's use of troops in suppressing Shays's Rebellion although the majority of Woburn's citizens opposed the use of troops. But his selection as one of the signers of Massachusetts's currency in 1780 indicates his high standing in the community. After the Continental currency became worthless, the Congress authorized the states to print their own paper money. One measure to reduce the chance of forgery was to require that the currency bear the signatures of two upstanding citizens and a guarantor. Baldwin was one of six citizens chosen for this role.

Baldwin was also a member of the American Academy of Arts and Sciences, and he published two papers under its auspices: "An Account of a Curious Appearance of the Electrical Fluid" and "Observations on Electricity and an Improved Mode of Constructing Lightning Rods." Between 1794 and 1804, Baldwin was manager of the Middlesex Canal project. As an engineer, Baldwin was instrumental in the construction of the canal, which was one of the earliest in the United States. Completed in 1803, the Middlesex Canal became a prototype for several others. Baldwin also developed the Baldwin apple in 1784.

John Barnhill

See also

Lexington and Concord; Massachusetts

References

Adams, Virginia H., and Matthew A. Kierstead. "Middlesex Canal Comprehensive Survey, Phase IV: Survey Report 1999." http://www.middlesexcanal.org/Phase_IV_Report.html, 1999.

Baldwin, Loammi. "An Account of a Curious Appearance of the Electrical Fluid." *Memoirs of the American Academy* 1 (1785): 257–259.

———. "Observations on Electricity and an Improved Mode of Constructing Lightning Rods." *Memoirs of the American Academy* 2(2) (1804): 96–104.

Fischer, David Hackett. *Paul Revere's Ride.* New York: Oxford University Press, 1994.

Galvin, John R. *The Minutemen: The First Fight; Myths and Realities of the American Revolution.* 2nd ed. New York: Pergamon-Brassey's, 1989.

"Loammi Baldwin." Virtualology: A Virtual Education Project, http://famousamericans.net/loammibaldwin/, 2001.

"Loammi Baldwin as a Signer of Massachusetts Paper Money." http://www.rootsweb.com/~nbstdavi/baldwincurrency.html, n.d.

Taylor, Norris. "Colonel Loammi Baldwin." http://members.tripod.com/~ntgen/bw/loammi.html, 1997.

Wilson, James Grant, and John Fiske. *Appleton's Cyclopedia of American Biography.* New York: Appleton, 1887–1889.

Bancroft, Edward (1744–1821)

Edward Bancroft, scientist, diplomat, and spy, was one of the most successful double agents of the war. He operated for British and American intelligence, motivated mostly by money, and his perfidy remained undetected until well after his death.

Bancroft, born in Westfield, Massachusetts, showed an early affinity for natural history, and while still a teenager he left America to pursue his studies. His travels brought him first to Surinam, where he worked for Englishman Paul Wentworth until 1766. Bancroft settled in London in 1767, quickly established himself as a physician, and published writings on natural history and an essay, "Remarks on the Review of the Controversy between Great Britain and Her Colonies," that was sympathetic to the colonies yet still supportive of Britain's claims. His work also brought him in contact with Benjamin Franklin, who befriended Bancroft and acted as his sponsor in European scientific circles.

When the war started, Franklin recruited Bancroft to spy for the Americans, under the cover of secretary to the Commission of United States to France. Franklin assigned Silas Deane, a commission member who had tutored Bancroft as a teen, to act as Bancroft's handler. Meanwhile, Wentworth, now working for British intelligence, learned of Bancroft's hiring and recruited him to pass information about Franco-American negotiations to the British.

While Bancroft worked for both sides, he clearly worked harder for the British, ostensibly because they paid more. England offered Bancroft an annual pension of £200, which was raised to £500. Initially Bancroft fed misinformation to Deane but, recognizing that this increased the likelihood of getting caught, began providing accurate but dated information to the Americans. Bancroft's work for the British proved more useful. The information that he channeled through Wentworth was generally accurate and current. Many French arms shipments were intercepted as a result of Bancroft's intelligence. He took great care in covering his actions. His messages to Wentworth, written under the name Dr. Edward Edwards, were usually in code and invisible ink, and Bancroft used a series of dead drops, such as a hollow tree in Paris's Tuileries Gardens, to send and receive messages.

Bancroft's greatest value to the British was in providing information about the negotiations between France and the American commission. Often his intelligence was so timely that the British knew of a confidential discussion before the French and American negotiators could inform their superiors of it. The Americans signed an alliance with France on 6 February 1778, but the British knew of the agreement long before it was formally announced, thanks to Bancroft.

Bancroft's actions during the war were motivated largely by money, not a loyalty to any one side. He regarded Franklin, and their friendship, as merely a source of income. Also, as hard as he worked to cover his actions, he worked just as hard to pressure his employers for greater pay. Bancroft also used his position as a spy to play the financial markets. He and Deane worked together on a scheme to use their inside knowledge to manipulate European markets by withholding intelligence or even passing misinformation. One such instance involved the defeat of General Burgoyne at Saratoga. Bancroft delayed passing the news to Wentworth so that he could take advantage of the expected drop in value in British funds once the news became public.

While Bancroft was never caught, several persons grew suspicious of his activities. Arthur Lee, a member of the American commission, challenged Bancroft's loyalties before Franklin and Deane but had no proof, and Deane staunchly defended Bancroft. King George III also grew suspicious of Bancroft's loyalties, commenting to William Eden that Bancroft was no more than a war profiteer.

It is possible that Bancroft was not completely successful in hiding his divided loyalties from Franklin. If Franklin did know of Bancroft's true nature, he never said so publicly, but he did allude to this knowledge. When a French noblewoman attempted to warn Franklin about Bancroft, Franklin replied that he was no fool and sometimes it was best to appear naive. Franklin may have known of Bancroft's work for the British and used him to pass misinformation.

Bancroft came close to blowing his cover in an event known as the John the Painter Affair in 1777. Bancroft and Deane arranged a plan for James Aitken to sabotage Royal Navy ships anchored at Portsmouth. The plan was a ruse to make money, as they also wrote letters about the plan that were intended to be intercepted by British intelligence. When Aitken's attack failed, he sought assistance from Bancroft. They met at a coffee shop near Bancroft's London apartment, and Bancroft was able to convince Aitken to name only Deane as a conspirator should he be caught. Aitken was promptly arrested, and Bancroft testified at his trial. Though Aitken lived up to his promise, British authorities were suspicious of Bancroft's connection to the affair, which forced Bancroft to leave London for full-time residence in Paris.

Bancroft continued to serve British intelligence until 1784, though his credibility and usefulness declined after the signing of the Franco-American Alliance in 1778. In 1782, he returned to America to gather intelligence, a trip he hoped would demonstrate his value to Britain so that he could keep his pension. Bancroft also continued to work with Deane, who was discharged from American service in 1778. Deane attempted to return from England to America in 1789 to clear his name but died shortly after boarding his ship. His death was officially ruled a suicide, but historian Julian Boyd advanced the theory that Bancroft poisoned Deane before he departed so that Deane would not reveal Bancroft's duplicity. The intriguing theory is based on Bancroft's medical knowledge and his role as Deane's physician, but it can probably never be proven.

After his discharge, Bancroft worked as a scientist in London until his death. The direct confirmation of his spying for Britain was not revealed until nearly seventy years after he died, at which time his grandson, General William G. Bancroft of the British Army, destroyed Bancroft's personal papers in a fit of anger.

Michael C. Miller

See also

Deane, Silas; Diplomacy, American; Diplomacy, French; Franco-American Alliance; Franklin, Benjamin; Wentworth, Paul

References

Bemis, Samuel Flagg. "British Secret Service and the French-American Alliance." *American Historical Review* 29 (1924): 474–495.

Boyd, Julian P. "Silas Deane: Death by a Kindly Teacher of Treason?" *William and Mary Quarterly* 16 (1959): 165–187, 319–342, 515–549.

Labaree, Leonard, William B. Willcox, et al. *The Papers of Benjamin Franklin.* 38 vols. to date. New Haven, CT: Yale University Press, 1952–.

Stevens, Benjamin Franklin. *Facsimiles of Manuscripts in European Archives Relating to America, 1773–1783.* London: Malby and Sons, 1889–1895.

Banneker, Benjamin (1731–1806)

The farmer and noted surveyor and astronomer Benjamin Banneker's natural gifts for scientific investigation demonstrated to his contemporaries that persons of African American heritage could make significant contributions to American society. Among his most famous achievements was his challenge to Thomas Jefferson to square the rhetoric of the Declaration of Independence with America's deep involvement in racial slavery.

The son of a freed slave father and mixed-race mother, Banneker was born in 1731 in Baltimore County, Maryland, on a one hundred-acre farm the family owned outright. Largely self-educated, he read literature, history, and mathematics in between his labors on his father's farm, where he resided until his death.

Banneker's mathematical skills soon put him in demand among his neighbors, for whom he kept accounts. Throughout adolescence he created numerous mathematical puzzles, and when he was twenty-one he constructed a working, striking clock made almost entirely of wood. The invention made him a local celebrity, and many came to see and admire the device. At maturity, he took over the family farm, raising tobacco, wheat, and corn; he also kept bees for honey. After the death of his parents, he lived alone on the farm, never marrying.

In 1771, as Banneker turned forty, the Ellicott family purchased a large estate next to his farm. Banneker became friendly with George Ellicott, the youngest son and an eager astronomer. Ellicott found a kindred spirit in Banneker, twenty years his senior, to whom he soon lent out books and a telescope. Banneker was immediately hooked on astron-

Benjamin Banneker, born a free African American in Maryland, became a self-taught mathematician, scientist, astronomer, and almanac maker. (North Wind Picture Archives)

omy and soon became largely nocturnal. Each night he gazed up at the sky, and he soon gained enough confidence in his new avocation to propose the theory that each star was a central sun around which planets surely circled.

After the Revolutionary War, Banneker's mathematical skills drew him to the attention of George's father, Andrew Ellicott III, the surveyor for the new nation's capital on the Potomac. For more than two months during the spring of 1791, the sixty-year-old Banneker served as Ellicott's assistant, slogging across difficult terrain by day and camping out at night as he surveyed the four 10-mile boundary lines. Utilizing many of the calculations that his assistantship had required, Banneker returned to his farm in April to create an almanac that compiled astronomical data and observations alongside literary and supplemental content supplied by his printer. It proved popular locally, and while it never made him rich, the almanac was issued annually until 1797.

Shortly before the publication of the almanac's first edition, Banneker sent a manuscript copy of his astronomical calculations to then Secretary of State Thomas Jefferson. Alongside the calculations he enclosed a 10,000-word letter outlining the discrepancies he perceived between the Declaration of Independence's egalitarian posture and the perpetuation of American slavery. The letter and Jefferson's sympathetic reply were soon published in a pamphlet, bringing Banneker some controversial fame as an African American of intellect and accomplishment. He thus became a figurehead for the cause of emancipation in the 1790s. Soon thereafter his declining health forced a retreat from public life. He died in his sleep at home on his farm a month short of his seventy-fifth birthday.

A divisive figure in the later years of his life, Banneker faced intimidation and threats of physical violence from proslavery neighbors and endured vandalism to his property after his pamphlet began to circulate. Yet in 1791, the annus mirabilis in which he surveyed the capital city, published his first almanac, and challenged Jefferson, one commentator preempted Banneker's later memorialists by placing him alongside the poet Phillis Wheatley and the essayist Ignacio Sancho as a leading example of the undeniable intellect of an enslaved race.

Richard J. Bell

See also

Jefferson, Thomas; Slaves and Free Blacks; Wheatley, Phillis

References

Bedini, Silvio A. *The Life of Benjamin Banneker: The First African American Man of Science.* Rev. ed. Baltimore: Maryland Historical Society, 1998.

Cerami, Charles A. *Benjamin Banneker: Surveyor, Astronomer, Publisher, Patriot.* New York: Wiley, 2002.

Graham, Shirley. *Your Most Humble Servant.* New York: Julian Messner, 1949.

Barbé-Marbois, François, Marquis de (1745–1837)

François Barbé-Marbois served as secretary to the French minister to the United States, the Chevalier de la Luzerne, during the Revolutionary War, as chargé d'affaires in America after the war, and as intendant (governor) of the French colony of St. Domingue (later Haiti) in the late 1780s. In 1803 Barbé-Marbois was the chief French negotiator of the Louisiana Purchase agreement.

Barbé-Marbois was born in 1745 in Metz, where his father was director of the royal mint, and entered the French diplomatic service as a young man. Barbé-Marbois's first major foreign post was secretary of the French legation to the Diet of the Holy Roman Empire at Ratisbon. There, in 1778, he and his superior, Luzerne, were successful in resolving the Bavarian succession crisis to France's satisfaction, and in 1779 the two were sent to America, Luzerne as French minister to the United States and Barbé-Marbois as secretary of the legation.

The intelligent and learned secretary had a gift for writing and was very popular in America. During his six years of service in the United States, beginning on his voyage across the Atlantic in company with Luzerne, John Adams, and young

John Quincy Adams, Barbé-Marbois wrote several letters to his fiancée in France, since published, that give a vivid picture of America and a view of France at the end of the old regime. Although he had a fiancée in France, he permitted himself relationships with certain American ladies, and on 17 June 1784, Barbé-Marbois married Elizabeth Moore of Philadelphia, the daughter of the locally prominent William Moore. When Barbé-Marbois dined with George Washington, the general congratulated him on his marriage as a sign of French attachment to the United States.

Barbé-Marbois remained in America from 1779 to 1785, and when Luzerne returned to France in 1784, Barbé-Marbois became chargé d'affaires, serving until he was made intendant at San Domingue, the largest and wealthiest French colony in the Americas, where he was an efficient and attentive governor. Upon his return to France at the end of 1789, he reentered the department of foreign affairs and was again sent, with the Duc de Nouville, on a mission to the Diet of the Holy Roman Empire and to Emperor Leopold. On his return to France, Barbé-Marbois was arrested, and when he was released he left government service and retired to Metz, where he farmed and was elected mayor.

Following the turmoil of the French Revolution, which claimed the lives of several of his friends and acquaintances from government service, Barbé-Marbois was again honored and brought into government service. In 1803 he became the principal French negotiator of the Louisiana Purchase and advised the Emperor Napoleon that France "should not hesitate to make a sacrifice of that which is about to slip from us." Napoleon replied by renouncing Louisiana and directing Barbé-Marbois to negotiate the treaty with the envoys of the United States.

Napoleon later rewarded Barbé-Marbois for his services, but after the emperor's defeat, Barbé-Marbois turned from a Bonapartist into a supporter of the Restoration and was well compensated. In 1815, now more than seventy years old, he was named minister of finance by Louis XVIII. Barbé-Marbois left the ministry in 1816 but served again under Charles X. Barbé-Marbois died in 1837 at the age of ninety-two.

Linda Miller

See also
Diplomacy, French; Luzerne, Anne-César de la

Reference

Chase, E. P., ed. *Our Revolutionary Forefathers: The Letters of François, Marquis de Barbé-Marbois.* New York: Duffield, 1929.

Barclay, Thomas (1728–1793)

Thomas Barclay, America's first consul to France and the first diplomat to negotiate an American treaty with a non-European power, was born in Strabane, Ireland. He migrated to Philadelphia, where he became a wealthy ship owner and merchant sometime before 1770, the year he married Mary Hoops of Philadelphia. With the outbreak of hostilities between the colonies and the mother country, he threw his full support behind the Revolutionary cause.

During 1774 and 1775, Barclay served as a member of Philadelphia's Committee of Correspondence, where he concerned himself with the situation in Boston following the Boston Tea Party and corresponded with other colonies in calling for the First Continental Congress. He was a leading member of the Committee of Inspection and Observation for the City of Philadelphia in 1775–1776. From 8 to 14 December 1776, George Washington stayed at Barclay's summer house (Summerseat), using it as his headquarters shortly before crossing the Delaware to attack Trenton and Princeton. The following year, Barclay served on the Pennsylvania Navy Board. As one of the original members of the Friendly Sons of St. Patrick, he served as its president from 1779 to 1781. And in 1780 he was one of the subscribers to the first Bank of Pennsylvania, giving £5,000 to help supply the Continental Army with provisions.

That same year, Congress appointed William Palfrey as American consul in France, but after his ship was lost at sea, Congress appointed Barclay, first as vice-consul on 26 June 1781 and, after it was certain that Palfrey had perished, as consul on 5 October. Barclay thereby became the first American consul to serve in a foreign land, arriving in France in late 1781. He was promoted to consul general in France on 2 January 1783. Congress also appointed Barclay a commissioner for the settling of American accounts in Europe on 18 November 1782, and he spent much time in Paris, Lorient, and Amsterdam obtaining provisions for the Revolutionary cause.

Barclay served as consul in France from 1781 to 1787, and although his personal difficulties with creditors caused the United States some embarrassment, he maintained a reputation for honesty and public service, as evidenced by the support of Thomas Jefferson and others after Barclay's arrest for debt in Bordeaux. In 1785 Barclay was designated by Jefferson and John Adams to negotiate a "treaty of amity and alliance" with the Sultan of Morocco. Barclay negotiated this treaty of friendship and commerce, also known as the Treaty of Marrakech, in 1786, and Congress ratified it on 18 July 1787. Today it is still in force, making it the oldest and longest-standing U.S. treaty with any foreign country.

Barclay returned to the United States in 1788. On 31 March 1791, Secretary of State Jefferson appointed Barclay consul to Morocco, and he departed shortly afterward. But Barclay died en route at Lisbon, Portugal, on 19 January 1793, apparently after a duel with a Spanish nobleman who had spoken insultingly of American womanhood. Barclay was buried at the British Protestant Episcopal Cemetery at Lisbon.

Michael Sletcher

See also

Adams, John; Congress, First Continental; Congress, Second Continental and Confederation; Continental Army; Correspondence, Committees of; Jefferson, Thomas; Washington, George

References

Campbell, John H. *History of the Friendly Sons of St. Patrick and of the Hibernian Society for the Relief of Emigrants from Ireland, March 17, 1771–March 17, 1892.* Philadelphia: Hibernian Society, 1892.

Congress of the United States. "On the Memorial of Mary, Widow of Thomas Barclay, Praying Compensation for Consular and Other Services Performed by Her Husband, January 8, 1808." P. 347 in *American State Papers,* Vol. 1, *Claims.* Washington, DC: Gales and Seaton, 1834.

Moffat, R. Burnham. *The Barclays of New York: Who They Are and Who They Are Not—and Some Other Barclays.* New York: Robert Grier Cooke, 1904.

Barlow, Joel (1754–1812)

Joel Barlow, one of the Hartford or Connecticut Wits, became an international entrepreneur, cultural leader, and sometime diplomat but left his mark as America's first epic poet.

Barlow was born in Redding, Connecticut, on 24 March 1754. Although his formal education included a brief period at the new Dartmouth College, it was at Yale College, as a member of the class of 1778, that he developed his lifelong interest in poetry. Barlow first wrote satirical verse and lyrical prose delivered at college commencements. Following graduation, he became chaplain of the Third Massachusetts Brigade and was secretly engaged to Ruth Baldwin of Connecticut, whom he married in 1781.

At the end of the war, Barlow opened a printing office in Hartford and embarked on his dream to become the epic poet of the new United States. Selecting as his theme the discovery of America, he published an epic poem in nine books, *The Vision of Columbus,* in 1787. Subscribers to the poem included George Washington, Benjamin Franklin, and Louis XVI.

In 1787, Barlow joined the Scioto Associates, a short-lived and dubious business enterprise to interest Europeans in the purchase of Ohio lands, and he sailed to Europe in 1788 to promote the venture. In Europe he continued to develop his literary, political, and social interests by meeting several prominent contemporaries, including William Blake, Thomas Paine, the Marquis de Lafayette, Joseph Priestley, and Mary Wollstonecraft. During the early days of the French Revolution, Barlow continued to write poetry as well as political and social propaganda and earned the distinction of being named a citizen of France. While on a tour to Savoy in 1793, he wrote and published the poem for which he is perhaps best known, "The Hasty Pudding."

In 1794 and 1795 Barlow amassed a considerable fortune while engaged in the shipping business in Hamburg. After the signing of the Jay Treaty, the Barlows returned to Paris, where Joel continued to develop his international connections and his fluency in foreign languages. Barlow was named U.S. minister to Algiers in 1796, where he successfully embarked on negotiations for a treaty to free the Mediterranean of Algerian pirates and ensure the release of more than one hundred Americans whom the pirates had seized. He returned to France in late 1797 and bought a house in Paris, where he became a patron of the arts and sciences and a friend and supporter of the inventor Robert Fulton, who lived with the Barlows for several years.

When the Barlows returned to the United States in 1804 and settled at their estate, Kalorama, they became active in Washington social and political circles. Several leaders of the American Revolution encouraged Barlow to write a history of the new nation, but he declined. He did, however, chronicle some events of the Revolutionary War in a revised version of his *Vision of Columbus,* which he published in 1807 as *The Columbiad.* And in 1811, James Madison called upon Barlow to resume his diplomatic efforts and negotiate a treaty with Napoleon. During this mission, Barlow traveled through Poland, where he contracted pneumonia and died on 26 December 1812.

Martha J. King

See also

Diplomacy, American; Paine, Thomas

References

Mulford, Carla J. "Joel Barlow." Pp. 166–168 in *American National Biography,* Vol. 2. New York: Oxford University Press, 1999.

Woodress, James. *A Yankee's Odyssey: The Life of Joel Barlow.* Philadelphia: Lippincott, 1958.

Zunder, Theodore Albert. *The Early Days of Joel Barlow, a Connecticut Wit.* New Haven: Yale University Press, 1934.

Barras, Jacques Melchoir, Comte de (1719–1793)

Jacques Barras was a distinguished French naval officer who fought in the campaigns of 1778 with Admiral d'Estaing, succeeded Ternay as commander of the squadron at Newport, delivered Rochambeau's artillery to Yorktown, and served during action at Gloucester, Virginia, and at St. Kitts against Admiral Hood.

Barras was born at Arles, in Provence, in 1719 to an old Provençal noble family. He joined the navy as a midshipman on 17 May 1734 and was promoted successively to lieutenant on 23 May 1754, captain on 15 January 1762, and squadron commander on 1 June 1778. As a lieutenant aboard the *Fier* (50 guns), he served in La Galissonière's squadron in 1756 and was present at the victory off Minorca against Admiral

Byng. Barras was aboard the *Souverain* (74 guns) in La Clue's squadron in 1759 when that ship narrowly escaped capture by the British and sought refuge at Rochefort.

Barras served with distinction in the American Revolutionary War. He was made squadron commander on 1 June 1778, replaced Breugnon, and took command of the *Tonnant* (80 guns). He went on campaign with d'Estaing aboard the *Zélé* (74 guns), leaving Toulon on 13 April and arriving in Delaware on 7 July, after which he took part in the blockade of Howe's squadron off Sandy Hook until 21 July. On 8 August Barras forced his way through the channel and dropped anchor off Rhode Island before confronting Howe's squadron on the following day. Barras later served in the action against Barrington off St. Lucia on 22 December. From 9 January to 23 March 1779, he safely escorted a convoy of fifty-nine merchant ships from Cap Français to La Rochelle. He distinguished himself as commander of the French squadron at Grenada on 6 July 1779 and in September of that year off Savannah.

In 1781 he was appointed by Castries, the secretary of the navy, to replace Ternay, then aboard the *Duc de Bourgogne* (80 guns), and arrived at Newport on 10 May aboard the frigate *Concorde.* A short time later Barras assumed command from Destouches, who had been acting as squadron commander after Ternay's death. Barras actively supported the Count de Grasse's plan against Cornwallis at Yorktown. On 25 August, eight ships under Barras, plus the vessels loaded with Rochambeau's heavy artillery and siege equipment, left Newport for Chesapeake Bay. After Grasse's victory on 5 September, the squadron entered the Chesapeake, where Barras distinguished himself in the action at Gloucester.

Barras was promoted to lieutenant general on 12 January 1782. He distinguished himself in the action off St. Kitts against Hood from 25 to 26 January 1782. His efforts contributed to the capture of that island as well as Nevis and Montserrat, at the last of which he supported the land operations conducted by the Count de Fléchin. Barras received the Grand Cross of Saint Louis in 1784. He was named vice admiral on 1 January 1792 by the Revolutionary government but refused to serve. He died the following year.

Patrick Villiers

See also

Estaing, Jean-Baptiste, Comte d'; Gloucester Point, Virginia, Action at; Grasse, François-Joseph-Paul, Comte de; Grenada, Battle of; St. Kitts, Battle of; St. Lucia, Naval and Military Operations against; Ternay, Charles Henri Louis; Yorktown Campaign

References

Clowes, William Laird. *The Royal Navy: A History from the Earliest Times to 1900.* 7 vols. London: Chatham, 1996.

Dull, John R. *The French Navy and the American Revolution: A Study of Arms and Diplomacy, 1774–1787.* Princeton, NJ: Princeton University Press, 1975.

Gardiner, Robert, ed. *Navies and the American Revolution, 1775–1783.* London: Chatham, 1996.

Barré, Isaac (1726–1802)

Born in Dublin in 1726, Isaac Barré was the son of a French Huguenot refugee family from La Rochelle. Although his parents intended him for the law, Barré left Trinity College, Dublin, for an ensign's commission in the British Army in 1746. He served with great competence in James Wolfe's regiment in the Louisbourg and Quebec Campaigns in Canada, during which he met his future patron, Lord Shelburne. A horrible wound received in the Battle of Quebec (1759) left Barré blinded in one eye and with a distinctive facial scar. He was at Wolfe's side when the general died during the battle.

Returning to England, Barré was promoted to lieutenant-colonel of the 106th Foot Regiment (Black Musketeers), who suppressed disturbances in Cornwall by the brigand tinners. He represented Chipping Wycomb (1761–1774) in the House of Commons through Shelburne's patronage. A masterful orator and skillful administrator, Barré served as adjutant-general and governor of Stirling in the Bute government but left his bureaucratic job under pressure from the new Grenville ministry in 1763. Originally an opponent of William Pitt, Barré became a strong Pitt supporter through their joint support of the radical politician John Wilkes. During the

Isaac Barré, who served in Parliament, opposed much of the legislation respecting taxation on the American colonists, who adopted for themselves Barré's term, "sons of liberty." (Library of Congress)

Stamp Act debates in the Commons, Barré coined the phrase "Sons of Liberty" and strongly opposed the government's method of taxing the American colonies, predicting rebellion if the colonies were forced to pay. He spoke against Townshend, characterizing the colonists as people who had fled British oppression and developed self-defense and sufficiency, rather than ungrateful children of the king. Barré also may have written the "Junius" letters, which appeared in 1768 as a harsh critique of the Tory ministry.

George III disliked both Wilkes and Barré and pushed for the latter's resignation from the army in February 1773. Subsequently, Barré served as a member of Parliament from Caine from 1774 to 1790. Despite Barré's support for the colonists and fierce criticism of Lord North, he ultimately voted to enforce the Boston Port Act, arguing that subordinate parliaments must obey the Westminster Parliament under the British Constitution. In 1782, his appointment as treasurer of the Royal Navy, with its large pension, sparked public criticism of Rockingham, and Barré was posted instead as clerk of the pells, then appointed paymaster-general under the subsequent Shelburne ministry. Completely blind by 1785, Barré retired from the House of Commons in 1790 and died at his Mayfair home on 20 July 1802. Three American cities are named in his honor: Barre, Massachusetts; Barre, Vermont; and Wilkes-Barre, Pennsylvania.

Margaret Sankey

See also

Boston Port Act; Petty-Fitzmaurice, William, 2nd Earl of Shelburne; Pitt, William, the Elder; Sons of Liberty; Wilkes, John

References

Alvord, Clarence. *Lord Shelburne and the Founding of British-American Goodwill.* London: Oxford University Press, 1926.

Britton, John. *Authorship of the Letters of Junius Elucidated.* London: J. R. Smith, 1848.

Miner, Sidney. *Colonel Isaac Barré, 1726–1802.* Wilkes-Barre, PA: Wyoming Historical and Geological Society, 1901.

Barren Hill, Pennsylvania, Action at (20 May 1778)

As his last military encounter in America, General Sir William Howe led 11,000 British troops against the Marquis de Lafayette's 4,000 American soldiers in an unsuccessful attempt to surround and capture the rebel force at Barren Hill, Pennsylvania, about halfway between Valley Forge and Philadelphia.

In the spring of 1778, Howe had resigned as commander in chief of the king's forces in America and was preparing to return to London. Sir Henry Clinton, his replacement, arrived in Philadelphia on 8 May, and three days later Howe formally handed over power to the new military chieftain. In reality, however, Clinton was awaiting Howe's departure before assuming active command. General George Washington was encamped at Valley Forge, about 20 miles west of Philadelphia, with the American army.

In an attempt to learn more about British intentions for the upcoming campaign, Washington ordered Lafayette, who was only twenty years old and had been in America less than a year, to venture over the Schuylkill River about 12 miles north of Philadelphia on the morning of 18 May. Lafayette's orders were to secure information, disrupt British communications, and shield the American encampment at Valley Forge should the enemy march in that direction. Proceeding with his men to Swede's Ford, Lafayette crossed the Schuylkill River and took position on the crest of Barren Hill. He posted his troops to cover all routes of approach to the camp and made sure that three fords across the Schuylkill were open should he need to retreat. Then he began scouting the British lines around Philadelphia and sending spies into the city to secure information.

The British, meanwhile, were honoring the departing General Howe with the Meschianza, a wild and elaborate celebration that began on 18 May and continued into the morning of the following day. During the party, Howe learned from scouts and Loyalists that the American force was encamped at Barren Hill and that Lafayette, "the Boy" as the British called him, was the commander. Discerning an opportunity to end his service with the capture of Lafayette, Howe determined to lead an expedition against the American encampment. He divided his men into three attacking columns, with the intention of encircling Lafayette with vastly superior forces on three sides and trapping him against the Schuylkill River. Howe would then attack and force Lafayette to surrender before Washington could come to his assistance.

General James Grant marched on 19 May, in command of 5,000 soldiers, with orders to proceed toward Whitemarsh, around Lafayette's left flank, and cut off the American retreat across the Schuylkill. Grant's men, the cream of the British Army, were the Queen's Rangers, the Guards, two light infantry battalions, three other regiments, and fifteen cannon. By the morning of 20 May, Grant had marched 20 miles and gotten into position, seizing all the vital roads without alerting Lafayette. Early that same morning Howe, accompanied by his brother, Admiral Richard Howe, and General Clinton, led 6,000 troops out of Philadelphia through Germantown and directly up the Ridge Road toward Barren Hill for a frontal assault. Along the way, General Howe dropped off General Charles Grey, with 2,000 grenadiers and a small troop of dragoons, with orders to take position on Lafayette's left flank without being detected. Grey also achieved his purpose. Howe's own column, however, was detected.

Lafayette had posted Captain Allan McLane and his partisan corps of 150 horsemen, along with 50 Oneida Indians, to patrol the Ridge Road south of the American camp. During the early morning of 20 May, McLane captured two British grenadiers who informed him of Howe's plans. Ordering a company of riflemen to retard Howe's approach, McLane rode quickly to Lafayette's camp. Just at daybreak, he arrived and spread the alarm, confirming what Lafayette had just learned from other sources. As the sleepy men were roused to arms and disposed in a defensive posture, they seemed on the verge of panic. Indeed, the situation was desperate. Lafayette, however, remained calm. He dispatched riders to seek help from Washington, 11 miles away at Valley Forge, only to have them return with news that Grant and Howe held the roads to Swede's, Blevin's, and Matson's fords. The Americans appeared to be cut off.

Just when all seemed lost, Lafayette learned from a scout that there was a road to Matson's Ford shielded from enemy observation. If Grant could be held in place, perhaps the Americans could escape. Lafayette organized a rear guard at St. Peter's Church to make Grant believe he was under attack. Meanwhile, with great discipline, the Americans began withdrawing while Lafayette remained behind with the rear guard. Grant was thrown into confusion by these maneuvers. When British officers saw the rebels withdrawing, they pleaded with Grant for permission to attack. He refused, believing that it was a ruse to draw his attention away from an impending assault. Lafayette soon managed to get his entire force across the Schuylkill and arrayed in strong defensive positions on the other bank. Grant finally pushed his men forward to Barren Hill and reconnoitered Lafayette's new position. Deciding that the enemy's retreat was a ruse to draw him into attacking strong rebel forces that must be lurking nearby, Grant withdrew, and Howe reluctantly ordered his troops back to Philadelphia. Grant's actions at Barren Hill were supported by Howe and Grey, although they were disappointed that Lafayette had escaped. Other British officers were less forgiving of their colleague, who had been bested by "the Boy." The Americans, of course, were delighted at the outcome.

Paul David Nelson

See also

Grant, James; Grey, Charles; Lafayette, Marquis de

References

Gottschalk, Louis. *Lafayette Joins the American Army.* Chicago: University of Chicago Press, 1937.

Jackson, John W. *With the British Army in Philadelphia, 1777–1778.* San Rafael, CA: Presidio, 1979.

Nelson, Paul David. *General James Grant: Scottish Soldier and Royal Governor of East Florida.* Gainesville: University Press of Florida, 1993.

———. *Sir Charles Grey, First Earl Grey: Royal Soldier, Family Patriarch.* Madison, NJ: Fairleigh Dickinson University Press, 1996.

Barrington, Samuel (1729–1800)

Samuel Barrington, a rear admiral in the Royal Navy at the beginning of the American Revolution, served competently but with little distinction against the French in the West Indies, commanding a squadron at the Battle of St. Lucia and holding subordinate rank at later actions fought off Grenada and St. Kitts. The fifth son of John, Viscount Barrington, Barrington entered the Royal Navy at the age of eleven and became a sloop captain in 1747. In the Seven Years' War he commanded the *Achilles* (60 guns), with which he captured the *Raisonnable* (64 guns) in 1759 and a large French privateer laden with supplies and commercial goods. He served in operations along the French coast and in 1760 was sent to North America with a squadron under Vice Admiral John Byron to reduce the fortress of Louisbourg. The following year Barrington took part in the operations against Belle Isle, off the French coast. When peace was concluded in 1763, Barrington had an almost unbroken record of service with the navy dating back to 1741.

Barrington's first service in the American Revolution came in 1777 when he commissioned the *Prince of Wales* (74 guns), stationed in the Channel Fleet. In January of the following year he was promoted to rear admiral and dispatched to the West Indies as commander of the Leeward Islands station. Barrington arrived at Barbados on 20 June 1778 shortly before the French declaration of war. His instructions ordered him to remain at his post, but on 12 September he received word from the lieutenant governor of Dominica that a strong French expedition had arrived and that the island would shortly fall. The estimate given for the force later proved rather an exaggeration, but the 2,000 French, having already left Martinique, did indeed capture the island. Based on these exaggerated reports of the strength of French forces, Barrington believed that he did not possess the numbers necessary to confront them and instead sailed to Antigua to prepare its defenses. He returned to Barbados after Commodore William Hotham arrived on 10 December with five small ships of the line, two frigates, and a convoy carrying 5,000 troops under General James Grant. Barrington, together with Hotham and Grant, decided to make an attack on St. Lucia and reached the Grand Cul de Sac on 13 December. Grant's troops went ashore and took the island without much resistance, though the French governor fled into the mountains to await relief.

No sooner had the island been secured, however, than a French fleet came into sight. This force was commanded by Admiral Jean-Baptiste d'Estaing, who had left Boston and sailed to Martinique practically parallel with Hotham's fleet, though neither side had known of the other's presence. Barrington had not anticipated the appearance of the French, and

Vice-Admiral Samuel Barrington. He served in the Seven Years' War (1756–1763) during which he took part in the expedition against Louisbourg. During the American Revolutionary War he fought in the West Indies and aided in the relief of Gibraltar in 1782. (Library of Congress)

his ships were not positioned for a proper defense. By morning, however, he had managed to establish a line across the opening of the bay, each end supported by guns mounted on the hills overlooking his anchorage. D'Estaing's ships formed into a line of battle, passed along Barrington's squadron (firing as they went), and proceeded out of the bay, repeating the same movement later in the afternoon. This action, however, proved indecisive, and on 18 December the French landed their troops at a point north of the bay and attempted several vain assaults on a hill defended by troops under Brigadier-General Medows. On hearing of the approach of a superior force under Vice Admiral Byron, d'Estaing withdrew with his remaining forces to Martinique. The French governor of St. Lucia thereupon had no choice but to surrender himself.

Byron, in fact, did not arrive at St. Lucia until 7 January 1779. He superseded Barrington, who became second in command of the West Indies fleet. In that capacity Barrington fought at Grenada on 6 July and in the defense of St. Kitts. Afterward he received permission to return home and in the spring of 1780 was offered command of the Channel Fleet. Owing to problems arising from a dispute between fellow officers (the Keppel-Palliser controversy) during the previous year, this new post was not an attractive one, and Barrington refused it in preference for the position of second in command under Admiral Francis Geary. When Geary resigned in August, Barrington refused to replace him, again insisting in a letter to the Admiralty that he would hold only the second most senior post. Geary actually relinquished command before the Admiralty had answered Barrington's letter, whereupon Barrington requested that Admiral Sir Thomas Pye assume command until the Admiralty's views were made known. This proposal prevented Barrington from any chance of further promotion while Lord North's government remained in office.

In April 1782, aboard the *Britannia,* Barrington again served in the Channel Fleet as second in command, then under Lord Howe. During Howe's temporary absence Barrington commanded off Ushant but again assumed the junior post when Howe returned. Barrington served in the relief of Gibraltar on 16–19 October and in the action against the Franco-Spanish fleets on 20 October. Afterward the fleet returned to Britain, and in February 1783 Barrington resigned his command. Four years later he was promoted to admiral and in 1790 was made second in command of the fleet again under Howe, under whose command he was to challenge Spain over the Nootka Sound incident involving Anglo-Spanish territorial disputes off the western coast of Canada. Hostilities did not result, however, and this proved Barrington's last occasion of service. Inexplicably, he did not hold command during the French Revolutionary Wars. Had Barrington not been superseded shortly after his independent command at St. Lucia, he might have distinguished himself during a period when the standards of officership among the senior ranks of the Royal Navy were low in relation to the standards of British naval campaigns before and since the American Revolution.

Gregory Fremont-Barnes

See also

British West Indies; Byron, John; Estaing, Jean-Baptiste, Comte d'; French Navy; French West Indies; Gibraltar, Siege of; Grenada, Battle of; Martinique, Battle of; Royal Navy; St. Kitts, Battle of; St. Lucia, Naval and Military Operations against

References

Clowes, William Laird. *The Royal Navy: A History from the Earliest Times to 1900.* 7 vols. London: Chatham, 1996.

Gardiner, Robert, ed. *Navies and the American Revolution, 1775–1783.* London: Chatham, 1996.

Morrissey, Brendan. *The American Revolution: The Global Struggle for National Independence.* San Diego, CA: Thunder Bay, 2001.

Barry, John (1745–1803)

A man of integrity, energy, and professional skill, John Barry ranks as one of the Continental Navy's greatest officers. He was also one of its most resourceful and ready-to-command officers of river barges when ships were not available and of troops on land when it was impossible to put out to sea, and he had the ability to win victories on land, river, or open water.

A native of Ireland, Barry immigrated to Philadelphia, where he became a respected merchant captain. In November and December 1775, he oversaw the outfitting of the Continental Navy's first warships. The following January, he supervised the construction of the Pennsylvania State Navy ship *Montgomery.* In March 1776, through the auspices of Congressman Robert Morris, Barry secured a captain's commission and command of the brigantine *Lexington* (14 guns). Over the next six months, Barry made two successful cruises in the *Lexington* but relinquished command of that vessel to take charge of the *Effingham,* one of four frigates then under construction in Philadelphia.

The *Effingham* was launched on 31 October 1776, but shortages of money, men, and stores prevented the frigate from ever getting to sea. In mid-December, Barry mustered a small force of sailors and mounted guns to help defend the American capital from British forces that had advanced in west New Jersey. He also served as an aide-de-camp in John Cadwalader's militia brigade and participated in the American victory at Princeton on 3 January 1777. When General Howe's army menaced Philadelphia again in September 1777, Barry moved the *Effingham* to a safe anchorage above the city near Bordentown, New Jersey, but the threat of enemy capture necessitated scuttling the frigate on 2 November. With no ship to command, Barry organized and led a small force of barges that plied the lower Delaware River in February and March 1778, disrupting the voyages of British supply ships.

John Barry's next command, the Continental frigate *Raleigh,* was brief and ended in disaster. Departing Boston on 25 May 1778, Barry soon found himself pursued by two enemy ships of superior force. Three days later, following a sharp engagement, he ran his damaged ship aground, compelled to abandon it to the enemy. Temporarily unable to offer Captain Barry another vessel, the Marine Committee granted him a furlough in January 1779. Barry returned to duty in October 1779 to command the *America* (74 guns), then under construction at Portsmouth, New Hampshire. His dissatisfaction with that assignment resulted in another furlough.

Recalled to duty in July 1780, Captain Barry assumed command of the frigate *Alliance* (36 guns). As captain of the *Alliance,* he performed some of his most noteworthy and important services to the Continental cause, including conveying American officials on important diplomatic missions to France and transporting desperately needed foreign loans in specie (coins) to America. Barry proved his mettle as a combat commander when the *Alliance* defeated HMS *Atalanta* and *Trepassey* on 28 May 1781 in a bloody engagement that left him severely wounded. The *Alliance*'s encounter with HMS *Sybil* on 10 March 1783 bears the distinction of being the last naval battle of the Revolutionary War. Barry's service in the Continental Navy came to a close when the *Alliance* was sold at public auction in August 1785.

Charles E. Brodine Jr.

See also

Continental Navy; Naval Operations, American vs. British

References

Clark, William Bell. *The Gallant John Barry, 1745–1803: The Story of a Naval Hero.* New York: Macmillan, 1938.

Clark, William Bell, et al., eds. *Naval Documents of the American Revolution.* 10 vols. to date. Washington, DC: Naval Historical Center, 1964–.

Ferguson, E. James, John Catanzariti, Elizabeth M. Nuxoll, Mary A. Y. Gallagher, Nelson S. Dearmont, et al., eds. *The Papers of Robert Morris, 1781–1784.* 9 vols. Pittsburgh: University of Pittsburgh Press, 1973–1999.

Bartlett, Josiah (1729–1795)

A medical doctor who served his province and state's troops before and during the Revolutionary War, a member of Congress, and a signer of the Declaration of Independence, Josiah Bartlett was a leader in New Hampshire politics for more than three decades.

Bartlett was born in Amesbury, Massachusetts, and apprenticed in medicine with a local relative. In 1750 he moved a few miles north to Kingston, New Hampshire, where he began his medical practice, married, and entered public life. From 1765 to 1775, Bartlett served as a member of New Hampshire's provincial assembly and as an officer in the colonial militia. Throughout this decade, however, Bartlett became increasingly hostile to the actions taken by the colony's last royal governor, John Wentworth. After Bartlett expressed sharp opposition to several royal policies, the governor removed him from his militia post. This only made Bartlett more willing to oppose the Crown. He attended the Revolutionary provincial congresses of 1774 and 1775, supported the seizure of Fort William and Mary in Portsmouth Harbor in December 1774, and accepted his appointment as a delegate to the Second Continental Congress, in which he served on several committees, notably those charged with naval and marine issues.

Throughout the next year, Bartlett's support for a total separation from Great Britain grew stronger. In July 1776, when the decision to declare American independence was made, the members of the Continental Congress voted in order of seniority within their delegations, proceeding from north to south. Thus Bartlett, as the senior New Hampshire delegate, cast the first vote in favor of the Declaration of Independence. And in August, when Congress was ready to sign the formally endorsed manuscript of the Declaration, Bartlett

Josiah Bartlett. Elected a member of the Continental Congress in 1775, he signed the Declaration of Independence, provided medical supplies to New Hampshire troops during the war, and served as a colonel of militia between 1777 and 1779. He helped draft the Articles of Confederation and later served as Chief Justice of New Hampshire. (Hayward Circer, ed., *Dictionary of American Portraits,* 1967)

became the second person to sign the document, after Congress's president John Hancock.

When Congress turned its attention to a plan of government for the former colonies, Bartlett served on the drafting committee and participated in the debates, in which he advocated a strong degree of state sovereignty. When just such a system was eventually devised in 1777, in the form of the Articles of Confederation, Bartlett was again one of the signers. Soon thereafter Bartlett returned to New Hampshire, in part to serve the medical needs of the militia in his home state. He tended to wounded New Hampshire soldiers after the Battle of Bennington in August 1777. Bartlett returned briefly to Congress in 1778 but spent most of the war years in New Hampshire, serving on the state's executive council and as a judge.

In 1782, Bartlett was appointed to New Hampshire's supreme court, of which he became chief justice in 1790. He was a strong supporter of the U.S. Constitution and presided over the state's ratifying convention in 1788. In 1790, Bartlett was chosen as "president" of New Hampshire, its chief executive officer, and continued in that capacity when it was relabeled "governor" in 1793, thereby becoming the first governor of post-Revolutionary New Hampshire. Bartlett died in May 1795, a year after leaving office.

William E. Doody

See also

Articles of Confederation; Bennington, Battle of; Congress, Second Continental and Confederation; Declaration of Independence; Declaration of Independence Signers; New Hampshire

References

Bartlett, Josiah. *The Papers of Josiah Bartlett.* Edited by Frank C. Mevers. Hanover: University Press of New Hampshire, 1979.

"Biography of Josiah Bartlett." Colonial Hall.com, http://www.colonialhall.com/bartlett/bartlett.php, n.d.

Daniel, Jere. *Experiment in Republicanism: New Hampshire Politics and the American Revolution, 1741–1794.* Cambridge: Harvard University Press, 1970.

Mevers, Frank C. "Bartlett, Josiah." Pp. 2:280–281 in *American National Biography.* Edited by John A. Garraty and Mark C. Carnes. New York: Oxford University Press, 1999.

Barton, William (1748–1831)

A Revolutionary officer whose claim to fame was the capture of Brigadier-General Robert Prescott, commander of British forces at Rhode Island. In 1775, Barton joined the Rhode Island militia and attained the rank of captain. On 19 August 1776 he was promoted to major. In 1777, he conceived his scheme of capturing Prescott. The year before, Prescott had been captured and exchanged for General John Sullivan. Prescott had made himself offensive to Americans through his arbitrary conduct in Rhode Island, quartering soldiers in farmhouses, demanding contributions, and acting insolently toward the citizenry.

In early July 1777, Barton carefully planned his operation, then chose forty-one men to assist him. On the evening of 4 July the force started out in whaleboats from Tiverton, proceeding to Bristol and then Warwick Neck. With muffled oars, Barton and his men rowed across Narragansett Bay on the night of 9 July and, after passing three British frigates unobserved, landed on the western shore of Rhode Island. Quietly and quickly, the party proceeded inland a mile to the house that Prescott used as his headquarters. They silenced the few sentries, broke in the door of Prescott's room, and seized the general. Hurrying him away half dressed, they rowed back across Narragansett Bay to Warwick and transferred him to the headquarters of General George Washington in New Jersey. Later, Prescott was exchanged a second time, for General Charles Lee. Prescott was soon promoted to major-general, but he did not escape the strictures of the British press for his humiliating capture.

Barton was promoted by Congress to lieutenant colonel and given a sword. He also received the thanks of the Rhode

Island General Assembly. He served as an aide-de-camp to General Nathanael Greene, then returned to regular duty. In 1778, Barton was wounded during the British retreat from Warren and was disabled for some time. A year later, he was appointed commander of a light corps that the Rhode Island General Assembly had just organized. He continued on active duty until the conclusion of the war.

In 1787, Barton was disappointed when the State of Rhode Island refused to send delegates to the Constitutional Convention, and he joined others in writing to support a revision of the Articles of Confederation. In 1790, he was a member of the state convention that finally ratified the U.S. Constitution. During these proceedings, he served as one of two monitors, chosen to make sure that the members attended to business. Later he settled on land in Vermont but refused to pay an assessment on the property, an infraction for which he was held prisoner for fourteen years in a Danville inn. In 1824–1825, during a visit to America, the Marquis de Lafayette paid the claim and set Barton free.

Paul David Nelson

See also

Articles of Confederation; Greene, Nathanael; Lee, Charles; Rhode Island; Sullivan, John

Reference

Diman, Jeremiah Lewis. *The Capture of General Richard Prescott by Lt.-Col. William Barton.* Providence, RI: S. S. Rider, 1877.

Basking Ridge, New Jersey, Action at (13 December 1776)

The action at Basking Ridge, New Jersey, on 13 December 1776 led to the capture of General Charles Lee by British forces under Lieutenant-Colonel William Harcourt. In the summer of 1776 George Washington's army was routed by William Howe's Anglo-German forces around New York City. On 10 November, Washington marched southward with the main Continental Army to counter Howe's threat to New Jersey, leaving Lee in command of a small army at White Plains, New York. As these operations unfolded, Lee grew suspicious that Washington was mishandling the army, and his worst fears seemed confirmed when the British captured Forts Washington and Lee on the lower Hudson River in mid-November. Hence, Lee began to vacillate in carrying out the commander in chief's orders. In late November and early December, as Washington retreated across New Jersey, he sent numerous letters ordering Lee to join the main army. By 4 December, Lee had finally crossed the Hudson River into New Jersey. But when he reached Morristown four days later, he contemplated independent actions against the British. By the night of 12 December he apparently had concluded reluctantly that he would join Washington and ordered John Sullivan, his second in command, to march next day toward Germantown.

On the evening of 12 December, for reasons unknown, Lee decided to stay at a tavern run by a widow in Basking Ridge, 3 miles from camp. He was accompanied by a guard of about fifteen men and four officers. On that same date, Lord Cornwallis, commanding the British vanguard at Pennington, realized that Lee's army posed a danger to his post. Not knowing where that army was, he determined to send Harcourt in search of it. Accompanied by Cornet Banastre Tarleton, three other officers, and twenty-five privates from his 16th Light Horse, Harcourt set off. As they approached the American army on 13 December, they captured two sentries, who informed them of Lee's whereabouts. Tarleton also captured a dispatch rider who provided the same information. Immediately, Harcourt galloped forward to surround the tavern.

On the morning of 13 December, Lee knew that his army was marching at about eight o'clock, but he lingered for two hours to do some paperwork. After Lee wrote Horatio Gates a letter condemning Washington for his military deficiencies, his quarters were suddenly attacked from two sides by Harcourt's troopers. From an upstairs window he saw his men routed, with two killed and two wounded. After enduring fifteen minutes of hostile fire he surrendered, after being promised that he would be well treated. Two of his officers escaped because the British did not adequately search the tavern. When Sullivan learned of Lee's capture, he dispatched a rescue party, but too late to stop Harcourt from safely delivering his prisoners behind British lines.

Paul David Nelson

See also

Fort Lee, New Jersey; Fort Washington, New York, Fall of; Lee, Charles; New Jersey, Operations in; Tarleton, Banastre

Reference

Alden, John Richard. *General Charles Lee: Traitor or Patriot?* Baton Rouge: Louisiana State University Press, 1951.

Baton Rouge, West Florida, Action at (August–September 1779)

The British fort at the town of Baton Rouge, West Florida (now Louisiana), was one of the westernmost and southernmost major military posts that Great Britain held in North America during the Revolutionary War, and its capture by Spanish forces in September 1779 greatly strengthened Spain's hold on the southwest border of British (and later American) territory.

The settlement and its nearby military post, founded by the French as part of its Louisiana colony, had passed to the

British and become part of the province of West Florida in the Treaty of Paris (1763). The boundary between British West Florida and Spanish Louisiana on the east side of the Mississippi River was located at Bayou Manchac, between Baton Rouge and New Orleans. Because of this proximity, Spanish Louisiana's governor, Bernardo de Gálvez, decided that the capture of Baton Rouge was his highest priority as soon as Spain became a belligerent in the Revolutionary War during the early summer of 1779.

To seize Baton Rouge, Gálvez organized a force during July and August of almost 1,000 men composed of regular Spanish soldiers, Louisiana militia forces, and Native American allies. These troops departed from New Orleans on 17 August 1779 and arrived at the small British cantonment known as Fort Bute, located on the north side of Bayou Manchac. This minor post fell quickly to the Spanish attackers on 7 September with hardly a shot fired. Gálvez then continued up the eastern bank of the Mississippi River until he arrived at Fort New Richmond, a British outpost located just south of Baton Rouge. Colonel Alexander Dickson commanded a well-fortified position that included heavy cannon designed to protect the fort against invasion, but Gálvez immediately began to lay an artillery siege, instructing his men to cut down many of the trees that obscured the attackers' clear view of the fort. This accomplished, a full-scale Spanish bombardment of the British fort began on 20 September. The cannonade was heavy. It quickly beleaguered Dickson's men, most of whom lost the will to fight. Dickson surrendered on the second day of the siege and agreed to terms that included the surrender of Fort Panmure, near Natchez. Gálvez, in turn, granted the British defenders their parole as he took possession of Baton Rouge.

The Spanish governor thereupon dispatched emissaries, including the American merchant Oliver Pollock, north to Natchez to inform the British soldiers and settlers there of the capture of Baton Rouge. The British commander promptly surrendered Fort Panmure at Natchez, and by the end of September 1779 the entire lower Mississippi River Valley had fallen under Spanish control.

Light Townsend Cummins

See also

Florida, East and West; Gálvez, Bernardo de; Spain

References

Cummins, Light Townsend. *Spanish Observers and the American Revolution, 1775–1783.* Baton Rouge: Louisiana State University Press, 1992.

Starr, J. Barton. *Tories, Dons, and Rebels: The American Revolution in British West Florida.* Gainesville: University Press of Florida, 1976.

Wright, J. Leitch. *Florida in the American Revolution.* Gainesville: University Press of Florida, 1975.

Baylor, George (1752–1784)

George Baylor was a brave and competent commander of Continental dragoons whose reputation was permanently tarnished when General Charles Grey ("No-Flint" Grey of Paoli fame) surprised and defeated him at Old Tappan, New Jersey, in 1778.

When the American Revolutionary War began in 1775, Baylor was elected to the Caroline County (Virginia) Committee of Safety. Using the influence of his father, John Baylor, young George secured an appointment as aide-de-camp to General George Washington and was promoted to lieutenant colonel in the Continental Army. He fought in the Battle of Trenton on 26 December 1776 and was selected by Washington to convey the news of victory to Congress. In a letter to Congress on 27 December, Washington commended Baylor for his spirited behavior and recommended that he be advanced in rank. Congress responded on 1 January 1777 by promoting Baylor to colonel, giving him a horse with cavalry accouterments, and suggesting that Washington give him command of a body of light horse. On 9 January 1777, Washington appointed Baylor commander of the 3rd Continental Dragoons, who were also known as "Mrs. Washington's Guards."

In the early morning of 28 September 1778, Baylor was encamped with his dragoons at Old Tappan, New Jersey, near the Hackensack River, about 2.5 miles from the main army. Apparently he had taken that exposed position to escape supervision by General Anthony Wayne, his immediate superior. But Colonel Baylor, who did post some night pickets, did not take adequate precautions against a surprise attack. General Charles Cornwallis was determined to trap him and assigned four British infantry regiments, including the 2nd Light Infantry, the 2nd Dragoons, and a party of Loyalists, to surround the Americans. General Grey led the main column in the attack. Using information from local Loyalists and quickly overwhelming the pickets Baylor had placed at a crossing of the Hackensack River, Grey's force quietly surrounded Baylor's men, who were sleeping in a house and two barns, at three o'clock in the morning. Raising a cheer, the soldiers attacked the unsuspecting Americans with bayonets without firing a shot. Baylor and his men, hardly awake, unarmed, and confronting enemy troops right on top of them, called for quarter. But the British soldiers, in the grip of a blood lust that Grey could not or would not control, refused quarter, and several Americans were massacred. Of the 104 men in Baylor's command, 16 were killed, 16 wounded, and 38 taken prisoner. Baylor himself was bayoneted in the lungs and captured but immediately paroled. The rest of Baylor's men escaped, but the British captured all of the Americans' horses and equipment.

On 19 October, when he was well enough to write to General Washington, Baylor defended his actions, hoping to persuade the commander in chief that he was not responsible for the bloody outcome at Old Tappan. Although some Americans criticized Baylor's conduct, Washington never reprimanded him for any supposed lapses in judgment during that fatal engagement. Later exchanged, Baylor commanded the 1st Continental Dragoons in the South. Even though he continued to suffer from his wound, he was a valuable officer and earned the praise of Henry Laurens for his soldiering. On 30 September 1783, Baylor was breveted to brigadier general. Soon thereafter he traveled to Bridgetown, Barbados, for his health but died in 1784.

Paul David Nelson

See also

Grey, Charles; Tappan, New Jersey, Action at

Reference

Baylor, Orval Walker, and Henry Bedinger Baylor. *Baylor's History of the Baylors.* [LeRoy, IL]: LeRoy Journal Printing Company, 1914.

Beattie's Mill, South Carolina, Action at (23 or 24 March 1781)

The Battle of Beattie's Mill, a military engagement between Patriot and Loyalist militia in upper South Carolina fought on either 23 or 24 March 1781 (sources disagree on the date), helped to maintain Patriot control of northwest South Carolina in the early spring of 1781 by discouraging the recruitment of Loyalist militia and forcing other Loyalist troops to remain near their base of operations at Fort Ninety-Six.

The Patriot victory at Cowpens, South Carolina, on 17 January 1781 prompted the main British force in the state, under General Charles Cornwallis, to pursue American General Nathanael Greene across North Carolina. Cornwallis won a bloody battle on 15 March 1781 at Guilford Courthouse, North Carolina, that cost him casualties of approximately a quarter of his command. As a result, Cornwallis withdrew his army to Wilmington, North Carolina, practically abandoning the interior of South Carolina and its string of British garrisons to Patriot assaults.

The British invasion of South Carolina in 1780 had initiated civil war conditions in the state, especially in the interior regions and along the frontier. Families and communities were roughly divided between Loyalists and Patriots. Each side turned to terror tactics to discourage the other from mobilizing militia and taking to the field. Many homes were burned and people murdered during the civil strife. Lord Francis Rawdon, the British commander at Camden, dispatched Loyalist militia and provincials into the South Carolina backcountry during March and April 1781 in order to discourage attempts to raise Patriot militia against the British cause. General Andrew Pickens, a South Carolina militia commander serving under General Greene, returned to the area with his force just prior to the Battle of Guilford Courthouse in order to protect homes and families from Loyalist raids. At the same time, Colonel Elijah Clarke, a Georgia militia commander, returned to South Carolina after recovering from wounds he suffered at the end of 1780.

The Patriots learned that seventy-five dragoons under Major James Dunlap had departed from the British fort at Ninety-Six, South Carolina, and were headed up the Little River into the backcountry. Clarke and 180 mounted militia moved to block the Loyalist unit. The Patriot force discovered Dunlap at Beattie's Mill and attacked his unit. The British offered a stubborn defense but lost thirty-four men before surrendering. The Patriots did not suffer any deaths in the battle.

Some Patriot accounts claim that Dunlap died in the attack, but Loyalist reports say that he was murdered by a Patriot militiaman in retaliation for the burning of homes in the area. Pickens agreed with the Loyalist side of the debate and sent a letter of regret to the British. Although he deplored the murder of Dunlap, Pickens did add the caveat that the British major had brought the wrath upon himself by burning Patriot homes. In fact, Dunlap had burned Pickens's own home in 1780 although the Patriot officer was on parole at the time. The remaining British prisoners were escorted to Virginia for internment. The engagement at Beattie's Mill secured the area between Augusta, Georgia, and Fort Ninety-Six for the Patriot cause.

Terry M. Mays

See also

Clarke, Elijah; Pickens, Andrew

References

Buchanan, John. *The Road to Guilford Courthouse: The American Revolution in the Carolinas.* New York: Wiley, 1997.

Ripley, Warren. *Battleground: South Carolina in the Revolution.* Charleston, SC: Evening Post, 1983.

Beaufort, South Carolina

See Port Royal, South Carolina, Action at

Beaumarchais, Pierre-Augustin Caron de (1732–1799)

Known today as the author of *The Barber of Seville* and *The Marriage of Figaro,* Beaumarchais was also a watchmaker, prominent businessman, spy for Louis XV and Louis XVI,

Pierre-Augustin Caron de Beaumarchais, a noted French playwright, founded a company called Rodrigue, Hortalez et Cie for the purpose of supplying weapons and materiel to the rebels beginning in the summer of 1776, well before France formally entered the war. (Library of Congress)

and arms dealer for the American revolutionaries through the cover of the firm of Rodrigue, Hortalez et Cie. Beaumarchais later supported the French Revolution, had to flee France but later returned, and was pardoned in 1796.

Beaumarchais, the son of an expert watchmaker, was born in Paris on 24 January 1732. He always remained attached to his family and protected it. After learning watchmaking, he worked in his father's workshop. Being quite skilled with his hands, in 1753 he invented a special watch mechanism, the plans for which the king's watchmaker, Lepante, tried to steal. Beaumarchais, however, won his case before the Academy of Sciences and was presented to the king and queen. He sold his invention quite profitably. Eager for power and money, and of respectable character, he threw himself successfully into business.

In 1755, he purchased the position of *contrôler clerc d'office de la maison du roi* (clerk of the office of the comptroller of the king's household) from M. Franquet while seducing Franquet's wife, Catherine Aubertin. When she became a widow the following year, he married her and took on the name Caron de Beaumarchais, after the name of one of his wife's properties. In 1757, he made contact with Le Normand d'Étoilles, a Parisian banker and husband of the Marquise de Pompadour, the king's mistress. Le Normand presented Beaumarchais to Louis XV's daughters (whom he taught to play the harp), but most importantly to his uncle, Pâris-Duverney, one of Paris's most important financiers. Beaumarchais grew rich very quickly, and in 1761 he bought the position of *conseiller secrétaire du roi* (counselor-secretary to the king), a post that made him a member of the nobility. In 1763, he became *lieutenant-général des chasses* (lieutenant general of the hunt), a position that gave him the authority to regulate hunting rights. Beaumarchais was married again in 1768 to a widow who died the following year.

In January 1773, Beaumarchais put on his drama, *The Barber of Seville,* a revolutionary piece both in content and form. To mollify Louis XV and also to avoid legal proceedings as well as to save his production, he became the king's spy in London.

Following the death of Louis XV, Louis XVI sent Beaumarchais on spying missions in 1775 and 1776, primarily in London. He resurrected previously conceived plans for an invasion of England and made contact with the American rebels. He sent the king several memoranda favorable to the insurgents and gained the confidence of Charles Gravier, the comte de Vergennes, the foreign minister, who proposed to the king that he entrust Beaumarchais with arms shipments to the Americans. On 10 June 1776, Vergennes gave Beaumarchais 1 million livres to secretly finance the rebels. Beaumarchais then created the firm of Rodrigue, Hortalez et Cie, which surreptitiously furnished arms to the Americans, though most of its business was conducted with French colonies. At the same time, Beaumarchais was a reporter in London with the *Courrier de l'Europe,* a medium through which he defended the cause of the insurgents. These assignments helped Beaumarchais, on 6 September, to win his legal case in the French parliament in Paris. The following month, he started his commercial firm and left for Le Havre to inspect the ships bound for the rebels. The years 1777 and 1778 were essentially tied up with the business of providing arms to the Americans. After the parliament of Aix-en-Provence issued a verdict in favor of Beaumarchais, La Blache accepted a final resolution in 1778 and compensated his adversary handsomely.

After the signing of the Franco-American Alliance on 6 February 1778, Beaumarchais continued his arms dealing with America but turned primarily to business with Santo Domingo and to the chartering of merchant ships for the king. At the same time, he occupied himself with drafting a law concerning the rights of authors of theater plays (1779) and wrote an edition of the works of Voltaire (1781–1790). Beaumarchais attained literary fame with *The Marriage of Figaro,* but Louis XVI insisted on major modifications. On 27 April 1784, the opening performance of *Figaro* was a triumph. On 19 August 1785, *The Barber of Seville* was performed at court, with Queen Marie-Antoinette playing the role of Rosine. In February 1786, Beaumarchais received 800,000 livres from the king as complete settlement for the losses sustained by his fleet in 1778 and 1779, with the provision that Beaumarchais would have to collect the rebels' debts. In 1787, Beaumarchais built, on borrowed money, a luxurious house near the Bastille and published the play *Tarare,* which was quite a success.

On 14 July 1789, Beaumarchais, a former commoner who had become a nobleman and who was one of the favorites of the court, nonetheless took the side of the revolutionaries in France. He returned to arms trafficking in November 1791, this time for the French army, and on 3 April 1792 signed a contract with the Dutch for the purchase of firearms from Holland. Although the Terror accused him of being a nobleman and arms trafficker, Beaumarchais did not hesitate to enter Paris, where he was declared innocent by the Comité du Salut Public (Committee of Public Safety). In 1794, Beaumarchais was nonetheless included on the list of persons who were forced to emigrate, and he went into exile in Hamburg. During this period, and specifically on 10 April 1795, Beaumarchais vainly attempted to recoup from the Americans the monies due to him. He was allowed to return to Paris on 5 July 1796. Worn out by this turbulent life and impoverished because of the failure of the Americans to pay him, he died from a stroke on 18 May 1799.

Patrick Villiers

See also

Gravier, Charles, Comte de Vergennes; Louis XVI, King of France; Rodrigue, Hortalez et Cie

References

Lafon, Roger. *Beaumarchais, le brillant armateur.* Paris: Société d'éditions géographiques, maritimes, et coloniales, 1928.

Larthomas, Pierre. *Beaumarchais, oeuvres.* Paris: Bibliothèque de La Pléiade, Gallimard, 1988.

Bedford and Fairhaven, Massachusetts, Raid on (6–7 September 1778)

The British expeditionary raid on Bedford and Fairhaven, Massachusetts, formed part of a broader British expedition to destroy American supplies and equipment located along the Massachusetts coast and on Martha's Vineyard.

The British, under Sir Henry Clinton, sought to strike against American and French forces at British-held Newport, Rhode Island, in fall 1778. French naval forces under the comte d'Estaing and American troops led by John Sullivan struggled to coordinate a siege of the British garrison commanded by Robert Pigot. Clinton's 5,000 men and 70 vessels sailed into Newport in early August but stood out to sea when the slightly superior French fleet under d'Estaing sailed toward them. A combination of foul weather, miscommunication between d'Estaing and Sullivan, and skilled British resistance turned back the Franco-American siege. On 1 September, Clinton and his force sailed into Newport and discovered that in the Battle of Rhode Island (28–29 August), Pigot and his men had repulsed a final assault from Sullivan's troops and the Americans had evacuated the area.

Believing that his expedition could further disrupt the Americans by destroying the privateering base of New London, Connecticut, Clinton directed his force toward the Connecticut coast on 2 September. During the next two days, Clinton consulted with General Charles "No Flint" Grey about the state of the expedition. Clinton and Grey determined that the force was not in the effective state of organization required for a strike at New London. Grey convinced Clinton, however, that the British expedition could conduct raids on smaller towns along the Massachusetts coast. As a result, Grey recommended a raid on Bedford and on Fairhaven, across the Acushnet River.

The raid began at 6:00 P.M. on 6 September and continued until the morning of 7 September. Grey's force included the 17th, 33rd, 42nd, 44th, and 64th Regiments along with grenadiers and light infantry. The raiders burned numerous buildings and nearly seventy naval and privateering vessels, many of which were under construction in the dockyards. The raid's success encouraged Grey to continue with an attack on Martha's Vineyard and furthered his reputation as a commander who did not hesitate to use harsh measures.

The Bedford-Fairhaven raid illustrated the beginning of a shift in British military policy during the war. By 1778, British strategy increased its reliance on coastal raids in the North, allowing for formal attacks and invasions in the South during the next three years of the war.

Daniel T. Miller

See also

Clinton, Henry; Estaing, Jean-Baptiste, Comte d'; Grey, Charles; Martha's Vineyard, Massachusetts, Raid on; Pigot, Robert; Rhode Island, Battle of; Sullivan, John

References

Allen, Gardner W. *A Naval History of the American Revolution.* 1913. Reprint, New York: Russell and Russell, 1962.

MacKenzie, Frederick. *The Diary of Frederick MacKenzie.* 1930. Reprint, New York: New York Times, 1968.

Tilley, J. A. *The Royal Navy in the American Revolution.* Columbia: University of South Carolina Press, 1987.

Belleville, South Carolina, Action at (21 February 1781)

The Battle of Belleville Plantation, also known as the Battle of Thomson's Fort, was an attempt by South Carolina militia general Thomas Sumter to capture a key British garrison in the backcountry. The actions around Belleville Plantation helped tie down British forces in South Carolina between the Patriot victory at Cowpens in January 1781 and the stalemate at Guilford Courthouse in March. The attack on the stockade also sparked a feud between Sumter and militia commander General Francis Marion. The British quickly complained to Marion that Sumter's men had killed British troops who were surrendering shortly after the engagement. The feud between Marion and Sumter would boil over later in the year at the Battle of Quinby Bridge.

In early 1781, the British controlled Charleston, Port Royal, and Georgetown on the coast and a string of forts in the South Carolina backcountry. Control of the territory that lay just a few miles beyond these forts was repeatedly contested by Patriot and Loyalist militia units. Sumter was on the offensive since the main British Army in the region was chasing General Nathanael Greene across North Carolina after the Patriot victory at the Battle of Cowpens on 17 January 1781. Sumter attempted to capture Fort Granby, South Carolina, on 19–20 February 1781. When this failed, a frustrated Sumter led his troops south and surprised the British garrison at Belleville Plantation the following day.

The Patriot forces drove the British into the stockaded buildings of the plantation and then attempted to burn them out. The British, however, managed to extinguish the flames and maintain sufficient firepower to thwart the Patriot attempt to drive them from the buildings. Sumter broke off the engagement, left a detachment to prevent the escape of the British, and withdrew the remainder of his force to regroup. The next day, when his men ambushed a twenty-wagon British supply train and captured all of the contents, some of the Patriot militia fired upon the surrendering British soldiers and killed several of them. The militia then loaded the supplies into boats because of flooding in the area and ordered the vessels moved to a point just above British-held Fort Watson, where Sumter would off-load them.

Sumter learned that Lord Rawdon, the British commander in South Carolina, was leading a large relief force to Belleville Plantation. Sumter gathered the detachment he had left to watch the plantation and withdrew to retrieve his supplies before heading deeper into the backcountry. But a Loyalist with the boats piloted the small convoy toward Fort Watson before the Patriots with him realized the situation. When the boats came within range of Fort Watson's guns, the Patriots escaped while the British retrieved their previously captured supplies. A disappointed Sumter then turned his attention to Fort Watson but failed to seize the post.

Terry M. Mays

See also

Cowpens, Battle of; Fort Granby, South Carolina; Fort Watson, South Carolina, Actions at; Greene, Nathanael; Guilford Courthouse, Battle of; Marion, Francis; Quinby Bridge, South Carolina, Action at; Rawdon, Francis; Southern Campaigns; Sumter, Thomas

Reference

Bass, Robert. *Gamecock: The Life and Campaigns of General Thomas Sumter.* 1961. Reprint, Orangeburg, SC: Sandlapper, 2000.

Bemis Heights, Battle of

See Saratoga Campaign

Bennington, Battle of (16 August 1777)

John Stark's American militia routed two detachments of British and German troops on 16 August 1777. British general John Burgoyne's attempt to acquire badly needed provisions and livestock resulted in a stinging defeat that helped set the stage for the decisive battles of Saratoga.

In July 1777, Burgoyne's 8,000-man army advanced south from Canada on Lake Champlain toward Albany, New York. There, Burgoyne intended to meet other British forces moving down the Mohawk Valley and up the Hudson River. On 5 July, Burgoyne forced the evacuation of Fort Ticonderoga without a fight. He pursued part of the American army to Skenesboro, New York, while other troops scattered the Patriots' rear guard, commanded by Colonel Seth Warner, at Hubbardton, Vermont, on 7 July. Rather than recalling his men to Ticonderoga where they could then advance up Lake George, Burgoyne opted to march to Fort Edward on the Hudson. This was a critical mistake. Burgoyne's army lacked an adequate number of draft animals, having received only one-third of the 1,500 horses that it had requested. The army also possessed too few wagons and carts, and those it did have were ill-constructed for the rugged, forested terrain. Philip Schuyler, the American commander in the North, exacerbated these obstacles by ordering soldiers to cut down trees to block the roads, destroy bridges, and redirect streams to flood the land. Schuyler also adopted a scorched earth strategy, whereby the colonists burned their crops and drove their livestock beyond Burgoyne's reach. The British advance slowed to a crawl, and Burgoyne did not reach the Hudson until 29 July, having covered only 23 miles in twenty-one days. This delay afforded the Americans time to regroup and strained Burgoyne's supply lines, which stretched to Canada.

Earlier that month, Baron Friedrich von Riedesel, who commanded the large German contingent of Burgoyne's army, suggested a raid into Vermont to procure horses, especially for his dismounted dragoons. On 31 July, facing increasing logistical problems, Burgoyne approved the plan and selected Lieutenant Colonel Friedrich Baum, a German officer who did not speak English, to command the expedition. Baum was to march toward Manchester and beyond, obtaining provisions and livestock, raising Loyalists, and creating a diversion by threatening the Connecticut River Valley. Colonel Philip Skene, the Loyalist proprietor of a large estate at Skenesboro and a

Battle of Bennington. Colonel John Stark, with a small body of New Hampshire militia, attacked and defeated a British, Loyalist, and Hessian force under Lieutenant Colonel Friedrich Baum, taking hundreds of prisoners and large stocks of weapons and ammunition. The battle deprived the British of almost 1,000 badly needed men during the Saratoga Campaign. (National Archives and Records Administration)

former British Army officer, was to assist Baum in his many assignments. Baum's force initially consisted of approximately 775 men: 374 German dragoons and grenadiers, 300 Loyalists, 50 British light infantry, and a collection of Canadians and artillerymen with two 3-pounder cannon. More than 100 Indians accompanied the expedition and ranged ahead of the main force, alarming the countryside.

While Burgoyne marched through the wilderness and planned Baum's operation, the newly independent state of Vermont called upon New Hampshire and Massachusetts for aid. On 18 July, New Hampshire authorized the raising of three militia regiments, totaling just under 1,500 troops, to assist its western neighbor and asked John Stark to command the brigade. Stark, a former member of Rogers's Rangers and a veteran of Bunker Hill and Trenton, had resigned his Continental Army commission earlier that year after being passed over for promotion. Stark agreed to serve, but only on the condition that he was answerable to New Hampshire, not the Continental Army. Volunteers quickly filled the new regiments, and Stark marched to Manchester in early August. There he conferred with Warner and Brigadier General Benjamin Lincoln, who was coordinating militia operations in the region. Stark reiterated his refusal to accept Continental authority but did agree to harass Burgoyne's flank. He then headed for Bennington, arriving on 8 August, where he was joined by growing numbers of his troops.

On 9 August, Baum marched from Fort Edward to Fort Miller, 7 miles to the south. Two days later he headed for Vermont, but, as he did so, Burgoyne changed his orders. Rather than marching to Manchester, the British general redirected Baum to Bennington. Intelligence reports indicated that the colonists had collected a large store of provisions and livestock there, including 1,300 horses. Failing to detect Stark, the same reports said that only several hundred militia guarded these valuable stores. After a short advance on 12 August, Baum departed early the next morning. Skirmishing with small detachments of militia and securing a number of livestock, Baum learned of Stark's presence, but he pushed on to Cambridge, New York.

Resuming his advance on 14 August, Baum encountered 200 of Stark's men near a mill at Sancoick, New York, about 9 miles from Bennington. Colonel William Gregg, the American commander, fired one volley and quickly withdrew, damaging a bridge as he retired. Briefly delayed while his men secured the mill and fixed the bridge, Baum sent a letter to Burgoyne apprising him of the situation. Baum then continued to march east while some of his troops and Indians rounded up livestock. Stark, having learned of Baum's presence the night before, requested that Warner and local militia join him at Bennington. He then marched from town and met Gregg, who informed him that the enemy was close behind. The two forces made contact along the Walloomsac River about 4 miles west of Bennington, just over the New York border. The German officer deployed for battle while Stark, wanting more information, withdrew to his camp a few miles away.

A steady flow of Loyalists, many without guns, had joined Baum over the past several days, bringing his force to nearly 1,200. However, his scouts reported that he faced a larger enemy. Baum therefore called for reinforcements and ordered his men to entrench. He constructed a redoubt facing northwest atop a steep bluff overlooking the Walloomsac and stationed 54 dragoons and some British light infantry there. Near the base of the hill, the rest of the British troops and some Germans defended a small breastwork with the two cannon overlooking a bridge. The Canadians manned several cabins on either side of this bridge, and several hundred Loyalists built a second redoubt on a small rise on the far side of the Walloomsac. Baum placed other detachments near the dragoon redoubt to protect his baggage and along the road on which he had advanced. Overall, his troops were widely scattered and could not support each other if attacked.

Heavy rain fell on 15 August, preventing a general engagement, but American skirmishers still inflicted 30 casualties, which disheartened Baum's Indians. Vermont and Massachusetts militia continued to arrive at Stark's camp, bringing his strength to around 2,000. The American general spent the day reconnoitering Baum's position and planning an elaborate attack to overwhelm him. Warner had arrived ahead of his regiment, and he helped Stark perfect his plan. Stark set the operation in motion the next day. He ordered 100 men to create a diversion in the open to conceal his real intentions. Meanwhile, Colonel Moses Nichols encircled Baum's left with 200 New Hampshire soldiers, while Colonel Samuel Herrick and 300 Vermonters enveloped his right. Colonels Thomas Stickney and David Hobart advanced toward the Loyalist redoubt with 300 men, while Stark personally led the assault on Baum's center. Nichols and Herrick needed time to reach their positions, however, so the attack did not begin until midafternoon.

Throughout the day, Baum's scouts detected troops moving into his rear, but he believed that they were Loyalists and so paid them little attention. He sent one cannon to the dragoon redoubt on request of its commander but did little else to prepare. Around 3:00 P.M. Nichols's troops opened heavy fire on the dragoon redoubt, signaling the attack to begin. The Americans, fortified by rum, struck Baum from all directions with great ferocity. Herrick and Nichols stormed the redoubt on the top of the hill and quickly sent its defenders fleeing toward the river. The Germans, encumbered by their heavy uniforms, were quickly run down. Many Indians and Canadians fled at the first fire, while Baum's other troops were overwhelmed by the attack's suddenness. The heaviest fighting took place at the Loyalist redoubt. A ravine hid the Americans as they advanced on the position, allowing them to get within a few feet of the works undetected. Many of the Loyalists were from the area and knew the men who now charged them. Neighbor fought neighbor in fierce hand-to-hand combat, and the Loyalists finally broke, just as Baum's other troops had. The Americans captured numerous soldiers along the banks of the Walloomsac, including the mortally wounded Baum. Estimates vary as to how long the fighting lasted during this first phase of the battle, but it was probably around one hour. Stark's men then scattered. Many were exhausted by the heat and fell out of line. Some scoured the field for prisoners and loot, while Stark sent others back to Bennington with long lines of captives.

The battle was not over yet. On 15 August, after receiving Baum's request for reinforcements, Burgoyne sent Lieutenant Colonel Heinrich Breymann and 642 men toward Bennington. Heavy rain and mud slowed his approach, but Breymann arrived at Sancoick the following afternoon. Because of an acoustic shadow, he did not hear the firing but learned of the battle from scattered survivors. Not knowing that Baum was already defeated, Breymann advanced several miles before coming under fire from a group of Americans behind a fence. The German troops easily brushed them aside and deployed for battle, supported by two cannon. Resuming the advance, Breymann next encountered a makeshift line that Stark had assembled. The Americans continued to fall back to higher ground before making a stand. Just then, Warner's regiment and some rangers, totaling 330 men, arrived on the field, stiffening Stark's line. The two sides battled until sunset, when the Americans managed to flank the Germans' left. Wounded in the leg and low on ammunition, Breymann ordered a retreat, but it turned into a rout as the Americans pursued. The Germans beat a parley to request terms, but the Americans misunderstood and continued to fire. The Germans fled into the growing darkness, and Stark soon halted the pursuit. He later claimed that none would have escaped if night had not fallen. As it was, Stark had won a signal victory. During the two engagements, the Americans killed 207 of the enemy; captured around 700, including 30 officers; and recovered four cannon and a large quantity of other military equipment. Estimates of American losses vary, but Stark put the figure at 30 dead and 40 wounded. Over the next several days, Baum's and Breymann's survivors trickled back to Burgoyne's army carrying the news of the disaster.

The Battle of Bennington marked a turning point in the campaign. The American victory seriously weakened Burgoyne by reducing his combat strength by nearly one-seventh. Without these losses, he may have been able to reach Albany or to return to Canada. Furthermore, the defeat denied his army the provisions and draft animals that it sorely needed. Finally, and most importantly, Bennington rejuvenated the colonists' efforts. Prior to the battle, Burgoyne's army had moved inexorably toward Albany, easily overcoming all resistance. Bennington demonstrated that the colonists could win and, in many respects, laid the groundwork for the American victory at Saratoga.

Michael P. Gabriel

See also

Burgoyne, John; Fort Edward, New York; Fort Ticonderoga, New York; German Mercenaries; Hubbardton, Battle of; Lincoln, Benjamin; Loyalist Units; New York, Operations in; Riedesel, Friedrich Adolph, Baron von; Sancoick, New York, Action at; Saratoga Campaign; Schuyler, Philip; Skene, Philip; Stark, John; Warner, Seth

References

Carrington, Henry B. *Battles of the American Revolution, 1775–1781.* 1876. Reprint, New York: Promontory, 1974.

Coburn, Frank Warren. *A History of the Battle of Bennington Vermont.* 2nd ed. Bennington, VT: Livingston, 1912.

Foster, Herbert D. "Stark's Independent Command at Bennington." *Proceedings of the New York State Historical Association* 5 (1905): 24–95.

Ketchum, Richard M. *Saratoga: Turning Point of America's Revolutionary War.* New York: Henry Holt, 1997.

Lord, Philip, Jr. *War over Walloomscoick: Land Use and Settlement Pattern on the Bennington Battlefield, 1777.* Albany, NY: State Education Department, 1989.

Morrissey, Brendan. *Saratoga 1777: Turning Point of a Revolution.* Oxford, UK: Osprey, 2000.

Ward, Christopher. *War of the Revolution.* 2 vols. New York: Macmillan, 1952.

Bermuda

Located in the western Atlantic Ocean, 600 miles east of South Carolina, Bermuda's isolation made its situation during the American Revolution a difficult one. The conflict first pushed the colony in the direction of its old commercial, cultural, and kinship connections to the American mainland. Then, as British military presence in the Atlantic grew and its army invaded the rebelling southern colonies in 1778 and 1780, Bermuda was pulled back toward the protection from attack, and from slave revolts, offered by Britain.

From the beginning of the conflict, the tiny island colony was divided by financial problems and insular politics, but its predominant trade patterns did not include New England, the early seat of conflict with Britain, and few Bermudans were concerned with the contentions there in the decade before war began. Bermuda was caught, however, between its vulnerability to British pressure due to its strategic location on major Atlantic shipping routes and its need for essential food from and commerce with the rebelling colonies.

The island's susceptibility to food shortages prompted the leading families to send an unofficial delegation to the Second Continental Congress, the only nonrebelling colony to do so. On 11 July 1775, this delegation petitioned for an exemption from America's upcoming embargo of all exports to nonrebelling colonies that would allow Bermuda to import food from North America. American sympathizers then orchestrated the theft on 14 August 1775 of more than one hundred barrels of gunpowder from the colony's powder magazine that were carried away on three American vessels to Philadelphia and Charleston. With this vital cargo Bermudans bought their exemption from the embargo but earned a reputation as supporters of the rebels.

In April 1776, congressional agent Silas Deane passed through Bermuda on his way to France. His friendly reception by Bermuda's merchant elite led him to believe that the colony ought to be secured forcibly for America, an idea repeated by the Marquis de Lafayette in 1779 and 1780 and considered by the Americans as late as 1781. Although Britain's Prohibitory Act of 1775 turned Bermuda's trade with America into smuggling, early in the war many merchants sold crucial salt, gunpowder, and fast Bermuda sloops to the rebel colonies.

From 1776 the increasingly regular presence of Royal Navy vessels and in 1778 the arrival of a garrison gradually dissuaded Bermudans from their illicit trade with America. The arbitrary application of military authority bred local discontent, but the arrival of several hundred Loyalist exiles, beginning in 1778, increased the influence of the pro-British element in Bermuda. The entry of traditional enemies France and Spain into the war in 1778 and 1779 further encouraged Bermudans to change their sympathies. By 1781, Bermuda's merchants, joining Loyalist exile families such as the Goodriches, turned their vessels from trade to privateering and transformed the colony into a highly effective base of attack on American shipping.

After the war, the Royal Navy established its largest fortified dockyard facility outside of Britain in Bermuda, thereby acknowledging the island's strategic importance as an Atlantic base. The impressive military presence and the reconfiguration of trade that resulted from the war thoroughly reoriented both the economy and the local society toward the British Empire.

Neil M. Kennedy

See also

Congress, Second Continental and Confederation; Deane, Silas; Loyalist Exiles; Privateering; Prohibitory Act

References

Bernhard, Virginia. *Slaves and Slaveholders in Bermuda, 1616–1782.* Columbia: University of Missouri Press, 1999.

Kerr, Wilfred B. *Bermuda and the American Revolution: 1760–1783.* Princeton, NJ: Princeton University Press, 1936.

Wilkinson, Henry C. *Bermuda in the Old Empire.* Oxford: Oxford University Press, 1950.

Bernard, Sir Francis (1712–1779)

Sir Francis Bernard, the royal governor of Massachusetts from 1760 to 1769, was born in Brightwell, Oxfordshire, the son of the Reverend Francis Bernard and Margaret Winlowe Bernard. Raised by an uncle following the early deaths of his parents, Bernard was educated at the Westminster School, Christ Church College, Oxford, and the Middle Temple, London, and was called to the English bar in 1737. In 1741, he married Amelia Offley, a cousin of William, Viscount Barrington, who served almost continuously as secretary of war from 1755 to 1778. Without this important family connection Bernard might have remained a well-educated but obscure barrister in the English provincial city of Lincoln. The financial pressure of a growing family, however, motivated Bernard to seek a lucrative office in America, and in 1758 Lord Barrington secured for him the governorship of New Jersey.

As governor, Bernard proved to be a capable, popular administrator, and his success in resolving many of the factional political disputes in the colony led to his promotion to the more important and potentially more lucrative post of governor of Massachusetts. His arrival in Boston in August 1760 coincided with an economic recession in that city, a situation that encouraged the meteoric rise of the radical lawyer and politician James Otis Jr. The postwar economic depression in Massachusetts following the end of the Seven Years' War increased popular support for Otis's attacks on the supposed aristocratic junta that controlled provincial affairs, headed by Thomas Hutchinson, the lieutenant governor of the colony. Bernard alienated Otis by appointing Hutchinson, a nonlawyer, to the post of chief justice, a position promised to Otis's father by Bernard's predecessor, Thomas Pownall. Nonetheless, Bernard, a basically decent if arrogant man, proved to be a popular governor until the Stamp Act crisis destroyed the delicate balance of Massachusetts's politics. In 1762, he supported a popular bill to increase the circulation of paper money, and his energetic efforts to replace the Harvard College library, which was destroyed in a fire in 1764, brought him many accolades. Bernard also designed the new Harvard Hall. Both his public statements and private correspondence to Lord Barrington indicate that he had serious misgivings about the Sugar Act and the Stamp Act, and he cautioned restraint in London as well as the need for colonial representation in the House of Commons.

These positions, however, were largely motivated by Bernard's realization that executive power in the colonies was weak, and from 1764 he bombarded officials in London with his ideas on administrative reform, which included the vacating of colonial charters, the transformation of the Massachusetts Governor's Council into an appointed body, and the creation of a colonial nobility. His views on colonial administration were later published in his *Select Letters on Trade and Government of America; and the Principles of Law and Polity, Applied to the American Colonies* (London, 1774). In 1765 he also began a campaign for his recall to London as a colonial constitutional expert to expedite such reforms.

Sir Francis Bernard, royal governor of Massachusetts, 1760–1769. His enforcement of the Stamp Act and other legislation rendered him unpopular in the colony, while his support for the Revolutionary idea that colonists should represent themselves in Parliament contributed to his recall by the British government. (*Francis Bernard,* painting by Giovanni B. Troccoli, 1925, Courtesy Commonwealth of Massachusetts Art Commission)

Unprepared for the outbreak of violence in Boston during the Stamp Act riots of August 1765, Bernard was powerless to enforce the Stamp Act and, fearing for his own personal safety, made preparations to flee Boston in October. Relieved by the repeal of the Stamp Act, he continued to suggest the necessity of colonial representation at Westminster, but he resisted the Massachusetts General Court's attempt to purge the Massachusetts Council of all executive officeholders as an act "to deprive [the government] of its best and most able servants whose only crime was their fidelity to the crown." Determined to implement the Townshend duties of 1767, Bernard informed his superior, Lord Hillsborough, Britain's secretary of state for the Southern Department, of the contents of the Massachusetts legislature's defiant circular letter of February 1768. Following the General Court's refusal to rescind its circular letter by a vote of 92 to 17 in June 1768, Bernard obeyed Lord Hillsborough's instructions and prorogued the legislature in July. Finding himself increasingly in conflict with Patriots in the colony following the disturbances arising from the seizure of John Hancock's sloop *Liberty,* Bernard sent letters to London suggesting the need for British troops in Boston to maintain order, a measure that "ought to have been done two years and a half ago." The British government did send the troops in, but the publication of several of Bernard's letters by the editors of the *Boston Gazette* in April 1769 ended his effectiveness as governor, and he was recalled to London.

As a mark of royal approbation Bernard was created a baronet in April 1769, but his departure from Boston in August was generally welcomed in London as well as in Massachusetts. Bernard would neither return to America nor gain another important colonial post. Awarded an honorary doctorate by Oxford University in 1772, he was appointed a commissioner of customs for Ireland in 1773; his duties were undertaken by a substitute while Bernard himself lived on an inherited estate in Aylesbury, Buckinghamshire. During the final imperial crisis initiated by the Boston Tea Party, Lord North consulted Bernard, and William Knox, an influential undersecretary at the American Department, attributed many of the provisions of the Massachusetts Government Act to Bernard's suggestions.

In increasingly ill health, Bernard was awarded a pension (which was rarely paid) in 1774. Following a series of seizures that had begun in 1771, he died at his home in Aylesbury on 16 June 1779. He was buried in the chancel of Aylesbury Church; his portrait, by John Singleton Copley, hangs in Christ Church College, Oxford. As governor of Massachusetts, Bernard exacerbated the growing conflict between Britain and her American colonies, but his actions alone, like those of other unpopular colonial governors, did not cause the American Revolution, which had deeper underlying causes.

Rory T. Cornish

See also

Adams, Samuel; Coercive Acts; Gage, Thomas; Hill, Wills; Hutchinson, Thomas; Massachusetts; Otis, James, Jr.; Pownall, Thomas; Stamp Act

References

Bailyn, Bernard. *The Ordeal of Thomas Hutchinson.* Cambridge: Harvard University Press, 1974.

Channing, Edward, ed. *The Barrington-Bernard Correspondence.* Cambridge: Harvard University Press, 1912.

Christie, Ian R., and Benjamin W. Labaree. *Empire or Independence, 1760–1776.* New York: Norton, 1976.

Fiore, Jordan D. "Sir Francis Bernard, Colonial Governor." *New England Social Studies Bulletin* 12 (1954): 13–18.

Nash, Gary B. *The Urban Crucible: Social Change, Political Consciousness and the Origins of the American Revolution.* Cambridge: Harvard University Press, 1979.

Biddle, Nicholas (1750–1778)

Nicholas Biddle was one of the most able and successful Continental Navy captains in the early years of the Revolutionary War at sea, and his death in battle was a considerable loss to the young nation's naval capacity.

Having served as a midshipman for three years before resigning his warrant on the eve of the War of Independence, Biddle was one of only a few American naval officers with Royal Navy experience. On 1 August 1775, the Pennsylvania Committee of Safety appointed Biddle to command the *Franklin,* one of a number of galleys the colony was building to defend the Delaware River. He resigned this commission four months later to accept command of the 14-gun brigantine *Andrew Doria* in the newly established Continental Navy. In mid-February 1776, Biddle participated in the navy's first fleet operation under the command of Commodore Esek Hopkins. The American fleet captured the Bahamian town of Nassau on 4 March, seizing military stores for the Continental cause. On the homeward voyage Biddle took part in his first sea action when Hopkins's fleet engaged HMS *Glasgow.*

Through the spring and summer of 1776, Biddle cruised in *Andrew Doria,* operating out of New London, Connecticut, and Newport, Rhode Island. During this time he captured and sent to port nine vessels as prizes, including two British transports. In September, Biddle arrived in Philadelphia to take command of the 36-gun *Randolph,* one of thirteen frigates whose construction Congress had authorized the previous December. Biddle spent the fall preparing the *Randolph* for sea. Slow recruiting, enemy warships off the Delaware Capes, and ice delayed the American frigate's departure until 6 February 1777. The *Randolph*'s first cruise terminated prematurely when, after several weeks at sea, the frigate lost both its fore and main masts. Through Biddle's skillful seamanship, however, the crippled American cruiser was able to sail safely to Charleston, South Carolina, on 11 March.

Necessary and extensive repairs to the *Randolph,* accidents (including two lightning strikes), and desertion and sickness among its crew kept the frigate idle for five months. On 1 September 1778, Biddle finally put to sea again. He returned to Charleston just five days later with four prize ships whose sale netted their captors more than $60,000. Biddle departed on his final cruise in the *Randolph* on 14 February 1778. Four vessels fitted out by South Carolina and placed under Biddle's command accompanied the Continental warship. The cruise came to a disastrous conclusion on 7 March, when Biddle's squadron encountered HMS *Yarmouth.* In an action fought at night, the *Randolph* and its much larger sixty-four-gun foe exchanged broadsides at close range. After a quarter hour of firing, an explosion on board the *Randolph* blew the frigate into fragments, killing Biddle and all on board except four crewmen. Biddle's death deprived the Continental Navy of an active and enterprising officer.

Charles E. Brodine Jr.

See also

Continental Navy; Naval Operations, American vs. British

References

Clark, William Bell. *Captain Dauntless: The Story of Nicholas Biddle of the Continental Navy.* Baton Rouge: Louisiana State University Press, 1949.

Clark, William Bell, et al., eds. *Naval Documents of the American Revolution.* 10 vols. to date. Washington, DC: Naval Historical Center, 1964–.

Biggin Church, South Carolina, Action at (16–17 July 1781)

The engagement at Biggin Church, South Carolina, was a confrontation between British Lieutenant-Colonel John Coates and Patriot militia as Coates attempted to withdraw his unit from Moncks Corner to British-held Charleston. British General Charles Cornwallis had marched his army north out of South Carolina in January 1781 in pursuit of General Nathanael Greene after the Battle of Cowpens. The British forces remaining in South Carolina garrisoned the major towns and a string of forts in an attempt to hold the state from the persistent Patriot militia. During the spring and summer of 1781, many British forts fell to Greene, who suddenly returned after Cornwallis marched his army to Wilmington, North Carolina, and then into Virginia. Other forts fell to the partisan commanders Thomas Sumter and Francis Marion.

Coates, the British commander at Moncks Corner, located north of Charleston, realized that he held an exposed position. Forts to the north and west had fallen, and Patriot forces roamed the countryside around him. Coates commanded approximately 700 men, with 150 of those being British regulars of his regiment.

Militia dragoons serving under Sumter cut the line of communications between Moncks Corner and Dorchester, the most direct route to Charleston. Coates then withdrew his force from Moncks Corner and established a camp at Biggin Church, a supply storage area located east of his original position.

Patriot militia units circled behind the church to destroy Wadboo Bridge, knowing that the British would have to cross it to reach Charleston. Coates deployed his dragoons during the night of 16 July 1781 to challenge the Patriot militia, but the Patriots held against the determined British attack. Coates then opted to destroy his supplies at Biggin Church, marched his infantry to Wadboo Bridge, and joined the action in the early hours of 17 July. British forces successfully pushed aside the Patriot militia and crossed the bridge. Coates continued his withdrawal toward Charleston and was engaged by the combined forces of Sumter and Marion at Quinby Bridge. If the Patriot militia had successfully destroyed Wadboo Bridge and encircled Coates at Biggin Church, the entire British regiment might have been forced to surrender, giving the Patriots a significant victory and demoralizing the British forces bottled up in Charleston by the Patriot advance. The British escape, however, gave new life to the spirited campaign against South Carolina's partisans. The ruins of Biggin Church still exist just outside of Moncks Corner.

Terry M. Mays

See also

Cornwallis, Charles; Cowpens, Battle of; Greene, Nathanael; Marion, Francis; Quinby Bridge, South Carolina, Action at; Southern Campaigns; Sumter, Thomas

Reference

Ripley, Warren. *Battleground: South Carolina in the Revolution.* Charleston, SC: Evening Post, 1983.

Billingsport, New Jersey, Attack on (2 October 1777)

Situated 12 miles below Philadelphia on the Jersey bank of the Delaware River, the redoubt at Billingsport guarded a double line of underwater obstructions (chevaux-de-frise) that blocked navigation up the river. Attacked in early October 1777, the undermanned and poorly constructed fort, vulnerable to landward attack, was abandoned by its defenders in the face of overwhelming enemy force. The attack on Billingsport was the first in a series of combined operations that enabled British land and naval forces to win control of the Delaware River by late November 1777, thus securing a waterborne line of supply for Sir William Howe's army in Philadelphia.

Shortly after he captured the Patriot capital, General Howe assigned Lieutenant-Colonel Thomas Stirling the task of capturing Billingsport. On 29 September, Stirling marched the 42nd and 10th Regiments and two 6-pounder field guns from Germantown to Chester, Pennsylvania, arriving at that port town the next day. At Chester, Stirling's force was augmented by the addition of the 71st Regiment and embarked in five warships commanded by Sir Andrew Snape Hamond. On 1 October, Hamond's squadron moved downriver, landing Stirling's detachment on the Jersey riverbank near Raccoon Creek, several miles below Billingsport, where the redcoats made camp and prepared for the next day's assault.

On the morning of 2 October, about 300 New Jersey militia under Brigadier General Silas Newcomb attempted to contest Stirling's advance on Billingsport but were soon routed. Recognizing that his garrison of 100 Pennsylvania militiamen was no match for a vastly superior foe, Colonel William

Bradford, Billingsport's commander, ordered the redoubt abandoned. His troops spiked the guns that could not be carried off, emptied the fort of its ammunition, and set fire to the barracks and bake house. Boats from the Pennsylvania State Navy evacuated the majority of Billingsport's defenders to Fort Mifflin. The British occupied the fort shortly after noon without suffering a single casualty.

Over the next four days, Stirling's men, assisted by marines and other personnel from Hamond's squadron, set about leveling the works at Billingsport. The American fleet repeatedly harassed these operations with offshore cannon fire. On 4 October, Hamond's vessels began the important work of clearing a passage through the chevaux-de-frise that blocked the shipping channel between Billings Island and Billingsport. They also began reembarking the majority of Stirling's command for transport across the river to Chester. The British set fire to the remaining structures at Billingsport on 6 October, thereby completing their demolition of the fort. That evening Hamond's squadron transported the last British troops across the river. On 20 October, Royal Navy vessels finally succeeded in clearing a passage through the underwater obstructions that the American redoubt had once guarded.

Charles E. Brodine Jr.

See also
Philadelphia Campaign

References

Jackson, John W. *The Pennsylvania Navy, 1775–1781: The Defense of the Delaware.* New Brunswick, NJ: Rutgers University Press, 1974.

Smith, Samuel S. *Fight for the Delaware, 1777.* Monmouth Beach, NJ: Philip Freneau, 1970.

Black Mingo Creek, South Carolina, Action at (28 September 1780)

The Battle of Black Mingo Creek, South Carolina, was a militia engagement between the Patriot leader Francis Marion and the Loyalist leader John Ball on 28 September 1780. Black Mingo Creek marked the return of Marion and the only viable Patriot military unit in the low country of South Carolina to the field in the fall of 1780. The skirmish boosted Patriot morale, encouraged recruitment to Marion's force, and diverted Loyalist militia from the harassment of Patriot settlements to a campaign against Marion.

The War of Independence had been going badly for South Carolina's Patriots in 1780. Charleston fell on 12 May, General Horatio Gates suffered a humiliating defeat at Camden on 16 August, and Patriot militia commander General Thomas Sumter nearly lost his life at the defeat of his force at Fishing Creek on 18 August. Loyalist militia units were rallying to the British cause as Patriot militiamen retreated and scattered to their farms.

Notwithstanding these setbacks, Marion scored two quick, small victories for the Patriot cause immediately after the Battle of Camden. Although these skirmishes, at Great Savannah and Blue Savannah, South Carolina, boosted Patriot morale during bitter times, many of the militiamen under Marion desired to return to their homes and be with their families during this period. Marion, recognizing this need in nonregulars, dismissed most of his force and withdrew into North Carolina with a small band of close followers. Loyalists took advantage of the recent British victories and began harassing pro-Patriot neighbors. When Marion heard of this, he returned from North Carolina and initiated a call for Patriot militia members to rally to him.

The British garrison at Georgetown, South Carolina, learned of Marion's return and dispatched two groups of Loyalist militia to prevent the Patriots from seizing arms. Ball led one Loyalist force consisting of fifty men and moved to Shepherd's Ferry on Black Mingo Creek. Marion, also with fifty men, opted to attack Ball's force and moved his troops to a bridge near Shepherd's Ferry. The creaking of the bridge planks as the horses crossed alerted a Loyalist sentry, who fired a warning shot. Marion divided his command into three groups and ordered an assault on the buildings thought to house the Loyalists. Ball, alerted by the musket shot, had moved his command into a nearby field. As the Patriots arrived, they were greeted by a sharp volley from the Loyalists. Marion's men recovered and were soon joined by the other Patriot groups, who then pinned the Loyalists against a swamp. The fifteen-minute engagement ended with the rout of the Loyalists, who retreated back to Georgetown. Patriot casualties numbered approximately ten while the Loyalists suffered approximately sixteen casualties. Marion also captured Ball's horse, named the animal "Ball," and rode it until the end of the war.

Terry M. Mays

See also
Blue Savannah, South Carolina, Action at; Camden Campaign; Charleston, South Carolina, Expedition against (1780); Fishing Creek, Battle of; Gates, Horatio; Great Savannah, South Carolina, Action at; Marion, Francis; Southern Campaigns; Sumter, Thomas

Reference

Bass, Robert. *Swamp Fox: The Life and Campaigns of General Francis Marion.* 1959. Reprint, Orangeburg, SC: Sandlapper, 1989.

Blackstock's, South Carolina, Action at (20 November 1780)

The engagement at Blackstock's, also known as Blackstock's Ford, occurred in upper South Carolina. The battle proved to be the first defeat for British Lieutenant-Colonel Banastre

Banastre Tarleton, a British cavalry officer in command of the Loyalist British Legion, suffered his first defeat at Blackstock's. (Library of Congress)

Tarleton, but it also ended the campaigning of the Patriot commander General Thomas Sumter for three months as he recovered from wounds suffered in the action.

Well into November 1780, Sumter and his 1,000-man militia unit combed north and central South Carolina in a campaign against Loyalist militia, following the 7 October Patriot victory over the Loyalists at Kings Mountain. A sharp engagement at Fishdam Ford, in which Sumter countered an attempt to kill or capture him, persuaded Lord Cornwallis that it was imperative to eliminate the threat posed by Sumter and his band. Cornwallis dispatched Tarleton with his dragoons and regular Highlanders to pursue and stop Sumter. Each commander was eager to engage the other, and on 20 November, Sumter moved his force onto a plantation owned by William Blackstock. Tarleton meanwhile abandoned his slow-moving infantry in order to increase his speed with 250 cavalry and mounted infantry to catch Sumter.

Sumter placed men in the plantation house and other buildings that were constructed of logs and offered good protection from musket fire. He deployed other men behind a log fence along the road. His flanks were protected by a river on one side and a rugged hill on the other. Tarleton realized that he faced a stout defensive position and opted to await the arrival of his infantry before attacking. Sumter, however, realizing that Tarleton had split his command, launched a quick attack to take advantage of the situation. Sumter ordered approximately 100 Patriot horsemen to turn the British right flank and attack from the rear. They successfully caught the British off guard and inflicted casualties among Tarleton's mounted infantry, who were now fighting on foot. The infantry reorganized, however, and counterattacked, driving the Patriot cavalry back toward Blackstock's with a bayonet charge. As the cavalry retreated, the pursuing British passed within range of the riflemen in the buildings, who poured devastating fire upon them, hitting three of the officers.

A second group of Patriot horsemen struck the British cavalry with greater success. They managed to move to within approximately seventy-five yards of the British and opened fire with buckshot. Some twenty dragoons were unsaddled by the volley before the rest counterattacked and drove the Patriots back to Blackstock's. Tarleton then ordered the dragoons forward to assist the infantry under fire from the buildings.

At the height of the engagement, Sumter moved too close to the British, who noticed his gold epaulets and fired a volley. Sumter's only defense was to turn his body so that he would not be hit squarely. Buckshot ripped into his right arm and part of his chest. He turned his horse and withdrew to rejoin his staff, whom he told to keep the news of his wounds secret so as not to alarm his troops and destroy their morale in the midst of the fighting. Sumter received medical attention that evening and was eventually evacuated for recovery.

While he recovered, Sumter turned over his command to militia Colonel John Twiggs. Tarleton eventually retreated and moved his troops 2 miles away to prepare for a second day of battle. However, Twiggs opted to remove his force from Blackstock's and withdraw from the area. Tarleton pursued the Patriots for two days but then abandoned the chase and returned south toward friendlier territory. Sumter's wounds, however, helped persuade his officers to dismiss their men home to their farms rather than continue the fight under a new commander. Although the Patriot leaders later reorganized their militia forces, Tarleton's pursuit had accomplished part of its goal—the removal of Sumter and his men from the field.

British losses at Blackstock's were quite high. The number of casualties differs greatly between sources but may have been as high as 92 dead and 100 wounded. Patriot losses, however, were reported as just 3 dead and only 4 wounded, including Sumter. Blackstock's became Tarleton's first defeat at the hands of Patriot forces, although he would not admit it later in life. His failure to crush the Patriot militia and prevent Sumter's escape served to bruise Tarelton's ego. Two months later he would again pursue a Patriot force, only to meet his greatest defeat at the Battle of Cowpens.

Terry M. Mays

See also
Cornwallis, Charles; Cowpens, Battle of; Fishdam Ford, South Carolina, Action at; Kings Mountain, Battle of; Southern Campaigns; Sumter, Thomas; Tarleton, Banastre

References
Bass, Robert. *Gamecock: The Life and Campaigns of General Thomas Sumter.* 1961. Reprint, Orangeburg, SC: Sandlapper, 2000.
Lumpkin, Henry. *From Savannah to Yorktown: The American Revolution in the South.* New York: Paragon, 1981.

Blackstone, Sir William (1723–1780)

An English jurist and professor of common law at Oxford University, Blackstone was the principal vehicle through which the English common law was transported and explained to late-eighteenth-century America.

In England, Blackstone gained renown while in his thirties for his ability as a lecturer, leading to his appointment in 1758 as the first Vinerian professor of English law at the University of Oxford. His *Commentaries on the Laws of England* (1765–1769), based on his Oxford lectures, was sold widely in America, both in English and American editions, before the Revolution. Blackstone was read by almost all jurists in eighteenth-century America and, perhaps more important, was well known to a wider politically active audience.

Blackstone's *Commentaries* was more than a legal text; it provided a systematic account of the history of the English government, or "constitution." Blackstone traced the English constitution from its early medieval origins to its eighteenth-century state, in which sovereignty resided with the King-in-Parliament. American writers, such as the youthful Alexander Hamilton, often referred to Blackstone, in part because his text was straightforward, lending itself to easy reference. Blackstone remarked that he wished to give "a general map of the law, marking out the shape of the country, it's connexions and boundaries, it's greater divisions and principal cities." Most frequently quoted by Americans during the Revolutionary era were passages from Book 1, *Rights of Persons* (especially its first chapter, "Of the Absolute Rights of Individuals"), and Book 2, *Rights of Things.*

Robert Bell published the first American edition of the *Commentaries* in Philadelphia in 1771–1772. Bell's edition, published by subscription, was an immediate success and soon became widely celebrated. Many other American editions followed. It was not until 1795–1796, with the publication of Zephaniah Swift's *A System of the Laws of the State of Connecticut,* that Americans had a native statement of a common-law tradition.

Some aspects of Blackstone's thought, however, received a mixed reception in Revolutionary America. Blackstone, like David Hume, thought that the power of the Crown to confer honors and privileges was a necessary check with which to control the people. Many Americans, such as Thomas Jefferson, disagreed. Others, such as James Wilson, came to question what they saw as Blackstone's conception of the law as an authority independent from, and superior to, its citizens. By the beginning of the nineteenth century, Blackstone's critics had increased in number, particularly as Jeremy Bentham's negative assessment became more widely held. Bentham regarded the *Commentaries* as "nonsense on stilts," arguing that Blackstone muddled common law and natural law. Nevertheless, the *Commentaries* was used widely as a textbook in America until the close of the nineteenth century.

Mark G. Spencer

See also
Hamilton, Alexander; Hume, David; Jefferson, Thomas; Wilson, James

References
Blackstone, William. *Commentaries on the Laws of England: A Facsimile of the First Edition of 1765–1769.* With an introduction by Stanley N. Katz. 4 vols. Chicago and London: University of Chicago Press, 1979.
Boorstin, Daniel J. *The Mysterious Science of the Law: An Essay on Blackstone's Commentaries.* 1941. Reprint, Boston: Beacon, 1958.
Lutz, Donald S. "The Relative Influence of European Writers in Late Eighteenth-Century American Political Thought." *American Political Science Review* 78 (1984): 189–197.

Bland, Richard (1710–1776)

Richard Bland, Virginian statesman and American constitutional spokesman, was born in Williamsburg, Virginia, the son of the planter politician Richard Bland and his wife Elizabeth Randolph Bland. Educated at the College of William and Mary, Bland, as befitted his status as a member of one of Virginia's elite families, served as a justice of the peace and colonel of the Prince George County militia. Elected to the House of Burgesses in 1742 and called to the Virginia bar in 1746, he established himself as one of Virginia's foremost constitutional experts. Serving continuously in the House until 1775, he took a leading part in protecting local colonial autonomy in matters regarding taxation throughout the 1750s. A conservative elder statesman, he was present at the October 1764 session of the House that dispatched petitions to London opposing the prospective Stamp Act, but he distanced himself from the passionate language of Patrick Henry and the Virginia Resolves.

The Resolves, together with the constitutional arguments in James Otis's *The Rights of the British Colonies Asserted and Proved* (November 1764), greatly irritated the Grenville ministry. In January 1765, that administration answered the colonists with Thomas Whately's *The Regulations Lately Made,* which defended the British notion that the colonies were virtually represented in the House of Commons. Bland framed his *An Inquiry into the Rights of the British Colonies* (1766) as a direct answer to Whately. His pamphlet, one of the most radical to appear in the 1760s, was widely read in the colonies and excerpted in several newspapers, but it was lost in the sea of pamphlets published during the Stamp Act crisis in London.

Basing his reasoning upon Lockean notions of natural rights, Bland argued that the original colonists who left England for America did not do so to become slaves. As their settlement in the colonies necessitated the creation of a new political compact, their colonial assemblies were thus based upon the two principles of "national freedom and independence." Believing the colonies to be sovereign in domestic, internal affairs, Bland further argued that their political link with Britain was with the king only and that any attempt by Parliament to tax the colonies internally was an "Act of Power and not Right." Implicit in Bland's constitutional position was the notion that the colonial assemblies were the equal of Parliament, and if their constitutional rights were encroached upon, the colonists had the right to rebel.

A reluctant rebel, Bland nonetheless supported Virginia's nonimportation agreement against the Townshend revenue acts in 1769, and in 1773 Bland was appointed a member of the House of Burgesses committee of correspondence with the other colonies. Bland also served reluctantly as a Virginia delegate to both the First and Second Continental Congresses. Accepting that a constitutional compromise had become impossible with Britain, he voted for Virginia's independence in May 1776 and supported the Declaration of Independence in July. As a member of Virginia's first House of Delegates, he was appointed to the committee that drew up the state's new constitution. Bland died in Williamsburg in October 1776.

Rory T. Cornish

See also

Congress, First Continental; Congress, Second Continental and Confederation; Declaration of Independence; Grenville, George; Henry, Patrick; Nonimportation Agreements; Otis, James, Jr.; Stamp Act; Townshend Acts; Virginia; Virginia Resolves

References

Bailyn, Bernard. *The Ideological Origins of the American Revolution.* 1967. Reprint, Cambridge: Harvard University Press, 1992.

Bland, Richard. *An Inquiry into the Rights of the British Colonies, Intended As an Answer to the Regulations Lately Made Concerning the Colonies, and the Taxes Imposed upon Them Considered.* London: John Almon, 1766.

Cornish, Rory T. *George Grenville, 1712–1770: A Bibliography.* London: Greenwood, 1992.

Bland, Theodorick (1742–1790)

A descendant of Pocahontas and of Virginia's early English settlers, Theodorick Bland was born on 21 March 1742 in Prince George County, Virginia. He grew up on a tobacco plantation owned by his aristocratic family and was sent to England in 1753 for his education. Bland graduated from the University of Edinburgh with a degree in medicine in 1763 and returned to Prince George County in 1764 to set up his practice. His own poor health led to his retirement from medicine in 1771 and the start of a new career as a gentleman tobacco farmer with an emerging interest in politics.

On 21 April 1775, Virginia's royal governor, Lord Dunmore, seized and locked away the better part of the province's gunpowder in Williamsburg, claiming that he feared a slave insurrection. Dunmore fled from Williamsburg two months later, summoning a naval squadron to nearby Chesapeake Bay to keep the peace. On 24 June 1775, Bland led some twenty men, including James Monroe and Benjamin Harrison Jr., into the deserted Governor's Palace, where they seized all the weapons they could find, both ceremonial swords and working firearms. Bland was in charge of distributing these weapons from the nearby powder magazine to any Virginia citizen who needed one.

On 13 June 1776, Bland became captain of the First Troop of Virginia Cavalry, and six months later, on 4 December, he was promoted to major of the Light Dragoons. Bland joined the American army on 31 March 1777 as colonel of the 1st Continental Dragoons and served in the New Jersey and Philadelphia Campaigns. His best-known combat role came on 11 September 1777, at the Battle of Brandywine in Pennsylvania, where he commanded his mounted troops on General George Washington's right flank. Bland, however, failed to adequately spy out the land and learn that the nearby creek could be forded by enemy troops. The faulty intelligence he delivered to Washington, along with contradictory reports from General John Sullivan, led to the American defeat at Brandywine.

On 5 November 1778, Washington ordered Bland to escort the so-called Convention Army, the British prisoners from the surrender at Saratoga, from New England to Charlottesville, Virginia, and Bland assumed command of the guard detail there in May 1779. This duty, however, was not to his liking, and he received permission to retire from the army in November.

Bland returned to his plantation, which had been looted by the British, and took up the role of legislator. He served as a delegate to Congress from 1780 to 1783 and served in the Virginia House of Delegates from 1786 to 1788. In 1786 he lost a contest for governor to Edmund Randolph. In 1788, as a member of Virginia's ratifying convention, Bland voted against adoption of the U.S. Constitution primarily because he felt that it gave the federal government too much power at the expense of the states. Virginia elected Bland to the first federal House of Representatives, but he died of influenza on 1 June 1790 before completing his term.

Kelly Hensley

See also
Brandywine, Battle of; Convention Army; Virginia
References
Boatner, Mark. *Encyclopedia of the American Revolution.* Mechanicsburg, PA: Stackpole, 1994.
Hagy, Mark R. "Portrait of a Virginia Antifederalist: Theodorick Bland, 1742–1790." *International Social Science Review* 71(3–4) (1996): 3–13.
Mattern, David. "Bland, Theodorick." Pp. 946–947 in *American National Biography,* vol. 2. New York: Oxford University Press, 1999.
Swem, Earl Gregg. "Bland, Theodorick." Pp. 356–357 in *Dictionary of American Biography,* vol. 1. New York: Scribner, 1928.

Blue Licks, Kentucky, Action at (19 October 1782)

On 19 October 1782, Kentucky frontiersmen were ambushed by pro-British Indian warriors at Blue Licks, Kentucky, and suffered a humiliating defeat. In August 1782, Tory Captain William Caldwell, Loyalist Simon Girty, and Alexander McKee crossed the Ohio River with 300 Indian warriors and on 15 August besieged Bryan's Station, near Lexington, Kentucky. Unable to compel its surrender, they withdrew on 18 August toward the Ohio River, making no attempt to disguise their march. At Bryan's Station, more than 200 militiamen, commanded by John Todd, Stephen Trigg, Daniel Boone, and others, quickly assembled. Refusing to heed Boone's advice to await reinforcements, 182 mounted men under Colonel Todd set out on 18 August to pursue their adversaries. Meanwhile, Caldwell and his party had arrived at the lower Blue Licks, crossed the Licking River, and arrayed themselves in ambush position.

On 19 August, the Kentuckians reached the Blue Licks and observed Indians on the north side of the Licking River. Boone, suspecting that the Indians were deliberately exposing themselves to lure an assault, pleaded with Todd to await reinforcements coming forward under Benjamin Logan. Apparently, at this point Major Hugh McGary accused Boone of cowardice, and Boone bristled that he was ready to fight, disadvantage or no. Others sided with McGary, and Todd, despite Boone's further pleas that he wait, decided to advance. Once across the Licking River, the Kentuckians moved forward in three columns for about a mile, with Boone commanding the left, Todd the center, and Trigg the right. A scouting party that included McGary and twenty-seven others led the way. Suddenly, the Americans were fired upon by Caldwell's concealed Indian warriors. All but three of the scouts were killed instantly; McGary was one of the few who survived.

Within seconds, Trigg's men on the right were fighting for their survival. They held their ground for about five minutes, but their flanks were enfiladed, their commander was killed, and they were practically annihilated. Shortly thereafter, the center under Todd also disintegrated. Todd and his men fled in disarray, leaving only the left flank under Boone still engaged. At McGary's urging, Boone was soon in headlong retreat, pursued by the Indians toward the Licking River. In the melee, Boone's son, Israel, was mortally wounded, and Boone was compelled to abandon Israel and flee for his life. Later that day, reinforcements under Logan met the retreating survivors and prepared to repel any pursuing warriors, but none followed. On 24 August, Logan and his men reclaimed the battlefield and the American dead, including Israel Boone. Seventy-seven Americans were killed, twelve were wounded, and eight were captured; most of the captives were burned alive. Seven of the Indians were killed, and ten were wounded; the rest escaped across the Ohio River.

Paul David Nelson

See also
Boone, Daniel; Girty, Simon; Kentucky; Native Americans
References
Adams, Michael C. C. "An Appraisal of the Blue Licks Battle." *Filson History Quarterly* 75 (2001): 181–203.
Cotterill, Robert S. "Battle of Upper Blue Licks (1782)." *Historical Quarterly* 2 (1927): 29–33.
Wilson, Samuel M. *The Battle of the Blue Licks, August 19, 1782.* Lexington, KY: n.p., 1927.

Blue Savannah, South Carolina, Action at (4 September 1780)

The Battle of Blue Savannah was a military engagement between the Patriot General Francis Marion and Loyalist militia who were hunting him after the Patriot victory at Great Savannah. The action at Blue Savannah boosted Patriot morale after a string of defeats in the spring and summer of 1780. Many recruits joined Marion's band as a result of the victory. The skirmish intimidated many Loyalist militia members and also prompted the British to intensify the hunt for Patriot militia in the field.

The war had been going badly for the South Carolina Patriot cause in 1780. Charleston fell on 12 May, the American General Horatio Gates suffered a humiliating defeat at Camden on 16 August, and the Patriot militia commander Thomas Sumter nearly lost his life at the defeat of his force at Fishdam Ford on 18 August. Loyalist militia units were rallying to the British cause as Patriot militia members retreated to their farms. Marion commanded the only viable Patriot military force south of the South Carolina up-country after August 1780.

Marion and approximately 50 Patriot mounted militia were in the swamps of eastern South Carolina after the action at Great Savannah. The British dispatched some 250 Loyalist militiamen to hunt him down. On 4 September 1780, a detachment of Marion's men stumbled upon 50 Loyalist mounted militia and initiated a charge to rout them. Major John James, the leader of Marion's advance detachment, recklessly continued the pursuit alone, calling out to nonexistent comrades to frighten the Loyalists he followed. The ruse worked, as most of the Loyalists scattered from the area. The Patriots captured 3 individuals who informed Marion that the other 200 Loyalists were only 3 miles away.

Marion and his main body continued their advance until they were surprised by the 200 Loyalist infantry who quickly and confidently formed a skirmish line. The Patriot leader realized the danger and withdrew into a swampy area with the Loyalists in hot pursuit. The Patriots reached an area of dense scrub pines and sandy ground along the Pee Dee River known as the Blue Savannah. Here, Marion doubled back and ambushed the Loyalists. The Loyalist force managed to fire one volley at the charging Patriots, dropping three of them and two horses. Although numerically superior to their attackers, the Loyalists were not able to organize a second volley due to the intensity of the attack. They turned and fled into the Little Pee Dee Swamp, where they were taunted by Marion's men patrolling along the edge of the swamp. Marion purposely kept the Loyalist casualties to a minimum in order to reduce the tensions caused by civil strife among South Carolinians. After the war, personal differences between Patriots and Loyalists would heal quicker if there were fewer deaths to remember. Patriot casualties included four wounded men; Loyalist casualties are not recorded, although they are known to have been also light.

Soon after the engagement, Marion released most of his men to return to their homes to avoid an impending British offensive to find them. Marion and a small group withdrew to North Carolina, but he would return to action within weeks at Black Mingo Creek.

Terry M. Mays

See also

Black Mingo Creek, South Carolina, Action at; Great Savannah, South Carolina, Action at; Marion, Francis

Reference

Bass, Robert. *Swamp Fox: The Life and Campaigns of General Francis Marion.* 1959. Reprint, Orangeburg, SC: Sandlapper, 1989.

Board of Trade

See Trade, Board of

Board of War

See War, Board of

Bonhomme Richard vs. *Serapis* (23 September 1779)

Key naval engagement of the American Revolutionary War fought off the English coast. One of the more sanguinary contests of the age of fighting sail, this American victory resulted in the enshrinement of John Paul Jones as one of the great heroes of U.S. naval history.

In November 1777 the thirty-year-old Captain Jones had sailed the 18-gun sloop of war *Ranger* to France with dispatches for the American commissioners there. In the spring of 1778 Jones and the *Ranger* carried the war to Britain. Operating from the French port of Brest, Jones took a number of British merchantmen; raided and burned the port of Whitehaven, England; and captured the 16-gun British sloop of war *Drake.* These events caused consternation in Britain and joy in America.

With the support of American Minister Plenipotentiary to France Benjamin Franklin, Jones then received command of the *Duc de Duras,* the largest ship to fight under the American flag during the Revolution. The French government had purchased this slow, fourteen-year-old, 900-ton East Indiaman in February 1779 and converted it into a warship. The French then loaned the vessel to the Americans. The ship was 145′ – 36′8″. Jones renamed the ship *Bonhomme Richard* (the French translation of *Poor Richard's Almanac*) in honor of his friend Franklin.

Jones wanted the *Bonhomme Richard* to mount what would have been a formidable battery of sixty-two guns: twenty-eight 18-pounders on the gun deck, twenty-eight 8-pounders on the upper deck, and six 8-pounders on the forecastle and quarterdeck. Although arrangements were made for the ship to carry sixteen 18-pounders on the gun deck, it went to sea with only six, and these were old. The ship's main strength was in twenty-eight 12-pounders on the upper deck. It also carried six 8-pounders—two on the forecastle and four on the quarterdeck—so that the ship mounted just forty guns. The *Bonhomme Richard* had a crew of 322 men, including a heavy complement of 140 French marines (60 would have been a normal number of marines on a French vessel of that size). Many of the crew were of French nationality, although all but 2 of the 26 officers were Americans.

On 14 August, Jones set sail from the French port of L'Orient with a small squadron of seven French and American ships, including two French privateers, on a two-month commerce-raiding cruise off the British coasts. The five navy vessels sailed under an agreement specifying that for the duration of the cruise they were considered to be Continental Navy warships and bound by its regulations. The French captains held commissions, issued by Franklin, as Continental Navy officers.

Bonhomme Richard vs. *Serapis.* This epic ship-to-ship engagement in British waters between Captain John Paul Jones and Captain Richard Pearson, marked by heroic conduct on both sides, is best known for Jones's refusal to surrender with the words, "I have not yet begun to fight." Ironically, after a lengthy fight at close quarters, the British vessel itself capitulated to Jones's crippled ship. (U.S. Navy)

The French privateers the *Granville* and the *Monsieur,* which had set out with the squadron, soon went their own way, and a French cutter, *Le Cerf,* became separated in fog. This left Jones with four ships: the *Bonhomme Richard;* the Continental Navy frigate the *Alliance* (36 guns) under Captain Pierre Landais, a Frenchman, but with an American crew; the *Pallas* (32 guns), an ex-privateer French frigate under Captain Denis Cottineau; and the *Vengeance* (12 guns), a French brig under Captain Philippe Ricot. During the next five weeks the squadron took a number of British merchantmen, including two supply vessels bound for America. By the third week of September, the squadron had sailed around the west coast of Ireland and the north coast of Scotland and then down the east coast of Scotland to the northeast coast of England as far as Hull before sailing north about 20 miles to rendezvous off Flamborough Head.

On the afternoon of 23 September the squadron was near Flamborough Head off the Yorkshire coast when it sighted a British convoy of forty-one merchantmen laden with naval stores from the Baltic and bound for the royal dockyards in southern England. Escorting the ships were the *Serapis* (44 guns), commanded by Captain Richard Pearson, and the armed ship the *Countess of Scarborough* (20 guns), under Captain Thomas Piercy. The *Serapis,* often identified as a frigate, was actually more powerful. At 886 tons and measuring 140′ – 38′, it was almost exactly the size of the *Bonhomme Richard.* The *Serapis* was also new, having entered service only the year before, and mounted forty-four guns: twenty 18-pounders on the gun deck, twenty-two 9-pounders on the upper deck, and two 6-pounders on the forecastle. The *Countess of Scarborough,* however, was a converted civilian sloop of light construction.

As Jones's squadron closed from the south, Captain Pearson placed his two warships landward in front of the merchantmen to allow them to escape. Jones ordered Captain Landais of the *Alliance* to attack the *Serapis* from its starboard side, while the *Bonhomme Richard* took up station on its port side. Cottineau's *Pallas* would engage the *Countess of Scarborough.* The *Vengeance,* armed only with 4-pounders, was to provide support as needed.

The battle between the *Bonhomme Richard* and the *Serapis* opened at 7:15 P.M., at a range of about 100 yards, and continued well into the night. The *Serapis* fired the first broadside, but each ship holed the other in the first exchange. The British fired a second broadside at only 20 yards. When the *Bonhomme Richard* returned fire, one and possibly two of its old 18-pounders blew up, probably from the strain of being double-shotted. In the explosion many of the crew were killed or wounded, and part of the ship's side was blown out. Jones then ordered the crew to abandon the other 18-pounders, leaving the *Bonhomme Richard* only 12-pounders against the main British battery of 18-pounders.

Sailing around the *Bonhomme Richard* at will, the *Serapis* then poured broadsides into the vessel, exacting a frightful toll. Soon the American ship was taking on water. The two vessels then became entangled. The British beat back an attempt by Jones to board, and the ships then came apart again. The *Bonhomme Richard* would not respond properly as Jones attempted to get in position to rake his opponent, and the two ships again collided. Jones then personally lashed the two vessels together, and grapples were thrown. The two ships were now starboard to starboard. Broadsides crashed out, and both crews fired small arms. Soon both vessels were on fire.

Meanwhile, the *Pallas* had taken the *Countess of Scarborough.* For reasons known only to Captain Landais, the *Alliance* had remained aloof from the action to this point but now appeared to fire three broadsides into the stern of the *Bonhomme Richard* and the bow of the *Serapis,* causing casualties on both ships. Both the *Bonhomme Richard* and *Serapis* were now virtual wrecks.

Asked to strike, Jones shouted in reply, "No, I'll sink, but I'll be damned if I will strike." His statement was recalled forty-six years later by retired Commodore Richard Dale, then sixty-five years old, as "I have not yet begun to fight." The battle had gone on for three hours, and despite horrific casualties both captains refused to strike. At this point the American side experienced a lucky turn when a seaman aboard the *Bonhomme Richard* succeeded in throwing a grenade down the main hatch of the *Serapis.* It set off cartridges below, putting the gun deck out of action. At 10:30, his main mast in danger of falling, Pearson surrendered. A total of 130 of the *Serapis*'s crew of 284 were either dead or wounded. The *Bonhomme Richard* sustained 150 casualties out of its crew of 322.

That night the victors cut away the main mast of the *Serapis* and put out fires aboard. All six vessels then got under way, but despite frantic efforts to save the *Bonhomme Richard,* it continued to take on water. On the morning of 25 September, Jones ordered the last of its crew transferred to the *Serapis.* The *Bonhomme Richard* sank shortly thereafter. The squadron then sailed to the Texel Roadstead, Holland.

Spencer C. Tucker

See also

Franklin, Benjamin; Jones, John Paul; Landais, Pierre

References

Boudriot, Jean. *John Paul Jones and the Bonhomme Richard.* Translated by David H. Roberts. Annapolis, MD: Naval Institute Press, 1987.

Morison, Samuel Eliot. *John Paul Jones: A Sailor's Biography.* 1959. Reprint, Annapolis, MD: Naval Institute Press, 1989.

Schaeper, Thomas J. *John Paul Jones and the Battle off Flamborough Head: A Reconsideration.* New York: Peter Lang, 1990.

Walsh, John E. *Night on Fire: The First Complete Account of John Paul Jones's Greatest Battle.* New York: McGraw-Hill, 1978.

Boone, Daniel (1734–1820)

The famed pioneer Daniel Boone served in the North Carolina militia during the French and Indian War (also known as the Seven Years' War), led settlers to the Kentucky frontier just as the American Revolution began, and got caught up in the struggle between settlers and Native Americans during the war.

Born on 22 October 1734 in Berks County, Pennsylvania, Boone was the son of Squire Boone, an English Quaker, and Sarah Morgan. The elder Boone, who was a weaver and tenant farmer, moved the family from the Pennsylvania frontier to the North Carolina backcountry in 1750, settling along the Yadkin River. The younger Boone likely had no formal education, but his brother Samuel's wife Sarah taught him to read and write. By his early teens, Boone had already developed some skill as a hunter and trapper and soon became a highly

Daniel Boone. A famous frontiersman, he served as a militia officer from Kentucky (then part of Virginia), making a name for himself as an Indian fighter. Taken prisoner by the Shawnee in 1778, he escaped and helped settlements prepare their defenses against attacks by Native Americans. (Library of Congress)

regarded backwoodsman and an excellent shot. In the process, he quickly came to love both the solitude of the wilderness and the challenge of the hunt.

In 1755, as a member of the North Carolina militia, Boone became a teamster in British General Edward Braddock's army that marched against the French at Fort Duquesne in western Pennsylvania. Boone fled with the other teamsters when the British forces were ambushed and decisively defeated. A year later, back in North Carolina, Boone married Rebecca Bryan, with whom he had ten children. Besides his hunting and trapping, he sought to make a living as a blacksmith and teamster, but increasing debts persuaded him to leave North Carolina. When his wife refused to move to Florida in 1765, Boone looked west. He had heard many glowing reports about the Kentucky Country, primarily from John Finley, a scout for Braddock's army. After an initial sojourn, Boone set out in 1769 on a two-year exploring and trapping expedition beyond the Cumberland Gap. Taken with the fertility of the bluegrass country along the Kentucky River, Boone led an abortive attempt to settle the area in 1773. The group of about fifty settlers returned to North Carolina after a force of Delaware, Cherokee, and Shawnee Indians captured and killed two in their party, including Boone's son James.

In 1775, Boone finally succeeded in relocating to Kentucky. Acting as an agent for North Carolina speculator Richard Henderson, Boone marked out the Wilderness Road, helped negotiate the purchase of Kentucky land from the Cherokees, and settled his family in Boonesborough. Once the Revolutionary War began, the British encouraged the trans-Appalachian tribes, who were already concerned with white encroachment, to resist the new settlements. In July 1776, a war party of Shawnees and Cherokees captured Boone's daughter Jemima and two other girls. Boone led a small party of men who rescued the girls three days later, an exploit that James Fenimore Cooper drew upon for his highly successful 1826 novel, *Last of the Mohicans.* In 1778, Boone and sixteen other men, who were making salt for the Boonesborough settlement, were captured by Shawnees. The Shawnees adopted into the tribe several of the captives including Boone, whom they renamed Sheltowee, or Big Turtle. Boone ingratiated himself with the Shawnees by persuading them that in the spring of 1779 he would help negotiate the surrender of the remaining Boonesborough settlers. Four months into his captivity, however, Boone learned of a Shawnee plan to attack Boonesborough and escaped. He traveled 160 miles in only four days to reach his settlement. Even though Boonesborough had only sixty able-bodied men, the settlers were prepared to resist an eleven-day siege. Some of the settlers were unhappy with Boone's relationship with the Shawnee tribe and charged him with treason in this episode, but a court-martial conducted by the Kentucky militia vindicated him.

Boone remained in the Kentucky Country until 1799. To support his large family, Boone tried surveying, running a tavern and a store, and speculating in land. He filed dozens of claims for thousands of acres, but the claims were so poorly drawn that he eventually lost virtually all the land in litigation with other claimants. Whenever circumstances and time permitted, Boone also returned to trapping and hunting. While he had a well-deserved reputation as a pioneer loner, Boone also often stepped forward as a community leader. He served as a deputy surveyor, coroner, and county sheriff. He also won election to several terms in the Virginia state assembly and served as a militia officer. In the latter capacity Boone participated in several Indian conflicts, including the battle at Blue Licks in 1782 that claimed his son Israel. But as his beloved Kentucky increased in population and he grew ever more frustrated with his lost land claims, Boone decided to accept an offer from the Spanish government to move to Missouri in 1799.

Besides granting him several thousand acres, the Spanish named Boone a syndic, or chief magistrate. His responsibilities included recommending applicants for land grants and supervising the surveys of the land. He settled in the Femme Osage district about 60 miles from St. Louis. Unfortunately for Boone, after the United States purchased the Louisiana territory in 1803, all Spanish land claims were subject to review, and his were not confirmed. Boone appealed to Congress, which in 1814 awarded him 850 acres. In his last years, even though well past seventy, Boone continued to hunt, trap, and explore. He even journeyed as far as Fort Osage (near present-day Kansas City), 250 miles west of St. Louis, and may have proceeded up the Missouri and Platte Rivers toward Yellowstone country. When at home, Boone grudgingly granted interviews to numerous inquisitive visitors eager to meet the famed pioneer. His wife Rebecca died in 1813, and Boone, shortly after sitting for the painter Chester Harding, died in the home of his son Nathan in St. Charles County, Missouri, in September 1820.

At his death, Boone was widely considered the nation's premier symbol of frontier independence. This notoriety was largely due to John Filson's best-selling 1784 book, *The Discovery, Settlement and Present State of Kentucke,* which had an appendix titled "The Adventures of Col. Daniel Boon." When Cooper began his successful Leatherstocking series of novels with *The Pioneers* in 1823, most readers understood that the backwoods hero, Nathaniel Bumppo, who kept moving farther west to avoid civilization was based on the recently deceased Boone. Boone remains for many America's most prominent frontier hero.

Larry Gragg

See also

Blue Licks, Kentucky, Action at; Cornstalk

References

Faragher, John Mack. *Daniel Boone: The Life and Legend of an American Pioneer.* New York: Holt, 1992.

Lofaro, Michael A. *The Life and Adventures of Daniel Boone.* Lexington: University Press of Kentucky, 1986.

Border Warfare (1775–1783)

Border warfare during the American Revolutionary War embraced a wide range of conflicts along the frontiers of most of the thirteen colonies/states between proindependence Americans, both soldiers and civilians, and British-allied Indian and Loyalist troops. Most of the engagements were relatively small, but from the Virginia and Kentucky frontier north to western New York, major conflicts began soon after Lexington and Concord and persisted until the Treaty of Paris in 1783.

Background. Warfare along the frontier areas of Britain's North American colonies was endemic through most of the seventeenth and eighteenth centuries, involving clashes between British and French or Spanish settlers as well as between British colonists and local Indian tribes. The American Revolution only served to exacerbate these well-established conflicts. Both British and American officials recognized the value of enlisting the Indian tribes living along the frontier. Each side had reservations about allying with the Indians and understood the propaganda value this would provide to the enemy, but each side also recognized the Indians' fighting skills, especially in wilderness areas, and their ability to cause fear in their opponents.

As part of the settlement that ended the French and Indian War (also known as the Seven Years' War) in 1763, the British had gained control of a huge territory that extended from the Mississippi River to the Appalachian Mountains. The Indians living there, particularly the Delaware, Ottawa, Miami, Shawnee, and Cherokee tribes, feared a massive influx of settlers from the thirteen British colonies. After the Indians forcefully communicated their concerns to the British government by staging Pontiac's Rebellion (1763–1766), the British responded by attempting to seal off the entire area, based on the guidelines in the Proclamation of 1763, from settlement by residents of the coastal colonies. As a result of this policy, the British were able to secure the support of many Indian peoples, not only those in the West but also the powerful Iroquois Confederacy (the Six Nations) of northern New York. Another point in favor of the British was their establishment in 1755 of a well-run Indian Department. The highly capable first Indian agent, Sir William Johnson, died in 1774, but his nephew, Colonel Guy Johnson, succeeded him in the Northern Department, while John Stuart served as the agent of Britain's Southern Department.

When the Revolutionary War began, each side initially preferred that the Indian tribes remain neutral for fear that any support from the Indians would provoke accusations of inciting native warriors against white settlers. The Americans, however, quickly realized that they were at a disadvantage on the frontier because the established Indian departments were British, while the Americans had no official relationship with the Indian leaders. The Continental Congress quickly set up its own Department of Indian Affairs and sent out commissioners to negotiate treaties with the various tribes and to argue that the quarrel now developing was strictly between white North American settlers and the British officials.

Britain's Indian agents initially promoted Indian neutrality but were not always successful in controlling either Indians or other British officials. In the summer before Lexington and Concord, Virginia's royal governor John Murray, Earl of Dunmore, provoked and won Dunmore's War against Shawnee and Delaware tribes in what is now West Virginia. In 1776, Cherokee Indians living along the frontiers of Virginia and North and South Carolina wanted to attack colonists who were aggressively moving into the area and sought the approval of John Stuart, superintendent of Britain's Southern Department. Stuart expressed his opposition, but the Cherokees went ahead with their attacks anyway. The three colonies raised militias in response, counterattacked effectively, and crushed the Cherokee effort, forcing them into a negotiated settlement.

In the North, both sides debated the use of Indians within their own commands. General Thomas Gage, the commander in chief of the British Army in North America from 1774 to 1775, wanted the Iroquois and other tribes to launch attacks along the New England frontier, a plan that was effectively opposed by General Guy Carleton, the governor of Canada. The Americans, for their part, considered using a tribe called the Stockbridge Indians to aid their efforts. In the end, however, it was the Indians themselves who decided to wage war against white settlers—and therefore against the rebelling Americans—on the New York and Pennsylvania frontiers. Thereafter the British used increasing numbers of Indians in brief raids and larger campaigns, both as scouts and warriors. The American forces, however, were never able to recruit a large number of Indian allies during the war. Too many Indians feared, with good reason, that an American victory would only open their lands to more aggressive settlement by farmers from the thirteen coastal colonies.

Whichever side they chose to support, however, both Indians and white settlers along the frontier had much to fear. Colonists who chose to remain loyal to the British were just as deeply caught up in the conflict as their Patriot neighbors. Many joined newly raised Loyalist regiments that fought alongside Indian raiders, even though some unlucky Loyalists were attacked by British-allied Indians by mistake. But so many Loyalists, especially in New York, had lost their lands and property to confiscation by state officials and local militia units that they considered the frontier raids on Patriot settlements to be just retribution for their losses. Even the late Sir William Johnson's house at Johnstown, New York, had to be abandoned to a band of proindependence militia. The most important areas of border conflict were the Kentucky, Ohio, and Illinois Countries well to the west and western New York and northern Pennsylvania closer to long-settled areas.

The West (Kentucky, Ohio, and Illinois). After the end of the French and Indian War, many white Americans settled illegally in the area now comprising Kentucky and West Virginia. This entire region was governed, at least in name, by the colony of Virginia. New settlements there, as well as others in Virginia itself and in the Carolinas, bore the brunt of the Indian raids of 1775–1777, which were organized and staged from the Ohio and Illinois Countries north of the Ohio River. The severity of these raids forced many of the settlers to gather in two larger settlements, Boonesborough and Harrodsburg, Kentucky, for protection.

Several of these Indian raids were organized by the British at Fort Detroit. Lieutenant-Colonel Henry Hamilton, the governor of Fort Detroit, was in theory the overall commander of British forces in the West. He provided aid to various Indian tribes in the form of weapons, ammunition, and rum. The Americans decided that the destruction of Fort Detroit was the key to breaking British control of the region. With the fort's destruction, the British would lose face with the Indians, thus providing the Americans with an opportunity to encourage their neutrality or even their alliance with American forces.

In late 1777, the Virginian George Rogers Clark, who had settled in Kentucky, decided to take matters into his own hands. Securing financial support from the state of Virginia, he launched an offensive operation against the Illinois Country. His first targets were three established French trading towns that could supply Indian raiding parties: Cahokia and Kaskaskia, along the Mississippi River, and Vincennes, on the Wabash River. Clark hoped that many of the French settlers would want to join him in fighting against the British (especially because America was just then seeking an alliance with France) or at least would choose to remain neutral. He also hoped to gain the support of various Indian tribes in the region. If all went according to plan, he would then march against Fort Detroit.

Clark recruited some 170 men from the frontier regions of Pennsylvania and Kentucky. In June 1778 they set off down the Ohio River and headed into the Illinois Country. Following an exhausting march, Clark's men seized Kaskaskia on 4 July 1778 without firing a shot, and the expedition immediately moved on to other settlements. By the end of August, Clark's force had seized the major trading and military posts in the region, including Cahokia, Prairie du Rocher, and Vincennes. Amazingly, they did not fire once during their sweep across the region, and no casualties occurred on either side during the campaign. While he waited for an expected British counterattack, Clark met with Indian and French leaders to try to win their support for the American cause. They expressed some interest in siding with the Americans, but neither French settlers nor Indians ever joined the Americans in significant numbers, and the best Clark could claim was that he had succeeded in keeping most of the region neutral for the time being.

When Hamilton received word of Clark's invasion, he launched an immediate counteroffensive. Assembling about 100 French militia, nearly 100 Indians, and only 30 British regulars, Hamilton set out in October 1778 to regain the lost posts in the Illinois Country. Clark, meanwhile, was encountering difficulties. His force, small to begin with, was getting steadily smaller as several of his men returned to Kentucky and Pennsylvania when their enlistment contracts ended. Clark, remaining with a small group at Kaskaskia, had to disperse his remaining forces among all the posts in the region that were under his control.

In December 1778, after a long and arduous march, Hamilton recaptured Vincennes from a small American garrison without firing a shot. The town's civilians promptly swore allegiance to the British Crown, and Hamilton prepared to move on to Kaskaskia. Clark, who by this time had only 100 men to oppose the British, marched 180 miles to Vincennes in midwinter to attack Hamilton, who then had just over 150 men. In late February 1779, the Americans reached Vincennes and tricked Hamilton into believing that they were a much larger force than they were. Many Indians and French militiamen now abandoned the British, and Hamilton, realizing that his position was precarious, surrendered and was sent to Virginia as a prisoner of war.

While Clark was successful in defeating Hamilton, he was unable to attack and destroy Fort Detroit, the main objective of his campaign. Because the main focus of the war remained on the eastern seaboard, Clark never received the required reinforcements to take Detroit. His forces remained on the defensive for the next three years, while Indian and Loyalist raids continued along the Ohio River Valley and into Kentucky. A stalemate ensued in the West, and Fort Detroit remained the central headquarters for British and Indian raids.

New York and Pennsylvania. While the fighting in the West was fairly sporadic, the struggle along the frontier in western New York and northern Pennsylvania was more intense and included larger numbers of warriors and soldiers. New York militia units were active in defending that state's advanced settlements, but the only major American expedition on the northern frontier was the Continental Army's campaign against the Iroquois Confederacy in 1779.

Just as Fort Detroit was the headquarters for British operations in the Illinois, Ohio, and Kentucky regions, Fort Niagara in western New York was the command center for the British war on the New York and Pennsylvania frontiers.

Indian tribes launched raids in the region from the beginning of the rebellion. Rebels and Loyalists often treated one another with exceptional cruelty in New York's Mohawk Valley. Many Indian warriors joined both General John Burgoyne and Lieutenant-Colonel Barry St. Leger in their New York Campaigns in 1777, but with the defeat of the British at Saratoga, local Indian, Loyalist, and British forces returned to a series of major raids. Major John Butler, a deputy superintendent in Britain's northern Indian department, created a British unit called Butler's Rangers by recruiting Loyalists who had been recently turned out of their homes by Patriot militia along the New York and New England frontier. This well-trained and well-led unit, the first of six and later ten companies of Loyalist infantry, led several of these raids. The British also trained a large corps of Indian warriors for the frontier war, under the command of the Mohawk Chief Joseph Brant. Brant was an excellent leader and understood the art of frontier warfare.

In the spring of 1778, both Brant's Indians and Butler's Rangers launched a series of well-planned and coordinated attacks. The focus for the 1778 campaign was the Wyoming Valley region of Pennsylvania, near Wilkes-Barre. Many of the settlers in the region, on becoming aware of the approach of the Indians and rangers, took refuge in the region's several forts. The raiders, numbering more than 1,000 men, arrived in the area in late June 1778. The American commander in the valley, Colonel Zeubulon Butler, had fewer than half that number of militia and local frontiersmen to deal with the British force. Colonel Butler made a major mistake in deciding to march his troops into the forest to confront the British and Indians. The raiders easily overwhelmed the American force and, in keeping with much of the fighting along the frontier, gave no quarter to the defeated enemy, who were almost completely destroyed. The British next turned their attention to burning farms and homesteads in a large radius surrounding the area of the battle.

The raiders then marched north to deal with settlements along the Mohawk River in New York. In the autumn of 1778, Butler and Brant launched devastating raids against the settlements at German Flats and Cherry Valley. Despite the rangers' and Indians' success in waging a devastating war, however, neither Brant nor Butler wanted to see civilians killed, and they attempted, although not always successfully, to keep the Indians from killing indiscriminately. Cherry Valley was one of their failures and involved a massacre of many civilians.

The successful British raids of 1778 forced General George Washington's hand in devising his strategy for the next year's campaign. Fort Pitt, at Pittsburgh, Pennsylvania, had a Continental Army garrison, but Washington decided that any effort by this garrison against Fort Detroit would have to wait. The Continental Army's first priority was to contend with the threat facing the New York and Pennsylvania frontiers. Washington's strategy of counterattack was to destroy as much of the Six Nations' homeland as he could reach. He decided to send two columns of Continental soldiers, one from Pennsylvania and the other from eastern New York, to burn and destroy the Indian villages. The columns were not strong enough to attack Fort Niagara itself, but Washington hoped to destroy the operational capabilities of the Indians and Loyalists for a number of years.

The Pennsylvania column, under the command of Major General John Sullivan, was the main Continental force. Sullivan, who understood the need in frontier warfare for flanking parties to protect his main force and for pioneers to build roads through the woods, was in command of five brigades of Continental soldiers. He left Easton, Pennsylvania, in May 1779. The New York militia commander, Brigadier General James Clinton, was in command of the second column, which moved west from the Cherry Valley region of New York. Both columns moved slowly due to difficult terrain. As the columns marched through Indian villages, they burned and destroyed all that was edible and worthy of the torch. The two columns met up on 22 August near Tioga, Pennsylvania.

Brant and Butler had their units shadow the American troops. They realized that the combined American column was too large for them to engage with the forces they had available. On 27 August, however, an Indian war council held at Newtown, New York, overruled both Brant's and Butler's defensive plans. Indian warriors wished to attack the American forces, and their views prevailed. The Indians and rangers moved out to ambush the American column. Contemporary reports estimated the British and Indian force at just under 1,000 men, while the Americans could muster 4,400. The two forces met on 30 August, but all element of surprise was lost when forward American scout units alerted Sullivan to the advancing British and Indian forces. Sullivan deployed his forces effectively in a flanking movement and overwhelmed the rangers and Indians. Newtown was more of a skirmish than a battle, as both the ranger and Indian units broke off the fight when they realized they were outflanked; casualties on both sides were minimal. The British, however, withdrew all the way to Fort Niagara, leaving all the land of the Six Nations open to Sullivan's depredations. The Americans laid waste to the region, destroying an estimated forty Indian villages and more than 100,000 bushels of grain.

While Sullivan's campaign in 1779 was successful, it did not end the Iroquois' ability to fight, and the war on the northern frontier continued. The Indians and Butler's Rangers continued their raids in western New York until the Treaty of Paris in 1783, and Americans continued to battle British and Indian forces in the Ohio Country for just as long. American settlements and forts all along the frontiers of New York, Pennsylvania, Virginia, and Kentucky were destroyed in a grinding war of attrition that consisted of endless raids and counterraids and continued to include occasional atrocities, of which the worst was probably the American massacre of peaceful Indians at Gnadenhutten in the Ohio Country in 1782.

Daniel Marston

See also

Boone, Daniel; Brant, Joseph; Brodhead, Daniel; Burgoyne, John; Butler, John; Butler, Walter; Cherokees, Operations against; Cherry Valley Massacre; Clark, George Rogers; Clinton, James; Continental Army; Forts, Western; German Flats, New York, Raid on; Gnadenhutten Massacre; Hamilton, Henry; Jefferson, Thomas; Johnson, Guy; Johnson, Sir William; Kentucky; Murray, John, Lord Dunmore; New York, Operations in; Newtown, New York, Action at; Pennsylvania; Proclamation of 1763; Saratoga Campaign; St. Leger Expedition; Stuart, John; Sullivan, John; Wyoming Valley, Pennsylvania

References

Abernethy, Thomas Perkins. *Western Lands and the American Revolution.* New York: Russell and Russell, 1958.

Alden, John Richard. *John Stuart and the Southern Colonial Frontier: A Study of Indian Relations, War, Trade, and Land Problems in the Southern Wilderness, 1754–1775.* 1944. Reprint, New York: Gordian, 1966.

De Vorsey, Louis, Jr. *The Indian Boundary in the Southern Colonies, 1763–1775.* Chapel Hill: University of North Carolina Press, 1966.

Graymont, Barbara. *The Iroquois in the American Revolution.* Syracuse, NY: Syracuse University Press, 1972.

Kelsay, Isabel T. *Joseph Brant, 1743–1807: Man of Two Worlds.* Syracuse, NY: Syracuse University Press, 1984.

Lowell, Harrison H. *George Rogers Clark and the War in the West.* Lexington: University Press of Kentucky, 1976.

Richter, Daniel K. *The Ordeal of the Longhouse: The Peoples of the Iroquois League in the Era of European Colonization.* Chapel Hill: University of North Carolina Press, 1992.

Richter, Daniel K., and James H. Merrell, eds. *Beyond the Covenant Chain: The Iroquois and Their Neighbors in Indian North America, 1600–1800.* Syracuse, NY: Syracuse University Press, 1987.

Boston, Massachusetts

In the 1760s and 1770s, the port city of Boston became the center and symbol of agitation against Britain's new imperial policies. The part the city would play in the Revolutionary movement cannot be separated from its social and economic identity. Indeed, Boston's participation in the American Revolution grew directly from its class structure and the city's participation in the world of transatlantic trade.

By the first half of the eighteenth century, the Boston wharves teemed with activity. Intertwined with the diverse markets of Britain's far-flung empire, Boston and its merchants sent lumber and naval stores to Europe, slaving ships to West Africa, and ships packed with fish from the cold New England waters to the southern colonies and the West Indies and received, in return, molasses produced by slaves for the New England rum industry. The social aggregate of the city reflected this heavy volume of mercantile activity. Shipbuilding played an integral part in the economy, and the port of Boston frequently played host to large numbers of sailors, known in the eighteenth century as Jack-Tars, who added an often tumultuous element to its working-class culture. The enormous wealth produced by the transatlantic trade also created a class of prosperous artisans whose craftsmanship served the needs of the town's elite. Silversmiths, such as Paul Revere, along with booksellers, goldsmiths, engravers, wig makers, japanners, and jewelers all flourished in the city. Amid the trappings of prosperity, a large number of poorer artisans lived outside the bright circle of abundance. The city also contained about 800 African Americans, most enslaved, who worked as household servants. A vast divide existed between the port's so-called better sort and meaner sort. In 1757, more than 1,000 of the city's 15,000 people were dependent upon the city's poor fund.

By midcentury, however, the divide between rich and poor was only one of Boston's difficulties. The town's economy began to stagnate, its problems sometimes exacerbated by British policies. The Royal Navy, in need of manpower to fight King George's War during the 1740s, swept the Boston wharves for Jack-Tars, dockworkers, and poor laborers to press into service. Fearful of being stripped of their crews by the "hot press" (the practice of abducting men in port towns and forcibly impressing them into the service of the Royal Navy, with no recourse to legal redress for the "pressed" man concerned) being carried on in Boston, many merchant ships avoided the otherwise busy port. Outrage at one particular press in 1747 led to a series of riots in which mobs broke windows at the home of the royal governor, William Shirley. Britain's involvement in imperial wars resulted in a general contraction of trade for many of Boston's merchants.

Boston's role as a center of trade also put some of its citizens at the forefront of the colonial protest movement. In 1764, Parliament passed the Sugar Act, which actually lowered duties but affirmed that customs officials must actually collect the full tax on the trade in molasses from the West Indies. In 1765, the Stamp Act levied taxes on everything from legal documents used by Boston merchants to the dice and playing cards of the working class. Drawing on a protest tradition that reached back to the "hot press" riots and beyond, a group of working-class Bostonians hung an effigy of Andrew Oliver, Boston's "stamp master," from an elm tree (the Liberty Tree) in the city's south end on 14 August 1765. That night, a large working-class crowd paraded the effigy through the streets and consigned it to a bonfire. Twelve days later, another crowd made up of the city's "lower sort" mobbed the home of Royal Governor Thomas Hutchinson in protest of his support for the Stamp Act.

The repeal of the Stamp Act in 1766 convinced many of the protest leaders in the new organization the Sons of Liberty,

Boston. The principal city of New England, it was the focus of commerce and Revolutionary agitation against Crown authority, largely the result of the unpopularity of the British garrison and the growing array of taxes imposed on the colonists. (National Archives and Records Administration)

which included Samuel Adams, John Hancock, and James Otis, that their tactics had proved an effective weapon. Following the passage of the Townshend Acts of 1767, the protest movement in Boston led the colonies in an economic boycott of British goods. Boston's town meeting circulated a pledge for citizens to sign in support of nonimportation. The mobbing of customs officials by dockworkers in the summer of 1768 further heightened tensions and brought twelve British warships and four regiments of British regulars to Boston. This strong show of military force quieted the city for a time, but ongoing conflict between the regulars and Boston's working class would lead to the Boston Massacre in March 1770. Leaders of the Sons of Liberty used the incident to rally Boston against British policies, and the eventual removal of British troops from the city seemed to be further proof of the effectiveness of protest.

Boston's reaction to the 1773 Tea Act revealed that class tensions remained strong. The Boston Tea Party in December seemed to many of the merchant class an example of proletarian rowdiness, though the elites who led the Patriot cause fully supported this action and worked hard to build coalitions with artisans and the "meaner sort." Some of the city's wealthy merchants, however, came to favor conciliation with the Crown after the so-called Coercive Acts closed the port of Boston to shipping in May 1774 and placed the entire province under tighter imperial control in August. British troops, now eleven full regiments, again marched in the streets of the city.

Following the clashes at Lexington and Concord in April 1775, General Thomas Gage, the royal governor of Massachusetts, called on Bostonians to surrender any guns in their possession or leave the city. Fearing retaliation and perhaps the coming siege by British troops, more than 12,000 refugees fled the city, and the population shrank from 15,000 to a mere 3,000. Loyalists made up the majority of those who remained.

Patriot militia surrounded Boston in the summer of 1775, entrenching the hills north and south of the city. In July, British troops won a costly victory when they drove Patriot forces from Breed's Hill, just east of Charlestown, in what would become known as the Battle of Bunker Hill. Beleaguered British forces remained in Boston through a long winter in 1775–1776, but in March 1776, when the Continental Army fortified Dorchester Heights with heavy cannon that threatened Britain's warships, British troops evacuated the city.

Boston would remain in American hands throughout the remainder of the war. As the only major American port that was never again seriously threatened by British capture, it often hosted warships of America's new ally, France. But the disruption of the war, following upon the occupation of 1774–1776, further damaged Boston's trade, some of which moved to nearby Salem, Massachusetts.

Daniel S. Poole

See also

Adams, Samuel; Administration of Justice Act; Boston, Siege of; Boston Massacre; Boston Port Act; Boston Tea Party; Bunker Hill, Battle of; Coercive Acts; Dorchester Heights, Massachusetts; Gage, Thomas; Hancock, John; Hutchinson, Thomas; Lexington and Concord; Loyalists; Massachusetts; Massachusetts Government Act; Nonimportation Agreements; Otis, James, Jr.; Quartering Acts; Sons of Liberty; Stamp Act; Townshend Acts

References

Brown, Richard D. *Massachusetts: A Concise History.* Amherst: University of Massachusetts Press, 2000.

Labaree, Benjamin. *Colonial Massachusetts: A History.* Millwood, NY: KTO, 1979.

Nash, Gary B. *The Urban Crucible: Social Change, Political Consciousness and the Origins of the American Revolution.* Cambridge: Harvard University Press, 1979.

Pencak, William. *War, Politics and Revolution in Provincial Massachusetts.* Boston: Northeastern University Press, 1981.

Boston, Siege of (19 April 1775–17 March 1776)

The pivotal siege of Boston by rebel colonists and militia derived from a continuation of the British victories at the skirmishes in Lexington and Concord. These three events became the initial engagements of the American Revolutionary War.

A siege is traditionally defined as one force cutting off another force's methods of communication with the outside world. However, Boston was only partially besieged because the Atlantic, its eastern boundary, allowed the seafaring British access and a means to communicate with the mother country via ships of the Royal Navy that controlled the harbor. At the time, Boston was a peninsula connected to the mainland by a long, narrow strip of land called the Neck. Boston was surrounded by rebels, known by those opposing the British as Patriots, from the west, north, and south.

Background. To understand the importance of the siege to the advent of the American Revolution, the chronology of events must be understood in the context of the times. Since the conclusion of the Seven Years' War (French and Indian War) in 1763, the colonists had held major grievances against British parliamentary rule and wanted them to be addressed. Parliament believed that the colonists should be financially responsible for their defense during the war, for the costs of waging war had caused extreme indebtedness for the mother country. However, the colonists deeply resented paying taxes to the mother country while being denied parliamentary representation that resulted in no control whatsoever over their own affairs.

The colonists eventually began to resent the overbearing, unbending British dominance. The fear that their liberty was at stake drove them to commit some desperate acts. Colonists seized and burned British ships. They responded to numerous British acts that would impede their livelihoods and freedoms. The Stamp Act of 1765, which implemented a tax on all paper goods, was a major cause of consternation. Another grievance was the Quartering Act of 1765 that allowed the billeting of troops in private homes, which the colonists believed was disproportionately allocated in some colonies. The Townshend Acts of 1767, named after Chancellor of the Exchequer Charles Townshend, aggravated the economic issues. The Tea Act of 1773 eliminated any profit for the colonial middlemen from the lucrative tea trade. By denying the middlemen income yet retaining the tax, the British stepped into a maelstrom from which there ultimately would be no escape. The colonists believed the acts to be unconstitutional. They retaliated by disallowing departure for British ships from New York. On learning of the future Tea Act, on 15 December 1773 some 150 men, masquerading as Mohawk Indians, dumped 340 tea chests, valued at nearly £10,000, from three ships into Boston Harbor. This episode became known as the Boston Tea Party. The British demanded restitution, but Bostonians refused to comply. Parliament closed the port of Boston, causing considerable hardship to the citizenry.

Even more drastic measures ensued with strict enforcement of the newly enacted Coercive Acts (also known as the Intolerable Acts) of 1774 that included the Tea Act, the Boston Port Act, the Massachusetts Bay Regulating Act, the Administration of Justice Act, and an amended Quartering Act. As a response to these acts, merchants, farmers, and whole villages began to prepare for a fight.

Colonial resistance also stemmed from the writings of Enlightenment philosopher John Locke, who had espoused the idea of removing a government that tyrannized its people. In *Two Treatises of Government* (1690), Locke had justified the Glorious Revolution in England that placed a king under the laws and subjected him to the powers of Parliament. Patrick Henry reiterated this idea with his rhetoric concerning the "tyranny" to which colonists were subjected; many influential colonists followed his line of thought.

Although not part of the Coercive Acts, the Quebec Act of May 1775 also aggravated the colonists because it extended British boundaries into the present-day midwestern United States and into Indian territory, which the colonists believed to be theirs. In addition, the act brought Roman Catholicism and the French language to the forefront. Colonists earnestly believed that the Church of England and the Roman Catholic Church would merge and deny them their religious freedoms.

Bunker Hill, during the early stages of the siege of Boston. British tactics on this occasion proved practically suicidal, with a disproportionate number of their officers falling to the accurate fire of defenders, who were admonished not to discharge their muskets until their target lay clearly in view. (National Archives and Records Administration)

To counter these British actions, colonists in some Massachusetts towns established conventions and organizations such as the Sons of Liberty. Networks of committees of correspondence cooperated in a joint reaction to British injustice. The First Continental Congress was established and convened in Carpenter's Hall in Philadelphia on 5 September 1774. The Congress's program was a combination of moderate and extreme solutions resulting in five major points that would likely resolve issues pertaining to British governance. These points surprised an incredulous Parliament, which deemed them anathema to its rights but was ready to give some concession with its Conciliatory Proposition that unfortunately came too late. Parliament had severely miscalculated the range of discontent brewing in the colonies.

By this time the people of Massachusetts understood that military action against the British would occur sooner rather than later. Consequently, the townspeople, farmers, and merchants had been drilling on village greens, gathering arms and gunpowder by various means, and training volunteers as minutemen, a term derived from their ability to be ready to fight on a minute's notice. The Continental Congress approved the fighting of a defensive war. All that was left was for the British to commence the fighting.

Lieutenant-General Thomas Gage, a brave, intensely loyal, highly experienced, steadfast, and competent military man, headquartered variously in Boston and New York, had been commander of British forces in the American colonies since 1763. Gage was particularly suited to the British military lifestyle, and his troops were extremely loyal to his leadership. Gage had served admirably in the Seven Years' War and obtained the position of governor of Massachusetts in 1774. As a free state, it was governed by a popularly elected provincial congress and had a committee of safety that included an organized armed resistance component. Gage's dispatches to Lord George Germain, the minister in charge of colonial affairs, describing the growing discontent were met with skepticism; Parliament responded with acrimony to his rather biased information.

Lexington. Massachusetts was under martial law. Gage was ordered by the British government to arrest the rebel leaders John Hancock and Samuel Adams for treason. After escaping from Boston, they initially hid from the British in

Siege of Boston, 1775 – 1776

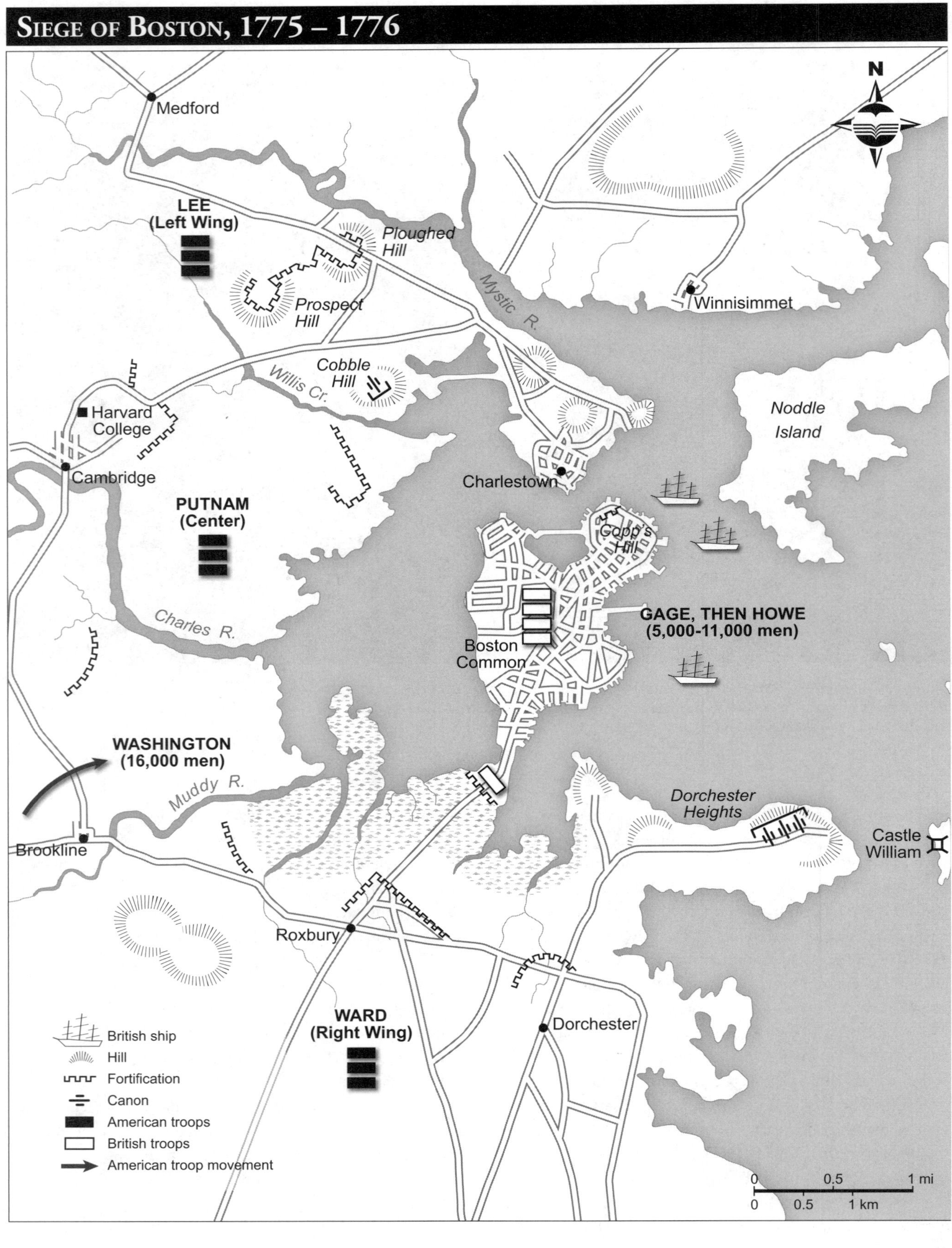
N
Medford
LEE
(Left Wing)
Ploughed
Hill
Prospect
Hill
Mystic R.
Winnisimmet
Cobble
Hill
Willis Cr.
Harvard
College
Cambridge
Noddle
Island
Charlestown
PUTNAM
(Center)
Copp's
Hill
Charles R.
GAGE, THEN HOWE
(5,000-11,000 men)
Boston
Common
WASHINGTON
(16,000 men)
Muddy R.
Dorchester
Heights
Castle
William
Brookline
Roxbury
WARD
(Right Wing)
Dorchester
British ship
Hill
Fortification
Canon
American troops
British troops
American troop movement
0
0.5
1 mi
0
0.5
1 km

Lexington. Gage learned that arms and ammunition were being accumulated in various strategic locations throughout Massachusetts, especially in Lexington and Concord, two small towns a few miles outside of Boston. The British government had ordered Gage to take decisive action and suppress rebellion in the colonies. However, the government had not sent the reinforcements Gage repeatedly requested simply because it did not believe the seriousness of the resistance he was facing. Eventually, 3,500 troops were sent, far fewer than Gage has requested. He bided his time to launch an attack mainly because he did not want to face a battle without an adequate number of troops.

Gage planned his attack on Lexington and Concord to commence on the evening of 18 April in order to surprise the towns and avoid major bloodshed. However, the noise made by the British alerted the rebels. That night Paul Revere and William Dawes rode throughout the countryside around Boston to warn Hancock and Adams about the British plans and simultaneously notify every household along the way about the impending attack. Gage's 800 troops, comprising six regiments and led by Colonel Francis Smith, were from the elite grenadier and flank companies of various British regiments. The advance party was led by Royal Marine Major John Pitcairn. The troops embarked onto their boats at 11:00 P.M. for what would become an exceedingly difficult march. They disembarked in knee-deep water at Charlestown, making their starched trousers soggy and difficult to walk in. The water was up to their waists while crossing the Charles River. Their packs, including musket and equipment, weighed more than sixty pounds. Moreover, they were forced to march under cover of darkness in unpleasant weather conditions. Smith sent for reinforcements from Boston because he anticipated heavy fighting.

The British were unaware that most of the ammunition and weaponry had already been removed from both towns. However, the rebels were ready to face the British. Some 77 militiamen waited for the British contingent on Lexington Green. After searching for Hancock and Adams to no avail, Pitcairn's 200-strong advance party was deployed into three lines facing the rebels. Pitcairn shouted, "Lay down your arms, you damned rebels, and disperse!" Parker ordered his men to withdraw, but the undisciplined, untrained rebels would not disarm. A shot rang out—to this day no one is certain from which side—that began the military phase of the American Revolution. This was the "shot heard 'round the world.'" The British then fired two volleys, after the second of which they launched a bayonet charge, causing the remaining militiamen to retreat. The result of this minor action was 8 militiamen killed and 10 wounded, while the British suffered 1 death. The British had cleared Lexington of rebels, re-formed, and marched another 14 miles toward Concord.

Concord. The weary troops reached Concord at 8:00 P.M. by which time the rebels surrounded the town with some six companies comprising minutemen and militia, led by Colonel James Barrett, who watched events unfold from a ridge just outside Concord. Only women and children remained in Concord. The British light infantry searched Barrett's house, where they believed supplies were stored, but found nothing. Meanwhile the grenadiers also searched the town and threw 100 barrels of flour, 500 pounds of shot, 17,000 pounds of fish, and 35,000 pounds of rice into the mill pond. The rebel gun carriages were set on fire, mistakenly leading Barrett to conclude that Concord was being razed. As Parker neared the North Bridge, the British fired; they were intentionally using balls, which killed, rather than powder, which would have only frightened. Parker returned fire, resulting in four British dead and eight wounded. Smith left Concord, taking his wounded in carriages that he hired for their protection.

The gauntlet. After the skirmishes in Lexington and Concord, the angered rebels, joined by some 4,000 enraged sympathizers from across New England, met at Meriam's Corner, the fork of the roads to Lexington and Bedford. They used a gauntlet strategy against the British during their 30-mile return journey to Boston. The exhausted, battle-weary British troops had marched 40 miles in two days, had fought two skirmishes, and had not slept for forty-eight hours. They were met by an undisciplined, unorganized, wholly spontaneous force, bound by neither a government nor a command system and unaided by an army, that shot at the bright red coats from ravines, farmhouses, stone fences, and trees. British flanking parties dispersed them momentarily, but the barrage of shots continued all the way to Lexington, where Pitcairn was joined at noon by 1,000 reinforcements who brought cannon and ammunition and took over the command. The rebels continued the ceaseless shooting. At Menatomy (present-day Arlington) each side lost 40 men. Percy headed for Charlestown. Every few miles the British would again disperse the rebels, but they would return to continue the incessant firing. Upon reaching Charlestown, the British were under the protection of Royal Navy guns. The rebels followed the British to Cambridge.

The return journey was a minor skirmish that had major repercussions. By the time the British reached Cambridge, they had lost 73 dead, 26 missing, 174 wounded, and 22 captured out of a total 1,800 men. The 4,000-strong rebel forces had lost 49 killed, 5 missing, and 4 wounded. The siege of Boston from the north, west, and south was led by General Artemas Ward, commanding a force of 8,000–12,000 undisciplined, untrained men serving as militia, and began on 19 April 1775.

The siege. The siege quickly became a stalemate because neither side wished to inflict further casualties. Bostonians

Royal Navy warships fill Boston Harbor on this British map of 1775. Tents on the west side of Boston symbolize General Thomas Gage's encampment. (Library of Congress, Geography and Map Division)

ing 140′ – 38′, it was almost exactly the size of the *Bonhomme Richard.* The *Serapis* was also new, having entered service only the year before, and mounted forty-four guns: twenty 18-pounders on the gun deck, twenty-two 9-pounders on the upper deck, and two 6-pounders on the forecastle. The *Countess of Scarborough,* however, was a converted civilian sloop of light construction.

As Jones's squadron closed from the south, Captain Pearson placed his two warships landward in front of the merchantmen to allow them to escape. Jones ordered Captain Landais of the *Alliance* to attack the *Serapis* from its starboard side, while the *Bonhomme Richard* took up station on its port side. Cottineau's *Pallas* would engage the *Countess of Scarborough.* The *Vengeance,* armed only with 4-pounders, was to provide support as needed.

The battle between the *Bonhomme Richard* and the *Serapis* opened at 7:15 P.M., at a range of about 100 yards, and continued well into the night. The *Serapis* fired the first broadside, but each ship holed the other in the first exchange. The British fired a second broadside at only 20 yards. When the *Bonhomme Richard* returned fire, one and possibly two of its old 18-pounders blew up, probably from the strain of being double-shotted. In the explosion many of the crew were killed or wounded, and part of the ship's side was blown out. Jones then ordered the crew to abandon the other 18-pounders, leaving the *Bonhomme Richard* only 12-pounders against the main British battery of 18-pounders.

Sailing around the *Bonhomme Richard* at will, the *Serapis* then poured broadsides into the vessel, exacting a frightful toll. Soon the American ship was taking on water. The two vessels then became entangled. The British beat back an attempt by Jones to board, and the ships then came apart again. The *Bonhomme Richard* would not respond properly as Jones attempted to get in position to rake his opponent, and the two ships again collided. Jones then personally lashed the two vessels together, and grapples were thrown. The two ships were now starboard to starboard. Broadsides crashed out, and both crews fired small arms. Soon both vessels were on fire.

Meanwhile, the *Pallas* had taken the *Countess of Scarborough.* For reasons known only to Captain Landais, the *Alliance* had remained aloof from the action to this point but now appeared to fire three broadsides into the stern of the *Bonhomme Richard* and the bow of the *Serapis,* causing casualties on both ships. Both the *Bonhomme Richard* and *Serapis* were now virtual wrecks.

Asked to strike, Jones shouted in reply, "No, I'll sink, but I'll be damned if I will strike." His statement was recalled forty-six years later by retired Commodore Richard Dale, then sixty-five years old, as "I have not yet begun to fight." The battle had gone on for three hours, and despite horrific casualties both captains refused to strike. At this point the American side experienced a lucky turn when a seaman aboard the *Bonhomme Richard* succeeded in throwing a grenade down the main hatch of the *Serapis.* It set off cartridges below, putting the gun deck out of action. At 10:30, his main mast in danger of falling, Pearson surrendered. A total of 130 of the *Serapis*'s crew of 284 were either dead or wounded. The *Bonhomme Richard* sustained 150 casualties out of its crew of 322.

That night the victors cut away the main mast of the *Serapis* and put out fires aboard. All six vessels then got under way, but despite frantic efforts to save the *Bonhomme Richard,* it continued to take on water. On the morning of 25 September, Jones ordered the last of its crew transferred to the *Serapis.* The *Bonhomme Richard* sank shortly thereafter. The squadron then sailed to the Texel Roadstead, Holland.

Spencer C. Tucker

See also

Franklin, Benjamin; Jones, John Paul; Landais, Pierre

References

Boudriot, Jean. *John Paul Jones and the Bonhomme Richard.* Translated by David H. Roberts. Annapolis, MD: Naval Institute Press, 1987.

Morison, Samuel Eliot. *John Paul Jones: A Sailor's Biography.* 1959. Reprint, Annapolis, MD: Naval Institute Press, 1989.

Schaeper, Thomas J. *John Paul Jones and the Battle off Flamborough Head: A Reconsideration.* New York: Peter Lang, 1990.

low on ammunition and completely lost firing discipline; many Patriots deserted due to exhaustion. For the third assault, Howe ordered his own exhausted men to remove their packs. This assault ultimately proved successful because the British brought forward the men of their reserve, and both flanks focused on Breed's Hill. When the Patriots' powder and ammunition supplies were depleted, the increasingly enraged British troops charged the defenses using bayonets, precipitating a Patriot retreat. Patriot losses totaled 140 dead, 271 wounded, and 30 taken prisoner. The British lost 226 men killed and 828 wounded. The entire battle had taken two and a half hours.

Although the British were victorious at Bunker Hill, the outcome left them no further ahead; the road to Charlestown and the surrounding area were still held by the Patriots. Moreover, a British breakout ceased to be an option as thousands of militia arrived from Massachusetts and neighboring colonies. Gage was recalled to England and left his post permanently in October 1775. Howe assumed command over the colonies, and Sir Guy Carleton became commander in chief of Canada, headquartered in Quebec.

Dorchester. The siege stalemated once again. Neither side was interested in more carnage. On 17 June 1775, Colonel George Washington was appointed as commander in chief of the Continental Army that had been created by the Continental Congress two days before. Washington's 17,000-strong army endured severe shortages of ammunition and weapons throughout his command. This continued until he received captured artillery from Fort Ticonderoga. Using a diversionary tactic by bombarding Dorchester, the Americans prepared their entrenchment on Dorchester Heights. Lines of defense were completed by 1,200 troops under General Thomas on the night of 4–5 March. Dorchester was seized, and Boston Harbor became untenable.

Thomas gave Howe an ultimatum: Patriot troops would destroy all the ships in the harbor, or the British could leave Boston in safety. Howe, unwilling to subject his troops to fighting in inclement weather and wanting to prevent casualties, chose the latter. On 17 March 1776, some 7,000 British and 1,000 Loyalists evacuated Boston and sailed to Halifax, Nova Scotia. The siege of Boston ended when Washington and the Continental Army entered the city.

The siege of Boston proved that the Americans could defy the world's most powerful army and demand their own interpretation of sovereignty. It fueled their resolve to continue resistance against the British and served to unify the colonies.

Annette Richardson

See also

Adams, John; Administration of Justice Act; Boston, Massachusetts; Boston Port Act; Boston Tea Party; Bunker Hill, Battle of; Burgoyne, John; Carleton, Guy; Clinton, Henry; Coercive Acts; Congress, First Continental; Continental Army; Dorchester Heights, Massachusetts; Fort Ticonderoga, New York; Gage, Thomas; Gridley, Richard; Hancock, John; Henry, Patrick; Howe, William; Lexington and Concord; Loyalists; Massachusetts Government Act; Minutemen; Pigot, Robert; Pitcairn, John; Prescott, William; Putnam, Israel; Quartering Acts; Revere, Paul; Smith, Francis; Sons of Liberty; Stamp Act; Tea Act; Townshend Acts; Ward, Artemas; Warren, Joseph

References

Alden, J. "Why the March to Concord?" *American Historical Review* 49 (April 1944): 446–454.

Andrews, Charles M. *The Colonial Background of the American Revolution.* New Haven, CT: Yale University Press, 1924.

Andrews, Joseph L., Jr. *Revolutionary Boston, Lexington and Concord: The Shots Heard Round the World.* Concord, MA: Concord Guides, 1999.

Bailyn, Bernard. *The Ideological Origins of the American Revolution.* 1967. Reprint, Cambridge: Harvard University Press, 1992.

Chidsey, Donald. *The Siege of Boston.* New York: Crown, 1966.

Elting, John R. *The Battle of Bunker's Hill.* Monmouth, NJ: Philip Freneau, 1975.

Frothingham, Richard. *History of the Siege of Boston and of the Battles of Lexington, Concord and Bunker Hill.* Boston: Little, Brown, 1849.

Ketchum, Richard. *Decisive Day: The Battle for Bunker Hill.* 1974. Reprint, New York: Henry Holt, 1999.

Maier, Pauline. *From Resistance to Revolution: Colonial Radicals and the Development of American Opposition to Britain, 1765–1776.* New York: Knopf, 1972.

Morrissey, Brendan. *Boston 1775: The Shot Heard around the World.* Oxford, UK: Osprey, 1995.

Boston Massacre (5 March 1770)

The Boston Massacre, a violent clash between British regulars and colonial civilians, was a pivotal event in the coming of the American Revolution. It permanently galvanized opposition to Crown policy in New England, fueled antiarmy sentiment throughout British North America, and pushed rebellious Americans closer to revolution.

Few people would have predicted this event at the beginning of the decade. In 1763 the Anglo-American victory over archrival France in the Seven Years' War suggested a bright future for the British Empire. That triumph removed France from competition for North America, made possible the expansion of British settlement west of the Appalachian Mountains, and bolstered the colonists' estimation of their future prosperity and importance. But the war with France also brought burdens. It saddled the victors with considerable debt, convinced British officials of the need to tighten imperial control, and reinforced the colonists' mistrust of regular soldiers in general and redcoats in particular.

As a consequence of all these factors, the end of the Seven Years' War brought important changes to the American colonies. During the next few years, Britain maintained thousands of expensive troops in North America, imposed a series

Boston Massacre. On 5 March 1770, growing tensions between Bostonians and British troops led to exchanges of insults before soldiers finally opened fire on a large mob, of whom five died of their wounds. The incident, which served as effective propaganda for Revolutionary agitators, played an important role in the movement toward general revolt. (National Archives and Records Administration)

of colonial taxes to reduce the burden of British taxpayers, and implemented measures to tighten governance throughout the region. These policies effectively ended several decades of so-called benign neglect—a phrase used by historians to describe the considerable autonomy heretofore enjoyed by the colonists. The Stamp Act, the Townshend Acts, and the presence of the king's troops, among other measures, provoked angry provincials to denounce and even openly defy royal policy. Because Bostonians engaged in a riot over the seizure of John Hancock's *Liberty* and appeared to both local customs officers and the royal governor, Sir Francis Bernard, to be out of control, British officials made the fateful decision to send redcoats into the city in 1768.

Beginning on 1 October, the 14th and 29th Regiments, along with soldiers from the 59th Regiment, disembarked in the Massachusetts capital. From the soldiers' first day ashore, they faced a well-organized opposition. The *Journal of the Times*, published by local radicals, regularly reported the various transgressions committed against Bostonians. By the end of October, the *Journal* alleged that British redcoats had abused the townspeople and subverted local government, that they were illegally billeted in the city, and even that they had attempted to incite a slave insurrection. The passage of time did little to alleviate tensions. The ongoing presence of the army provided a daily reminder that soldiers were there to coerce colonists rather than to protect them. Furthermore, morale was low among the troops, and desertion was common. By the winter of 1770, tensions ran high, and confrontations between soldiers and civilians became more common.

The gradual easing of winter brought no relief. On Friday, 2 March, fights erupted between Boston ropemakers and British soldiers, some of whom sought part-time employment when not on duty. On Monday, 5 March, the crisis that had been brewing finally boiled over. Multiple altercations occurred that snowy day, but the catalyst for the massacre took place in front of the customhouse on King Street (now State Street). There a lone sentry, Private Hugh White, stood guard. At about 8:00 P.M. he tried to settle an argument with a wig maker's apprentice by striking the young man in the head with his musket. Immediately a crowd gathered and grew larger as a nearby church bell mysteriously tolled and a voice cried "Fire!" Dozens, if not hundreds, of people trudged through snow and ice and joined the angry crowd surrounding White. Captain Thomas Preston, a corporal, and six privates arrived to provide support. The eight soldiers formed an arc next to Preston and eventually loaded their weapons before a throng that threw insults, snowballs, and sticks. Preston and Private Hugh Montgomery received blows, and someone again cried "Fire!" The soldiers discharged their muskets into the crowd. Five townspeople lay dead or mortally wounded: Patrick Carr, Samuel Maverick, Samuel Gray, James Caldwell, and Crispus Attucks, a mulatto of African and Natick Indian descent who was also known as Michael Johnson.

In the wake of the Boston Massacre, as the radicals immediately dubbed it, Lieutenant Governor Thomas Hutchinson agreed to remove the troops from the city to Castle William in the harbor. Captain Preston, his soldiers, and four civilians were subsequently arrested and jailed until their trials late in 1770. In a fine irony, the moderate Patriot Robert Treat Paine and the conservative Samuel Quincy prosecuted the soldiers, while the more radical John Adams and Josiah Quincy Jr. (Samuel's younger brother) argued on their behalf. The defense prevailed. In the first trial the jury acquitted Preston, and in the second trial the jury found all but two of the soldiers not guilty. Privates Hugh Montgomery and Matthew Kilroy were convicted of manslaughter. But the court reduced their sentences to branding on their thumbs after the two were able to plead clergy, a medieval law that gave special consideration to people who demonstrated their literacy—a curious outcome considering that Kilroy appears to have been unable to write his name.

The so-called massacre had a significant impact on the colonies and the Anglo-American relationship. In Boston, which annually commemorated the event, it further galvanized opposition to British imperial policies. For the next thirteen years, until Britain finally recognized America's independence, prominent speakers met on the anniversary of the massacre to praise the town's martyrs and denounce British tyranny. To Bostonians, the massacre confirmed the British government's determination to ensure the colonists' subordination, even by force. It also reinforced the antiarmy sentiment that was growing in popularity in many colonies. Annual speakers commonly emphasized the political oppression and moral degradation that invariably accompanied standing armies. That was a powerful message that influenced the Revolutionary generation as it formed its own armies and went to war with Britain in 1775.

Mark Thompson

See also

Adams, John; Gage, Thomas; Hutchinson, Thomas; Quincy, Josiah, Jr.; Stamp Act; Townshend Acts

References

Adams, John. *Legal Papers of John Adams,* Vol. 3, *The Boston Massacre Trials.* Ed. L. Kinvin Wroth and Hiller B. Zobel. Cambridge: Harvard University Press, 1965.

Shy, John. *Toward Lexington: The Role of the British Army in the Coming of the American Revolution.* Princeton, NJ: Princeton University Press, 1965.

Wemms, William. *The Trial of the British Soldiers, of the 29th Regiment of Foot.* 1807. Reprint, Miami, FL: Mnemosyne, 1969.

Zobel, Hiller B. *The Boston Massacre.* New York: Norton, 1970.

Boston Port Act (March 1774)

The first of the so-called Intolerable or Coercive Acts, the Boston Port Act was introduced into Parliament on 14 March 1774. It effectively closed the port of Boston to all commerce and was designed to punish the people of Boston and Massachusetts. Together, the Boston Port Act and the other Coercive Acts were directly responsible for moving the American colonies to open rebellion.

By 1770 the imperial crises stemming from the Stamp Act (1765) and the Townshend Acts (1767) had subsided. Successive ministries had retreated from efforts to tax the colonies after being met with stiff protest and resistance in America, as well as sympathetic protests from British merchants, but Parliament never totally backed down. The Declaratory Act of 1766, passed after the repeal of the Stamp Act, upheld the principle that Parliament had supreme legislative authority in the colonies. And when Parliament repealed the Townshend duties, it retained the tax on tea—and that would prove most important.

Parliament had not backed down from its philosophical position, and neither had the Americans. The period between the repeal of the Townshend duties and the passage of the Tea Act was indeed a time of relative calm, but colonial radicals, locally organized as the Sons of Liberty, remained ever watchful. Storm clouds began to gather again in 1773, when Lord North, British prime minister, introduced the Tea Act in an effort to aid the ailing East India Company.

The Tea Act allowed the East India Company to sell its tea directly to the colonies without having to pay any duties in England. Even though East India tea was still subject to the remaining Townshend duty on tea, the company could now undercut the price of smuggled tea from foreign competitors. Moreover, only select American merchants would be allowed to sell the tea. In Massachusetts, the five authorized merchants were all friends or close relatives of the detested royal governor, Thomas Hutchinson. Upon learning of the scheme, many in Massachusetts reacted with outrage. They saw it as a deliberate effort to entice them into submitting to and paying the Townshend duty, which they believed was an illegally imposed parliamentary tax. Radicals such as Samuel Adams and the Sons of Liberty had a new grievance to seize upon, and they wasted little time.

In other colonies, too, many people protested and tried to resist the implementation of the Tea Act. In several places, such as Charleston, South Carolina, radicals attempted to prevent the tea from being unloaded. The most drastic resistance measure, of course, took place in Boston on 16 December 1773. That night, members of the Sons of Liberty dressed as Indians and dumped approximately 340 chests of East India tea into Boston Harbor.

By January 1774 word of the Boston Tea Party reached London. This time the colonists had gone too far. The Bostonians had again defied Parliament and wantonly destroyed private property in the process. Both in the government and among the people at large, the resolve to punish the colonies stiffened. Thus, the ministry decided both to punish Boston and Massachusetts and to set an example of what would happen to other colonies that showed such defiance. Out of this sentiment were conceived the Coercive Acts, the first of which was the Boston Port Act.

The bill required that the port of Boston be closed to both overseas and coastal shipping until "peace and obedience to the laws" was restored, so that "the trade of Great Britain may be safely carried on there, and his Majesty's customs duty collected." It would be at the discretion of the Privy Council to decide when these terms had been met and when the harbor could be reopened. The bill was to take effect on 1 June 1774, which would perhaps give the colonists time to come into compliance and make amends by paying back the cost of the destroyed tea.

The Boston Port Act was a severe measure that would cripple Boston's economy, but Lord North felt it totally justified. Addressing Parliament on 14 March as he introduced the measure, he argued that the bill would put an end to the disturbances in America and secure the dependence of the colonies on the Crown. He said that British commerce was not safe in Boston Harbor and that the unruly Bostonians deserved to be severely punished. This was, he said, the third time that customs officers had been prevented from doing their duty in Boston, and since the local authorities had "been asleep" while all this happened, it was not unreasonable for the ministry to seek justice by punishing the entire town. Furthermore, Boston had been the ringleader in all riots for the previous seven years (since the Stamp Act was passed). The bill, Lord North argued, would be a test for Boston.

Not everyone in Parliament agreed. The Earl of Chatham (William Pitt the Elder), Edmund Burke, and Charles James Fox led the opposition, arguing that such harsh measures would only inflame the colonies to resistance on an unprecedented scale. Yet, a vast majority of Parliament approved the measure, which George III signed in short order.

As Chatham and Fox predicted, the Boston Port Act and the successive Coercive Acts set off a firestorm of protest, beginning in Boston but quickly spreading to several other colonies. Samuel Adams condemned the Boston Port Act, saying that "for us to reason against such an act would be idleness. Our business is to find means to evade its malignant design. The inhabitants view it not with astonishment, but with indignation." For radicals such as Adams, the bill finally provided proof that there indeed was a conspiracy among corrupt British ministers to subject the colonies to despotism. Soon other colonies, seeing what might happen to them, joined the protest. In Philadelphia, a meeting of freeholders on 20 June declared the act unconstitutional and called for a congress of delegates from all colonies to meet.

Even earlier, however, on 24 May, the Virginia House of Burgesses resolved that 1 June (the day the act was to take effect) was to be a day of prayer and fasting. The governor, Lord Dunmore, was outraged and dissolved the burgesses, who then proceeded to meet illegally at the Raleigh Tavern in Williamsburg. There they called for intercolonial nonimportation and a continental congress to meet in Philadelphia. Finally, the burgesses sent their resolves to the other colonial assemblies, all of which, except Georgia, eventually elected delegates to the First Continental Congress, which would vote to impose nonimportation as the burgesses recommended. Thus the Boston Port Act and the other Coercive Acts, far from having the intimidating effect that Lord North intended, united Britain's North American colonies in a way that no imperial measure had ever done before.

Aaron J. Palmer

See also

Boston, Massachusetts; Burke, Edmund; Coercive Acts; Fox, Charles James; Massachusetts; North, Lord Frederick; Pitt, William, the Elder; Tea Act

References

Ammerman, David. *In the Common Cause: American Response to the Coercive Acts of 1774.* New York: Norton, 1975.

Brown, Richard D. *Revolutionary Politics in Massachusetts: The Boston Committee of Correspondence and the Towns, 1772–1774.* Cambridge: Harvard University Press, 1970.

Cobbett, William. *Cobbett's Parliamentary History of England from the Norman Conquest in 1066 to the Year 1803.* London: R. Bagshaw, 1806.

Gipson, Lawrence Henry. *The Coming of the Revolution, 1763–1775.* New York: Harper and Row, 1954.

Labaree, Benjamin Woods. *The Boston Tea Party.* New York: Oxford University Press, 1964.

Maier, Pauline. *From Resistance to Revolution: Colonial Radicals and the Development of American Opposition to Britain, 1765–1776.* New York: Knopf, 1972.

Thomas, Peter D. G. *Lord North.* New York: St. Martin's, 1976.

Boston Tea Party (16 December 1773)

Early on the evening of 16 December 1773, thousands of Bostonians and other colonists from neighboring towns poured out of a large gathering at Old South Meeting House shouting, "Boston Harbor a tea pot tonight," "the Mohawks are come," and other rallying cries. They swarmed down through the narrow streets to Griffin's Wharf, where two merchant vessels were moored (a third was anchored close by). When the crowd reached the waterfront, a band of fifty or sixty men, roughly disguised as Indians, climbed aboard the vessels. There they hoisted out 340 chests of tea, most weighing nearly 400 pounds; broke them open with hatchets; and dumped the contents into the waters of Boston Harbor. This event, known ever after as the Boston Tea Party, precipitated consequences that inexorably led to the outbreak of the War for American Independence at Lexington and Concord sixteen months later.

At the end of the Seven Years' War in 1763 the British Parliament adopted a new policy of taxing its American colonies to help defray the costs of their administration and defense. Almost immediately colonists objected to this innovation, insisting that they should be taxed only by their own provincial legislatures, not by Parliament where they were not represented. After one ministry repealed the unpopular Stamp Act in 1766, Parliament adopted the Townshend Acts, levying duties on tea and a few other commodities imported into America. Again the colonists protested, and this time most of the merchants in the leading seaports agreed not to import any goods from England until Parliament repealed the act. Much of their effort focused on dutied tea, which many Americans stopped drinking altogether, while others switched to tea smuggled in from Holland.

So successful was the boycott of British goods that in the spring of 1770 Parliament was forced to repeal most of the duties, retaining only the one on tea to uphold its power of taxation. In turn, the merchants rescinded their nonimportation agreements while generally continuing their ban on tea, and there ensued a three-year period of relative calm in relations between Britain and its North American colonies. Meanwhile, however, the East India Company, which monopolized the importation of tea into Great Britain, was accumulating an enormous surplus due to lagging sales. In 1773, Parliament permitted the shipping of company tea directly to American ports, bypassing British middlemen and refunding the import tax levied in Britain, enabling the company to compete with smuggled tea. But the head of the ministry at that time, Lord North, insisted on retaining the hated colonial tea duty despite the warning from an opposition spokesman that "if he don't take off the duty they won't take the tea."

In the autumn of 1773 word reached America of the East India Company's intention to send more than two thousand

Boston Tea Party. In protest against the Tea Act of 1773, which imposed unpopular taxes on a heavily consumed commodity, colonists disguised as Mohawk Indians boarded three British East Indiamen and cast more than 300 chests of tea into the harbor. The following year Parliament replied with the Intolerable Acts. (Library of Congress)

chests of dutied tea to Boston, New York, Philadelphia, and Charleston. Opposition in all four ports quickly focused around two themes: first, that submission to dutied tea would pave the way for Parliament to levy other taxes in the future, and second, that permitting the East India Company to establish a monopoly in tea would open the door for the company to monopolize other aspects of colonial trade. The colonial governors at New York, Philadelphia, and Charleston were reluctant to intervene to protect the importation of tea in the face of staunch public opposition, and the tea consignees in those ports resigned their commissions. Charleston's tea was ultimately impounded at the customhouse, and at both Philadelphia and New York the ships were forced to return to England with their cargoes.

But at Boston the situation was very different. There the royal governor, American-born Thomas Hutchinson, had no intention of giving in to demands that Boston's tea ships be sent back to England. For one thing, the East India Company had appointed two of his sons as consignees, and they stood to profit from the sale of its tea. Second, Hutchinson and the leader of the opposition, Samuel Adams, had been bitter enemies for years, and the governor had old scores to settle. He was confident that should matters come to a head, he would have the support of numerous British soldiers, naval vessels, and other royal officials stationed in Boston. For their part, local Patriots had been roundly criticized throughout the continent for the large amount of dutied tea that had landed at Boston over the past three years, despite their efforts to ban it. The fact that the Hutchinsons and their fellow consignees were the worst violators of the tea boycott gave the Patriots a score of their own to settle. A showdown in Boston over the East India Company's tea was all but inevitable.

On 28 November, the first of the tea vessels, the *Dartmouth,* entered the port of Boston, to be joined a few days later by the *Eleanor* and the *Beaver,* carrying altogether 340 chests of dutied tea. (A fourth vessel, the *William,* was wrecked on Cape Cod.) The law required that cargo owners pay all customs duties within twenty days of entering a port or face seizure of their goods. If that should happen, the Patriots feared, the tea would quickly find its way into the hands of the consignees, who would put it up for sale. The deadline for payment was 17 December. The Patriot leaders called for public meetings on 29 and 30 November, which were attended by more than 5,000 people from Boston and its surrounding communities. They demanded that the tea be returned to London without payment of the duties, but Hutchinson and the consignees had already left town to avoid such intimidation. They were content to let the clock run out, knowing that the vessels could not get out by the fort on Castle Island without a pass from the governor. Having failed to persuade Hutchinson and the consignees to give in, the Patriots had the vessels brought up to Griffin's Wharf, where they placed armed guards on board to prevent the tea from being unloaded clandestinely.

In mid-December the Patriots assembled two more mass meetings, again with more than 5,000 people packing the pews and aisles of the Old South Meeting House and spilling outside. On the afternoon of 16 December, the second assemblage, with Samuel Adams presiding, made one final effort to have the tea returned. William Rotch, the young captain of the *Dartmouth,* was dispatched to deliver the demand to the governor at his country estate in Milton. A last-ditch effort at compromise fell through. Hutchinson refused to grant a pass by Castle Island, and shortly after dark the forlorn ship captain returned empty-handed to the Old South Meeting House. It looked as though Hutchinson was on the verge of winning a major victory.

But suddenly from the gallery came a war whoop, answered by similar cries from a small group of men standing by the doorway and disguised as Indians. Followed by thousands of ordinary citizens, they rushed to the waterfront, boarded the vessels, and destroyed the tea. At first no one would admit taking part in this momentous event, but the passage of time has since revealed that among the "Indians" were members of Boston's Committee of Correspondence, the grand lodge of Masons, the Long Room Club, and other groups of political activists, including residents from outlying towns, some from as far away as Maine. A few were merchants or other prominent citizens such as Paul Revere, William Mollineux, and Dr. Thomas Young, but most were artisans and apprentices.

"This is the most magnificent Movement of all," John Adams pronounced in his diary the next day. "This Destruction of the Tea is so bold, so daring, so firm, intrepid and inflexible, and it must have so important Consequences, and so lasting, that I cant but consider it as an Epocha in History." Events would soon demonstrate the accuracy of Adams's prediction. As news of Boston's action spread rapidly down the Atlantic seaboard, carried by Revere and other post riders, it generated a fresh wave of unity throughout the continent that would pave the way for a congress of all the colonies nine months later.

By far the most significant consequence of the Boston Tea Party was the reaction it provoked in Great Britain. In the weeks after learning of the tea's destruction, the British ministry read reports and heard testimony from Governor Hutchinson, General Thomas Gage, and other royal officials who had witnessed the events in Boston. Realizing the difficulty of singling out individual perpetrators for prosecution, the ministry instead decided to punish Bostonians as a whole. Not only was such a policy easier to execute, but it gave vent to Britain's long-festering anger with Massachusetts Bay. The ministry was determined to distinguish Boston from the other ports—New York, Philadelphia, and Charleston—that had also rejected dutied tea but by less violent means. In the end, the ministry proposed and Parliament adopted the Boston Port Act, which closed the port of Boston and moved its customhouse affairs to Plymouth, and three additional Coercive Acts, the most important of which altered the charter of Massachusetts Bay to give royal officials more control over the rebellious province.

John Adams was right in pronouncing the Boston Tea Party an "epocha," by which he meant that it would mark the beginning of an entirely new era in the relationship between the mother country and its American possessions. Before the Boston Tea Party, most Americans would have continued to accept British rule, perhaps for decades to come. But Boston's bold act of defiance drove the ministry to adopt punitive measures that Patriots in all of the colonies could not accept. In the months that followed passage of the Coercive Acts, colonists closed ranks and made common cause with the beleaguered town of Boston.

Benjamin W. Labaree

See also

Adams, Samuel; Boston, Massachusetts; Boston Port Act; Coercive Acts; Hutchinson, Thomas; Massachusetts; Tea Act

References

Adams, John. *Diary and Autobiography of John Adams.* Edited by L. H. Butterfield. 4 vols. Cambridge: Harvard University Press, 1961.

Ammerman, David. *In the Common Cause: American Response to the Coercive Acts of 1774.* New York: Norton, 1975.

Brown, Richard D. *Revolutionary Politics in Massachusetts: The Boston Committee of Correspondence and the Towns, 1772–1774.* Cambridge: Harvard University Press, 1970.

Labaree, Benjamin Woods. *The Boston Tea Party.* New York: Oxford University Press, 1964.

Boudinot, Elias (1740–1821)

Elias Boudinot, president of the Continental Congress under the Confederation, director of the U.S. Mint, and founder of the American Bible Society, was the son of Elie Boudinot and Catherine Williams, the daughter of a planter. Elie Boudinot, of Huguenot descent, at one point owned large tracts of land in what is now Bergen County, New Jersey, and was a silversmith.

Elias grew up in Philadelphia in a house just down the street from Benjamin Franklin, and his father's business was adjacent to Franklin's printing shop. The elder Boudinot was a staunch Presbyterian and had Elias baptized by none other than the celebrated evangelical preacher and promoter of the Great Awakening movement in the colonies, George Whitfield. In 1752, Boudinot's family moved to Princeton, New Jersey, after his father had become owner of a newly discovered copper vein near New Brunswick. By 1760, the younger Boudinot had joined the New Jersey bar and, through his sister's marriage, become the brother-in-law of the prominent Princeton lawyer Richard Stockton, who would sign the Declaration of Independence. Soon thereafter, Boudinot moved to Elizabeth Town (now Elizabeth), New Jersey, where he married and opened his own law office.

In 1774, Boudinot joined the Patriot movement and became a member of the local committee of correspondence; he also took in young Alexander Hamilton as a boarder. After Lexington and Concord, Boudinot became a member of the provincial congress of New Jersey, and the next year saw him trying to protect his small town from General William Howe's army, which controlled New York Harbor and nearby Staten Island. When General George Washington lost the Battle of Long Island in August 1776, Elizabeth Town was evacuated, and Boudinot moved to a home he had previously purchased in Basking Ridge, New Jersey.

In April 1777, Washington asked Boudinot to become commissary of prisoners (with a little additional spying duty). American prisoners were then living in deplorable conditions behind the British lines; Boudinot's job became negotiating with the British for prisoner exchanges and seeing to it that the British actually gave the American prisoners the blankets and other supplies Boudinot bought for them. He was also involved in the treatment of British soldiers taken prisoner, whom the Americans had scattered in camps in the various states. While still at that post, Boudinot was elected to Congress by the New Jersey legislature. He did not attend Congress immediately because he needed to arrange some prisoner exchanges and visit America's most famous prisoner, General Charles Lee, whose release he eventually secured. In July 1777, Boudinot left the army for the Continental Congress. Boudinot went to Congress as much to settle his own personal accounts with that body as to represent his state, for the central government owed him considerable sums for his expenses.

In 1778 and 1779 Boudinot largely returned to the private practice of law, but in 1780 a British raid on Elizabeth resulted in the burning of a Presbyterian church, and there were rumors that Boudinot's family was an objective of the raid. In 1781, Boudinot's brother-in-law, Stockton, died of wounds he received while he was a British prisoner; Stockton was perhaps the best-known abused prisoner of war during the entire conflict. In 1781, Boudinot returned to the Continental Congress.

Boudinot had speculated in land in the West, partially in the area around present-day Dayton, Ohio. In the Congress he met James Madison, one of the most outspoken enemies of the speculators. Their personality clash was to echo through most of the early Federal period. In 1781, after Yorktown, Boudinot had planned to return to his home, but the New Jersey legislature reappointed him to Congress, where he was put on several committees, including one to design the present Great Seal of the United States. In November 1782, Boudinot was chosen by Congress to be its presiding officer, which made him president of the young nation at the formal end of the war.

In 1783 Congress was generous in spirit—it released Cornwallis and thanked the departing French army—but financially bankrupt. Even as word arrived from Europe that America's diplomats had reached a preliminary agreement with the king's envoys on peace terms, word also came of a potential Continental Army mutiny over Congress's failure to pay the soldiers. On 11 April 1783, Boudinot, as president of Congress, signed the ratification of the preliminary peace treaty ending the Revolutionary War. That, however, still did not pay the soldiers. They marched on Philadelphia in June, and after a tense standoff and the departure of the soldiers, Congress moved to Boudinot's old haunt, Princeton, where they met in Nassau Hall, the chief building on the college campus. In the fall, Boudinot signed the resolutions disbanding the army and proclaiming a national day of thanksgiving.

On 2 November 1783, Boudinot's term of office expired; he had asked New Jersey not to reelect him to Congress. He returned to an Elizabeth that was greatly changed by the war. Boudinot again turned his attention to land speculation in the West, and while he was thus engaged the new federal Constitution was written in Philadelphia in 1787, without the benefit of his experience. In March 1789, Boudinot was elected to the House of Representatives as one of four at-large members from New Jersey, and in April he welcomed Washington as the general passed through Elizabeth on his way to New York to be sworn in as president. In Congress, Boudinot drafted the rules for the first session of the House of Representatives.

In 1790, Boudinot became one of the first members of the bar of the U.S. Supreme Court. The same year he received an honorary degree from Yale, his only academic achievement. He also became one of the founders of the Society for Useful Manufactures, set up to exploit the Great Falls at Paterson, New Jersey. In 1795 he became director of the U.S. Mint in Philadelphia and continued at that post into the Jefferson administration. After retiring, Boudinot presided at meetings of the American Bible Society. He died in August 1821 and is buried at St. Mary's Church in Burlington, New Jersey.

John David Healy

See also

Congress, Second Continental and Confederation; New Jersey; Prisoners of War

References

Boyd, George Adams. *Elias Boudinot, Patriot and Statesman.* Princeton, NJ: Princeton University Press, 1952.

Thayer, Theodore. *In Old Elizabethtown.* Elizabeth, NJ: Grassman, 1964.

Whisenhunt, Don. *Elias Boudinot.* Trenton: New Jersey Historical Commission, 1976.

Bougainville, Louis-Antoine de (1729–1811)

Louis-Antoine de Bougainville, born in Paris on 11 November 1729, was a representative in the Paris Parlement, a Black Musketeer, a mathematician, an aide-de-camp to General Louis-Joseph Montcalm, and an officer in the navy. In the late 1760s and early 1770s he commanded a voyage around the world aboard the *Boudeuse.* In 1778–1779, he served with Admiral Jean-Baptiste d'Estaing and later distinguished himself at Grenada and in the Chesapeake, though he was much criticized for his conduct at the Battle of the Saintes. He was made a vice admiral in 1792 and later became a senator, and then a count, under Napoleon's regime.

The son of a solicitor in the Chatelet, Bougainville studied law before becoming a lawyer in the Paris Parlement. He later became a soldier in the Black Musketeers. After the publication of his notable *Traité de Calcul Intégral* (Treatise on Integral Calculus), he left for London in 1754 to become a secretary in the French Embassy and became a member of the Royal Society. In 1756, he was promoted to captain in the Dragoons and went with his regiment to Canada. He participated in the defense of Fort Carillon (Ticonderoga) and in the capture of Fort William Henry (August 1757). As aide-de-camp to Colonel Montcalm, Bougainville's conduct at the Battle of the Plains of Abraham (1759) was called into question. From North America he went to serve in the campaign in Germany.

On 15 June 1763 Bougainville joined the navy as a ship's captain. He armed two vessels at St. Malo and founded the Acadian colony in the Falkland Islands in February 1764. He handed those islands over to Spain in June 1767. Louis XV rewarded this soundness of his diplomacy by entrusting Bougainville with the command of the frigate *Boudeuse* and the supply ship *Etiole,* with which to explore the Pacific. Bougainville followed, without being aware of it, the same route taken a few months earlier by the Englishman Samuel Wallis, who discovered Tahiti in 1767. Bougainville encountered the island in April 1768 and wrote an Eden-like description of it, naming it "La Nouvelle Cythère," a reference to the Greek island of Cythera, in legend the birthplace of the goddess Aphrodite (Venus).

Bougainville's travels led him to Samoa, the New Hebrides, New Guinea, and the Moluccas. He returned triumphantly to St. Malo on 16 March 1776. This extensive voyage befitted an eighteenth-century philosopher such as himself. For the next 200 years, Europe was able to draw on Bougainville's travels as a utopian concept of happiness and as a justification for colonialism. Bougainville's expedition was the last one headed by a humanist: with Captain James Cook came the era of the specialists.

Bougainville left Toulon in April 1778 aboard the *Guerrier* (74 guns). Promoted to squadron commander in 1779, he participated with d'Estaing in the American War of Independence and was present at the capture of Grenada and the siege of Savannah. He laid up at Rochefort on 9 December 1779, his squadron having suffered forty-five dead and seventy-five sick or wounded. Bougainville did not receive a new command until 1781, when he hoisted his flag in the *Auguste* (80 guns) in François de Grasse's squadron. On 29 April, Bougainville engaged Samuel Hood's squadron but was put under arrest by de Grasse for not having executed his orders. Tobago was captured on 2 May 1781. Bougainville, who was the first commander under de Grasse to cast off from his anchorage on 5 September 1781, confronted Hood's *Barfleur* and played a major role in de Grasse's victory over Admiral Graves in the Second Battle of the Chesapeake Capes.

After the fall of Yorktown, Bougainville participated in the escort of colonial convoys to France and in the capture of St. Kitts (also know as St. Christopher Island). Stressing to his superiors the state of fatigue of the crews, he fought valiantly on the morning of the Battle of the Saintes (12 April 1782) but then abandoned de Grasse, who was consequently beaten. After the war a court-martial found Bougainville guilty, but he received only a reprimand.

When appointed vice admiral in 1790 and commander of the Brest squadron, Bougainville decided to resign. He refused the post of *ministre de la Marine* (secretary of the navy) in 1792. He took refuge near Coutances in Normandy and was arrested in 1793 during the Terror but was saved by Robespierre's death. Napoleon heaped honors on Bougainville, making him a senator and count of the empire. He was also a member of the Legion of Honor. After Trafalgar, he presided over the *conseil de guerre* (war council). He died in Paris on 31 August 1811.

Patrick Villiers

See also

Chesapeake, Second Battle of the; Estaing, Jean-Baptiste, Comte d'; Grasse, François-Joseph-Paul, Comte de; Grenada, Battle of; Saintes, Battle of the; St. Kitts, Battle of

References

Bougainville, Louis-Antoine de, Comte. *The Pacific Journal of Louis-Antoine de Bougainville, 1767–1768.* Translated and edited by John Dunmore. London: Hakluyt Society, 2002.

Martin-Allanic, Jean Étienne. *Bougainville: Navigateur et les découvertes de son temps.* 2 vols. Paris: Presses Universitaires de France, 1964.

Ross, Michael. *Bougainville.* London: Gordon and Cremonesi, 1978.

Bouillé, François-Claude-Amour, Marquis de (1739–1800)

Cousin of the Marquis de Lafayette, soldier, governor of Guadeloupe and then of the (French) Windward Islands, the Marquis de Bouillé played a crucial role in the conquest of the British Antilles and was a faithful supporter of Louis XVI during the French Revolution.

Born at Cluzel-Saint-Eble in 1739, Bouillé was a native of the Auvergne region, like his cousin Lafayette. Bouillé was promoted to colonel in 1761, then governor of Guadeloupe in 1768–1769. On 15 March 1777, he became commander in chief in the Windward Islands and governor of Martinique. He was very supportive of the American rebels and authorized the sale of prizes captured by American privateers. He captured Dominica from the British on 7 September 1778 and participated in the capture of Grenada, in the course of which he fell out with Admiral Jean-Baptiste d'Estaing. Bouillé recaptured St. Eustatius from the British on 26 November 1781 and, together with Admiral François de Grasse, seized Tobago in February 1782.

Bouillé was promoted to lieutenant general, then placed in command of the French forces meant to invade Jamaica, though this expedition never materialized. He returned to France in May 1783. He was *commandant militaire* (military commander) of Alsace and Lorraine in 1789, then commanding general of the Army of the Meuse and Moselle. As a supporter of Louis XVI, he participated in organizing the king's escape to Varennes. When this failed, Bouillé joined the French royalist army in exile. He died in London in 1800.

Patrick Villiers

See also

British West Indies; Dominica, First Battle of; Estaing, Jean-Baptiste, Comte d'; French West Indies; Grasse, François-Joseph-Paul, Comte de; Grenada, Battle of; St. Eustatius, Operations against

Reference

Villiers, Patrick. *Le commerce colonial atlantique et la guerre d'indépendence des États-Unis d'Amérique, 1778–1783.* New York: Arno, 1977.

Bound Brook, New Jersey, Action at (13 April 1777)

On 13 April 1777, Major General Benjamin Lincoln, in camp at Bound Brook, New Jersey, was surprised and routed by British troops under the command of Lord Charles Cornwallis. During the early months of 1777, General George Washington and his army were encamped at Morristown, New Jersey, with detachments posted near British lines. One of Washington's advance posts was on the American right flank at Bound Brook, guarding a pass through the Wachtung Mountains that offered access to Morristown. There, Lincoln commanded about 500 men, only 7 miles up the Raritan River from Brunswick, where the British commander in chief, General Sir William Howe, had stationed 8,000 British and Hessian troops under the command of Cornwallis. Lincoln's orders from Washington were to harass the British and to guard the mountain pass.

As spring came on, both Lincoln and Cornwallis increased their raids against each other, and finally Cornwallis tired of the rebels' attacks. In February, Howe had informed Cornwallis that he could strike at rebel posts nearby as soon as the weather permitted. Hence, on the evening of 12 February, Cornwallis, with General James Grant as second in command, set out for Bound Brook in two columns consisting of five battalions of British infantry and Carl von Donop's jaegers—4,000 men in all. Cornwallis's column marched on the right of the Raritan River while Grant came forward on the opposite side, so that the two columns could converge on the American post. Advancing near Lincoln's camp without being detected by American pickets, the British and Hessian soldiers lay quietly with their weapons until dawn on 13 April, when they attacked on signal.

Lincoln and his men were immediately in danger of being trapped by Cornwallis's threatening columns. The American pickets fled in terror without alerting the camp, and the British were very near Lincoln's headquarters before he was even aware of their approach. With no time to reflect on the best course of action, Lincoln rallied his men, guided them through British musket fire, and escaped. The Americans lost about 60 casualties (some taken prisoner) plus 3 cannon; much camp equipment; 200 cattle; some sheep and hogs; large quantities of rum, flour, and bread; and all Lincoln's personal papers. General Nathanael Greene hurried reinforcements from Middlebrook shortly after breakfast. Cornwallis and Grant withdrew, and the Americans reoccupied the post.

Because of his calm and decisive leadership, Lincoln had averted a catastrophe; nobody blamed him for the mishap. Washington referred to Lincoln's losses as trifling. As a consequence of the raid, however, Washington did reduce the number of his detached posts to prevent any further losses and to make it easier to respond when the British commenced their anticipated spring campaign.

Paul David Nelson

See also

Cornwallis, Charles; Donop, Carl von; German Mercenaries; Greene, Nathanael; Grant, James; Lincoln, Benjamin; Morristown, New Jersey, Continental Army Winter Quarters; New Jersey, Operations in

References

Mattern, David. *Benjamin Lincoln and the American Revolution.* Columbia: University of South Carolina Press, 1995.

Nelson, Paul David. *General James Grant: Scottish Soldier and Royal Governor of East Florida.* Gainesville: University Press of Florida, 1993.

Boycotts (1765–1776)

The word "boycott" first appeared in 1880 in Ireland, according to the *Oxford English Dictionary.* But the practice of trying to achieve a political objective by refusing to buy goods or services from a local tradesman, a major import merchant, or a whole country was basic to the growing success of the Revolutionary movement in North America from the Stamp Act crisis until independence. And the use of the term for various nonimportation and nonconsumption agreements of the 1760s and 1770s in North America, and at other times in other places, has long been common among both historians and the general public.

America's Revolutionary boycotts against British imperial policy included the rebelling colonies' three major nonimportation movements—protesting the Stamp Act (1765–1766), the Townshend duties (1768–1770) and dutied tea (through 1774), and the Coercive Acts (1774–1776)—but the practice was broader than nonimportation. Local nonconsumption agreements had a more popular appeal than nonimportation, because virtually any freeman, and on occasion freewomen as well, whether a craftsman, farmer, or housewife, could pledge not to consume a product without having either the money or the connections to be able to import any goods directly from Britain.

Such protests were appealing in nearly every British colony. Widespread, if largely uncoordinated, popular boycotts first appeared in reaction to the Townshend duties of 1767. In Massachusetts, a nonconsumption agreement spread from Boston to several smaller towns, inland as well as coastal. In the southern colonies, which had relatively few major ports and where much of the population was quite remote from major import merchants, nonconsumption spread deeply into the backcountry. Whether nonconsumption appealed more to a Calvinist, covenant-based stoicism, as in New England, or to a more secular self-denial with roots in stoical images of the Roman world, as in many colonies North and South, the agreements generated a deep Patriotic fervor.

A limitation on the effectiveness of the economic boycott in Revolutionary America may have been the slowness of leaders to understand how potent a weapon it could be. The first extended nonimportation movement, against the Townshend duties of 1767, gradually failed, both because the merchants in the several major ports did not coordinate their actions and also, one suspects, because nonimportation did not provide the great majority of the population with a way to join the protest. In several colonies, many nonmerchants eagerly embraced the popular substitution of nonconsumption, but in 1770 they found themselves powerless to influence the merchants, who controlled and ultimately abandoned nonimportation when Parliament repealed all the Townshend duties except the one on tea.

The leaders of America's Revolutionary movement did not repeat this mistake in 1774. When they decided that they must oppose the Coercive Acts with a massive economic boycott, they recruited supporters everywhere, and in great numbers. In city after city, artisans were invited to join merchants in planning nonimportation. And in October 1774, when the First Continental Congress devised the Continental Association, a comprehensive nonimportation plan for every colony, they entrusted the association's enforcement to new Committees of Observation, Inspection, and Correspondence in every legal locality that wished to participate, be it a city, town, or county. Hundreds of localities responded, choosing perhaps 7,000 freemen to serve on local committees from Maine to South Carolina (Georgia joined the association in 1775). Many more performed the symbolic act of signing the Continental Association. And in Edenton, North Carolina, several women also signed the plan, an event immortalized in a satiric print by an English artist.

This superbly coordinated boycott, unlike the more ragged efforts of 1768–1770, did not persuade the British government to make the slightest alteration in its policy. But it did something far more important. It created a massive Revolutionary leadership that prepared the thirteen rebelling colonies for independence.

Richard Alan Ryerson

See also

Boston, Massachusetts; Congress, First Continental; Continental Association; Correspondence, Committees of; Massachusetts; New York City; Nonimportation Agreements; Philadelphia; Sons of Liberty; South Carolina

References

Ammerman, David. *In the Common Cause: American Response to the Coercive Acts of 1774.* New York: Norton, 1975.

Countryman, Edward. *A People in Revolution: The American Revolution and Political Society in New York, 1760–1790.* Baltimore: Johns Hopkins University Press, 1981.

Maier, Pauline. *From Resistance to Revolution: Colonial Radicals and the Development of American Opposition to Britain, 1765–1776.* New York: Knopf, 1972.

Nash, Gary B. *The Urban Crucible: Social Change, Political Consciousness and the Origins of the American Revolution.* Cambridge: Harvard University Press, 1979.

Ryerson, Richard A. *The Revolution Is Now Begun: The Radical Committees of Philadelphia, 1765–1776.* Philadelphia: University of Pennsylvania Press, 1978.

Brandywine, Battle of (11 September 1777)

The Battle of Brandywine was one of the largest battles of the American Revolution, but its outcome was not as decisive as the British would have liked. They succeeded in defeating, but not in routing, the American forces. As they had in the New York Campaign, the American forces withdrew to fight another day.

During the early summer of 1777, the main American army, under the command of General George Washington, and the British Army, under the command of General Sir William Howe, carried out a series of marches and countermarches. The two armies were stationed in southern New York and northern New Jersey. Howe crossed over to New Jersey on 17 June in an attempt to force battle, but Washington was not willing to engage unless conditions were favorable. At the same time, a second British force was marching south from Lake Champlain toward Albany. Washington was unsure of Howe's plans and feared that Howe would march north toward Albany to combine forces with the British from Lake Champlain.

Howe's strategy was, in fact, to move either over land or by sea against Philadelphia, the capital of the thirteen colonies. Following his failed attempt to goad Washington into battle, in early July Howe withdrew his forces from New Jersey and headed for Staten Island, where the army boarded ships and transports waiting in New York Harbor. Once embarked the army waited two weeks for orders, while Washington and his staff tried to figure out what would happen next. On 23 July the ships sailed. Washington and part of his forces proceeded toward central New Jersey, while other units were sent north to reinforce the defense against British forces heading toward Albany. Washington was unsure of where the British planned to land, but intelligence indicated that their destination might be Philadelphia.

British vessels were sighted on the Delaware River on 29 July, lending credence to Washington's suspicions. He moved his troops toward Philadelphia. Howe, meanwhile, received faulty intelligence that American forces had reached Delaware and feared that Wilmington and the northern Delaware River were strongly fortified. The Delaware River had already been strongly fortified between Chester and Philadelphia. Howe decided to withdraw his fleet to the Chesapeake River. They waited another three weeks, then set sail up the Chesapeake.

When Washington received word of Howe's approach from the Chesapeake, he moved his army to protect the area south of Philadelphia, toward Wilmington. American forces marched through Philadelphia on 24 August, and British forces landed at the top of Chesapeake Bay the next day at a place named Head of Elk, only 55 miles from Philadelphia.

Howe bided his time in beginning the march toward Philadelphia and the main American army. His troops had been cooped up aboard ships for more than a month. Reorganization took time; units had to be brought up to strength. British forces totaled around 13,000 men, while Washington's forces totaled nearly 15,000 men, of which two-thirds were Continental regulars. Washington sent a brigade of light

Battle of Brandywine. During his march on Philadelphia in the autumn of 1777, British General William Howe encountered George Washington with a mixed army of Continentals and militia at Brandywine Creek. Although the Americans offered a respectable degree of resistance, they suffered from a poor understanding of the local geography, thus enabling Howe to outflank them. The resulting American defeat slowed, but failed to stop, the British occupation of Philadelphia, America's capital and largest city. (Library of Congress)

infantry, under the command of Brigadier General William Maxwell, to report on British movements. Forward elements of Maxwell's brigade located British columns near Cooch's Bridge. After a short but lively engagement, the Americans withdrew.

Washington decided to deploy his forces in a defensive position on the main road to Philadelphia. His troops began to reach the area on 9 and 10 September. He chose a position at Chadds Ford along the Brandywine Creek. Washington decided on the place because of the defensive possibilities offered by the terrain. The valley of the creek was deep, and the creek itself could only be forded in certain places. The surrounding heights overlooked both sides of the creek. Washington decided to rest most of his defense on the central Chadds Ford position, on the eastern bank of the creek.

He divided his forces into five divisions. Major General Nathanael Greene, Major General William Stirling, and Major General Adam Stephen commanded the divisions stationed near Chadds Ford. Maxwell with his light troops was stationed on the main road due west of Chadds Ford as a delaying force. A brigade of Pennsylvania militia was deployed to the south at Pyle's Ford, under the command of Brigadier General John Armstrong. The right flank of the American position, 5 miles to the north of Chadds Ford, was weakly defended by units under the command of Major General John Sullivan. Small detachments from Sullivan's forces were deployed farther north to cover other fords across the creek. Sullivan's troops had not carried out adequate reconnaissance of their area before the British forces arrived, and this negligence was to have consequences for the battle's outcome.

Howe and his forces arrived in the area on 10 September. British forward units were sent on reconnaissance missions to ascertain American positions in the area. Various small-scale skirmishes took place as units encountered each other. Local Loyalists also contacted senior British commanders to provide information on the area's roads and terrain as well as the Americans' whereabouts. Howe soon realized that the area around Chadds Ford was heavily defended but also learned that the fords to the north were not so well protected. As he had in the Battle of Long Island, Howe decided to use a flanking movement and feint frontal attack to knock the American forces off balance.

On 10 September Howe issued orders to his brigade commanders. Lieutenant-General Baron Wilhelm von Knyphausen, with 5,000 men from the 1st and 2nd (British) Brigades, three battalions of Hessians, riflemen, and the

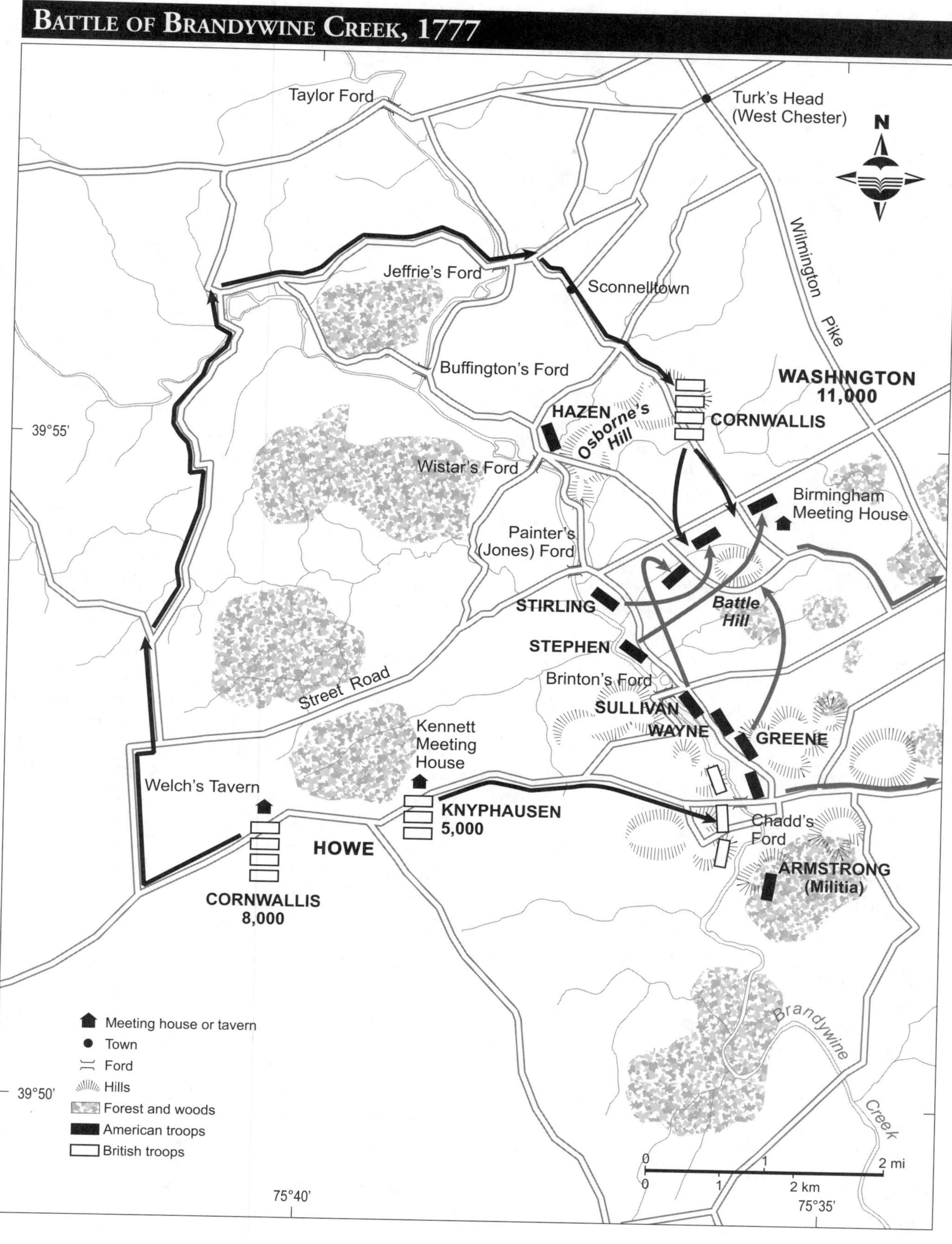
Battle of Brandywine Creek, 1777
Taylor Ford
Turk's Head
(West Chester)
N
Jeffrie's Ford
Sconnelltown
Wilmington Pike
Buffington's Ford
WASHINGTON
11,000
HAZEN
Osborne's Hill
CORNWALLIS
39°55'
Wistar's Ford
Birmingham
Meeting House
Painter's
(Jones) Ford
STIRLING
Battle Hill
STEPHEN
Street Road
Brinton's Ford
SULLIVAN
WAYNE
GREENE
Kennett
Meeting
House
Welch's Tavern
KNYPHAUSEN
5,000
Chadd's
Ford
HOWE
ARMSTRONG
(Militia)
CORNWALLIS
8,000
Brandywine
Creek
Meeting house or tavern
Town
Ford
Hills
Forest and woods
American troops
British troops
39°50'
0
1
2 mi
0
1
2 km
75°40'
75°35'

(Loyalist) Queen's Rangers, was to advance toward Chadds Ford. This force would constitute the feint attack to draw off the American forces. Howe and Lieutenant-General Lord Charles Cornwallis, with 8,000 troops of the 3rd and 4th Brigades and composite units of Hessian and British grenadiers, were to march some 18 miles in a flanking movement, if possible without being detected, and smash into the American right flank. This second column would represent the main body of the British attack.

The British troops began their respective marches before dawn on 11 September. Knyphausen's troops marched due east. The first reports of British movements reached Washington by 8:00 A.M., when the American picket at Anvil's Tavern was attacked. No casualties were reported, as the troops in the tavern had made a hasty retreat. The British continued to march toward Chadds Ford. Forward units of Maxwell's brigade stationed at Kennett Meeting House, 3 miles west of Chadds Ford, engaged and eventually repulsed advance units of the enemy on the opposite side of the creek. The battle continued until Maxwell's troops were outnumbered by the arrival of Knyphausen's full column. After two hours, Maxwell ordered his men to fall back, and Knyphausen resumed his advance toward Chadds Ford. A mile west of the ford, Maxwell, with the remainder of his light infantry, attempted to inflict more damage upon the British columns. The British and their Hessian support had to clear Maxwell's troops from hill positions overlooking the valley. After about an hour's fighting, Maxwell was finally forced to withdraw to the opposite bank, assuming a new position with Greene's division.

With this success, Knyphausen was in control of the hills on the western side of the creek overlooking the valley. He was ordered to march and countermarch his troops on the hills to make his columns appear to be the main British force. The elevation of the British position made it impossible for the Americans to discern that Knyphausen's brigade was only a small part of the British force. Knyphausen also set about creating batteries of artillery to bombard the American positions in the valley below. Both sides exchanged cannon fire, with little damage to either.

Howe, Cornwallis, and the flanking column were also on the move, marching north up the Great Valley Road. At 11:00 A.M. the British column was approaching Jeffries' Ford, and forward units of Sullivan's troops began to report British troop movements north of their positions. Sullivan immediately sent an aide to Washington's command post to report the approach of the enemy columns. Washington, however, dismissed the reports and did nothing.

Only after the lull in the fighting near Chadds Ford did Washington begin to pay attention to reports of a British column to the north. Inspecting these, he decided on a bold plan. If the reports were true, he could attack Knyphausen's column and destroy it, as it must be unsupported. He ordered Greene to advance across the creek and attack the British positions. Greene's troops cleared some of the British forward positions but were ordered to withdraw when Washington received a third set of intelligence reports from Sullivan. This report, contradicting those sent earlier, described a second British force to the north. A scout who had been on the western side of the creek had seen no sign of British troops to the north. Assuming this report was correct meant that Greene's troops were potentially vulnerable to the entire British force. Believing this report, Washington had no choice but to withdraw Greene's troops and await a British attack across Chadds Ford.

By 2:00 P.M. Sullivan had received still more news of the elusive British forces. The latest reports indicated that a large body was indeed bearing down on Sullivan's positions from Jeffries' Ford, as indicated by earlier reports. Sullivan immediately advised Washington of the latest developments, forcing Washington to decide hastily what to believe. Washington ordered Sullivan to move his troops from the creek to the north and also directed troops under the command of Generals Stephen and Stirling to move from Chadds Ford to the north in order to create a defensive line near the Birmingham Meeting House. Sullivan's troops would take considerable time to wheel into position, and information on the size of the flanking British force was still lacking.

Stirling's troops created a defensive line on the western side of the road, with the meetinghouse in the center. Stephen's troops created a second defensive line on the meetinghouse's eastern side. The British approached over Osborne's Hill, giving Howe and Cornwallis the opportunity to observe the American lines forming a mile off. The British deployed from column into line formation and began to march down the hill toward the American lines. The 3rd (British) Brigade was held in reserve, and Howe remained on the hill to direct the attack.

Sullivan and his troops moved into the area, on the left of Stirling's lines, as the British light troops and American forward troops began to skirmish. The British immediately put pressure on Stirling's left flank. Meanwhile, Sullivan's troops ran into a British formation while they were still in column formation. The British seized the opportunity to attack and threw Sullivan's troops into disorder. The British next turned their attention to the right flank of Stephen's troops.

The various skirmishes gave way to the main battle, which finally commenced at 4:00 P.M. The American flanks were under considerable pressure and were being pushed into the center by the British attack. With no support, the center itself eventually collapsed under a bayonet charge. The Americans withdrew to a position in the rear, half a mile away.

Howe moved his headquarters to the meetinghouse as the focus of battle shifted to new American lines at Battle Hill. The British lines moved against the remnants of Sullivan's, Stirling's, and Stephen's troops on Battle Hill. Washington and his staff also moved to Battle Hill to assess the situation.

Before he moved, Washington ordered Greene and his division to move from Chadds Ford to Battle Hill to reinforce the crumbling American lines. The American positions on Battle Hill were becoming untenable.

When Greene arrived with his troops in the area of Battle Hill, he formed a line at Sandy Hollow, to the rear of the American positions. His men were tired after the march from Chadds Ford. The American forces who had already fought in the actions at Birmingham Meeting House and Battle Hill withdrew through Greene's line positioned at Sandy Hollow. The British came hard on the heels of the American withdrawal from Battle Hill, and Greene and his troops were able to deliver a devastating volley of fire. This stopped the British, but only for a moment; they came on again almost at once, obliging Greene to withdraw before a force that vastly outnumbered his own.

When the fighting at Birmingham Meeting House commenced, Knyphausen also began to move against Chadds Ford. Greene's withdrawal left only a small American force to hold Chadds Ford, but Maxwell's and Wayne's troops attempted to forestall the British advance. The American troops were compelled to withdraw from in front of Knyphausen's brigade as Cornwallis's troops approached from the north. Although they withdrew from the field, the Americans did not run; they retreated in fairly orderly fashion toward Chester.

The British achieved a victory at Brandywine, but the flanking attack and the heavy fighting at the Birmingham Meeting House, Battle Hill, and Sandy Hollow had left them unable to follow the American withdrawal and completely destroy Washington's forces. The Americans are estimated to have lost about 300 killed, 600 wounded, and 400 taken prisoner. British losses are estimated at just under 100 killed and about 400 wounded.

The British had successfully carried out a difficult flanking movement (known as oblique order) during the morning and early afternoon of the battle. British discipline on the march and in battle helped Howe and his commanders win the day. While Washington and Sullivan are partly responsible for the loss—due to lack of intelligence and reconnaissance on the American right flank—the Americans fought well against the British. In his official report to Congress, Washington noted this intelligence failure as a major cause of the defeat, but the ability of the Americans to cope with complicated linear maneuvers also deserves comment, as it highlighted the new American professionalism. Washington chose an excellent defensive position, and aside from the destruction of Sullivan's column, the Americans successfully regrouped into new defensive positions and delivered a devastating volley against the British. Cornwallis and Howe pointed out in their reports the ability of the Americans to deploy for battle. The Americans were able to fight through most of the day and to hold their ground; this steadfastness proved too tiring for the British, who were consequently unable to follow up their victory. Morale was high enough in the American units to prevent a speedy and disorganized withdrawal that could have proven costly for Washington's army and may have possibly even led to a full-scale rout. Instead, the Americans emerged with their forces largely intact and ready to continue the conflict.

Daniel Patrick Marston

See also

Alexander, William; Cooch's Bridge, Delaware, Action at; Cornwallis, Charles; German Mercenaries; Greene, Nathanael; Howe, William; Knyphausen, Wilhelm, Baron von; Long Island, Battle of; Loyalist Units; Maxwell, William; Stephen, Adam; Sullivan, John

References

André, John. *Major André's Journal: Operations of the British Army under Lieut. Generals Sir William Howe and Sir Henry Clinton.* Tarrytown, NY: New York Times, 1968.

Black, Jeremy. *War for America: The Fight for Independence.* Stroud, UK: Alan Sutton, 1991.

Canby, Henry S. *The Brandywine.* New York: Farrar and Rinehart, 1941.

Carrington, Henry B. *Battles of the American Revolution, 1775–1781.* 1876. Reprint, New York: Promontory, 1974.

Conway, Stephen. *The War of American Independence, 1775–1783.* London: Arnold, 1995.

Ewald, Johann. *Diary of the American War: A Hessian Journal.* New Haven, CT: Yale University Press, 1979.

Greene, Francis V. *The Revolutionary War and the Military Policy of the United States.* New York: Scribner, 1911.

Higginbotham, Don. *The War of American Independence: Military Attitudes, Policies, and Practice, 1763–1789.* New York: Macmillan, 1971.

Mackesy, Piers. *The War for America, 1775–1783.* 1965. Reprint, Lincoln: University of Nebraska Press, 1993.

Reed, John F. *Campaign to Valley Forge: July 1 to December 19, 1777.* Philadelphia: University of Pennsylvania Press, 1965.

Smith, Samuel. *The Battle of Brandywine.* Monmouth Beach, NJ: Philip Freneau, 1976.

Ward, Christopher. *War of the Revolution.* 2 vols. New York: Macmillan, 1952.

Wood, W. J. *Battles of the Revolutionary War, 1775–1781.* Chapel Hill, NC: Algonquin, 1990.

Brant, Joseph (1742–1807)

A powerful and dynamic Mohawk chief, Joseph Brant (whose Indian name was Thayendanegea, or He Places Two Bets) was born along the Ohio River during a hunting trip in 1742. Following his father's early death, he inherited his father's position as Mohawk chief. His mother later married an Indian known to the whites as Brant. Exactly when he adopted the name Joseph is not known, though it may have been at about this time.

Joseph Brant, a leading Mohawk chief, conducted numerous raids against Patriot frontier settlements, most notably in the Wyoming and Cherry Valleys, often with Loyalist aid. His warriors also participated in the fighting at Oriskany during the Saratoga Campaign of 1777. (National Archives and Records Administration)

At age thirteen young Brant joined Sir William Johnson's expedition to Lake George. Johnson, who was the common-law husband of Brant's older sister, Molly, took a liking to the young man and sent him to school. Brant attended a charity school for Native Americans in Lebanon, Connecticut, where he learned to speak English and studied the rudimentary elements of Western history and thought. His education and position allowed him to become an interpreter for the Anglican missionary John Stuart, with whom he worked to translate the Anglican prayer book and the Gospels into his native Mohawk language. In 1765 Brant joined the Episcopal Church, married, and fathered a son and daughter. Following the death of his wife, he married her half sister.

Brant accompanied Johnson during his Niagara expedition of 1759. No doubt due largely to his mentor's influence, Brant became a staunch supporter of the British, on whose side he fought during Pontiac's Rebellion. Brant's loyalty to the Crown never wavered. He traveled to England in 1775 and was presented to King George III. Upon his return, he persuaded four of the six nations in the Iroquois Confederacy to support the British cause (the Tuscaroras and Oneidas elected to ally themselves with the American colonies). Under Brant's charismatic leadership, the four nations of the Iroquois Confederacy inflicted a reign of terror across the northeastern frontier throughout the Revolution. Brant commanded native troops in the Battle of Oriskany on 6 August 1777 and in other actions along the Susquehanna River.

Brant is primarily known for his leadership during the Cherry Valley Massacre of 11 August 1778. He and his troops, primarily Indians but also including Loyalist forces under Colonel William Butler, attacked the fort and town at Cherry Valley, New York. The attackers killed more than 30 men, women, and children and took more than 71 prisoners in the raid. Brant withdrew his forces before the colonial reinforcements arrived the next day, but his actions at Cherry Valley brought general retribution to the entire region peopled by the Iroquois tribes. Major General John Sullivan led an expedition of more than 3,700 men against the Iroquois, destroying villages and fields. Indian raids continued until the end of the war in the region, but the Iroquois Confederacy did come to an end after the signing of the Treaty of Fort Stanwix in 1784.

After the war, Brant attempted to place himself as the representative of all of the British-allied tribes and secured land rights for himself and others in present-day Ontario. He continued to press his people to move closer to the British culture and adopt Christianity and British schooling practices. Brant died on 24 November 1807 on the Grand River in Ontario.

Kelly Hensley

See also

Cherry Valley Massacre; Johnson, Sir William

References

Brandt, Joseph. *Joseph Brandt Papers.* Chicago: University of Chicago Press, 1977.

Kelsay, Isabel. *Joseph Brant, 1743–1807: Man of Two Worlds.* New York: Syracuse University Press, 1986.

Briar Creek, Battle of (3 March 1779)

The British victory in the Battle of Briar Creek in March 1779 permitted the restoration of royal government in all of Georgia from that point on the Savannah River to the Atlantic coast.

Disappointed at the failure of large numbers of Loyalists to join him in Augusta, Georgia, and threatened by the arrival just across the Savannah River of 1,200 North Carolina troops under General John Ashe, British Lieutenant-Colonel Archibald Campbell abandoned his two-week occupation of

Augusta on 14 February 1779 and marched 25 miles to a camp at Boggy Gut on the Savannah River. His situation remained perilous. Ashe's North Carolinians, combined with General Andrew Williamson's South Carolina militiamen and Georgia's Continentals under General Samuel Elbert, formed a force of more than 2,000 men. Ashe assumed command of the entire force and ordered a pursuit of Campbell. In addition, farther south on the South Carolina side of the Savannah River, General Benjamin Lincoln's main army of some 4,000 men camped at Purrysburg, and General Griffith Rutherford had around 800 men at Black Swamp.

Campbell continued his retreat to Hudson's Ferry, below Briar Creek. On 20 February 1779, Lieutenant-Colonel James Mark Prevost, brother of General Augustine Prevost, the commanding British officer in Georgia, reached Campbell's camp and announced that he was now in charge of Campbell's 71st Highland Regiment and provincials, a force somewhat smaller than Ashe's. Campbell willingly released command and briefed Prevost on his situation. He predicted that Ashe would continue his pursuit as far as Briar Creek, and he showed Prevost how he might "amuse" Ashe by a demonstration against his front while most of the army circled around behind the rebel camp. Campbell then retired to Savannah on 26 February and began the business of setting up civil government, naming James Mark Prevost acting governor until the arrival from England of Governor James Wright.

To confront the British, Lincoln convened a council at Black Swamp on 1 March 1779 and decided to reinforce Ashe at the Briar Creek encampment. Ashe assured Lincoln that his position was secure. On 2 March, the British began a demonstration directly in front of Ashe's camp while Colonel Prevost with 900 men crossed upper Briar Creek and, on 3 March, approached the American position from the rear. Continental Colonel Leonard Marbury's rear guard raised the alarm at the British approach. Ashe's drums beat the long roll as his men took a position flanked by Briar Creek on one side and the swamps of the Savannah River on the other. His North Carolina militia formed the right and center, General Elbert's Georgians the left.

The British launched their assault at 3:00 P.M. on 3 March. Ashe later testified that his men did not stand for five minutes before beginning a panicked rout. Elbert's Georgians stood and fought but were all killed or captured. Many of the Americans drowned trying to swim across the Savannah River. A court-martial assembled by Lincoln blamed Ashe for not taking necessary precautions against a surprise attack but acquitted him of any lack of personal courage.

Edward J. Cashin

See also

Ashe, John; Augusta, Georgia, Operations at; Campbell, Archibald; Georgia; Lincoln, Benjamin

References

Campbell, Colin, ed. *Journal of an Expedition against the Rebels in Georgia in North America under the Orders of Archibald Campbell, Esquire, Lieutenant Colonel of His Majesty's 71st Regiment, 1778.* Darien, GA: Ashantilly, 1981.

Cashin, Edward. *The King's Ranger: Thomas Brown and the American Revolution on the Southern Frontier.* Athens: University of Georgia Press, 1989.

Jones, Charles C., Jr. *The History of Georgia.* 2 vols. Boston: Houghton, Mifflin, 1883.

Bristol, Rhode Island, Raid on (25 May 1778)

In the spring of 1778, British and Hessian troops raided the seaport town of Bristol, Rhode Island, destroying several houses and buildings and taking a number of residents prisoner. Located on the eastern shore of Narragansett Bay, Bristol faced the constant threat of attack during much of the Revolutionary War because of the British occupation of nearby Newport, Rhode Island's principal seaport and commercial center. Although spared the ordeal of British occupation, many of Bristol's residents experienced the destruction of their homes and property during the raid, which demonstrated the vulnerability of coastal towns that supported the cause of American independence.

Around daybreak on the morning of 25 May, a combined British and Hessian force of 500 men landed at Bristol and marched to the neighboring town of Warren. Their mission was to destroy a flotilla of flat-bottomed boats in the Kickemuit River at Warren. The boats were used by American forces for transporting men and supplies around Narragansett Bay and were thought to be part of an upcoming American expedition against the British in Newport. After setting fire to the boats, the British and Hessians returned to Bristol.

Marching down Hope Street, they set fire to eighteen houses, St. Michael's Episcopal Church, and several smaller buildings. The houses and buildings belonged to Bristol residents who were known to be prominent Patriots or were used as barracks and storage facilities for American forces. The British believed that the crypt underneath the church housed a storage site for arms and a powder magazine. Approximately thirty townspeople were taken prisoner during the raid.

Soon after the British and Hessian soldiers had landed in Bristol, local residents sent word of the raid and a call for help to Major General John Sullivan, the Continental Army commander in Rhode Island. News of the raid reached Sullivan's headquarters in Providence around eight o'clock in the morning. Sullivan ordered local militia under the command of Colonel William Barton to set out for Bristol in order to harass and delay the British and Hessians until Continental troops could arrive. The militia briefly engaged the British rear as it was departing Bristol. Four Americans, including Barton, were wounded along with several British soldiers. The British and Hessian force and the prisoners departed by water at Bristol Ferry, on the narrow channel between Bristol and Aquidneck Island (the island on which Newport is located), and returned to the British base at Newport before any Continental troops arrived. The Bristol residents captured during the raid were later released in a prisoner exchange with the British.

William P. Leeman

See also

Barton, William; German Mercenaries; Rhode Island; Sullivan, John

References

Howe, George. *Mount Hope: A New England Chronicle.* New York: Viking, 1959.

McLoughlin, William G. *Rhode Island: A History.* New York: Norton, 1978.

Munro, Wilfred H. *The History of Bristol, R.I.: The Story of the Mount Hope Lands, from the Visit of the Northmen to the Present Time.* Providence: J. A. and R. A. Reid, 1880.

Britain

See Great Britain

British Army

Reviled by many nineteenth-century historians, particularly in the United States, the British soldier of the American Revolutionary War has, for the most part, received rather a poor billing at the hands of students of military history, notwithstanding a generally admirable record in the war. Reasonably becoming in his conduct though occasionally prone to excess, the British soldier displayed exceptional courage and discipline and submitted to extreme hardship with little complaint. When the war ended, the redcoat returned home under very unusual circumstances in the history of the British Army: defeated, in spite of many battlefield victories, in stark contrast to the more usual tradition of eventual victory after initial disaster.

Until 1763 the British Army helped defend the thirteen American colonies against the French in Canada and served on the frontiers against the Indians. With the conquest of Canada, however, and the final ejection of the French from North America, the army rapidly became an unpopular institution. Billeted among the population and perceived by many American colonists as expensive and a bad influence on the populace of the garrison towns, particularly Boston, the British Army found itself even more unpopular as a result of its unenviable responsibility for having to quell civil disturbances. As such, the army was viewed as a nuisance at best and an oppressive occupying force at worst.

In stark contrast to its continental European counterparts, the British Army was a small institution, as the bulk of the nation's defense expenditure and resources went to the Royal Navy—the country's first line of defense and the basis for the protection of its maritime trade. At the outbreak of war the army numbered around 48,500 men, with just over 11,500 of these stationed in North America. The remaining 37,000 men formed garrisons in England, Ireland, Scotland, the West Indies, Africa, Minorca, India, and Gibraltar. By the middle of 1776 the number in America had increased to 27,000 men, reaching a maximum strength of 56,000 in 1781, by which time the army's total strength worldwide stood at 110,000.

Small though these numbers were by European standards, the military authorities in London still experienced great difficulties recruiting sufficient men to bring the army up to required strength. This was the consequence of two factors: dreadful service conditions—whether at home or on campaign—and the fact that the lower classes, the prime source of recruits, often supported the Americans' struggle for independence and were thus loath to serve against a people whom they regarded as fellow Englishmen.

Low pay numbered among the more unpopular aspects of the conditions of service. The lowest rank received less than one shilling a day, and with the usual deductions for equipment, clothing, replacements for lost property, and other costs, the ordinary man in the ranks had hardly enough to live on, much less take part in any form of entertainment that cost money. Ordinary civilian laborers or semiskilled craftsmen were often much better off than soldiers, and what plunder there was to be had on the battlefield and on the march naturally became highly sought after. If men thought themselves poorly paid, other forms of recognition were nonexistent: neither bravery nor even simple service on campaign was as yet rewarded in the form of medals or decorations.

Soldiers were also often abused and ridiculed by the populace as a burden on the public purse at best and as natural enemies of public liberty at worst—evidence that memories of Cromwell's regime more than a century before had not entirely faded. Finally, and most obviously, army life offered tangible danger and often death from wounds or disease in a far-off land. All of these circumstances explain why officers were reluctant to retire old soldiers, however unfit or inefficient they might be, since they were difficult to replace. It is thus unsurprising that the government was not particular about the type of recruit required to fill the ranks of the army.

Unattractive as the prospects for ordinary soldiers were, all sorts of means were devised to maintain numbers. Some

British infantry advance against the American redoubt at the Battle of Bunker Hill, 17 June 1775. Though highly trained and disciplined, even the most determined troops faltered under the destructive hail of fire directed against them by entrenched colonial militia. (Library of Congress)

were "enlisted" by press gangs and kidnapping parties, while genuine volunteers were often those facing unemployment and near starvation in civilian life. Recruiting sergeants glamorized life in the ranks, regaled men with stories of adventure overseas, and offered the newly enlisted soldier an attractive uniform and a handsome bounty. Glory in battle, free food and accommodation, and long-term employment in an age bereft of practically any relief for the poor offered, in the end, some compensation. The lure of a £3 bounty for enlistment for the ordinary foot regiments and £6 for the Guards was also tempting, but much of it was frittered away by the new recruit in the first few days after "taking the King's shilling." Normally, Roman Catholics were not sought to fill the ordinary ranks—and both the law and army regulations explicitly banned them from the officer corps—but the pressing need for men led to the system being relaxed for the rank and file. Drastic measures were sometimes used, the authorities often resorting to drawing upon convicts as a ready source of young men and a means of alleviating prison overcrowding. Indeed, at least three regiments were almost entirely composed of prisoners. In pressing times, military authorities sometimes resorted to taking soldiers long since pensioned off after lengthy service or previously discharged as invalids.

Notwithstanding these various expedients, the Crown had to raise mercenary troops—eventually 30,000 of them—from among the smaller German principalities and even approached Tsarina Catherine of Russia for 20,000 mercenaries (though no agreement was concluded). Large numbers of Scots came forward, partly to relieve poverty, but mostly because entrenched military traditions and respect for the profession of arms—especially in the Highlands—made service more attractive than in England. At the beginning of the war, age limits for recruits stood at seventeen to forty-five years old, with service for five years or until the end of hostilities. But even these standards were relaxed as the conflict dragged on.

Once enlisted, a recruit had to face the long journey across the Atlantic, often in dreadful conditions and lasting from four to six weeks, before arrival at Boston, New York, Newport, or Halifax. Desertion was high, both in Britain and in America. The death sentence awaited anyone caught deserting, but a strong financial incentive encouraged men to take the risk, for a greedy (and fearless) recruit could enlist in one regiment and claim his bounty before absconding to another town, where he could enlist under another name and thus claim another bounty. If he chose to desert in America, language posed no barrier to swift integration, and anonymity (at least in the cities) and the chance to settle down in a new land and make a fresh start certainly attracted some soldiers.

The basic unit of the British Army was the regiment. A soldier identified with it as his adoptive family. To his regiment the soldier was usually exceedingly loyal, proud of its record in battle and of its history, which was regularly commemorated by its members in rituals and social occasions of various kinds. Nearly all units in America were infantry. The mainstay of practically every army before and since has consisted of the foot soldier, and the North American terrain did not suit cavalry and artillery nearly so well. At the time of the American Revolution, a British infantry regiment was composed of about 450 men: eight companies of ordinary musketeers plus one company of grenadiers deployed on the right and one company of light infantry on the left.

These two flanking companies were considered the elite of the regiment. Grenadiers were chosen from among the tallest, strongest men and were often used to lead a charge, especially of fortified positions. Although they no longer hurled grenades at close range, as had their predecessors under the Duke of Marlborough at the beginning of the century, the designation of "grenadier" remained, and these men continued to represent the cream of each regiment.

The light company troops were drawn from smaller, independent-minded, more nimble men used for skirmishing. These had been employed in small numbers during the Seven Years' War (1756–1763) and thus were not an entirely new innovation. Nevertheless, the British Army was not yet truly adept at this form of fighting and would not attain expertise in skirmishing until the era of reforms inaugurated by Sir John Moore at the beginning of the Napoleonic Wars a generation later. Still, there were new units, such as the 60th Foot, that carried rifles and wore forest green uniforms—an early instance of camouflage—to counter concealed American sharpshooters in an era otherwise noted for its sartorial splendor of garishly colorful and impractical uniforms. The adoption of the rifle was a matter of necessity, for many American backwoodsmen were armed with the famous Pennsylvania version of that weapon and were accustomed to frontier living and fighting conditions in forests or on broken ground. Rifles were much slower to load but were several times more accurate than the standard smoothbore musket.

Only two regiments of cavalry—the 16th and 17th Light Dragoons—served in America, with a tiny strength of about 230 men each, though Loyalist units operating with British regulars were often mounted. The Royal Artillery supplied a complement of batteries, but like the cavalry, the drivers with their guns limbered often had to struggle over primitive roads and trails and experienced difficulty obtaining supplies of ammunition and fodder, thus rendering them less effective. These physical and logistical handicaps meant that these arms were not as well represented in America as on European battlefields.

Artillery pieces were very heavy: a 6-pounder with its carriage weighed between 850 and 1,200 pounds and required six horses and a requisite amount of forage. The average number of guns was about three pieces for every 1,000 men, with batteries mounting four 3-pounder or 6-pounder brass guns (cannon), but some with ordnance firing as heavy as a 12-pound round shot (today popularly known as a cannonball). Round shot was the usual form of ordnance. It contained no charge inside; as a solid iron sphere, it simply bowled over men and horses, creating gaps in the enemy ranks that were sometimes several files deep. Rapid in flight though a round shot might be, a careful observer could track its course, and a soldier finding himself a potential target could virtually dodge this deadly projectile if he was nimble enough and stood in isolation. For those standing shoulder to shoulder in the ranks—as the tactics of the day dictated—there was no escape, and sergeants and officers regarded as cowards those who "ducked" to avoid enemy fire. Round shot in flight was lethal enough, but in dry conditions it often bounced or bounded along the surface of the ground for considerable distances, with its greatest effective range about 1,000 yards.

Cavalry constituted the smallest arm of British forces in America. The most important function of the cavalry was the charge, particularly on the wide-open battlefields of the Low Countries, France, and Germany. Rough terrain and forests in North America usually precluded the use of the mounted arm in this way, and in any event cavalry were never present in sufficient numbers to operate as the shock troops that they functioned as in Europe. Patrolling and scouting were thus paramount. However, intelligence gathering, essential to any army, was poor, since British forces suffered from an acute shortage of cavalry. Indeed, on many occasions the lack of horses compelled cavalry troopers to serve on foot. While mounted, the Light Dragoons in the American theater of operations carried a flintlock carbine with a twenty-nine-inch barrel, a pair of pistols, and a curved sword used for slashing rather than the heavier, straight saber used by their counterparts in the "heavy" regiments.

The very rigid class system that pervaded eighteenth-century British society was reflected in the officer corps of the army even more powerfully than in civilian life. Commissions were obtained almost exclusively through purchase, which meant that families with sufficient wealth were able to buy responsible positions in the army for sons who were often as young as fourteen years old. The lowest officer rank was an ensign in the infantry and cornet in the cavalry; men so commissioned had to wait for a vacant lieutenancy to become available in order to receive promotion. This was possible through a promotion higher up the ranks, which in turn left room for the advancement of a junior officer. No commissions could be purchased in the artillery, where technical expertise was required. The opportunity for advancement was more rapid in wartime for the obvious reason that a soldier could distinguish himself in battle and thus become eligible for a brevet appointment. More commonly, of course, vacancies appeared as the result of fellow officers' deaths. This was particularly so after the Battle of Bunker Hill, where infantry officers were shot down in disproportionately large numbers by rebel militia who designated them as special targets.

Officers certainly held privileged positions, but on the other hand they were expected to lead from the front and consequently bore the brunt of the fighting, and thus faced the greatest risks. The higher ranks were often mounted and, being easily distinguishable, were easy targets. They were also set apart from the men in the ranks because they carried swords and wore a different hat and a more resplendent uniform, complete with gold braid. Apart from the Royal Military Academy at Woolwich, which trained officers in the artillery, there were no formal military colleges at the time for new officers. They consequently took the field with no formal military training and were therefore obliged to obtain what advice there was to be had from those already serving. The Royal Military Academy at Sandhurst was still a generation in the future.

Nearly all officers, particularly in the higher ranks, were classed as gentlemen, a designation that implied well-educated men of independent means who were loyal to the king and for whom service to the nation was the natural responsibility of their privileged position in society. This system was by definition entirely undemocratic and did not even benefit from a merit structure, yet it functioned surprisingly well since such men, accustomed to a strict social hierarchy, were used to giving instructions to their social inferiors and regarded command of troops as a natural extension of what already existed in civilian society, albeit not quite as rigidly. An officer corps drawn from the social elite was all the more natural in light of the fact that men suited to becoming officers were generally accustomed to handling weapons on the hunt and, similarly, could ride and maintain a horse—an expensive commodity in the eighteenth century. They were also expected to supply, at their own expense, their weapons and uniforms and maintain a high standard of appearance. This lavish expenditure ensured that only men of means could maintain the standards and lifestyle expected of an officer.

Securing a commission from the ranks was almost impossible. If an able soldier did manage this, he normally remained in a static position as a junior officer, lieutenant, or captain for the remainder of his career, not having the necessary funds to achieve promotion through the purchase of a commission. This left a fighting force top-heavy with a high proportion of inexperienced teenagers and old men as junior officers. A proper system of promoting good officers through merit, rather than through financial status, was not to appear for another century.

This was very much the age of the amateur. There was no organized mess; officers amused themselves by drinking and gambling, much like the troops and often at the expense of military responsibilities. Officers had little contact with their men and frequently neglected their duties. It was commonplace, for instance, for regimental colonels to be absent from regiments serving in the field due to parliamentary responsibilities back in Britain.

Uniforms were elaborate and often impractical in campaign conditions. The nature of the eighteenth-century battlefield partly explains the brightness of uniforms, which were not simply the product of the sartorial splendor of the era but performed the vital function of identification on battlefields obscured by the thick white smoke produced by musket and artillery fire. The infantry wore the famous scarlet jacket, hence the nickname "redcoat" attributed to the British soldier. He also wore a felt hat, coarse linen shirt, and waistcoat. Tight-fitting white breeches were worn in summer, tan in winter. Over these garments the men wore black or white gaiters that, depending on the season, were buttoned up to the knee. British soldiers were well equipped insofar as they carried all that was required on campaign, but their uniforms were ill-suited to both the North American climate and topography. The tight-fitting uniform proved particularly uncomfortable in the humidity of an American summer, especially in the South. In short, the uniform was a magnificent sight on the battlefield and parade ground, but the wearer could not have been comfortable, especially on the march.

If his uniform was not enough of a nuisance, the infantryman was burdened with all manner of paraphernalia, including a musket, bayonet, cartridge pouch, water bottle, knapsack, and a haversack in which he kept his rations—usually of sufficient bread, flour, and biscuits for four days' consumption. His rations could also include cheese, rice, oil, pork, beef, and oatmeal. With sixty rounds of ammunition and all his other equipment, the infantryman's burden weighed about sixty pounds. On campaign, of course, difficulties of supply made modification and improvisation of his uniform and equipment necessary, and resourceful soldiers acquired local materials whenever possible. It was not long into a campaign before the appearance of the troops became rather different from that seen back home.

Once in the army the recruit resigned himself to iron discipline under threat of the lash. A soldier's waking hours were occupied by guard duties, cleaning, repairing equipment, and four hours of drilling every day except Sundays. The eighteenth century was a period notorious for heavy drinking by all sections of society, and soldiers, who had to endure months of boredom in the absence of fighting, were often half drunk on the parade ground, sometimes with their officers and noncommissioned officers drilling them while in a similar state of inebriation. Soldiers with wives and children did not see them for years, if ever again, and written permission was required from officers for ordinary ranks to marry. All but a handful of wives remained in Britain; only six wives per company were usually permitted to accompany their husbands on campaign. Such women washed clothes, tended to the sick and wounded, and supplemented their income by selling food or clothing. Thus, conditions for the rank and file were not high, and these "dregs of society," as they were sometimes described, had little opportunity for improving their lot in life.

Infantry tactics of the period depended almost entirely on their weapons' capabilities, the standard firearm being the Brown Bess musket, in use since the Duke of Marlborough's time and the most effective handheld weapon in the world at that time. This was a single-shot, smoothbore flintlock firearm, loaded down the muzzle, that could be supplemented with a socket bayonet fitted to the muzzle. The Brown Bess, which fired a round lead ball approximately three quarters of an inch in diameter and about one ounce in weight, inflicted hideous wounds. The musket ball itself was contained with its charge of powder in a paper cartridge, the end of which the soldier bit off with his teeth in order to prime the charge. His musket weighed about fourteen pounds, with a barrel measuring either forty-two or forty-six inches long.

The Brown Bess suffered from several deficiencies, especially in the rain. When wet, an infantryman's powder became unusable. Even high wind posed problems, since it could blow the priming out of the pan. In either case, the soldier was left with a weapon that could only be crudely wielded as a club or used to thrust with the bayonet. As the bayonet did not interfere with loading (being fitted by a ring around the muzzle), it was customary for the infantry to go into battle with bayonets fixed. Even in the best conditions—on a clear, windless, dry day—the flintlock musket was hopelessly inaccurate at all but the closest ranges. Even a veteran soldier was unlikely to strike a target more than 100 yards away, as his weapon had no rifling (a series of grooves in the barrel that enabled the ball to spin, thus increasing its accuracy). With a smooth rather than rifled bore, the ball assumed an erratic path from the moment it left the barrel. Beyond 200 yards a volley was effectively wasted.

The slow rate of fire posed another problem with the weapon. The process of loading and firing was cumbersome and therefore time-consuming; even an experienced soldier seldom discharged his weapon more than three times a minute. The pace was set by the officers, who shouted commands—an altogether noisy, frightening, not to mention exceedingly lethal business. The process of loading and firing by platoons involved twelve separate commands, or evolutions, endlessly drilled into the soldier so that he performed these essential functions almost by instinct. Even if he carried out all these maneuvers correctly, his musket was liable to misfire due to exposure to moisture or become clogged with burnt powder. Worst of all, a soldier might fail to realize that his weapon had misfired and continue to ram a second or third round down the barrel. Under these circumstances, once discharged the weapon was likely to explode in the firer's face, causing frightful burns and mutilation, if not death to himself and sometimes to his comrades immediately beside him.

These various limitations naturally dictated the tactics of British (and indeed all other European) infantry of the eighteenth century. To compensate for inaccuracy, soldiers were deployed in long, two-rank lines, shoulder to shoulder (known as close order), with officers immediately at hand so their orders could be heard and steadiness maintained. The objective of such a formation was to strike and repel enemy units through frequency of fire. Thus, the secret to success lay not in accuracy but in discipline. Troops had to maintain their nerve under imminent threat of death; they had to offer a steady rate of fire amid the screams of the wounded, the shouts of the officers, and the deafening roar of the muskets discharged immediately beside and behind them. And if this was not enough to unnerve a man, it all took place amid acrid smoke obscuring his vision and with round shot hurtling through the ranks. In short, if a regiment could keep up a more concentrated hail of shot than its immediate opponents, it was more likely to prevail.

British troops were renowned throughout Europe for their ability to carry out these functions methodically, a fact partly attributable to their study of Prussian methods developed by the tactical genius of Frederick the Great. Troops were also trained to move and fight in line and column and to march and wheel in exact cadence. All this was of course well and good on the parade ground, but in the heat of battle officers and noncommissioned officers had to sometimes literally beat the men with the flats of their swords to steady the ranks and maintain regular fire. Little attempt, however, was made at maneuvering for advantage once on the battlefield. Both sides normally proceeded to deliver deadly close-range volleys at one another until one side began to falter. When a man fell—and frequently whole files fell amid what amounted to two firing squads pitted against each other—those who remained standing were expected to methodically close the gaps and carry on with the fusillade. A bayonet charge generally decided the issue, though troops seldom actually came to physical blows with their weapons: one side usually broke and ran before contact was made.

Almost no attention or resources were devoted to the injured; hospitals in the field were akin to butchers' shops, with the chances of survival for the severely wounded greatly diminished by the doctors' ignorance of the causes of infection or even basic hygiene. Fallen soldiers staggered or crawled to the rear if they could; otherwise, they lay where they fell, hoping that drummer boys would take them away, laid across two muskets or a makeshift stretcher. No horse-drawn ambulance service existed, nor was there any formal procedure for the evacuation of the wounded. Even when they received medical attention, there was no triage or any concept of giving priority to the most seriously wounded. Patients were generally seen in the order in which they arrived, though rank could take precedence. Musket balls and artillery shell fragments had to be probed for and extracted from the body, or the resulting infection usually proved fatal. If a projectile smashed an extremity, amputation was nearly always standard procedure, barring which the likely onset of gangrene would soon kill the victim.

Surgeons were shockingly few in number and consequently constantly overworked; during and after combat they were usually unable to cope with their regiment's casualties. Nor were surgeons particularly well regarded. Their low social standing reflected an age in which the medical profession had yet to attain general respectability; indeed, that change was not to come about for more than two generations. Medical staff attempted to offer help under extremely difficult conditions while equipped with crude and inadequate medical supplies. In fact, a surgeon had to supply his own medical instruments. Knives, bone saws, bandages, ointments, splints, and other equipment were always scarce, and during surgery frequent use was made of the same sponge for a succession of patients. This practice, in combination with the absence of antiseptics, led to many wounds becoming infected. Proper anesthetics were unknown at this time; the only recourse available to the wounded soldier facing the surgeon's knife was a bullet on which to bite or raw spirits to render him semiconscious. Not surprisingly, a large number of men died of shock during such an ordeal.

The importance of fatalities resulting from combat should not be overemphasized, however. For more than a century after the American Revolutionary War, the overwhelming majority of British soldiers still succumbed to disease, not to wounds received in combat. This was particularly so in the West Indies; being transferred there was tantamount to a death sentence. Yellow fever, malaria, typhoid, cholera, and other diseases, tropical or otherwise, dispatched thousands of men without so much as an enemy in sight. The real tragedy was that during this period, there was no understanding that a regiment ought to have been withdrawn, at least temporarily, from such inhospitable places at certain times of the year. Nor was it properly understood that regiments unaccustomed to the conditions and climate of the Caribbean should not be exposed to its rigors during the hotter months of the year. In short, ignorance of the causes of—much less cures for—such diseases led to thousands of noncombat deaths.

Although the British Army may rightly claim to have constituted one of the leading military institutions of the late eighteenth century, also important are the causes of its greatest defeat—against the American colonists. Failure cannot be attributed to a want of courage or training on the part of officers and men. Their conduct at Bunker Hill offers the seminal example of the doggedness and discipline shown by British soldiers at the time. Moreover, British troops almost invariably succeeded in the pitched battles of the war. In the army's two great disasters—at Saratoga and at Yorktown—these capitulations were due less to any inadequacies of the British troops themselves than to the lack of supplies and poor planning by senior officers in the first case and to poor planning and extremely faulty cooperation between the army and navy in the second. Foreign intervention also played a crucial role in British defeat—a fact that has been played down in American historiography.

Other factors help explain the failure of the British Army to secure victory. Immense physical obstacles in the form of vast distances, poor roads, dense forests, and extreme temperature took a heavy toll on the troops. Poor and insufficient food sapped energy and morale, exacerbated by sparsely populated areas that could not support the needs of the troops. Unlike Europe, the American colonies possessed no large fortified towns whose possession secured control over a wide area to the garrison. There was no sense of clear strategy on a grand scale, leaving the men at the bottom to fight battles that consistently defeated American forces but ultimately reduced British numbers until the army could not carry out what faulty plans strategists in London had formulated. Finally, most senior commanders had learned their trade on the battlefields of Europe during the Seven Years' War. Such men, schooled in traditional eighteenth-century warfare, found it difficult to adapt formal, linear tactics to the special circumstances of North America, with no lines of fortresses, primitive or nonexistent roads, vast distances, and the absence of large population centers capable of providing supply, entertainment, billeting, and transport for large numbers of troops.

Gregory Fremont-Barnes

See also
Continental Army; French Army; German Mercenaries; Loyalist Units; Musket; Rifle
References
Buckley, Roger. *The British Army in the West Indies: Society and the Military in the Revolutionary Age.* Gainesville: University Press of Florida, 1998.
Curtis, Edward. *The Organization of the British Army in the American Revolution.* New Haven, CT: Yale University Press, 1926.
Fortescue, John. *The War of Independence: The British Army in North America, 1775–1783.* London: Greenhill, 2001.
Frey, Sylvia. *The British Soldier in America: A Social History of Military Life in the Revolutionary Period.* Austin: University of Texas Press, 1981.
Holmes, Richard. *Redcoat: The British Soldier in the Age of Horse and Musket.* London: HarperCollins, 2001.
Houlding, J. A. *Fit for Service: The Training of the British Army, 1715–1795.* Oxford, UK: Clarendon, 1981.
Kemp, Alan. *The British Army in the American Revolution.* London: Almark, 1973.
May, Robin, and Gerry Embleton. *The British Army in North America, 1775–1783.* Oxford, UK: Osprey, 1997.
Mollo, John. *Uniforms of the American Revolution.* New York: Sterling, 1991.
Reid, Stuart. *British Redcoat, 1740–93.* Oxford, UK: Osprey, 1997.
———. *King George's Army, 1740–93.* 2 vols. Oxford, UK: Osprey, 1995.
———. *Redcoat Officer, 1740–1815.* Oxford, UK: Osprey, 2002.
Shy, John. *Toward Lexington: The Role of the British Army in the Coming of the American Revolution.* Princeton, NJ: Princeton University Press, 1965.

British Navy

See Royal Navy

British Parliament

Parliament is the bicameral national legislature of Great Britain (from 1707 consisting of England, Wales, and Scotland; Ireland, though a British possession, had its own parliament in Dublin). Origins of Parliament can be traced to the medieval period of English history when a council of lords, known as the Curia Regis, acted as advisors to the king. This advisory council evolved into the upper chamber of today's Parliament, the House of Lords. The lower chamber, the House of Commons, originated in the thirteenth century from periodic meetings of knights and burgesses. The first Parliament was called in 1265 and in succeeding centuries gained greater governmental power at the expense of an ever-weakening monarchy. The power struggle between Parliament and the monarchy was settled in 1689 when the English

William Pitt, 1st Earl of Chatham (1708–1778), speaking in the House of Lords. (Library of Congress)

Bill of Rights was passed by Parliament, effectively placing the sole power of policymaking in the hands of the elected body.

The strength of Parliament's unity was tested during the eighteenth century as competing factions within the legislative body debated the future of the American colonies. During this era, governmental power was shared more evenly between Parliament, the monarchy, and an emerging prime ministerial office, with each attempting to take a more guiding role in policy. The debates in government focused on a few main issues: an attempt to increase revenue for the Crown, military garrisons in the colonies, and the delicate balance of adequate representation in government.

Upon his ascension to the throne in 1760, King George III, feeling as though the monarchy's power was slipping through his grasp, focused his political strategy on destroying the system of cabinet government and taking more power for the Crown. He was against any reform in Parliament, the emancipation of Roman Catholics, and the relaxation of the Irish commercial laws and was steadfast in his opposition to concessions to the American colonies. George Grenville, prime minister from 1763 to 1765 and a narrow-minded constitutional formalist, echoed the king's attitude toward the colonies. Combining the offices of prime minister and chancellor of the Exchequer, he focused much of his efforts on economic objectives such as raising revenue and controlling trade to the colonies.

Grenville was the scourge of American political rights. He argued that virtual representation in Parliament required the colonists to compensate the Crown for benefits received, such as defense and trading rights. Under Grenville's leadership, Parliament passed the Stamp Act in 1765 to help defray the war debt accumulated while fighting France for control of North America. Following shortly on the heels of the Stamp Act, Parliament, under the leadership of Charles Townshend, British chancellor of the Exchequer, passed the Townshend Acts that imposed taxes to balance the British budget. Both the Townshend duties and the Stamp Act caused voracious debates not only in the chambers of Parliament but also across Britain and in the American colonies.

The average Briton agreed that the colonists should contribute to the Crown, but there were others who were not as convinced of Parliament's policies concerning the colonies. Debates arose regarding the right of Parliament to levy internal versus external taxes on the colonies. Unlike Grenville and Townshend, who had ultimate faith in Parliament's sovereign powers, William Pitt the Elder, prime minister from 1757 to 1761 and from 1766 to 1768, and political philosopher Edmund Burke argued that the government was not infallible and was in fact at odds with the will of the populace. Burke's pamphlet *Thoughts on the Cause of the Present Discontents* (1770) argued that although the actions of both the monarchy and Parliament were not against the letter of the constitution, they violated the spirit of the document by upsetting the delicate balance shared between England and her American subjects. Unrepresentative government, Burke argued, was dangerously at odds with the manifest will of the people. Both Burke and Pitt sought to bridge the widening gap between the English government and the colonies by restoring a mutual confidence between them.

Many of the same arguments made by Burke and Pitt were echoed on the other side of the Atlantic. Most fervent of these was the contention that the taxes levied upon the American colonies were not used to limit trade or to fund the protection of the colonies as Parliament had declared; instead, they were a means to increase internal revenue for the Crown. For the colonists, the power to tax was the power to destroy.

The colonies, after years of intermittent and inefficient control by the British, had become self-governing and self-regulating with regard to their internal affairs. Unlike the British Parliament, representation in the colonial legislatures was apportioned on a territorial basis, constantly adapting to suit the changing conditions in each colony. The colonists held fervently to the system of actual representation, something they did not have in Parliament. American statesman James Otis, an ardent supporter of colonial rights, argued in the 1765 Stamp Act Congress that Americans were not bound to yield obedience to laws they had no share in creating: no taxation without representation.

The debates over colonial taxation created two factions. The first supported the rights and will of the people and was advocated for by Pitt, Burke, and Otis. In opposition, Grenville, Townshend, and King George III argued for the infallibility of the English Crown and Parliament. British imperial policy ignored the efforts made by its challengers. Without political recourse in London, the American colonists acted in retaliatory response with riots, protests, and boycotts. The seed of the American Revolution was sown.

See also

Burke, Edmund; George III, King of England; Otis, James, Jr.; Pitt, William, the Elder; Pitt, William, the Younger; Stamp Act; Townshend, Charles; Townshend Acts; Wilkes, John

References

Channing, Edward. *A Students' History of the United States.* New York: Macmillan, 1902.

Smith, Goldwin. *A History of England.* 3rd ed. New York: Scribner, 1966.

Webb, R. K. *Modern England: From the 18th Century to the Present.* New York: Dodd, Mead, 1968.

British West Indies

The thirteen rebelling colonies in North America comprised only half the colonies of British America in 1776. The majority and wealthiest of the other colonies were in the Caribbean (Antigua, Barbados, Dominica, Grenada, Jamaica, Montserrat, Nevis, St. Kitts, St. Vincent, Tobago, and Tortola). Britain persisted in the war for America at least partly in the belief that the loss of the thirteen colonies might also entail the loss of the British West Indies and the rest of the British Empire. George III and his ministers regarded the possession of the island colonies as essential for generating the wealth to wage the war and to sustain national greatness. As France prepared to enter the war in alliance with the United States, the British government agonized over whether to abandon the war in America to launch offensive operations in the Caribbean.

The islands were closely associated with the mainland colonies by their proximity and trade. They shared similar political developments, including the rise of elected assemblies, and a similar political ideology to North America. Their plantation system was analogous to the economies of the southern mainland colonies, especially that of South Carolina. Yet when revolution came, the majority of the white island colonists did not side with their compatriots on the mainland. The divergence was anticipated in the 1760s. West Indians not only lobbied for the Sugar (Revenue) Act—the first direct imperial tax in America—but also campaigned for

Siege of the British fort on Brimstone Hill, on St. Kitts. In January 1782 Admiral François de Grasse landed 8,000 troops at Basseterre and proceeded to reduce the island's defenses, taking Brimstone Hill three weeks later. (Library of Congress)

higher duties after 1764 as a way of excluding cheaper French sugar from the North American market. In contrast to all the thirteen mainland colonies, Jamaica and Barbados submitted to the Stamp Act. There were Stamp Act riots on St. Kitts and Nevis, but they only occurred after threats of what amounted to an economic boycott by the mainland Patriots. These smaller islands risked a famine and the associated danger of a slave rebellion if they complied with the Stamp Act.

After the repeal of the Stamp Act in 1766, the British West Indies remained aloof from the growing imperial crisis until the eve of the Revolutionary War. Parochial disputes about the corporate privileges of the island assemblies transcended the larger imperial crisis in the British West Indies. In contrast to the political crisis in North America, imperial tensions in the islands did not mount to a climactic breakdown between the legislatures and the governors in the 1770s. West Indians conspicuously failed to join the pamphlet campaign against Britain. They did not set up extraparliamentary opposition groups, and they made no attempt at federation. Like the American Loyalists, they objected to imperial taxes but believed in obedience to authority. They sought to direct the internal affairs of their colonies and obtain local autonomy within the British Empire. They specifically denied claims of coequality between their assemblies and Parliament. They continued to affirm their belief in parliamentary sovereignty at the time of the Declaration of Independence.

The difference in their reaction to imperial policies from the mainland colonies was due partly to the eighteenth-century sugar revolution that made the British West Indies economically dependent on Britain. Sugar was the primary produce of the British West Indies. For most of the eighteenth century, the island colonies were unable to compete with the price of rival French sugar. So great was the price differential that the British West Indies rapidly lost its market share to the French in both Europe and North America. Only the monopoly of the British market enabled West Indians to flourish. The labor-intensive requirements of sugar and the profits of sugar planting were the primary reasons for the increasing proportion of black slaves. Slavery also made the white colonists militarily dependent on Britain. The white colonists encouraged the presence of metropolitan troops and petitioned for larger peacetime garrisons.

The immense wealth derived from the sugar plantations enabled elite planters to return home to Britain to escape the

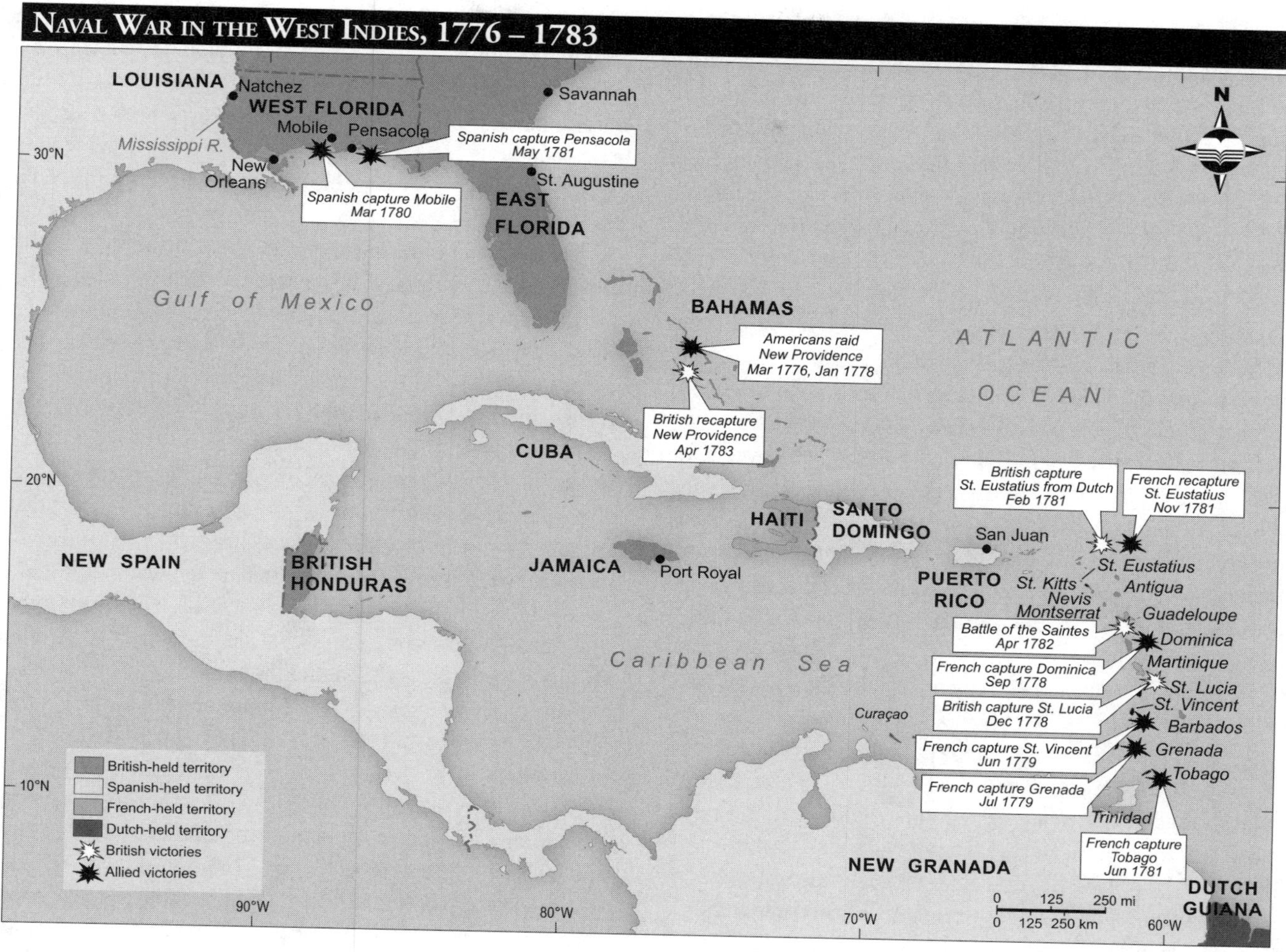

uncertainty of life in the tropics, where they were exposed to high mortality rates, hurricanes, slave revolts, and the threat of foreign conquest. The absence of so many sugar tycoons hindered the development of infrastructure, such as schools and colleges, within the islands, and this reinforced the tendency of the planters to return to Britain. The development of a white settler society was additionally hindered by high mortality rates, low fertility rates, and unbalanced sex ratios that kept the white population small in relation to that of North America. The geographical isolation of the islands also restrained the development of a political federation within the British West Indies. In an era when a British identity was often defined in opposition to the national character of the French, the white colonists identified with Britain for protection against the threat of French expansion in the Caribbean.

The British West Indies stood to gain nothing from the American Revolutionary War. They dreaded the onslaught of a conflict in which the colonies were wrenched apart in what contemporaries termed a civil war. West Indians wanted most of all to maintain the integrity of the empire, and they blamed extremists on both sides for disrupting the peace. The onset of the Revolutionary crisis occasioned a shift in the political posture of the islands and their London lobby. Toward the end of 1774, the island assemblies and the West India lobby in London belatedly tried to intervene to avert war and keep the empire intact. The Jamaica assembly petitioned the king in words and sentiments that were almost indistinguishable from those of the Patriots in North America. However, these intercessions avoided reference to constitutional issues because opinion remained divided about the relative merits of the arguments. Furthermore, these futile protests were not the climax of a cumulative opposition movement but rather a spontaneous reaction to the threat of losing their trade with North America together with the associated fear of a slave rebellion. The planters and their lobbyists consequently interceded in a vain attempt to persuade the British government to adopt a more conciliatory policy toward North America, both to prevent the imminent breakup of the empire and to win themselves a reprieve from the economic sanctions imposed by Congress.

Whatever their various opinions of the merits and causes of the dispute, the planters became increasingly hostile to a conflict in which they had nothing to gain and much to lose. They felt themselves neglected and defenseless. With the entry of France into the war, the white colonists felt vulnerable to the external threat of foreign conquest and to the internal threat of a slave rebellion. British military resources were overstretched in the West Indies. The French conquered seven British islands, beginning with Dominica in 1778, then Grenada and St. Vincent in 1779, Tobago in 1781, and Montserrat, Nevis, and St. Kitts in 1782. The inadequacy of imperial protection and the shortage of food heightened fears of slave rebellion. The inadequacy of imperial protection also necessitated arming unprecedented numbers of slaves and free blacks who became active participants in the war as soldiers, militiamen, sailors, laborers, pioneers, guards, and nurses. The black acquisition of these roles challenged white racial assumptions that denied the capacity of blacks to possess the traits of honor and courage, which were the qualities of a good soldier.

The growing opposition of the planters to the war was also a consequence of the lowest plantation profits of the century. The interruption of trade by enemy privateers and fleets aggravated the rise in plantation expenses; higher freight rates, shipping shortages, convoy delays, and increased insurance rates led to severe financial losses for many individuals. The loss of the rum market in North America was not compensated by the opening of new markets among the British Army or in Ireland. Of greater significance was the loss of North American imports of foodstuffs and lumber, which soon caused inflated prices and conditions of famine. The latter was most pronounced in the Leeward Islands, where a fifth of the slave population died in Antigua. The interruption of the slave trade and the rising cost of living increased the cost of free labor and of slave hire. British import duties on sugar and rum rose to pay the escalating costs of the war. The planters were sensitive to any rise in costs because they needed to maximize profits to pay off loans to metropolitan merchants. Planters were unable to control the majority of their expenses except for local taxes intended to defray defense expenditures.

British defense interests in the Caribbean deflected resources from the war in North America. Naval ships were used to convoy trade against American privateers beginning in 1776. Following the declaration of war by France in 1778, Britain temporarily subordinated military activities in North America to objectives in the Caribbean. The British relinquished Philadelphia in June 1778 to free troops for the conquest of St. Lucia. Sir Henry Clinton blamed the absence of these troops for his subsequent failure to engage the Continental Army aggressively. Between 1778 and 1780, six new regiments were sent to the Caribbean but none to Clinton in North America. The exceptionally high rate of mortality from malaria and yellow fever in the Caribbean was a drain on British manpower in both the army and navy. The stipulation in the contracts of German mercenaries that they could not serve in the Caribbean meant that more of them served in America, while only British troops could serve in the Caribbean. British fears of slave revolts in the Caribbean may also have restrained the use of black troops and slaves on a more ambitious scale in North America.

The diversion of resources for the British conquest of the Dutch island of St. Eustatius in 1781, which contributed to the British failure to intercept the French fleet, had momentous strategic consequences in the British defeat at Yorktown. The defense of the British West Indies thereafter overshadowed the North American theater in the final phase of the Revolutionary War. The rumor of the loss of St. Kitts haunted the last three weeks of the government of Lord North (February–March 1782). It fed fears among wavering independent members that the ministry was incapable of saving the rest of the empire and justified the warnings of opposition members that Britain risked the loss of the West Indies. In April 1782, however, the great naval victory of Admiral Sir George Rodney over the French at the Battle of the Saintes in the Caribbean enabled the British to salvage most of their empire outside of the United States at the Treaty of Paris in 1783. They obtained the return of all their former colonies in the West Indies except Tobago.

It was only after the American Revolution that West Indian elites began to question parliamentary supremacy and even to threaten rebellion. They developed various strategies of opposition to imperial policies that they had conspicuously failed to use between 1763 and 1774. This was symptomatic of the way in which the war had isolated the islands and contributed to the creolization of their societies. The planters had emerged from the war embittered by its cost and seeming futility. The changed circumstances of the postwar era left the planters on the defensive against imperial measures prejudicial to their interests. They were resentful when the British government prevented a full resumption of their prewar trade with the United States. However, the planters began to lobby more aggressively against the imperial government primarily because of the success of the metropolitan antislavery movement and the possibility of parliamentary intervention against slavery.

The American Revolution weakened the foundations of slavery in the British Caribbean but not because of economic decline, since plantation profits revived after the war. The republican ideology of the American Revolution placed a premium on the value of liberty, which itself helped foster the metropolitan antislavery campaign. The Revolutionary rhetoric was also appropriated by free blacks in their postwar campaign for civil rights and by slaves in their struggle for freedom. Free blacks utilized the circumstances of the war to assume visible roles as peasant farmers, soldiers, and religious evangelists who undermined the racial assumptions that supported slavery. The number of free blacks increased owing to postwar manumissions that again weakened the grip of slavery.

The influence of the West India lobby that defended slavery in London began to diminish as it was forced to adopt more confrontational tactics in the postwar years and was no longer able to rely on a discrete insider relationship with government. The division of British America helped the cause of abolitionists in both Britain and the United States by halving the number of slaves remaining within the British Empire and leaving slavery a peculiar institution of the South within the United States.

Andrew Jackson O'Shaughnessy

See also

French West Indies; Jamaica; West Indies

References

Carrington, Selwyn H. H. *The British West Indies during the American Revolution.* Dordrecht, Holland: Foris, 1988.

Greene, Jack P. "Liberty, Slavery and the Transformation of British Identity in the Eighteenth-Century West Indies." *Slavery & Abolition* 21 (2000): 1–31.

O'Shaughnessy, Andrew. *An Empire Divided: The American Revolution and the British Caribbean.* Philadelphia: University of Pennsylvania Press, 2000.

Sheridan, Richard B. "The Crisis of Slave Subsistence in the British West Indies during and after the American Revolution." *William and Mary Quarterly,* 3rd ser., 33 (1976): 615–641.

Whitson, Agnes. "The Outlook of the American Colonies on the British West Indies, 1760–1775." *Political Science Quarterly* 45(1) (March 1930): 56–86.

Brodhead, Daniel (1736–1809)

Daniel Brodhead was a capable Continental Army officer who in 1779 led a successful expedition against the Seneca Indians in the Allegheny Valley. In his youth, Brodhead had a reputation among his neighbors on the Pennsylvania frontier as an Indian hater. By 1773 he was a prosperous merchant in Reading, Pennsylvania, serving as deputy surveyor general of the province. In 1774 he helped found the Bucks County Committee of Correspondence. In May 1775 he organized a rifle company and joined the Continental Army at the siege of Boston, and in 1776 he was elected to the Pennsylvania Convention.

Brodhead was commissioned a lieutenant colonel of the Pennsylvania Rifle Regiment on 13 March 1776 and fought in the Battle of Long Island on 17 August. Afterward he was appointed acting commander of his regiment and on 25 September was transferred to the 3rd Pennsylvania Battalion. After fighting in a number of skirmishes around New York, he was promoted to colonel of the 8th Pennsylvania Regiment on 12 March 1777. Brodhead served under General Benjamin Lincoln in New Jersey and fought at Bound Brook on 13 April. In the last four months of 1777, he led his regiment in battles at Brandywine, Paoli, Germantown, and Whitemarsh. On 8 March 1778, he was ordered to join Brigadier General Lachlan McIntosh at Fort Pitt in western Pennsylvania.

During the following winter, Brodhead commanded Fort McIntosh, on the Ohio River, while General McIntosh conducted ineffectual operations against Detroit. Brodhead soon complained to General George Washington that McIntosh was incompetent, and on 5 March 1779, Washington appointed Brodhead to replace McIntosh at Fort Pitt. On 11 August, in cooperation with General John Sullivan, who was attacking the Iroquois in western New York, Brodhead commanded an expedition of some 600 men up the Allegheny River to assault Seneca villages. Without losing a single man, he marched almost 400 miles, destroyed ten villages and 600 acres of corn, and captured much booty. He returned to Fort Pitt on 14 September and later that month concluded a treaty with the Delaware Indians. Washington congratulated Brodhead for these successes, and Congress voted its thanks.

On 17 January 1781, Brodhead took command of the 2nd Pennsylvania Regiment and in April conducted operations against the Delaware Indians. By October 1781 he was unpopular with Colonel John Gibson and other officers at Fort Pitt. Charged with malfeasance, Brodhead was removed from command by Washington on 6 September 1781 and ordered to join the main army in New York. Brodhead demanded a court-martial and was acquitted on 28 February 1782. At Washington's behest, Brodhead was breveted to brigadier general on 30 September 1783. He lived at Milford, Pennsylvania, after the war and was an ardent Federalist. In 1790 the Pennsylvania General Assembly appointed him state surveyor general. At the time of his death in 1809, he was admired as an officer and businessman.

Paul David Nelson

See also

Border Warfare; Boston, Siege of; Brandywine, Battle of; Brodhead Expedition; Fort McIntosh, Pennsylvania; Germantown, Battle of; Long Island, Battle of; McIntosh, Lachlan; Paoli, Battle of; Sullivan, John; Sullivan Expedition; Whitemarsh, Pennsylvania, Action at

References

Appel, John C. "Colonel Daniel Brodhead and the Lure of Detroit." *Pennsylvania History* 38 (1971): 265–282.

Buck, Solon, and Elizabeth Hawthorn Buck. *The Planting of Civilization in Western Pennsylvania.* [Pittsburgh]: University of Pittsburgh Press, 1939.

Brodhead Expedition (August–September 1779)

From 11 August to 14 September 1779, Colonel Daniel Brodhead led a destructive expedition against Indians in the Allegheny Valley, in support of General John Sullivan's invasion of the Iroquois country. Throughout the Revolution, American settlements on the frontiers of Pennsylvania and New York were the targets of attacks by Loyalists and Indians. On 27 February 1779, Congress directed George Washington to launch punitive attacks against frontier Indians and the British post of Fort Niagara. Brodhead, commander at Fort Pitt, was to first strike north, his force of more than 600 men destroying Indian villages and crops along the way. He was then supposed to direct his march to Genesee, where he would rendezvous with Sullivan and assist in an attack on Fort Niagara.

Departing Fort Pitt, Brodhead proceeded into country that was almost impassable due to rough terrain and thick forests. In the midst of these harsh surroundings, on 15 August his advance party of twenty-five men, under Lieutenant John Harding, surprised a Seneca war party. When the Senecas stripped themselves for action, brandishing their tomahawks, Harding and his party attacked with fury. Soon the Indians broke and ran, some plunging into the river, others escaping through the thick underbrush. Five were killed, and there were no losses among Harding's men. By this time, Brodhead had deployed, as a precaution, his whole army for battle, but this skirmish was the only resistance that he met during the entire campaign.

That same day, Brodhead's expedition reached Buchan, Pennsylvania, where the commander deposited all his army baggage under guard. Proceeding to the Seneca settlements, about 20 miles farther on, the Americans burned eight abandoned towns and threw the Indians' military gear into the Allegheny River. Over the next three days Brodhead's troops cut down 600 acres of corn, piled it in heaps, and burned it. Proceeding on toward Genesee, Brodhead came within 50 miles of his destination but decided to turn back because he was unfamiliar with the territory and had no guides to lead him through. On his return march, his soldiers burned the old Indian towns of Conauwago and Mahusquachinkocken. They arrived back at Fort Pitt on 14 September, laden with plunder and proudly displaying the scalps they had taken from their enemies. In the course of thirty-three days, Brodhead had marched almost 400 miles without the loss of a single man, perhaps a record in the Revolution. For his exploits, Congress thanked him and Washington congratulated him warmly.

Although Brodhead's expedition produced no smashing military triumph, the Americans considered it a success. Brodhead's projection of American power into seemingly impenetrable country had shown the Indians that none of their towns were secure. More importantly, Brodhead found awaiting him at Fort Pitt a delegation of Wyandot warriors who sued for peace because their dream of an Iroquois alliance was permanently shattered by his and Sullivan's successes.

Paul David Nelson

See also

Border Warfare; Brodhead, Daniel; Sullivan, John; Sullivan Expedition

References

Brady, William J. "Brodhead's Trail up the Allegheny, 1779." *Western Pennsylvania Historical Magazine* 37 (1954): 19–31.

Buck, Solon, and Elizabeth Hawthorn Buck. *The Planting of Civilization in Western Pennsylvania.* [Pittsburgh]: University of Pittsburgh Press, 1939.

Brown, John (1744–1780)

A native of Massachusetts and a lawyer before the Revolution, John Brown saw extensive service as a Revolutionary soldier and died in battle. A graduate of Yale in 1771, he became a lawyer and opened a law office in Caghnawaga (now Johnstown), New York, in 1772. A year later he was appointed king's attorney. Shortly thereafter, he moved to Pittsfield, Massachusetts. On 30 June 1774 he was appointed to the Pittsfield Committee of Correspondence and in October was elected to the provincial congress. Boston Patriots dispatched Brown to Montreal in February 1775 to encourage rebellion among Canadians. Passing Fort Ticonderoga, at the south end of Lake Champlain, he was impressed with its strategic importance and urged its seizure upon his return to Massachusetts in March 1775. On 10 May, he took part in the capture of the fort and was chosen to deliver the news to Congress.

On 6 July 1775, Brown was commissioned a major in the Pittsfield militia and for the next month scouted into Canada and commanded gunboats on Lake Champlain. In September he joined Ethan Allen in a failed attempt to seize Montreal; when Allen was captured, his supporters charged Brown with not giving him adequate support. On 19 October, Brown and James Livingston captured Fort Chambly on the Sorel River, seizing six tons of gunpowder. Brown and Colonel James Easton overwhelmed enemy fieldworks dominating the St. Lawrence River on 19 November and captured a British flotilla fleeing from Montreal. Brown was with the American army that besieged, fought for, and retreated from Quebec in the winter of 1775–1776. During that time he fell out with General Benedict Arnold, and for a year he and Arnold hurled accusations at each other. On 1 August 1776, Brown was promoted to lieutenant colonel in the Continental Army, and in early 1777 he participated in military operations around Lake George. In February 1777, rather than serve under Arnold, Brown resigned his commission, returned to Pittsfield, and published handbills against his nemesis.

In the summer of 1777 Brown returned to military service when General John Burgoyne invaded upstate New York. Elected colonel of a Berkshire militia regiment, in September Brown seized Fort George, then led an attack on British outworks near Fort Ticonderoga, capturing 293 enemy soldiers and liberating 100 American prisoners. He served in the American army on the Hudson River until Burgoyne's surrender on 17 October and then returned to his law practice. In 1778 Brown was in the state legislature and a year later was appointed county judge. He returned to arms in the fall of 1780, marching to oppose Sir John Johnson and Joseph Brant in the Mohawk Valley. On 19 October, he fell into an ambush near Stone Arabia, New York, and was killed, along with 40 of his men.

Paul David Nelson

See also

Allen, Ethan; Arnold, Benedict; Brant, Joseph; Burgoyne, John; Canada, Operations in; Chambly, Quebec, Action at; Fort Ticonderoga, New York; Johnson, Sir John; Montreal, Operations against; Quebec, Siege of

References

Bellesiles, Michael A. *Revolutionary Outlaws: Ethan Allen and the Struggle for Independence on the Early American Frontier.* Charlottesville: University of Virginia Press, 1993.

Howe, Archibald. *Colonel John Brown, of Pittsfield, Massachusetts: The Brave Accuser of Benedict Arnold.* Boston: W. B. Clarke, 1908.

Sturtevant, Walter B. "John Brown's Raid, September, 1777." *Infantry Journal* 36 (1930): 475–485.

Brown, Thomas (1750–1825)

To follow the career of Thomas Brown is to discover the course of the Revolutionary War on the southern frontier. Brown emigrated from England with the intention of becoming a gentleman farmer and instead emerged as one of the best-known Loyalists who fought along with British-allied Indians.

Brown arrived in Georgia in November 1774 in answer to Governor James Wright's invitation to settle on Georgia's ceded lands, territory acquired from the Creek and Cherokee Indians in 1773. Brown brought with him some seventy indentured servants and founded the settlement of Brownsborough on the forks of the Kiokee Creek in the Georgia backcountry. Wright promptly named him a magistrate.

Brown's arrival, however, coincided with the rise of Revolutionary fervor in the colony. Georgians who met in a provincial congress in January 1775 were too divided to take a firm stand on opposition to British measures. But when a second congress assembled in July, the delegates adopted the Continental Association, which authorized the selection of local committees to monitor the banning of all trade with Britain. The association had been framed in October 1774 by the First Continental Congress, which Georgia, alone among the thirteen ultimately rebellious colonies, had not attended.

In Augusta, Georgia, Brown denounced the Continental Association and attempted to form a counterassociation. The rumor spread that he was the illegitimate son of Lord North, come to spy on the Americans. On 2 August 1775, the Augusta committeemen, calling themselves the Sons of Liberty, visited Brown at his residence to force him to swear to uphold the ban on trade. He vainly asked for liberty to follow his own conscience. Brown was bludgeoned, burned, and carted around Augusta. When Brown recovered he attempted to rally Loyalists in the South Carolina up-country, but Governor Lord William Campbell, himself under virtual arrest by the Revolutionary faction, advised against a premature uprising.

Brown avoided arrest by fleeing to British East Florida in January 1776 and unveiling a plan of counterattack to Governor Patrick Tonyn of that province. Georgians were deathly afraid of a major Indian uprising, and Brown believed that bringing the Creeks and Cherokees into action on the frontier in combination with the landing of British regulars on the coast would quickly end the rebellion. Brown, who had little knowledge of local Native Americans, volunteered to go into the Indian country to recruit his allies. Tonyn enthusiastically supported the plan and conferred upon Brown a commission as lieutenant-colonel with authorization to raise a troop of Loyalist rangers to ride with the Indians.

After spending most of 1776 among the Creek villages, Brown returned to Florida in 1777 to lead his rangers in repelling an invasion by Georgia troops. During the winter of 1777–1778, Brown's East Florida Rangers stationed themselves at Fort Tonyn on the St. Marys River and from there conducted cattle raids into southern Georgia. On 12 March 1778, Brown staged his most daring escapade; with 100 rangers and a band of Indians, he swam across the quarter-mile-wide Altamaha River and captured Fort McIntosh. That post commanded the routes to the backcountry, and Brown's agents ventured into the Carolina up-country to recruit hundreds of Loyalists in anticipation of a British invasion. Lord George Germain, prodded by Tonyn, had finally decided to test the Southern Strategy outlined by Brown to Tonyn.

General Sir Henry Clinton in New York chose Lieutenant-Colonel Archibald Campbell to lead the invasion of the Georgia coast and sent instructions to the Indian agent John Stuart in Pensacola to bring down the Indians upon the frontier. Campbell was authorized to restore royal government in Georgia, and his 3,000-man army easily overwhelmed General Robert Howe's Savannah garrison on 28 December 1778. General Augustine Prevost, with his Royal American troops, marched up from Florida, accompanied by Brown's East Florida Rangers. On 22 January 1779, Campbell began his march to Augusta with the expectation of meeting Indian allies. During the march, Brown was wounded in an attempt to rescue Loyalists imprisoned in the Burke County Jail.

On 31 January 1779, British troops occupied Augusta. Before the Indians arrived, however, rebel reinforcements from North Carolina threatened Campbell, and a group of

Loyalists advancing to join him were defeated at Kettle Creek, Georgia, on 14 February 1779. But this did not deter Campbell from proclaiming the restoration of royal rule and then handing over the command of his troops to Lieutenant-Colonel James Mark Prevost, who soon turned on the pursuing Patriot forces and routed them at Briar Creek on 3 March 1779.

On 25 June 1779, following the death in Pensacola that March of Stuart, Indian superintendent of the Southern Department, Germain appointed Brown to supervise the Creek and Cherokee Indians. Before Brown learned of his new responsibility, his rangers helped repulse the Franco-American attack upon Savannah in October 1779. After the fall of Charleston to British forces on 12 May 1780, American resistance collapsed over most of coastal Georgia and South Carolina. Brown and his men, now known as the King's Rangers, garrisoned the up-country town of Augusta, the scene of Brown's torture in 1775 at the hands of the local Sons of Liberty. There he stored Indian supplies and invited the Indians to visit him.

In September 1780, however, the Indian supplies lured several hundred Georgians under Lieutenant Colonel Elijah Clarke to attack Augusta and besiege Brown, his rangers, and their Indian friends in the fortified Mackay house. After a four-day battle, British reinforcements drove off the raiders. Brown then constructed a defense works called Fort Cornwallis, only to be besieged again in the spring by Georgia militia under Clarke, South Carolina militia under Andrew Pickens, and Continental soldiers under Lieutenant Colonel Henry "Light-Horse Harry" Lee. Brown was forced to surrender on 5 June 1781, after a bitterly fought two-week battle.

Brown was sent to Savannah under parole but was later exchanged. He raised another troop of rangers and in 1782 engaged in skirmishes with American troops under General Anthony Wayne. When Savannah surrendered to Wayne on 14 July 1782, Brown and his rangers accompanied Georgia refugees to East Florida. With the return of Florida to Spain by treaty in 1783, many local Loyalists left for Nova Scotia or the West Indies. Brown finally settled into the life of a gentleman planter, his first objective in coming to America, in the Bahamas. He died on the island of St. Vincent at the age of seventy-five on 3 August 1825.

Edward J. Cashin

See also

Augusta, Georgia, Operations at; Campbell, Archibald; Clarke, Elijah; Georgia; Prevost, Augustine; Savannah, Georgia, Allied Operations against; Savannah, Georgia, British Capture of; Wayne, Anthony

References

Cashin, Edward. *The King's Ranger: Thomas Brown and the American Revolution on the Southern Frontier.* Athens: University of Georgia Press, 1989.

Olson, Gary D. "Thomas Brown, Partisan, and the Revolutionary War in Georgia, 1777–1782." *Georgia Historical Quarterly* 44 (Spring 1970): 1–19; (Summer 1970): 183–208.

Searcy, Martha Condray. *The Georgia-Florida Contest in the American Revolution, 1776–1778.* Tuscaloosa: University of Alabama Press, 1985.

Browne, Montfort

See New Providence, Bahamas, Attacks on

Brunswick, New Jersey

See New Brunswick, New Jersey

Bull, William, Jr. (1710–1791)

The last lieutenant governor and acting governor of colonial South Carolina, William Bull Jr. was born at his family's plantation, Ashley Hall, near Charleston (then known as Charles Town), South Carolina, on 24 September 1710. He was the son of William Bull Sr., who was lieutenant governor of South Carolina from 1737 to 1743, and Mary Quintyne Bull.

In 1734, the younger Bull became the first native-born American of European extraction to earn a medical doctorate from the University of Leyden in Holland. Upon his return to South Carolina, he purchased a tract of land along the Port Royal River and established himself as both a planter and a politician. He began his political career as a member of the Commons House from 1736 to 1749, serving as Speaker of the House during 1740–1742 and 1744–1749. First appointed lieutenant governor of South Carolina in 1759, he served as acting governor of the colony during 1760–1761, 1764–1766, 1768–1771, and 1773–1775 as well as during the British occupation in 1781–1782. Despite showing sympathy for the Revolutionary cause, he remained a Loyalist and departed permanently for England in December 1782.

Early on, Bull proved to be a shrewd politician in his dealings with the Indians. In 1751 he helped negotiate a treaty between the Catawba and the Iroquois tribes, who had been at war with each other since 1745. He also helped conclude the Cherokee War of 1760–1761. The South Carolina Commons House was initially hostile to Bull's moderate-toned peace plan, but he managed to pass the plan despite opposition. He would exercise the same temperate behavior in his dealings with both the British government and the Commons House of South Carolina over the highly unpopular Stamp Act, the Townshend Acts, and the Tea Act, attempting to enforce the new statutes while easing the burdens they placed on South Carolinians.

Bull was also an advocate of a strong public education system and attempted to establish a College of Charles Town in 1770. This proposal initially floundered for lack of money, and Bull would not get to see his idea come to fruition while lieutenant governor. After his final departure for England, however, the passage of South Carolina's 1785 College Act enabled the permanent establishment of the College of Charles Town. In 1772, Bull also made a donation of £150 to the College of Philadelphia in Pennsylvania.

The British recaptured Charleston in the spring of 1780, and Bull resumed his position as lieutenant governor early the following year. But his tenure was to be brief, and the area under his authority shrank steadily as the British Army gradually surrendered every part of South Carolina beyond the Charleston area. Just two weeks before the British evacuated Charleston, Bull sailed for England, where he died in London on 4 July 1791.

Daren Swanick

See also

Charleston, South Carolina, Expedition against (1780); Cherokees, Operations against; Loyalists; South Carolina

References

Bull, Kinloch, Jr. *The Oligarchs in Colonial and Revolutionary Charleston: Lieutenant Governor William Bull II and His Family.* Columbia: University of South Carolina Press, 1991.

Weir, Robert M. *Colonial South Carolina: A History.* Columbia: University of South Carolina Press, 1997.

Bull's Ferry, New Jersey, Action at (20–21 July 1780)

In mid-July 1780, General Anthony Wayne conducted a raid into an area known as the English Neighborhood, south of Fort Lee, New Jersey, and unsuccessfully attacked a British blockhouse at Bull's Ferry on the Hudson River. Only days earlier, General George Washington had solicited advice from his officers on American operations for the summer of 1780, and Wayne had responded from his camp at Totowa, New Jersey, on 19 July. He would forage for horses and cattle and lure British troops into an ambush when they responded to his operations. Washington approved the plan on 20 July. That evening, Wayne marched with 2,000 men to New Bridge on the Hackensack River, where he encamped. The following day he crossed the river and arrayed two regiments in concealment to ambush enemy troops, should they land to cut him off. With the remainder of his men, he marched southward toward Bull's Ferry, dropping off two more covering forces to protect his route of return.

As Wayne approached the Bull's Ferry blockhouse, he discovered the strength of the post. It was garrisoned with 70 soldiers and Loyalist militiamen and protected with an abatis, a stockade, and rock cliffs next to the Hudson River. Undaunted, he ordered two regiments to fire on the blockhouse while he positioned four cannon at close range. Then he commenced a furious hour-long bombardment that had little effect on the logs of the blockhouse. Realizing that he could not carry the place by storm and learning that the enemy was preparing to land 3,000 troops somewhere north of his position, he ordered his men to cease their attacks and march in that direction, but they did not disengage until 3 of them had been killed crossing the abatis. As he withdrew, he burned some boats in the Hudson River and drove off a large herd of cattle.

Marching swiftly toward Fort Lee, Wayne hoped to catch the British landing party in a cross fire. But the enemy detected his ruse and refused to disembark. He now withdrew his troops, fearing that he might be cut off from his retreat across the Hackensack River bridges. When he reached Totowa, he wrote to Washington to report on his expedition. Noting that sixty-four of his men had been killed or wounded, he praised his soldiers for their bravery under fire. He was sorry, however, that the operation had not achieved as much as he and Washington had hoped. Washington agreed, fearing that it had been mostly a wasted effort. Other Americans were more critical, complaining that Wayne had rushed into a useless operation merely to embellish his own military reputation. His British foes mercilessly derided him. Major John André, in a poem titled "Cow Chase," parodied Wayne as a cowardly, drunken cowboy. In response, Wayne began exaggerating his accomplishment, claiming that his attack had thwarted enemy plans to attack Rhode Island.

Paul David Nelson

See also

André, John; Fort Lee, New Jersey; Wayne, Anthony

Reference

Nelson, Paul David. *Anthony Wayne: Soldier of the Early Republic.* Bloomington: Indiana University Press, 1985.

Bulltown Swamp, Georgia, Action at (19 November 1778)

The engagement at Bulltown Swamp occurred during a British campaign from East Florida into coastal Georgia. Patriot militia fought a delaying action against the British forces moving northward toward the port town of Sunbury, Georgia.

A Patriot offensive into East Florida from Georgia floundered in July 1778 due to the climate, logistical problems, and personal issues among the commanders. Meanwhile, British commanders discussed a new strategy in the stalemated war against their American colonies. Sir Henry Clinton, with the encouragement of Secretary of State Lord George Germain, opted to shift the focus of the British military to the southern colonies, where he believed that London would find more sympathy and support among the local population. In response, British forces planned assaults against Sunbury and Savannah, Georgia, during the late fall of 1778. The operation called for Colonel Archibald Campbell to sail from New York with 2,000 British soldiers and land near Savannah. Meanwhile, General Augustine Prevost would launch a two-pronged offensive north from East Florida toward Sunbury. The first group, led by his brother Lieutenant-Colonel Mark Prevost, marched into Georgia along the coast. This force consisted of 100 British regulars and approximately 300 Native Americans and Loyalist militia. Lieutenant-Colonel L. V. Fuser commanded an expedition of 500 men who would sail to the Sunbury area and join Lieutenant-Colonel Prevost in a final assault on the town and Fort Morris.

The land expedition under Lieutenant-Colonel Prevost moved into Georgia and began apprehending known Patriots and plundering Patriot-owned plantations as they moved northward. Patriot mounted militia, under the command of Colonel John Baker, engaged Prevost at the general location where the Savannah and Darien roads crossed Bulltown Swamp. On 19 November 1778, the small group of Patriot mounted militia (the exact number of men is unknown) conducted a delaying operation against the 400 British regulars, Native Americans, and Loyalist militia marching northward with Prevost. Three Patriots, including Baker, were wounded in the skirmish. British casualties, if any, are not known. The Patriot force withdrew northward, and the British continued their advance toward Sunbury.

At Newport Bridge, also known as Riceborough Bridge, Patriot militia conducted a second delaying action. The number of Patriot militia is not known, but they were too small of a force to offer more than a token resistance before withdrawing northward. Colonel John White, commanding the Patriot forces stationed at Sunbury, marched approximately 100 Continentals and militia, with two small artillery pieces, westward and established a position at Midway Meeting House to counter Prevost. A small band of Patriot mounted militia under Major William Baker rode southward to harass the British as they approached a breastwork established by White. Prevost encountered White's men on 24 November 1778 at Midway, Georgia. Following this engagement and a temporary withdrawal by Prevost, British forces seized Savannah in December 1778.

Terry M. Mays

See also

Alligator Creek, East Florida, Action at; Midway, Georgia, Action at; Prevost, Augustine

References

Coleman, Kenneth. *The American Revolution in Georgia, 1763–1789.* Athens: University of Georgia Press, 1958.

Stevens, William Bacon. *A History of Georgia.* Savannah, GA: Beehive, 1972.

Bunker Hill, Battle of (17 June 1775)

The Battle of Bunker Hill was the first pitched battle of the American Revolution. In the wake of Lexington and Concord, some 20,000 New England troops fortified Charlestown peninsula, overlooking Boston, from which they were driven off by the British but at huge cost.

On 12 June 1775, the governor of Massachusetts, Lieutenant-General Thomas Gage, declared martial law and offered pardons to all those who had borne arms or otherwise participated in the events during and after 19 April, with two exceptions: John Hancock and Samuel Adams. Meanwhile, Gage and three major-generals who had recently arrived from England—William Howe, Henry Clinton, and John Burgoyne—planned a four-pronged attack on Dorchester Heights, Roxbury, Charlestown, and Cambridge scheduled for Sunday, 18 June. With so many spies among the civilian population of Boston, word inevitably reached the Massachusetts Committee of Safety, and on 15 June it resolved to occupy Bunker Hill on the Charlestown peninsula and also the hills behind Dorchester. Ironically, none of this reached Gage, as the Committee of Safety had sent his chief informant, Dr. Benjamin Church, to Philadelphia with dispatches deemed too secret to be entrusted to anyone else.

Artemas Ward, commander of the New England Army of Observation, convened a council of war on 16 June. Ward was not convinced of his army's capabilities, but after two months of keeping the king's troops penned inside Boston, Ward's subordinates were more aggressive and confident. Prominent among them was Israel Putnam of Connecticut, recently made a brigadier-general, who argued that the army would fight well as long as it was behind fortifications, saying: "Americans are not at all afraid of their heads, though very much afraid of their legs; if you cover these, they will fight for ever." Despite his misgivings, Ward accepted the view of the majority and sent four infantry regiments—about 1,000 men—supported by two small cannon to occupy high ground on the Charlestown peninsula overlooking the town itself and the entrance to Back Bay.

At about 9:00 P.M. on 16 June, the majority of the troops, led by William Prescott and Richard Gridley of Massachusetts (the army's only engineer), left Cambridge Common. En route, they stopped to pick up several wagons full of entrenching tools guarded by some Connecticut troops from Putnam's own regiment, under Thomas Knowlton, and a surprise addition to the party—Putnam himself. With everything ready, the contingent crossed Charlestown Neck onto the peninsula. However, on arriving at Bunker Hill, the actual lay of the land and the lack of written directions from the council of war led to a long argument between Putnam and

Battle of Bunker Hill. In the first and bloodiest battle of the Revolutionary War, British troops crossed Boston Harbor to confront a force of New England militia entrenched on a small peninsula opposite the city. General William Howe's men only drove off the defenders after three frontal assaults in which they suffered horrific casualties—almost 40 percent of their force. This painting, John Trumbull's *Death of General Warren,* is the finest image of the Battle of Bunker Hill and is an important American historical and patriotic painting. It was painted several years after the event, but Trumbull was himself a participant at the battle. (National Archives and Records Administration)

the Massachusetts officers as to where the fortification should be constructed. The result was a compromise decision to place the main work on Breed's Hill, with supporting works only on Bunker (known at the time as Bunker's) Hill. Gridley marked out an area about 130 feet square with a redan (a triangular projection) facing east, toward Charlestown, and a narrow gorge on the opposite side to provide easy access for reinforcements. The work began at midnight and, despite the exposed position and closeness of the guard boats in the harbor, there were no alarms raised. (Several British sentries heard the digging but did not report it and mentioned it only in passing conversation the next day.) It is now impossible to know for certain if the fortification of Breed's Hill was a mistake by Prescott; deliberate disobedience by him and others, possibly encouraged by Putnam; or the actual intention of Ward and his subordinates.

At 4:00 A.M., the British ship *Lively* (20 guns) spotted the earthworks on Breed's Hill and opened fire, while the *Glasgow* (20 guns) swung round to prevent further troop movements across Charlestown Neck. By 9:00 A.M., the Copp's Hill battery was also bombarding the American positions. Gage and the major-generals were all in agreement that the works posed a threat but offered an opportunity for offensive action, as they were incomplete and isolated from the main enemy works around Cambridge. The quickest approach would be by water, but there were only enough boats to carry just over 1,000 troops. Moreover, as these were not purpose-built, flat-bottom transports, but plain rowing boats with crews of varying quality and no special facilities for artillery or horses, it was vital to choose a landing site that allowed these vessels to come in close enough to land guns but still return quickly to collect a second wave. Moulton's Point offered an open, gently sloping beach and a road of sorts, and it was also sufficiently far from Breed's Hill to prevent a sortie by the defenders that might overwhelm the first wave before the second could arrive.

The plan of battle, once all the troops were ashore, was to ignore the redoubt and swing around it to capture Bunker Hill and Charlestown Neck, thus isolating the defenders on Breed's Hill. Howe would command the main force while Clinton supervised the reinforcements back in Boston. The first wave—six battalions, six extra flank companies, and twelve pieces of artillery—was to leave from the Long Wharf and the North Battery; two other battalions would remain in reserve at the North Battery, while the rest of the garrison was to come to a state of readiness. As the assault and any follow-up operations might take some time, blankets and three days' rations would be issued, but the troops would not take their packs. Howe and the senior Royal Navy officer, Samuel Graves, then went aboard the 64-gun *Somerset* to direct operations. However, the ebb tide meant that the water was too shallow, and Graves had to transfer men from his three largest ships—the *Somerset,* the *Boyne* (70 guns), and the *Preston* (50 guns)—into the smaller elements of his fleet. The *Falcon* (14 guns) joined the *Lively,* which was still warping slowly toward Moulton's Point, while the *Symmetry* (18 guns) and two gondolas—manned by sailors but with Royal Artillery gun crews and officers—went to help the *Glasgow* stop reinforcements from crossing Charlestown Neck. All this time, the Copp's Hill battery maintained a steady fire on the redoubt, scoring several hits but causing little damage due to the extreme range and the thickness of the earthworks.

Up on Breed's Hill, thirst and hunger (few men had brought any water or food) and lack of sleep were creating problems. The first salvo from the *Lively* had killed one man, at which point many others stopped work to bury him and not a few took the chance to leave. The activity visible over in Boston contrasted worryingly with the empty slopes of Bunker Hill, and some men began to wonder if they had been betrayed. When the ships had begun firing, Putnam rode over from Cambridge to see what was happening and then came back to report to Ward, who faced a difficult decision. Gage could strike anywhere, so Ward could not commit his main force; nevertheless, he saw that Prescott was isolated and ordered three Massachusetts regiments to each send several companies to occupy Charlestown.

Back on Breed's Hill, by 1:00 P.M., Prescott and his men—and the huge audience on Boston's rooftops and the hills around the harbor—observed two columns of boats approach from the North Wharf and head for the peninsula. At the same time the British bombardment increased in intensity: the *Lively,* the *Falcon* and the *Spitfire* (6 guns) raked Moulton's Point; the *Symmetry* and the two gondolas swept Charlestown Neck; the *Glasgow* fired into the houses of Charlestown; and the 24-pounders on Copp's Hill engaged the redoubt (the distance and elevation of Breed's Hill put the works beyond the range of the ships' broadsides). The only reply was a few salvos from Gridley's two 4-pounders in the redoubt.

Ward was now being pressed by the Committee of Safety to send more troops to help Prescott. He dispatched two New Hampshire and nine Massachusetts regiments, with two more companies of artillery, while the remainder of his command formed a defensive line to the east of Cambridge. John Stark's New Hampshire regiment was found to be short of ammunition; the men were quickly issued ball and loose powder, but Stark then had a frustrating wait while these were made up into cartridges before he could begin the hour-long march to Charlestown Neck. Meanwhile, Prescott had become aware of a 200-yard gap between the breastwork and the Mystic River. He ordered Knowlton to move up to Moulton's Point and oppose the landing, but the gunners attached to the Connecticut man withdrew to Bunker Hill and only returned when Putnam threatened to kill their commanding officer (later on, they would leave for good, abandoning their guns). Realizing that his force was too weak to attack, Knowlton formed his men behind a rail fence, creating a wall with rails from other fences nearby and bales of hay from the fields. Prescott then sent out two more parties to observe the British landings but heard nothing more from either. Still more of his men went missing while supposedly taking the entrenching tools back to Bunker Hill for safe keeping. Around 3:00 P.M., Stark arrived at Charlestown Neck to find five Massachusetts regiments that Ward had sent earlier halted and blocking the road, unwilling to brave the British bombardment. He promptly marched his regiment, and Reed's, around them and across the Neck without loss.

About the time Stark was crossing the Neck, Howe was landing with the second wave at Moulton's Point and sending out four light infantry companies to cover the deployment of his main body in three lines atop Moulton's Hill. The enemy position seemed stronger than it had from Boston, occupying an almost continuous 600-yard line from Charlestown to the Mystic River, and with reserves already amassing on Bunker Hill. Howe immediately ordered up reinforcements and had his artillery bombard the redoubt. He also asked for the two gondolas to row all the way around from the Mill Pond at Charlestown Neck into the Mystic River (which, unfortunately, required them to row against the tide and put them out of action for the rest of the day). He then turned to the ground to his front, which appeared to comprise open fields, clumps of trees, and some brick kilns.

However, prior to that day, nobody in Gage's headquarters had felt the need to survey the peninsula in any detail, and the long grass hid a rocky, uneven surface, crossed by gulleys and stout fences that would only be revealed as his troops advanced. To make matters worse, there were no horses for Howe or his staff, preventing him from inspecting the field more closely (a move that might well have revealed the wide gap in the left of Prescott's line). As luck would have it, that gap was soon filled, and by the most competent regimental commander in Ward's army. Stark's and Reed's regiments joined Knowlton at the rail fence and spilled over onto the beach, with its nine-foot-high embankment. The men quickly constructed a wall of stones, while Stark set up aiming points some fifty yards to their front.

The American line was now complete and may have numbered as many as 4,000 men—almost twice Howe's force. In Charlestown itself, covering the right flank of the redoubt on

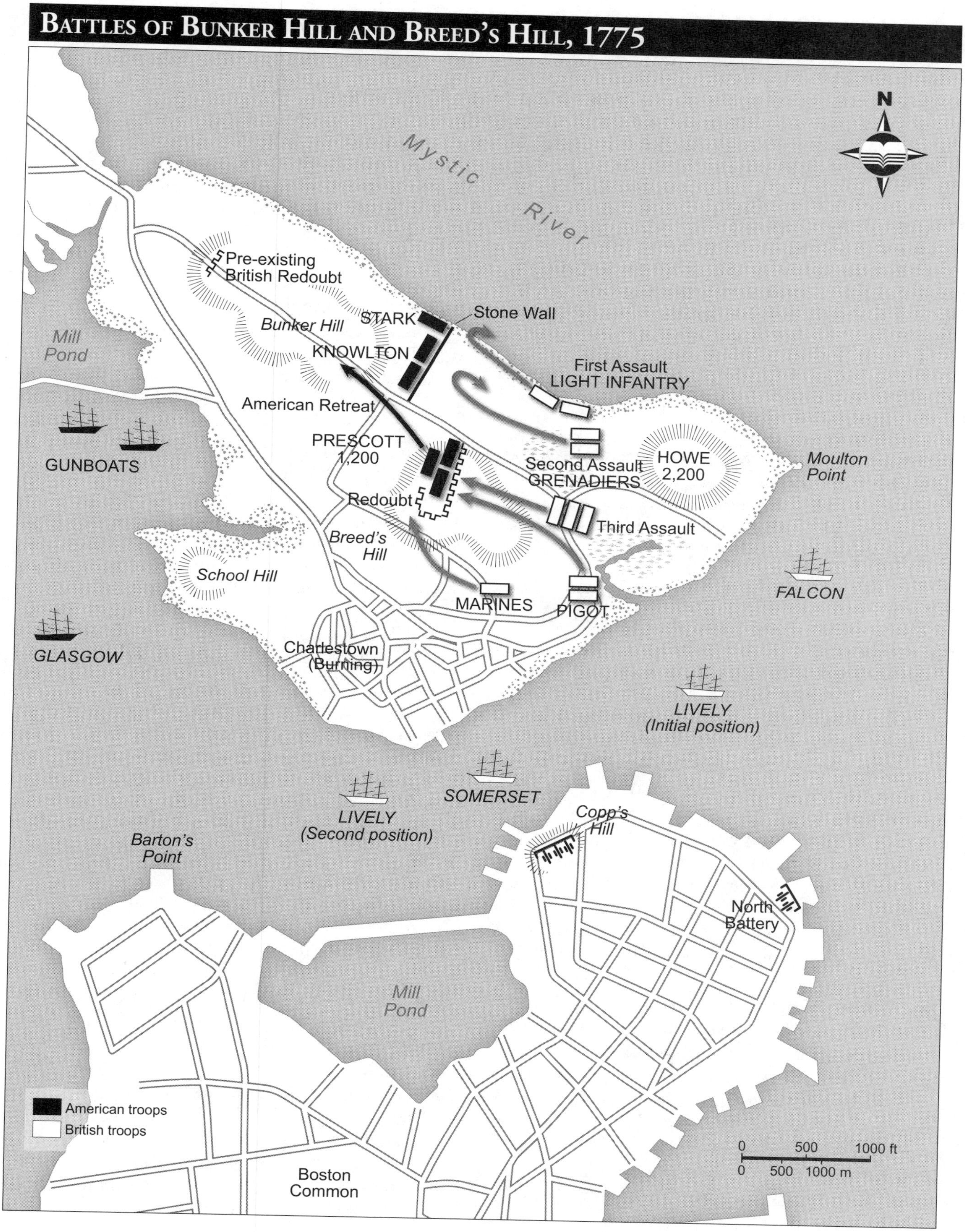

Battles of Bunker Hill and Breed's Hill, 1775

N
Mystic River
Pre-existing British Redoubt
Bunker Hill
STARK
Stone Wall
KNOWLTON
Mill Pond
First Assault
LIGHT INFANTRY
American Retreat
GUNBOATS
PRESCOTT
1,200
Second Assault
GRENADIERS
HOWE
2,200
Moulton Point
Redoubt
Third Assault
Breed's Hill
School Hill
MARINES
PIGOT
FALCON
GLASGOW
Charlestown (Burning)
LIVELY (Initial position)
SOMERSET
LIVELY (Second position)
Copp's Hill
Barton's Point
North Battery
Mill Pond
American troops
British troops
0 500 1000 ft
0 500 1000 m
Boston Common

Breed's Hill, were several detachments of Massachusetts men, probably equal to two regiments. In the redoubt itself and in a breastwork that stretched 100 yards beyond it to the north, covering its left flank, were almost three full regiments of Massachusetts troops, commanded by Prescott. Both the breastwork and the redoubt were rough and incomplete but were still around six feet high with a ditch in front and a firing platform inside. To their north were three flèches (triangle-shaped earthworks) hastily constructed from fence rails and some fences and trees lining a road. These were defended by detachments from at least three more Massachusetts regiments. Then came the rail fence, manned by Knowlton's company of Connecticut men, and Reed's New Hampshire regiment with two guns. Finally came Stark's own regiment, covering the shore of the Mystic River. Although Putnam was struggling to control the hordes of deserters, stragglers, and genuinely bemused on Bunker Hill, some men were still drifting forward, including two major generals—Joseph Warren and Seth Pomeroy—whose commissions had not yet been confirmed but who offered their services as volunteers to Prescott and then Stark.

Howe organized his command into two wings—right and left—with the heavy guns remaining on Moulton's Hill and only the lighter 6-pounders advancing with the infantry. By now, he must have realized that he was outnumbered and therefore had to clear the peninsula by dusk; with time running out, he had no alternative but to attempt a frontal assault. He would command the right wing against the rail fence. Brigadier-General Robert Pigot, whose force was still coming ashore, would lead the left wing in a feint against Charlestown and the redoubt in order to pin down their garrisons.

However, as Pigot's men deployed, marksmen in Charlestown opened up on them, and Howe immediately sent orders to the Royal Navy squadron to set the town alight. By 4:00 P.M., it was burning fiercely. Howe then ordered his own wing to advance. Completely unaware of Stark's wall, Howe sent the Light Battalion, under Alured Clark of the 23rd Foot, to outflank the rail fence. The battalion moved in fours along the beach, as four 6-pounders, protected by some grenadiers from the 35th Foot, attempted to breach the rail fence in preparation for a frontal assault by the Grenadier Battalion—led by Howe in person—followed by the 5th Foot and 52nd Foot. With the defenders of the rail fence fixed on the frontal assault, the light infantry would take them in the rear, and Howe's entire wing would then turn left and roll up the whole of the enemy line.

As Clark's battalion, led by the light company from his own regiment, reached Stark's marker, the New Hampshire men opened fire, mowing them down. With no room to deploy, the light companies of the 4th Foot and 10th Foot struggled over the bodies but were shot down. Eventually, the battalion fell back, leaving ninety-six troops dead or wounded on the beach. To their left things were little better, if slightly less bloody. It was only half a mile from Moulton's Hill to the rail fence, but frequent halts were needed for the guns to fire and to negotiate obstacles. As the Grenadier Battalion approached the rail fence, Howe regretted assigning their pioneers (who could have helped clear their line of march) to the artillery. As the grenadiers climbed a fence some ninety yards in front of Knowlton, some of his men (or Reed's) opened fire, but the range was too great to cause many casualties—the real damage was that the grenadiers halted to return the fire. The 5th Foot and 52nd Foot quickly caught them up, and as the three battalions crowded together, the attack lost its momentum and the men had to be pulled back out of range to re-form.

Howe rethought his plan; he now knew that the beach was defended, but the enemy's weak point was still his left. He ordered the light infantry to attack the rail fence while his grenadiers attacked the flèches—this time with closer support from the guns, which had drifted too far to the left due to the rough ground. After a short break, the line advanced again, but this attack was another disaster, being hit by a succession of volleys over a period of thirty minutes. The artillery support never appeared, as the 6-pounders had been resupplied with 12-pounder ammunition, and attempts to return the fire by the infantry collapsed as officers fell everywhere (all twelve of Howe's staff were hit, though he was unscathed) and some light and grenadier companies were reduced to single figures. Howe pulled back again to reassess his position: more Americans were amassing on Bunker Hill—some advancing, others building defensive works—and soon they would be too numerous to dislodge, perhaps even numerous enough to drive Howe off the peninsula. He ordered Clinton to send over reinforcements and prepared for one last assault.

To Howe's left, Pigot had made his feint, with the 38th Foot and 43rd Foot advancing against the redoubt and breastwork, while the 47th Foot and 1st Marines circled around to the south. The troops opened fire at more than 100 yards and did little damage but did succeed in encouraging Prescott's men to fire back, using up their smaller amount of ammunition. Prescott moved around the redoubt, ordering his men to hold their fire until the British were within 30 yards, supposedly saying, "Don't fire 'til you see the whites of their eyes." (This order has also been attributed to Putnam during the same battle; in both cases, it is often suggested that the speaker actually coined the phrase. However, the phrase was, in various forms, an apparently commonplace instruction to those using the relatively inaccurate firearms of the eighteenth century.) As Pigot's men approached a second time, the Americans unleashed a volley that forced the British back out of range. The 47th Foot and the 1st Marines also had to withdraw after running up against a large detachment of Massachusetts troops who had fortified a stone barn after being forced out of Charlestown by the fires.

As the crowds in Boston watched both British wings retreating and the horde of casualties falling back to Moulton's Point, Clinton responded to Howe's request for reinforcements. Asking Burgoyne to make his apologies to Gage, he took the 2nd Marines and 63rd Foot across to Charlestown peninsula, landing under a heavy fire that wounded several men in the leading boats. As he landed, he organized the remaining men to guard the beaches and as many walking wounded as he could find into an ad hoc army. As Clinton moved forward to support Pigot, the 47th Foot and 1st Marines finally cleared the enemy marksmen from the outskirts of Charlestown and captured the stone barn, while Howe's right formed up for one more attack on the rail fence.

On the American side, Knowlton's and Reed's men were forced to raid the pockets and cartridge boxes of the dead to find more rounds, while in the redoubt Prescott broke open the cartridges meant for the cannon and handed out the coarse powder. Nobody had sent food, water, or ammunition to the troops on Breed's Hill all day; Ward was now trying desperately to get supplies forward, but nobody was willing to take wagons across Charlestown Neck, much less to Breed's Hill (the few supplies that did get over were consumed by those on Bunker Hill). Even the men Ward had sent forward had still not arrived. Several colonels were later court-martialed for cowardice as a result, although in fairness Ward had no staff and no maps, so some who were unfamiliar with the area may easily have become lost.

Once reinforcements reached Bunker Hill, few officers had the leadership abilities to take them farther; stray shots claiming the occasional victim further demoralized the men, and only small groups reached Breed's Hill, mostly reinforcing the flèches, which were nearest. In terms of manpower, Ward had now committed every man and gun and could do nothing to support his right wing if the British attacked across Boston Neck toward Roxbury. Luckily, Gage was in no position to do any such thing—even if he had been aggressive enough to contemplate it. Apart from a regiment of light dragoons still recovering from their Atlantic crossing, his only reserve was the brigade of Lord Hugh Percy, which had only replaced its losses from 19 April the previous day with drafts of raw recruits fresh from England.

Back on Moulton's Hill, Howe had a new plan. The surviving light infantry—no more than 150—would engage the defenders of the rail fence with long-range musketry. Meanwhile, the 6-pounders would advance, their right flank protected by the light infantry, to enfilade the breastwork as the 5th Foot attacked the flèches and the grenadiers and 52nd Foot assaulted the northern half of the breastwork. At the same time, Pigot would attack the southern half of the breastwork and the front of the redoubt with the 38th Foot and 43rd Foot, while the 47th Foot and the 1st Marines would sweep around and storm the south and west sides of the redoubt. Once in possession of Breed's Hill, Howe could face any counterattacks or any advance on Bunker Hill as he wished. With the 6-pounders now correctly supplied, the end was swift (as, in truth, it should have been originally). The breastwork was swept clean of defenders, who either fled or retired into the redoubt. The same thing occurred at the flèches, while over at the rail fence Stark knew that he had to cover Prescott's retreat but could also see that he was in danger of being cut off. If he considered a counterattack against the weakened light infantry, he quickly discounted it because of having to cross the same rough terrain as his enemy and with men who were much less adept at maneuvering in the open under fire.

In the redoubt, Prescott's men held their fire until the British were twenty yards away, then unleashed a volley that brought down several officers but could not stop the regulars from entering the work. Almost simultaneously the breastwork was captured by the 52nd Foot, who came under a heavy cross fire from the flèches and the north face of the redoubt. Three captains climbed onto the parapet of the redoubt; they were shot down almost at once, but their men followed and burst into the redoubt, bayoneting the defenders. Meanwhile, the 1st Marines and the 47th Foot swarmed across the ditch and into the south side of the redoubt, despite having been disordered by hedges and fences and losing several officers, including John Pitcairn, second in command during the Concord raid, who received a fatal wound and collapsed into the arms of his son. Attacked from three sides, Prescott ordered his men to retire through the gorge at the rear face of the redoubt; as they left, British volleys and bayonets struck their backs, one bullet killing Warren. (The story that the redoubt was held by only 150 men, who were only defeated because their ammunition ran out, is simply not true.) Seeing Prescott fall back, Stark also retired, taking the one serviceable gun remaining, after a tussle with the 5th Foot.

Although the reserves on Bunker Hill alone still outnumbered Howe, panic took over as the battle they had avoided all afternoon suddenly came inexorably nearer. Clinton arrived at the redoubt and took over the pursuit from the weary Howe, pausing only to post 100 of his walking wounded from the beach in the redoubt to provide a rallying point if anything should go wrong. As Clinton moved forward toward Bunker Hill, the enemy divided into fleeing masses, and a group of Massachusetts and Connecticut troops tried heroically to cover their retreat. Formed up behind a low, stone wall, they traded volleys for several minutes with the three light companies of Pigot's reserve (reducing one company to just 5 men) before withdrawing, fence by fence, across Charlestown Neck.

Although fresh units were still arriving from Cambridge, even those keen to get forward could not pass the horde streaming in the opposite direction as the *Glasgow* and the *Symmetry* sprayed Charlestown Neck with grapeshot. Putnam finally accepted defeat and rode away, carrying valuable entrenching tools (probably the only ones saved that day). As Clinton reached the Neck, Howe ordered him to halt, as his force was too depleted, especially in officers, to carry the fight to the Americans. Fortified posts were set up to cover the road across the Neck and the north end of the Mill Dam. It was still only 5:00 P.M.

Unshaken by the chaos, Ward arranged the remaining Connecticut regiments to cover the retreat, and that evening Putnam had them build another fort on Winter Hill, just west of the Neck. One unit occupied some houses and opened up a sporadic fire until a 12-pounder sent forward by Howe drove them away, supported by broadsides from the *Glasgow*. Clinton's rapid advance had also trapped large numbers of Americans on the peninsula (one pair killed an officer of the 38th Foot and his servant who thought they were surrendering), and mopping up continued for several days.

Back at Moulton's Point, the *Somerset* had landed barrels of water as the boats ferried the wounded back to Boston. They included George Harris, captain of the 5th Foot's grenadier company, who would use mirrors to watch surgeons trepanning his skull to remove a bullet from his brain. Many of the enlisted men had severe leg wounds, caused by the Americans' use of scrap metal, nails, and glass, that would require amputation. Though often explained as an act of desperation by men out of regular ammunition, it stretches credulity to the limit that such items would be lying around in fields (especially pastures used to graze livestock) in any quantity, let alone in the amounts apparently used on the day.

In a battle lasting barely ninety minutes, Howe, with up to 3,500 men, of whom no more than 1,500 were engaged at any time—and in an area covering less than half a mile square—lost 226 dead and more than 900 wounded. This staggering figure represented almost half those engaged (the oft-quoted figure of 1,054 casualties excludes the wounded from the 38th Foot—which had the most dead of any British unit—usually estimated at more than 100). The losses in officers, 19 dead and 70 wounded, were particularly severe and would represent one-quarter of all British officer casualties in the Revolution. The Americans, who had up to 10,000 men—of whom no more than 2,000 were engaged at any time—lost between 400 and 600, mostly in the retreat; Massachusetts lost 115 dead, 305 wounded, and 30 captured (most of whom were also wounded), while Stark reported 19 dead and 74 wounded from his and Reed's regiments. Knowlton's losses are unrecorded but were probably negligible. In one category, though, American losses heavily outweighed those of the British—hundreds of men simply went home during and after the battle. The various provincial governments took prompt steps to return many of them, but for the moment their absence added to Ward's already dangerous weakness.

On 18 June, Howe burned the houses west of Charlestown Neck to protect working parties from sniper fire. Both he and Clinton urged Gage to proceed with the plan to occupy Dorchester Heights while the opposition was still weak (in fact, Ward had just taken 1,000 men from Thomas to strengthen his own left), but Gage did nothing until 24 June. On that day, a force comprising three gondolas, the 2nd Marines, the 63rd Foot, and the flank companies of the 64th Foot were detailed to storm the heights, supported by a diversionary attack from Charlestown peninsula and an artillery bombardment of Roxbury from Boston Neck. Inevitably word got out, and Gage called off the attack at the last moment (the bombardment of Roxbury went ahead but did no damage). Ward had learned of the assault and had reinforced Thomas, but Thomas had still not fortified the heights and would have been forced to fight Gage's troops in the open. Instead, Howe established a permanent camp on Charlestown peninsula, as both Gage and the provincial congress sent dispatches to London giving their own versions of a battle fought between two raw and inexperienced armies and won by superior leadership and discipline, but at a crippling cost both numerically and psychologically.

It has long been fashionable to criticize almost every aspect of the British plans that day. Some armchair strategists have argued that occupying Charlestown Neck would have resulted in a bloodless victory. However, the south side was impracticable since the mill dam and marshes would have prevented the boats from getting close enough to land artillery, while a landing on the north side would have involved a long row up the Mystic River (completely uncharted, due to an oversight by the Royal Navy) against the tide. Any landing site had to be close enough to prevent the first wave being left unsupported in close proximity to a numerically superior enemy while the boats returned to collect the second wave. The wharves and jetties of Charlestown could have offered a better beachhead but would have brought vulnerable boats full of troops within range of the redoubt's guns. The British would then have had to fight their way through the town, negating their superior maneuverability.

Mother Nature also helped the Americans on that day: the weather was dry and clear, with light westerly breezes alternating with flat calms—almost the exact opposite of what the Royal Navy needed for its understrength crews to maneuver around Charlestown and give supporting fire to Howe. The tides were equally unfavorable; the time taken to assemble the troops meant that the flood tide was lost and the boats had to be rowed against the current. Fear, dense smoke from hundreds of black-powder weapons, and the claustrophobic nature of the fighting around the redoubt, all recorded in contemporary accounts, have created the myth that the action took place in a heat wave. In fact, humidity was low, and the temperature was recorded as 64°F that morning, reaching the mid-80s by the afternoon—a typical June day in Boston.

Howe's battlefield tactics are also frequently denigrated, but in fact he correctly identified the weak points of his opponents' line and attacked them. Had his artillery not let him down (bringing the wrong ammunition) or fate not brought Stark—one of the few competent American officers—to the most vulnerable part of the line at just the right moment, either of Howe's first two attacks would have cleared the field. Such a comprehensive defeat might well have caused a major morale failure in the Continental forces; even if it had not, the absence of massive British casualties might well have led to a more aggressive approach from Howe during the New York Campaign the following year.

Brendan D. Morrissey

See also

Boston, Siege of; Burgoyne, John; Clinton, Henry; Dorchester Heights, Massachusetts; Gridley, Richard; Howe, William; Lexington and Concord; Percy, Hugh; Pigot, Robert; Pitcairn, John; Prescott, William; Putnam, Israel; Reed, Joseph; Stark, John; Ward, Artemas; Warren, Joseph

References

Carrington, Henry B. *Battles of the American Revolution, 1775–1781.* 1876. Reprint, New York: Promontory, 1974.

Elting, John. *The Battle of Bunker's Hill.* Monmouth Beach, NJ: Philip Freneau, 1975.

Fleming, Thomas J. *Now We Are Enemies: The Story of Bunker Hill.* New York: St. Martin's, 1960.

Frothingham, Richard. *History of the Siege of Boston and of the Battles of Lexington, Concord and Bunker Hill.* Boston: Little, Brown, 1849.

Ketchum, Richard. *Decisive Day: The Battle for Bunker Hill.* 1974. Reprint, New York: Henry Holt, 1999.

Morrissey, Brendan. *Boston 1775: The Shot Heard around the World.* Oxford, UK: Osprey, 1995.

Ward, Christopher. *War of the Revolution.* 2 vols. New York: Macmillan, 1952.

Wood, W. J. *Battles of the Revolutionary War, 1775–1781.* Chapel Hill, NC: Algonquin, 1990.

Burgoyne, John (1723–1792)

A British Army officer and dramatist, John Burgoyne was one of the most flamboyant and interesting figures in the War for American Independence. His significance in that conflict derives not from his brilliance or high accomplishment as a soldier but from his defeat as commander of an Anglo-German army that capitulated to General Horatio Gates at Saratoga in 1777. Burgoyne may have been a more accomplished playwright than general, for he achieved considerable fame in London as a dramatist after the war.

Burgoyne was born at Park Prospect, Westminster, London, on 4 February 1722. He attended Westminster School, where he became the intimate friend of James Stanley-Smith, Lord Strange, son of the eleventh Earl of Derby, who was head of the powerful Stanley family. This connection proved to be important and beneficial later in Burgoyne's life. In 1737 Bur-

Major-General John Burgoyne. Arriving in Boston in 1775, he witnessed the assault on Bunker Hill before later bringing British reinforcements to the garrison at Quebec in the spring of 1776. His own campaign in the Hudson Valley in 1777 ended in complete disaster and culminated in the surrender of his army at Saratoga. (Library of Congress)

goyne began his military career as a subbrigadier in the 3rd Horse Guards and three years later was promoted to cornet in the 13th Light Dragoons. He was promoted to lieutenant in the same regiment in 1741.

In 1743 Burgoyne eloped with Lady Charlotte Stanley, the fifteen-year-old daughter of the Earl of Derby. Angry with the new Mrs. Burgoyne, Lord Derby grudgingly gave her a small dowry and refused to have anything more to do with her or her husband. With his wife's money, in 1745 Burgoyne purchased a junior captaincy in the 13th Dragoons. For the next two years he and his wife lived in London, where Burgoyne drank and gambled in the most fashionable gentlemen's clubs. But in 1747 he was so overwhelmed by gambling debts that he was forced to sell his commission. The Burgoynes then moved to France and settled into a quiet life in the countryside near Chanteloup, the estate of François Joseph, Duc de Choiseul. Burgoyne became acquainted with the duke's son, Etienne François, comte de Stanville; learned French; read French literature; and studied French military institutions. In 1750, Burgoyne and his wife traveled through Europe and then settled in Rome. Their only child, Charlotte Elizabeth, was born in 1754; she died ten years later.

In 1755 the Burgoynes decided to return to England, despite family difficulties. Fortunately for them, Lord Derby and Burgoyne reconciled their differences, and Lady Charlotte was provided with an annuity of £400 and a guarantee of £25,000 on her father's death. Moreover, in 1757 Lord Derby was instrumental in securing for his son-in-law a captaincy in the 11th Dragoons. In May 1758 Burgoyne exchanged his captain's rank for a lieutenant-colonelcy in the prestigious 2nd (Coldstream) Foot Guards. He seems to have participated in expeditions to Rochefort in September 1757 and St. Malo in June 1758. He definitely was involved in the expeditions against Cherbourg in August 1758 and St. Malo in September 1758. In the latter operation, which turned into a disaster for the British, Burgoyne distinguished himself under intense fire during the withdrawal. In August 1759 he was selected by Prime Minister William Pitt to raise a regiment of light cavalry, which joined the service as the 16th Light Dragoons and became informally known for a time as "Burgoyne's Light-Horse."

In February 1761 part of Burgoyne's regiment was selected to go on an expedition to Belle Ile on the coast of Brittany. Being a colonel, Burgoyne could not command a detachment and so accompanied the expedition as a volunteer. On 30 March 1761 he was elected to Parliament for Midhurst, Sussex, but was too involved in his military career to assume his seat. In May 1762 he arrived in Portugal, serving under Count la Lippe with the local rank of brigadier-general. Given command of an Anglo-Portuguese brigade of about 3,000 men, on 27 July Burgoyne led his brigade in a dawn attack on the Spanish town of Valencia de Alcántara. He destroyed a Spanish regiment and captured a general, thereby earning the praise of King José of Portugal and la Lippe. On 5 October, Burgoyne's subordinate, Lieutenant-Colonel Charles Lee, stormed and captured the fortified Portuguese town of Villa Velha, thus adding luster to Burgoyne's military reputation. As a reward for his Iberian service, Burgoyne was promoted to colonel of the 16th Light Dragoons in late 1762 and to colonel commandant in March 1763. In February 1766, as a mark of favor from the king, Burgoyne's regiment was designated "royal" and named the "Queen's Light Dragoons." He was appointed governor of Fort William in October 1769 and promoted to major-general on 25 May 1772.

During this time, Burgoyne was a parliamentary spokesman for the government. Regarding American affairs, he took a hard line toward the colonies, voting against repeal of the Stamp Act and in favor of the Declaratory Act. In 1768 he was elected as a member of Parliament for Preston in a viciously contested race. Later convicted in court of attempting to incite violence during the campaign, he was fined £1,000. Burgoyne represented Preston for the rest of his life. In 1772 he strongly condemned the alleged misconduct of Robert, Lord Clive, who was accused of peculation during his service in India and almost impeached. Meanwhile, Burgoyne hobnobbed with high society in London, frequenting the most fashionable clubs and gambling outrageously. An amateur actor, he also tried writing plays. He wrote *Maid of the Oaks* in 1774, satirizing English social mores, and staged it in June at the wedding of Lord Strange's son. David Garrick, an outstanding theater manager and actor, staged the play at Drury Lane in November of that year.

In April 1775 Burgoyne, despite his claim that he found it distasteful to fight those whom he considered fellow Englishmen, found himself bound by loyalty to the king to participate in the suppression of the rebellion in America. Burgoyne was sent with two other major-generals, Sir William Howe and Henry Clinton, to assist Lieutenant-General Thomas Gage in Boston. Burgoyne spent the summer and fall complaining bitterly about his enforced inactivity and criticizing his commander in chief. Wishing for an independent command, Burgoyne wrote letters to the ministry in London advocating a grand strategy that in broad form would be adopted in 1777. He also corresponded with Lee, whom he had commanded in Portugal and who now was a general in the Continental Army. Their exchange of letters quickly degenerated into a propaganda battle. Burgoyne composed bombastic proclamations for Gage and in the autumn wrote a farce, *The Blockade of Boston,* that was staged at Charlestown in January 1776. By that time Burgoyne had returned home in disgust to lobby for an independent command.

In early 1776, at the request of Lord George Germain, secretary of state for the colonies, Burgoyne drafted a memorandum on how his country should prosecute the war. He proposed that one army should drive southward from Montreal through Lake Champlain while another should advance up the Hudson River from New York City to converge at Albany. On the tactical level, he suggested that the British Army employ more light infantry forces and artillery. Although he did not secure his much-desired independent command, Burgoyne did receive orders to lead an army in relief of General Sir Guy Carleton, governor-general of Canada, who was then besieged in Quebec. With the local rank of lieutenant-general, Burgoyne was appointed second in command to Carleton for the anticipated campaign against the Americans in upstate New York. With sadness Burgoyne left his ailing wife, who survived his departure by only two months. He sailed for Canada on 7 April 1776, arriving with his army on 1 June.

During the summer and fall of 1776, Carleton drove the retreating American army out of Canada, engaged in a shipbuilding contest on Lake Champlain, overwhelmed an American flotilla at Valcour Island (11–13 October), and advanced to Crown Point, New York. In all these operations Burgoyne played only a minor role, leading no troops in action and advancing his men only after Carleton opened the way. Although Burgoyne felt that he was not being given opportunities to prove himself and his ideas in battle, he was supportive of his commanding officer throughout these maneuvers. In late October, Carleton decided to terminate the campaign

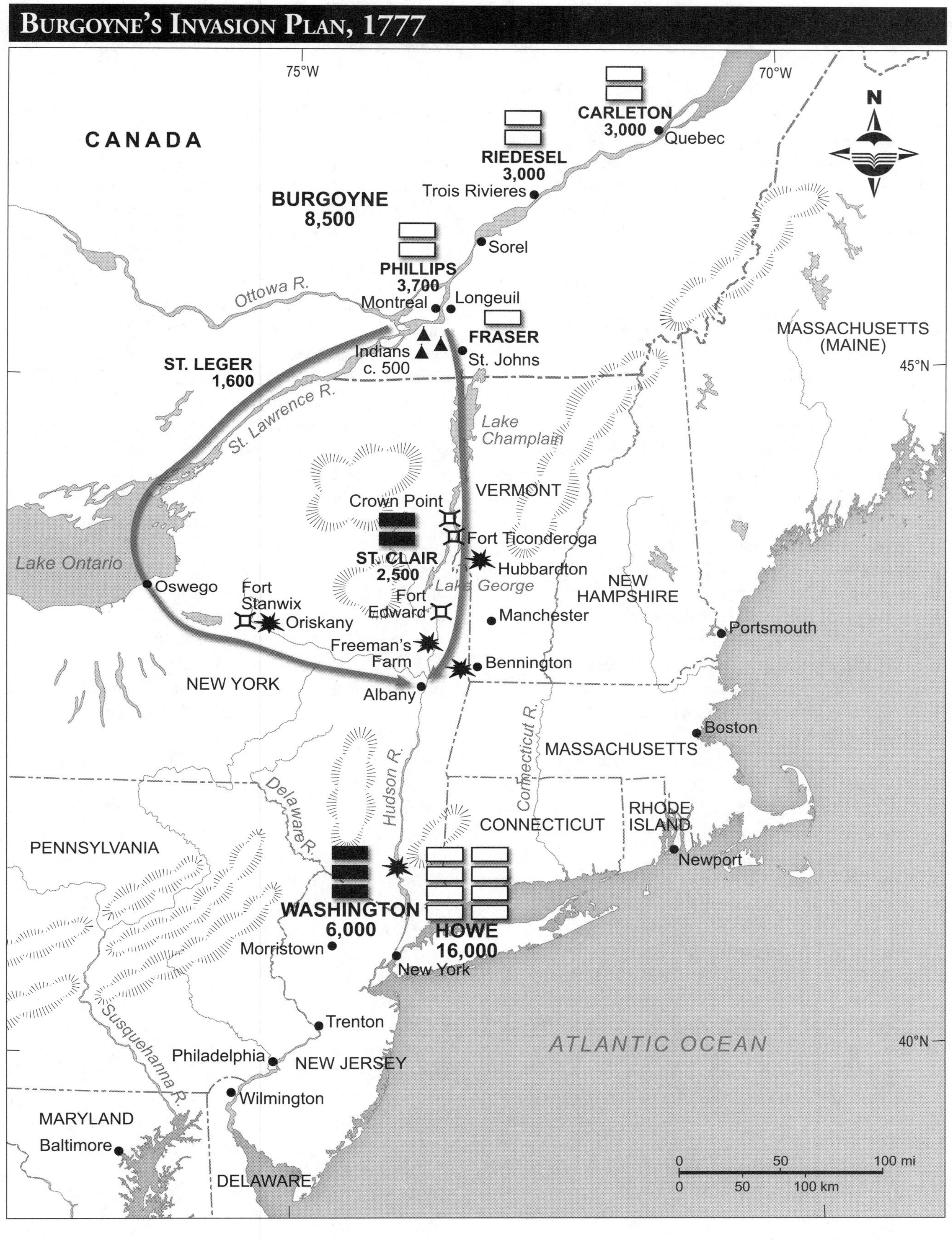
BURGOYNE'S INVASION PLAN, 1777
75°W
70°W
N
CANADA
CARLETON
3,000
Quebec
RIEDESEL
3,000
Trois Rivieres
BURGOYNE
8,500
Sorel
PHILLIPS
3,700
Ottowa R.
Montreal
Longeuil
FRASER
Indians
c. 500
St. Johns
ST. LEGER
1,600
MASSACHUSETTS
(MAINE)
45°N
St. Lawrence R.
Lake
Champlain
VERMONT
Crown Point
Fort Ticonderoga
ST. CLAIR
2,500
Hubbardton
Lake Ontario
Oswego
Fort
Stanwix
Oriskany
Fort
Edward
Lake George
Manchester
NEW
HAMPSHIRE
Portsmouth
Freeman's
Farm
Bennington
NEW YORK
Albany
Boston
MASSACHUSETTS
Connecticut R.
Delaware R.
Hudson R.
CONNECTICUT
RHODE
ISLAND
PENNSYLVANIA
Newport
WASHINGTON
6,000
HOWE
16,000
Morristown
New York
Trenton
Susquehanna R.
ATLANTIC OCEAN
40°N
Philadelphia
NEW JERSEY
Wilmington
MARYLAND
Baltimore
DELAWARE
0
50
100 mi
0
50
100 km

without attacking Fort Ticonderoga, at the south end of Lake Champlain, and withdraw back into Canada for the winter. Burgoyne strongly opposed these decisions, urging Carleton to carry out a full-scale offensive or at least to make a powerful feint against Ticonderoga. After the withdrawal, Burgoyne wrote to Clinton and complained that Carleton was endangering "the fruits of our summer's labor and autumn victory." With Carleton's permission, Burgoyne departed for Britain in mid-November, carrying to the government Carleton's recommendations for the campaign of 1777.

Learning on his arrival in London that Germain intended to replace Carleton with a new commander in Canada, Burgoyne began lobbying for the position. Subverting Carleton's proposals, Burgoyne drafted his "Thoughts for Conducting the War from the Side of Canada," which was accepted by the government. Going further, on 18 March 1777 he got himself appointed commander of Carleton's army in Canada. Burgoyne proposed to lead it down Lake Champlain to Albany while a division of Howe's army in New York would move northward and effect a junction, hopefully isolating New England from the other American colonies. In the meantime, a smaller body of troops under Colonel Barry St. Leger would act as a diversion in the Mohawk River Valley. On 6 May, Burgoyne arrived at Quebec and replaced Carleton, who, despite the severe rebuff from London, subsequently gave his former subordinate full support during the campaign. In June, Burgoyne collected 10,500 British and German troops and 140 pieces of artillery at St. John's, south of Montreal, then sailed down Lake Champlain toward Fort Ticonderoga.

On the morning of 6 July, Burgoyne occupied Ticonderoga without firing a shot, the American garrison having fled the night before toward Castleton and Hubbardton, Vermont. King George III offered Burgoyne a knighthood for this service, but he rejected it. He did, however, accept promotion to permanent lieutenant-general on 29 August. Pursuing the Americans southward, Burgoyne's victorious army swept aside the rebels and pushed toward the Hudson River. At that point, however, he inexplicably decided to send his army over land to Fort Edward rather than advancing by water up Lake George. He was also impeded in his advance by bringing along a mistress, an extensive wardrobe, and copious supplies of champagne. As a result, the Americans were given time to collect their wits and their troops to impede his slow progress up Wood Creek. Specifically, the forces of Major General Philip Schuyler, the American commander, felled trees across paths that Burgoyne's troops were obliged to use, destroyed bridges, and dammed Wood Creek with boulders to flood the vicinity. It consequently took Burgoyne's army twenty days to advance 20 miles from Skenesborough to Fort Edward on the Hudson River.

With his supply situation becoming desperate by 11 August, Burgoyne sent Lieutenant-Colonel Friedrich Baum, later reinforced by Lieutenant-Colonel Heinrich von Breymann, to forage around Manchester, Vermont. On 16 August at the Battle of Bennington, these two forces were defeated by American militiamen under Brigadier Generals John Stark and Seth Warner. Burgoyne lost about 900 men during the operation—a tenth of his entire army. Shortly thereafter, he learned that St. Leger's expedition had begun withdrawing from Fort Stanwix on 22 August and would offer him no support. Still refusing to retreat, Burgoyne crossed the Hudson River to the west bank on 15 September and advanced southward toward Bemis Heights. There, Major General Gates, who had replaced Schuyler as American commander, had constructed elaborate defensive fortifications with the assistance of Colonel Thaddeus Kosciuszko, a Polish military engineer, and ensconced an army of about 8,000 men to await Burgoyne's arrival. On 19 September, at the Battle of Freeman's Farm, Burgoyne attacked Gates's position in a three-pronged assault. In a fierce action, Burgoyne took possession of the contested ground but suffered about 550 casualties, which he could not replace. Had he attacked again the following day, he might have broken the American lines. Instead, Burgoyne fortified his position and waited until 7 October, when he launched another assault against Gates's position at Bemis Heights. British troops were driven back to their lines, and Burgoyne's most capable officer, Brigadier-General Simon Fraser, was killed.

Having learned that his supply lines to Canada were endangered by American militia forces operating in his rear, Burgoyne began retreating on 8 October. Four days later he realized that he was surrounded and cut off from any hope of outside assistance. Opening negotiations with Gates, he parleyed with the American general for a few days. On 17 October, Burgoyne bowed to the inevitable, signing a convention and surrendering his army. Ten days later, he and his disconsolate troops started a journey to Massachusetts, reaching Cambridge on 7 November. Burgoyne spent the winter doing whatever he could to make captivity comfortable for himself and his troops. Although not formally exchanged until 1781, he was allowed to depart for Britain on 15 April 1778 and arrived in London in mid-May. There he proved a great embarrassment for Lord North, now prime minister, and Germain, who were attempting to suppress any parliamentary inquiry of Burgoyne's conduct in America for fear that it would weaken the war effort. But when Burgoyne appeared in Parliament on 26 May, a motion was introduced to form a committee to examine the terms of the Saratoga convention.

Burgoyne defended himself in the ensuing debate and then had his speeches published for public consumption. Nevertheless, opposition politicians such as Charles James Fox used the occasion to attack the government—particularly Germain. Burgoyne demanded a court of inquiry into his conduct and also a court-martial, but both were blocked by the king and Germain, who wanted him returned to America as an unexchanged prisoner of war. Burgoyne was not sent to America, but in 1779 he was stripped of his colonelcy in the 16th Light Dragoons and of his governorship of Fort William. He retained only his rank in the army. In 1780, Burgoyne published his own version of events, *A State of the Expedition from Canada,* in which he vindicated his actions in America. He also joined the parliamentary opposition, led by Fox, Edmund Burke, and Richard Sheridan. When Lord Rockingham came to power in 1782, Burgoyne was appointed commander in chief in Ireland, colonel of the 4th Foot (the "King's Own"), and created an Irish privy councilor. The government fell after only a year, and Burgoyne was stripped of all his titles.

Afterward, Burgoyne tended to distance himself from politics, although as an opposition member he chided the prime minister, William Pitt the Younger, by composing the satirical *Westminster Guide.* In 1787, Burgoyne helped manage the impeachment of Warren Hastings for supposed malpractice as governor-general of India. Turning more to the cultivation of his literary interests, Burgoyne developed a considerable reputation as a man of letters. He wrote a libretto for two comic operas, one of which was *The Lord of the Manor,* produced by Garrick at the Drury Lane Theater. In 1785 Burgoyne translated the libretto for the opera *Richard Coeur de Lion,* and a year later he wrote *The Heiress,* which became a great success, moving through ten English editions in a year and appearing in translation in French, German, Italian, and Spanish. All of Burgoyne's plays were collected and published in 1808. In his last years he formed a liaison with Susan Caulfield, an actress, and together they had four children. The eldest of these, John, was eventually knighted and became famous in the Crimean War. Burgoyne died of the gout at the height of his literary fame and is buried in Westminster Abbey.

Paul David Nelson

See also

Bennington, Battle of; Canada, Operations in; Carleton, Guy; Clinton, Henry; Convention Army; Fort Ticonderoga, New York; Gage, Thomas; Gates, Horatio; Germain, Lord George; Howe, William; Kosciuszko, Thaddeus; Lee, Charles; North, Lord Frederick; Pitt, William, the Elder; Pitt, William, the Younger; Prisoners of War; Saratoga Campaign; Schuyler, Philip; St. Leger Expedition; Stark, John; Valcour Island, Battle of; Warner, Seth

References

Billias, George A. "John Burgoyne: Ambitious General." Pp. 142–192 in *George Washington's Opponents: British Generals and Admirals in the American Revolution.* Edited by George A Billias. New York: Morrow, 1969.

Bird, Harrison. *March to Saratoga: General Burgoyne and the American Campaign, 1777.* New York: Oxford University Press, 1963.

Burgoyne, John. *A State of the Expedition from Canada: As Laid before the House of Commons by Lieutenant-General Burgoyne, and Verified by Evidence; With a Collection of Authentic Documents, and an Addition of Many Circumstances Which Were Prevented from Appearing before the House by the Prorogation of Parliament; Written and Collected by Himself.* London: J. Almon, 1780.

DeFonblanque, Edward B. *Political and Military Episodes in the Latter Half of the Eighteenth Century: Derived from the Life and Correspondence of the Right. Hon. John Burgoyne, General, Statesman, Dramatist.* London: Macmillan, 1876.

Glover, Michael. *General Burgoyne in Canada and America: Scapegoat for a System.* New York: Atheneum, 1976.

Hargrove, Richard J. *General John Burgoyne.* Newark: University of Delaware Press, 1983.

Howson, Gerald. *Burgoyne of Saratoga: A Biography.* New York: Times Books, 1979.

Hudleston, F. J. *Gentleman Johnny Burgoyne: Misadventures of an English General in the Revolution.* Garden City, NY: Garden City Publishing, 1927.

Lewis, Paul. *The Man Who Lost America: A Biography of Gentleman Johnny Burgoyne.* New York: Dial, 1973.

Lunt, James. *John Burgoyne of Saratoga.* New York: Harcourt Brace Jovanovich, 1975.

Mintz, Max M. *The Generals of Saratoga: John Burgoyne and Horatio Gates.* New Haven, CT: Yale University Press, 1990.

Nelson, Paul David. *General Sir Guy Carleton, Lord Dorchester: Soldier-Statesman of Early British Canada.* Madison, NJ: Fairleigh Dickinson University Press, 2000.

Nickerson, Hoffman. *The Turning Point of the Revolution, or Burgoyne in America.* Boston: Houghton Mifflin, 1928.

Pancake, John S. *1777: The Year of the Hangman.* University: University of Alabama Press, 1977.

Styles, Showel. *Gentleman Johnny.* New York: Macmillan, 1962.

Burke, Edmund (1729–1797)

Edmund Burke was a British statesman, political writer, and journal editor whose writings circulated widely in Revolutionary America. In the 1770s, Americans were familiar with Burke's political thought, which they read favorably in part because they saw him as an opposition writer and kindred spirit. Colonial writers mined Burke's *Speeches* for gems they could use in defending the Revolutionary cause. Beginning in the 1780s, American historians used material in Burke's *Annual Register* to construct their accounts of the Revolution. By the 1790s, many Americans were less inclined to think of Burke as an ideological ally, particularly because of his critical *Reflections on the French Revolution.*

Burke was born in Dublin to a Protestant father and Catholic mother, a circumstance that may have instilled in him a disposition toward religious toleration that his early schooling with a Quaker teacher probably reinforced. Burke entered Trinity College in 1743 and earned his bachelor's degree in 1748. In 1750 he studied law, which did not hold his attention. In 1756, Burke published two books. *A Vindication of Natural Society, in a Letter to Lord ———, by a Late Noble Writer,* was a parody of parts of Bolingbroke's writings, although some of Burke's readers missed his irony. Burke's *Philosophical Inquiry into the Origin of Our Ideas on the Sublime and Beautiful* was a study of aesthetics that had a significant circulation in Britain and Germany but not in America. Burke's early interest in things American was evident, however, in *An Account of the European Settlements in America,* a publication on which Burke appears to have worked with his cousin, William Burke, in the late 1750s and early 1760s.

Burke's most significant writings on America resulted from his political career. Not until late 1765, when he was in his midthirties, did he become a member of Parliament, after having served as private secretary to Lord Rockingham. In 1769, Burke published *Observations on a Late Publication Entitled "The Present State of the Nation,"* a pamphlet that was highly critical of George Grenville and the Stamp Act. A propagandist for the Rockingham Whigs, Burke wrote that the Stamp Act would have "let loose that dangerous spirit of disquisition, not in the coolness of philosophical inquiry, but inflamed with all the passions of a haughty, resentful people, who thought themselves deeply injured, and that they were contending for everything that was valuable in the world." Burke maintained that real consequences and practical circumstances ought to be at the forefront of Britain's policy toward her American colonies:

> Whoever goes about to reason on any part of the policy of this country with regard to America upon the mere abstract principles of government, or even upon those of our own ancient constitution, will be often misled. Those who resort for arguments to the most respectable authorities, ancient or modern, or rest upon the clearest maxims drawn from the experience of other states and empires, will be liable to the greatest errors imaginable. The object is wholly new in the world. It is singular; it is grown up to this magnitude and importance within the memory of man; nothing in history is parallel to it. All the reasonings about it that are likely to be at all solid must be drawn from its actual circumstances.

Appointed agent for the province of New York in 1771, Burke, in his major parliamentary speeches published as *Mr. Burke's Speech on American Taxation* (1774) and *Mr. Burke's Speech on Moving His Resolutions for Conciliation with the Colonies* (1775), argued against taxing the American colonists who, he said, had come to value liberty highly as a result of their particular history. And even though Burke defended the Declaratory Act of 1766, which asserted the right of Parliament to legislate for the colonies, he recognized that the colonists "had a beneficial right to the maintenance and proper administration of that authority." Burke saw as well that to argue for taxation of the colonies was to take a position that was unnatural and certain to fail, and he couched his position in terms that appealed to many Americans in the 1770s: "It is not what a lawyer tells me I *may* do, but what humanity, reason, and justice tell me I ought to do."

Modern scholars differ on how best to interpret Burke's political writings, and contemporaries seldom, if ever, appreciated Burke's intricacies. In America, his support of the Revolutionary cause was especially well known, and the "celebrated Mr. Burke" was seen by many to be, like David Hume, a true friend of liberty and of America. Moses Mather, a New England minister, described Burke in *America's Appeal to the Impartial World* (1775) as one of the "illustrious patriots . . . whose names and memories no distance of place or time, will be able to obliterate from the grateful minds of the Americans"—an assessment that proved to be overly optimistic.

Burke's writings influenced Revolutionary America in other ways as well. As editor of the *Annual Register,* a publication that gave extensive consideration to American topics, Burke may have reached more American readers after independence than he had through the publication of his speeches in the early 1770s. Prominent American historians, such as David Ramsay in his *The History of the American Revolution* (1789) and Mercy Otis Warren in her *History of the Rise, Progress, and Termination of the American Revolution* (1805), borrowed heavily from the *Annual Register,* sometimes without saying so, perhaps because by the 1790s Burke's reputation in America was on the decline. Unlike Joseph Priestley and Richard Price, who also supported the American Revolution and with whom Burke is often compared, Burke denounced the French Revolution in his *Reflections on the Revolution in France* (1790), which was reprinted in America by Hugh Gaine in 1791. Because of Burke's harsh criticism of the French Revolution, he fell out of favor with America's more liberal republican revolutionaries in the 1790s, including Thomas Jefferson and Thomas Paine. Ultimately, however, that same criticism would make him a favorite of more conservative Americans, especially in the twentieth century.

Mark G. Spencer

See also

Declaratory Act; Grenville, George; Hume, David; Price, Richard; Priestley, Joseph; Ramsay, David; Stamp Act; Warren, Mercy Otis

References

Dreyer, Frederick. *Burke's Politics.* Waterloo, Ontario: Wilfrid Laurier University Press, 1979.

Kramnick, Isaac. *The Portable Edmund Burke.* New York: Penguin, 1999.

Lock, F. P. *Edmund Burke,* Vol. 1, *1730–1784.* Oxford: Oxford University Press, 1998.

Burke, Thomas (1747?–1783)

Thomas Burke was born in Ireland but came to America as a teenager and became one of North Carolina's most distinguished delegates to the Continental Congress. He is most closely associated with the issue of state sovereignty. Scarred by smallpox and possessing only one good eye, Burke cut an arrogant, unmistakable path through political circles during his short life.

Burke practiced law in Norfolk, Virginia, and Hillsborough, North Carolina, and attracted attention for his criticism of Great Britain during the Stamp Act controversy before he was twenty years old. While still in his twenties, he helped draft North Carolina's state constitution in 1776 and then became North Carolina's fourth representative to the Continental Congress, replacing William Hooper in 1777.

Burke's arrival in Congress coincided with several debates about the extent of congressional authority. Distrustful of central government, he typically sided with state governments and pressed for few additions to Congress's growing list of wartime powers. Indeed, he argued that Congress should not even have the power to arrest army deserters but should leave the matter to state officials. James Wilson of Pennsylvania, however, contended that desertion must be handled by Congress and the Continental Army, and his views prevailed. In April 1777 during debates on John Dickinson's draft of the Articles of Confederation, Burke once again urged that state governments should be supreme. Fearing that Article III might be construed as giving Congress supreme authority in the new confederated government, he proposed an amendment stipulating that the states retain their sovereignty, freedom, and independence as well as all powers not explicitly granted to Congress in the new document. Burke's views were congruent with those of many radical Whig thinkers of the day, who saw all governments as tending toward corruption when granted too much power, and his Irish background made him distrustful of faraway governments that were less responsive to the people than local authorities. After his struggles on the deserter issue, Burke may have anticipated more debate on the topic, but only James Wilson and Richard Henry Lee spoke at length in favor of the original Article III. Eventually, eleven states voted in favor of Burke's proposal (Virginia was opposed, and New Hampshire was divided), and the amendment became Article II of the Articles of Confederation, ultimately adopted by all states in 1781. Although Burke would make many other contributions through debate in the Congress, the guarantee of state sovereignty in the new confederation stands as his greatest legislative achievement.

Burke worked tirelessly during the next four years, futilely pressing for an end to the circulation of worthless congressional paper money and urging his state to reconsider its stance on western land concessions. He recorded his views on the tangled Deane-Lee Affair in a poem titled "An Epistle." He also helped draft preliminary peace terms in 1779 when the tide of war started to favor America. He supported the demand for free navigation of the Mississippi River, but on the issue of fishing rights off the Grand Banks, he took a less aggressive stance. He did not think it worthwhile to prolong the war in order to gain fishing rights for the New England states, but again he was outvoted. Burke's tenure in Congress was contentious and frequently found him on the losing side of many a debate, but he doggedly held fast to his vision of a free America.

The longer he served in Congress, however, the more Burke appeared to entertain the possibility that a central authority might be trusted with more power. A few months before leaving Philadelphia, he voted for two measures that would substantially increase Congress's authority: the first would allow Congress to oversee the commercial regulations of each state, and the second would give Congress the power to levy a 5 percent duty on imported goods, a source of revenue that would free Congress from requesting funds from the states. Only the second proposal received enough votes to pass, although it was not ratified by the states. By 1781, when Burke left Congress to become governor of North Carolina, he had become more nationalist in his approach to government, though he is best remembered as an ardent supporter of state power.

Burke's governorship was fraught with danger and disappointment. Only four months into his new post, he was captured by Loyalists who raided the state capital at Hillsborough and was taken to South Carolina, where he was paroled on condition that he would not leave James Island in Charleston Harbor. Hearing rumors that Loyalists planned to assassinate him, Burke broke his parole and returned to North Carolina, where he resumed his work as governor. But his violation of his parole disgraced him in the eyes of North Carolina voters, who turned him out of office in 1782. He retired to his farm, Tyaquin, and died there in 1783. Had he lived longer, Burke might have regained some of the stature he lost in the last two years of his life. Ever a Patriot, Burke's contributions in the Continental Congress marked him as the most distinguished delegate of the seventeen men who served on behalf of North Carolina.

Sally E. Hadden

See also

Articles of Confederation; Congress, Second Continental and Confederation; Hillsborough, North Carolina, Raid on; North Carolina

References

Burke, Thomas. *The Poems of Governor Thomas Burke of North Carolina.* Edited by Richard Walser. Raleigh, NC: State Department of Archives and History, 1961.

Morgan, David T., and William J. Schmidt. *North Carolinians in the Continental Congress.* Winston-Salem, NC: John F. Blair, 1976.

Rakove, Jack. *The Beginnings of National Politics: An Interpretive History of the Continental Congress.* New York: Knopf, 1979.

Rankin, Hugh F. *The North Carolina Continentals.* Chapel Hill: University of North Carolina Press, 1971.

Burr, Aaron (1756–1836)

Aaron Burr, who became a highly partisan and eventually notorious figure in the party battles that dominated America's early national period, was a dedicated, successful, and uncontroversial officer in the Continental Army during the Revolutionary War.

Born in 1756 in Newark, New Jersey, Burr was the son of Aaron Burr Sr., a Presbyterian minister and president of the College of New Jersey (now Princeton University), and Esther Edwards, daughter of the famed theologian Jonathan Edwards. Both parents died within two years of Burr's birth, and he was raised by an uncle, Timothy Edwards. Burr entered the College of New Jersey in 1769 at the age of thirteen and graduated in 1772. In 1774, after a brief attempt to pursue the family profession by studying theology, he turned his attention to the law, but his studies were cut short by the opening of the Revolutionary War.

When Burr heard of the conflict at Lexington and Concord in April 1775, he decided to join the Continental Army in Cambridge, Massachusetts. He volunteered to join General Benedict Arnold's expedition through the Maine wilderness to Canada (September–November 1775). In December 1775, General Richard Montgomery was impressed enough by Burr's abilities to appoint him his aide-de-camp with the rank of captain; Burr was with Montgomery when the general fell during the American attack on Quebec on 31 December 1775.

In May 1776, Burr left the American army in Canada and headed south in search of new military opportunities. In June, he accepted a place on Washington's staff but left after roughly ten days, possibly unsatisfied with the slow pace at headquarters. By the end of that month, however, he was aide-de-camp to General Israel Putnam with the rank of major. Burr served with Putnam during the Battle of Long Island on 27 August 1776 and played a large role in the rescue of American troops trapped at Brooklyn Heights on 29 August. In June 1777, the Continental Congress commissioned Burr a lieutenant colonel in the Continental Army and assigned him to the regiment of Colonel William Malcom near Poughkeepsie, New York. Malcom must have been impressed with the young officer, because when the colonel went home on a family visit, he left Burr in command. Burr performed admirably, increasing the size of the regiment and successfully leading it against Loyalist raiders.

Burr and his regiment spent the winter of 1777–1778 at Valley Forge with Washington's army and fought at the Battle of Monmouth the following June. For a short time in 1778, Burr acted as a sort of intelligence agent for General Washington, collecting information on British movements around New York City, but left within a few months, probably due to ill health. Burr was next given the difficult task of commanding troops patrolling the contested ground between the American and British lines in Westchester County, New York, but in March 1779, after roughly two months of this service, he resigned his commission, sick and exhausted. His last military action during the Revolution was an impromptu defense of New Haven, Connecticut, in July 1779, during which he arranged a hasty defense of the town against a British raid, using local militiamen and Yale College students.

Aaron Burr. Serving in the invasion of Canada and at Long Island, he led a brigade at the Battle of Monmouth, after which he publicly supported Charles Lee during his court-martial. Burr is best known for his duel with Alexander Hamilton and his various alleged conspiracies to create a separate nation out of the western states of the Union. (Library of Congress)

For the next several years, Burr devoted himself to the practice of law and to his family. In 1782, he married Theodosia Prevost, a widow ten years his senior, who bore him a daughter, also named Theodosia, in 1783. The next year he began his public career by winning election to the New York Assembly, and several years later, in 1789, he was appointed state attorney general. Thereafter his career became more national, as he served in the U.S. Senate, became a power in the new Republican-Democratic Party in the late 1790s, and was elected vice president to President Thomas Jefferson in 1801. In 1804, Burr unsuccessfully sought New York's governorship and soon thereafter killed Alexander Hamilton in a duel (July 1804). Public hostility to this act and to Burr's alleged involvement in an attempt to set up a separate empire in America's southwest in 1805–1806, for which he was tried and acquitted in 1807, drove him to Europe, but he returned in 1812 and spent his last years in New York.

Joanne B. Freeman

See also

Arnold, Benedict; Canada; Hamilton, Alexander; Jefferson, Thomas; Montgomery, Richard; Putnam, Israel

References

Lomask, Milton. *Aaron Burr,* 2 vols. New York: Farrar, Straus and Giroux, 1979, 1982.

Parmet, Herbert, and M. B. Hecht. *Aaron Burr: Portrait of an Ambitious Man.* New York: Macmillan, 1967.

Bushnell, David (1740–1826)

Known as the Father of Submarine Warfare, inventor David Bushnell devoted his time and personal assets to developing methods to deliver and explode underwater mines to use against the Royal Navy during the War for Independence.

When Bushnell entered Yale in 1771, he brought with him preliminary designs for both an underwater mine and a submarine, and he used his time as a student to experiment with underwater demolition. He also worked on his plans for a submarine as a means to deliver the mines. With help from his brother Ezra, Bushnell worked on building the submarine at their family home in Saybrook, Connecticut, so that he could keep his plans a secret from the British.

By the summer of 1776, Bushnell successfully tested the submarine, which he called the *Turtle,* as it resembled two tortoise shells pasted together. The *Turtle* had its first mission on 6 September 1776 when it attacked the flagship of the British fleet, HMS *Eagle,* anchored near Manhattan. Piloted by Sergeant Ezra Lee, the *Turtle* was able to approach the *Eagle* undetected but was unable to affix the explosive to the warship's hull. Lee then detonated the explosive underwater before returning to port, thus proving that Bushnell's concept was feasible.

The *Turtle* made two more unsuccessful attacks near Fort Washington on the Hudson River. As American forces retreated upriver, the sloop carrying the *Turtle* was sunk on 9 October 1776 near Dobb's Ferry. Bushnell reportedly returned to salvage the submarine, but the vessel's fate is unknown. After the loss of the *Turtle,* Bushnell returned to Saybrook to concentrate on improving underwater mines. His first mine attack was against the frigate *Cerberus,* which had anchored in Black Point Bay between Saybrook and New London. His mine did destroy a schooner that had pulled alongside the *Cerberus.*

On 5 January 1778, Bushnell unleashed another mine attack in what became known as the Battle of Kegs on the Delaware River. His new weapons had spring-lock mechanisms that were designed to detonate on impact. The mines were conveyed to their targets by buoys that resembled kegs. When the attack came, most of the British ships had left the river, but the mines were successful in scaring the British into ordering the Royal Navy to shoot any strange object floating near any British ship.

On 6 May 1778, British forces captured Bushnell but did not know who he was, and he was released shortly after his capture. He later received a commission as captain in the Corps of Sappers and Miners, but he did not have another opportunity to use his underwater demolition experience. After the war Bushnell disappeared from Saybrook, Connecticut, but reappeared in the 1790s as Dr. David Bush in Georgia, where he remained until his death.

Michael C. Miller

See also

Continental Navy; Naval Operations, American vs. British

References

Grant, Marion H. *The Infernal Machines of Saybrook's David Bushnell: Patriot Inventor of the American Revolution.* Old Saybrook, CT: Bicentennial Committee, 1976.

Wagner, Frederick. *Submarine Fighter of the American Revolution: The Story of David Bushnell.* New York: Dodd, Mead, 1963.

Butler, John (1728–1796)

John Butler spent most of his life on the New York frontier, where he became best known as the leader of the Loyalist partisan force Butler's Rangers. His military service began during the French and Indian War (1754–1763), continued with Colonel Barry St. Leger's invasion of the Mohawk Valley in 1777, and culminated in the leadership of his own unit in a series of savage raids along the New York and Pennsylvania frontiers.

Born in New London, Connecticut, in 1728, Butler grew up in the Mohawk Valley and entered military service at an early age. At the outbreak of the French and Indian War, he joined British General Sir William Johnson's expedition against Crown Point and fought at the Battle of Lake George on 8 September 1755. Butler then served under General Robert Abercromby at Fort Ticonderoga, where British forces were defeated on 8 July 1758. Butler then fled to another command and was present at the capture of Fort Frontenac in Kingston on 27 August 1758. Butler later served again under Johnson, first in operations around Fort Niagara in June–July 1759 and then at Montreal in September 1760.

Butler fled north to Canada at the start of the American Revolutionary War and worked for a time as a British Indian agent.

The Loyalist John Butler fought alongside British forces that invaded New York in 1777 and then formed Butler's Rangers, a Loyalist unit that joined Native Americans to attack the New York frontier. (Canadian Heritage Gallery ID#21678)

Anxious to return south, he offered his services to St. Leger in the unsuccessful invasion of the Mohawk Valley and siege of Fort Stanwix (present-day Rome, New York) in July and August 1777. Butler fought in the British-Indian victory at Oriskany on 6 August but was later forced to retreat to Canada with St. Leger's British forces. In 1778, Butler was commissioned a major in the British Army and raised a force of Loyalist partisans known as Butler's Rangers. His unit fought along the New York and Pennsylvania frontiers and earned for themselves a reputation for savagery. Butler led merciless raids into the Wyoming Valley near Wilkes-Barre, Pennsylvania, in the summer of 1778 and fought a sharp engagement at Newtown, near Elmira, New York, on 29 August 1779. In October 1780 he led a series of brutal raids in the Schoharie Valley, New York.

When it was clear that the British had lost the war, Butler fled from New York to Canada one last time in 1783. He resumed his work in Britain's Office of Indian Affairs and later became a commissioner at Niagara. Butler died at Niagara on 14 May 1796.

Andrew B. Godefroy

See also

Butler, Walter; Fort Stanwix, New York; Newtown, New York, Action at; Oriskany, Battle of; Schoharie Valley, New York; St. Leger Expedition; Wyoming Valley, Pennsylvania

References

Cruikshank, E. A. *The Story of Butler's Rangers and the Settlement of Niagara.* Owen Sound, Ontario: Lundy's Lane Historical Society, 1975.

Swiggett, H. *War Out of Niagara: Walter Butler and the Tory Rangers.* 1933. Reprint, Port Washington, NY: I. J. Friedman, 1963.

Butler, Richard (1743–1791)

A competent Continental Army officer during the Revolution, Richard Butler also served the early American republic as an Indian commissioner and soldier on the frontier. Born in Dublin, Ireland, and raised in Lancaster, Pennsylvania, he was an ensign in General Henry Bouquet's army during Pontiac's Rebellion in 1763 and later became a successful Indian trader. In 1775, Butler was appointed Indian agent in the Northwest Territory by Congress. On 5 January 1776, he was commissioned captain in the 2nd Pennsylvania Battalion. He was promoted to major of the 8th Pennsylvania Regiment on 20 July and to lieutenant colonel on 12 March 1777. He fought at Bound Brook on 13 April and was promoted to colonel of the 9th Pennsylvania Regiment on 7 June.

Later in 1777, Butler marched northward and joined Colonel Daniel Morgan's rifle corps as lieutenant colonel and second in command. In September and October, Butler fought in the battles of Freeman's Farm and Bemis Heights and then rejoined Washington's army. Butler's 9th Pennsylvania Regiment served under General Anthony Wayne's command in the Battle of Monmouth on 28 June 1778 and was in a skirmish at Kingsbridge, New York, on 30 September. Wayne praised Butler for his conduct in the storming of Stony Point on 16 July 1779. In January 1781 Butler assisted Wayne in suppressing a mutiny in the Pennsylvania line. Joining the Marquis de Lafayette in Virginia, Butler fought at Spencer's Ordinary on 26 June and was present at the British surrender at Yorktown on 19 October. He served with Wayne in Georgia in 1782 and on 30 September 1783 was breveted to brigadier general.

In March 1784, Congress again appointed Butler an Indian commissioner in the Northwest Territory. Over the next two years he and other commissioners dictated three treaties to the Indians that forced them to cede huge tracts of land to the United States. Congress appointed Butler superintendent of Indian Affairs for the Northern District in August 1786, and two years later he was commissioned a justice of the Court of Common Pleas for Allegheny County, Pennsylvania. In 1790 he was elected to the Pennsylvania Senate as a representative from Pittsburgh. The following year, he chaired an inquiry that exonerated Brigadier General Josiah Harmar of blame for defeat by Indians during an expedition against the Northwest tribes. Immediately thereafter Butler was appointed second in command with the rank of major general in Arthur St.

Clair's army, which was ordered to suppress those Indians. Butler quarreled with St. Clair over how the expedition was carried out as the army marched northward into Ohio. Chafing from this feud, when Butler learned on 3 November 1791 of an impending Indian assault, he did not inform St. Clair. When the Indians attacked the following day, Butler commanded the army's right wing and fought bravely but was mortally wounded. He insisted on being left behind when the Americans fled in disarray. Indian warriors killed Butler by a tomahawk blow to the head and ate his heart. Wayne's army recovered Butler's body on 25 December 1793 and buried him on the battlefield.

Paul David Nelson

See also

Bound Brook, New Jersey, Action at; Harmar, Josiah; Kingsbridge, New York, Actions around; Lafayette, Marquis de; Monmouth, Battle of; Morgan, Daniel; Mutiny, Continental Army; Saratoga Campaign; St. Clair, Arthur; Stony Point, New York, Capture of; Wayne, Anthony; Yorktown, Virginia, Siege of

References

Green, Thomas Marshall. *Historic Families of Kentucky.* Cincinnati: R. Clarke, 1889.

Sword, Wiley. *President Washington's Indian War: The Struggle for the Old Northwest, 1790–1795.* Norman: University of Oklahoma Press, 1985.

Butler, Walter (1752?–1781)

Walter Butler was born about 1752 near Johnstown, New York. He was the son of the Loyalist leader John Butler, who served as Sir William Johnson's Indian agent in the Mohawk Valley. The younger Butler also served as a Loyalist officer during the American Revolutionary War, notably as the leader of Butler's Legion. An aggressive soldier perhaps best known through the exploits of his fictionalized persona in the early-twentieth-century novels of Robert Chambers, Butler fought at Montreal (1775) and Oriskany (1777) and led a series of raids throughout the Mohawk Valley (1778–1780). His most aggressive attack was the Cherry Valley Massacre of 11 November 1778.

Butler received his education in Albany, New York, with the intention of becoming a lawyer. He showed great promise in his studies and opened a practice soon after completing school. At the same time, he joined his father's militia company as an ensign in 1768.

The outbreak of the Revolutionary War put an end to Butler's law practice, however, and he fled with his family and other Loyalists into Canada. There he was commissioned an ensign in the 8th (King's) Regiment and soon after fought his first engagement at Montreal in September 1775. Butler showed equal promise as a soldier, successfully leading an enveloping force attack against Ethan Allen on 25 September.

Butler accompanied his father on Colonel Barry St. Leger's invasion of northern New York and fought at Oriskany on 6 August 1777. When his father raised Butler's Rangers after Oriskany, Walter resigned his commission in the 8th Regiment and transferred to his father's Loyalist unit. Promoted to captain, Butler volunteered to lead a recruiting expedition behind enemy lines and was captured by Continental troops at Shoemaker's Tavern in the Mohawk Valley. Rather than being charged with attempting to enlist Loyalist supporters, he was tried for espionage by a court-martial under Lieutenant Colonel Marinus Willett, convicted, and sentenced to hang. His execution was stayed only after several American officers, including General Philip Schuyler, petitioned for his reprieve. Butler was instead imprisoned at Albany but soon managed to escape and rejoin British forces in Canada in April 1778. There he regained his commission and formed his own irregular Tory unit, just as his father had done.

Under Butler's command, Butler's Legion carried out a number of savage attacks, including the infamous Cherry Valley Massacre on 11 November 1778. Accompanied by an Indian raiding party led by Joseph Brant, Butler completely surprised the local outpost commander, Ichabod Alden, and took his town by storm. Attacking at the breakfast hour, Butler's forces killed Alden before he could reach the fort, and a subsequent incident sparked the Indians to lay waste to the town, slaughtering the men, women, and children. It is unclear who was actually controlling the Indian raiding party—Butler or Brant—but history has charged Butler with the responsibility for the massacre, just as his father has been remembered for vicious raids in the Wyoming Valley. From then on, Butler became known as the Terror of the Mohawk Valley.

Butler was heavily engaged in opposing the Sullivan-Clinton campaign of 1779 and continued raiding in the Mohawk Valley through 1780 and 1781. In October 1781, he participated in a raid near West Canada Creek in the Mohawk Valley. As the party engaged in destruction and burning on 30 October, it was counterattacked by a larger force of Continental Army soldiers and militia led by Butler's former would-be executioner, Willett. A running fight ensued, and Butler and the other men were pursued for some time until they were finally overtaken at a ford across West Canada Creek. Willett later recorded in his memoirs that Butler was shot in the head as he tried to cross the creek, but legend offers another version of his death. According to one account, Butler cried for quarter, but an Oneida Indian cried in return that he would give Butler "Cherry Valley quarters" and promptly tomahawked and scalped Butler where he lay wounded and exhausted. As historical evidence for this engagement is sparse, it is difficult even to suggest which version of events may be correct.

In upstate New York, circulation of the news of Butler's death coincided with that of Cornwallis's earlier surrender at

Yorktown. In a single day, two threats to the Patriot population of the Mohawk Valley were gone, and residents undoubtedly breathed a sigh of relief.

Andrew B. Godefroy

See also

Brant, Joseph; Butler, John; Cherry Valley Massacre; Montreal, Operations against; Oriskany, Battle of; St. Leger Expedition; Willett, Marinus

References

Cruikshank, E. A. *The Story of Butler's Rangers and the Settlement of Niagara*. Owen Sound, Ontario: Lundy's Lane Historical Society, 1975.

Graymont, Barbara. *The Iroquois and the American Revolution*. Syracuse, NY: Syracuse University Press, 1972.

Kelsay, Isabel T. *Joseph Brant, 1743–1807: Man of Two Worlds*. Syracuse, NY: Syracuse University Press, 1984.

Swiggett, H. *War Out of Niagara: Walter Butler and the Tory Rangers*. 1933. Reprint, Port Washington, NY: I. J. Friedman, 1963.

Byron, John (1723–1786)

Born on 8 November 1723 at his family's estate near Newstead Abbey, John Byron was the second son of the fourth Baron Byron. While still a teenager, he was made a midshipman in the Royal Navy and sailed aboard the *Wager* in Admiral Lord Anson's famous cruise during the War of Austrian Succession. Byron was shipwrecked off the Chilean coast in May 1741 and after much hardship reached Britain in 1745. He published an account of his adventures in 1768.

In 1764, Byron was appointed captain of the frigate *Dolphin*. He undertook a secret two-year exploration of the South Pacific, a cruise that earned him the nickname "Foul Weather Jack." The exploration yielded very little, and Byron returned home to receive his next assignment, governor of Newfoundland. He was promoted to rear admiral in March 1775 and then vice admiral in June 1778.

Succeeding Admiral Richard Howe, Byron led a poorly organized relief fleet to North America in the summer of 1778. Encountering en route one of the worst Atlantic gales on record, his fleet was so battered and dispersed that he could not commence operations until October. Almost immediately another storm hit as soon as he left New York Harbor, and the resulting damage delayed his deployment for another eight weeks. He finally set sail for the West Indies on 13 December. On 6 July 1779, with a force of twenty-one ships, he chased and engaged a numerically superior fleet under Admiral Jean-Baptiste d'Estaing off Grenada, but by attacking in a piecemeal fashion, Byron's efforts were thwarted and his force suffered heavily. Fortunately for Byron, d'Estaing, for reasons that are not clear, withdrew instead of seeking to engage in a general action, a circumstance that also certainly preserved Byron's fleet from decisive defeat. After requesting recall owing to poor health, Byron left the West Indies for Britain on 10 October, passing command to Rear Admiral Sir Peter Parker.

Andrew B. Godefroy

See also

Estaing, Jean-Baptiste, Comte d'; Grenada, Battle of; Howe, Richard; West Indies

References

Graham, G. S. *The Royal Navy in the War of American Independence*. London: HMSO, 1976.

Syrett, David. *The Royal Navy in American Waters, 1775–1783*. Brookfield, VT: Gower, 1989.

Tilley, J. A. *The Royal Navy in the American Revolution*. Columbia: University of South Carolina Press, 1987.

C

Cadwalader, John (1742–1786)

A prominent native of Philadelphia with strong family connections in Maryland, John Cadwalader served in the Revolution as a militia officer and was highly regarded as a businessman, soldier, and polished gentleman. In 1775 he was a man of wealth and social prominence who heartily supported popular opposition to Britain's attempts to coerce the colonies. He served on the Philadelphia Committee of Safety and was appointed captain of the City Troop, also known as the Silk Stocking Company. He soon became colonel of a Philadelphia battalion and in 1776 was promoted to brigadier general of the Pennsylvania militia. In late December 1776 he was ordered by General George Washington to ferry 1,500 militiamen across the Delaware River in support of the Continental Army's operations against Trenton, New Jersey. Although ice in the river impeded Cadwalader's movements, he did get across in time to fight in the Battle of Princeton on 3 January 1777. Washington then recommended to Congress that Cadwalader be promoted to brigadier general in the Continental Army, but Cadwalader declined the offer because he believed that the war was almost at an end. In September 1780, he wrote to Washington that he regretted this decision.

When General Sir William Howe invaded Maryland and Pennsylvania from Chesapeake Bay in September 1777, Cadwalader mobilized militiamen on Maryland's eastern shore to assist Washington. Cadwalader fought as a volunteer in the battles of Brandywine and Germantown and during the following winter engaged in guerrilla warfare against enemy foraging parties in eastern Pennsylvania. After the British evacuated Philadelphia on 18 June 1778, he organized Philadelphia volunteers and joined Washington in harassing General Henry Clinton's march across New Jersey toward New York. On 4 July, Cadwalader fought a duel with General Thomas Conway, who he believed was involved in a conspiracy to remove Washington from command of the Continental Army. Cadwalader wounded Conway in the mouth and neck, wounds that initially appeared to be mortal. Conway recovered, however, and later wrote to Washington and apologized for criticizing him.

Even though Cadwalader had won Washington's respect as an officer and a gentleman, his role in the Revolution now came to an end as the fighting shifted to other theaters. Later Cadwalader moved to Maryland and was elected to the state legislature. In his last years he became embroiled in a controversy with General Joseph Reed. When the "Brutus Letter," which was critical of Reed's conduct during the Trenton Campaign, was published in 1782, Reed believed that Cadwalader had written it. When Reed publicly accused Cadwalader of authorship in 1783, Cadwalader in some heat wrote *A Reply to General Joseph Reed's Remarks,* refuting the charges. In 1785, Cadwalader, along with John Beale Bordley and Samuel Powel, founded the Philadelphia Society for the Promotion of Agriculture, America's first agricultural society. The society encouraged American farmers to adopt the English practice of intensive cultivation rather than employing extensive farming methods. Cadwalader died in Kent County, Maryland, in 1786.

Paul David Nelson

See also

Brandywine, Battle of; Conway, Thomas; Conway Cabal; Germantown, Battle of; Princeton, Battle of; Reed, Joseph; Trenton, Battle of

References
Heathcote, Charles. "General John Cadwalader: A Sturdy Pennsylvania Military Officer and Devoted to General Washington." *Picket Post* 70 (1960): 4–9.
Ketchum, Richard M. *The Winter Soldiers.* Garden City, NY: Doubleday, 1973.

Camden, Baron
See Pratt, Sir Charles, 1st Earl Camden

Camden Campaign
In April 1780, Major General Benjamin Lincoln, at the head of 3,371 Continental and militia troops in Charleston, South Carolina, was besieged by British troops and in danger of capitulation. General Sir Henry Clinton, with 8,500 British, Hessian, and Loyalist soldiers, had maneuvered Lincoln into Charleston and was fast cutting off the Americans from outside support. Responding to Lincoln's difficulties, General George Washington ordered Major General Johann de Kalb to march south with 1,400 Delaware and Maryland Continentals to reinforce the American army in Charleston. When Kalb arrived in Petersburg, Virginia, on 6 June, he learned that Lincoln had surrendered the city and its garrison on 12 May. Hence, he reluctantly assumed military command in the Southern Department, but he did not relish his new responsibilities. He marched on into North Carolina and finally encamped at Coxe's Mill on Deep River, all the while encouraging Congress to appoint another officer to supersede him in the South.

The congressmen were amenable to Kalb's request, and a few were anxious to appoint Major General Horatio Gates. They were aware that General Washington wanted to send Major General Nathanael Greene to the South, but they had other ideas. These small-government legislators favored Gates because he agreed with their views on states' rights and also because on 7 March he had written them a seven-page letter outlining a plan of defense for the southern states. On 13 June 1780 Gates was appointed by Congress to take command in the South, and on 25 July he superseded Kalb at Coxe's Mill. Gates found the army in deplorable condition, suffering from a shortage of rations and a deficiency of every species of military provision. The Delaware and Maryland Continentals, three small artillery companies, and a cavalry corps of 60 men under Colonel Charles Armand were at Coxe's Mill. North Carolina militiamen under Major General Richard Caswell, about 1,200 strong, were encamped at Moore's Ferry on the Yadkin River, and nearly 1,500 Virginia militia were at Deep River. The main cavalry forces under Colonels Anthony White and William Washington were at Halifax, trying to recover after being mauled by Lieutenant-Colonel Banastre Tarleton's British Legion, the famous Green Dragoons, at Moncks Corner on 14 April and Lenud's Ferry on 6 May.

After the fall of Charleston, British forces quickly took control of South Carolina and Georgia. Clinton dispatched three columns of troops to seize Camden and Ninety-Six in upper South Carolina and Augusta in Georgia. On 5 June, Clinton departed for New York, leaving General Lord Charles Cornwallis in command of the South, with Charleston as his headquarters. When Gates arrived at Coxe's Mill, he found awaiting him a report from General Thomas Sumter, a partisan officer, describing the British dispositions and giving the number of British troops at Camden as 700, commanded by Lieutenant-Colonel Francis Rawdon. Gates was assured that if American forces could reach Camden within fifteen days, Rawdon's garrison could be easily overrun. Thus, on 27 July Gates decided, to the astonishment of Colonel Otho Williams and other American officers, to march in a direct line toward Camden rather than take a more westward route where supplies would be plentiful.

Gates's decision for haste was uncharacteristic, for normally he was a prudent and careful officer. A number of factors besides Sumter's letter contributed to Gates's decision, although that was probably the most weighty one. First, he believed that Rawdon, a young officer, could be easily dealt with. Second, Gates had been stung two years before at Saratoga, New York, by criticisms of his cautious generalship, even though he had forced General John Burgoyne to surrender. Third, Gates learned that Caswell was about to attack opposing forces on Lynches Creek, South Carolina, and was pleading for assistance. Therefore, in early August Gates had to rush to Caswell's assistance. Marching westward, Gates left behind the demoralized cavalry units of White and Washington. Not only did Gates refuse to await their reorganization or give them any assistance, but he pointedly let it be known that he did not consider cavalry to be very useful in the southern theater of operations.

Gates's poorly supplied, ragged, and weak troops marched for the next two weeks through a region of pine barrens, sand hills, and swamps peopled by Loyalists. They had covered only 120 miles, often sustained by nothing more than Gates's promises that plentiful supplies of rum and rations were somewhere ahead. The troops suffered terribly, living on green peaches and raw corn, while Gates pleaded with Governor Thomas Jefferson of Virginia to send food to his half-starved fellow citizens. In the area of intelligence, at least, Gates was not deficient, despite his neglect of the cavalry. Mounted irregulars commanded by Colonel Francis Marion of South Carolina provided him with information as he entered that state. Also, Caswell and General Griffith Rutherford informed him that Rawdon

The Battle of Camden. General Horatio Gates, with a mixed force of Continentals and militia, and General Charles Cornwallis, with an army of British regulars, unexpectedly clashed in a bloody engagement that left three-quarters of the Americans killed, wounded, or captured. The battle ended in a rout of the American forces, and Gates himself fled the field. (National Archives and Records Administration)

was moving his troops northward out of Camden and taking a defensive position on Lynches Creek. On 3 August, Gates detached a force under Sumter toward the Wateree River below Camden, under orders to disrupt Rawdon's supply lines and capture provisions.

Despite Gates's dismissive assessment of Rawdon, the young officer was a decisive and intelligent soldier and had no intention of waiting meekly for the Americans to attack him at Camden. He had under his command three times the number of troops that Sumter had estimated and disposed them to the best advantage. Rawdon recognized the need to concentrate forces at Camden, but he kept small garrisons at Hanging Rock and Rocky Mount to fend off Sumter's attempts to get around him and attack his supply lines. Sumter attacked Rocky Mount on 1 August and five days later Hanging Rock but was repulsed. Rawdon next threw Caswell's North Carolina militia into confusion by feigning an attack at Lynches Creek, then withdrawing. Caswell joined Gates's army on 7 August. Four days later, Rawdon took a defensive post at Little Lynches Creek, 15 miles northeast of Camden, barring Gates's passage across a bridge. Although locally outnumbered by the Americans, Rawdon occupied a good defensive post. Nevertheless, he was in danger of being outflanked on his left, thus allowing Gates to seize Camden and throw the British situation in upstate South Carolina into turmoil.

Discovering that Rawdon's position was too strong for a frontal assault, Gates did indeed try a flanking maneuver to the British left, and he may have intended a decisive action. If so, he negated any possibility of success by acting in broad daylight and losing the element of surprise. Rawdon hastily fell back to Camden, using Tarleton's Legion to cover his withdrawal. He also pulled his forces out of Hanging Rock and Rocky Mount, thus allowing Sumter to seize these positions. Sumter asked Gates for reinforcements to cut off the British line of retreat south of Camden and on 14 August received a body of 100 Continentals and 300 North Carolina militia under Lieutenant Colonel Thomas Woolford. By that date Gates had reached Rugeley's Mill, a few miles north of Camden, where he was joined by 800 Virginia militia under General Edward Stevens. Gates now believed, inexplicably, that he had collected 7,000 troops. When Colonel Williams gave him the more accurate figure of 3,052, Gates was disappointed but enigmatically remarked that they were "enough for our purpose."

Gates did not divulge his purpose to Williams, but apparently it was to move quickly into a defensive post just north

Battle of Camden, 1780

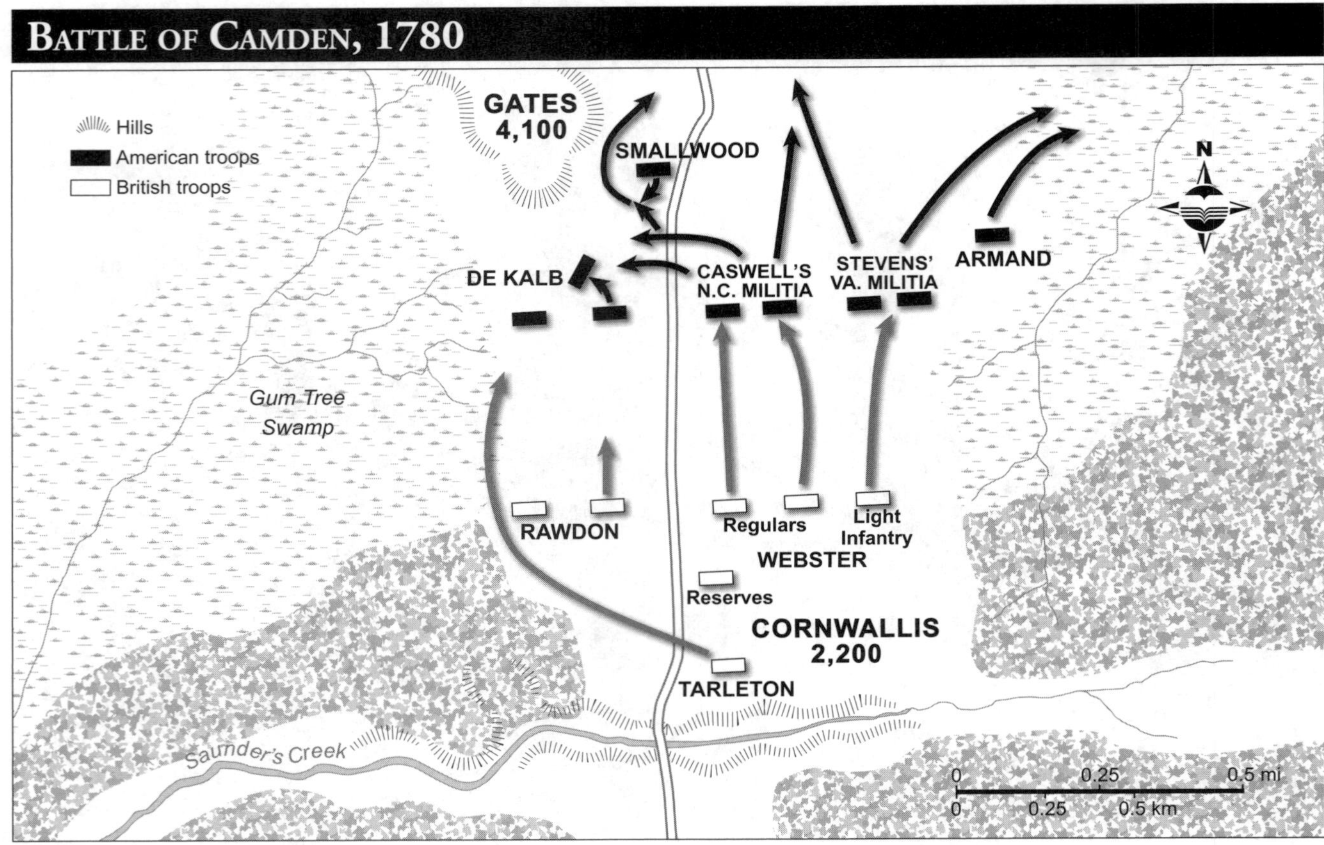

of Camden and compel the British to either attack at a disadvantage or retreat. That was what Gates told at least one of his officers at the time and also told Congress later. Such a plan would repeat his successful conduct against Burgoyne. It would explain his neglect of cavalry, the absence of his usual caution, and his weakening of the American army by detaching reinforcements to Sumter in the face of a British army. It would also explain his decision to march southward on the night of 15 August, to the amazement of Tarleton, "in the neighbourhood of an enterprizing enemy." Gates did indeed march, and almost blindly, even though more than half his army was raw militia and a night maneuver was difficult under the best of circumstances. He had sent Colonel Christian Senff, an engineer, to choose the defensive ground that his army would occupy, and he wanted to reach that position and construct earthworks before being detected by his opponent. Gates's officers agreed with his decision, not believing any more than he did that the British would try to fight outside Camden.

Unknown to Gates, however, Cornwallis had joined the British Army at Camden with reinforcements on 13 August and quickly decided that he should not await an American advance. By sheer coincidence, he too decided that he would resort to the unusual recourse of a night march on 15 August. At least he had the excuse that his men were mostly regulars or seasoned Loyalist veterans and were disciplined enough to carry out a difficult night march. His army numbered 122 officers and 2,117 men and consisted of parts of the 23rd, 33rd, and 71st Regiments; the Volunteers of Ireland; Tarleton's British Legion; two North Carolina Loyalist regiments; a small detachment of Royal Artillery; and a pioneer unit of 26 men. By ten o'clock on the evening of 15 August, both armies were marching toward each other, after Gates had taken the precaution of sending all his baggage wagons to the Waxhaw settlements, about 30 miles north of Camden. Before the march, the Americans were debilitated by the effects of consuming molasses instead of rum, for while the latter, dispensed in moderation, could enliven the spirits of the troops, molasses eaten in large quantities induced diarrhea. Many of the soldiers, the Virginians in particular, were exhausted from lack of sleep and food. But Gates was confident that he would be able to rehabilitate his troops once they reached their defensive post.

At about midnight, American scouts under Armand and British scouts under Tarleton blundered into each other, about halfway between Camden and Rugeley's Mill. Armand later observed bitterly that his men were unnecessarily exposed by Gates's night maneuver. In a sharp clash with Tarleton's dragoons in the dark, the Americans broke and ran, leaving Gates entirely without cavalry. Tarleton kept his legion of 289 men intact. When Gates was told that Cornwallis was in his front, he was astonished but felt that he had no choice but to fight. At least the ground was favorable for battle, with swamps protecting both his flanks. At daybreak, Cornwallis began disposing his line of battle. On his extreme right, he placed the Loyalist light infantry and then the troops of the 23rd and 33rd Regiments, all under the command of Lieutenant-Colonel James Webster. On Cornwallis's left, near the road, he put the Volunteers of Ireland and beside them the infantry of the British Legion and the North Carolina volunteers. The British left was under the command of Rawdon. In the center rear, Cornwallis placed the 71st Regiment as a reserve, and he posted Tarleton's cavalry on the right behind the fighting line.

As Gates observed the British dispositions, he made a decision that was fatal to his army and to his military reputation. Logically, he should have posted his best troops on his left to confront the hardened British regulars of the 23rd and 33rd Regiments and put his militia on the right to meet Cornwallis's Loyalist units. Instead, Gates ordered the Delaware and Maryland Continentals under Kalb to the right wing and posted the Virginia and North Carolina militias in the center and on the left, facing the 23rd and 33rd Regiments. As a reserve, Gates placed part of the Maryland regiment 200 yards behind his line and deployed six cannon in pairs of two along his front. He established his command post 600 yards behind his front and awaited Cornwallis's first move. After about two hours of skirmishing as the two armies moved into position, Cornwallis opened the battle by ordering his regulars on the right to advance. Williams, observing this maneuver and believing it to be merely an adjustment of the opposing line, rode to Gates's headquarters and urged the American general to order the Virginia militia under Stevens to advance. Gates agreed, thus giving his only order of the entire battle.

The order was a mistake, for both Gates and Williams were sadly deluded in believing that raw militiamen could charge regulars with good effect. As the Virginians advanced, they found before them not a disorganized body of troops readjusting their battle line but troops charging in their direction, firing and yelling as they came. The Virginians, stricken with panic, immediately threw down their loaded muskets and fled in terror, sweeping the North Carolinians with them. At that point, Cornwallis sent Tarleton's Legion charging down upon the unprotected flank of the Maryland Continentals, which immediately gave way, and ordered Rawdon to send the rest of his line into action against Kalb's Delaware regulars. Gates was appalled that one whole wing of his line had disintegrated. Riding into the midst of the retreating militiamen, he strove with Caswell's assistance to rally the broken ranks. Threatened with capture by Tarleton's cavalry, Gates withdrew from the battlefield and attempted twice more to stop the panic-stricken citizen-soldiers. Gates now believed, as he later told Congress, that the Maryland and

Horatio Gates lost much of his reputation as the victor at Saratoga in 1777 as a result of his disastrous defeat and hasty retreat at the Battle of Camden in 1780. (Library of Congress)

Delaware Continentals had also been overrun, so that he felt he had no choice but to ride to Charlotte, 60 miles away, and attempt a reorganization of his army there. With Tarleton's cavalry bedeviling him, he rode with all haste for his destination and finally retreated all the way to Hillsborough.

Despite Gates's belief that the Continentals had been destroyed, they were in fact fighting the entire British Army with desperate courage and determination. Ordered by Kalb to come forward, the Maryland reserves under the command of Williams attempted to shore up the American left after the militia's departure. Cornwallis turned Webster's regulars against the Marylanders, and a bitter fight ensued.

Twice the Continentals were forced back, and twice they rallied before finally being driven from the field. Williams, rather than accompanying them, joined other Americans in hand-to-hand combat that was still going on to his right. Kalb, unhorsed and bleeding from a number of wounds, including a saber cut on his head, refused to surrender without orders from Gates. Kalb rallied his men and led a counterattack but fell with a mortal wound. Tarleton meanwhile returned from his pursuit of the militia and struck the Americans from the rear. At that point organized Patriot resistance ceased, as the soldiers fled for their lives.

A few Americans rallied under Armand at Rugeley's Mill and tried to protect the baggage train from Tarleton's Legion. Most, however, were pursued by Loyalist troopers—against whom they could offer no opposition—to Hanging Rock before the horsemen stopped from exhaustion. Tarleton then rallied his legion and on 18 August, at Fishing Creek, routed Sumter's militiamen in a humiliating defeat. Gates's defeat at Camden was far worse. He had lost about 250 men killed and 800 wounded, and his army had simply ceased to exist. Cornwallis had suffered 68 killed and 256 wounded. The road now seemed open for the British to march northward without hindrance. But Cornwallis had his own problems to contend with, such as sickness in the army, the summer heat, and partisan operations against his supply lines. With the assistance of Marion, Sumter, and Colonel Andrew Pickens, Gates was given time to recoup his losses, while Cornwallis sat immobile in camp at Waxhaw Creek. Gates's military reputation was ruined. Ridiculed for leaving his army engaged on the battlefield and riding 200 miles in three days to Hillsborough, he was relieved of command by Congress on 5 October and superseded by Greene on 2 December. By that time, Gates had rebuilt his shattered army until it presented, according to Tarleton, a tolerable appearance. It was these troops whom Greene led so successfully against the British in the southern campaigns of 1781.

Paul David Nelson

See also

Augusta, Georgia, Operations at; Charleston, South Carolina, Expedition against (1780); Cornwallis, Charles; Fishing Creek, Battle of; Gates, Horatio; Greene, Nathanael; Hanging Rock, South Carolina, Action at; Jefferson, Thomas; Kalb, Johann, Baron de; Lenud's Ferry, South Carolina, Action at; Lincoln, Benjamin; Marion, Francis; Moncks Corner, South Carolina, Action at; Pickens, Andrew; Rawdon, Francis; Rocky Mount, South Carolina, Action at; Saratoga Campaign; Southern Campaigns; Sumter, Thomas; Tarleton, Banastre; Washington, William; Webster, James; Williams, Otho

References

Bass, Robert. *Gamecock: The Life and Campaigns of General Thomas Sumter.* 1961. Reprint, Orangeburg, SC: Sandlapper, 2000.

———. *The Green Dragoon: The Lives of Banastre Tarleton and Mary Robinson.* 1957. Reprint, Orangeburg, SC: Sandlapper, 2003.

Carrington, Henry B. *Battles of the American Revolution, 1775–1781.* 1876. Reprint, New York: Promontory, 1974.

Johnson, William. *Sketches of the Life and Correspondence of Nathanael Greene.* Vol. 1. Charleston, SC: A. E. Miller, 1822.

Landers, H. L. *The Battle of Camden, South Carolina, August 16, 1780.* Washington, DC: U.S. Government Printing Office, 1929.

Lumpkin, Henry. *From Savannah to Yorktown: The American Revolution in the South.* New York: Paragon, 1981.

McCrady, Edward. *The History of South Carolina in the Revolution, 1775–1780.* 1901. Reprint, New York: Russell and Russell, 1969.

Morrill, Dan L. *Southern Campaigns of the American Revolution.* Baltimore, MD: Nautical and Aviation Publishing Company of America, 1993.

Nelson, Paul David. *General Horatio Gates: A Biography.* Baton Rouge: Louisiana State University Press, 1976.

———. "Major General Horatio Gates as a Military Leader: The Southern Experience." Pp. 132–158 in *The Revolutionary War in the South: Power, Conflict, and Leadership.* Edited by W. Robert Higgins. Durham, NC: Duke University Press, 1979.

Pancake, John S. *This Destructive War: The British Campaign for the Carolinas, 1780–1782.* University: University of Alabama Press, 1985.

Tarleton, Banastre. *History of the Campaigns of 1780 and 1781, in the Southern Provinces of North America.* 1787. Reprint, New York: New York Times, 1968.

Ward, Christopher. *War of the Revolution.* 2 vols. New York: Macmillan, 1952.

Wickwire, Franklin, and Mary Wickwire. *Cornwallis: The American Adventure.* Boston: Houghton Mifflin, 1970.

Campbell, Archibald (1739–1791)

Born in Scotland, Archibald Campbell entered the army in 1757. He served throughout the French and Indian War and was wounded during the campaign against Quebec in 1758. In 1775 Brigadier-General Simon Fraser raised a new regiment of Highlanders to serve against the American rebels, and Campbell was chosen as lieutenant-colonel of the second battalion. When his ship accidentally landed at Boston, then in rebel hands, he was made a prisoner but was released the next year in exchange for Ethan Allen. Campbell was promoted to brigadier-general and given command of an expedition against Savannah, which Campbell captured, together with numerous cannon and substantial stores, at a trifling cost to himself.

Campbell's exploits in Georgia had meanwhile impressed the king, who made him governor of Jamaica in July 1781 and a major-general in November of that year. The post was one of great responsibility, for the French had designs on Britain's sugar islands and managed to take Tobago, St. Eustatius, St. Kitts, Nevis, and Montserrat. The defense of Jamaica, Britain's most important West Indian possession, therefore took on a particularly critical significance. Campbell's preparations, including the raising of black units, proved so extensive that the French under the Marquis de Bouillé could not contemplate an attack without the assistance of additional troops; thus, the island remained in British hands. In the meantime, Campbell was assiduous in supplying intelligence, supplies, and troops to British commanders in America and a portion of his garrison to operate as marines aboard Admiral Sir George Rodney's ships, thus contributing to Rodney's success against Admiral de Grasse. In 1785 Campbell returned home from Jamaica and received a knighthood. In the same year, he was appointed governor and commander in chief at Madras. He settled amicably the debts owed by the

Nabob of Arcot to the East India Company, a success that helped sustain the British defense of his territory.

Gregory Fremont-Barnes

See also

Allen, Ethan; British West Indies; Fraser, Simon; Grasse, François-Joseph-Paul, Comte de; Jamaica; Rodney, George; Savannah, Georgia, British Capture of; West Indies

Reference

Fortescue, John. *The War of Independence: The British Army in North America, 1775–1783.* London: Greenhill, 2001.

Campbell, John (1753–1784)

The son of Lord Stonefield and Lady Grace Stuart, sister of the Earl of Bute, John Campbell became an ensign in the 37th Foot in 1771. He fought in the American Revolutionary War for a brief time before being taken prisoner. He was exchanged and continued service in America until 1781, when as a colonel he went to India and fought in command of the 42nd Highlanders in the Second Mysore War against Hyder Ali. At the head of the 42nd, Campbell took the fort at Annanpore, but British mismanagement of the campaign by Brigadier-General Richard Matthews led to a series of disasters that obliged the army to seek refuge at the coastal town of Mangalore, the main outlet to the sea for Mysore. Owing to Matthews's recall and the illness of another superior officer, Campbell, now a lieutenant-colonel, was left in charge of the city's defense.

When Tipu Sultan, Hyder's son and successor, captured Bednar on 3 May 1784, he followed up his success with a rapid move against Mangalore in the belief that news of the fall of Bednar would induce the small garrison to capitulate. Campbell, however, refused to be discouraged, and on 6 May, 12 miles from the fort, he shocked his opponent by attacking and defeating the detachment sent against him, seizing all its artillery. Tipu, outraged, assembled his entire force for a siege against the city. Campbell had at his disposal a mere 600 men of the 73rd Foot and 1,400 sepoys. Tipu, on the other hand, possessed a massive force of 140,000 Mysorean infantry and cavalry, supplemented by 400 French under General David Charpentier de Cossigny.

Campbell refused a summons to surrender, unknowingly consigning himself and the garrison to what would become a long and miserable experience of hunger and continuous combat. The Mysoreans soon breached the walls with siege guns, yet their repeated and desperate assaults were consistently repulsed with serious losses. Fighting continued in the trenches outside the city walls for nearly two months until Cossigny informed Campbell by letter that hostilities had ceased in the Carnatic as a result of the conclusion of peace in Europe. The French then induced Tipu to agree to an armistice that included the guarantee of food supplies to the garrison.

Tipu nevertheless failed to honor the agreement and, notwithstanding peace negotiations then under way between the British authorities in India and the Mysorean leader, the latter renewed the siege of Mangalore. In the end, the garrison, ravaged by scurvy and starvation and down to half strength, had no choice but to surrender on 30 January 1784, although Campbell secured a condition that permitted his men safe transport to Tellicherry, a point to the south on the Malabar coast. Campbell was universally praised for his gallant efforts, but he died at Bombay the following month from the effects of exhaustion and starvation.

Gregory Fremont-Barnes

See also

India, Operations in

Reference

Fortescue, John. *The War of Independence: The British Army in North America, 1775–1783.* London: Greenhill, 2001.

Campbell, John, 4th Earl of Loudoun (1705–1782)

John Campbell, 4th Earl of Loudoun, was commander in chief of British armed forces in America from 1756 to 1758, during the French and Indian (Seven Years') War. His strategy against France led to a number of defeats. He was also high-handed in his dealings with colonial officers, and his insistence on quartering his troops in American homes soured the colonists' relations with the Crown, convincing many that they would never be treated equally within the British Empire.

Campbell came from a wealthy Scottish family and was the heir to the title of Loudoun. During the Jacobite rebellion in Scotland in 1745, he led a regiment, raised in his family name, to repress the uprising. Loudoun did not distinguish himself during the campaign, but he gained promotion through family influence and in 1756 was appointed commander of all British troops in North America and governor of Virginia. He reached America when the war with French and Indian forces had been raging for two years. He had little idea of American affairs and was insensitive to the colonists' commitment to autonomy for themselves and their colonial governments. He also believed in the superiority of British troops and was not prepared to listen to the advice of colonial officers. He ignored George Washington's advice to reinforce the forts held by the British in the West and, as a result, Fort Oswego was quickly lost. While Loudoun was at Albany, he further alienated Washington and other officers by breaking an agreement that colonial militias should not be placed under direct British command. Loudoun proposed to break the deadlock in the West by launching an attack on the French fort at Louisbourg on Cape Breton Island. This attack failed, with the British force withdrawing in the face of a superior French fleet. While Loudoun was leading this campaign, the French overran Fort William Henry on Lake George. Soon thereafter, Loudoun was recalled from America.

It was not Loudoun's military failure, however, that had the greatest effect on America but rather his insensitive demands on the colonists. He believed that the colonies should bear the brunt of the cost of the war and should be expected to pay for new barracks to quarter his troops. If no such accommodation was available, he insisted that the troops should be billeted in private residences, and he was prepared to use the threat of martial law to enforce his position. This could not have happened in England, and many colonists saw it as a sign that they would never achieve equality as subjects of the British Crown. In order to ensure that he had sufficient troops for his Louisbourg Campaign, Loudoun also organized a campaign of impressment in New York that led to the enlistment of a quarter of the male population. Benjamin Franklin criticized Loudoun for his lavish lifestyle. The commander had little regard for the ideas or cultures of New England's latter-day Puritans or Pennsylvania's Quakers, two groups that were essential to his success. When he departed for Britain, Loudoun was a widely detested figure in the American colonies.

Ralph Baker

See also
Quartering Acts

Reference

Anderson, Fred. *Crucible of War: The Seven Years' War and the Fate of Empire in British North America, 1754–1766.* London: Vintage, 2001.

Campbell, William (1745–1781)

A rough Virginia frontiersman, William Campbell was a Continental Army officer who treated Loyalists harshly and led American militiamen to victory in the Battle of Kings Mountain in 1780. An imposing man with sandy hair, blue eyes, and a fiery temper, Campbell was appointed justice of the peace of Fincastle County, Virginia, on 6 July 1773, and in the following year he served as a militia captain in Lord Dunmore's War. On 20 January 1775, Campbell and his Fincastle County neighbors protested Britain's violation of colonial liberties. As captain of a militia company under Colonel William Woodford, Campbell helped defeat Lord Dunmore, the royal governor, in 1775. On 3 February 1776, Campbell was appointed captain in the 1st Virginia Regiment, Continental Army, commanded by Colonel Patrick Henry, and he and Henry became close friends.

On 9 October 1776, Campbell resigned his captaincy so that he could defend his frontier homeland against Cherokee raids. He was appointed commissioner to draw a boundary line between Virginia and the Cherokee Nation in 1777 and again served as justice of the peace. That same year he was appointed lieutenant colonel of the 10th Regiment of Virginia Militia; three years later he was promoted to colonel of the regiment. Ruthlessly suppressing Loyalists, he destroyed or confiscated their property and executed perhaps a dozen without trial. In 1779 he helped defeat Loyalist threats to the lead mines in Montgomery County, Virginia. In early 1780 he was elected to the Virginia assembly and on 15 June was appointed commander of troops to fight the Cherokees in Tennessee. Before he could execute his orders, he once more had to suppress Loyalist attempts to capture the lead mines.

In the fall of 1780, Campbell learned that Loyalist militia forces commanded by Major Patrick Ferguson were threatening western North Carolina. In late September, Campbell marched with Washington County, Virginia, militia to a rendezvous with other militia units from Virginia and North Carolina at Sycamore Shoals on the upper Watauga River. Chosen by the other militia leaders to command their army, he surrounded the Loyalists in their strong defensive position on Kings Mountain on 7 October. Audaciously, he led his men on a charge up the slopes, using trees and rocks as cover. Ferguson was killed, the Loyalists surrendered, and Campbell was praised by Congress and the Virginia Senate for his triumph.

In 1781, Campbell joined General Nathanael Greene's army in fighting Lord Charles Cornwallis in the South. Campbell skirmished with British cavalry at Wetzell's Mill, North Carolina, on 6 March and nine days later fought under the immediate command of General Henry "Light-Horse Harry" Lee at Guilford Courthouse, where Greene praised Campbell for his bravery. Elected again to the Virginia legislature, he did not serve, for on 14 June 1781 he was appointed a brigadier general of militia. He joined the Marquis de Lafayette's army in eastern Virginia but in July was stricken with fever and chest pains. Campbell died on 22 August 1781 in Hanover County and was interred with full military honors.

Paul David Nelson

See also
Ferguson, Patrick; Lee, Henry

Reference

Riley, Agnes Graham. *Brigadier General William Campbell, 1745–1781.* Abingdon, VA: Historical Society of Washington County, Virginia, 1985.

Canada

Canada's historical background greatly influenced the decision of its people to remain in the British Empire during the American Revolution. The region's relationship to the Revolution grew out of its role in a century of global rivalries

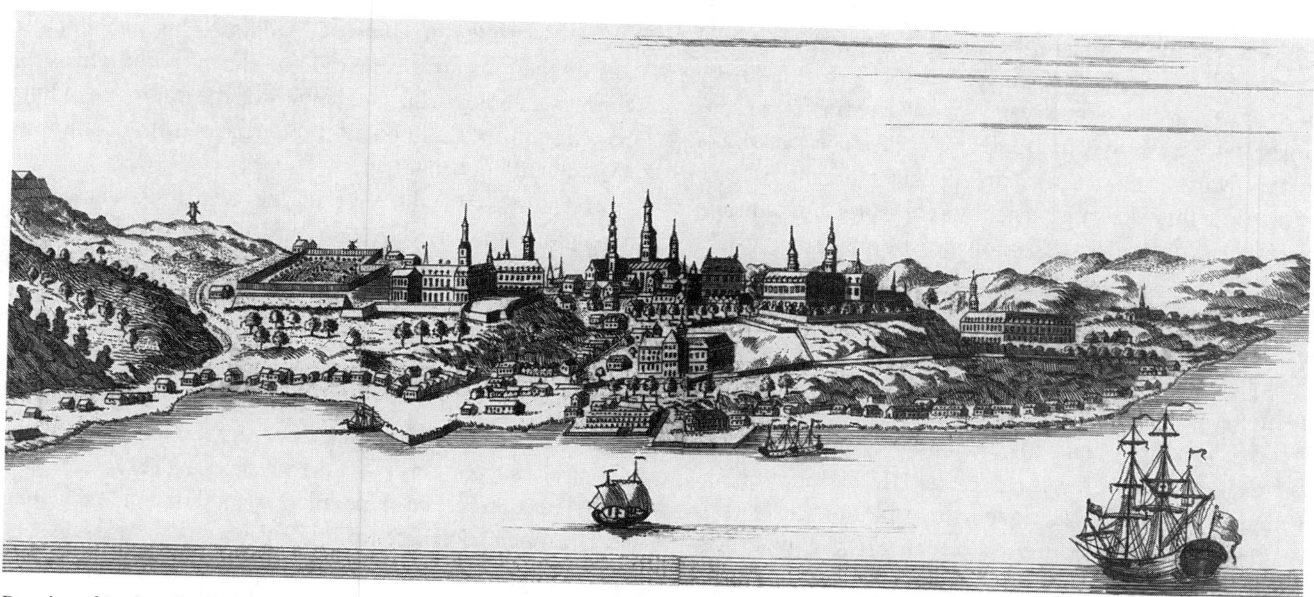

Drawing of Quebec City from the personal collection of Jean-Baptiste Vimeur, the comte de Rochambeau. (Library of Congress, Geography and Map Division)

between Britain and France. After Britain conquered Canada in 1763, British conciliatory policies toward the French-speaking Canadians and the Roman Catholic Church effectively kept Canada from joining the rebelling thirteen colonies just a dozen years later. As a result of the American Revolution, not only did the United States emerge from those thirteen colonies, but a distinct Canadian identity arose to resist the force of American nationalism.

French settlement of the territory that became the foundation of modern Canada began in 1608, at Quebec City; the colony was known as New France. But France did little to encourage large-scale immigration, and by the 1660s the population of New France numbered only 3,000. Most population growth thereafter came from natural increase, not immigration. New France was incorporated as a French province, complete with French legal and political institutions and the French feudalism of its seigneurial system. The French government gave major land grants in New France along the St. Lawrence River to favored seigneurs, who administered local affairs and were bound to the Crown. French settlers, known as the habitants, managed the estates of the seigneurs and served as tenant farmers. Unlike the English North American colonies, which provided many opportunities for social mobility, New France, like its parent, remained a class-ridden society. Agriculture composed a significant proportion of the economy of New France. The habitants grew wheat as their primary crop, supplemented by peas, oats, barley, rye, and corn. The chief commercial value of French Canada, however, was its fur trade. This became a source of conflict with Britain, which controlled the fur trade in Hudson's Bay to the north and had its eye on the trade in New France.

For nearly a century the dynastic wars of Europe had extended to North America, under different names, as Britain and France competed for global supremacy. The War of the League of Augsburg (1689–1697) between William III and Louis XIV became King William's War in British North America. The War of the Spanish Succession (1702–1713), which was fought to decide whether Louis XIV's grandson would become king of Spain, was Queen Anne's War to British Americans. The War of the Austrian Succession (1740–1748), which began with Frederick the Great of Prussia's invasion of Maria Theresa's Habsburg domain, was King George's War across the Atlantic. And the Seven Years' War (1756–1763), which eventually involved a rematch between Austria and Prussia, actually began in the Ohio Valley in 1754 and became locally known as the French and Indian War.

During each of these conflicts, Britain and France enlisted the aid of the indigenous peoples of North America; the French solicited the Algonquians, while the British courted the Iroquois. The settlers of the North American colonies were also subject to the whims of European diplomacy. In 1748 Britain handed back the French fortress at Louisbourg on Cape Breton Island, which had been captured by a combined British-American force, in exchange for Madras in India, causing much bitterness in New England against the British government. Another egregious example was the expulsion of the French settlers of Acadia in present-day Nova Scotia in 1755 by the British. The concerns of either British or French colonists, or of the indigenous peoples, counted for little in European capitals during these wars for empire.

After seventy years of North American conflict between Britain and France, General James Wolfe defeated General

Louis-Joseph de Montcalm-Gozon at Quebec in 1759, and Canada fell to Britain the following year. In 1763 the Treaty of Paris, which ended the Seven Years' War, transferred control of New France to Britain and greatly increased the size of British North America. Britain quickly reorganized New France into the colony of Quebec by a royal proclamation and sought to mold its new possession into the image of its established royal colonies to the south. James Murray, the first British governor of Quebec, was given instructions to establish the Anglican Church while providing toleration to the Catholic Church. Britain also provided for an elected government for Quebec, with the ultimate goal of assimilating French-speaking Canadians. Britain's hope for French assimilation, however, was based upon the assumption that the French population would remain stable or even decrease as a result of immigration back to France, while the Protestant British population would increase as a result of emigration from Britain. None of these developments occurred. The French remained in Canada and grew rapidly by natural increase, as they had been doing for more than a century, while no more than 200 mostly mercantile British families immigrated to Montreal, so the British government had to change its policy.

In 1774, the Quebec Act superseded the Proclamation of 1763. Murray had quickly come to oppose Britain's assimilation policy for Quebec as he saw tensions rise between French Canadians and British settlers who desired nothing less than the complete religious, social, and political marginalization of the French. In 1765, General Sir Guy Carleton replaced Murray and continued his policy of protecting the interests of the French Canadians. In the early 1770s Carleton returned to England to lobby for a conciliatory policy in Quebec out of sheer pragmatism, just as British leaders such as Charles Fox and Edmund Burke were urging reconciliation with the uneasy thirteen colonies to the south. In this difficult situation, Carleton hoped to secure the loyalty of Quebec in enforcing British imperial policy. After extensive hearings before the House of Commons and despite strong opposition from business interests, Carleton's plan materialized into the Quebec Act in 1774.

The Quebec Act openly accommodated the culture and aspirations of the French-speaking inhabitants of Canada. The act protected the seigneurial system and the privileged status of the Roman Catholic Church and recognized the legal system of Quebec instead of imposing English common law. The act did not allow for an elected legislature, as the Proclamation of 1763 had done, but Roman Catholics were allowed to hold public office by taking a special oath. And to the dismay of the British colonies to the south, the act expanded the province to include the Ohio Valley. Despite objections by Fox and Burke that the Quebec Act did not instill the virtues of the British Constitution in Quebec, the act effectively protected the status of French Canadians. This did much to ensure their loyalty during the American Revolution, as the thirteen colonies, which had inherited the traditions of English common law and constitutional rule, were breaking away from the mother country.

Yet it was the attempt of the British Parliament to strengthen the imperial bond in English-speaking North America that sparked the American Revolution. After Britain had expelled France from North America, British policy makers concluded that since the war was fought for the safety of the North American colonists, they should shoulder part of the responsibility in paying for their own defense and submitting to new trade and settlement regulations that would secure the empire. A succession of British ministries in the 1760s exacerbated tensions between the colonies and London to the point that reconciliation became difficult and finally impossible.

Even before armed conflict between Britain and her colonists broke out at Lexington and Concord in 1775, America's leaders hoped to persuade French-speaking Canada to join them in resisting British power. The First Continental Congress issued a manifesto to the people of Quebec, urging them to join the American cause and send delegates to the Second Continental Congress at its meeting in Philadelphia in May 1775. The Canadians, however, declined the invitation, and Congress's three-man delegation to Canada, headed by Benjamin Franklin and sent the following spring, had no more success. From the beginning of the rebellion, Canada's habitants were ambivalent about joining the thirteen colonies. And although several hundred French-speaking volunteers did fight with American forces against the British Army during the war, the great majority of Quebec's people remained neutral in the struggle for two reasons: The influential Roman Catholic clergy were beholden to Britain, especially after the passage of the Quebec Act, for their continued dominance in Canada's religious and cultural life, and the French-speaking population feared becoming a linguistic and cultural minority on an overwhelmingly English-speaking continent.

The recently organized, mostly English-speaking colony of Nova Scotia also declined an offer to send delegates to the Continental Congress, largely for economic reasons. Even though many New Englanders had recently settled in Nova Scotia, there was little connection between them and the colonies from which they had come. Nova Scotia's economy was more closely linked with London than with the thirteen colonies. In the new port of Halifax, which the British were spending money developing as a military and naval center, the mercantile class had no dispute with the Navigation Acts passed by Parliament. And unlike several of the thirteen colonies, Nova Scotia felt no resentment at being sealed off from the western frontier, as imposed by Britain's Proclamation of 1763, because the colony was still lightly settled, and any pressures for new settlement could be met within the

Benedict Arnold leads troops through Skowhegan Falls, Maine, en route to Canada. (Library of Congress)

Maritime region. For different reasons, neither Quebec nor Nova Scotia saw any advantage in joining the thirteen colonies in their rebellion against Britain.

As the American Revolution developed into a full-scale war, Canada became the bastion of British loyalty in North America, and its conquest became a war aim of the Continental Congress. Quebec and Montreal were safe ports where the British could build up large arsenals and from which they could easily strike New York and New England. General George Washington also saw the British presence in Canada as a threat and was concerned that the Britons would inflame Native Americans against the colonies. The first engagements of the war outside eastern Massachusetts took place in northern New York and its border with Canada. On 10 May 1775, three weeks after the Battle of Lexington and Concord, a New England force under Ethan Allen and Benedict Arnold launched a surprise attack on Fort Ticonderoga. Their success boosted the morale of the Continental Army, and American forces moved farther north toward Canada by capturing the small garrison at Crown Point shortly thereafter. Canada appeared to be open to an American invasion.

In June 1775, the Continental Congress ordered General Philip Schuyler to march an army into Canada. As Schuyler moved north from Crown Point, Arnold was to advance through Maine to Quebec. General Richard Montgomery, a former British Army officer living in the province of New York, joined Schuyler's force of some 1,500 men in late August, took command in mid-September, and placed Fort St. John, on the Richelieu River, under siege. St. John fell on 2 November 1775, opening the way to Montreal.

Carleton, meanwhile, was hastily mustering troops for the defense of Montreal. He could perhaps have employed some 500 Indian warriors from northern New York, led by Guy Johnson, Britain's Indian superintendent for the Northern Department, and this was a force that General Thomas Gage hoped Carleton would use to attack the New England frontier. But Carleton distrusted Indian warriors and rebuffed Johnson's offer. Instead, Carleton was hoping that the seigneurs and the clergy, whose loyalty he helped buy with the Quebec Act, would deliver to him the troops necessary to defend Canada. The bishop of Quebec did issue a statement threatening excommunication to anyone who aided the rebels, but Carleton's hopes were in vain. The habitants, who bore the brunt of British taxation in Quebec, refused to take up arms for the British, and the Americans seized Montreal on 13 November 1775.

The city of Quebec was the Americans' next and greatest target. In December 1775, Arnold's force, marching north from Maine, joined Montgomery's small army west of the city. A desperate New Year's Eve assault by some 900 Americans on the fortified city, defended by at least as many British and French, failed completely, and Montgomery was killed. With its army now beginning to suffer from disease, especially smallpox, as well as the bitter weather, America's invasion of Canada was badly stalled.

In May 1776, the British brought several thousand fresh troops to Quebec and began driving the disease-ridden Americans back up the St. Lawrence River. On 8 June 1776, they defeated General John Sullivan's force at Trois-Rivières, and the Americans abandoned Montreal and retreated back to Lake Champlain, losing all of their gains of the previous ten months. Carleton now built small warships to seize control of the lake, while Arnold built other small vessels to oppose him. On 11 October 1776, Carleton's flotilla defeated Arnold off Valcour Island, and the Americans fell back to Fort Ticonderoga at the southern end of the lake. Carleton, deciding not to press on as winter approached, returned to Canada.

In 1777, the British made a grand attempt to conquer America from Canada. General John Burgoyne brought some 8,000 British, German, and Indian warriors down Lake Champlain to cut off New England from the rest of the colonies and link up his force with General William Howe's army in the Hudson River Valley. But the total lack of Howe's cooperation led to Burgoyne's surrender at Saratoga and put Britain on the defensive. For the rest of the war, Canada played no important role in British military strategy, and the Americans, after considering another invasion in 1778, left their northern neighbors alone until the conclusion of peace.

As the war came to an end, both British and American leaders faced the question of what to do with the Loyalists in the thirteen colonies. Perhaps 250,000 British colonists, about a sixth of the white population in the rebelling colonies, still supported the Crown. As the colonies declared their independence, those who remained loyal to Britain suffered all kinds of persecution and discrimination, including removal from public office, disfranchisement, punitive taxation, the loss of legal rights, the confiscation of property, imprisonment, and banishment (and in the case of a few spies, even execution). By 1777, every state except South Carolina and Georgia regarded anyone who supported the British as a traitor. In the same year, Congress recommended the confiscation of Loyalist estates, which was already under way in several states.

As life under the new regime became intolerable for many Loyalists, perhaps 80,000 persons in all, the only alternative was to leave for Britain, Canada, or other British colonies. After Yorktown, when American independence looked assured, the majority of Loyalists who considered emigration looked to Canada. Only the elite seriously considered returning to Britain, especially London, where the cost of living was prohibitive. Canada, with a climate that was comparable to at least that of the northern British colonies, offered a semblance of their previous lives and allowed them to remain British subjects in North America.

By the end of the Revolutionary War, the Loyalists had established two large communities in Canada. Nova Scotia, which initially had the larger community, took in about 35,000 Loyalists in 1782 and 1783, mostly from New York City. Carleton, who by then was commander in chief of the British Army in North America, and was stationed in New York until the final evacuation (in November 1783), interceded on the Loyalists' behalf by writing to Governor John Parr of Nova Scotia to secure 500 acres of land for each Loyalist family, 300 acres for each single man, 2,000 acres for each church, and 1,000 acres for each school.

Parr was saddled with the responsibility of providing this land. Loyalists settled all along the coasts of the Maritime Provinces, founding communities along the Bay of Fundy, Cape Breton Island, and the Atlantic coast. Life in these new settlements was difficult for Loyalists, and the provision of supplies by the British government was uneven. Moreover, the earlier settlers of Nova Scotia had little regard for these United Empire Loyalists. To ease this massive influx, Britain created the province of New Brunswick, on the Bay of Fundy's unsettled west shore in 1784, as a site for new Loyalist settlements, with Thomas Carleton, Guy's brother, as its first governor.

The second largest group of Loyalists settled in Quebec. These settlers founded communities in southern and western Quebec along the St. Lawrence River, on the northern shores of Lake Ontario and Lake Erie, and on the Niagara and Detroit Rivers. Those who settled in Quebec received some compensation from the British government consisting of land and supplies, based on their civilian or military rank, but the Quebec Act forbade them the representative government and justice under English common law they had enjoyed before the Revolution. Soon they pressured the British government for the same rights they once held in the thirteen colonies, which necessitated the creation of a new colony. The solution was found in the British Parliament's Constitutional Act of 1791, also known as the Canada Act, that divided Quebec into two provinces. Lower Canada remained a largely French-speaking province with 100,000 French Canadians and 10,000 English-speaking Canadians, while Upper Canada consisted of an English-speaking majority of 20,000 and would become the present-day province of Ontario. Representative government was provided to both provinces. The Canada Act prepared the way for the foundation for modern Canada.

Although such an outcome was never intended by the Founding Fathers of the United States of America, the foundations of the modern Canadian state emerged from the years immediately prior to and during the American Revolution. British conciliatory gestures to the French Canadians ensured their loyalty, while Britain's harsher policies alienated its English colonists. The American invasion of Canada during the Revolutionary War and then the massive influx of Loyalist refugees helped to forge a Canadian identity that would have to come to terms with both its French and British heritages. It was from these events that Canada emerged as a culture and nation that remained distinct from its neighbor to the south.

Dino E. Buenviaje

See also

Arnold, Benedict; Burgoyne, John; Carleton, Christopher; Carleton, Guy; Carleton, Thomas; Congress, First Continental; Congress, Second Continental and Confederation; Crown Point, New York; Fort Ticonderoga, New York; Loyalists; Montgomery, Richard; Quebec, Siege of; Quebec Act; Schuyler, Philip; Sullivan, John; Trois-Rivières, Action at; United Empire Loyalists; Valcour Island, Battle of

References

Bradley, A. G. *The United Empire Loyalists: Founders of British Canada.* London: Thornton Butterworth, 1932.

Brown, Wallace. *The Good Americans: The Loyalists in the American Revolution.* New York: William Morrow, 1969.

Conway, Stephen. *The War of American Independence, 1775–1783.* London: Arnold, 1995.

Coupland, Sir Reginald. *The Quebec Act: A Study in Statesmanship.* Reprint. Oxford: Oxford University Press, 1968.

Lawson, Philip. *The Imperial Challenge: Quebec and Britain in the Age of the American Revolution.* Montreal: McGill-Queen's University Press, 1990.

McNaught, Kenneth. *The Penguin History of Canada.* London: Penguin, 1989.

See, Scott W. *The History of Canada.* Westport, CT: Greenwood, 2001.

Wrong, George M. *Canada and the American Revolution: The Disruption of the First British Empire.* New York: Macmillan, 1935.

Canada, Operations in (1774–1778)

In the first year of the war, the Americans unsuccessfully attempted to expand the Revolution's base of support and secure the northern frontier by seizing Canada.

Throughout autumn 1774 and into spring 1775, the First and Second Continental Congresses appealed to the Canadians to adopt their cause and send delegates to Philadelphia. Intelligence reports suggested that many Canadians supported their neighbors to the south and doubted Britain's ability to defend the province. Still, the French-Canadian upper class and the clergy favored the British largely because of the 1774 Quebec Act, which recognized Catholicism and secured the elite's status.

On 10 May 1775, Benedict Arnold and Ethan Allen captured Fort Ticonderoga on Lake Champlain. Over the next eight days, the Americans also seized Crown Point and raided the British fort at St. John's, Quebec, on the Richelieu River, capturing valuable military supplies and a schooner. The colonists now controlled Lake Champlain, but Congress hesitated to proceed farther, not wanting to jeopardize reconciliation with Britain. Congress also remained uncertain whether the Canadians would welcome American troops. By late June, however, the colonists learned that the governor-general of Canada, Sir Guy Carleton, was gathering troops and ships at St. John's to attack the New York and New England frontier. Therefore, on 27 June Congress authorized an invasion of Canada.

Major General Philip Schuyler assembled troops and supplies at Ticonderoga throughout the summer. On 28 August, Brigadier General Richard Montgomery, who assumed command for the ailing Schuyler, led 1,200 men northward. Encamping at Île-aux-Noix, 12 miles south of St. John's, on 4 September, Montgomery made two unsuccessful attempts to take the fort. By 17 September, he managed to isolate St. John's, which guarded Montreal 20 miles to the northwest, and began siege operations. For the next seven weeks, Major Charles Preston and his British and Canadian garrison grimly hung on, while Montgomery contended with torrential rains, a lack of ammunition and provisions, and unruly troops. As Montgomery laid siege to St. John's, Allen attempted to raise Canadians to assist him.

On 25 September, Allen foolishly attacked Montreal without informing other nearby American detachments and was quickly defeated. Allen and about 30 of his men were captured, and 6 were killed. The defeat raised British morale but failed to break the American grip on St. John's. On 17 October, Montgomery sent troops to capture Chambly, a British outpost 6 miles north of St. John's. Chambly surrendered the following day, yielding 88 prisoners and a rich cache of military stores, including more than six tons of gunpowder. With this gunpowder and now reinforced to 2,400 soldiers, Montgomery intensified his efforts. On 30 October, an American detachment at Longueuil, south of Montreal, repelled Carleton's attempt to relieve the beleaguered garrison. Two days later Montgomery unleashed a punishing artillery barrage that prompted Preston to surrender on 3 November. During the siege, the Americans killed or wounded 40 and captured 600, at a cost of 20 dead. Montgomery's victories at Chambly and St. John's wrecked the only two British regiments in the St. Lawrence Valley but consumed much of the campaign season, as the weather had turned markedly colder. Although Preston lost the battle, he helped win the campaign for Britain.

Capitalizing on his success, Montgomery quickly sent part of his army down the Richelieu River to prevent Montreal's garrison from escaping to Quebec. The rest of his troops marched to Montreal, which Carleton evacuated without a fight on 11 November. Montgomery's troops entered the city two days later. On 19 November, Carleton's flotilla surrendered at the mouth of the Richelieu, having failed to pass the

The death of Brigadier General Richard Montgomery during the storming of Quebec. Despite insufficient numbers with which to make an assault viable, Montgomery knew that he must nevertheless face the risks before the enlistment period of his troops expired. (National Archives and Records Administration)

American batteries there. The governor escaped by disguising himself as a civilian, but the colonists still captured eleven ships and 150 soldiers. Over the next two weeks, Montgomery reorganized and resupplied his army. Many troops wanted to return home as their enlistments neared expiration, and only 800 reenlisted. The Americans also managed to raise several hundred Canadians.

While Montgomery moved against St. John's and Montreal, George Washington sent Arnold through the Maine wilderness to Quebec. Washington hoped that Arnold could take the city easily, as Carleton deployed most of his forces against Montgomery. Leaving from Cambridge, Massachusetts, Arnold proceeded to Fort Western (then Massachusetts, now Maine) and advanced up the Kennebec River with 1,100 men on 25 September. The Americans badly underestimated the distance to Quebec and the hardships they would encounter. Their poorly constructed bateaux leaked heavily, ruining provisions, and the men struggled through icy water. In late October, 300 soldiers turned back, taking most of the remaining provisions with them, but Arnold, facing starvation, pushed on to the Chaudière River. He eventually procured food from the local inhabitants, and his 600 gaunt survivors reached the St. Lawrence River opposite Quebec in mid-November. Crossing the river, Arnold sent messengers to Montgomery and unsuccessfully called upon Quebec to surrender. He then retreated to Pointe-aux-Trembles to await Montgomery, who arrived on 1 December with 300 men.

The combined American force, supported by several hundred Canadians, arrived at Quebec three days later and blockaded the walled city. Carleton could field 1,800 troops, but only 70 were regulars. The rest were a collection of British and Canadian militia of dubious loyalty and some sailors. Throughout the month, Montgomery repeatedly tried to induce the British governor to surrender. The American general also bombarded the city, but his light artillery caused little damage. Carleton wisely chose not to venture outside of his fortifications and awaited relief from Britain. Smallpox broke out in the American army, and Arnold's enlistments expired at the end of the year. Faced with this situation, Montgomery launched a two-pronged assault on the night of 30–31 December that was repelled with heavy losses. The Americans had 48 killed, including Montgomery; 34 wounded; and 372 captured. British casualties were 5 dead and 14 wounded.

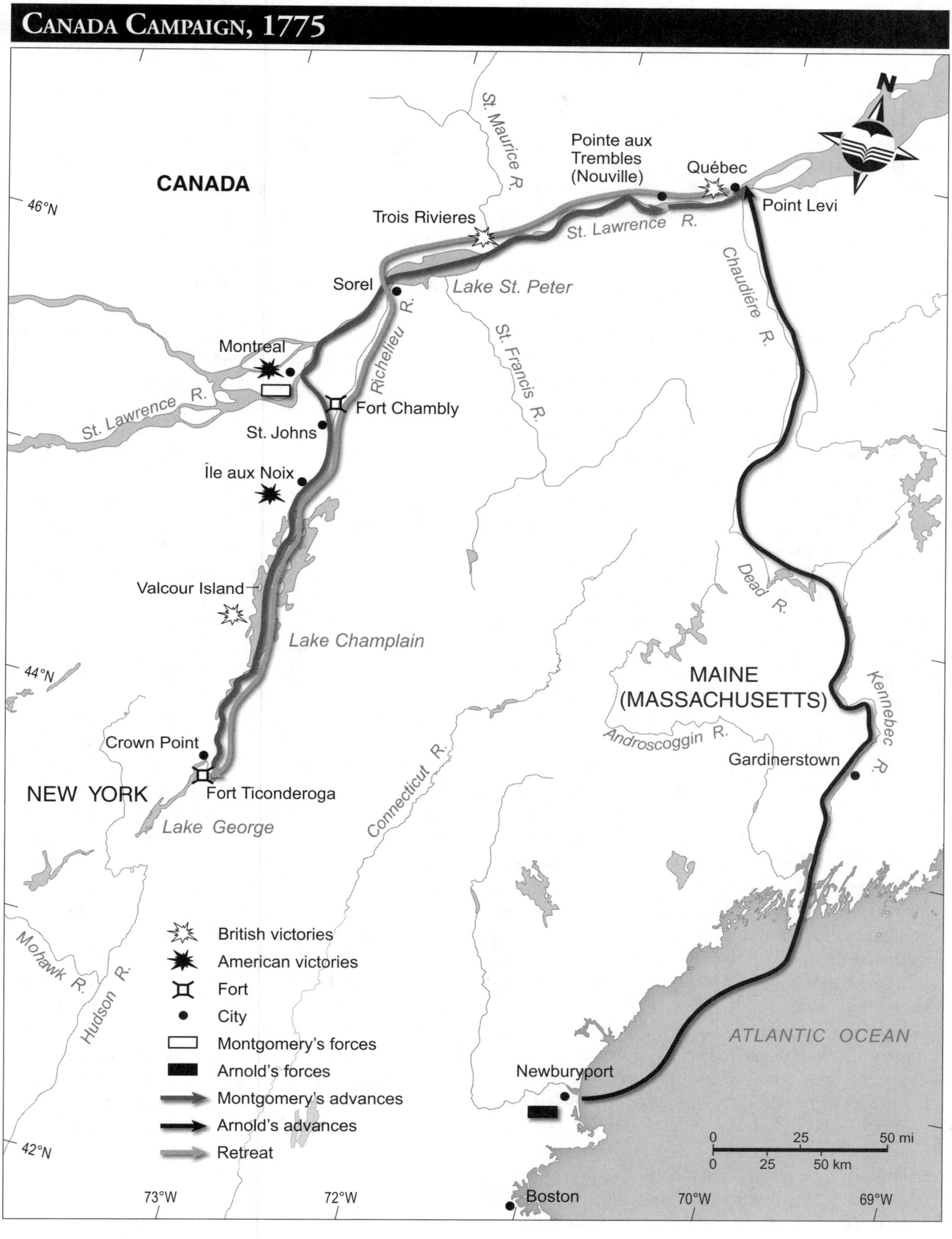
Canada Campaign, 1775
CANADA
St. Maurice R.
Pointe aux
Trembles
(Nouville)
Québec
Point Levi
Trois Rivieres
St. Lawrence R.
Chaudiére R.
Sorel
Lake St. Peter
Richelieu R.
St. Francis R.
Montreal
St. Lawrence R.
Fort Chambly
St. Johns
Île aux Noix
Valcour Island
Lake Champlain
Dead R.
MAINE
(MASSACHUSETTS)
Kennebec R.
Androscoggin R.
Gardinerstown
Crown Point
Fort Ticonderoga
NEW YORK
Lake George
Connecticut R.
Mohawk R.
Hudson R.
British victories
American victories
Fort
City
Montgomery's forces
Arnold's forces
Montgomery's advances
Arnold's advances
Retreat
ATLANTIC OCEAN
Newburyport
Boston
0 25 50 mi
0 25 50 km
46°N
44°N
42°N
73°W
72°W
70°W
69°W
N

Arnold, shot in the leg, gamely maintained the blockade throughout the winter. He and his Canadian allies repeatedly skirmished with pro-British inhabitants. The largest of these engagements occurred on 25 March at St. Pierre du Sud on the south bank of the St. Lawrence, where an American and Canadian detachment routed Loyalist militiamen who were marching to Quebec. Still, the inhabitants slowly turned against Arnold's men as the Americans' strength ebbed. The Americans further alienated the Canadians by requisitioning provisions with increasing frequency and paying for them with questionable paper money. In spring 1776, Congress sent a committee composed of Benjamin Franklin, Charles Carroll, and Samuel Chase to investigate affairs in Canada, but it could do little more than report on a rapidly deteriorating situation.

On 6 May, the first detachments of 13,000 British and German troops commanded by Major-General John Burgoyne arrived at Quebec. Carleton immediately attacked the besieging Americans, now led by Brigadier General John Thomas. Ravaged by smallpox and a chronic shortage of everything, the colonists hastily retreated to Deschambault, 45 miles west of Quebec, abandoning large amounts of equipment and stores. Remaining there for a week, Thomas retired to Sorel at the mouth of the Richelieu and then to St. John's. Against Burgoyne's more aggressive counsel, Carleton cautiously pursued, allowing the Americans to withdraw, but their position in Canada continued to worsen. On 19 May, a British and Indian force from Oswegatchie captured 400 colonists at the Cedars, 40 miles west of Montreal. They then ambushed a relief column and took another 100 prisoners before returning to Oswegatchie, when Arnold approached with a large force.

By early June, the Americans controlled only Montreal and St. John's, but Congress had rushed reinforcements northward. General John Sullivan, who replaced Thomas after he died from smallpox, led nearly 7,000 men back to Sorel. On 6 June, Sullivan received intelligence that only 800 British troops held Trois-Rivières, about halfway between Montreal and Quebec, and he ordered General William Thompson to counterattack with 2,000 troops. Thompson landed near the town two days later but quickly became lost in an impenetrable swamp. When the Americans finally emerged hours later, British warships on the St. Lawrence fired upon them, as Carleton's army had arrived. The British easily repelled the disorganized American attack on the town. Thompson's men retreated into the forest, and Carleton moved to cut off their escape. He landed troops upriver, while additional soldiers blocked a bridge across the Rivière du Loup, the only other escape route. At the last minute Carleton recalled this detachment and allowed the Americans to escape. The governor favored a reconciliation with the colonists and thought that he lacked the provisions necessary to feed thousands of prisoners. Still, he inflicted around 400 casualties, of whom 236 were prisoners, including Thompson. Carleton lost 8 killed and 9 wounded.

Carleton advanced to Sorel, while Sullivan, convinced that Canada was lost, began to retreat. On 14 June, Carleton ordered Burgoyne to drive the Americans south toward St. John's with 4,000 troops, while Carleton sailed to Longueuil with the rest of the army. There, he intended to land his troops and rapidly march southeast to St. John's, enveloping the Americans. Winds delayed Carleton's ships, however, and gave the Americans time to evacuate Montreal and reach St. John's. On 19 June, the colonists abandoned St. John's, taking four warships with them. These vessels allowed them to retain control of Lake Champlain. Halting briefly at Île-aux-Noix, the Americans soon resumed the retreat to Ticonderoga, from where Montgomery had begun the invasion ten months earlier. Despite other rumors and false starts, most notably in March 1778 under the Marquis de Lafayette, they would not invade Canada again during the Revolutionary War.

Some historians have argued that the American expulsion from Canada was ultimately a blessing in disguise. The colonists lacked the resources to conduct major operations both in Canada and the lower thirteen colonies. The Canadian defeat allowed the colonists to focus on the most important theater of the war. The invasion also had more positive long-term consequences. The early victories boosted the colonists' morale and bought the Revolution valuable time by preventing the British from attacking the northern frontier. This allowed Washington to concentrate his efforts and resources on the main British Army in Boston.

Additionally, the invasion complicated British planning by forcing it to divert 13,000 troops to Canada. That Britain deployed such strength makes it questionable whether the Americans could have held Canada permanently. Still, the invasion prevented those troops from being sent against the thirteen colonies in 1776. Similarly, the fear of a future invasion caused Britain to keep a large garrison in Canada—soldiers who might have been better employed elsewhere—throughout the Revolutionary War. Furthermore, American control of Lake Champlain, even after the Americans returned to Ticonderoga, caused Carleton to spend much of the summer and early autumn of 1776 building warships. When the governor finally advanced in October, it was too late in the season to capture Ticonderoga and Albany and cooperate with Major-General William Howe's army in the Hudson Valley. This failure allowed the Americans to continue the war effort for another year and helped lay the foundation for the decisive Saratoga Campaign of 1777.

Michael P. Gabriel

See also

Allen, Ethan; Arnold, Benedict; Burgoyne, John; Canada; Carroll, Charles; Carleton, Guy; Chambly, Quebec, Action at; Chase, Samuel; Crown Point, New York; Diseases; Fort Ticonderoga,

New York; Franklin, Benjamin; Lafayette, Marquis de; Lake Champlain, Operations on; Montgomery, Richard; Montreal, Operations against; Quebec, Siege of; Saratoga Campaign; Schuyler, Philip; St. John's, Actions against; Sullivan, John; Thomas, John; Thompson, William; Trois-Rivières, Action at

References

Gabriel, Michael P. *Major General Richard Montgomery: The Making of an American Hero.* Madison: Fairleigh Dickinson University Press, 2002.

Gabriel, Michael P., and S. Pascale Dewey, eds. *Quebec during the American Invasion, 1775–1776: The Journal of François Baby, Gabriel Taschereau, and Jenkin Williams.* East Lansing: Michigan State University Press, 2005.

Lanctot, Gustave. *Canada and the American Revolution, 1774–1783.* London: Harrap, 1967.

Roberts, Kenneth Lewis. *March to Quebec: Journal of the Members of Arnold Expedition.* 1945. Reprint, Rockport, ME: Down East Books, 1967.

Smith, Justin H. *Our Struggle for the Fourteenth Colony: Canada and the American Revolution.* 2 vols. 1907. Reprint, New York: Da Capo, 1974.

Stanley, George. *Canada Invaded, 1775–1776.* Toronto: Canadian War Museum, 1973.

Ward, Christopher. *War of the Revolution.* 2 vols. New York: Macmillan, 1952.

Canajoharie, New York, Raid against (2 August 1780)

In the summer of 1780, the Mohawk Chief Joseph Brant led a party of Loyalists and Native Americans in a raid that destroyed the settlement at Canajoharie, New York. Raiding by Loyalists and Native Americans in the Mohawk Valley occurred for much of the Revolutionary War in an effort to drive the settlers away and deprive the Patriot armies of local food supplies.

In 1780 the Patriots needed to supply the frontier garrison at Fort Stanwix. The supply convoy was gathering at Fort Plank to make the trip to Fort Stanwix. Brant become aware of the convoy, and a rumor spread on the frontier that he planned to intercept it. To protect the convoy, the Patriots called out additional militia from the Mohawk Valley. Instead of attacking the convoy, however, Brant led his party around the well-protected area through which the convoy was traveling and moved lower down the Mohawk Valley to strike the Canajoharie settlement and nearby Fort Plank.

Brant split his party into two parts, sending one against the settlement and the other against the fort. The first raiding party managed to get into position to launch the attack without alerting the settlers, but some of the Native Americans were too eager and prematurely began their assault. This alerted the settlers, and many were able to escape to the fort. With the fort alerted to his presence, Brant was unable to capture it, but since most of the local militia was away helping guard the convoy, the garrison was only strong enough to defend the fort. This allowed Brant to burn the Canajoharie settlement, destroying the grain that was being harvested and killing or driving off the livestock.

Probably less than thirty Patriots were killed, but forty to sixty settlers, mostly women and children, were taken prisoner. Some accounts claim that Brant released many of the women and children. The militia from lower down in the valley was called out upon seeing the smoke from the burning buildings and moved slowly toward the scene of the raid, allowing Brant to retire from the Canajoharie area without being attacked.

Dallace W. Unger Jr.

See also

Brant, Joseph; Fort Stanwix, New York; Loyalists; Native Americans

References

Edmonds, Walter D. *Drums along the Mohawk.* 1937. Reprint, Syracuse, NY: Syracuse University Press, 1997.

Kelsay, Isabel T. *Joseph Brant, 1743–1807: Man of Two Worlds.* Syracuse, NY: Syracuse University Press, 1984.

Mays, Terry M. *Historical Dictionary of the American Revolution.* Historical Dictionaries of War, Revolution, and Civil Unrest Series, no. 7. Lanham, MD: Scarecrow, 1999.

Stone, William L. *Life of Joseph Brant-Thayendanegea: Including the Border Wars of the American Revolution, and Sketches of the Indian Campaigns of Generals Harmar, St. Clair, and Wayne, and Other Matters Connected with the Indian Relations of the United States and Great Britain, from the Peace of 1783 to the Indian Peace of 1795.* Vol. 2. 1838. Reprint, New York: Kraus, 1969.

Cane Creek, North Carolina, Action at (13 September 1781)

In the actions at Cane Creek, North Carolina, also known as the Battle of Lindley's Mill, a 1,000-man Loyalist force was withdrawing with more than 200 prisoners after an extremely successful raid on Hillsborough, at the time the capital of North Carolina, when they were attacked by 400 Continental soldiers in Chatham County.

The Loyalist force, under the command of Colonel David Fanning and Colonel Hector McNeill, and their prisoners, including Governor Thomas Burke, had traveled nearly 20 miles from Hillsborough and had begun to cross the Stafford Branch where it enters Cane Creek, near a mill owned by a Quaker, Thomas Lindley. The Patriots, led by General John Butler and Colonel Robert Mebane, issued musket fire from a short distance east on a low ridge overlooking the crossing. The initial attack surprised and pinned down the Loyalists, killing McNeill and seven others.

Fanning quickly pulled back from the creek but then crossed the branch at another location with some of his men and attacked the Continentals' flank. The action raged for nearly four hours and left the Continentals with twenty-five men dead, ninety wounded, and ten captured. The Loyalists suffered twenty-seven casualties. Fanning was badly wounded and had to be left behind along with sixty of the ninety wounded Loyalists. Command of the Loyalists passed to Lieutenant-Colonel Archibald McDugald, Major John Ranes, and Lieutenant-Colonel Archibald McKay, who eluded further pursuit on their march to Wilmington, North Carolina.

Mark Speltz

See also

Burke, Thomas; Butler, John; Fanning, David; Hillsborough, North Carolina, Raid on

References

Arthur, Billy. "The Midnight Ride of Alexander Mebane." *Our State* 67 (August 1999): 18–20.

DeMond, Robert O. *The Loyalists in North Carolina during the Revolution.* Durham, NC: Duke University Press, 1940.

Cape St. Vincent, Battle of (16 January 1780)

The Battle of Cape St. Vincent, also known as the Moonlight Battle, occurred off the Spanish coast and was fought between Admiral George Rodney, escorting supplies to Gibraltar—then under siege by Spanish land and naval forces—and a Spanish fleet under Commodore Don Juan de Yardi.

In October 1779 Rodney was placed in command of the Leeward Islands station in the West Indies. Although originally Rodney was only to take four or five ships with him, the Admiralty decided to use the opportunity of his departure to put under his command a large force, consisting of his own ships and others detached from the Channel Fleet, to convoy vessels carrying supplies and troops intended for Gibraltar and Minorca. Rodney sailed from Plymouth on 29 December with twenty-two line of battle ships, fourteen frigates and smaller craft, and a huge number of supply ships and transports carrying provisions, ammunition, troops, and merchandise intended for the West Indies and Gibraltar. On 7 January the ships bound for the West Indies separated with an escort of one ship of the line and three frigates. On the following day, a Spanish squadron of twenty-two ships was sighted and chased, and the entire force was captured in the course of the day. Only seven were warships, the remainder being merchantmen carrying supplies for the Spanish fleet at Cadiz. These were sent to aid the beleaguered garrison at Gibraltar, where such captured naval stores and other provisions would be of considerable use.

Shortly thereafter news arrived of a Spanish squadron having been sighted near Cape St. Vincent. Rodney passed the Cape on 16 January, and at 1:00 P.M. a Spanish squadron of eleven ships of the line and two small frigates was sighted. Rodney immediately pursued, ordering his ships to engage the enemy as they reached the sternmost vessel and in a manner that would put his own ships between the Spanish and their supposed destination, Cadiz, 100 miles to the southeast. Rodney had some advantages in pursuit, his crews possessing superior seamanship skills and his vessels benefiting from copper bottoms, making it difficult for an enemy not so fitted either to overtake its opponents or escape from them.

Shortly after 4:00 P.M. the four leading British ships engaged the Spanish and forty minutes later the *Santo Domingo* (70 guns) blew up, killing its entire crew. At 6:00 P.M. another vessel surrendered. Darkness had fallen by then, but fighting continued until 2:00 A.M., when the leading Spanish vessel struck its colors. Six of the eleven Spanish ships of the line were taken, one was destroyed, and four escaped. The captured vessels were the *Fenix* (80 guns), the flagship under Admiral Don Juan de Langara; the *Monarca* (70 guns); the *Princessa* (70 guns); the *Diligente* (70 guns); the *San Julian* (70 guns); and the *San Eugenio* (70 guns). The last two were driven ashore and abandoned, though one may have been recovered by the Spanish. Rodney brought the other four into Gibraltar, and all were eventually commissioned into the Royal Navy. The sea was very turbulent during the night, with high winds continuing into the following day. During this period several of Rodney's ships were at considerable risk of grounding on the shoals off San Lucar and were not out of danger until the morning of 18 January.

This action was a great credit to Rodney, who surprised the Spanish with double the force and ensured that, through the careful placing of his own vessels, his opponents did not escape. He did this at considerable risk to himself, sailing close to the shore and under difficult weather conditions. There was originally some question as to whether Rodney should open an engagement as sunset approached, but the fact that he did rendered the victory all the more complete. The captures taken on 8 and 16 January were welcome news to the garrison at Gibraltar, which eagerly received the seized provisions in addition to those from Britain itself. The fact that Rodney also had ships of the line as prizes contributed all the more to raising the morale of the defenders.

The news of Rodney's success was enthusiastically welcomed in Britain, where the government had received considerable public criticism for its lack of preparedness. At Cape St. Vincent, Rodney not only secured more captured vessels than in any other single action of the two previous wars, but he did so in close proximity to Admiral Don Louis de Cordova's superior fleet at Cadiz, which consisted of twenty Spanish and four French ships of the line. Cordova, in fact, never attempted to threaten Rodney during the eighteen days that the British were to remain in the vicinity of Gibraltar. Rodney's storeships carried on to Minorca under convoy.

When they returned the admiral left for the West Indies on 13 February.

Gregory Fremont-Barnes

See also

Gibraltar, Siege of; Naval Operations, British vs. Spanish; Rodney, George; Royal Navy; Spain; West Indies

References

Clowes, William Laird. *The Royal Navy: A History from the Earliest Times to 1900.* 7 vols. London: Chatham, 1996.

Gardiner, Robert, ed. *Navies and the American Revolution, 1775–1783.* London: Chatham, 1996.

James, William. *The British Navy in Adversity: A Study of the War of American Independence.* 1926. Reprint, New York: Russell and Russell, 1970.

Syrett, David. *The Royal Navy in European Waters during the American Revolutionary War.* Columbia: University of South Carolina Press, 1998.

Tilley, J. A. *The Royal Navy in the American Revolution.* Columbia: University of South Carolina Press, 1987.

Carleton, Christopher (1749–1787)

Christopher Carleton was a British Army officer who had a great admiration for American Indians and led a raid against Patriot settlers on Lake Champlain in 1778. Born in Newcastle-upon-Tyne in England, he was the second son of William Carleton, elder brother of the soldiers and governors Sir Guy Carleton and Thomas Carleton. On 29 July 1763 at the age of fourteen, Christopher Carleton was appointed lieutenant in the 31st Regiment. Serving in America, he lived among the Indians and adopted their customs, a practice that continued as late as the beginning of the Revolutionary War. He painted his face, wore a ring in his nose, had himself tattooed, and took an Indian wife. He later asserted that his time among the natives was the happiest of his life, but he soon abandoned Indian ways, perhaps because of pressure from his distinguished uncles, more likely because his health was not robust enough to sustain the lifestyle. In 1770 he married Anne Howard, daughter of Thomas Howard, 2nd Earl Effingham, after she had rejected his uncle, Guy Carleton. Subsequently, Guy Carleton married Anne's sister, Maria Howard.

Christopher Carleton was promoted to captain-lieutenant on 25 December 1770 and to captain on 25 May 1772. Early in the Revolution, he served in Canada as aide-de-camp to his uncle, Governor-General Guy Carleton. Christopher Carleton led troops during General John Burgoyne's expedition in 1777 and on 14 September was promoted to major of the 29th Regiment. Carleton was a spy in the Mohawk Valley in early 1778 and apparently a successful one, for the Marquis de Lafayette placed a bounty of fifty guineas on his head. In October 1778 Canadian Governor-General Frederick Haldimand appointed Carleton commander of an expedition on Lake Champlain against rebel inhabitants living along the shores. His orders were to destroy enemy supply depots, provisions, and animals as well as boats, sawmills, and gristmills. Additionally, he was to take prisoner all men who had sworn allegiance to Congress and disperse women and children with orders not to return. He was given command of a flotilla consisting of the warships *Carleton* and *Maria* and a number of small craft, 354 British troops and militiamen, and 100 Indians.

On 24 October, Carleton's expedition departed Île-aux-Noix in the Richelieu River, sailing south up Lake Champlain. After exercising his troops in woodland fighting, he began raiding on 31 October. He directed small parties against both individual homesteads and enemy blockhouses, capturing rebels and destroying their stores. Although American defenders fired upon his troops at various places, he acted with near impunity, raiding as far south as Chimney Point, Vermont, on West Bay. On 12 November, he returned to Île-aux-Noix and reported to Haldimand that he had captured 39 prisoners and destroyed four months' provisions for 12,000 rebel troops. His expedition was hailed by Canadian and British leaders as a major success. He served in Quebec after the Revolution and was promoted to lieutenant-colonel on 19 February 1783. He died four years later at Quebec.

Paul David Nelson

See also

Burgoyne, John; Carleton, Guy; Lafayette, Marquis de; Lake Champlain, Operations on

Reference

Washington, Ida H., and Paul A. Washington. *Carleton's Raid.* Canaan, NH: Phoenix Publishing, 1977.

Carleton, Guy (1724–1808)

Sir Guy Carleton, 1st Baron Dorchester, an important soldier-statesman in the formative years of British Canadian history, is remembered for his distant and reserved personality, his military and political abilities, and his occasional ruthlessness. A member of an old Anglo-Irish family, he joined the British Army on 21 May 1742, enrolling as an ensign in the 25th Regiment. On 1 May 1745, he was promoted to lieutenant in the same regiment. He was aide-de-camp to the Duke of Cumberland in 1747 and fought at Bergen op Zoom in the Netherlands. On 22 July 1751, Carleton was appointed lieutenant of the 1st Foot Guards. Upon the recommendation of his friend Lieutenant-Colonel James Wolfe, Carleton became military advisor to Charles Lennox, third Duke of Richmond, in early 1753. With the duke's patronage, Carleton assumed the lieutenant-colonelcy of the 1st Foot Guards on 18 June 1757.

In 1758, Carleton was aide-de-camp to Prince Ferdinand during operations in Germany and was appointed lieutenant-colonel of the 72nd Regiment. When Wolfe organized his

Major-General Sir Guy Carleton. As governor of Quebec and commander of British forces in Canada in 1775, he defended Quebec against the Americans and pursued their army back to New York. His push up Lake Champlain came to a halt with the onset of winter. And in 1777 John Burgoyne replaced Carleton as head of British forces in the north. (Library of Congress)

campaign against Quebec in early 1759, he commissioned Carleton as quartermaster-general of the army, with the rank of colonel in America. During the campaign, Carleton distinguished himself as quartermaster, military engineer, and commander of an elite grenadier corps. He fought bravely in the Battle of the Plains of Abraham on 14 September, suffering a head wound and the loss of his friend Wolfe, who died in battle. Returning to Britain, Carleton served in March 1761 as a brigadier-general in the expedition to Belle Isle, off the French coast, where he was wounded. He was promoted to colonel on 19 February 1762 and joined the Earl of Albemarle's expedition against Havana as quartermaster-general with the local rank of brigadier-general. On 22 July, Carleton was slightly wounded while leading a successful attack against a Spanish post in Cuba.

On 7 April 1766, Carleton was appointed lieutenant governor of Quebec. Although he was not commissioned governor until 12 April 1768, he acted as governor from the outset with the support of London officials. Sailing into New York on 21 August 1766, he consulted with General Thomas Gage, commander in chief of North America, and finally arrived at Quebec on 22 September. On 3 October, he was appointed brigadier-general in America, a temporary rank only effective on that continent. Governing with the assistance of his council, Carleton quickly asserted control over its members, and although some thought his actions arbitrary, his superiors in London supported him. He paid attention to encouraging the fur trade and unsuccessfully battled against the fee system used to pay government officials. As a military man, he attempted to improve Quebec's defenses.

Carleton protected the French Canadians against what he called commercial adventurers from Britain. When Parliament began discussing the reorganization of Quebec's government in 1767, he supported the French cultural heritage and encouraged laws to protect it. In 1770 he took a leave of absence and returned to Britain to present his views. He was promoted to colonel of the 47th Regiment on 12 April 1772, and on 22 May he married Lady Mary Howard, with whom he had eleven children. In 1774, Parliament approved the Quebec Act, incorporating most of Carleton's recommendations. He returned to Quebec on 18 September 1774.

In the summer and fall of 1775, as Revolutionary unrest grew in the lower thirteen colonies, American rebels invaded Quebec. Carleton tried to mobilize the old French citizens, but they would not help him, and he refused to use Indians, whose methods he found ruthless and distasteful. General Richard Montgomery advanced up Lake Champlain toward Montreal, while General Benedict Arnold approached Quebec through Maine. Carleton attempted to defend Montreal but was thrown back toward Quebec with Montgomery in pursuit. He arrived at Quebec just before Arnold invested the city. On 31 December, Carleton defeated an American attempt to capture Quebec in which Montgomery was killed and Arnold was wounded. Rescued on 6 May 1776 by the arrival of reinforcements from Britain, Carleton learned that on 1 January he had been promoted to full general in America.

By 19 June 1776, Carleton had pushed the rebels, who were severely weakened by smallpox, completely out of Canada, allowing them to escape in hopes that if he showed leniency they would cease their rebellion. Some of his own officers were disgusted with this policy. During the summer, Carleton organized a fleet on Lake Champlain in order to invade upstate New York. On 11–12 October, he attacked and destroyed an American flotilla commanded by Arnold at Valcour Island and Split Rock and then approached Fort Ticonderoga. Deciding that it was too strong to assault and that the season was too late to continue the campaign, Carleton withdrew his army into Canada.

When Lord George Germain, British colonial secretary, learned of Carleton's decision, he was dismayed and appointed General John Burgoyne to replace Carleton as army commander during the next year's campaign. Before this decision, Carleton was given the Order of the Bath on 7 July 1776 for his defense of Quebec and on 29 August was promoted to lieutenant-general in the British Army, a position carrying higher authority than his previous ranks that had only been effective in America. But when Carleton learned of Germain's decision to place Burgoyne in command in the spring of 1777, he resigned his governorship and asked to be relieved, although he supported Burgoyne during the summer. When Burgoyne was defeated at Saratoga in October, Carleton was not blamed in London. He returned to Britain in July 1778, where he lived quietly as a gentleman, keeping up his political connections and waiting for a new appointment.

This finally came on 18 February 1782, when Carleton was appointed to succeed General Henry Clinton as commander in chief in America and was dispatched to New York, where he arrived on 5 May. Still hoping to persuade the Americans to remain within the British Empire, he was dismayed to learn in August that Britain had agreed to American independence. Although he asked to be relieved on 14 August, he was persuaded to remain and effect the withdrawal of British troops and Loyalists. Over the next few months, despite enormous logistical difficulties, he dispatched 30,000 soldiers and 27,000 refugees from America. He departed New York on 5 December 1783. He was welcomed in London by politicians and the king, and his advice was solicited about the reorganization of Canada to accommodate the large influx of Loyalists. Upon his suggestion, new provinces were created: New Brunswick was created out of Nova Scotia, and Cape Breton Island and St. John's (later Prince Edward) Island were made subprovinces. In 1784 Carleton was appointed governor of Quebec, Nova Scotia, and New Brunswick. On 21 April 1786, he was created 1st Baron Dorchester, in recognition of his military contributions.

Carleton arrived at Quebec on 23 October 1786 and continued to advocate the interests of the French inhabitants. At the same time, he sympathized with the new Loyalist community. Since numerous language and cultural differences separated these groups, Parliament, with Carleton's approval, divided the region into Upper Canada, largely English-speaking, and Lower Canada, mostly old Quebec, in 1791. He returned to Britain in 1791 and on 12 October 1793 was promoted to full general. Back in Quebec by 1793, he dealt successfully with problems caused by the French Revolution and less so with military and diplomatic tensions between the United States and Britain. In 1794, he adopted a tone of belligerence toward America that seemed to threaten war and was mildly rebuked by Henry Dundas, the home secretary. Angrily, Carleton requested permission to resign, and in May 1796 he was replaced. He and his family were shipwrecked on their way home and had to be rescued. In his last years he lived as a landed gentleman, keeping up his interest in military affairs. He had been appointed colonel of the 15th Dragoons in 1790. In March 1801 he transferred to the colonelcy of the 27th Light Dragoons and in August 1803 to the 4th Dragoons. He died in Maidenhead, Berkshire, in 1808.

Paul David Nelson

See also

Arnold, Benedict; Burgoyne, John; Canada; Canada, Operations in; Carleton, Christopher; Carleton, Thomas; Clinton, Henry; Fort Ticonderoga, New York; Gage, Thomas; Germain, Lord George; Lake Champlain, Operations on; Montgomery, Richard; Quebec, Siege of; Quebec Act; Saratoga Campaign; Valcour Island, Battle of

References

Bowler, R. Arthur. "Sir Guy Carleton and the Canadian Campaign of 1776 in Canada." *Canadian Historical Review* 55 (1974): 131–140.

Bradley, Arthur G. *Sir Guy Carleton (Lord Dorchester).* Toronto: University of Toronto Press, 1907.

Nelson, Paul David. *General Sir Guy Carleton, Lord Dorchester: Soldier-Statesman of Early British Canada.* Madison, NJ: Fairleigh Dickinson University Press, 2000.

Smith, Paul H. "Sir Guy Carleton: Soldier-Statesman." Pp. 103–141 in *George Washington's Opponents: British Generals and Admirals in the American Revolution.* Edited by George A. Billias. New York: Morrow, 1969.

Carleton, Thomas (1735–1817)

Thomas Carleton, a British Army officer who served during the Revolution, later served as the first governor of New Brunswick. He was eleven years younger than his more famous brother, Guy Carleton. In 1753 Thomas Carleton joined the 20th Regiment as a volunteer. He was commissioned an ensign in 1755 and later that year was promoted to lieutenant and appointed adjutant. He was in the Rochefort expedition in 1757 and the expedition against St. Malo in 1758, during the Seven Years' War. He fought at Minden in 1759 and Wesel and Campen in 1760. He was promoted to captain in 1759 and was appointed aide-de-camp to Lord Frederick Cavendish in 1761. From 1765 to 1769 Carleton served at Gibraltar. Breveted a major in 1773, he obtained leave the following year to fight with the Russian army against Turkey. After spending the winter in St. Petersburg, he returned to Britain in 1775.

In 1776, Carleton was commissioned a lieutenant-colonel of the 19th Regiment and ordered to Quebec. He arrived on 6 May and was appointed quartermaster-general by his brother. Carleton was next promoted to lieutenant-colonel of the 29th Regiment on 21 August. In September he led an Indian advance guard up Lake Champlain and was wounded during the naval action in mid-October 1776 at Valcour Island. Little is known of his activities for the subsequent six years, though he appears to have served under his brother.

He returned to Britain in 1782 but was ordered to New York in the summer of that year, rejoining his brother who now was commander in chief of the British Army in North America. On 20 November 1782 he was appointed colonel of the 29th Regiment. With his brother's patronage, he was appointed governor of the newly created province of New Brunswick on 16 August 1784. His title was changed to lieutenant governor on 20 May 1786 owing to a reorganization of the province by London that placed New Brunswick under the control of Guy Carleton, but this new title represented scarcely any diminution of power. Also in 1786, with his brother's assistance, Thomas Carleton was appointed commander of troops in the Maritime Provinces.

Carleton arrived at St. John's (then Parr Town), New Brunswick, on 21 November 1784 and was enthusiastically welcomed by the inhabitants. With the assistance of his council, which was dominated by Loyalist elites, he organized the government. A man of generous and humane instincts, he tried to treat all parties with impartiality, but his own Anglo-Irish and military background inclined him to sympathize with the Loyalists. The development of New Brunswick was strongly influenced by this alliance. He gave much attention to getting Loyalists settled on their lands. At the same time, he tried to act justly toward the Acadians. Although he was promoted to major-general in 1793, lieutenant-general in 1798, and general in 1803, his hopes for a more important military command never materialized. He was also disappointed at New Brunswick's slow growth and at the demands of some of the settlers for an assembly, and over time his critics grew in number. In 1803 he took a leave of absence to Britain and never returned, although he continued to hold the office of lieutenant governor until his death in 1817.

Paul David Nelson

See also

Carleton, Christopher; Carleton, Guy; Lake Champlain, Operations on; Valcour Island, Battle of

Reference

Nelson, Paul David. *General Sir Guy Carleton, Lord Dorchester: Soldier-Statesman of Early British Canada.* Madison, NJ: Fairleigh Dickinson University Press, 2000.

Carlisle Peace Commission (1778)

The Carlisle Peace Commission, formed in April 1778, was an attempt by Great Britain to reach a negotiated end to the war without granting full independence to the rebellious colonies.

After General John Burgoyne surrendered at Saratoga on 17 October 1777, Parliament and, in particular, Lord North, the prime minister, were concerned that the American victory might prompt France to ally with America. The news troubled many as the first sign that Britain might actually lose the war. On 7 December 1777, William Eden wrote North a letter suggesting that a new pacification plan be brought before Parliament, and North agreed. When news of the impending Franco-American Alliance became public, King George III, hesitant to reconcile with the colonies, finally agreed to the plan. On 11 February 1778, North presented a "Plan of Conciliation with America," which became the Conciliatory Acts, largely written by Eden.

The acts changed the way Britain viewed the colonies. The most important aspect of the acts was the repeal of all the offending laws enacted since 1763, effectively ending all British taxation of North America. The acts also allowed for American representation in Parliament, British representation in the colonial assemblies, and the removal of all British armed forces from the colonies during peacetime. Finally, the acts called for the creation of a new peace commission to negotiate with the colonies on these points. The new commission replaced the existing and ineffective Howe Peace Commission, led by brothers Admiral Lord Richard Howe and General Sir William Howe.

Eden was responsible for selecting members of the commission. His first appointee was Frederick Howard, 5th Earl of Carlisle, a twenty-something gambler and privy councilor to the king. Carlisle had already planned a trip to America and may have been chosen to appease the influential Lord Gower, his father-in-law. Eden wanted Richard Jackson as the next member, but Jackson had concerns about the orders of the commission and declined the appointment. George Johnstone, a retired naval officer and member of Parliament, became Jackson's replacement on the advice of the king. To fill out the commission, Eden selected the Howe brothers, representing the Royal Navy and the British Army, to meet with the commissioners in America and Adam Ferguson to serve as secretary. Eden pressed for the commissioners to be given ambassadorial rank, with all associated honors and pay, but the king rejected the idea.

The commission received its instructions on 12 April 1778. Much of the instructions repeated clauses in the Conciliatory Acts, including the repeal of all taxation laws. The commissioners were also instructed to offer trade protection from the Royal Navy once peace was established, the removal of all British troops, and a promise that Britain would not change colonial governments without their consent. There was no need to demand a repeal of the Declaration of Independence, as any agreement would nullify the document. If Congress balked at negotiations, the instructions gave the commission the authority to deal with individual colonies.

The members of the commission, particularly Eden, believed that the plan would not work unless it was accompanied by a significant show of force. Lord George Germain assured them that the navy would be reinforced and remain on the offensive, but he sent secret orders to Sir Henry Clin-

Carlisle Peace Commission (1778). British political cartoon depicting three members of the Continental Congress standing beneath palm trees, outlining their demands for peace to three members of a British peace commission: the Earl of Carlisle, Baron Auckland, and George Johnstone. Lord Bute stands between the two groups. (Library of Congress)

ton, commander of British forces in America, to withdraw from Philadelphia, and even from New York if necessary, and to refrain from any offensive operations. Germain felt that British forces were needed to face Britain's new enemy, France. These orders, withheld from the commission, essentially undercut any chance of successful negotiations. After a series of meetings with Lord North, Eden and Carlisle became suspicious, and rightfully so, that North himself had little faith in the commission.

On 16 April, the commissioners set sail for America aboard the *Trident,* almost two months after the Conciliatory Acts were sent to the colonies. While they were at sea, Germain redeployed British troops and established a defensive strategy in the rebellious colonies. Back in Parliament, opposition members, led by Charles James Fox, accused the North ministry of forcing the Conciliatory Acts through Parliament and making fools out of the members of the House of Commons. Publicly, North defended his policy and said that he thought the commission would succeed. Conciliation, however, was never a unanimous plan, and after the signing of the Franco-American Alliance, it became even less certain. British military strategy and parliamentary politics alike appeared to doom the commission from the start.

The commissioners, though possibly suspicious that they did not have the government's full support, proceeded with guarded optimism. Johnstone proposed the plan that the commission would follow, the "Heads of Accommodation," which he based on a letter he received from his brother William Pulteney. In March, Pulteney had met with Benjamin Franklin in Paris and was convinced that the Americans would accept a negotiated peace, especially if they were promised seats in Parliament. The commissioners agreed to make a strong pitch, offering all they were authorized to offer to the American Congress at the onset of negotiations.

During their crossing the commissioners heard from a passing ship that the Howe brothers were in Philadelphia, so they agreed to head there. When they arrived on 6 June, however, Clinton was already withdrawing British forces. The sight of a "fleeing army" angered the commissioners. Their first report to Germain stated that the commission could have successfully persuaded the Americans to separate from the French alliance had one more strong military push taken place. Immediately upon arriving in Philadelphia, the commission changed shape as Admiral Howe refused his appointment (because he was not in charge) and General Howe returned to England. Clinton became the sole member representing the military, but he was a member in name only, as he was soon overwhelmed with the British withdrawal and other military duties.

On 9 June, the commission's chair sent a letter to Congress along with another copy of the Conciliatory Acts. Carlisle's letter was full of kind words for the Americans but was hostile to France. He hoped to encourage America to reconcile with Britain in light of a possible European war. Peace was not dependent on Britain alone, he argued, but on America's love of country. The letter pleaded that America should avoid an unnatural foreign alliance but maintain a firm and perpetual coalition with the parent state. If America allied with France, America would become a dangerous enemy and would be treated as such.

Congress read the letter, in part, on 13 June but stopped when reaching the part that was derogatory to France. Congress finished reading on 16 June and drafted a reply, stating that it would meet with the commission only after British forces withdrew and Britain recognized American independence. Before receiving Congress's reply, the commissioners left Philadelphia for New York. The commission finally received the reply on 30 June and responded with a second letter offering conditional independence. Congress ignored the second letter. Based on Congress's response and the fact that the Continental Army was still in the field, the commissioners wrote a second report to Germain stating that unless Britain was willing to take the offensive, the commission would be unable to negotiate. The commission also requested permission to return home at each member's discretion.

Once it became clear that traditional negotiations were untenable, Johnstone decided to try other means. He believed that some congressmen could be coerced or bribed, and he sent letters to Robert Morris and Colonel Joseph Reed hinting at possible rewards if there was a quick end to the war. When Reed reported the overture to Congress, it resolved to ignore all future commission correspondence. On 11 August, Congress further resolved to have absolutely no dealings with Johnstone or with the commission as long as Johnstone was a member. Johnstone resigned his commission on 26 August and published a rebuke to Congress's charges in *The New York Gazette* on 28 September. When he returned to England, he had his first ever audience with the king and denied any wrongdoing. Clinton, Carlisle, and Eden, for their part, denied any knowledge of Johnstone's actions and intent. The commission urged Congress not to break off talks based on Johnstone's actions.

Johnstone's possible bribery attempt was likely not an isolated action. Eden, when he prepared the budget for the commission, included provisions for contingent secret service money, approved by North and the king, to be used for bribery and other commission needs. And two secret service agents—John Berkenhout, a physician and acquaintance of Arthur Lee, and John Temple—traveled to America to assist the commission. Temple, a Boston native, was highly paid to use all of his influence to assist in the negotiations. He convinced many rebels that he favored America's position, and he traveled freely. He remained in America after the commission left but concluded that there was little Britain could do to stave off defeat. Berkenhout also traveled extensively and, based on discussions during his excursion, concluded that there was no reason the British should not rout Washington's army. The Supreme Executive Council of Pennsylvania jailed Berkenhout when he was in Philadelphia as the members attempted to ascertain why he was there.

After realizing that negotiations with Congress would be fruitless, the commission attempted to appeal to the American public by publishing Britain's peace offer and all their correspondence. The commission incorrectly believed that Congress was not acting based on the will of the people. On 7 August 1778, the commission made its last demand on Congress by asking for the return of Burgoyne's army to Britain, under the terms of the Saratoga Convention, but Congress refused. On 3 October, Carlisle issued a "Manifesto & Proclamation," an appeal to different groups and individuals to speak against Congress and for peace. The manifesto stated that the commission had offered everything the colonies asked for when the war started and that its members could not believe that Congress was acting for the people. Carlisle expected little from the appeal but felt that he had to try something. The manifesto also served as notice that the commission was leaving America, and if America remained obstinate, only great calamity would follow. Congress responded by urging all state authorities to arrest anyone carrying the manifesto as an act of sedition.

On 27 November 1778, the commission left America aboard the *Roebuck,* landing at Portsmouth on 20 December. Though the commission was a complete failure, the commissioners were well received and rewarded. Carlisle became president of the Board of Trade and eventually lord-lieutenant of Ireland. Johnstone became commodore of a fleet stationed in Lisbon, Portugal. And Eden, disgusted with the current government, refused a seat in the House of Commons but did secure a pension for his wife.

It was hardly surprising that the commission failed as it did. Few people expected it to amount to much, including those who sent it to America. Perhaps the biggest problem with the commission was timing. All the aspects of the Conciliatory Acts and points of negotiation by the commission were the very things the rebellious colonies wanted in 1775 and what some American Patriots may have still wanted before Saratoga. But by 1778 this was not enough. The commission came about as a recognition that Toryism had failed, at least in regard to the American colonies, and the only way Britain could hold on to those colonies was through some concept of federalism. By the time the North ministry and the king recognized this, however, it was too late. Even the delay between the passing of the Conciliatory Acts and the commission's arrival in America proved costly. Congress had not heard word from France in over a year and had no clue about how negotiations were proceeding. Copies of the Conciliatory Acts, shipped immediately after they passed though Parliament, arrived in America well before news of the alliance with France, and Congress agonized over how to receive the upcoming commission. If the commissioners had also sailed in February instead of April, they too would have beat the news of the alliance, which arrived in May, and would have encountered a different Congress. Once the alliance with France became official, commission activities likely only encouraged Americans to remain united and independent.

Michael Miller

See also

Clinton, Henry; Eden, William; Franco-American Alliance; Germain, Lord George; Howe, Richard; Howe, William; Howe Peace Commission; Johnstone, George; North, Lord Frederick

References

Bemis, Samuel F. *The Diplomacy of the American Revolution.* 1935. Reprint, Bloomington: University of Indiana Press, 1957.

Brown, Alan S. "The British Peace Offer of 1778." *Papers of the Michigan Academy of Science, Arts and Letters* 40 (1955): 249–260.

Howard, George James, et al. *The Manuscripts of the Earl of Carlisle, Preserved at Castle Howard.* London: Eyre and Spottiswoode, 1897.

Ritcheson, Charles. *British Politics and the American Revolution.* 1954. Reprint, Westport, CT: Greenwood, 1981.

Van Doren, Carl. *Secret History of the American Revolution: An Account of the Conspiracies of Benedict Arnold and Numerous Others from the Secret Service Papers of the British Headquarters in North America.* New York: Viking, 1941.

Carmichael, William (1735?–1795)

William Carmichael assisted America's first diplomats in Paris and Madrid, and as America's chief envoy to Spain for more than a dozen years during and after the war, he was involved in several important negotiations. But his career, spent largely in one of the more challenging European capitals for any American, held more frustrations than triumphs.

Born at Round Top, the family home near Chestertown, Maryland, Carmichael was the son of William Carmichael, a Scottish immigrant, and Ann Brooke, a niece of Richard Bennett, one of the wealthiest landowners in Maryland. Carmichael studied law, was admitted to the bar, and practiced in Centerville, Maryland.

Following the outbreak of the American Revolution, Carmichael, then visiting London, met Silas Deane, secret agent of the Continental Congress sent to France to procure military aid, and Deane appointed Carmichael as his private secretary in August 1776. In this role, Carmichael assisted the American commission in France (Deane, Benjamin Franklin, and Arthur Lee) in their efforts to enlist European aid for the American cause. Carmichael supervised the shipment of French muskets and supplies to the American army that proved crucial to the American victory at Saratoga in October 1777, and he convinced the Marquis de Lafayette to join the American cause. In November 1777 the Continental Congress appointed Carmichael as official secretary to the American commission in France, but he never accepted the post, and in May 1778 he returned to the United States.

Upon his return, Carmichael soon faced private accusations that he was a double agent. His frequent complaints regarding the lack of reimbursement for his own funds that he had advanced on the public account and his relationship with Joseph Hynson, a British agent, caused Lee and the French foreign minister, the comte de Vergennes, to question Carmichael's loyalty. To be sure, the British secret service did try to employ Carmichael as a spy, but there is no clear evidence that he was a double agent. Such rumors nonetheless persisted as Lee criticized Carmichael for circulating reports of dissension in the American commission and showing confidential dispatches to Deane. In early 1778, however, there was relatively little suspicion of Carmichael, and his services to the American commission in France were deemed satisfactory.

Carmichael served as a delegate in the Continental Congress from Maryland from November 1778 to September 1779, when Congress appointed him secretary of the American legation in Spain under John Jay. Personality differences, failure to attain the objectives of their mission, and personal quarrels soon produced a stormy relationship between the two men. Carmichael viewed Jay as authoritarian and vain; Jay distrusted Carmichael because of his gregariousness and questionable past. Frustration in dealing with the Spanish Court, which refused to recognize American independence, grant Americans navigation rights on the Mississippi River, or accept American territorial claims in the Old Southwest, as well as constant money problems only aggravated these differences. Furthermore, in disputes with the American minister, Carmichael sided with Conrad-Alexandré Gérard, the French minister to the United States; Henry Brockholst Livingston, Jay's brother-in-law; and Lewis Littlepage, Jay's insubordinate protégé. Jay might have overlooked Carmichael's personal manner and disloyalty had he not had serious reservations about Carmichael's official conduct. Carmichael often assumed greater authority than was properly his, talked more freely than seemed prudent, and handled funds improperly. Jay, believing that Carmichael was a spy, would not allow Carmichael's secretary to copy confidential reports, but without any hard evidence of treason Jay could not demand Carmichael's dismissal.

During the war years, Carmichael had little success in promoting American interests in Spain. To be fair, no American diplomat could have gained much in Madrid at any point between the late 1770s and the early 1790s because Spain feared the impact of the American Revolution on her empire in the Western Hemisphere. Reaching Madrid before Jay, Carmichael did persuade King Charles III and his foreign minister, the comte de Floridablanca, to negotiate with the American minister, but they declined to formally receive the legation. By 1782, Jay had only secured $200,000 in Spanish loans, and Spain had not recognized American independence. Upon leaving Madrid in May 1782 to join the American Peace Commission in Paris, Jay appointed Carmichael acting chargé d'affaires (1782–1790).

When acting on his own, Carmichael proved valuable to the American cause as an additional intelligence channel for the Continental Congress in Europe. He cultivated the friendship of ministers and leading men of Spain and the diplomatic corps in that country to report on the activities of British agents in Spain (the Hussey-Cumberland negotiations of 1779–1780), military objectives (especially Spain's obsession with regaining Gibraltar), and mediation efforts. In 1783, Carmichael, aided by Lafayette, gained a certain recognition from the Spanish government by being invited to attend a diplomatic dinner, an honor rarely accorded to any diplomat below the rank of minister. In April 1790, Carmichael finally received his formal commission as American chargé d'affaires at Madrid, which he held until 1794.

Unfortunately, this proved to be the pinnacle of Carmichael's diplomatic career. He failed to secure compensation for American claims against Spain, a significant reduction of Spanish duties against American ships, or much aid from Spain in obtaining the release of American prisoners in Morocco. Perhaps Carmichael's greatest fault as a diplomat is that he appeared to be so enthralled by the Spanish Court's courteous treatment of him and its expressions of sympathy for the American cause that he believed Spain was sincere in its friendship toward the United States.

Eventually Carmichael failed to maintain his diplomatic correspondence, and with his health much impaired, in January 1791 he asked to return to America. Secretary of State Thomas Jefferson rejected the request and, in March 1792, directed Carmichael to join William Short, then American minister resident at The Hague, to negotiate a treaty with Spain that would grant Americans navigation rights on the Mississippi River, grant a port of trade at the mouth of the river, and fix the U.S.-Florida boundary. Carmichael participated in these negotiations from March 1793 to May 1794, when he was recalled. Spain eventually accepted all of the American demands in Pickney's Treaty (1795). Meanwhile, Carmichael's planned return to America was delayed by the onset of winter, and he died in Madrid on 9 February 1795.

Dean Fafoutis

See also

Congress, Second Continental and Confederation; Deane, Silas; Franklin, Benjamin; Jay, John; Lafayette, Marquis de; Lee, Arthur; Spain

References

Coe, Samuel Gwynn. *The Mission of William Carmichael to Spain.* Baltimore, MD: Johns Hopkins University Press, 1928.

Crompton, Samuel Willard, "William Carmichael." Pp. 406–407 in *American National Biography,* Vol. 4. Edited by John A. Garraty and Mark C. Carnes. New York: Oxford University Press, 1999.

Streeter, Floyd B. "The Diplomatic Career of William Carmichael." *Maryland Historical Magazine* 8(2) (1913): 119–140.

Wharton, Francis, ed. *The Revolutionary Diplomatic Correspondence of the United States.* 6 vols. Washington, DC: U.S. Government Printing Office, 1889.

Carrington, Edward (1748–1810)

Edward Carrington, a Virginia lawyer and planter, was an important officer in General Nathanael Greene's Southern Army and the first U.S. marshal for Virginia under the federal government.

Carrington was born on 11 February 1748 in Cumberland County, Virginia. He practiced law while he managed his family's plantation. At the outbreak of the Revolutionary War, Carrington joined the First Continental Artillery, where he earned the rank of lieutenant colonel, and distinguished himself at the Battle of Monmouth (28 June 1778). In 1780 he transferred to the Southern Army to serve as quartermaster general. In December 1780, Greene directed Carrington to reconnoiter the roads and river crossings that would allow rapid army movement through North Carolina into Virginia. This policy was rendered doubly necessary when the Americans learned in 1781 how easily the British Army could march through North Carolina into the Virginia low country. Greene's order to Carrington was to explore the Dan, Yadkin, and Catawba Rivers and to make himself thoroughly acquainted with the streams into which they discharged. Carrington executed the order effectively.

Carrington first accompanied Greene to Richmond after the organization of the Southern Department, then joined the commanding officers at the Battle of Cowpens (17 January 1781) and remained with them through the Battle of Guilford Courthouse (15 March 1781). Carrington's light corps helped cover Greene's rear on the rapid retreat northward in February 1781, and he provided boats to pass to safety over the River Dan.

Later in the southern campaign, Carrington was ordered to take artillery and baggage back to Rugly's Mills, and he delivered them just in time for the Battle of Hobkirk's Hill (25 April 1781). He also saw action at the siege of Yorktown in September–October 1781. On one occasion he met with the British representatives to discuss an exchange of prisoners. And in 1781, General George Washington put him in charge of selling goods and property confiscated by the Continental Army.

After the war, Carrington returned to his law practice and became involved in politics. He was a delegate to the Continental Congress from Virginia in 1785–1787 and an occasional visitor to Mount Vernon. Carrington's wife and the wife of John Marshall, who became chief justice of the Supreme Court in 1801, were sisters, so the Carringtons were frequent visitors to the Marshall home in Richmond as well. Carrington himself was initially suggested for a federal judicial post, but in 1789 President Washington appointed him as the first U.S. marshal for Virginia. In March 1791, however, he was appointed as the supervisor of the revenue for Virginia, which was a more lucrative job than marshal. He held this office until 1794.

As president, Washington often sought Carrington's advice on public opinion and on appointments. In the mid-1790s, the president offered Carrington the posts of attorney general and then secretary of war, both of which he declined. In 1798, on the recommendation of Washington and Alexander Hamilton, the War Department appointed Carrington quartermaster of the army that the Adams administration began to raise during its Quasi-War with France. And in 1807, Carrington was the foreman of the jury that acquitted Aaron Burr of treason in the trial presided over by his wife's brother-in-law, Chief Justice Marshall. Carrington died in Richmond on 28 October 1810 at the age of sixty-two.

Linda Miller

See also

Continental Army; Greene, Nathanael; Southern Campaigns

Reference

Boatner, Mark. *Encyclopedia of the American Revolution.* Mechanicsburg, PA: Stackpole, 1994.

Carroll, Charles (1737–1832)

Charles Carroll, generally identified as "of Carrollton" to distinguish him from his relatives, is most commonly remembered as the last living signer of the Declaration of Independence. He was also the only Roman Catholic signer. As America's most prominent Catholic revolutionary, Carroll's commitment to the cause helped overturn the civil disabilities suffered by Catholics in his native colony of Maryland.

Unlike many of his fellow revolutionaries, Carroll spent most of his early life overseas. He was born in Annapolis, Maryland, on 19 September 1737 but was educated by Jesuits in France and later studied law in London. After spending seventeen years abroad, Carroll returned to Maryland in 1765. The passage of the Stamp Act in that year and the Townshend Acts in 1767 created a dangerous tension between Great Britain and her colonies. Since, as a Catholic, Carroll was prohibited by Maryland law from holding public office, he at first watched the nascent Revolutionary events from the sidelines. He would first enter the political fray not as an officeholder but as a newspaper writer. The occasion was Maryland's fee controversy.

Charles Carroll, who represented Maryland in the Second Continental Congress, was the only Roman Catholic to sign the Declaration of Independence. A confirmed Federalist, he served on the Board of War and helped write the Maryland constitution. (Bettman/Corbis)

The issue of fees erupted in 1770 when judges who handled land transactions continued to collect revenue even though the Maryland Assembly had not renewed legislation to that effect. The proprietary governor of Maryland, Robert Eden, announced that fees would continue to be collected according to the 1763 schedule. This unpopular measure was supported in a series of essays written by Daniel Dulany and published in the *Maryland Gazette* in early 1773.

The same newspaper soon published a defense of the more popular legislative position written by "First Citizen." Over the course of five months, in a series of lengthy and learned essays, "First Citizen"—who turned out to be Carroll—emerged as a popular hero. It soon became apparent that Carroll's arguments against the governor's measure helped the opposition win the election for the Maryland Assembly in May 1773.

The year 1774 marked the beginning of Carroll's life as a revolutionary. The city of his birth, Annapolis, appointed him to its Committee of Correspondence. He was also elected to Maryland's first Revolutionary convention, which began acting as the provisional government. In this convention Carroll served on a number of committees. Later in the year Annapolis and surrounding Anne Arundel County appointed him to a local committee that was responsible for enforcing the Continental Association, which the First Continental Congress had approved in October. Annapolis and Anne Arundel County later sent Carroll to Philadelphia to attend Congress as an unofficial delegate. His commitment to the American cause quickly became apparent. From Philadelphia, Carroll wrote to his father that he would "either endeavor to defend the liberties of my country, or die with them: this I am convinced is the sentiment of every true and generous American."

In early 1776, Congress sent Carroll to Canada on an important diplomatic mission; his task was to persuade the Canadians to join the American cause. Congress chose Carroll because, like nearly all Canadians, he was a Catholic and spoke French fluently. On this mission, he was joined by his cousin, Father John Carroll (who would later become America's first Catholic bishop), Samuel Chase, and Benjamin Franklin. But this strong delegation could not persuade the Canadians to reject British rule.

Upon his return from Canada, Carroll set out to persuade Maryland to change its instructions to its delegates in the Continental Congress. Maryland's delegates in Philadelphia had been instructed to vote against independence, but a determined Carroll soon succeeded in getting these instructions changed. His commitment to independence led Maryland to elect him to Congress in the summer of 1776. Although he missed the vote for independence in July, he was among the delegates who assembled for the formal signing of the Declaration of Independence on 2 August 1776. Years later, he would say that when he signed the Declaration of Independence, he contributed not only to "our independence of England but the toleration of all sects professing the Christian religion and communicating to them all equal rights."

While no evidence exists to prove that Carroll was cognizant of this idea on that fateful day in August 1776, his involvement in Revolutionary politics did help pave the way for freeing Catholics from civil disabilities in Maryland. In November 1776, Carroll played a major role in Maryland's Constitutional Convention. That body produced a constitution and a Declaration of Rights that granted full political participation to Catholics. Carroll himself immediately took advantage of this new right by seeking and winning election to the Maryland Senate, where he served from 1777 to 1801.

Carroll also supported the new U.S. Constitution. He declined an opportunity to be a delegate at the Constitutional Convention, but from 1789 to 1792 he did serve in the U.S. Senate. In the early nineteenth century he reduced his involvement in public life but remained active in business, and in 1828 the ninety-year-old patriarch helped break ground for the Baltimore and Ohio Railroad—a symbolic act that inaugurated another revolution in the United States.

In the 1820s and 1830s Americans were realizing that the Revolutionary generation was passing away. With the deaths of both Thomas Jefferson and John Adams on 4 July 1826, Carroll, the last living signer, became a celebrated national figure. He died at age ninety-five on 14 November 1832.

Christopher J. Young

See also

Canada; Congress, First Continental; Congress, Second Continental and Confederation; Continental Association; Declaration of Independence; Declaration of Independence Signers; Dulany, Daniel, Jr.; Eden, Robert; Maryland; Religion

References

Hoffman, Ronald, with Sally D. Mason. *Princes of Ireland, Planters of Maryland: A Carroll Saga, 1500–1782.* Chapel Hill: University of North Carolina Press, 2000.

Maier, Pauline. *The Old Revolutionaries: Political Lives in the Age of Samuel Adams.* New York: Knopf, 1980.

Malone, Dumas. *The Story of the Declaration of Independence.* New York: Oxford University Press, 1975.

Onuf, Peter S., ed. *Maryland and the Empire, 1773: The Antilon-First Citizen Letters.* Baltimore, MD: Johns Hopkins University Press, 1974.

Catherine II, Empress of Russia (1729–1796)

Catherine II, born Sophie Friederike Auguste von Anhalt-Zerbst and best known as Catherine the Great, ruled Russia from 1762 until her death in 1796. During her reign, Russia made significant territorial gains within Western Europe (through the three partitions of Poland) and Southern Europe (at the expense of the Ottoman Empire). The diplomatic importance and influence of Russia grew considerably during this period. The prospect of an independent United States of America did not directly threaten Russian interests; indeed, it opened up the possibility of increased exports of Russian raw materials, particularly naval stores, to North America. Catherine's attitude toward the American Revolutionary War was, however, primarily governed by what she perceived to be Russia's territorial and diplomatic interests within Europe at the time.

In the 1760s, Catherine's foreign minister, Count Nikita Panin, had established a loose alignment of powers including Russia, Britain (through a trade treaty), Prussia, Denmark,

Catherine II, tsarina of Russia. Catherine declined George III's request for the use of Russian troops in the suppression of rebellion in America on the grounds that it might involve Russia in an unwanted, general European war. Instead, in 1781 she offered to mediate a treaty of peace between the contending parties. (Library of Congress)

Sweden, Poland, and Saxony. This so-called Northern System was intended to counter the power of France and Austria and maintain a balance of power within Europe. When tension grew in its North American colonies, Britain originally hoped for Russian support. In 1775 Britain even attempted to hire some 20,000 Russian troops to be used against the colonists. Catherine's rather sharp refusal of this proposal in September was governed not only by her determination that Russia should not appear to be subservient in any way to Britain but also by her more pressing and immediate foreign policy concerns over Russia's boundary disputes with Prussia regarding Poland (the first partition of Poland had taken place in 1772).

By 1779, Britain was prepared to give Russia a subsidy in the event of a Russo-Turkish war in return for Russian naval assistance against France. Catherine had recently reached an agreement with the Turks and refused this offer. She rapidly became concerned, however, about the British policy of detaining all neutral ships bound for France and confiscating naval stores as contraband. The Russian merchant navy was, in fact, very small, but Russian goods carried in Dutch ships were condemned despite earlier treaties that did not regard naval stores as contraband. The presence of an American privateer in the North Sea in August 1778 was regarded as a threat to Anglo-Russian trade.

Catherine saw that the American Revolutionary War, and the subsequent war between Britain and France, had opened up opportunities for the export of Russian naval stores to all the belligerents, and she wished to encourage the growth of Russian trade and the merchant navy. She also wanted to assert Russian diplomatic influence in Europe, and the issue of neutral shipping provided her with an ideal opportunity to do so without risking armed conflict. In 1780, Catherine proclaimed the principles that should govern the rights of neutral shipping and proposed the formation of a league of neutral nations (the League of Armed Neutrality), comprising at first Russia, Denmark, Sweden, and the Dutch Republic. The league was not overtly anti-British, but it certainly challenged the right of the Royal Navy to interfere with neutral trade and was perceived in Britain as an unfriendly organization.

Catherine also involved Russia in abortive attempts to mediate between the belligerents. In 1779, Panin, who was hostile to Britain at the time and believed that an independent American nation could bring commercial benefits to Russia, proposed that Russia should act as mediator between Britain and the colonists and between Britain and France. Both Britain and France ignored his initiative. The following year, Panin proposed that each North American colony should be allowed to decide whether it wanted independence from Britain and suggested a conference to discuss the matter. This proposal was now greeted with some enthusiasm in France, where the war with Britain was draining the nation's finances. Britain, however, first tried to delay the calling of the conference and then, by the summer of 1781, simply stopped proceedings by refusing to deal directly with the colonists.

The League of Armed Neutrality was formally set up in February 1780 by Russia, Sweden, and Denmark; the Dutch Republic agreed to join in December 1780, followed by Prussia, Portugal, and Austria. Meanwhile, Britain declared war on the Netherlands, which kept that nation out of the league. And Panin's policies were now weakened by his waning position at the Russian court. Russia and Austria signed a secret alliance in May 1781 that committed both countries to expansion at the expense of the Ottoman Empire and signified a fundamental change in the orientation of Russian foreign policy. Russia abandoned its Northern System, Catherine dismissed Panin in September 1781, and Count Grigory Potemkin now dominated foreign policy. The mission of the American diplomat Francis Dana to St. Petersburg in the summer of 1781 to seek recognition and a commercial alliance with Russia became an embarrassing failure.

It was now in Russia's interest that Britain and France should be so exhausted by their conflict that they not be in a position to restrict Russian expansion. Catherine refused an offer by Britain of the island of Minorca in return for military support but agreed to act as mediator between Britain and the Dutch Republic in 1782. Although the mediation failed, it demonstrated again Catherine's determination that Russia should play a dominant diplomatic role in international affairs without becoming embroiled in a war that brought her no obvious advantages. In fact, when the American Revolutionary War ended in 1783, Catherine did have to postpone her more ambitious plans for expansion into the Balkan Peninsula, but this did not prevent her acquisition of the Crimean Peninsula that year.

Janet Hartley

See also

Dana, Francis; Diplomacy, American; Diplomacy, British; Diplomacy, French

References

Griffiths, David. "Mediation as a Diplomatic Weapon: Russian Attempts to Mediate among the British, the Dutch and Even the Americans, 1781–3." Pp. 19–31 in *Reflections on Russia in the Eighteenth Century*. Edited by J. Klein, S. Dixon, and M. Fraanje. Cologne, Vienna: Böhlau Verlag, 1999.

———. "Nikita Panin, Russian Diplomacy, and the American Revolution." *Slavic Review* 28 (1969): 1–24.

Madariaga, Isabel de. *Britain, Russia, and the Armed Neutrality of 1780: Sir James Harris's Mission to St. Petersburg during the American Revolution*. New Haven, CT: Yale University Press, 1962.

———. *Russia in the Age of Catherine the Great*. London: Weidenfeld and Nicholson, 1981.

Chambly, Quebec, Action at (16–18 October 1775)

The engagement fought at Chambly in the province of Quebec consisted of the siege and capture of a British-held fort of minor strategic significance but containing large quantities of vital military stores.

Fort Chambly was built by the French in 1709, during their wars with the Iroquois, to protect Montreal and guard the portage around the Chambly rapids. Standing on the west bank of the Richelieu River, the square, stone-built bastion with its sixteen-foot-high walls was defensible only against musketry and light artillery, and by 1775 it was no more than a warehouse for the much larger British post at St. John's, 12 miles to the south. The governor of Quebec, Sir Guy Carleton, believed the fort impregnable as long as St. John's held out, as the latter would prevent an enemy force bringing up artillery heavy enough to breach Chambly's walls. On that basis, he garrisoned the fort with just eighty-three officers and men of the 7th Foot, under Major Joseph Stopford, plus five artillerymen.

However, the first weeks of the American invasion showed that both posts could be bypassed with ease. As the Separate Army under Richard Montgomery invaded Canada in mid-September 1775, Major John Brown with 135 Continentals slipped around St. John's and ambushed a British supply train about 2 miles north of Chambly. Brown and Ethan Allen later marched around Chambly to Longueuil and Laprairie to launch their ill-advised attack on Montreal on the night of 25 September. After their defeat, the area remained quiet until the night of 16–17 October, when Brown returned with 50 men, to be joined by another 350 (mostly locally recruited Canadians) led by James Livingston, and two bateaux each armed with 9-pounder cannon, which had been slipped past St. John's under Jeremiah Duggan, a Quebec barber.

Early the next day, the bombardment began; although this did little more than damage one of the fort's chimneys, Stopford surrendered on 18 October. More serious than the loss of the fort, though, was the large quantity of stores it contained: 80 barrels of flour, 134 barrels of pork, 3 mortars, 6 tons of gunpowder, 125 firearms, and 6,500 cartridges—all items in which Montgomery's army was seriously lacking. (While the failure to destroy the stores was inexcusable, in Stopford's defense it should be noted that in 1760, the French had surrendered the fort without a shot being fired due to their lack of confidence in the walls, and little—if anything—had been done to strengthen them in the intervening fifteen years.) After the surrender, the eighty-eight-strong British garrison, together with thirty women and fifty-one children, were taken south by boat and deliberately paraded past St. John's to demoralize its garrison and cheer the besiegers, who had hitherto been hampered by bad weather and lack of supplies. The captured colors of the 7th Foot were sent to Congress and are still on display today at West Point.

After the siege, Chambly reverted to its previous role as a storehouse but was also used by the Americans to imprison any Canadians they considered hostile to the Revolution. During the retreat of the American forces in May and June 1776, the senior American general, John Thomas of Massachusetts, died of smallpox at Chambly.

Brendan D. Morrissey

See also

Allen, Ethan; Brown, John; Canada, Operations in; Carleton, Guy; Montgomery, Richard; Montreal, Operations against; St. John's, Actions against; Thomas, John

References

Hatch, Robert. *Thrust for Canada: The American Attempt on Quebec, 1775–1776*. Boston: Houghton Mifflin, 1979.

Lanctot, Gustave. *Canada and the American Revolution, 1774–1783*. London: Harrap, 1967.

Stanley, George. *Canada Invaded, 1775–1776*. Toronto: Canadian War Museum, 1973.

Champe, John (1752–1798)

John Champe, a native of Loudoun County, Virginia, and a sergeant major of cavalry in the Continental Army, spent seven months behind British lines in one of the most ambitious intelligence operations of the American Revolution: the attempted capture of Benedict Arnold.

Shortly after the discovery of Arnold's treason and his defection to the British in September 1780, General George Washington was troubled by the possibility of there being other British spies in his command. He was particularly concerned with persistent rumors that additional senior Continental Army officers were also aligned with British interests. While there were other unsuccessful attempts to capture Arnold, the plan proposed to Washington by Major Henry "Light-Horse Harry" Lee was arguably the most elaborate: Champe, Lee's own sergeant major, would pretend to desert to the British ranks. Once behind British lines, Champe would arrange the kidnapping of Arnold, who would then be delivered to General Washington to face punishment for his treason.

Washington approved the plan but insisted that Arnold not be killed or injured in carrying it out, even at the risk of allowing Arnold to escape. From Washington's perspective, public punishment was the operation's sole objective. Washington also ordered Champe, if the opportunity presented itself, to attempt to determine if other Continental officers might be collaborating with the British. Based on the information gathered by Champe, Washington hoped to establish the innocence of Continental Army generals Horatio Gates and Arthur St. Clair, both of whom had been suspected of complicity with the British.

Champe's mission posed considerable personal risks. No one besides Washington, Lee, and Champe could know of the scheme, and as Champe "deserted" he would have to avoid Lee's own guards as well as horse and foot patrols and irregular scouting parties. Nevertheless, late on the evening of 20 October 1780, Champe deserted the American camp at Tappan, New York, on horseback and began his journey to New York City, where Arnold was known to be living. Half an hour later Champe's absence was discovered and reported to Lee, who delayed the pursuit as long as he possibly could without arousing suspicion. A little after midnight, troops started after the supposed deserter.

With his pursuers rapidly closing on him, Champe realized that he would never reach New York on horseback and instead rode toward the British patrol boats in Newark Bay near Brown's Ferry. When his pursuers were within 200–300 yards of him, he dismounted, ran across the meadows, and plunged into the bay. Hearing Champe's cries for help, a British galley sent a boat for him, fired upon his pursuers, and took him into custody, where he was sympathetically received.

Champe was escorted to the headquarters of the British commandant of New York, General Sir Henry Clinton. There Champe presented a letter from the captain of the galley detailing the circumstances surrounding his defection. During a preliminary round of questioning, Champe explained that his was not an unusual circumstance in that following the example set by Arnold, a certain widespread spirit of defection was present in the Continental troops. To support this opinion, Champe indicated that he was led by his own observations and particularly by his knowledge of the discontent that continued to plague his own cavalry corps. He evidently impressed his British interrogators with his story, for duly noted in a large folio book were his size, place of birth, form, and countenance; the color of his hair; the corps in which be had served; and remarks illustrating his conformity to the British position. After the preliminary interrogation was concluded, he was sent to the office of the British commander in chief.

Clinton treated Champe kindly and spoke with him for more than an hour, asking him many leading questions: What were the proper inducements to encourage defections from the Continental Army? What other Continental officers were suspected by Washington of being traitors? Did the soldiers in Washington's command agree with Washington's suspicions? Did Washington remain popular in the army, or was his reputation falling? To the various questions, many of which were far beyond the knowledge of a sergeant major of cavalry, Champe answered warily, relying instead on his own circumstances and pressing the argument that by exploiting measures to encourage desertion, the British could decimate Washington's ranks, as even whole corps sought to follow Arnold's lead.

At the conclusion of their conversation, Clinton presented Champe with a few guineas and recommended him to Arnold, who was then engaged in raising an American legion in the service of King George. Since Arnold's legion was largely comprised of deserters and Loyalists, he was immediately interested in Champe and the manner of his escape through Continental Army lines. Arnold was also intrigued to learn how his own example, as Champe's story suggested, had spurred Champe and prompted numerous others to ponder desertion from Washington's army.

Arnold proposed that Champe join his legion, offering him the same rank he had held in the Continental Army and promising further advancement when merited. After initially expressing some concern about being executed as a traitor if captured by Continental forces, Champe accepted appointment as sergeant major of Arnold's American Legion. Now wearing a British uniform and having freedom of movement in British-occupied New York, Champe quickly made contact with two of Washington's secret agents and laid plans for Arnold's capture.

The plot called for the abduction of Arnold from New York City, after which he would be conveyed to American lines. The abduction might well have succeeded, but on the night that the operation was to take place, Arnold moved his quarters to another part of the city to better oversee the embarkation of the American Legion for its expedition to Virginia. In preparation for the expedition, Arnold, fearing that if the members of the legion were left on shore many of them might desert, transferred them, including Champe, from their barracks to one of the British ships, where they remained until reaching the Virginia coast. Unable to get Arnold in a position where he could be abducted, Champe continued his clandestine investigation, moving with the British to Petersburg, where in May 1781 he deserted the British ranks and rejoined the American forces under General Nathanael Greene, who immediately provided Champe with a horse and money and sent him to General Washington.

While the abduction of Arnold failed, Champe's efforts were not in vain. His investigations determined that there was no evidence that other American officers were collaborating with the British, thus securing the vindication of Gates, St. Clair, and numerous other Continental officers. Washington discharged Champe for fear that he might be captured by the British and, if recognized, executed as a spy. Champe returned to his home in Loudoun County. He died near Morgantown in present-day West Virginia in 1798.

Brett F. Woods

See also

Arnold, Benedict; Clinton, Henry; Gates, Horatio; Lee, Henry; St. Clair, Arthur

References

Arnold, James R. "Northern Virginia Patriot: The Adventures of John Champe of Loudoun County." *Northern Virginia Heritage* 8 (February 1986): 11–14, 20.

Central Intelligence Agency. "Intelligence Operations." http://www.cia.gov/cia/publications/warindep/intellopos.html.

Lee, Henry. *Memoirs of the War in the Southern Department of the United States.* 1812. Reprint, New York: New York Times, 1969.

Charles City, Virginia, Action at (8 January 1781)

The surprise British attack on Virginia militiamen at Charles City Court House was one of several engagements in the James River Valley in January 1781 that would throw Virginians into a state of fear and confusion that would continue for much of the year and finally end only with Yorktown.

In December 1780, British Commander Sir Henry Clinton ordered General Benedict Arnold to head to Virginia and lead a series of raids on the Patriots along the James River. This was the first command that Arnold had received since going over to the British side. Clinton gave Arnold 1,600 troops, including the Queen's Rangers, a Tory regiment under the command of the able British officer Sir Henry Graves Simcoe. Clinton told Arnold to destroy all military stores he came upon in Virginia, rally Loyalist support throughout the Tidewater, and cut off the aid flowing to the army of General Nathanael Greene in the Carolinas.

While Arnold was eager to take his first command in the field, he had a difficult time getting his men to the James. Several ships that carried 400 of his men were blown off course in bad storms in the Atlantic. Arnold and the main body of the army finally reached Hampton Roads on 30 December 1780. Four days later, they anchored off of Jamestown Island and came under fire from Patriot artillery at Hood's Point. Simcoe and 130 rangers landed on shore, and the Virginians fled from their fortification. Arnold and his company next headed up the river, landing at the Byrd estate at Westover. By 5 January 1780, they had marched to Richmond. Simcoe's Rangers quickly routed 200 militiamen that Governor Thomas Jefferson had collected to defend the city. Arnold offered to spare Richmond if the governor allowed British ships to come up the James and carry off the tobacco stored there. Jefferson refused, and Arnold promptly burned all the warehouses along with several other buildings.

On 8 January, Arnold's force headed back down the James. They stopped at the estate of Benjamin Harrison at Berkeley. Arnold ordered his men to strip the house of all its furniture, draperies, clothes, and paintings and to burn them on the lawn. Arnold's men also used the cattle for target practice and then took 40 slaves and all the horses with them to Westover. Upon arriving back at the Byrd estate, Arnold sent Simcoe on a reconnaissance mission to Long Bridge on the Chickahominy River. Simcoe learned that Thomas Nelson, commander of the Virginia militia, was a few miles to the west near Charles City Court House. Late in the evening, a slave taken prisoner by the British led Simcoe and 40 rangers back up the James. The British surprised 150 Virginia militiamen encamped for the night at Charles City Court House. They killed 2 and took several others prisoner. Many Virginians escaped to Nelson and the main body of the militia a few miles away, while others headed east to Williamsburg to warn of the possible attack of the British. Simcoe did not head east but instead returned to Westover with prisoners and more horses. The raids of Arnold and Simcoe along the James had been so successful that General George Washington sent three Continental regiments to Virginia under the command of the Marquis de Lafayette.

Mary Stockwell

See also

Arnold, Benedict; Jefferson, Thomas; Lafayette, Marquis de; Simcoe, John Graves; Virginia

Reference

Selby, John. *The Revolution in Virginia, 1775–1783.* Williamsburg, VA: Colonial Williamsburg Foundation, 1988.

Charles III, King of Spain

See Spain

Charleston, South Carolina, Expedition against (1776)

Expecting local support from Loyalists, the British government, against the advice of General William Howe, the commander in chief, planned an invasion of the Carolinas in early 1776. Troops under Major-General Lord Cornwallis and Lieutenant-General Sir Henry Clinton assembled at Cork, Ireland, at the close of 1775 and sailed the following January in a fleet under Commodore Sir Peter Parker. Having encountered rough seas, the expedition reached Cape Fear, North Carolina, in May and was met by 2,000 additional troops from New York under Howe. The Loyalists duly opened resistance but were soon crushed at Moore's Creek Bridge, and in light of the large number of Patriot forces, Clinton decided to scrap his original plans. Instead, he chose to launch an attack on Charleston, South Carolina. On 1 June 1776 the fleet left Cape Fear and arrived off Charleston three days later.

The Americans had already taken some measures in preparing a defense. At the mouth of the harbor lay two islands, Sullivan's to the north and James to the south. Charleston Bar also lay to the south of the entrance. At the southern end of Sullivan's Island the rebels established a hastily built post, Fort Sullivan (later changed to Fort Moultrie), that commanded the harbor entrance together with Fort Johnson on James Island. Fort Sullivan was constructed of palmetto logs bolted together to form a square with bastions at each angle. Inside, another row of logs was laid parallel to the outside walls, with the space between the walls filled with sand to absorb the shock of artillery fire. On 4 June, when the fleet under Parker appeared, the south and west walls of the fort were incomplete, while the north and east sides were only seven feet high, though designed to resist land assault. The fort's complement of artillery consisted of thirty-one 18- and 9-pounders, twenty-one of which faced south. A traverse within the fort built from east to west offered protection to the gunners from behind, but any vessels that could run past the fort and anchor above it could enfilade the position and render it untenable. Unknown to Parker, the commander, Colonel William Moultrie, had only twenty-eight rounds of ammunition—fewer than one round per piece.

Parker hoped to attack the fort by a coordinated land and sea operation. On 7 June, having made soundings, he anchored his transports and frigates inside the bar, and two days later Clinton disembarked 500 men on Long Island, just north of Sullivan's Island and east of the city. All the troops had been landed by 15 June. Clinton believed that he could ford a small inlet separating the two islands, but subsequent investigation revealed that even at low tide the water was seven feet deep, and there were no boats to effect a crossing. This left Parker with the single option of bombarding Fort Sullivan by sea.

Unfavorable winds delayed the attack until 28 June, during which time the Americans continued to improve their

Attack by a Royal Navy squadron on Fort Sullivan during the British expedition against Charleston in 1776. The spongy palmetto logs and soft earth used in the construction of Colonel William Moultrie's improvised fort provided unexpected protection from cannon fire. (Library of Congress)

SIEGE OF CHARLESTON, 1780

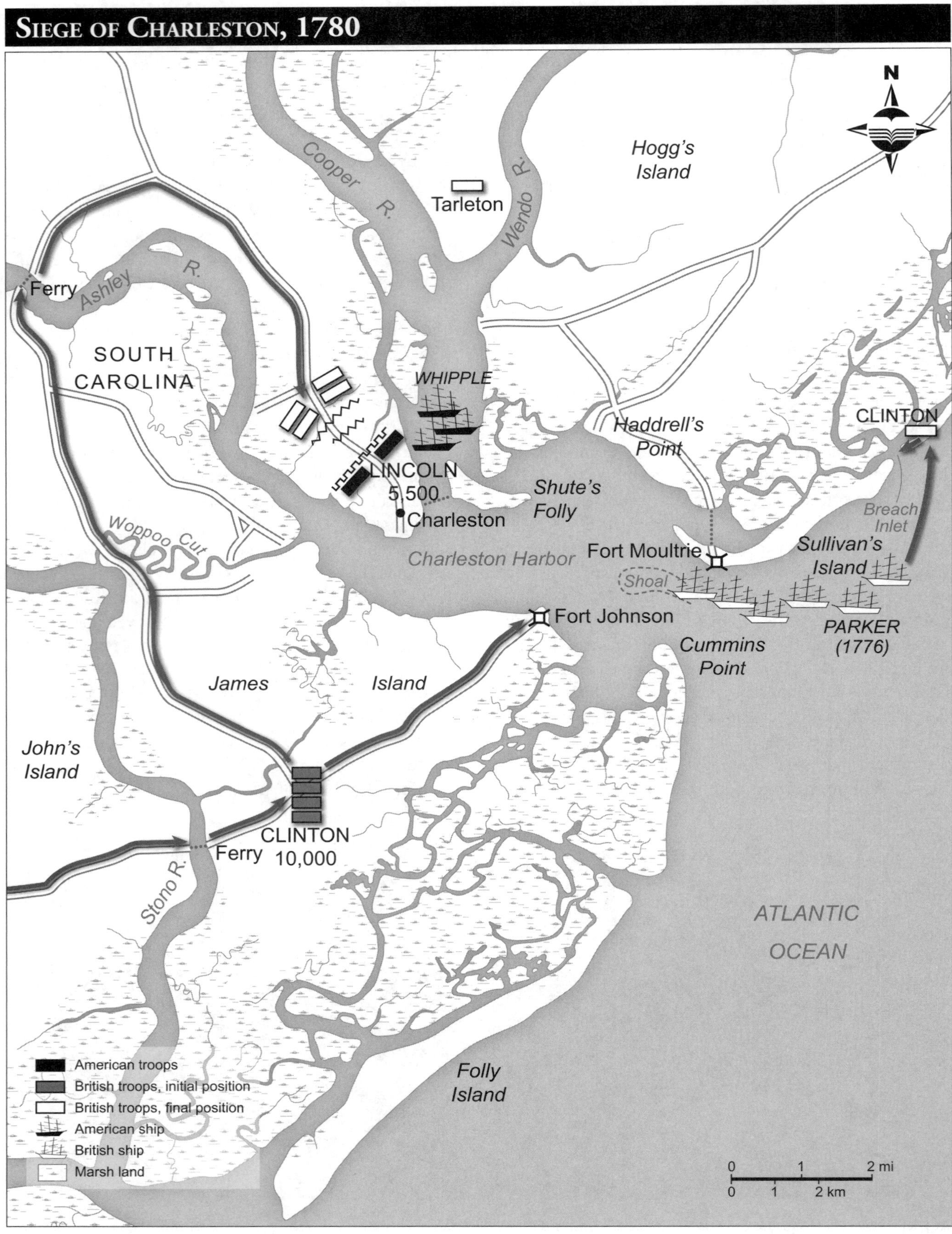
N
Hogg's Island
Cooper R.
Tarleton
Wendo R.
Ferry
Ashley R.
SOUTH CAROLINA
WHIPPLE
Haddrell's Point
CLINTON
LINCOLN 5,500
Shute's Folly
Charleston
Breach Inlet
Woppoo Cut
Fort Moultrie
Sullivan's Island
Charleston Harbor
Shoal
Fort Johnson
PARKER (1776)
Cummins Point
James Island
John's Island
CLINTON 10,000
Ferry
Stono R.
ATLANTIC OCEAN
Folly Island
American troops
British troops, initial position
British troops, final position
American ship
British ship
Marsh land
0 1 2 mi
0 1 2 km

defenses. The British plan was to bombard the main face of the fort with the 50-gun *Bristol* and *Experiment,* the frigates *Active* and *Solebay* (both 28 guns), and a bomb ship, the *Thunderer* (8 guns). Meanwhile, three other vessels were to pass the fort and anchor up the channel to the west, where they could block any attempts by the defenders to use fire ships against Parker's larger vessels, while simultaneously offering enfilading fire against the main American battery. Two 28-gun frigates, the *Actaeon* and the *Syren,* together with the corvette *Sphinx* (20 guns), were to fulfill this task.

Shortly after 11:00 A.M. the ships reached their appointed places and began an accurate and regular fire at about 350 yards. This distance, however, proved too great to permit the use of grapeshot in addition to round shot, and the fort's palmetto construction easily absorbed the shock of the balls. Although the bomb ship managed well-directed fire into the fort, the shots fell harmlessly into the morass in the center of the work. Fire ceased entirely, however, when the mortar bed collapsed during the bombardment.

The Americans meanwhile returned fire and, though short of ammunition and powder, managed to achieve extraordinary accuracy against the *Experiment,* which lost twenty-three killed and sustained fifty-six wounded. Worse still, when the *Bristol*'s spring was shot away, the ship shifted with its stern facing the fort, whose raking fire caused severe losses. After the crew made three attempts to replace the spring, the *Bristol* managed to correct its position, but not before it had lost forty killed and seventy-one wounded, including Parker himself. The other vessels lost one dead and fourteen wounded. The Patriots at the fort lost thirty-seven killed and wounded, mostly by shots passing through the embrasures.

The British suffered further frustration when it was discovered that the three ships meant to anchor west of the fort in order to enfilade its front had never reached their designated places: the riggings of the *Syren* and *Sphinx* had become fouled before the two ships ran aground on a shoal. They managed to withdraw a few hours later when the tide rose, but the *Actaeon,* also aground, failed to refloat and was set on fire and abandoned by its crew. The Americans managed to board the *Actaeon* before it blew up and took away its colors, which had been carelessly left behind.

The British bombardment nevertheless continued until after dark, the relative silence of the Patriots' guns suggesting that they had been silenced when, in fact, Moultrie merely wished to conserve his meager supply of ammunition. However, with visibility impaired by darkness, his ammunition low, his crew wearied, and his losses heavy, Parker gave the order to withdraw at around 9:00 P.M. Instead of resuming the attack, he repaired his ships and sailed, together with the transports, to New York, where the expeditionary force arrived on 4 August. So disappointing was the result of this expedition that the British would not make another attempt to take Charleston for three years.

Gregory Fremont-Barnes

See also

Charleston, South Carolina, Expedition against (1780); Clinton, Henry; Cornwallis, Charles; Howe, William; Moore's Creek Bridge, North Carolina, Action at; Moultrie, William

References

Clowes, William Laird. *The Royal Navy: A History from the Earliest Times to 1900.* 7 vols. London: Chatham, 1996.

Gardiner, Robert, ed. *Navies and the American Revolution, 1775–1783.* London: Chatham, 1996.

Lumpkin, Henry. *From Savannah to Yorktown: The American Revolution in the South.* New York: Paragon, 1981.

Morrill, Dan. *Southern Campaigns of the American Revolution.* Baltimore, MD: Nautical and Aviation Publishing Company of America, 1993.

Ward, Christopher. *War of the Revolution.* 2 vols. New York: Macmillan, 1952.

Charleston, South Carolina, Expedition against (1780)

The British expedition against Charleston (known as Charles Town during the Revolution) in 1780 culminated in the siege and capture of the city and commenced major British operations in the South. The siege of Charleston was the longest formal siege of the war on the North American continent and the largest single operation in South Carolina.

The success of their forces in Georgia in 1779 and their belief that the rebellious southern colonies possessed a substantial number of Loyalists prompted Lord George Germain and Sir Henry Clinton to shift their strategy southward. They saw the capture of Charleston, the most important city and port in the southern colonies, as the key to victory in the Carolinas. Reinforcements from Britain in late summer 1779 and the strategic evacuation of the post at Newport, Rhode Island, in the fall gave Clinton the men he needed to make the attempt. The arrival of a French fleet off the Georgia coast delayed the expedition, but news that Savannah had held against a combined French and American siege induced him to proceed.

On 26 December 1779, more than ninety transports departed New York with 7,258 men. British units that embarked included the 7th, 23rd, 33rd, 63rd, and 64th Foot; a battalion of the 71st Regiment; a detachment of the Royal Artillery; a squadron of the 17th Light Dragoons; two battalions of light infantry; and two battalions of grenadiers. The Hessians consisted of the von Huyn regiment, a detachment of Hessian jaegers, and four battalions of Hessian grenadiers. The Loyalists included Lord Cathcart's Legion (the British Legion), American Volunteers, and New York Volunteers. Vice Admiral

Sketch of Charleston, South Carolina, during the siege of 1780. More than 6,000 British troops, arriving by sea from New York, landed south of the city, joined later by other contingents. Finding themselves encircled and subjected to an intense bombardment, the 5,000 defenders under General Benjamin Lincoln surrendered on 12 May in the worst American defeat of the war. (Naval Historical Center)

Marriot Arbuthnot commanded the transports, five ships of the line, one 50-gun ship, two 44-gun ships, four frigates, and two sloops. Success at Charleston would require close cooperation between the Royal Navy and the British Army.

Severe winter storms scattered the fleet as it sailed southward, and several ships were lost including the *Russia Merchant,* which carried much of the army's ordnance, and the *Defiance,* one of the ships of the line. Many vessels sailed into the Gulf Stream and were pushed far off course. The lengthened voyage caused provisions to run short on the vessels, and many of the horses died or had to be thrown overboard, a circumstance that would seriously affect the army once on land. By the beginning of February, however, most of the ships had reached the rendezvous point at Tybee Island, off Savannah, Georgia.

After sending ashore the cavalry to collect new horses and a detachment under Brigadier-General James Paterson to make a diversion toward Augusta, Clinton and Arbuthnot sailed with the rest of the troops toward Charleston. Transports sailed into the North Edisto River on 11 February 1780, and troops disembarked that evening and the following day on Simmons (now Seabrook) Island. Over the next several days, British soldiers established positions across neighboring Johns Island.

Twice previously the British had threatened Charleston: the disastrous attack on Sullivan's Island in 1776 and General Augustine Prevost's move against the town in May 1779. Both Charleston and the Continental Congress anticipated a renewed effort against the city, and in the wake of the failed Franco-American attempt to recapture Savannah, Major General Benjamin Lincoln, commander of the Southern Department, entreated Congress for additional aid for the southern states. Congress responded in November by sending south the North Carolina Continental troops from Washington's army as well as the frigates *Providence, Boston,* and *Queen of France* and the sloop of war *Ranger,* from the Continental Navy. Washington, eager to help his subordinate, ordered the Virginia Continental Line and Baylor's Light Dragoons south as well. The warships arrived in Charleston in December, but several months passed before the soldiers reached the city.

Still, throughout the British effort against Charleston, Lincoln believed that he had too few troops to engage the British outside the city's defenses. At the time the British landed, Lincoln had under his command approximately 1,000 Continental infantry, 250 cavalrymen, and 2,000 militia. Numerically inferior, he chose to keep the bulk of his force in Charleston but sent the cavalry west of the Ashley River to harass the British advance.

Clinton wished to move against the city by marching across the sea islands and then advancing up the Ashley River and across it to the Charleston peninsula. Supported by the Royal Navy, his troops crossed from Johns Island to James Island on 24 February. They could proceed no farther, however, until Admiral Arbuthnot pushed ships over Charleston Bar, a large sandbank that protected the entrance to the harbor.

Lincoln hoped that Commodore Abraham Whipple, commander of the small American fleet, would station his warships so as to defend the ship channel at the primary crossing point over the bar. Based on the opinions of his officers and the harbor pilots, however, Whipple determined that such a position was impracticable and instead moved his vessels near Fort Moultrie. Consequently, Royal Navy warships, including the 50-gun *Renown,* 44-gun *Roebuck,* 44-gun *Romulus,* four frigates, and a sloop of war, crossed the bar unopposed on 20 March. Outgunned by the British ships, Whipple retreated with his own vessels to the safety of the Cooper River. They took post behind a boom, stretched between the town and Shutes Folly, that was held in place by a line of sunken hulks.

The Royal Navy's success in crossing the bar allowed Arbuthnot to send boats and men to Clinton for the advance to Charleston. When reinforcements under Brigadier-General Paterson arrived, Clinton sent a force up the Ashley River to

Drayton Hall. From there, on the morning of 29 March, Royal Navy sailors ferried the British and Hessian troops to the east bank of the river. This division included two battalions of British light infantry; two battalions of British grenadiers; the 7th, 33rd, and 71st Regiments; four battalions of Hessian grenadiers; and the detachment of jaegers. Upon landing, they faced only a few scattered shots from an American patrol.

Lincoln still wished to keep the bulk of his limited force in Charleston, but on the morning of 30 March he sent out his light infantry under Lieutenant Colonel John Laurens to reconnoiter and prevent the British from advancing too quickly toward the city. Laurens's men skirmished with the enemy throughout the day but eventually retreated within the American defenses that evening.

On the outskirts of Charleston, the Americans had constructed a potent defense-in-depth. A central hornwork consisting of two bastions connected by a wall, or "curtain," lay astride the main road leading into town, and Lincoln's engineers later enclosed them to form a citadel. To the front of the hornwork lay a line of redoubts and batteries connected by a parapet that stretched across the peninsula from the Ashley River to the Cooper River. Two rows of abatis stood before this line. Finally, the Americans had dug a canal across the neck, which was fed by tidal creeks. A dam on the Cooper River side allowed the garrison to control the depth of the water in the canal. A redoubt on the American right protected this dam, while a half-moon battery on the left covered the canal on the Ashley River side. Fort Moultrie protected the entrance to Charleston Harbor, while fortifications at Lempière's Point (Hobcaw) and Haddrell's Point defended the Cooper River.

British working parties broke ground for the first parallel on the night of 1 April, approximately 800–1,000 yards from the American defenses, constructing three redoubts before daybreak without interruption from the garrison. Although their own batteries were incomplete, the Americans fired more than thirty shots at the enemy works throughout the following day. That number increased substantially over the next several days. Beginning on the night of 5 April, British galleys in the Ashley River and batteries west of the river fired several shots into Charleston, but until they completed their batteries in the first parallel the British could make no impression on the American lines.

The garrison's morale soared on 7 April, when the Virginia Continentals arrived to reinforce them (the North Carolinians had reached the city on 3 March). This addition gave Lincoln approximately 4,500 men. The celebration in Charleston, however, was short-lived. The following day, Arbuthnot sailed nine warships and two transports past Fort Moultrie and anchored them safely off Fort Johnson. Fort Moultrie's artillery fired furiously at the British vessels but only inflicted minor damage on them. The only ship lost was a third transport, which Royal Navy sailors destroyed when it ran aground. With British ships now at anchor in the harbor, Charleston was cut off by sea.

Although their batteries were unfinished, Clinton and Arbuthnot elected to summon the town to surrender on 10 April. Lincoln rejected their request that he surrender the city, responding to the British commanders that "sixty days have passed since it has been known that your intentions against this town were hostile in which time has been afforded to abandon it, but duty and inclination point to the propriety of supporting it to the last extremity." Three days later, British batteries in the first parallel began to fire upon Charleston and its defenses. The two sides cannonaded each other for the next month.

To keep open the communication with the South Carolina backcountry, Lincoln sent his cavalry under Brigadier General Isaac Huger to the upper reaches of the Cooper River. Clinton realized that he would have to deal with that force before sending his own troops across the Cooper to cut off the garrison's escape route. Early on the morning of 13 April, Lieutenant-Colonel Banastre Tarleton and the British Legion attacked the American cavalry at Biggin's Church near Moncks Corner and completely routed them. The British victory opened the way for Lieutenant-Colonel James Webster to lead a detachment of 1,500 troops east of the Cooper River. British reinforcements, which arrived in the Stono River on 18 April, allowed Clinton to strengthen the force east of the Cooper to 2,300 men. He appointed Lord Cornwallis to command the detachment. While Cornwallis and Webster attempted to cut off Charleston by land, Clinton hoped that Arbuthnot would send ships into the Cooper River itself to complete the investiture. Arbuthnot's failure to do so, however, frustrated Clinton throughout the siege.

By 17 April, however, the British had pushed forward-approach trenches (trenches dug in zigzag fashion, in the direction of a besieged city, off of which parallel trenches could then be dug and siege guns emplaced) on Charleston Neck and completed a second parallel 750 feet from the American canal. Lincoln, recognizing the impending danger, convened a council of war of his officers on 21 April to discuss the garrison's situation. Some officers, such as Brigadier Generals Lachlan McIntosh and William Moultrie, favored evacuating the army; others, such as engineer Colonel Jean Baptiste Joseph, the Chevalier de Laumoy, believed that they should offer terms of capitulation to the British. Acting Lieutenant Governor Christopher Gadsden and members of South Carolina's Privy Council starkly opposed an evacuation, and some civilian officials threatened that if it were attempted they would "open the gates to the enemy" and assist them in attacking the retreating troops. In the face of such pressure, Lincoln and his officers decided to offer terms of capitulation rather than withdraw from the town. The terms offered, which included allowing the American army to march into the backcountry and American ships to go to sea unmolested, were summarily rejected by Clinton and Arbuthnot.

With the American proposals turned down, the siege continued. British engineers extended their approach trenches toward Charleston, and a third parallel was commenced within 800 feet of the American line of redoubts and batteries on 21 April. With the British pressing ever closer to the American works, small arms and grapeshot took on an increasingly important role, and casualties mounted. Hessian jaegers were particularly effective against American artillerymen, shooting them down as they attempted to service their guns.

A sortie early in the morning of 24 April, led by Lieutenant Colonel William Henderson of the South Carolina Continentals, temporarily disrupted work on the British lines but failed to halt it altogether. The following night, British soldiers in the third parallel mistakenly believed that another sortie was taking place and retreated to the rear; many were killed or wounded when their comrades in the first and second parallels mistook them for attacking Americans and fired upon them.

Sent south by the Continental Congress, Brigadier General Louis Lebegue du Portail arrived in the garrison on 25 April. After examining Charleston's fortifications, du Portail declared them untenable and recommended an immediate evacuation. Lincoln called another council of war to discuss the matter, and the officers determined that evacuation was impracticable. Any hope of evacuation faded completely on 27 April when Lieutenant Colonel François Malmédy retreated with his detachment from the works at Lemprière's Point on the east bank of the Cooper River, which kept open the garrison's communication with the South Carolina backcountry.

Malmédy had abandoned Lemprière's Point because he believed that Cornwallis would soon attack his position. Cornwallis had no such intention, but troops under his command now ranged throughout the region east of the Cooper to prevent an escape by Lincoln's army. At Lenud's Ferry on 6 May, Tarleton's cavalry again routed the American cavalry, demonstrating the supremacy the British had attained in the area.

On the neck, British working parties strengthened the third parallel and extended it on the left toward the dam that controlled the depth of the water in the canal. On 1 May, they cut the dam and began to drain the canal. Meanwhile, Clinton continued to press Arbuthnot to push ships into the Cooper River and complete the investiture of Charleston, but Arbuthnot was now engaged in other operations. In early May, he sent seamen and marines under Captains Charles Hudson and John Orde to Sullivan's Island to seize weakened Fort Moultrie. Lieutenant-Colonel William Scott, the fort's commander, vowed to hold out when Hudson demanded a surrender but relented when Hudson declared that he would storm it and put all within to the sword. Militarily the fort's loss meant little since British warships had already passed it, but psychologically it was a major blow to the Charleston garrison.

Fort Moultrie's surrender and the British victory at Lenud's Ferry afforded Clinton another opportunity to call upon the garrison to capitulate, which he did on the morning of 8 May. Clinton initially gave Lincoln until eight o'clock that evening to respond, but Lincoln's need to consult with his officers and the civilian officials and the subsequent negotiations extended the truce into the following day.

Lincoln's proposed articles of capitulation included the surrender of the Continental soldiers as prisoners of war, while the city, its fortifications, and the warships were to be turned over to the British. Lincoln insisted, however, that the militia in the garrison be allowed to return to their homes. Meanwhile, civilians who wished to retire from the city would have twelve months to depart. Negotiations eventually broke down over the status of the militia. Clinton allowed that they could return to their homes, but he was equally insistent that they do so as prisoners of war on parole.

When the two sides failed to reach an accommodation, hostilities recommenced on the night of 9 May. The Americans fired first, launching solid shot and shells from more than 180 pieces of cannon. The British responded in kind, and the cannonade continued until 11 May. By then, the morale of the militia in the garrison had lessened considerably. Lincoln received several petitions from them in which they outlined their understanding that negotiations with Clinton had broken down over their classification as prisoners on parole. The militiamen now informed Lincoln that such an arrangement was perfectly acceptable to them. Gadsden sent Lincoln a letter that contained similar sentiments.

The situation of the garrison was now critical. The militia had lost the will to fight, Royal Navy vessels lay at anchor in the harbor, the British works on Charleston Neck were now only yards from their defenses, and enemy troops blocked their escape routes east of the Cooper River. Lincoln had little choice but to surrender the town.

On the afternoon of 11 May, Lincoln sent a message to Clinton requesting the terms that the British commander had been willing to grant three days earlier. Although Clinton responded that the Americans were not deserving of such terms after rejecting them, he agreed to offer them again.

The formal surrender of the town took place on 12 May. Lincoln had requested the honors of war for the garrison, asking that they advance from their works with colors flying and their drums beating a march. Clinton insisted, however, that their colors be cased, and he denied them the honor of playing a British march. The Continental troops piled their arms between the hornwork and the canal, while the militia surrendered within the American fortifications.

The surrender of Charleston was the largest defeat for the Americans during the Revolution. Lincoln surrendered to Clinton approximately 6,000 men, including 3,465 officers and enlisted men of the Continental Army. The Americans also suffered 89 killed and 138 wounded. British losses were 76 killed and 189 wounded for the army and 23 killed and 28 wounded for the navy.

Despite their overwhelming victory at Charleston, the British soon found that the rest of South Carolina would not be pacified so easily. Although many South Carolinians took oaths of allegiance in the wake of the city's surrender, others, such as Francis Marion and Thomas Sumter, continued to take the field and harass the British. The campaign against Charleston commenced major British operations in the South, a circumstance that would draw increasing numbers of British troops to a theater where land operations in North America would reach their dramatic conclusion the following year.

Carl P. Borick

See also

Biggin Church, South Carolina, Action at; Charleston, South Carolina, Expedition against (1776); Charleston, South Carolina, Raid on; Clinton, Henry; Gadsden, Christopher; Germain, Lord George; Lenud's Ferry, South Carolina, Action at; Lincoln, Benjamin; McIntosh, Lachlan; Moultrie, William; Prevost, Augustine; Siege Warfare; Tarleton, Banastre; Webster, James; Whipple, Abraham

References

Allaire, Anthony. *Diary of Lieutenant Anthony Allaire.* New York: New York Times and Arno, 1968.

Borick, Carl. *A Gallant Defense: The Siege of Charleston, 1780.* Columbia: University of South Carolina Press, 2003.

Bulger, William T. "The British Expedition to Charleston, 1779–1780." PhD diss., University of Michigan, 1957.

Clinton, Henry. *The American Rebellion: Sir Henry Clinton's Narrative of His Campaigns, 1775–1782, with an Appendix of Original Documents.* Edited by William B. Willcox. New Haven, CT: Yale University Press, 1954.

Ewald, Johann. *Diary of the American War: A Hessian Journal.* New Haven, CT: Yale University Press, 1979.

Moultrie, William. *Memoirs of the American Revolution.* 1802. Reprint, New York: New York Times, 1968.

Russell, Peter. "The Siege of Charleston: Journal of Captain Peter Russell, December 25, 1779 to May 2, 1780." *American Historical Review* 4(3) (1899): 478–501.

Taliaferro, Benjamin. *The Orderly Book of Captain Benjamin Taliaferro, 2nd Virginia Detachment, Charleston, South Carolina, 1780.* Edited by Lee A. Wallace. Richmond: Virginia State Library, 1980.

Tarleton, Banastre. *History of the Campaigns of 1780 and 1781, in the Southern Provinces of North America.* 1787. Reprint, New York: New York Times, 1968.

Uhlendorf, Bernhard A., trans. and ed. *The Siege of Charleston with an Account of the Province of South Carolina: Diaries and Letters of Hessian Officers from the von Jungkenn Papers in the William L. Clements Library.* University of Michigan Publications on History and Political Science, vol. 12. Ann Arbor: University of Michigan Press, 1938.

Charleston, South Carolina, Raid on (1779)

In May 1779, Major-General Augustine Prevost marched on Charleston to keep American forces from threatening Georgia. British successes at Savannah in December 1778 and Briar Creek in March 1779 had given them firm control of Georgia and prompted American Major General Benjamin Lincoln, the new commander of the Southern Department, to attempt to drive them out of that state.

The American army in South Carolina numbered approximately 5,000 militia and Continentals. Lincoln proposed to move the bulk of this force up the Savannah River and then to Augusta. From there, they would drive into the Georgia backcountry. Originally intending to leave 1,000 men each at Black Swamp and Purrysburg on the lower Savannah to protect against a British incursion into South Carolina, Lincoln ultimately left only 1,200 at the two posts.

Advancing up the Savannah River on 20 April 1779, Lincoln left Brigadier General William Moultrie in command at Purrysburg. On 29 April, Prevost, in an attempt to draw Lincoln's attention from Georgia, crossed the Savannah at Purrysburg with more than 3,000 men. With too few troops to stop Prevost, Moultrie immediately fell back toward Charleston, destroying the bridges he had used to cross the rivers as he went. He also sent several messages to Lincoln entreating him to return to South Carolina.

The Americans had recently improved the defensive works before Charleston, and Governor John Rutledge had brought additional militia into the town. However, Moultrie found the city in a panic when he arrived on 7 May. Word spread quickly that Prevost's troops were plundering farms and plantations on their march from Georgia. Many in the garrison doubted that they could hold out against the British.

Prevost's advanced guard appeared before Charleston on 10 May, and the rest of his army came up the following day. Rutledge, believing the British force to be much larger than his own force, suggested to Moultrie that they parley with the enemy. Although Moultrie was confident that they could defend the city, Rutledge and several members of the South Carolina Privy Council convinced him to send a message to Prevost asking what terms he would grant the garrison.

Prevost's brother, Lieutenant-Colonel Mark Prevost, responded on 11 May that any in the town who did not wish to receive the king's peace and protection would be treated as prisoners of war, and he reminded them of the horrors that an assault on their works would bring. Despite the opposition of Moultrie and other officers, the civilian officials decided to propose the neutrality of South Carolina for the rest of the war in exchange for the security of Charleston. When the British received this proposition on 12 May, however, Lieutenant-Colonel Prevost replied that they had not come in a legislative capacity but only in a military one and that their business was with Moultrie as military commander. Upon hearing this, Moultrie informed his officers and the civilian officials that they would "fight it out." He sent word to Prevost and prepared the garrison for action.

The following morning, 13 May, the garrison of Charleston discovered that the British had withdrawn during the night. Prevost had intercepted a message from Lincoln that indicated he was returning to Charleston from Georgia, and the British general did not want to be trapped between the two American forces. Prevost retreated first to James Island and then to Johns Island, eventually falling down to Beaufort after the action at Stono Ferry. Although his army was unable to take Charleston, Prevost had achieved his objective of keeping Lincoln from making progress against Georgia.

Carl P. Borick

See also

Briar Creek, Battle of; Georgia; Lincoln, Benjamin; Moultrie, William; Prevost, Augustine; Rutledge, John; Savannah, Georgia, British Capture of; Stono Ferry, South Carolina, Action at

References

Borick, Carl. *A Gallant Defense: The Siege of Charleston, 1780.* Columbia, University of South Carolina Press, 2003.

Clinton, Henry. *The American Rebellion: Sir Henry Clinton's Narrative of His Campaigns, 1775–1782, with an Appendix of Original Documents.* Edited by William B. Willcox. New Haven, CT: Yale University Press, 1954.

McCrady, Edward. *The History of South Carolina in the Revolution, 1775–1780.* 1901. Reprint, New York: Russell and Russell, 1969.

Moultrie, William. *Memoirs of the American Revolution.* 1802. Reprint, New York: New York Times, 1968.

Charlotte, North Carolina, Action at (26 September 1780)

A modest town of twenty houses in 1780, Charlotte was the county seat of Mecklenburg County, North Carolina. Named for Great Britain's Queen Charlotte (of Mecklenburg, Germany), it was settled largely by Scots-Irish Presbyterians who avidly supported the Revolution.

With much of South Carolina under British occupation in the summer of 1780, General Lord Charles Cornwallis next prepared to invade North Carolina. On 26 September, his army advanced on the town. About 120 American militia and dragoons under Colonel William Richardson Davie were waiting. The Americans had taken up their position behind a stone wall near the courthouse, at the intersection of Trade and Tryon streets. Knowing they could not hold off the main British Army, they only hoped to harass and delay their advance.

The British approached from the southeast, pushing back American pickets. Near the courthouse they deployed for battle. Dragoons from the British Legion under the command of Major George Hanger charged twice but were repulsed. Light infantry under Lieutenant-Colonel James Webster then arrived, and with Cornwallis himself on the scene, they pushed the Americans back.

American losses were around thirty, with fifteen British casualties. Their occupation of Charlotte was disappointing to the British, however, as the local residents did not embrace royal forces warmly. Cornwallis referred to the region as a "hornets' nest" of rebels, and Charlotte treasured the epithet into the twentieth century, naming the city's professional basketball team the Hornets.

When news of the disastrous defeat of the large Loyalist force at Kings Mountain arrived early in October, Cornwallis felt compelled to fall back to Winnsboro, South Carolina, and delay his invasion of the northern province. British forces chose instead to winter at Winnsboro and prepare to resume their march in the spring, a plan that was interrupted when the American victory at Cowpens in January brought Cornwallis back into the field against the Continental Army.

Robert M. Dunkerly

See also

Cornwallis, Charles; Davie, William Richardson; Southern Campaigns; Webster, James

References

Boatner, Mark. *Encyclopedia of the American Revolution.* Mechanicsburg, PA: Stackpole, 1994.

———. *Landmarks of the American Revolution.* Mechanicsburg, PA: Stackpole, 1973.

Charlottesville, Virginia, Raid on (3–4 June 1781)

The cavalry raid conducted by Lieutenant-Colonel Banastre Tarleton almost captured the entire Virginia legislature, including Governor Thomas Jefferson. On 1 June 1781, Tarleton learned from a captured dispatch that the Virginia legislature was at Charlottesville—some 60 miles from the army of Lord Charles Cornwallis. Tarleton set out early on 3 June with 180 cavalry from the (Loyalist) British Legion and the 17th Light Dragoons and 70 mounted infantry from the 23rd Foot. The column was spotted that afternoon by John Jouett, a captain of militia, who rode off to give the alarm.

Tarleton reached Louisa Court House at 11:00 P.M., where he rested for three hours before resuming the march. Around dawn Tarleton destroyed twelve wagons carrying 1,000 muskets and clothing for General Nathanael Greene's army, then about 6 miles from Charlottesville, before dividing his own force in two. Leading one column himself, Tarleton headed for the home of Dr. Thomas Walker (not to be confused with the Montreal merchant of the same name) and captured Colonel John Simms, a member of the state legislature, and two brothers of General Thomas Nelson.

While Tarleton allowed his men an hour's rest for breakfast, Jouett had reached Jefferson, who was playing host to the Speaker of the legislature and most of the members. The politicians headed for Staunton with no time to spare. As Jefferson's wife and children left in a carriage, some of Tarleton's dragoons were riding up the road to the house. Jefferson himself apparently walked through the grounds, picked up his horse from the local blacksmith, and escaped with his family.

Meanwhile, the second column, under Captain David Kinlock, had reached the house of John Walker, brother of Thomas. There, Kinlock captured his own cousin Francis, a member of the legislature—a feat he had predicted before leaving Britain. The column then forded the Rivanna River, dispersing some militia, and rode on up the hill into Charlottesville but found it empty. The next day, some militia marched into Staunton with a message from Baron von Steuben; the politicians fled once more and would not return for several days.

After destroying more military supplies and tobacco, Tarleton rejoined Cornwallis on 9 June at Elk Hill, about 30 miles from Charlottesville. Despite capturing up to seven members of the legislature (according to different accounts), he has been criticized for the delay at Walker's house. However, given that his men and horses had covered 60 miles in twenty-four hours in extreme heat, a rest must have been essential.

Brendan D. Morrissey

See also

Cornwallis, Charles; Greene, Nathanael; Jefferson, Thomas; Nelson, Thomas; Point of Fork, Virginia, Raid on; Steuben, Friedrich von; Tarleton, Banastre

References

Bass, Robert D. *The Green Dragoon: The Lives of Banastre Tarleton and Mary Robinson.* 1957. Reprint, Orangeburg, SC: Sandlapper, 2003.

Lossing, Benson J. *The Pictorial Field Book of the Revolution.* 1951. Reprint, Rutland, VT: Tuttle, 1972.

Scotti, Anthony. *Brutal Virtue: The Myth and Reality of Banastre Tarleton.* Bowie, MD: Heritage Books, 2002.

Tarleton, Banastre. *History of the Campaigns of 1780 and 1781, in the Southern Provinces of North America.* 1787. Reprint, New York: New York Times, 1968.

Chase, Samuel (1741–1811)

Samuel Chase was a lawyer, a Revolutionary leader, a Maryland delegate to the Continental Congress, and a signer of the Declaration of Independence. He was known as the "Maryland Demosthenes" because of his ability to deliver impassioned, persuasive, and presumably loud speeches.

Samuel Chase. A prominent lawyer from Maryland, he was a member of the Sons of Liberty and publicly supported various forms of protest and agitation. In addition to serving as a member of both the First and Second Continental Congresses and signing the Declaration of Independence, he served on the Committee of Safety, in the first Maryland Convention, and on the Committee of Correspondence. (Collection of the Supreme Court of the United States)

Chase was born on 17 April 1741 in Somerset County, Maryland. His father was an immigrant from England who served as Episcopal rector of St. Paul's parish in Baltimore. Chase was educated in the classics by his father. In 1759, he began the study of the law in the offices of Hammond and Hall of Annapolis and was admitted to the bar in 1761.

In 1764, Chase was elected to the Maryland Assembly. He served in that body until 1788. He was an early supporter of colonial rights and was aligned with the opponents to Maryland's royal governor. At one point, Chase voted for legislation that regulated the salaries of clergy in the colony, thereby effectively reducing his father's income. Chase also became active in the Sons of Liberty, and his protests against the Stamp Act soon attracted the attention of the mayor and aldermen of Annapolis, who denounced Chase as a "busy, restless incendiary, a ringleader of mobs, a foul-mouthed and inflaming son of discord."

Chase became a member of Maryland's Committee of Correspondence in 1774 and was chosen as a delegate to the First

Continental Congress. A member of the Maryland provincial convention that met in 1775, Chase also served on the Council of Safety. In Congress, Chase took a radical position against the British, arguing that only a complete embargo of British goods into North America would cause the mother country to listen to American grievances. Congress elected Chase to a committee to seek foreign alliances and on 15 February 1776 appointed him to a special commission to travel to Canada to win its French Catholic population over to the American side. The commission included Benjamin Franklin, Charles Carroll of Carrollton, and Carroll's cousin John, a Catholic priest. The party left Philadelphia on 25 March and reached Montreal on 29 April but was unsuccessful and returned to Philadelphia in early June. The commission's report to Congress detailed the failure of its mission and outlined the problems that Americans faced in their military invasion of Canada.

Soon after returning to Philadelphia, Chase traveled to Maryland to conduct a vigorous campaign to get Maryland's provincial convention to change its instruction opposing complete independence. After helping to convince the convention to change its position, Chase rode 150 miles in two days to vote in favor of the Declaration of Independence and signed it on 2 August.

Chase was continually returned to Congress through 1778. An active member, he served on twenty-one committees in 1777 and on thirty in 1778. One of the most important committees on which he served drafted Congress's reply to the peace proposals of Britain's Carlisle Commission in 1778. He also worked to block congressional attempts to remove General George Washington as commander in chief of the Continental Army. Because of Chase's loyalty and support, he earned Washington's respect.

Chase's congressional career ended suddenly in 1778. Using information he obtained as a member of Congress, he joined with others to speculate on the flour market in advance of the arrival of the French fleet. The group calculated that the presence of the French army would increase demand for flour. Alexander Hamilton, writing as "Publius" in the *New York Journal,* attacked Chase for engaging in the financial arrangement. Because of his involvement in the scandal, Maryland failed to reappoint Chase to Congress. He returned to Baltimore to continue his law practice, speculate in land ventures, and try to restart his political career.

In 1783, Maryland's governor sent Chase to England to try to recover funds owed the state by the Bank of England. Although unsuccessful in his financial mission, he succeeded in meeting famous British politicians such as Edmund Burke. Upon Chase's return to Maryland, his friends encouraged him to move permanently from Annapolis to Baltimore, which he did in 1786. In 1788 Chase became chief judge of the Baltimore City Court, and in 1791 he was appointed chief judge of the Maryland General Court while continuing to hold his position on the Baltimore bench. His time on the state bench was stormy. Chase was not concerned with the feelings and rights of others, and in 1794 a grand jury in Baltimore accused him of overreaching his authority by censuring a sheriff and not summoning a jury. He was also accused of violating the Maryland Bill of Rights by holding two judicial appointments. But nothing came of the grand jury's charges.

Chase opposed the new national Constitution and was one of eleven delegates to the Maryland ratifying convention who voted against the document. His opposition to the new structure of government stemmed from his republican ideals; he feared that the Constitution placed too much power in the hands of rich merchants who would use it against the masses. After the Constitution was ratified, Chase was appointed to a special committee to write a proposed Bill of Rights in order to limit the powers of the national government.

Despite his initial opposition to the Constitution, however, Chase became a Federalist by the mid-1790s. Historians differ on the reasons for Chase's political conversion. President Washington, overlooking Chase's vocal opposition to the Constitution and possibly remembering Chase's support of Washington's command of the army in Congress during the war, nominated the Marylander to a seat on the U.S. Supreme Court on 26 January 1796. Even as the newest justice, Chase exerted significant influence on the Court. At the time, each justice read his opinion, with the most recently appointed justice speaking first. In several cases, the justices who followed Chase did nothing more than state their agreement with his opinion. He established the judicial precedent defining a federal direct tax as either a poll or a land tax, a ruling that guided judicial decisions until 1895. He also wrote the opinion establishing the supremacy of treaties over state laws, an important principle of constitutional law. A Chase opinion established the fact that ex post facto laws applied to criminal cases only, not to civil cases. He argued in a dissenting opinion that the Court did not have jurisdiction over common-law crimes but could act only when Congress enacted specific legislation, a view that the Court adopted in 1812.

Chase attracted controversy throughout his political and judicial career, and he is primarily remembered as the first Supreme Court justice to be impeached. In 1800, Thomas Jefferson was elected president. As the leader of the Republicans, Jefferson disliked the idea of judges being appointed for life. He feared that under such a system the judiciary might become too powerful. In a number of cases Chase heard as a circuit judge, he strongly expressed his Federalist opinions from the bench. For this reason, Jefferson encouraged the House of Representatives to impeach Chase.

The House passed articles of impeachment on 12 March 1804. In the Senate, all nine Federalist senators voted to acquit Chase, and his attorney, Luther Martin, was able to convince six Republican senators to vote with the Federalists, so the vote for conviction fell short of the two-thirds majority needed. Chase remained on the Court, but he played a smaller role than he had in the 1790s. He died in Baltimore on 19 June 1811.

John David Rausch Jr.

See also

Carroll, Charles; Congress, First Continental; Congress, Second Continental and Confederation; Constitution, United States, Ratification of; Franklin, Benjamin; Sons of Liberty; Stamp Act

References

Ellis, Richard E. *The Jeffersonian Crisis: Courts and Politics in the Young Republic.* New York: Norton, 1974.

Elsmere, Jane Shaffer. *Justice Samuel Chase.* Muncie, IN: Janevar, 1980.

Haw, James, Francis F. Beirne, Rosamond R. Beirne, and R. Samuel Jett. *Stormy Patriot: The Life of Samuel Chase.* Baltimore: Maryland Historical Society, 1980.

Sanderson, John. *Biography of the Signers of the Declaration of Independence,* Vol. 9. Philadelphia: R. W. Pomeroy, 1820.

Chatham, William Pitt, 1st Earl of

See Pitt, William, the Elder

Cherokees, Operations against (1760–1761, 1773–1774, 1776–1777, 1779–1780, and 1782)

The Cherokee Nation, formidable before the American Revolution, strongly supported the British during the conflict in an effort to stop the encroachment of European settlers upon their lands. But the Cherokees emerged from the Revolutionary War a weakened people, unable to resist continued pressure from white settlers that eventually drove them from the region.

The Cherokee Nation sprawled over the mountain country from North and South Carolina and northern Georgia to the future state of Tennessee. The Lower Towns clustered in up-country South Carolina east of the Appalachian Mountains. The Middle Towns or Settlements occupied the fertile valley of Cowee along the northward-flowing Little Tennessee River and the southern-flowing tributaries of the Savannah River. The Overhill Settlements lay to the west of the mountains.

Colonial South Carolinians regarded the rivers flowing south and east out of the Cherokee country as a potential avenue of invasion by the Louisiana French and their Indian allies. To prevent this, in 1756 Governor James Glen persuaded the Overhill chieftains to allow him to build Fort Loudoun on the Little Tennessee River. During the French and Indian (Seven Years') War, the Cherokees joined the French, attacked the fort, and massacred most of the garrison. That episode launched three decades of sporadic warfare between the Cherokees and the white settlers. In 1760 and 1761, British expeditions devastated the Lower and Middle Towns but could not penetrate the Overhill Settlements.

This intermittent warfare interfered with the Cherokees' usual hunting, and they became heavily indebted to their suppliers. Their traders, in turn, owed money to the merchants in England and Scotland. An arrangement was made whereby the Cherokees exchanged land in northern Georgia for the royal government's assumption of the Cherokee debt. The Treaty of Augusta in 1773 confirmed the cession. The land in question, however, was also claimed by the Creek Nation, and warriors from the Lower Creek towns raided frontier settlements in Georgia during the winter of 1773–1774. Governor James Wright disappointed settlers by declining to demand further land cessions as a condition of peace. The perception that the royal government favored the interests of Indian traders over those of the settlers had much to do with the growth of the Revolutionary movement in the Georgia and Carolina backcountry.

Although the British Proclamation of 1763 prohibited colonial settlement west of the Appalachians, hardy pioneers moved into the Watauga and Holsten river valleys in the Cherokee Overhill country. Speculators met with Cherokee chieftains in March 1775 and claimed that the Indians had ceded a huge territory amounting to the future state of Kentucky and much of middle Tennessee. Dragging Canoe, son of the Cherokee leader Attakullakulla, showed his disgust with the proceedings by leaving the conference in a fury and later led a secessionist movement westward to the Chickamauga River. John Stuart, the Indian superintendent, declared the transaction illegal, and the chiefs claimed that they had been duped. Nevertheless, the interlopers remained on the Watauga and Holsten Rivers.

The Revolutionary movement in the South gathered strength in 1775, fueled partly by a false rumor that Stuart intended to launch an Indian war upon the frontier settlements. By the late summer of 1775, Loyalists and Patriots engaged in armed conflict in the South Carolina backcountry. Some of the Loyalist partisans, notably Thomas Brown, borrowed upon the rumor to suggest a strategy of using Indians on the frontier in conjunction with the landing of British troops on the coast to crush the rebellion. The plan received the approval of the royal governors of South Carolina, Georgia, and East Florida and finally of Britain's war minister, Lord George Germain.

Stuart commissioned his brother Henry to deliver twenty-one horse loads of ammunition to the Cherokees by way of a fifty-five-day journey from Pensacola through the Chickasaw country to the Overhill Settlements. He did not intend to instigate an Indian war, but he wanted the Cherokees to be armed and ready in case they were called upon by the British military. The delivery of ammunition, subsequent Cherokee raids against frontier settlements, and the coincidence of a British naval attack upon Charleston in June 1776 convinced Carolinians of the truth of the rumor of an imminent Indian attack.

Continental General Charles Lee ordered a three-pronged attack upon the Cherokees from the militia of South Carolina, North Carolina, and Virginia. In August 1776, South Carolina General Andrew Williamson led 1,000 South Carolinians in the destruction of the Lower Towns. In September, Williamson's troops joined General Griffith Rutherford's North Carolinians in a devastating expedition against the Middle Settlements. Finally, in October, Virginians under General William Christian approached the Overhill Settlements along the western side of the mountains and destroyed many of those towns.

A delegation of older chiefs signed a peace treaty with the Carolinians at DeWitt's Corner, South Carolina, on 20 May 1777. Dragging Canoe and many of the younger warriors, however, continued hostilities. In April 1779, Virginia's Governor Patrick Henry organized a punitive invasion of the Chickamauga country. Although it seemed that Cherokee resistance was finally crushed, the reoccupation of Georgia and South Carolina by the British Army between 1778 and 1780 and the resumption of British supplies of ammunition caused isolated bands of Cherokees to resume their struggle against the frontier settlements. Cherokees fought alongside Brown's King's Rangers at Augusta in September 1780 in a four-day battle to repulse Lieutenant Colonel Elijah Clarke's Patriot raiders, and Cherokee warriors harassed Clarke's retreating Georgians as they made their way back to the mountains.

As he moved into the South Carolina backcountry, British General Lord Charles Cornwallis initially disdained the use of Indians in warfare. After the Loyalists' defeat at Kings Mountain in October 1780, however, Cornwallis ordered Brown, Stuart's successor as Indian superintendent, to launch Cherokee attacks on the Watauga and Holsten settlements. The raids caused the mountain men under John Sevier and Arthur Campbell to retaliate against the Indian villages, destroying 1,000 houses and burning 50,000 bushels of corn. And even as the British prepared to evacuate Georgia in 1782, Thomas Brown ordered his deputy, Thomas Waters, to recruit the Cherokees for new raids upon the Georgia backcountry. Clarke chased Waters and his Indian allies down to Florida, and South Carolina's Andrew Pickens led another attack on the Cherokee Middle Settlements.

The final withdrawal of the British from Florida subsequent to the treaty of peace in 1783 forced the Cherokees to conclude peace at the cost of the surrender of large tracts of land in both South and North Carolina. Having learned the bitter lesson of the futility of warfare against white settlers, the Cherokee Nation would try another tactic to hold on to its land. Over the next fifty years, the Cherokees adopted several basic features of European-American civilization, including farming and writing. Even these alterations, however, could not stop the inexorable invasion of aggressive American settlers, and in the 1830s the Cherokees had to abandon the Southeast entirely and embark on their Trail of Tears to Oklahoma.

Edward J. Cashin

See also

Brown, Thomas; Clarke, Elijah; Cornwallis, Charles; Lee, Henry; Pickens, Andrew; Rutherford, Griffith; Sevier, John; Stuart, John; Williamson, Andrew

References

Brown, John P. *Old Frontiers: The Story of the Cherokee Indians from Earliest Times to the Date of Their Removal to the West, 1838.* Kingsport, TN: Southern Publishers, 1938.

Hatley, Tom. *The Dividing Paths: Cherokees and South Carolinians through the Era of Revolution.* New York and Oxford: Oxford University Press, 1993.

O'Donnell, James H., III. *The Cherokees of North Carolina in the American Revolution.* Raleigh: North Carolina Department of Cultural Resources, Division of Archives and History, 1976.

———. *Southern Indians and the American Revolution.* Knoxville: University of Tennessee Press, 1973.

Cherry Valley Massacre (11 November 1778)

The Cherry Valley Massacre was probably the most notorious encounter between Patriot settlers and Loyalist and Iroquois raiders on the New York frontier. The massacre was the culmination of the increasingly destructive and bloody warfare that plagued the frontier along and south of the Mohawk Valley throughout 1778. Cherry Valley was an important settlement because of its strategic position at the headwaters of the Susquehanna River, a position in which a strong enough Patriot force could bar the passage of Loyalist and Indian raiding parties moving east from Fort Niagara by way of the Genesee, Chemung, and Susquehanna Rivers.

Throughout the spring and summer of 1778, Loyalist rangers and Iroquois warriors conducted a series of successful raids, including the Wyoming Valley Massacre and the destruction of German Flats, on the Pennsylvania and New York frontiers. The Patriots quickly retaliated by burning several Indian towns along the Susquehanna River. In late October, Colonel Walter Butler decided to attack Cherry Valley before winter set in and organized a force of 250 Loyalist rangers and 400 Iroquois, mostly Senecas but with a small number of Mohawks led by Joseph Brant. While marching toward Cherry Valley, Brant and Butler quarreled. Brant was reluctant to serve under Butler, who was commanding his first expedition, and nearly left the enterprise. Though persuaded to remain, Brant exercised no authority over the raid.

The Patriots understood the strategic importance of Cherry Valley, and in the summer of 1778 they constructed Fort Alden to protect the settlement, garrisoning the fort with 450 militiamen. They undercut this precaution, however, by placing the fort under the command of Colonel Ichabod Alden, a Massachusetts officer with no frontier experience. On 8 November, a messenger from Fort Stanwix warned Alden that a raid on Cherry Valley was imminent. Alden dismissed the warning. Such alarms were common, and the fact that the raid was to occur at the beginning of winter, a season when the Indians normally returned home, convinced Alden that the message was a false rumor. The colonel refused to allow the town's residents to take refuge in the fort, but he did send out a scouting party to watch for enemy movements.

On 9 November, Butler's command, moving through cold weather and snow, encountered Alden's scouts. The scouts had not expected to find an enemy force out in such weather and spent the night curled around a fire, a mistake that allowed Butler to capture them all. They divulged the strength of the garrison at Fort Alden and the fact that the garrison's officers slept outside of the fort in private homes. Armed with this information, Butler planned to attack Cherry Valley before dawn on 11 November, hoping to capture the officers and then the fort. The evening before the attack, while still 6 miles from Cherry Valley, the Iroquois refused to march any farther and forced Butler to encamp for the night, delaying the assault until after eleven o'clock the following morning.

As they approached the town, the Iroquois made another error when they shot at two woodcutters. Although one man was killed, the other escaped and warned Alden of the approaching enemy force. Alden, then at the home of Robert Wells with his second in command, Lieutenant Colonel William Stacey, dismissed this warning as well, insisting that the Indians were just stragglers and not a threat. At that moment, the Loyalists and Iroquois charged into the town. Butler led most of the rangers and Mohawks toward the fort while ordering the Senecas and fifty rangers to attack the surrounding homes and capture or kill the garrison's officers.

Butler had no intention of committing a massacre, but he failed to comprehend the temper of the Iroquois, especially the Senecas. They sought revenge for the destruction of the Indian towns along the Susquehanna River, and they were especially angry that a Patriot officer captured at Wyoming Valley and later paroled by the British had participated in those attacks. Furthermore, they were incensed that the Patriots referred to the Wyoming action as a massacre. It was quite obvious to Brant that the Senecas were planning to do more than just kill soldiers, but he was unable to prevent the atrocities.

From the moment the raid commenced, Butler lost control of the Senecas. These Iroquois first descended upon the Wells home, where the worst butchery occurred. The raiders killed Alden, captured Stacey, and then slaughtered the Wells household, including Wells, seven family members, and three servants. Following this, the Indians and a few rangers swept through the rest of the town looting, burning, killing, and mutilating. By the end of the day, they had killed fifteen soldiers and thirty-two civilians, mostly women and children, and captured seventy-one. Most of the town was destroyed.

The massacre prevented Butler from assaulting the fort because it tied down more than half of his force, leaving him with fewer soldiers than the Patriots had inside the bastion. The garrison, stunned by the ferocity of the attack and lacking its commanding officers, made no effort to launch a counterattack. Two days later, after convincing the Iroquois to release all but ten of the captives, Butler abandoned his attempt to capture Fort Alden and withdrew to Fort Niagara.

Coming near the end of a year that had seen several bloody frontier raids, few major Continental Army engagements since the indecisive Battle of Monmouth in June, and the disastrous attempt to take Newport, Rhode Island, in August, the Cherry Valley Massacre received tremendous public attention. The event, coupled with the earlier raids of that year, convinced many families to abandon the frontier and compelled Congress to undertake the Sullivan expedition in 1779 to destroy the military capacity of the Iroquois. Word of the massacre even reached England, where opposition leaders in Parliament used it to attack Lord North's conduct of the war.

David Work

See also

Atrocities; Border Warfare; Brant, Joseph; Butler, Walter; German Flats, New York, Raid on; North, Lord Frederick; Sullivan Expedition; Wyoming Valley, Pennsylvania

References

Goodnough, David. *The Cherry Valley Massacre, November 11, 1778: The Frontier Atrocity That Shocked a Young Nation.* New York: Franklin Watts, 1968.

Kelsay, Isabel T. *Joseph Brant, 1743–1807: Man of Two Worlds.* Syracuse, NY: Syracuse University Press, 1984.

Van Every, Dale. *A Company of Heroes: The American Frontier, 1775–1783.* New York: Morrow, 1962.

Chesapeake, First Battle of the (16 March 1781)

The First Battle of the Chesapeake, also known as the action off Cape Henry, or the Virginia Capes, was a naval encounter resulting from Vice Admiral Mariott Arbuthnot's attempt to seek control of Chesapeake Bay over a numerically superior French fleet. In the opening months of 1781, Major-General Lord Cornwallis undertook operations in the Carolinas and sent a raid against Richmond, Virginia, and the surrounding area. The Americans, under General George Washington, persuaded the French naval commander at Newport, Commodore

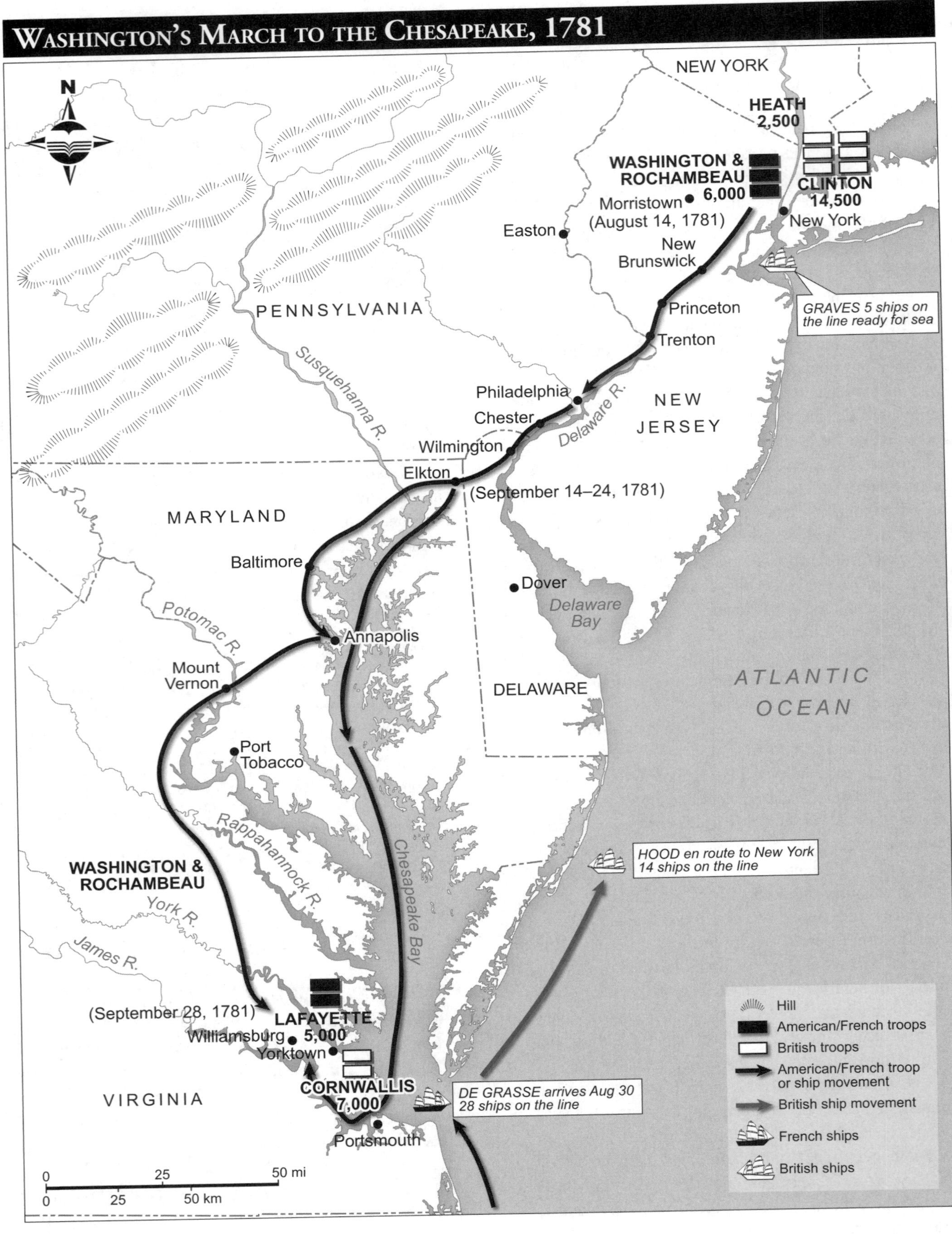
WASHINGTON'S MARCH TO THE CHESAPEAKE, 1781
N
NEW YORK
HEATH
2,500
WASHINGTON &
ROCHAMBEAU
6,000
CLINTON
14,500
Morristown
(August 14, 1781)
New York
Easton
New
Brunswick
Princeton
GRAVES 5 ships on the line ready for sea
PENNSYLVANIA
Trenton
Susquehanna R.
Philadelphia
NEW
JERSEY
Chester
Delaware R.
Wilmington
Elkton
(September 14–24, 1781)
MARYLAND
Baltimore
Dover
Delaware
Bay
Potomac R.
Annapolis
Mount
Vernon
DELAWARE
ATLANTIC
OCEAN
Port
Tobacco
Rappahannock R.
Chesapeake Bay
HOOD en route to New York
14 ships on the line
WASHINGTON &
ROCHAMBEAU
York R.
James R.
(September 28, 1781)
LAFAYETTE
5,000
Williamsburg
Yorktown
CORNWALLIS
7,000
VIRGINIA
DE GRASSE arrives Aug 30
28 ships on the line
Portsmouth
Hill
American/French troops
British troops
American/French troop or ship movement
British ship movement
French ships
British ships
0 25 50 mi
0 25 50 km

Charles René, Chevalier Destouches, to assist in the rebel defense by conveying ships and troops to Chesapeake Bay. However, a recent storm had damaged the British squadron under Arbuthnot after it had left Gardiner's Bay, and Destouches, though he was in port during the gale, was hesitant to embark under such adverse circumstances. Therefore, on 9 February he dispatched only one 64-gun ship and two frigates from Newport, Rhode Island, the main French anchorage. On reaching the Chesapeake, the French took the *Romulus* (44 guns) before returning to Newport on 25 February. Thus, by the end of the first week of March, there were no French ships on Chesapeake Bay.

At the same time, Arbuthnot believed that the French were making ready to leave Gardiner's Bay in force, which in fact they did on 8 March. After carrying out what repairs he could, Arbuthnot put to sea the next day, and the day after that he received intelligence of French movements and proceeded to the entrance of the Chesapeake, thus making it possible to follow his opponents. Intelligence received on 13 March informed him of the French course, and with strong winds and the advantage of copper-bottomed ships, Arbuthnot managed to catch up with Destouches three days later. The French were only a league away to the northeast, 40 miles from Cape Henry, the southernmost point of the entrance to the bay. A frigate had spotted Destouches, but otherwise thick haze obscured the French from view.

Arbuthnot immediately sailed in the direction of the French, and before long both squadrons observed each other. Each force consisted of eight ships of considerable armament and a number of smaller vessels. Arbuthnot had one 98-gun ship, three 74-gun ships, four 64-gun ships, one 50-gun ship, and four frigates. Destouches commanded one 84-gun ship, two 74-gun ships, four 64-gun ships, one 44-gun ship, and three frigates. Destouches maneuvered to windward between 8:00 and 9:00 A.M., and the two opposing squadrons then sought to gain the weather gauge. The haze persisted in obscuring vision on both sides, while shifting winds made maneuver a difficult business. Around midday, the wind blew to the northeast and, owing to superior handling, by 1:00 P.M. Arbuthnot managed to reach the French while on the port tack. The rival squadrons stood in line of battle, heading east-southeast amid increasingly squally conditions and heavy seas.

With his rear now exposed to an enemy capable of overtaking him, Destouches took the defensive measure of wearing his squadron and reversing in succession. He also chose to forgo the usual advantage of the weather gauge and maneuvered to leeward. His rationale was sound: the prevailing conditions of wind and sea and the inclination of the ships would allow him, with the British on his weather side, to make use of the guns on the lower deck, whereas Arbuthnot could not do so without flooding the deck through the open ports. Destouches could therefore enjoy the advantage of increased firepower, as the heaviest guns always occupied the lowest deck. To accomplish this Destouches altered course, his ships passing in succession on a southward course that took them across the head of Arbuthnot's column before assuming a parallel course to leeward of the same.

Apparently satisfied to engage the French in this position, Arbuthnot proceeded until 2:00 P.M., when he signaled for the column to wear. Once on a parallel course with the French, his ships stood down and opened the engagement at 2:30, but not before the three ships in the lead took raking fire as they tacked. Being the first to come into action, these vessels also suffered severe casualties and damage to their sails and rigging. Moreover, by failing to alter the signal from "line" to "close action," his squadron became confused. The French profited by this situation; passing the three crippled ships in the van of Arbuthnot's line, they fired in succession before wearing and making an easterly course, leaving the scene of the fighting.

Arbuthnot wished to pursue and issued orders to that effect, but two vessels of the van, the *Robust* and the *Prudent,* had suffered so severely from the final broadsides delivered by the succession of ships that had passed them that they stood practically dead in the water. The only three-decker in the squadron, the *London* (98 guns) had lost its main topsail yard. Pursuit was therefore considered impossible, and Arbuthnot made sail for Chesapeake Bay on a fair wind, having lost 30 men killed and 73 wounded. The French, in turn, sailed for Newport, with losses of 72 killed and 112 wounded.

Although both sides had eight ships, the British enjoyed a numerical advantage in guns. This fact and the fact that Arbuthnot neglected to fly the signal for close action—thereby leaving several vessels a fair distance from the French—indicate the extent of the British admiral's mistakes on this occasion. Arbuthnot may be justly criticized for not taking on the French in an aggressive manner, though, in fairness, he was still practicing the naval tactics of a previous generation.

Destouches, on the other hand, conducted himself with tactical adeptness. With inferior firepower, he inflicted considerable damage through sound thinking and maneuver. Had he attempted to profit from his advantage, Destouches might have won command of Chesapeake Bay. He had, however, conformed to orthodox French philosophy, which dictated that unless the enemy could be thoroughly destroyed, it was prudent to break off action until a future occasion provided better chances for doing so. This strategy made the decisive defeat of the French an elusive object for British commanders throughout the war, they themselves being hidebound by naval tactics which mitigated against decisive victory. Nevertheless, with the French headed for Rhode Island, the British could reestablish control of the Chesapeake—a vital waterway for landing, embarking, and supplying troops. With the French temporarily at sea, General Sir

Henry Clinton had been able to send 2,000 reinforcements to General Benedict Arnold in Virginia. They arrived in Lynnhaven Bay on 26 March, ten days after the naval battle off the Chesapeake, and from there marched to Portsmouth, Virginia.

Gregory Fremont-Barnes

See also

Arnold, Benedict; Cornwallis, Charles; Clinton, Henry; Naval Operations, British vs. French

References

Clowes, William Laird. *The Royal Navy: A History from the Earliest Times to 1900.* 7 vols. London: Chatham, 1996.

Gardiner, Robert, ed. *Navies and the American Revolution, 1775–1783.* London: Chatham, 1996.

James, William. *The British Navy in Adversity: A Study of the War of American Independence.* 1926. Reprint, New York: Russell and Russell, 1970.

Syrett, David. *The Royal Navy in European Waters during the American Revolutionary War.* Columbia: University of South Carolina Press, 1998.

Tilley, J. A. *The Royal Navy in the American Revolution.* Columbia: University of South Carolina Press, 1987.

Chesapeake, Second Battle of the (5 September 1781)

The Second Battle of the Chesapeake was a naval action fought off the mouth of the Chesapeake Bay on 5 September 1781 in which a French fleet beat back a British fleet that might have brought rescue to Major-General Charles Cornwallis's beleaguered British Army at Yorktown. Though only the lead elements of the two fleets were actually engaged, the battle proved the most significant naval encounter of the war, leading directly to Cornwallis's surrender six weeks later.

The battle is also called the Battle of the Virginia Capes, from the nautical bounds of Capes Charles and Henry that form its mouth. A previous action, fought six months earlier, is called the First Battle of the Chesapeake. In this earlier encounter the results were quite different, the British managing to win control—if only temporarily—of the Chesapeake.

Thereafter, in spring 1781, it was the convergence of British land forces on Virginia that set up the decisive naval battle that occurred in September. First, British amphibious raids—conducted under Brigadier-General Benedict Arnold, who had shifted sides the year before—hit points along the tidal rivers. Other British forces followed, eventually to include Cornwallis's army that marched up from the Carolinas and established a base at Yorktown. The American commander in chief, Lieutenant General George Washington, meanwhile continued to press his French counterpart, Lieutenant General Jean-Baptiste Vimeur, the comte de Rochambeau, for a combined French and American attack against the principal British base of New York. But New York was held by the most substantial assemblage of British troops in America under British commander in chief Lieutenant-General Sir Henry Clinton. No attack there seemed likely to succeed unless it could receive the substantial support of French sea power.

Such sea power—in the form of a French fleet of twenty-eight ships of the line, commanded by the comte de Grasse—was, as Washington and Rochambeau learned in August, indeed on its way and already in the West Indies. Rather than coming north to support an attack on New York, however, de Grasse would come only as far as the Chesapeake and would there ride out the hurricane season. Aware from intelligence that a French fleet was on its way to North American waters, the British secretary of state for war in London, Lord George Germain, assured Clinton and Cornwallis that such a fleet posed them no real threat. There was little chance, he wrote to them, that de Grasse would be able to sail north past the British fleet commanded by Admiral Sir George Rodney in the West Indies. What Germain could not know, however, was that Rodney, who was ill, would have to take sick leave in Britain. In addition, recent movements would so disperse their ships that the British would forfeit to the French—if only for the critical moment—command of the sea in American waters.

Meanwhile, de Grasse's promised arrival in the Chesapeake galvanized Washington into a new plan. Abandoning his original idea of going to New York, he decided instead to move against Cornwallis at Yorktown. Washington and Rochambeau turned their armies south, moving as rapidly as possible to link up with de Grasse. De Grasse himself sailed north from the West Indies early in August, choosing a dog-leg route off the Cuban and Florida coasts. A week later, a squadron of fourteen British warships, under Rear Admiral Sir Samuel Hood, also sailed north but by a more straight-away course. Hood thus reached the Chesapeake ahead of de Grasse. But there was a price to be paid for winning this race as well as for the dispersal of British ships. Finding the bay empty as yet of French masts, Hood, rather than lingering to try to cover Cornwallis ashore at Yorktown with a force half the size of de Grasse's, saw no choice but to sail north and seek help. De Grasse's fleet arrived after Hood's departure and sailed into the bay unimpeded.

As arranged, French transports began ferrying Washington's and Rochambeau's troops into position to lay siege to Yorktown. Arriving at New York, Hood came under the command of his senior in rank Rear Admiral Thomas Graves. The news that the French squadron based at Newport, Rhode Island—which included eight ships of the line under the comte de Barras—had just put to sea forced the British to do likewise. Graves's and Hood's fleet, now numbering nineteen ships of the line, headed south for the Chesapeake.

Ships of the line on parallel courses engage one another in the Second Battle of the Chesapeake in September 1781. The painting wrongly depicts the British ships flying the Union Jack, when in fact it was not adopted until 1801. (U.S. Navy)

On 5 September, a French frigate brought de Grasse, his own fleet lying at anchor in the bay, news of the British approach. Though enjoying an obvious edge over the British in number of ships, de Grasse's situation was less favorable than it appeared. First, substantial numbers of crewmen were ashore, acting to support the land operations against Yorktown. With no time to recall them, his ships were left seriously undermanned—to the point that some would be unable to fire off a full broadside. Second, the approaching British fleet enjoyed the tactical advantage of the weather gauge—the favorable, windward position that gave the attacker the ability to initiate action. Third, given the suddenness of the British approach, de Grasse would have little chance of getting his ships formed up to sail out in the sort of tight, well-ordered formation called for in the standard, line-ahead naval tactics of the day. Yet de Grasse decided to give battle, his fleet standing out of the bay for open sea. Certainly the bay offered little in the way of maneuver room, but de Grasse was influenced by another factor as well: his knowledge that de Barras could arrive at any moment, and with him and his Newport squadron the heavy siege artillery essential if Cornwallis's fortifications were to be pounded into submission. De Grasse thus needed to draw the British away so that de Barras might have a chance to make a run into the bay.

The two fleets continued on their respective courses, de Grasse's ships sailing east but in some disarray, Graves and Hood coming down from the north and enjoying the weather gauge. Graves, though outnumbered twenty-four French ships (de Grasse had dispatched four to cover the approach to Yorktown) to his own nineteen, never for a moment hesitated in his decision to press home the attack. In the early afternoon the British fleet had to shift course to aim for the lead element, or van, of de Grasse's formation, still heading east. This maneuver put the two fleets on a converging course, with the British angling in from the northwest. But there was confusion in the British line. Graves, in command and a third of the way back from the lead ship but well ahead of Hood, raised two signals at the same time. One signal ordered "close action"; the second specified "line ahead at half a cable." To Hood—and doubtless many of the captains as well—these signals appeared contradictory. "Close action" dictated that each ship should bear down upon the enemy line by the most direct course possible. "Line ahead at half a cable," on the other hand, meant something quite different. Rather than individual maneuvers carried out in order to close on the enemy's fleet, the "line ahead" signal meant to do just that: maintain the line-ahead formation. Each ship should carry on in its assigned position within the formation specified (at intervals of half a cable between ships)—not turn and maneuver so as to engage the enemy as each captain could best manage. The ships could not comply with both signals at the same time. Certainly the Royal Navy's tactical doctrine,

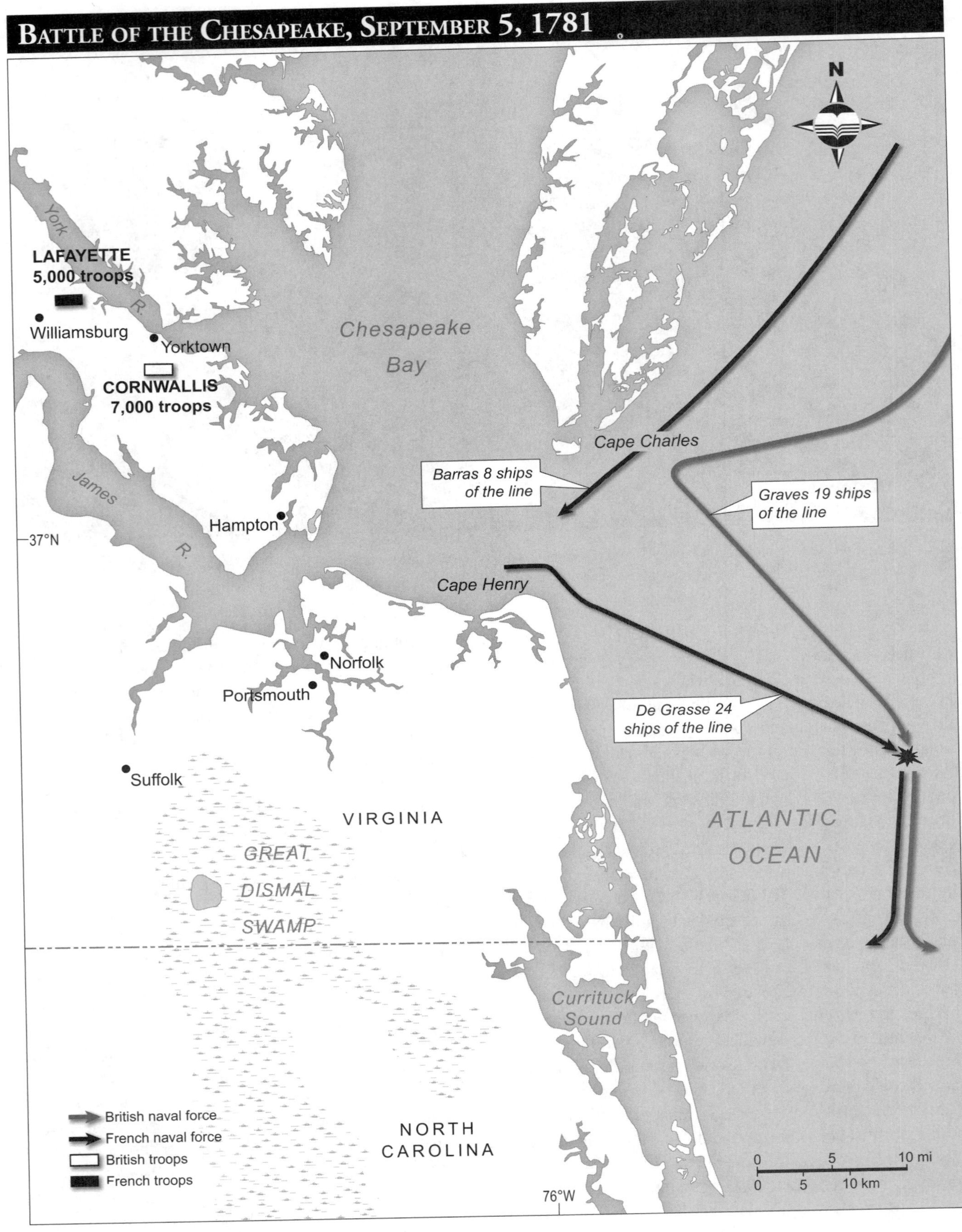

Battle of the Chesapeake, September 5, 1781
N
York R.
LAFAYETTE
5,000 troops
Williamsburg
Yorktown
CORNWALLIS
7,000 troops
Chesapeake
Bay
Cape Charles
Barras 8 ships
of the line
Graves 19 ships
of the line
James R.
Hampton
37°N
Cape Henry
Norfolk
Portsmouth
De Grasse 24
ships of the line
Suffolk
VIRGINIA
ATLANTIC
OCEAN
GREAT
DISMAL
SWAMP
Currituck
Sound
British naval force
French naval force
British troops
French troops
NORTH
CAROLINA
0
5
10 mi
0
5
10 km
76°W

the official document titled *Fighting Instructions,* left no doubt that the line-ahead formation was the prescribed way of employing ships of the line in battle.

The result—whether from confusion or Hood's rigid adherence to tactical doctrine—was that only the van and not the rest of Graves's fleet, the portion following behind Hood in the line, would actually engage the French. The battle began when the two vans converged on each other around 4:00 P.M. British gunners were trained to shoot on the downward roll of the ship, French gunners just the opposite. The French approach—facilitated by the fact that their own ships were sailing on the lee rather than the weather gauge and thus naturally heeled over—enabled them to shoot into the British rigging and there do considerable damage to masts, sails, and yards. At length Graves finally hauled down the signal for maintaining the line, but by then it was too late; the French fell off to the south, still maintaining their own formation. The battle went on in this way until sunset, with just the two vans engaged but the rest of the two fleets out of range of each other, still continuing on in two more or less parallel lines. By the end of the action the British had lost more than 300 men and the French about 200, but the British had been greatly shot up in their rigging. In the days ahead Graves tried again to bring the French to battle but could not, being foiled either by weather or by de Grasse's adroit maneuvering. In all this de Barras managed to arrive with perfect timing, slipping into the bay with the all-important guns. His ships now brought de Grasse's total to thirty-six sail of the line, impossible numbers for Graves to take on with his battered nineteen. He at length sailed north to New York to effect repairs, planning to return and resume the fight as soon as possible.

A British relief force that included Clinton and 6,000 troops as well as Graves's repaired ships thus departed New York on 19 October. But they were too late. Isolated and cut off from relief, Cornwallis could not prevail against the superior American and French forces besieging him from the landside and surrendered his army that same day. The Second Battle of the Chesapeake was a turning point, ending major fighting in America and setting in motion the peace negotiations that terminated the war.

John W. Gordon

See also

Arnold, Benedict; Barras, Jacques Melchoir, Comte de; Chesapeake, First Battle of the; Clinton, Henry; Cornwallis, Charles; French West Indies; Germain, Lord George; Grasse, François-Joseph-Paul, Comte de; Graves, Thomas; Hood, Samuel; Rodney, George; Vimeur, Jean-Baptiste, Comte de Rochambeau; West Indies; Yorktown, Virginia, Siege of; Yorktown Campaign

References

Clowes, William Laird. *The Royal Navy: A History from the Earliest Times to 1900.* 7 vols. London: Chatham, 1996.

Gardiner, Robert, ed. *Navies and the American Revolution, 1775–1783.* London: Chatham, 1996.

James, William. *The British Navy in Adversity: A Study of the War of American Independence.* 1926. Reprint, New York: Russell and Russell, 1970.

Larrabee, Harold A. *Decision at the Chesapeake.* London: William Kimber, 1965.

Syrett, David. *The Royal Navy in American Waters, 1775–1783.* Brookfield, VT: Gower, 1989.

Tilley, J. A. *The Royal Navy in the American Revolution.* Columbia: University of South Carolina Press, 1987.

Church, Benjamin (1734–1778?)

The physician and traitor Benjamin Church was the son of Benjamin Church, an auctioneer, and Hannah Dyer. Born in Newport, Rhode Island, the younger Church was raised in Boston, where he attended Boston Latin School. Following his graduation from Harvard College in 1754 he studied medicine, and in March 1757 he was appointed surgeon of the Massachusetts vessel of war, the *Prince of Wales.* After a brief service, Church traveled to London, where he continued his medical studies and met his bride-to-be, Sarah Hill. Returning to Boston in 1759, he entered private practice, providing medical services and free smallpox inoculations to the poor.

By 1768, Church had become active in Boston politics, serving on several committees including the town's Committee of Correspondence. He wrote and delivered the annual Boston Massacre oration on 5 March 1773, and in 1774 he was chosen as one of Boston's delegates to the Massachusetts Provincial Congress. On 16 May 1775, the Provincial Congress sent Church to Philadelphia to petition the Continental Congress for permission to establish a new Massachusetts government. The members of Congress were so impressed with Church's patriotism that on 25 July 1775 they appointed him the first director-general of the Continental Army Hospital in Cambridge.

After a short but controversial directorship, Church resigned on 20 September 1775. Nine days later he was arrested on charges of treason stemming from an intercepted letter in Newport. The enciphered letter, addressed to British Major Maurice Cane, aide to British commander General Thomas Gage, outlined the Continental Army's strengths and the distribution of its forces. Church admitted that he had written the letter but declared that his intent was to confuse the enemy and avert further attacks by exaggerating the Continental Army's power. He was brought before a military tribunal headed by Commander in Chief George Washington on 4 October. The tribunal found him guilty of communicating with the enemy but believed that the punishments outlined by the Articles of War did not fit the magnitude of the crime. The tribunal's members referred the case to the Massachusetts House of Representatives, which expelled Church from the legislature and had him arrested. At the same time, Washington petitioned the Continental Congress to revise the Articles of War with regard to treasonous activities. On 7 November, Congress amended the articles, making espionage an offense punishable by death. Church remained in custody at various locations until 9 January 1778, when the Massachusetts House ordered him exiled to the West Indies. He was sent to the island of Martinique aboard the schooner *Welcome,* but the ship was lost at sea during a violent storm.

Bernadette Zbicki Heiney

See also

Boston, Massachusetts; Boston Massacre; Continental Army; Correspondence, Committees of; Smallpox; Washington, George

References

French, Allen. *General Gage's Informers: New Material upon Lexington and Concord.* Ann Arbor: University of Michigan Press, 1932.

Kiracofe, David James. "Dr. Benjamin Church and the Dilemma of Treason in Revolutionary Massachusetts." *New England Quarterly* 70(3) (1997): 443–462.

Clapp's Mill, North Carolina, Action at (2 March 1781)

The relatively little-known fight at Clapp's Mill, North Carolina, was the first of a series of small encounters between General Nathanael Greene's Continental Army of the South and General Charles Cornwallis's British troops. The two forces had been maneuvering for some time looking for favorable opportunities for a major engagement. Greene's army depended in large part on support from the North Carolina militia, so he felt that he must fight soon before their enlistment terms expired.

On 2 March 1781 near Clapp's Mill in Alamance County, Colonel Henry Lee's dragoons clashed with a force under Lieutenant-Colonel Banastre Tarleton. Accompanying Lee were Virginia riflemen under Colonel William Campbell and South Carolina militia led by Colonel Andrew Pickens.

The main American army was positioned behind Lee, drawn up in three lines of battle. Cornwallis's force was also present behind Tarleton, ready to advance. The brief skirmishing convinced Tarleton that the Americans were in a strong position. After failing to dislodge the American forces, Tarleton fell back. Cornwallis did not press the attacks, and both armies moved away, only to meet again two weeks later at Guilford Courthouse.

The Americans suffered only eight casualties at Clapp's Mill, and the British suffered about twenty. Details of the battle remain sketchy, and conflicting accounts make it difficult to reconstruct the event. Although a small skirmish, Clapp's Mill had the potential to escalate into a large engagement if the British had pushed forward. Instead, the decisive battle of the campaign was fought later at Guilford Courthouse.

Robert M. Dunkerly

See also

Campbell, William; Lee, Henry; Pickens, Andrew; Southern Campaigns; Tarleton, Banastre

References

Barefoot, Daniel. *Touring North Carolina's Revolutionary War Sites.* Winston Salem, NC: John F. Blair, 1998.

Conrad, Dennis, et al., eds. *The Papers of General Nathanael Greene.* 13 vols. Chapel Hill: University of North Carolina Press, 1976–2005.

Clark, Abraham

See Declaration of Independence Signers

Clark, George Rogers (1752–1818)

George Rogers Clark, frontiersman and Revolutionary soldier, seized control of the Northwest during the Revolution and laid the groundwork for the British cession of the territory to the United States in the Treaty of Versailles on 3 September 1783. Born in Virginia to Scottish immigrants, Clark was a robust man, six feet in height, with dark, flashing eyes and red hair. In his youth he studied surveying and read history and geography. He traveled by flatboat down the Ohio River in 1772 and established a homestead at the mouth of the Kanawha River. In 1774, he served as a captain of Virginia militia in Lord Dunmore's War but saw no fighting. A year later, he set out for Kentucky on a surveying trip for the Ohio Company. Establishing himself among the few settlers in the region of present-day Kentucky, he worked to establish orderly government. At the outbreak of the Revolution, he and his neighbors declared for the Patriot cause. By 1776, they were under attack by Indians from north of the Ohio River who were encouraged by Lieutenant Governor Henry Hamilton at Detroit.

In the summer of 1776, Clark traveled east to Williamsburg, Virginia, where he petitioned Governor Patrick Henry and the Virginia Assembly for assistance in defending Kentucky. In response, the government created Kentucky County in December and gave Clark 500 pounds of gunpowder. After his return home in March 1777, he was appointed major of militia, with orders to defend Kentucky. Fending off Indian attacks during the summer and fall, he became convinced that Americans ought to wrest the Northwest Territory from British control. In October, he again returned to eastern Virginia and persuaded the governor and the legislature to

George Rogers Clark. As a result of his successful campaigns in the West, American representatives at the peace talks in Paris were able to secure for an independent United States the substantial expanse of territory that lay between the Ohio and Mississippi Rivers. (Library of Congress)

accept his idea. He was promoted to lieutenant colonel in the Virginia State Line, and in the spring of 1778 he organized an army of 175 men near Louisville.

On 28 June, Clark launched his march across the Illinois Country toward Kaskaskia. He arrived at the town on the evening of 4 July, surprising the garrison and forcing its capitulation. With the assistance of friendly inhabitants, he quickly sent detachments to Vincennes and Cahokia, and he convinced local Indians to join him. He also established cordial relations with Spanish authorities at St. Louis. Hamilton, alarmed at Clark's successes, marched on 7 October with a force of 500 British regulars, French militia, and Indians to retake the Illinois posts. He forced the tiny American garrison at Vincennes to surrender on 17 December, then suspended operations for the winter. On 29 January 1779, Clark, who was then at Kaskaskia, learned of Hamilton's success and decided to retake Vincennes immediately. He set out on 5 February with 170 men, and after an arduous march of almost 200 miles through freezing water and marshy plains, he arrived at Vincennes on 23 February and forced Hamilton to surrender two days later.

Over the next three years, Clark operated mostly from Fort Nelson at the Falls of the Ohio, trying to capture Fort Detroit while fending off British attempts to regain control of the Illinois Country. Although he never mobilized the resources to seize Detroit, he was successful in keeping control of his conquests. In the summer of 1780, he thwarted four British attacks west of the Appalachians, the most ambitious of which was Colonel Henry Bird's attempt to capture Fort Nelson. Clark retaliated by successfully attacking Shawnee Indians on the Little Miami River. In 1781, while he was in Virginia seeking more military assistance, he was involved in a skirmish with British regulars. Commanding 250 men, he ambushed a part of General Benedict Arnold's invading force at Hood's Ferry in early 1781, killing 17 and wounding 13 before he had to give way to a British bayonet charge. Back in Kentucky and promoted to brigadier general, he led an expedition against Shawnee Indians at Chillicothe on 4 November 1782.

After the Revolution, Clark served for a number of years on the Federal Board of Commissioners, supervising the allotment of lands in the Illinois Country to Virginia's Revolutionary veterans. In 1786 he was one of three commissioners who concluded the Treaty of Fort McIntosh with the Indians north of the Ohio River. Soon it was clear that the treaty was ineffective, and Clark led an expedition in the fall of 1786 and early 1787 against the Wabash Indians, during which he confiscated goods from Spanish merchants in Vincennes. When his men mutinied, he had to call off the attack, and his reputation sank to a low ebb. The master intriguer James Wilkinson, taking advantage of the situation to remove a perceived rival to his own preferment, successfully campaigned to destroy Clark's credibility. For the remainder of his life, Clark was out of favor with the governments of both the United States and Virginia and was constantly harassed by creditors. Although he claimed unpaid obligations of $20,000 for his services during the Revolution, he could collect nothing.

In an attempt to restore his fortunes, Clark tried to get permission from Spanish authorities to found a colony in Spanish Louisiana. Having no success, he set out to found a colony near Natchez without Spain's consent but was stymied when President George Washington issued a proclamation banning the scheme. In 1793, Clark accepted a French commission as a major general to lead an American filibustering campaign against Spanish territory. When the American government insisted that he cease and desist, he refused and lived for a time in St. Louis. In 1803, he settled at Clarksville in the Northwest Territory (now in Indiana) and drank to excess. After suffering a stroke and the amputation of his right leg in 1809, he moved to his sister's home near Louisville. Belatedly, in 1812, the General Assembly of Virginia, in recognition of his

George Rogers Clark's Campaign, 1778 – 1779

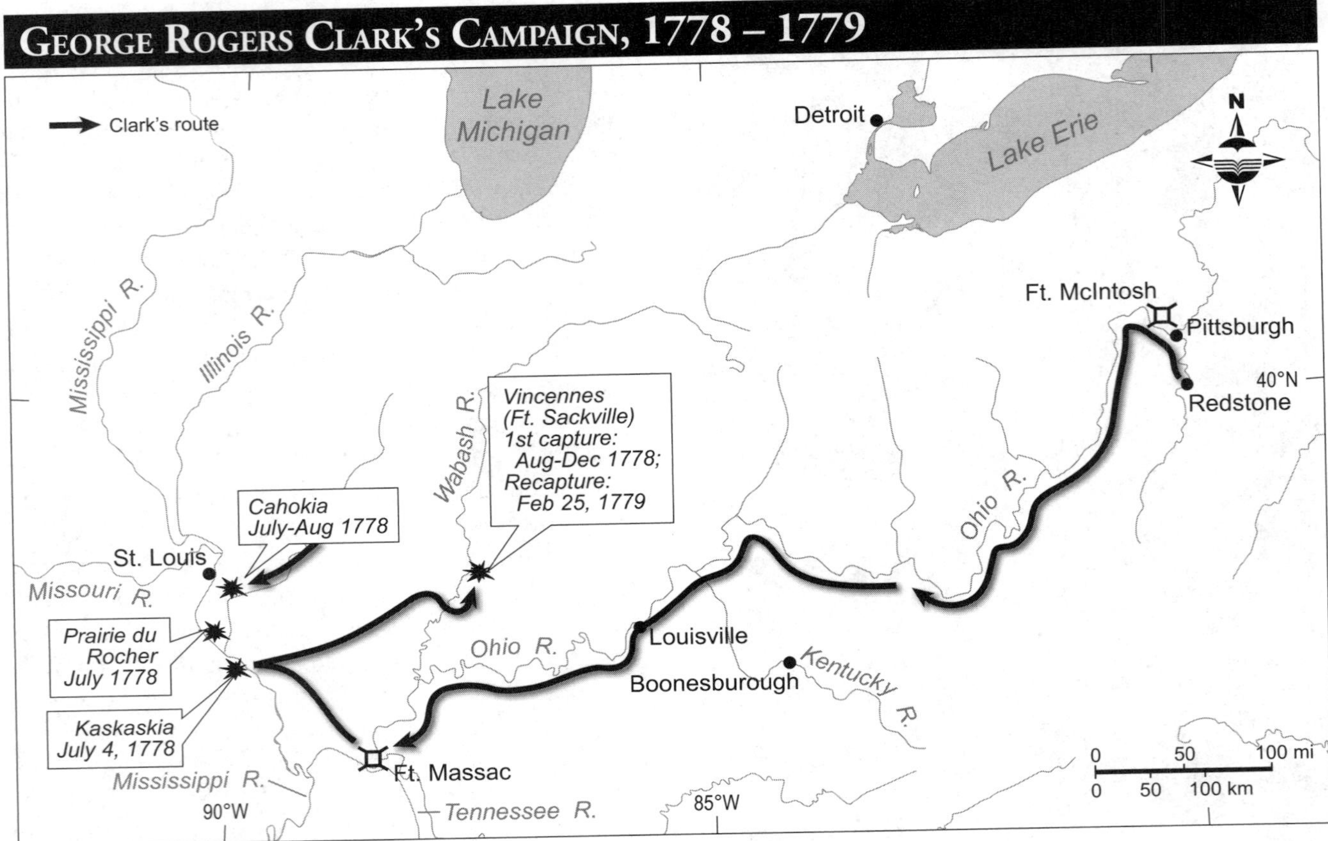

services in the Revolution, voted to award him with a sword and half pay of $400 per year. Clark died in 1818 as the result of another stroke.

Paul David Nelson

See also

Arnold, Benedict; Hamilton, Henry; Henry, Patrick; Kaskaskia, Illinois, Capture of; Kentucky; Northwest Territory; Versailles, Treaty of; Vincennes, Illinois Country, Captures of; Wilkinson, James

References

Bakeless, John. *Background to Glory: The Life of George Rogers Clark.* Philadelphia: Lippincott, 1957.

Bodley, Temple. *George Rogers Clark: His Life and Public Services.* Boston: Houghton Mifflin, 1926.

Butterfield, Consul W. *History of George Rogers Clark's Conquest of the Illinois and Wabash Towns, 1778 and 1779.* Columbus, OH: F. J. Heer, 1904.

Lowell, Harrison H. *George Rogers Clark and the War in the West.* Lexington: University Press of Kentucky, 1976.

Clarke, Elijah (1742–1799)

Elijah Clarke is one example of a military leader who rose from obscurity to prominence during the American Revolution.

Clarke, who was probably born in North Carolina, was one of the restless pioneers who settled on Georgia's so-called Ceded Lands north of Augusta in 1773. Creek Indian raids kept the frontier in turmoil during the winter of 1773–1774 and caused backcountry Georgians to look to the king for protection. Clarke's name was on the 24 August 1774 list of those who opposed the Revolutionary movement. The perception that Governor James Wright preferred the continuation of the Indian trade over the acquisition of additional Indian lands for settlement, however, soon turned many backcountry Georgians against the government.

In 1776, Clarke was elected captain in the militia of his district, and in 1777 the Ceded Lands became Wilkes County. During that year Clarke's troopers defended the county against raids by the Coweta Creeks. By 1778, Clarke had risen to the rank of lieutenant colonel and led his men in an attempted invasion of Florida. Clarke suffered a leg wound in a fight with Lieutenant-Colonel Thomas Brown's Loyalist rangers and British regulars at Alligator Creek, Florida, on 30 June 1778.

Clarke returned to Wilkes County in 1778 and posted men at strategically located forts. On 31 January 1779, a British army under Lieutenant-Colonel Archibald Campbell occupied Augusta and called upon backcountry people to join him. A band of around 700 Loyalists from South Carolina under Colonel John Boyd entered Wilkes County on their way to Augusta. Clarke, with reinforcements under Colonels John Dooley and Andrew Pickens, intercepted and defeated the Loyalists at Kettle Creek on 14 February 1779. This victory persuaded Campbell to abandon Augusta and retreat down the Savannah River.

When Charleston fell to the British in May 1780, the British again advanced up the Savannah River to Augusta, and most Georgians took the oath of allegiance to the king. Clarke and thirty or so of his followers preferred exile in the North Carolina mountains. From there Clarke conducted raids into Loyalist territory in South Carolina. Clarke's mounted militia fought Colonel Alexander Innes's South Carolina Royalists at Woffords Ironworks on 7 August and at Musgroves Mill on 17 August. Both Clarke and Innes were wounded in the latter engagement, but Clarke's wounds did not prevent him from rallying some 600 of his former Wilkes County militia and attacking Augusta on 14 September. After a four-day battle, Clarke was forced to retire to the mountains, with Cherokee warriors harassing his forces on the way.

In May 1781, Clarke returned to lay siege to Augusta and was joined by Andrew Pickens's Carolina militia and Continental cavalry under Lieutenant Colonel Henry Lee. On 5 June, the British commander Lieutenant-Colonel Thomas Brown, another settler on Georgia's Ceded Lands before the war, surrendered his garrison. The Georgia legislature promoted Clarke to the rank of colonel in August 1781. During the last two years of the war, Clarke engaged in sporadic forays into Indian country.

After the war, Clarke never really settled down to civilian life. During the next decade he continued to engage the Creek Indians in skirmishes. In 1794 he enlisted in a bizarre scheme hatched by the controversial French emissary Edmond "Citizen" Genet in which Clarke, as a general in the French army, would lead a French-inspired invasion of Florida. When that plan collapsed, Clarke decided to cross the Oconee River into Indian territory and inaugurate the short-lived Trans-Oconee Republic. He died in 1799.

Edward J. Cashin

See also

Augusta, Georgia, Operations at; Brown, Thomas; Cherokees, Operations against; Kettle Creek, Battle of

References

Cashin, Edward. *The King's Ranger: Thomas Brown and the American Revolution on the Southern Frontier.* Athens: University of Georgia Press, 1989.

Davis, Robert S., Jr. "Clark (Clarke), Elijah." Pp. 1:190–192 in *Dictionary of Georgia Biography.* 2 vols. Edited by Kenneth Coleman and Charles Stephen Gurr. Athens: University of Georgia Press, 1983.

Murdoch, Richard K. "Elijah Clark and the Anglo-American Designs on East Florida." *Georgia Historical Quarterly* 35 (1951): 174–190.

Cleveland, Benjamin (1738–1806)

Benjamin Cleveland earned his nickname "Terror of the Tories" for his aggressive pursuit of Loyalists before and during the American Revolution. He made his most noteworthy contribution at the Battle of Kings Mountain.

Born in Orange County, Virginia, Cleveland early on acquired a reputation as a rowdy individual, if not an outright ruffian. He wasted much of his youth in gambling and fighting, and his education was minimal. He married Mary Graves in 1758 before leaving Virginia for North Carolina. She supposedly civilized him, but she could not domesticate him. In 1765 he followed his wife's father to newly opened lands in western North Carolina, but even with his father-in-law's assistance, he failed to make a go of farming, not having the predisposition for agriculture.

Cleveland preferred hunting in the Indian lands that lay just beyond the edge of civilization. In 1772 he and four others went on a long hunt to Kentucky. Cherokee Indians robbed them of all their possessions, including their weapons, and ordered them home. Cleveland then began a career as a surveyor and became active in local affairs.

As early as 1774, Cleveland, a lieutenant in the militia, was an outspoken critic of British taxes. In 1775 he formed his own Patriot band and began pursuing Loyalists. In 1776 he was variously a member of the Committee of Safety and a leader in the effort to cow Cherokees who had been roused by the British, and he won promotion to captain. In 1777 he took the lead in forming Wilkes County, and in 1778 he became colonel of the county militia. He served in North Carolina's House of Commons in 1778 and its Senate in 1779. In the county, he was presiding justice of the Court of Pleas and Quarter Sessions and had a reputation for meting out harsh rulings. He continued his attacks on the Loyalists, sending parties into the mountains to break up Tory bands who committed murder and arson and stole horses, among other offenses. Cleveland reputedly hanged more Loyalists than any other individual in America. Supposedly, he once forced a Loyalist to cut off his own ears rather than hang—without evidence or trial.

At the Battle of Kings Mountain on 7 October 1780, Cleveland showed his personal courage as the Americans won an overwhelming victory. In the battle's aftermath, more than thirty Loyalists were condemned to die. Nine were hanged; the others were reprieved. The Tories had in the past burned houses, assaulted women, killed noncombatants, and generally engaged in the brutalities that characterized the southern theater—on both sides. The hangings were retaliation for the British hanging of eleven Americans at Fort Ninety-Six, South Carolina. The Battle of Kings Mountain established relative order to western North Carolina, but the war continued. At its end, Cleveland moved to South Carolina, where Cleveland County was named for him. He died at the breakfast table in October 1806.

John Barnhill

See also
Kings Mountain, Battle of; Loyalists; North Carolina

References

Arthur, John Preston. *Western North Carolina: A History from 1730 to 1913.* 3rd ed. Johnson City, TN: Overmountain, 1996.

Ashe, Samuel, Stephen B. Weeks, and Charles L. Van Noppen, eds. *Biographical History of North Carolina from Colonial Times to the Present.* Vol. 5. Greensboro, NC: Charles L. Van Noppen, 1906.

Cleveland, Vikki L. Jeanne. *Deeds of Glory: A Biography of Colonel Benjamin Cleveland,* http://www.angelfire.com/il/ClevelandFamilyChron/ColBen.html, 1993.

Clinton, George (1739–1812)

George Clinton served as the first governor of the independent State of New York under its new constitution from 1777 to 1795 and again from 1801 to 1804. He was one of three exceptionally effective governors—along with Jonathan Trumbull of Connecticut and William Livingston of New Jersey—who served as chief executives through virtually the entire Revolutionary War and, in Clinton's case, far beyond that conflict. He was also, along with Virginia's Patrick Henry and Massachusetts's John Hancock, one of the most popular governors in America during the Revolutionary era.

Clinton was born in 1739 in Little Britain, Ulster County, on what was then the New York frontier. He studied law in New York City under the eminent William Smith and returned to Ulster, where he farmed and practiced law. Clinton became clerk of the Ulster County Court in 1759, a sinecure he retained for the rest of his life. During the French and Indian (Seven Years') War, he served aboard a privateer in the Caribbean and fought as a subaltern in the militia during the campaign against Quebec. In 1770 he married Cornelia Tappen, thus connecting him to a prominent Ulster County Dutch family and securing a solid base of political support.

Clinton became a Patriot leader during the events leading to the Revolution and served in New York's Provincial Assembly, in the Provincial Congress, and in the Second Continental Congress, where he was an outspoken radical who opposed reconciliation and supported the Declaration of Independence. After being commissioned brigadier general commanding the militia brigade of Ulster and Orange counties, he left Congress before the New York Provincial Congress authorized its delegates to vote for independence. In August 1776 and January 1777, his command expanded to include the Westchester and Dutchess county militias, respectively. He was assigned the duty of fortifying the Highlands of the Hudson to block British navigation up the river, and in March 1777 Congress commissioned him a brigadier general in the Continental Line with command over Forts Montgomery and Clinton on the west bank of the Hudson.

George Clinton. He served as a representative for New York in the Second Continental Congress before leaving Philadelphia to command American troops along the Hudson River in 1776. He resumed his political life as governor of New York in July 1777, but was unable to halt the British advance north up the Hudson River in October of that year. (Library of Congress)

In July 1777 Clinton was unexpectedly elected both governor and lieutenant governor of New York under the newly adopted state constitution. He kept the former position and resigned the latter. The aristocratic General Philip Schuyler, the expected gubernatorial winner, grudgingly pledged support to Clinton, stating: "[his] family and connections do not entitle him to so distinguished a predominance." However, Schuyler admitted of Clinton: "[he is] virtuous and loves his country, has abilities and is brave." From this time forward, however, Clinton and Schuyler (who was later assisted by his powerful sons-in-law Alexander Hamilton and Stephen Van Rensselaer) were political enemies.

So long as the Revolutionary War was in progress, Clinton, like several other strong governors—Hancock in Massachusetts, Trumbull in Connecticut, Livingston in New Jersey, and Henry in Virginia—worked effectively with Congress, General

George Washington and the Continental Army, and state militia commanders to oppose and ultimately defeat Great Britain. With the coming of peace, however, Clinton perceived that New York was threatened by the actions of Congress and some of the neighboring states. While remaining strongly committed to the thirteen-state union, Clinton and his advisors advocated policies that benefited New York over the Confederation. When stronger powers for Congress would benefit New York—powers that would assist Congress in foreign affairs, especially in its efforts to remove British trade restrictions—Clinton endorsed such measures. In purely domestic matters, however, the governor put New York's concerns above all others. Later, Hamilton would refer to the governor's policies as "Clintonism." The success of Clintonism was manifested in 1786 when Clinton ran unopposed for a fourth consecutive three-year term as governor. Schuyler, who had unsuccessfully challenged Clinton's reelection in 1780 and 1783, sought in 1786 to convince John Jay, the Confederation's secretary of foreign affairs, to run for governor, but Jay understood that Clinton had done an admirable job and was unbeatable.

An increasingly well-organized statewide party, which became the core of New York's Republican (or Democratic-Republican) Party of the 1790s, backed the governor on issues dealing with the secession of Vermont from New York, the treatment of Loyalists and returning Loyalist exiles, the state's western lands, the British forts in northwestern New York, the generation of revenue through a state tariff, the restoration of a devastated economy through the use of a state loan office that issued paper money, and the payment of bounties and subsidies on various agricultural and manufactured goods. The state debt was funded with paper money that retained its par value, and much of the federal debt owed by New Yorkers was assumed by the state, making New York a creditor of the Confederation. By 1787, when other states eagerly welcomed the newly proposed U.S. Constitution in the hope that it would restore economic prosperity to the depression-ravaged country, New York was well along the road to recovery.

Governor Clinton's followers saw the new federal Constitution as another effort by non–New Yorkers and by anti-Clintonians within New York to unseat the governor and establish a more aristocratic government. A large majority of New Yorkers were prospering, and they liked the transformation of New York into the Empire State. Clintonism peaked in April 1788 when two-thirds of the delegates elected to New York's ratifying convention initially opposed the adoption of the U.S. Constitution. Clinton led the state's Antifederalists, writing the six "Cato" newspaper essays that instigated a lively public debate over the Constitution, and then served as president of the state's ratifying convention. Shortly after New Hampshire and Virginia became the ninth and tenth states to ratify the Constitution in June 1788, New York's Antifederalists, with Clinton's tacit consent, acquiesced to the emerging national decision. But in ratifying the Constitution, the state convention unanimously adopted a circular letter to the other states, signed by Clinton, that advocated a general convention of the states to propose constitutional amendments.

Clinton's opposition to the unamended Constitution catapulted him onto the national scene as the most prominent Antifederalist candidate for vice president in 1788–1789. Washington, a personal friend and business associate, would have been comfortable with Clinton as vice president, but Hamilton, who had strenuously opposed Clinton's postwar policies, lobbied unceasingly in New York and several other states against Clinton's candidacy. In New York, the legislature was to choose the presidential electors. The Federalist-controlled senate opposed the more numerous assembly's plan to select the electors by joint ballot. Because neither house would compromise, New York did not participate in the first presidential election, thereby denying Clinton a foundation to mount a campaign for the vice presidency. He received only three electoral votes, all from Virginia.

George Clinton, a delegate from New York to the Second Continental Congress, took up command of the defenses along the Hudson River but was unable to stem the British advance north from New York in 1777. (National Archives and Records Administration)

With the popularity of the newly ratified Constitution, Federalists saw an opportunity to gain control of New York's government in the spring elections of 1789. They chose the Clintonian Robert Yates, a state Supreme Court justice since 1777 who had voted against ratification in the state convention, to run against Clinton. The governor barely won reelection. Yet by 1791, Clinton had formed a new coalition that included many of his longtime supporters, the powerful Livingston family, and the supporters of Aaron Burr. This alliance maneuvered in the state legislature to defeat Schuyler's reelection to the U.S. Senate in 1791, replacing him with Burr.

Clinton again seemed to be a logical vice presidential opponent to Adams in 1792. Although Burr made a strong challenge, Thomas Jefferson and James Madison supported Clinton's candidacy. On 16 October 1792, Republican leaders from New York, Pennsylvania, Virginia, South Carolina, and perhaps Georgia met in Philadelphia and endorsed Clinton. His candidacy, however, was damaged by his controversial gubernatorial reelection to a sixth term in the spring of 1792, which was accomplished only by disallowing the votes of three counties on technicalities. In the national contest Clinton received the unanimous electoral votes of New York, Virginia, North Carolina, and Georgia but only one of fifteen Pennsylvania votes. He lost his bid for the vice presidency to Adams by a vote of 74 to 50.

In 1795, after eighteen years as governor, Clinton retired to private life. A year later, he refused an offer by Republican leaders to stand again for vice president. In the spring of 1800, however, Burr coaxed him out of retirement with the argument that New York's presidential electors would probably determine the presidential election later in the year. Since the electors were to be chosen by the state legislature, which would probably be controlled by whichever party won the New York City seats, it was imperative to run the most popular Republican candidates in this traditionally Federalist stronghold. Reluctantly, the thoroughly upstate leader Clinton stood for and was elected an assemblyman from New York City.

Clinton and Burr were the only serious Republican candidates for the vice presidency in 1800. While Clinton agreed only halfheartedly to stand for the position, Burr ardently sought and won the nomination. When Jefferson and Burr received the same number of electoral votes, Burr quietly attempted to win the election in the House of Representatives. Clinton and Hamilton, both of whom distrusted Burr, joined in opposing his election.

In 1801, Vice President Burr seemed ready to run for governor. To thwart him, Clinton agreed to stand for governor again and was elected. After serving as a figurehead for the three-year term dominated by his nephew DeWitt Clinton, George Clinton again attempted to retire, but President Jefferson asked Clinton to serve as his vice president. In February 1804, the Republican congressional caucus nominated Clinton for the position. In June 1804 the states adopted the Twelfth Amendment to the Constitution. Clinton became the first Republican candidate to run specifically for the vice presidency, and the Republican ticket overwhelmed its Federalist opponents by an electoral vote of 162 to 14.

In January 1808, the Republican congressional caucus nominated Secretary of State Madison for president and Clinton for vice president. Clinton's supporters, most of whom boycotted the meeting, condemned the caucus and strenuously worked for his election as president. Although strongly opposed to the administration's foreign policy and its failure to mobilize for war, Clinton remained silent. He did not declare himself a candidate for president, but he did not withdraw his name from consideration. At the same time, he neither accepted nor declined the caucus's vice presidential nomination. New England Federalists also considered endorsing Clinton as their presidential candidate, hoping that he would end the embargo on American trade. Republican electors, particularly in Virginia, had qualms about voting for Clinton as vice president because, in their judgment, he had turned his back on the party's nomination. Not wanting to diminish respect for the congressional caucus, however, Madison's backers supported Clinton. Madison won the presidential election by a vote of 122 to 47, and Clinton was reelected vice president by a vote of 113 to 47.

Throughout his tenure as vice president, Clinton opposed the foreign and defense policies of Jefferson and Madison. Many opponents of those policies clustered around Clinton, but he was too old and ill to provide effective leadership. Nor was he well suited to be vice president. He knew little about the protocol of presiding over the Senate, and his performance paled when compared with his masterful predecessor, Burr. On several occasions, however, Clinton cast the tie-breaking vote in the Senate, most significantly on 20 February 1811 when he voted against rechartering the Bank of the United States. Clinton died in office in Washington, D.C., on 20 April 1812 and was buried in the Congressional Cemetery. In 1908 his remains were reinterred in the cemetery of the Old Dutch Church in Kingston, New York.

John P. Kaminski

See also

Burr, Aaron; Constitution, United States; Constitution, United States, Ratification of; Hamilton, Alexander; Jay, John; New York, Province and State; Schuyler, Philip; Smith, William, II

References

Hastings, Harold, ed. *Public Papers of George Clinton.* 10 vols. New York: State of New York, 1899–1911.

Kaminski, John P. *George Clinton: Yeoman Politician of the Young Republic.* Madison, WI: Madison House, 1993.

Spaulding, E. Wilder. *His Excellency George Clinton: Critic of the Constitution.* New York: Macmillan, 1938.

Young, Alfred F. *The Democratic Republicans of New York: The Origins, 1763–1797.* Chapel Hill: University of North Carolina Press, 1967.

Clinton, Henry (1730–1795)

General Sir Henry Clinton served in the American colonies from 1775 to 1782, except for a brief return to London in the spring of 1777. He was second in command to General William Howe until the latter's resignation in 1778, when Clinton became commander in chief, a position he held until his resignation was accepted in the spring of 1782.

Clinton was born in 1730, probably on 16 April, the son of a naval captain, George Clinton. Henry's mother was the daughter of a general. She had six children, but Henry was the only surviving son. He had some powerful connections: he was a nephew of the 8th Earl of Lincoln and a first cousin of the 2nd Duke of Newcastle. George Clinton (who should not be confused with the governor of New York by the same name) moved his family to that colony in September 1743. Thus Henry Clinton began his military career in colonial New York.

Clinton served for a year in the militia on Manhattan and the following year was commissioned a captain. In 1749, he sailed for England to look for advancement and sought the help of the 1st Duke of Newcastle. In November 1751, Clinton was commissioned a lieutenant in the 2nd (Coldstream) Guards. By 1756 he had obtained a post as aide-de-camp to Sir John Ligonier (in 1757 Lord Ligonier was made commander in chief of the British Army). In 1758, Clinton became a lieutenant-colonel in the 1st Regiment of Foot Guards. Two years later his regiment was sent to Germany to serve under Lord Granby. Clinton obtained Granby's permission to volunteer for service in the allied corps commanded by Charles, Hereditary Prince of Brunswick (later Duke of Brunswick). Clinton became the prince's aide-de-camp. Both men were wounded at the Battle of Friedberg in 1762. Clinton won promotion to full colonel on 24 June 1763. He returned to England and in 1764 became groom of the bedchamber to William Henry, the Duke of Gloucester, a position Clinton held for many years.

In 1767 he married Harriet Carter, whose parents were of the landed gentry. They had five children. She died in 1772 at age twenty-six, eight days after the birth of her second daughter. Harriet's death was a devastating blow to Clinton. He brought his wife's family into his house: her father became like a second father to Clinton, and her two sisters took charge of rearing the children.

Meanwhile, Clinton's career had advanced with his promotion to major-general in 1772, just a few months before his wife's death. He was also elected as a member of Parliament. He set out on a six-month trip to the Balkans to observe Russian preparations for war against the Turks. Upon his return, he was almost at once involved in a parliamentary election as a candidate for one of the Duke of Newcastle's boroughs.

Lieutenant-General Sir Henry Clinton, commander in chief of British forces in North America (1778–1782). Although he forced the surrender of an entire American army at Charleston in 1780, he was blamed for the capitulation of his own subordinate, General Charles Cornwallis, at Yorktown the following year. (Library of Congress)

Although successful in the election, Clinton's political career was interrupted when his regiment was ordered to North America in February 1775. On 20 April he left from Portsmouth aboard the *Cerberus.* Generals William Howe and John Burgoyne were on the same ship. They landed in Boston on 25 May.

It was there in North America that Clinton's military career began to unfold. He stressed the point that unlike most British officers, he had received his early experience in campaigns in Germany. As a strategist, he had a sharp appreciation that Britain could best win in the colonies by making good use of the navy and that the best base of operations would be Manhattan and the Hudson River, not Boston. As a tactician, he leaned toward enveloping his adversary with attacks from two or more directions rather than by frontal assault. This type of thinking can be seen time and time again in North America, beginning at Breed's Hill at the Battle of Bunker Hill.

Clinton proposed landing in the front and rear of Breed's Hill to cut off the rebels' escape. His advice was not heeded. Instead, the British launched two frontal assaults that cost them half of their force in killed and wounded. Clinton intervened at a critical moment to lead a final (and successful) attack against Breed's Hill and then up Bunker Hill. He later advised the seizure of Dorchester Heights, which overlooked the city of Boston—and on which the rebels would later mount artillery dragged down from Fort Ticonderoga. Again his advice was ignored, and his prediction that the rebels could force the British to evacuate Boston was fulfilled.

In September 1775 Clinton became second in command when Howe superseded General Thomas Gage as commander in chief in North America. At first Howe and Clinton were on good terms, but that situation would change. Indeed, the cordiality and generosity of their relationship began to deteriorate within a few short months. Much of the problem was Clinton's personality, which was prickly and quarrelsome. He saw injury and insult where there was none and typically blamed others when things went wrong. He could see strategic factors clearly, and his tactical planning was often superior to that of others. But he wanted to give advice as a subordinate, and he sulked when his advice was not taken.

As commander in chief, Clinton's planning became cautious, unlike what it had been as a subordinate. This factor owed to a certain lack of assurance and self-confidence in his personality. Over a prolonged period he quarreled with almost all the officers of equivalent or junior rank with whom he served. Indeed, Clinton's inability to work well with other officers doomed many of his superior plans to failure. This behavior, too, would become habitual in his career.

In October of 1775 the British government decided to send an expedition to the southern colonies to support the Loyalists in an attempt to reestablish royal government. For the expedition, Howe appointed Clinton to lead a force of 1,200 to 1,500 men to the Cape Fear River in North Carolina. There he was to meet with a naval force and troops coming from Britain.

Success of the expedition depended on exquisite timing, which of course was difficult to establish across an ocean and in an age of sail. Clinton and his force left Boston on 20 January 1776. After shipboard consultations in New York Harbor with colonial delegations and with the Virginia governor at Hampton Roads, Clinton went south to Cape Fear. There he discovered that the Loyalist Highlanders from the backcountry had risen prematurely and been destroyed at Moore's Creek Bridge.

Now Clinton's force waited for the British fleet, under Admiral Sir Peter Parker, to appear off Charleston Bar, which it did on 1 June. General Charles Cornwallis, who was eight years younger than Clinton, was commander of the troops sent from Britain. After consultations, the decision was made to land on Long Island, to the north of Sullivan's Island, where the pilots assured them that the channel to its south was only eighteen inches deep. In fact, the water was seven feet deep, and the landing was a disaster for the British. After sustaining a battering from American guns, the grounded ships, which the tide finally refloated, reembarked the troops and returned to New York. It had been Clinton's first independent command. He wanted to be certain that he was not saddled with responsibility for the fiasco and began a letter-writing campaign.

Meanwhile, Howe, who had evacuated Boston, planned to attack the rebels on Long Island, New York. He would sail to New York, where he would meet Clinton's force and an army sent from Britain. By August 1776, Howe had 30,000 regulars, backed by ten ships of the line and twenty frigates under Admiral Richard Howe, his older brother. General Howe had landed his 9,000 troops on Staten Island, where he was joined by the reinforcements from Britain as well as Clinton's small force and Parker's fleet. The British outnumbered General George Washington's forces three to two and controlled the water on all sides of Manhattan. The Americans were in desperate straits.

By 22 August, Howe had concentrated his forces on Long Island. He actually adopted most of Clinton's plan of attack, which was for a double envelopment that would surround the rebels in their location in Brooklyn. Although the attack achieved what was intended, Howe did not press it, instead insisting on a siege. Then two days later the weather turned against the British, and a fog allowed the rebel army to escape from Brooklyn to Manhattan. Now Clinton once more pressed for an envelopment movement that would cut off the rebels' retreat via northern Manhattan and enable the British to capture the American army. His plan was rejected. The British took the ground (Manhattan), but the American army remained a force with which Howe would have to contend.

In December, Clinton took charge of an expedition against Newport, Rhode Island, that was intended to gain a secure anchorage for the British fleet. Strangely, he made no effort to employ the envelopment method that he had urged in the past. The rebels escaped to the north. A Christmas Eve snowstorm ended all further winter hostilities.

Clinton now returned to England, intending—as he saw it—to set the record straight with regard to Sullivan's Island. Since the king would not allow Clinton to resign, he wanted some reward to show that he enjoyed the government's commendation. The government agreed to a solution with Clinton: if he would return to America as second to Howe and not publish his account of Sullivan's Island (which was critical of the Royal Navy's role), he would be awarded a knighthood. On 11 April 1777 while still in London, Clinton received his knighthood.

He sailed for New York on 29 April and arrived in early July. By then Howe had changed his plan of attack on Philadelphia from an overland to a seaborne campaign. Worse, from Clinton's point of view, was his discovery that Howe was leaving him to defend New York and adjacent posts with a force of only 7,700 men, half of them provincials. With Howe's army taking a roundabout route to Philadelphia by sea, Washington would be free to attack either New York or Burgoyne up the Hudson.

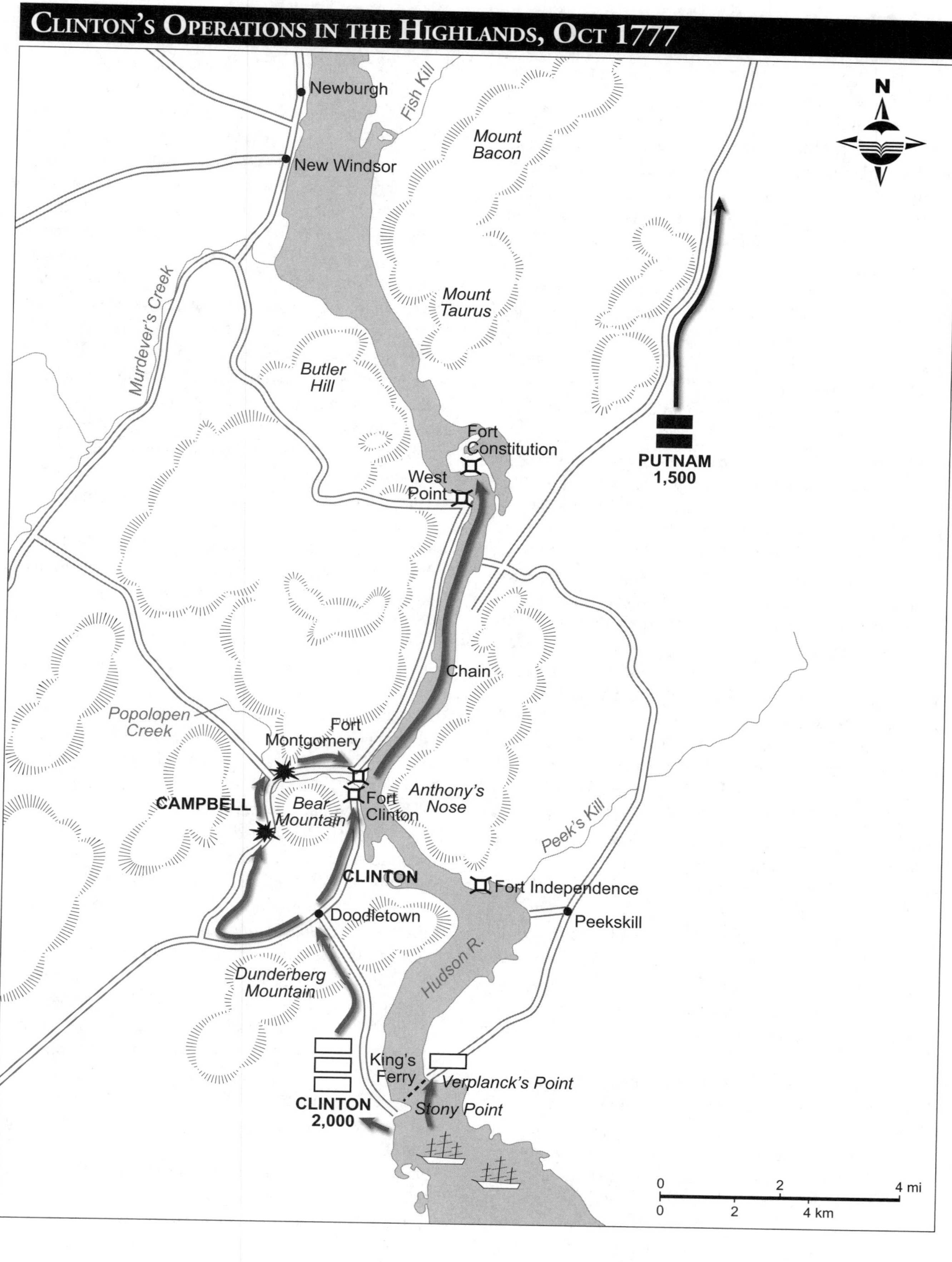
Clinton's Operations in the Highlands, Oct 1777
N
Newburgh
Fish Kill
Mount Bacon
New Windsor
Mount Taurus
Murdever's Creek
Butler Hill
Fort Constitution
West Point
PUTNAM 1,500
Chain
Popolopen Creek
Fort Montgomery
CAMPBELL
Bear Mountain
Fort Clinton
Anthony's Nose
Peek's Kill
CLINTON
Fort Independence
Doodletown
Peekskill
Hudson R.
Dunderberg Mountain
King's Ferry
Verplanck's Point
Stony Point
CLINTON 2,000
0 2 4 mi
0 2 4 km

On 16 August, Burgoyne lost 500 of his regulars at the Battle of Bennington. Clinton viewed the defense of New York as his chief obligation. He could not afford to send troops away unless Burgoyne requested aid. Burgoyne did just that, but too late for Clinton to render successful aid. When Burgoyne's request came, Clinton had at last received the long-expected reinforcements from Europe. He moved with commendable speed to put 3,000 troops on shipboard under a force commanded by Commodore William Hotham. The British forces reached their objective—the forts in the Highlands on the western side of the Hudson River—and took both forts, winning the Highlands by 6 October. However, Burgoyne sued for peace on 14 October and surrendered his entire force three days later. On the same day Clinton received orders from General Howe to send 4,000 troops to him at once. Clinton returned to New York and asked Howe for leave. But he was too late, since four days before Howe had already submitted his own resignation.

On 4 February 1778 Lord George Germain wrote to accept Howe's resignation and to tell Clinton that he was now commander in chief. As commander, Clinton put bold moves behind him. His position would be further imperiled by the French announcement of its Treaty of Amity and Commerce with the United States on 13 March. Since Spain was expected to enter the war on France's side, British naval superiority in American waters became dubious. The first lord of the Admiralty, John Montagu, Lord Sandwich, was committed above all else to the defense of the Channel and was loath to detach ships from the Home Fleet. Soon the loss of naval superiority in America would spell defeat for Britain.

On 8 May 1778, Clinton arrived in Philadelphia to carry out the evacuation of that capital city. So many Loyalists took passage to New York on the transports that there remained too little space for the army, cavalry horses, baggage, and supplies. Clinton therefore marched to New York. He also delayed sending expeditions, amounting to 8,000 troops, to St. Lucia and Florida, which was fortunate for the British.

The retreat from Philadelphia began on 18 June. The baggage train was 12 miles long. On 28 June Clinton fought the Battle of Monmouth against Washington's forces. Heat and exhaustion were the arbiters of the conflict, which was indecisive. It was the only battle in which Clinton commanded. The British continued their march to Sandy Hook and were ferried to New York by 5 July.

Once Admiral Jean-Baptiste d'Estaing arrived at Rhode Island at the end of July, the next several months were filled with naval maneuvering. On 3 November, Clinton sent Major-General James Grant with 5,000 men, escorted by Hotham, to the British West Indies, where in December they invested St. Lucia just before the arrival of d'Estaing.

The year 1779 was one of relative inactivity, but it was full of portent for the future. Both Cornwallis and Admiral Marriot Arbuthnot (with whom Clinton would quarrel) arrived at New York, and Clinton decided upon the assault on Charleston, which would divide the British Army into two parts at the same time that the British lost naval control.

Clinton joined Arbuthnot at Sandy Hook on 25 December 1779, and the fleet put to sea the next day. After a stormy passage, they reached Simmons Island, southwest of Charleston, on 14 February 1780. Now Clinton revealed the same sort of tactical planning that he had recommended for Manhattan: Charleston was in many ways analogous in that the city proper was at the end of a long, thin neck and surrounded by water. The army landed and marched around to come upon Charleston Neck from the north. There Clinton erected siege lines that prevented an escape by the "back door" (which had happened on Manhattan). The navy would prevent escape or resupply by the "front door." After bombardments of the city by the British, the American commander, General Benjamin Lincoln, surrendered on 12 May. For Clinton, this was a triumph. On 3 June, he issued a proclamation requiring everyone to take an oath or be treated as a rebel. Then he sailed north, leaving Cornwallis in command in the south.

Over the course of the next year, Clinton tried in vain to win support for his opinions from Germain, feuded with Arbuthnot, and had little communication with and even less control over Cornwallis. Indeed, Clinton did not make clear to Cornwallis what he wanted. Finally, in July 1781, Clinton's order to take a post at the Chesapeake reached Cornwallis. At the same time, in June, Clinton urged Admiral George Rodney, who was in the British West Indies, to come north to command the fleet in American waters, but Rodney was ill and went home to England. Thus, Arbuthnot was succeeded by Admiral Thomas Graves rather than by the more aggressive Rodney. The road to Yorktown was now marked out.

The French naval forces under François de Grasse and Jacques de Barras had joined in the Chesapeake. Washington and the comte de Rochambeau were marching toward Yorktown, though Cornwallis did not know it. In the middle of September, at the urging of Lieutenant-Colonel Banastre Tarleton, Cornwallis planned an attack to break out of his box, but at that very moment he received Clinton's letter that relief would arrive soon. Clinton had no great sense of urgency because he said that Cornwallis had enough provisions to hold out until the end of October. But his fortifications were not sufficiently finished to hold out that long. Rear Admiral Robert Digby, senior to Graves and intended as successor to Arbuthnot, arrived on 24 September but insisted that Graves retain command for the coming effort. Meanwhile, the fleet continued to refit. Just as the fleet left Sandy Hook, on 19 October, Cornwallis surrendered. The shooting war was over.

Not over, however, was Clinton's battle of the pen. While still in New York, he had published a pamphlet containing his correspondence with Cornwallis. In Britain in 1783, he had published his *Narrative of His Campaigns,* which was an attempt to justify his military campaigns. Then he fought another paper battle against the commissioners of Public Accounts, whose praise of the economy of Cornwallis's military system marked by implication, Clinton thought, the laxness of his own.

Clinton's military career was over. In the spring of 1782 he received Germain's dispatch accepting his resignation. His successor, Sir Guy Carleton, arrived on 5 May. Clinton's appointment as governor of Gibraltar in May 1794 was one that he never went to take up, citing reasons of health. He died in England in December 1795.

Mary B. Wickwire

See also

Barras, Jacques Melchoir, Comte de; Bunker Hill, Battle of; Burgoyne, John; Carleton, Guy; Charleston, South Carolina, Expedition against (1776); Charleston, South Carolina, Expedition against (1780); Clinton-Cornwallis Dispute; Cornwallis, Charles; Dorchester Heights, Massachusetts; Estaing, Jean-Baptiste, Comte d'; Fort Ticonderoga, New York; Gage, Thomas; Germain, Lord George; Grant, James; Grasse, François-Joseph-Paul, Comte de; Graves, Thomas; Howe, Richard; Howe, William; Hudson River and the Hudson Highlands; Lincoln, Benjamin; Long Island, Battle of; Monmouth, Battle of; Moore's Creek Bridge, North Carolina, Action at; New York, Operations in; Rhode Island, Battle of; Rodney, George; St. Lucia, Naval and Military Operations against; Tarleton, Banastre; Vimeur, Jean-Baptiste, Comte de Rochambeau; Yorktown, Virginia, Siege of; Yorktown Campaign

References

Billias, George A., ed. *George Washington's Generals and Opponents: Their Exploits and Leadership.* Reprint. New York: Da Capo, 1994.

Bowler, R. Arthur. *Logistics and the Failure of the British Army in America, 1775–1783.* Princeton, NJ: Princeton University Press, 1975.

Christie, Ian R. *The End of North's Ministry, 1780–1782.* London: Macmillan, 1958.

Clinton, Henry. *The American Rebellion: Sir Henry Clinton's Narrative of His Campaigns, 1775–1782, with an Appendix of Original Documents.* Edited by William B. Willcox. New Haven, CT: Yale University Press, 1954.

Stevens, Benjamin F., ed. *The Campaign in Virginia: An Exact Reprint of Six Rare Pamphlets on the Clinton-Cornwallis Controversy.* 2 vols. London: n.p., 1888.

Syrett, David. *Shipping and the American War, 1775–83: A Study of British Transport Organization.* London: Athlone, 1970.

Valentine, Alan. *Lord George Germain.* Oxford: Oxford University Press, 1962.

Willcox, William B. *Portrait of a General: Sir Henry Clinton in the War of Independence.* New York: Knopf, 1964.

Clinton, James (1733–1812)

James Clinton, a brigadier general in the Continental Army, was born in Little Britain, Ulster County, New York. As a militia captain in the French and Indian War, he served in the campaign against Fort Frontenac in 1758. By 1775 he was a lieutenant colonel and represented Ulster County in New York's First Provincial Congress in May. In March 1776 he was commissioned colonel in the New York line and served in the disastrous Canada Campaign. After returning to New York, he was commissioned brigadier general in the Continental Army in August 1776. For a time, he assisted his younger brother George in fortifying the Hudson Highlands and then was assigned to Albany under General Philip Schuyler. Schuyler told General George Washington: "[I have] a high Respect for [Clinton], as a Friend and a Citizen; and althou' I believe him to be a brave Officer, yet he is amazingly slow and I believe no Disciplinarian."

James Clinton. A brigadier general in the Continental Army, he received a bayonet wound during his unsuccessful defense of Fort Montgomery on the Hudson River in 1777. He played a significant part in Sullivan's expedition against the Iroquois in 1779 and led the brigade at the siege of Yorktown that received the captured British colors. (National Archives and Records Administration)

When George Clinton was elected governor of New York in 1777, James, against the wishes of Schuyler, was reassigned to defend the Highlands. Alexander Hamilton, although recommending Clinton for the position, concurred with Schuyler's concern over Clinton's lack of energy. When Governor Clinton rejoined the army temporarily to resist Sir Henry Clinton's assault up the Hudson in October 1777, James Clinton commanded Fort Clinton while his brother commanded Fort Montgomery, both on the west bank of the

Hudson on opposite sides of Popolopen Creek. When attacked by an overwhelming force of Britons, Hessians, and Loyalists, the 600 American defenders (mostly militia, half of whom had no firearms) fought stubbornly and then evacuated. Despite a bayonet wound, James Clinton was able to escape under cover of darkness.

In November 1778, Clinton was ordered to Albany to fight against Indians and Loyalists harassing the frontier. From May through November 1779 he was second in command to Major General John Sullivan in the punitive campaign against the Iroquois in western New York. The joint expedition fought no major battles with the Indians, led by Joseph Brant, and their Loyalist allies, but on its 140-mile march west to the Genesee River and return through the Finger Lake area, the American force destroyed forty Iroquois towns and their crops, livestock, and orchards and so disrupted the Indians that their marauding attacks on the frontier ended, at least temporarily. Quartermaster General Nathanael Greene reported that the expedition had "returned victorious almost without seeing an Enemy."

In 1780 Clinton assumed command of the Northern Department of the army, headquartered at Albany, which protected the northern New York frontier from Indian and Loyalist attacks. In 1781 he led a brigade of more than 1,100 men to Virginia, where he was attached to Major General Benjamin Lincoln's division at the siege of Yorktown. Clinton's brigade received the surrendered British colors. Clinton protested in 1782 when Congress twice passed him over for promotion even though he was the ranking brigadier general. By a general order of Congress in 1783, he was breveted a major general.

After the war, Clinton went back to Ulster County and farmed; he resided in New Windsor and owned thirteen slaves. In 1785 he served on the commission to settle the boundary dispute between New York and Pennsylvania. Three years later, representing Ulster County in the state convention, he voted against ratifying the proposed U.S. Constitution. As a supporter of his brother, he served for a time in both the state assembly and senate in the late 1780s. By this time his son, DeWitt Clinton, had become secretary to the governor. James Clinton died in Ulster County in 1812.

John P. Kaminski

See also

Brant, Joseph; Canada, Operations in; Clinton, George; Clinton, Henry; Fort Clinton, New York; Fort Montgomery, New York, Assault on; Greene, Nathanael; Hamilton, Alexander; Hudson River and the Hudson Highlands; Lincoln, Benjamin; Schuyler, Philip; Sullivan, John; Yorktown, Virginia, Siege of

References

Diamant, Lincoln. *Chaining the Hudson: The Fight for the River in the American Revolution.* Secaucus, NJ: Lyle Stuart, 1989.

Twohig, Dorothy, et al. *The Papers of George Washington: Revolutionary War Series,* Vol. 8. Charlottesville: University of Virginia Press, 1985–.

Clinton-Cornwallis Dispute (1781–1784)

Military strategy was the major point of contention between Sir Henry Clinton, British commander in chief of the British forces in America (1778–1782), and Lord Charles Cornwallis, his second in command. The root of the discord stemmed directly from Cornwallis's belief that he was the better general and that British victory would be achieved if he was given the freedom to conduct the war as he saw fit. Clinton, for his part, regarded his subordinate as prone to taking risky and unnecessary gambles. These differences of opinion led to quarrels, insulting letters, and bitter feelings between the two generals during and after the war.

Shortly after taking command, Clinton evacuated Philadelphia and concentrated his forces at New York. From his base of operations, he launched a successful attack on the southern colonies in 1780. Soon after the fall of Charleston, South Carolina, in May, Clinton returned to New York, leaving Cornwallis in command of the area with orders to hold Georgia and South Carolina. In November 1780, however, Cornwallis invaded North Carolina, and in June 1781 he marched his troops into Virginia.

Once in Virginia, Cornwallis tried to persuade Clinton to evacuate New York and concentrate the entire British Army in Virginia as well. Clinton did not agree. Instead, he ordered Cornwallis to move his army to Yorktown. In September, Cornwallis became trapped as George Washington and the French coordinated a successful land and sea attack. Heavy bombardment, which reduced Yorktown to rubble, led to a British surrender on 19 October. Ironically, the surrender took place on the same day that Clinton and 7,000 British troops set sail in an attempt to relieve Cornwallis. By the time Clinton arrived on 24 October, however, it was too late. The British defeat at Yorktown turned out to be the last major land battle of the American Revolution.

After the war, a pamphlet battle ensued in which each general blamed the other for the British defeat at Yorktown. After the defeat, Clinton resigned and was replaced by Sir Guy Carleton. Parliament began a formal inquiry into the Yorktown fiasco, and since Clinton had been the commanding general in the colonies during the defeat, he was held responsible for the failure. On the other hand, Cornwallis, the general who surrendered at Yorktown, was not held responsible, and the British government continued to place Cornwallis in positions of trust. In the years that followed, Cornwallis served as governor-general and viceroy of India and lord-lieutenant and commander in chief in Ireland. In 1792 he was created a marquis.

The Clinton-Cornwallis controversy raised several questions: Was Cornwallis's decision to invade Virginia in disregard of Clinton's orders to hold Georgia and South Carolina? Was Clinton's decision not to reinforce Cornwallis in Virginia, at the expense of evacuating New York, a mistake? Was the decision to make Yorktown Cornwallis's headquarters a mistake? Was Cornwallis constrained by Clinton to occupy Yorktown? Was the British defeat at Yorktown Clinton's fault because he delayed in coming to Cornwallis's aid?

Any historian who writes about this time period must contend with these questions. However, in more than two centuries of examination, historians have failed to come to a consensus. Consequently, the pamphlet dispute that began between Clinton and Cornwallis so many years ago has been transformed into an ongoing dispute among historians. The central question still remains the same: Who should be held responsible for the British defeat?

Rolando Avila

See also

Carleton, Guy; Charleston, South Carolina, Expedition against (1780); Clinton, Henry; Cornwallis, Charles; Southern Campaigns; Yorktown, Virginia, Siege of; Yorktown Campaign

References

Chidsey, Donald Barr. *Victory at Yorktown.* New York: Crown, 1962.
Fleming, Thomas. *Liberty: The American Revolution.* New York: Viking Penguin, 1997.
Stevens, Benjamin F., ed. *The Campaign in Virginia: An Exact Reprint of Six Rare Pamphlets on the Clinton-Cornwallis Controversy.* 2 vols. London: n.p., 1888.

Clymer, George (1739–1813)

A merchant, member of the Continental Congress, signer of both the Declaration of Independence and the U.S. Constitution, and a member of the first U.S. Congress, George Clymer, a Pennsylvania native, was one of the wealthiest figures of the Revolutionary era and one of the principal financiers of the American Revolution. Clymer earned his fortune through a successful shipping business headquartered in Philadelphia. As a merchant, he was hostile to the frequent British efforts to control the colonial economy through taxes, tariffs, and restrictions on trade. This hostility eventually translated into a keen desire for independence and a major involvement in the establishment of the new nation. Without the financing of individuals such as Clymer, the success of the Revolutionary War would have been in serious doubt.

Beginning in the early 1770s, Clymer began to take an active role in Pennsylvania's colonial government, in which he displayed an increasingly separatist attitude. In 1775, as Pennsylvania's government became radicalized, Clymer joined its Committee of Safety and quickly became the key member of this small body, which essentially ran the province in its last year before independence. In the same year he was appointed one of the two Continental treasurers responsible for managing the finances of the Continental Congress. In 1776, he was elected to Congress, where he became a part of the Pennsylvania delegation's one-vote majority that approved the Declaration of Independence. During the war with Britain, he helped to organize financial support for the army and continued to manage the fiscal affairs of the Continental Congress.

After the American victory, Clymer was one of the delegates chosen to represent Pennsylvania in the Constitutional Convention, where he was considered part of the nationalist faction that supported increased federal power and included fellow Pennsylvanians James Wilson, Benjamin Franklin, Gouverneur Morris, and Robert Morris. While Clymer does not figure prominently in the accounts of the convention debates, his financial expertise and political experience surely influenced the other delegates. Once the Constitution had been approved by the convention, Clymer became one of the members of the Pennsylvania convention that considered and ratified the document. While his fellow signer Wilson took the lead in making speeches that promoted ratification in Pennsylvania, Clymer helped organize support among the merchants and financial leaders in Philadelphia and its vicinity.

William E. Doody

See also

Congress, Second Continental and Confederation; Constitution, United States; Declaration of Independence Signers; Pennsylvania; Wilson, James

References

Bradford, M. E. *A Worthy Company: Brief Lives of the Framers of the United States Constitution.* Marlborough, NH: Plymouth Rock Foundation, 1982.
Grundfest, Jerry. *George Clymer: Philadelphia Revolutionary, 1739–1813.* New York: Beaufort Books, 1982.
Ryerson, Richard A. *The Revolution Is Now Begun: The Radical Committees of Philadelphia, 1765–1776.* Philadelphia: University of Pennsylvania Press, 1978.

Cochran, John (1730–1807)

A doctor in the Continental Army and a close associate of Dr. William Shippen, John Cochran joined Shippen in proposing a reform of the army medical services and became chief of the army's medical services toward the end of the American Revolutionary War.

Cochran was born to Irish parents in Sadsbury, Pennsylvania, in 1730. He began his education with Dr. Francis Allison; studied medicine with doctors in Lancaster, Pennsylvania; and increased his medical expertise by serving with the British Army as a surgeon's mate during the Seven Years' War. Cochran married in 1760 and moved to New Brunswick, New Jersey, in 1763, where he helped found the New Jersey Medical Society in 1766.

At the beginning of the Revolutionary War, Cochran joined the Continental Army as a doctor. The army's medical services at the beginning of the war were a mess. The situation was not helped by the fact that the first head of the medical services, Dr. Benjamin Church, turned out to be loyal to the British. His replacement, Dr. John Morgan, became involved in fights between individual regimental surgeons and supervisory personnel, such as himself, over who should control the medical services. Morgan was replaced by Dr. William Shippen, who also spent a lot of time and energy fighting both the regimental doctors and Dr. Benjamin Rush, his rival for the position.

On 14 February 1777, Cochran and Shippen submitted a plan they had developed for reorganizing the Continental Army's medical department. Congress approved the plan on 7 April 1777 and appointed Cochran physician and surgeon general in the Middle Department. There Cochran focused on his duties as a medical director and not on political maneuvering like some of the other physicians. For the remainder of the war he labored to improve the operations of military hospitals and the conditions of the sick and wounded. On 17 January 1781, Congress promoted him to the top position in the medical services of the Continental Army. On 11 April 1783, Cochran resigned his post and left the army.

After the war Cochran moved to New York City, and in 1790 President George Washington appointed him to the position of commissioner of loans. Cochran later suffered a stroke and retired to Palatine, New York, where he died in 1807.

Dallace W. Unger Jr.

See also

Church, Benjamin; Continental Army; Morgan, John; Rush, Benjamin; Shippen, William

References

Blanco, Richard L., ed. *The American Revolution, 1775–1783: An Encyclopedia.* New York: Garland, 1993.

Boatner, Mark. *Encyclopedia of the American Revolution.* Mechanicsburg, PA: Stackpole, 1994.

Purcell, L. Edward. *Who Was Who in the American Revolution.* New York: Facts On File, 1993.

Coercive Acts (March–June 1774)

The Coercive Acts, also known as the Intolerable Acts, were a series of punitive acts passed by Parliament between March and June 1774 in response to the Boston Tea Party. They represented Britain's immediate and forceful attempt to quell the continued colonial opposition to imperial policy and demonstrated a hardening of British attitudes toward American recalcitrance. Although intended to isolate and subdue malcontents in Boston as an example to all other British colonies, the Coercive Acts effectively rallied British North America to the plight of Massachusetts, undermined royal authority in a dozen colonies, and eventually provoked open rebellion.

British political cartoon, circa 1774, shows Bostonians held captive in a cage suspended from the "Liberty Tree." Three British sailors standing in a boat feed them fish in return for a bundle of papers labeled "Promises." Around the tree and in the background are cannons and British troops. (Library of Congress)

When reports of the Boston Tea Party reached London in January 1774, many British officials were outraged. On 7 March 1774, a royal message to Parliament called for a more vigorous execution of the law and a more secure dependence of the colonies on the mother country. Unable to prosecute those directly responsible for the Boston Tea Party because of a lack of evidence, Prime Minister Lord North decided to punish both the port of Boston and the province of Massachusetts with several new statutes. Despite warnings from several members of Parliament, notably William Pitt the Elder and Edmund Burke, that punitive legislation would unite the colonies behind Massachusetts and that the measures proposed were harmful and oppressive of American rights, a large majority of Parliament supported the passage of North's legislation.

The first law to be introduced and passed, in March 1774, was the Boston Port Act. This closed the port of Boston, beginning 1 June 1774, to all commercial trade except for necessary food and fuel for the city's inhabitants carried by vessels involved in the coastal trade and military supplies for British troops. The Royal Navy would enforce the law until compensation was paid to the East India Company for the tea thrown into Boston Harbor. Parliament stipulated that the harbor would remain closed until the government decided that the province had sufficiently obeyed the law and that trade could enter the port safely. The Boston Port Act effectively threatened Boston's economic survival because of the city's almost total reliance on shipping and commerce. An additional cause of concern for the colonists was the arrival of a new royal governor of Massachusetts to enforce the law: the commander of British forces in North America, General Thomas Gage.

Parliament passed two more acts in May 1774. The Massachusetts Government Act, the most radical of all the Coercive Acts, unilaterally altered the province's 1694 charter to bring its government more effectively under royal control. It ended the right of the province's lower house to nominate members of the Governor's Council, which would be henceforth appointed by the Crown; expanded the power of the governor to appoint and remove judges, sheriffs, and other law enforcement officials without the consent of the council; restricted town meetings to convening only once a year and only to elect their provincial representatives and pass their annual budgets, unless granted permission by the governor to meet at other times and for other purposes; and granted the power to summon juries, which had been exercised by locally elected constables, to the appointed sheriffs. Through this bill, Parliament effectively curtailed the power of local government and increased the governor's ability to suppress disorder and enforce British authority.

The third new law was the Administration of Justice Act. This measure stated that any British official or soldier who was charged with a capital offense committed while enforcing the authority of the Crown, including suppressing riots, could be extradited, by the authority of the governor, to England or to another colony in order to ensure a fair trial. The colonists saw this act as granting royal officials and military officers a free hand in imposing their will and ensuring that their oppressive actions would go unpunished.

The last of the Coercive Acts proper was a revision of the Quartering Act of 1765. The initial act had required each colonial government to provide sufficient housing and supplies for British troops stationed within its province. The revised act of June 1774 augmented the responsibility of every province and was potentially more intrusive. It stated that if a province did not provide suitable barracks or that if the quarters that were provided were too distant from any scenes of disturbance or disorder, troops would be quartered in conveniently located uninhabited buildings for as long as necessary. The act did not require the billeting of soldiers in occupied private homes, as many colonists claimed. However, Americans detested the Quartering Act and viewed it as an unjust indirect tax and a violation of their personal property rights.

An additional act, the Quebec Act, is sometimes included among the Coercive Acts, although it was not primarily intended to punish or control British colonists. Passed by Parliament in June 1774 to better organize and administer Canadian territory, the statute extended the boundaries of the province of Quebec southward to the Ohio River and westward to the Mississippi River. The act was an attempt by Parliament to replace a vast military district that had existed since Britain's conquest of Canada in 1760 with a civil government. It established a governmental structure controlled by a governor and council appointed by the Crown; recognized French civil law, not English common law, as the province's legal foundation; and granted Catholics full civic rights. Many Protestant colonists, particularly in New England, bitterly opposed the act and further resented the British. British colonists deemed the measure threatening and despotic because the province lacked a representative assembly and its new borders essentially nullified the western land claims held by Massachusetts, Connecticut, and Virginia in the Ohio River Valley.

The colonial response to the Coercive Acts strengthened colonial unity and deepened the imperial crisis. Most American colonists believed that in passing the statutes, Parliament had gravely overstepped its authority and violated the natural rights of the colonists. Support for Massachusetts grew throughout the colonies, which sent food and supplies to Boston. The severity of the acts enabled radicals to coordinate and orchestrate the opposition to British authority through local committees of correspondence and provincial legislatures and conventions. These activities resulted in the First Continental Congress, in which delegates from twelve colonies met in Philadelphia to discuss ways of reversing the policy of the British government, with particular attention to the Coercive Acts. Following the lead established by the Suffolk Resolves in Massachusetts and resolutions in Virginia, Congress created the Continental Association to boycott British goods and agreed to the use of local militia to protect colonial rights by military means if necessary until the Coercive Acts and other imperial laws were repealed.

Peter S. Genovese Jr.

See also

Administration of Justice Act; Boston Port Act; Boston Tea Party; Congress, First Continental; Continental Association; Massachusetts; Massachusetts Government Act; North, Lord Frederick; Quartering Acts; Quebec Act; Suffolk Resolves

References

Ammerman, David. *In the Common Cause: American Response to the Coercive Acts of 1774.* New York: Norton, 1975.

Brown, Richard D. *Revolutionary Politics in Massachusetts: The Boston Committee of Correspondence and the Towns, 1772–1774.* Cambridge: Harvard University Press, 1970.

Reich, Jerome R. *British Friends of the American Revolution.* Armonk, NY: M. E. Sharpe, 1998.

Tiedemann, Joseph S. *Reluctant Revolutionaries: New York City and the Road to Independence, 1763–1776.* Ithaca, NY: Cornell University Press, 1997.

Coffin, John (1756–1838)

John Coffin, a Loyalist officer during the American Revolution and later a general in the British Army, was born in Boston, Massachusetts, the son of Nathaniel Coffin, the last receiver general and cashier of His Majesty's Customs in Boston. The Coffins were descended from a royalist officer, Tristram Coffin, who had immigrated to Nantucket after the English Civil War. John's younger brother, Isaac Coffin (1759–1839), entered the Royal Navy in 1773, eventually becoming an admiral, baronet, and member of the House of Commons.

John Coffin went to sea at an early age, and in 1775 he commanded a ship that brought a British regiment to Boston. Following his gallant service as a volunteer at Bunker Hill in June 1775, General Thomas Gage appointed him an ensign and later a lieutenant. Moving to New York in March 1776, Coffin raised a Loyalist regiment, the King's Orange Rangers, and fought at the battles of Long Island (1776) and Germantown (1777). Transferring to the New York Volunteers in 1778, he accompanied the unit to the South where he commanded its light infantry company at the capture of Savannah, Georgia, in December of that year. Coffin next raised a company of Loyalist cavalry and fought with great distinction at Hobkirk's Hill in April 1781 and at Eutaw Springs the following September. After the British surrender at Yorktown, Coffin, who had a price on his head, escaped through American lines and made his way to New York City. Promoted to major of the King's American Regiment, a unit placed on the regular establishment as the 4th American Regiment, he sailed with his regiment to Nova Scotia in December 1782. When the regiment was disbanded in October 1783, he was placed on half pay.

Awarded land grants in New Brunswick, Coffin and his South Carolina wife, Ann Mathews, established a large estate in King's County. A member of both the provincial assembly and the King's Council of New Brunswick, Coffin rose through the seniority system to become a lieutenant-general in the British Army in 1809. During the War of 1812 he raised the New Brunswick Fencibles but saw no action. When Coffin died in June 1838, he was the oldest general in the British Army. A distinguished Loyalist junior officer in the American Revolution, his loyalty to the king was never in doubt. Coffin's eldest son, Guy Carleton Coffin, became a general in the Royal Artillery, while two other sons, John and Henry Coffin, became admirals in the Royal Navy.

Rory T. Cornish

See also

Associated Loyalists; Bunker Hill, Battle of; Eutaw Springs, Battle of; Gage, Thomas; Germantown, Battle of; Greene, Nathanael; Hobkirk's Hill, Battle of; Long Island, Battle of; Savannah, Georgia, British Capture of; Southern Campaigns; Yorktown, Virginia, Siege of

References

Pancake, John S. *This Destructive War: The British Campaign for the Carolinas, 1780–1782.* University: University of Alabama Press, 1985.

Stark, James H. *The Loyalists of Massachusetts and the Other Side of the American Revolution.* 1907. Reprint, Bowie, MD: Heritage Books, 1988.

Combahee River, South Carolina, Action at (27 August 1782)

The engagement at Combahee River was a skirmish between British troops foraging for food and a Continental force based southwest of Charleston, the last British post in South Carolina. By 1782 the remaining British forces in South Carolina were penned up in Charleston, while the Southern Continental Army of General Nathanael Greene controlled virtually all the territory outside of the city. On 27 August 1782, the British dispatched between 300 and 500 men in eighteen small vessels to the head of the Combahee River, approximately 50 miles southwest of Charleston, to seize rice and other crops that the locals had refused to sell to them. Good intelligence sources within Charleston alerted the Patriots, and General Mordecai Gist moved approximately 300 infantry and cavalry to intercept the British.

The British landed on the south bank of the Combahee River to forage. Most of the crops in the area, however, had already been acquired by Patriot forces operating out of Georgia. The British found little edible food and could not cross to the north bank to continue their search because of the presence of Gist's men. Gist, on the other hand, lacked the means to cross the river and attack the British force at that point. He ordered his cavalry to cross a bridge located 10 miles upriver and circle behind the British while dispatching Colonel John Laurens and forty of his infantry with an artillery piece downstream to ambush the British boats if they withdrew from the area. The British watched the movement of the Patriot units from their vessels.

The Patriot infantry sent to ambush the British boats delayed at a local plantation for several hours before continuing their march, while the British, accurately guessing Gist's intentions, slipped downstream after dark. At the bend in the river where the Patriot force had planned its ambush, the British landed a force of 140 men and marched inland. As the Patriot troops approached, the British sprang their own ambush. Colonel Laurens, at the head of his column, fell when the British fired their first volley. The British troops captured the artillery piece and its crew, and the remainder of the Patriot force retreated from the site. The arrival of Gist with his main force saved the retreating Patriots from potential disaster. Gist's men repulsed the advancing British, who then withdrew to a small log breastwork they had constructed earlier near the river. There the British soldiers awaited the expected Patriot assault against their position. Gist did assault the position, but the British successfully repulsed the attack, withdrew to their vessels, and continued downriver. Patriot losses included 2 men killed, 19 wounded, and 3 missing. British losses are not known. The Patriot force held the field, but the British had successfully given them a bloody nose before withdrawing their force and sailing back to Charleston.

Terry M. Mays

See also

Fair Lawn Plantation, South Carolina, Action at

Reference

Ripley, Warren. *Battleground: South Carolina in the Revolution.* Charleston, SC: Evening Post, 1983.

Committee of Secret Correspondence

See Secret Correspondence, Committee of

Conanicut Island, Rhode Island, Actions at (1775–1779)

Conanicut Island, also known as Jamestown Island, was the site of several significant military actions during the Revolutionary War. The island is strategically located at the entrance to Narragansett Bay, Rhode Island, where it controls the approaches to both Newport and the entire upper part of Narragansett Bay, including Providence. The inhabitants of the island's most important settlement, Jamestown, recognized this and constructed earthworks and two batteries, Fort Dumpling and Conanicut Battery at Beaverneck.

At the outbreak of the war, the entrance to the bay was patrolled by HMS *Rose* (20 guns), whose commander, Captain James Wallace, was still bitter over the seizure and burning of the revenue cutter the *Gaspée* by Rhode Islanders in 1772 and was intent on punishing the colonists. The British first retaliated by kidnapping the Providence merchant John Brown and seizing the local flour vessels the *Abigail* and the *Diana.* On 15 June 1775, Rhode Island's Commodore Abraham Whipple, commanding the *Katy* (6 guns) and the sloop *Washington* (6 guns), engaged the armed British packet vessel *Diana.* After a short gun battle, the *Diana*'s master ran the ship aground on Conanicut Island. The Americans refloated the *Diana,* and the ship had the distinction of being one of the first British prizes taken by the rebels. The Rhode Island vessel *Katy* was later purchased by the Continental Congress and became the *Providence.*

Wallace next demanded that the locals sell supplies to his vessels. They refused and evacuated all their livestock off Conanicut Island. In response, Wallace bombarded the nearby towns of Bristol and Stonington. On 7 December 1775, a British fleet arrived at Narragansett Bay and occupied Newport. Three days later, 200 British and Hessian troops landed on Conanicut, marched across the island burning homes and businesses in Jamestown, and caused nearly half the island's residents to flee to the mainland.

On 29 July 1778, a French fleet commanded by Admiral Jean-Baptiste d'Estaing arrived off Conanicut, causing the alarmed British forces at Newport to scuttle five frigates and several other vessels to block shipping channels and add guns and crews to their garrison. D'Estaing landed 4,000 French troops on Conanicut Island, but before they could attack Newport the British fleet arrived and the French reembarked. Poor weather prevented an engagement of the two fleets. In December 1778, the British occupied Conanicut and took control of its batteries. They remained until 25 October 1779, when they destroyed their fortifications and abandoned the island.

Robert S. Abbott

See also

Gaspée Incident; Newport, Rhode Island, Naval Operations against; Royal Navy; Washington's Navy; Whipple, Abraham

References

"A Brief History of Jamestown and Newport, Rhode Island: The Eighteenth Century," http://www.jamestown-ri.info/18th_century_history.htm.

Coggins, Jack. *Ships and Seamen of the American Revolution.* 1969. Reprint, Mineola, NY: Dover, 2002.

James, William. *The British Navy in Adversity: A Study of the War of American Independence.* 1926. Reprint, New York: Russell and Russell, 1970.

Rhode Island Department of Environmental Management. "Fort Wetherill State Park," http://www.riparks.com/fortwetherillhistory.htm.

Rider, Hope S. *Valour Fore & Aft.* Newport, RI: Seaport 76 Foundation, 1978.

Concord, Massachusetts

See Lexington and Concord

Confederation Congress

See Congress, Second Continental and Confederation

Congress, First Continental (5 September–26 October 1774)

The First Continental Congress, which met in Philadelphia in September 1774, was a gathering of representatives of twelve of the thirteen colonies that would soon form an independent United States of America. This body was the first American institution to exercise any authority over the several colonies and communities in North America, through its Continental Association. It was also the first in a series of American congresses that have extended, with no break greater than one year, from 1774 to the present. In short, the First Continental Congress laid the groundwork and set the fundamental precedent for America's first national government.

Congress's immediate task was to develop an effective response to the British Parliament's passage of the Coercive (or Intolerable) Acts, which were primarily designed to get firm control over and punish Massachusetts for the Boston Tea Party. At the direction of their several colonies, however, the congressmen quickly decided to address the concerns of all the colonies in regard to every British executive action and parliamentary legislation since 1763 that they perceived as a threat to their liberties and rights as subjects of the British Empire. Congress addressed this challenge by devising America's first comprehensive system of economic sanctions, setting dates for ending all imports from, and later all exports to, Britain, and creating the Continental Association to carry out those sanctions. Congress also approved the Demand for the Redress of Grievances: Declaration and Resolves, its official statement of the rights of British Americans and the manner in which those rights had been violated by the British government. Congressional delegates also prepared several addresses to the people of Great Britain, the American people, King George III, and the people of Quebec. Finally, they agreed to meet again in May 1775 if the concerns of the American people were not met.

The immediate cause for convening the First Continental Congress was the need to respond to the Coercive Acts passed by the British Parliament in the spring of 1774, including the Boston Port Act, which closed the port of Boston until the town's inhabitants paid for the tea the Patriots had destroyed in December 1773; the Administration of Justice Act; a new Quartering Act; and finally, the Massachusetts Government Act, which unilaterally altered an eighty-year-old charter to give the British government greater political control of its most rebellious province. Many colonists were also upset by the recent Quebec Act (June 1774), which extended that province's boundaries south and west into territory claimed by several colonies and granted not only toleration to the Catholic inhabitants but important privileges to the Catholic Church, a cause of concern to Britain's Protestant North American subjects. A more general reason for convening the Congress was the distress that the colonists felt at threats to several of their rights and liberties by British executive proclamations and parliamentary statutes dating back to the end of the French and Indian (Seven Years') War in 1763.

The First Continental Congress. Convened in September 1774 at Carpenter's Hall, Philadelphia, it consisted of delegates from twelve of the thirteen colonies who sought to address various of the colonists' grievances with Britain, beginning with the Intolerable Acts. (Library of Congress)

Congress opened on 5 September 1774, with forty-five members representing eleven colonies. North Carolina's delegates had not yet arrived, and Georgia chose not to send representatives. Additional members from several colonies soon arrived, and on 14 September, North Carolina's delegates completed the Congress. The selection process for the delegates varied from colony to colony. Colonial legislatures chose the delegates in several colonies, but in others, where the royal governor had dismissed the legislature, Revolutionary congresses performed this task. The members arrived with commissions from their colonies and general instructions that directed them to consult with delegates from the other colonies to determine the best course for asserting their rights as British citizens. The instructions from New Hampshire, Massachusetts, Virginia, and Pennsylvania also mentioned a desire to reestablish the colonies' earlier peaceful relationship with Britain. Most of the commissions implied the colonies' allegiance to the Crown but did not state this outright.

Nearly every colony sent its most distinguished and talented leaders to Philadelphia, and some have argued that the First Continental Congress was the greatest concentration of political ability in the American Revolution. Nearly all of the members would play important roles in their colonies and states during the Revolution, and many went on to become leaders in the new American republic. Among the most important delegates were Samuel Adams and John Adams from Massachusetts; Silas Deane and Roger Sherman from Connecticut; John Jay from New York; John Dickinson and Joseph Galloway from Pennsylvania; Thomas Johnson and Samuel Chase from Maryland; Patrick Henry, Peyton Randolph, and George Washington from Virginia; and John Rutledge from South Carolina. Only two of these men, Joseph Galloway, who became a leading Loyalist in the spring of 1775, and Peyton Randolph, who died suddenly of apoplexy later that year, were not among America's leaders at the signing of the Declaration of Independence.

Congress's first order of business was the selection of its meeting place and its leadership. In an immediate show of independence, the delegates chose Carpenter's Hall instead of Pennsylvania's State House (later known as Independence Hall), which had been offered by Joseph Galloway, Speaker of the conservative Pennsylvania Assembly. They named Peyton Randolph, the highly respected Virginia lawmaker, as their president and Charles Thomson, a key leader of Philadelphia's Revolutionary movement, as their secretary. This immediately signaled a division in Congress, as Galloway and Thomson (who was not a member of Congress) were on opposite ends of the spectrum in Pennsylvania's efforts to confront British authority.

The congressional delegates quickly decided that their debates would be secret and immediately confronted their first major disagreement, over the relative strength of large and small colonies in voting. Virginia's delegates argued that it would be unfair to their people and those of the other more populous colonies to have their will thwarted by a group of smaller colonies whose combined population might not equal even one of the larger colonies. Henry viewed this particular congress as unique and held that the equal-vote procedure of previous intercolonial gatherings, the Albany Congress of 1754 and the Stamp Act Congress of 1765, could not be used as precedents. In arguing for a one delegate, one vote rule, Henry declared: "the distinctions between Virginians, Pennsylvanians, New Yorkers, and New Englanders, are no more. I am not a Virginian, but an American." Representatives from the smaller colonies replied that each colonial government was independent of the others and deserved to have an equal vote. Congress adopted this rule after it decided that it could not find any satisfactory method for determining what should be the voting strength for each colony. The decision served as a precedent for the Second Continental Congress and the Confederation Congress.

Early in Congress's proceedings, events outside the chamber began to foretell the future. The members were first alarmed by a rumor that the British had bombarded Boston, which turned out to be false. This temporary distress and the question of opening sessions with a prayer led to one of Congress's more interesting episodes. The problem of religious diversity among the delegates led to the belief that opening with a prayer was impractical until Samuel Adams rose and said that "he was no bigot, and could hear a prayer from a gentleman of piety and virtue, who was at the same time a friend to his country." The next day, Philadelphia's Reverend Jacob Duché, an Anglican, read from the thirty-fifth Psalm during the opening prayers. The Scripture's focus on retribution reportedly had a strong impact on the delegates.

On 7 September, Congress formed its first committee, on colonial rights, with two members from each colony. Among its most important members were John and Samuel Adams, Jay, Caesar Rodney of Delaware, and Richard Henry Lee of Virginia. On 24 September, Congress decided to limit its consideration to rights that had been violated since 1763, putting off older issues to a future date. Congress's second committee, on trade and manufactures, had one member from each colony, the most prominent of whom were Chase and Henry.

On 17 September, Congress dealt with what became known as the Suffolk Resolves. These were resolutions recently adopted by citizens of Suffolk County, Massachusetts (Boston and environs), who pledged to resist British authority by whatever means were necessary within the law to preserve their rights as subjects of the empire. After some debate, Congress accepted the resolves. But as the month continued, Congress began to put in place its own economic strategy for dealing with Britain. On 22 September, it requested that merchants delay ordering British goods. On 27 September, the delegates went further by passing a nonimportation agreement and setting 1 December 1774 as its effective date. And on 30 September, Congress set 10 September 1775 as the date to end all exports of staple goods to Great Britain and the West Indies if its grievances were not addressed.

On 28 September, Galloway presented Congress with a different option for ending the crisis: a political union between Britain and America that centered on a permanent intercolonial American legislature. Under Galloway's plan, the king

PHILADELPHIA.

In CONGRESS, Thurſday, September 22, 1774.

RESOLVED,

THAT the Congreſs requeſt the Merchants and Others, in the ſeveral Colonies, not to ſend to Great Britain any Orders for Goods, and to direct the execution of all Orders already ſent, to be delayed or ſuſpended, until the ſenſe of the Congreſs, on the means to be taken for the preſervation of the Liberties of *America,* is made public.

An Extract from the Minutes,
CHARLES THOMSON, *Sec.*

Document from the First Continental Congress requesting merchants and others to refrain from purchasing goods from Great Britain. (Library of Congress)

would appoint a president-general who would act as the chief executive for British North America. The legislature would be a council of delegates chosen by the several colonial assemblies for three-year terms. This council would meet every year and would have the rights and privileges of the British House of Commons, including the election of its own Speaker. The royally appointed president and the elected council would act like a national government in colonial matters. Galloway did not regard the council as an entirely independent body; rather, he saw it as an inferior but distinct branch of the British Parliament. Both the American council and the British Parliament could originate legislation for America, but it would require passage by both bodies to become law. The major exception was for bills in the American council that granted aid to the king in times of war, which would not require acceptance by Parliament. Galloway's plan of federal union was not completely original; it bore a striking similarity to the Albany Plan of Union, originally proposed in 1754 by his longtime Pennsylvania ally, Benjamin Franklin. While Galloway freely admitted that his plan was not perfect, he believed that it offered an alternative to using economic sanctions for ending the crisis.

This plan was hotly debated in Congress. Among those who found the idea acceptable or of interest were Jay and Edward Rutledge. Among its opponents was Henry, who expressed fears of an intercolonial American legislature. These fears foreshadowed his concerns, nearly fourteen years later during the debates over ratification of the U.S. Constitution, regarding a powerful federal government. In the end, delegates who opposed Galloway's plan were able not only to defeat it but to have it expunged from the official minutes of Congress. With this defeat, America turned resolutely away from accommodation with Britain and embraced open economic warfare to gain its rights in the British Empire.

On 14 October 1774, Congress approved its general statement of American rights that became known as its Declaration and Resolves. The related issues of colonial rights and the proper role of the British government in America were hardly new to any of the delegates. Well before the Stamp Act crisis of 1765, some colonists had been trying to define a better relationship between North America and Britain. By 1774 in Philadelphia, British North Americans felt ready to claim numerous rights as subjects of the British Empire. They were especially "entitled to life liberty & property, and they ha[d] never ceded to any sovereign power whatever, a right to dispose of either without their consent." Emigrants from Britain, they argued, were still entitled to the rights of British subjects; emigration did not deprive them of those rights. They also asserted the popular right of participation in the government and declared that because the colonists were not represented in Parliament, they had the right to self-government through their own assemblies in matters of taxes and internal affairs.

They did accept the role of Parliament in regulating, but not taxing, commerce to secure wealth for the empire.

In its resolves, Congress claimed for Americans the privilege of being tried by their peers. It insisted on the benefits of laws that existed at the time of the creation of the colonies and claimed an entitlement to the "immunities and privileges" granted by the royal charters and colonial laws. The resolves argued for the right to assemble and to petition the king. They asserted that the maintenance of an army without the consent of the local legislature was illegal and that the colonies' royally appointed councils were a violation of the British constitution because they prevented a separation of the legislative and executive branches. Congressional delegates then listed many of the acts they considered to be unconstitutional infringements on their rights, including the Coercive Acts and the Quebec Act. They concluded by publicly stating the means they had chosen to respond to these provocations: nonimportation, nonconsumption, nonexportation, and addresses to the people of North America, the people of Britain, and the king.

On 20 October 1774, Congress approved its economic strategy, the Continental Association. The methods chosen for implementing the association's core tactics—nonimportation, nonconsumption, and nonexportation—would be critical to its success. Congress had to reach several compromises among its members to make economic sanctions workable. Nonimportation was to begin first; American merchants were to immediately cease all importing from Britain. The delegates further agreed not to import goods made in Britain but exported to a third location. And they added slaves to those items not to be imported and agreed to end their involvement in the slave trade after that date. Nonconsumption—the ceasing of all retail purchases of British imports—was to begin on 1 March 1775. Nonexportation to the British Isles and the West Indies was the tactic held off the longest, until 10 September 1775, after the middle and southern colonies' staple crops—wheat, tobacco and rice—could be shipped to Britain and Europe to improve the colonies' financial position. It is significant that among the fifty-two signers of the Continental Association were men from a wide political spectrum. Not only did radical leaders such as John and Samuel Adams and moderates such as Jay, Chase, and George Washington sign but also conservatives such as Galloway and Isaac Low, although both Galloway and Low soon became Loyalists.

Simply passing the Continental Association, however, was not going to force Britain to comply with America's demands. Congress needed to gain public support, not only at home in its members' own colonies but among friends in Britain, by clarifying its position while trying to limit the growth of any opposition. To achieve these goals, Congress passed a petition to the king and a series of addresses to what it considered to be its most important audiences.

On 21 October, Congress approved its Address to the People of Great Britain, which outlined the colonists' concerns regarding taxes and government: "*Know then,* That we consider ourselves, and do insist, that we are and ought to be, as free as our fellow-subjects in Britain, and that no power on earth has a right to take our property from us without our consent." Congress accepted the role of the British government in the regulation of colonial trade but rejected both direct taxation and the use of import duties as a method of raising revenue. It also expressed concerns about bad colonial governors and recent British policy toward Quebec. But the address sought to strike a conciliatory tone toward the British people: "We believe there is yet much virtue, much justice and much public spirit in the English nation—To that justice we now appeal." And while the members of Congress regretted that their economic measures would hurt fellow subjects in the mother country, they hoped that the British people would see the need for such actions and intercede with Parliament in order to "save the violated rights of the whole empire."

On that same day Congress approved its Memorial to the Inhabitants of the Colonies, which outlined the members' developing list of grievances against British laws and declared: "the immediate tendency of these statutes is, to subvert the right of having a share in legislation, by rendering Assemblies useless." It further argued: "under the pretense of governing them, so many new institutions, uniformly rigid and dangerous, have been introduced.... By order of the King, the authority of the Commander in chief, and under him, of the Brigadiers General, *in time of peace,* is rendered *supreme* in all civil governments, in America; and thus an uncontrollable military power is vested in officers not known to the constitutions of these colonies." This memorial became a detailed indictment of British policy toward the American colonists after the French and Indian War and a justification of Congress's policy choices for dealing with the crisis.

In their address to King George III, the delegates argued: "we ask but for peace, liberty, and safety. We wish not a diminution of the prerogative, nor do we solicit the grant of any new right in our favor." They ultimately requested action to grant them redress of their grievances in return for which the colonists would be loyal subjects of the British monarchy. On 25 October, Congress ordered that its address be sent to the colonial agents for presentation to the king. The next day, the delegates authorized the submission of their address to the press for publication, along with their statement of the colonists' grievances.

Also on 26 October, Congress passed its Address to the Inhabitants of Quebec, a bid to gain the French colonists as allies in their struggle with Britain. They declared: "after a gallant and glorious resistance ... we rejoiced in the truly valuable addition [of Canada to the British Empire] ... expecting, as courage and generosity are naturally united, our brave enemies would become our hearty friends," and went on to discuss the rights of all citizens in the empire. They used the writings of the French philosopher Baron de Montesquieu to further the discussion, showing that for the sake of liberty judges must be separated from the legislative and executive branches, something the English colonists did not see in Quebec. They then cited the example of the Swiss cantons as a possible model for Catholic-Protestant cooperation.

With its work done, the First Continental Congress adjourned on 26 October 1774, having agreed on 22 October to convene a second congress on 10 May 1775, if the colonists had not yet received the desired redress of their grievances.

Donald E. Heidenreich Jr.

See also

Adams, John; Adams, Samuel; Administration of Justice Act; Albany Congress; Alsop, John; Bland, Richard; Boston Port Act; Chase, Samuel; Coercive Acts; Congress, Second Continental and Confederation; Continental Association; Dickinson, John; Duane, James; Franklin, Benjamin; Gadsden, Christopher; Galloway, Joseph; Harrison, Benjamin, V; Henry, Patrick; Jay, John; Lee, Richard Henry; Livingston, Philip; Livingston, William; Massachusetts Government Act; McKean, Thomas; Paca, William; Paine, Robert Treat; Quartering Acts; Quebec Act; Randolph, Peyton; Rodney, Caesar; Rutledge, Edward; Rutledge, John; Sherman, Roger; Stamp Act; Stamp Act Congress; Suffolk Resolves; Sugar Act; Tea Act; Thomson, Charles; Washington, George

References

Adams, John. *Diary and Autobiography of John Adams.* Edited by L. H. Butterfield. 4 vols. Cambridge: Harvard University Press, 1961.

Ammerman, David. *In the Common Cause: American Response to the Coercive Acts of 1774.* New York: Norton, 1975.

Barger, B. D. *Lord Dartmouth and the American Revolution.* Columbia: University of South Carolina Press, 1965.

Burnett, Edmund Cody, ed. *The Continental Congress: A Definitive History of the Continental Congress from Its Inception in 1774 to 1789.* New York: Norton, 1964.

———, ed. *Letters of Members of the Continental Congress.* Vol. 1. 1921. Reprint, Gloucester, MA: Peter Smith, 1963.

Ford, Worthington Chauncey, ed. *Journals of the Continental Congress,* Vol. 1, *1774.* Washington, DC: U.S. Government Printing Office, 1904.

Jensen, Merrill, ed. *English Historical Documents,* Vol. 9, *American Colonial Documents to 1776.* New York: Oxford University Press, 1964.

Library of Congress. *American Memory.* http://memory.loc.gov/ammem/index.html.

Montross, Lynn. *The Reluctant Rebels: The Story of the Continental Congress, 1774–1789.* New York: Harper, 1950.

Rakove, Jack. *The Beginnings of National Politics: An Interpretive History of the Continental Congress.* New York: Knopf, 1979.

United States Congress. *Biographical Dictionary of the United States Congress, 1774 to Present.* http://bioguide.congress.gov/biosearch/biosearch.asp.

United States House of Representatives. *Commemoration Ceremony in Honor of the Two Hundredth Anniversary of the First Continental Congress in the United States House of Representatives.* Washington, DC: U.S. Government Printing Office, 1975.

Congress, Second Continental and Confederation (1775–1788)

The Second Continental Congress quickly evolved into the first national government of the United States. For more than thirteen years it directed the Revolutionary War to a successful conclusion, framed the nation's first structure of national government, concluded peace with Britain, established relations with several European nations, directed the early development of the country's western lands, and presided over the troubled postwar economy until the United States decided that it needed a more powerful national government.

In the First Continental Congress (September–October 1774) American colonial representatives discussed grievances against the British government and planned a united response to British policy. Although some delegates were dissatisfied with the limited action taken by that body, the Congress had set a precedent for joint action, developed common coercive economic action through its Continental Association, and agreed to convene a second congress in May 1775 if Britain had not recognized America's grievances. The First Continental Congress also revealed divisions among the colonists, and Georgia had not even sent a delegation. Some of the members were beginning to favor independence from Great Britain, although they could not say this in public, while more moderate representatives ardently sought reconciliation with London. These divisions carried over into the Second Continental Congress, but events soon shifted the momentum in favor of independence-minded delegates.

The Second Continental Congress convened on 10 May 1775 in Philadelphia, and the Battles of Lexington and Concord in late April soon compelled the delegates to approve strong measures against what they perceived to be British provocations. The members first reelected Peyton Randolph of Virginia as their president, the post he had held in the First Continental Congress, but Randolph quickly resigned to return to Virginia and serve as Speaker of its Revolutionary legislature. On 24 May, Congress elected John Hancock of Massachusetts as its president, a position he would hold until 1777. In this Congress, as in its predecessor, each colony had one vote in deciding all issues, but the colonies (and the states that succeeded them) sent delegations of from two to eight members, largely depending on the size of their populations. From the opening month of the Second Continental Congress, the delegates included many influential political leaders, including Samuel and John Adams, John Dickinson, Benjamin Franklin, John Jay, Thomas Jefferson, Richard Henry Lee, and George Washington. Each of the first five presidents of the federal government of the United States—Washington, John Adams, Jefferson, James Madison, and

The Second Continental Congress votes for independence in 1776. The congress served as the national government during and after the Revolutionary War and drafted the Articles of Confederation, which were ratified by all states by 1781. (National Archives and Records Administration)

James Monroe—was a delegate to the Second Continental Congress at some point in its history.

Initially the Congress, like its predecessor, had few real powers. It could not pass legislation or levy taxes and had no executive branch or treasury. The body could only recommend actions to the individual colonial governments. But as armed conflict with Britain grew, Congress gained increasing power and influence. In one of its first actions, Congress voted to table any discussion of the Conciliatory Proposition that had been offered—to the several colonies, not to Congress—by Britain's prime minister, Lord North, in February. This offer was regarded as a scheme to divide the colonies and as totally inadequate to restore America's lost liberties.

The move to arms quickly gained momentum. On 15 May 1775 Congress voted to put the colonies in a state of defense and soon thereafter agreed to raise a standing army of 20,000 men. On 14 June, Congress authorized the first muster of troops under its direct authority and created the Continental Army, which was at first largely composed of the Massachusetts militiamen besieging Boston. These forces were taken over from the control of that province's Revolutionary government. On 15 June, the body appointed Washington as commander in chief of its new army. Washington promptly resigned his seat in Congress and for the next eight years served in the field. On 13 October, Congress voted to arm a ship and appointed a Marine Committee, thereby laying the foundation for the Continental Navy. The fleet was continuously expanded, and on 10 November 1775 Congress authorized the formation of two marine battalions to be deployed with the naval forces.

In turning to armed resistance, Congress was keenly aware of the value of public opinion and directed Jefferson to prepare the Declaration of the Causes and Necessity of Taking Up Arms (6 July 1775), which was distributed throughout the colonies to rally the public to the cause. But in deference to moderates in Congress, the body authorized Dickinson to draft its Olive Branch Petition (5 July 1775) to George III, who had refused to receive a similar appeal from the First Continental Congress. In this last address to Britain's king, Congress pledged America's loyalty to the Crown and asked the monarch to end the fighting until solutions could be found to resolve the conflict between the colonies and the mother country.

Most of the delegates believed that the Olive Branch Petition would fail, and they began to lay the groundwork for independence, without openly admitting they were doing so.

In fact, George III rejected the petition, ordered an additional 20,000 troops sent to America, and in August 1775 declared the colonies in open rebellion. In response, Congress decreed that each colony should resist any effort to force it to submit to royal authority or to pay taxes to the Crown. Furthermore, Congress resolved that Americans should provide no provisions to British troops and that no American ships should be used to transport British forces or supplies.

By the summer of 1775 the governments of several colonies, including New York and Massachusetts, called on Congress to take on more of the functions of a national government. The government of New York wanted Congress to establish a national tribunal, and several delegations called for a national body to issue bills of credit to finance military operations and build a navy. Congress had begun in May to issue paper currency to pay for military expenses and the costs of the national legislature and, over the course of the next year, issued four emissions of continental paper money. Congress would continue to issue continental currency until January 1779, emitting a total of $240 million in paper bills, mostly in denominations of $1, $2, $3, $5 and $10. Franklin designed the first images on the currency, and Paul Revere made the first plates. Congress attempted to utilize coinage as well; in February 1777 a committee recommended the creation of a mint, but the high projected costs killed the proposal. Instead, another committee was tasked to determine the value of British, Spanish, and French coins in relation to the continental dollar. Several states, including New York, did produce coins that made their way into circulation.

Nevertheless, throughout the war, Congress was constrained by a lack of funds. It passed budgets and divided the costs among the states, depending on the value of each state's land. To pay its share of the national budget, each state could draw on its own tax receipts or levy new taxes. But the states could not be forced to make their payments, and few actually met their obligations in full, which left Congress in a perpetual state of financial crisis. The value of the continental dollar was supposed to be backed by future tax and tariff revenues coming into Congress, but slow state payments and rapid inflation quickly eroded the value of the currency. The notes were also easily copied, and counterfeit bills became quite common. By 1780 the continental currency had fallen to one-fortieth of its initial value. This was especially problematic, because by 1779 the annual budget of Congress had risen to $60 million. In order to stabilize the currency, Congress chartered the Bank of North America in Philadelphia in 1781. Congress also had difficulty borrowing money, and the state legislatures proved to be unwilling to lend the national government funds because they faced their own fiscal problems as they tried to pay their militiamen and state officials.

To secure private loans, Congress authorized the establishment of loan offices in several of the major states, but relatively few loans were originated through these offices. This hampered another congressional program to raise money by lotteries since the payouts for the lotteries were in loan office certificates. Since there were few loans, the amount one could win from a congressional lottery was minimal, and the lottery plan was eventually abandoned. The most significant impact of the fiscal problems of Congress was on the nation's military capacity. Because of a lack of funds, projected military campaigns in 1778 had to be abandoned.

Congress's last hope of acquiring additional funding was from foreign sources. In March 1776, Congress dispatched Silas Deane to France to gain French military, political, and economic support. But French and later Spanish sources provided only about $4 million in loans and subsidies during the early years of the war. Although this figure would increase, it remained a fraction of the money needed to oppose the British Army. For the entire conflict, France, America's only formal ally, provided a total of about $8 million in loans and subsidies; Spain, which would not ally with the United States, provided only about $645,000. In 1779, Congress voted to send Henry Laurens to The Hague to negotiate a loan from the Dutch, but Laurens's capture by the British in 1780 ended his mission. John Adams, however, began the same work in Holland in 1780, and in 1782, with Congress's finances in chaos, he secured the first installment in some $12 million in loans and a Treaty of Amity and Commerce between the two countries.

More important to Congress than economic aid in the early years of the war were diplomatic recognition and military support. Following Deane's mission, Congress sent several delegations to Europe to garner support for the new nation. The most successful was the commission to France headed by Franklin. He proved immensely popular with the French elite and was able to negotiate the Franco-American Alliance in February 1778 following the British defeat at Saratoga. Missions to various German and Italian states and to Russia from 1777 to 1783 were unsuccessful, and America's mission to Spain was more frustrating than rewarding. Beginning with Adams's mission to Holland, however, several American diplomats were eventually able to negotiate commercial treaties with the Netherlands (1782), Sweden (1783), Prussia (1785), and Morocco (1786).

Congress also hoped to promote insurrection against the British in other colonies, or at least to cultivate public sentiment in these regions, and appointed committees to draft letters to Canada, British West Florida, and the British Caribbean islands to explain and justify its resistance to British rule. Its most important initiative, in the spring of 1776, was to send a delegation to Canada (which the Americans had already invaded in the fall of 1775) to try to persuade French Canadians to join the rebellion. This effort failed, but several hundred Canadians did travel south to join Americans in their armed struggle against Britain. Congress also

Raising the first flag at Independence Hall, Philadelphia, circa 1776–1777. The Second Continental Congress was the first to meet in the hall, commencing on 10 May 1775, less than a month after the clash at Lexington and Concord. (National Archives and Records Administration)

instructed representatives of the various colonies to begin negotiations with Native American tribes in an attempt to convince them to remain neutral in the conflict. Finally, in defiance of the Navigation Acts, the delegates authorized American ports to be opened to trade with all nations.

The first great test of Congress's leadership was the issue of independence. Beginning early in 1776 and aided by Thomas Paine's advocacy of independence in January in America's first best-seller, the pamphlet *Common Sense,* Lee, Patrick Henry, and John Adams led the campaign in Congress for full separation from Great Britain. A large group of moderates, led by Dickinson, opposed this decision to the last moment. As fighting in New England and in Canada continued through the winter and spring of 1776, the delegates began considering a formal break with Britain. On 7 June, Lee, seconded by John Adams, introduced a resolution declaring independence. Following two days of intense debate, Congress tasked a committee to draft a declaration for consideration by the full house. The committee's members, John Adams, Jefferson, Franklin, Robert Livingston, and Roger Sherman, chose Jefferson to write the first draft. The committee made a few minor changes, but the document presented to the full Congress was essentially Jefferson's work.

The declaration, which incorporated many of the sentiments expressed in nearly two years of congressional declarations and featured the arguments of the British political philosopher John Locke, was presented to the full Congress on 28 June. Spirited debate and editing of Jefferson's draft began on 1 July, and initially nine colonies voted in favor of the declaration, two opposed it, one delegation was divided, and one abstained. On 2 July, twelve delegations voted for independence; New York abstained. Congress declared the measure passed, and after final editing, the Declaration of Independence was approved on 4 July. The Declaration added new responsibilities for Congress, including increased pressure to secure a military victory to confirm this radical decision.

Both Congress and the Continental Army now faced their greatest difficulties. British victories in New York and New Jersey persuaded Congress to relocate briefly in late 1776, and General William Howe's invasion of the Delaware Valley forced the delegates to flee Philadelphia for Lancaster and then York, Pennsylvania, in 1777. Congress returned to Philadelphia when the British left the city in 1778 and remained there for the duration of the war, now operating under its first formal frame of government.

Even as Congress debated the Declaration of Independence, it appointed a committee chaired by Dickinson to develop a plan for a union of the states, the first constitution for the new nation. The committee's proposed draft of the Articles of Confederation for the United States of America was fully debated in Congress and finally approved on 15 November 1777. To be formally effective, the Articles had to be ratified by each of the thirteen states, and Congress urged the states to take action by 10 March 1778. Most states quickly approved the new constitution, but Maryland refused to ratify the Articles of Confederation until March 1781 because of land disputes with neighboring states. But the Second Continental Congress, which now became in effect the Confederation Congress, officially began operating under the Articles in 1778 and continued to do so until the U.S. Constitution became effective in 1789.

Congress was granted the power to regulate foreign relations under Article 9 of the Articles of Confederation and used this authority to try to gain diplomatic recognition by the major European powers. While France and Spain were anxious to see America defeat their old enemy, Great Britain, they were unwilling to commit to the American cause until they could be reasonably sure of victory. American envoys quickly convinced the French to open their ports to American privateers and merchants, but it took the American victory at Saratoga in 1777 to persuade the French court to recognize and ally with the new country. Spain and the Netherlands soon became involved in the struggle with Britain but would not recognize America until after the war was over. Congress's greatest international triumph after the Franco-American

Alliance of 1778 was the Peace of Paris, negotiated with Great Britain in 1782 and formally concluded in 1783. But this victory owed more to the dogged determination of John Adams, Franklin, and Jay than to any support or guidance they received from Congress.

Under the Articles of Confederation, the national government was composed of a unicameral legislature with no executive branch. Congress's elected president served as a coordinator and advocate for legislation but lacked any real political power. Several presidents had to rely on their personal reputations and prior influence to lead effectively, and the office did attract some of the nation's strongest early leaders. Hancock (1775–1777) and Lee (1784–1785) were particularly effective chief executives. Other wartime presidents included Laurens, Jay, Samuel Huntington of Connecticut, and Thomas McKean, a leader in both Pennsylvania and Delaware. Most presidents after Yorktown—John Hanson of Maryland, Elias Boudinot of New Jersey, and Thomas Mifflin of Pennsylvania, and Nathaniel Gorham of Massachusetts, Arthur St. Clair of Pennsylvania, and Cyrus Griffin of Virginia toward the end of the old Congress—were less commanding figures trying to lead an often demoralized national legislature.

The Confederation Congress had the power to declare war and make treaties and alliances, but it could not force the states to respect or comply with those treaties. It could request men from the states for the Continental Army but could not establish a standing army in peacetime. Congress also had the power to regulate coinage and to issue bills of credit and borrow money, but it could not levy taxes. Finally, Congress was tasked to oversee relations with Native Americans and to settle disputes between the individual states, areas in which it had some success.

Congress's central weaknesses were its lack of a strong executive, its difficulty in enacting legislation, and its inability to enforce legislation. Each state received one vote in deciding every issue, and the approval of all legislation required a three-fourths majority of nine states. Any amendments to the Articles required the unanimous consent of the thirteen states. The national government could adjudicate interstate disputes but lacked any true judicial branch. Finally, the inability of Congress to levy taxes was a constant problem for the national government until the adoption of the U.S. Constitution.

To compound its problems, there were continuing tensions between Congress and the military leadership during the Revolution. Most members of Congress had an abiding mistrust of a standing army. They feared that senior military officers might use their power to undermine Congress or even to establish a dictatorial government. Hence, Congress jealously guarded its control of the military and elected and dismissed most generals and senior officers. This led to political battles as state delegations sought to promote their own officers and stifle the aspirations of others. Congress also controlled the pay and supply of the Continental Army. It established the Board of War to oversee the procurement and delivery of supplies to the troops, but the board had little power and faced a variety of obstacles in its efforts to support the army. Congress even set some military objectives during the conflict. In 1779 financial constraints caused Congress to order General Washington to act on the defensive only for the remainder of the year. Congress also drew up the first Articles of War in 1775 for the Continental Army, which it revised a year later. The rules were based on those of the British Army and established military courts-martial. But Congress also maintained the supremacy of civilian judicial bodies over many crimes, including capital offenses.

Of all of the political influences that Congress exerted on the Continental Army, none caused more problems than those involving the issue of pay. The Continental Army was paid differently than the state militias, and state soldiers usually received better and more regular pay. The pay differential was so pronounced that Congress had to pass a special supplemental pay increase for officers in the Continental Army in 1776. Throughout the war there was constant agitation over the issue of pensions. Regular officers in the army wanted half pay for life once the war ended, a common practice in British and European armies. Congress balked at such a long-term financial commitment, but by 1780 the morale of officers was so low that they were resigning in large numbers, and Washington said that if this continued he could not sustain the war effort. Congress relented and on 21 October 1780 passed legislation giving the officers half pay for life.

Low pay among enlisted soldiers caused other problems. Several units mutinied, and some states took advantage of the low salaries to lure soldiers away from the Continental Army into their militias. By the end of the war only the force of Washington's will kept both officers and men from open rebellion. And when the army was demobilized in 1783, it was done in such a haphazard manner that ex-soldiers seeking pay or other benefits engaged in sporadic revolts. The traditional civilian mistrust of a standing army and the actions of the soldiers at the war's end led the Confederation Congress to refuse to maintain a national army throughout the remainder of its existence.

The problems of the Confederation Congress did not cease at the end of the Revolutionary War but instead grew worse as the national government confronted growing questions about its ability to govern. By 1783, there was increasing sentiment to change the Articles of Confederation. The inability of Congress to force several states to pay their portions of the national debt they had incurred during the Revolution and its lack of authority to levy taxes constrained its ability to deal with the problems facing the new nation. In October 1781, Congress requested $8 million from the states, but by the formal end of the war in 1783, the states had paid only $1.5 million. By 1786, the national government had revenues of only $370,000 and a national debt of $35 million. The requirement that amendments to the Articles of Confederation receive unanimous consent destroyed efforts in 1782 and 1786 to grant Congress an independent revenue. By 1786, Congress was on the verge of bankruptcy, and armed insurrections, such as Shays's Rebellion that broke out in Massachusetts that fall, convinced many Americans of the need for a standing army. In September 1786, delegates from five states gathered to discuss the crisis at Annapolis, Maryland, where Alexander Hamilton called for a convention to thoroughly reform the Articles of Confederation.

Congress, desperate to receive more power and authority, issued a formal call for a general meeting, and the Philadelphia Convention opened on 25 May 1787. Twelve states sent delegates; only Rhode Island boycotted the convention. Among the delegates, the Federalists, led by Hamilton and Madison, and strongest in several of the larger states advocated a powerful central government. The Antifederalists, a distinct minority at Philadelphia, sought minor changes in the Articles of Confederation but adamantly opposed the establishment of a federal government, which they believed would lead to tyranny. Two main plans were proposed, the Virginia Plan, favored by the most ardent Federalists from the larger states, and the New Jersey Plan, favored by spokesmen from the smaller states. The Great Compromise, which gave large states proportional representation in the House of Representatives and small states an equal voice in the Senate, finally resolved an issue that had frustrated both the First and Second Continental Congresses since 1774.

In the ensuing struggle for ratification, eleven states approved the Constitution in time for new national elections in the fall of 1788, the last year in which the gradually failing Confederation Congress could secure a quorum. The new national government, with full independent taxing powers, went into operation in April 1789. It quickly persuaded North Carolina later that year and largely coerced Rhode Island in 1790 to join the federal union, with its new powerful bicameral Congress.

Tom Lansford

See also

Adams, John; Adams, Samuel; Articles of Confederation; Congress, First Continental; Constitution, United States; Constitution, United States, Ratification of; Constitutions, State; Continental Army; Continental Navy; Currency, American; Deane, Silas; Declaration of the Causes and Necessity of Taking Up Arms; Declaration of Independence; Dickinson, John; Diplomacy, American; Diplomacy, French; Federalist Papers; Franco-American Alliance; Franklin, Benjamin; Hamilton, Alexander; Hancock, John; Jay, John; Jefferson, Thomas; Laurens, Henry; Lee, Richard Henry; Madison, James; North, Lord Frederick; Northwest Territory; Olive Branch Petition; Philadelphia; Privateering; Randolph, Edmund Jennings; Randolph, Peyton; War, Board of; Washington, George; Yorktown, Virginia, Siege of; Yorktown Campaign

References

Bemis, Samuel F. *The Diplomacy of the American Revolution.* 1935. Reprint, Bloomington: Indiana University Press, 1957.

Benton, Wilbourn, ed. *1787: Drafting the U.S. Constitution.* 2 vols. College Station: Texas A&M University Press, 1986.

Bonwick, Colin. *The American Revolution.* Charlottesville: University of Virginia Press, 1991.

Davis, Derek. *Religion and the Continental Congress, 1774–1789: Contributions to Original Intent.* New York: Oxford University Press, 2000.

Furgang, Kathy. *The Declaration of Independence and Richard Henry Lee.* New York: Rosen, 2002.

Henderson, H. James. *Party Politics in the Continental Congress.* New York: McGraw-Hill, 1974.

Hoffman, Ronald, and Peter J. Albert, eds. *Diplomacy and Revolution: The Franco-American Alliance of 1778.* Charlottesville: University of Virginia Press, 1981.

Horsman, Reginald. *The Diplomacy of the New Republic, 1776–1815.* Arlington Heights, IL: Harlan Davidson, 1985.

Jensen, Merrill. *The Articles of Confederation: An Interpretation of the Social-Constitutional History of the American Revolution, 1774–1781.* Madison: University of Wisconsin Press, 1940.

———. *The New Nation: A History of the United States during the Confederation, 1781–1789.* 1950. Reprint, New York: Knopf, 1965.

Montross, Lynn. *The Reluctant Rebels: The Story of the Continental Congress, 1774–1789.* New York: Harper, 1950.

Rakove, Jack. *The Beginnings of National Politics: An Interpretive History of the Continental Congress.* New York: Knopf, 1979.

Robson, Eric. *The American Revolution in Its Political and Military Aspects, 1763–1783.* London: Batchworth, 1955.

Varg, Paul. *Foreign Policies of the Founding Fathers.* East Lansing: Michigan State University, 1963.

Connecticut

Connecticut was never the seat of war during the American Revolution, but the relatively small state made a large contribution to the war effort, providing arms, manpower, provisions, and several important leaders—in the army, politics, and even the arts—to support America's struggle for independence. While the British Army firmly controlled the New York City area and at times seized large parts of New Jersey, Pennsylvania, and Rhode Island during the war, Connecticut remained free from British occupation throughout the conflict. The absence of British troops, except for brief raids on half a dozen communities on or near the coast, allowed the state to aid the American forces with foodstuffs and weapons. The onset of the American Revolution also produced a modest political revolution in Connecticut. Prior to the conflict, residents from western Connecticut held political power within the colony. By 1766, individuals of eastern Connecticut gained power, and they remained dominant for the duration of the war.

Connecticut's resistance to British rule began soon after the conclusion of the French and Indian (Seven Years') War.

View toward Canaan and Salisbury, Connecticut, circa 1789. (Library of Congress)

Connecticut had played an important role in that war by providing financial contributions and manpower, and its inhabitants viewed their efforts as a major factor leading to the defeat of the French in North America. But the end of hostilities caused Connecticut to enter into a severe depression. By 1764 many farmers lacked a market for their agricultural products because militiamen and British troops no longer needed their crops, and the farmers' plight soon affected the colony's merchants. When the merchants could not collect the farmers' outstanding debts, they failed to meet their obligations to merchants and manufacturers in other northeastern colonies. By the mid-1760s a majority of Connecticut's farmers and merchants had declared bankruptcy.

When the British government passed the Sugar Act of 1764, which imposed duties on molasses, refined sugar, and wine, Connecticut's inhabitants protested that the legislation would damage its trade with the West Indies. Governor Thomas Fitch declared that the act would add to the colony's economic distress by forcing merchants to trade solely with British sugar islands. This would make trading with the West Indies less profitable because British sugar was more expensive than French sugar, and the British islands were not a major source of specie for the colony, which was always short of hard cash. In a letter to the British Parliament, Fitch concluded that the act was unjust. The residents of Connecticut also voiced their opposition toward the new legislation, but the British government remained indifferent to the colonists' views and did not reconsider the act.

In March 1765 the British government enacted another revenue measure, the Stamp Act, that required printed documents such as legal contracts, newspapers, and marriage licenses to bear a stamp or be printed on stamped paper available from royal stamp distributors. Connecticut's inhabitants immediately expressed their opposition to the legislation to their General Assembly, which established a committee to write a report expressing the colony's objection to the act. The report maintained that the British government did not have the authority to impose such taxation because residents of Connecticut lacked representation in Parliament and noted that the colony's seventeenth-century charter granted the General Assembly the sole authority to pass legislation. But again, Parliament disregarded the colonists' views and put the Stamp Act into effect on 1 November 1765.

In Connecticut, the attempt to enforce the Stamp Act led to immediate political unrest. The roots of this turmoil stemmed from the manner in which different colonists responded to the act. A majority of the residents in western Connecticut expressed moderate and reasoned views regarding the Stamp Act. Fitch stated that the colonists had a right to express their discontent regarding the legislation, but he asserted that they needed to end their protests once Parliament had decided to enforce the measure. Jared Ingersoll, who had been appointed the stamp distributor in New Haven, believed that the colonists would better serve their interests if they merely accepted the measure and was convinced that if they refused, they would alienate Connecticut's governor, military personnel, and customs collectors.

But while western Connecticut took a moderate stand on the Stamp Act, residents in eastern Connecticut expressed outrage at Parliament's actions. Residents of New London, Lebanon, and Windham denounced the moderation of western Connecticut and burned an effigy of Ingersoll in protest. When Easterners condemned the attitudes of Westerners, however, they were not merely ridiculing them for their stance on the Stamp Act. The residents of eastern Connecticut were giving vent to years of frustration at Westerners defeating them on issues regarding paper money, religious revivalism, and territorial expansion. The Easterners now began using popular outrage over the Stamp Act to undermine the influence of the Westerners in their colony's government.

In the summer of 1765, Eliphalet Dyer of Windham, Jonathan Trumbull of Lebanon, Captain Hugh Ledlie of Windham, Colonel Israel Putnam of Pomfret, and Major John Durkee of Norwich met to discuss both the colony's sectional division and its response to British policy. At the meeting they formed the Sons of Liberty. This organization worked to convince Connecticut's inhabitants that their liberties could only be protected if they removed the colony's Tory officeholders, most of whom resided in western Connecticut, and replaced them with Patriots from eastern Connecticut.

The Sons of Liberty directed their initial efforts against Ingersoll. They believed that by removing him from the General Assembly, they could limit western influence in the legislature and intimidate other moderates. In September 1765, Ingersoll planned to travel to Hartford for a meeting of the General Assembly, which would discuss a proposal to send representatives to the upcoming Stamp Act Congress in New York City. Believing that Ingersoll would oppose sending delegates to the Stamp Act Congress, nearly 500 Sons of Liberty surrounded him in Wethersfield and demanded that he resign from the legislature. Fearing that they would become violent if he refused their demands, Ingersoll agreed. With Ingersoll unable to express his views, the General Assembly voted in favor of sending delegates to the Stamp Act Congress.

In the spring of 1766, the Sons of Liberty turned against Fitch. The Easterners opposed him because of his stance on the Stamp Act; although the governor viewed the act as unjust, he upheld its enforcement. The Sons of Liberty campaigned to defeat Fitch in the upcoming election by appealing to the colonists' distress over Connecticut's economic troubles. The Easterners asserted that if the colonists voted for Fitch in the upcoming election, he would not only infringe upon their freedoms and liberties but would also remain indifferent to their economic plight. The Sons of Liberty also declared that they supported candidates who would prevent further British tyranny within the colony. Their campaigning worked. In the election of 1766 Easterners gained control of both the colony's upper legislative house and the governorship, and they remained in control of Connecticut throughout the Revolutionary era.

Connecticut now adopted a firm Patriot stance in its relations with Britain. While there were few direct confrontations with British authority in Connecticut until the mid-1770s, the Sons of Liberty enforced a boycott of tea following the passage of the Tea Act, and the colonists firmly supported the Patriots who dumped tea into the Boston Harbor in December 1773. Thereafter, Governor Trumbull and other Easterners in control of Connecticut pushed the colony toward a full confrontation with Britain. In 1774, Connecticut's General Assembly passed several resolutions in support of the Patriot position. It repudiated the Coercive Acts, which closed the port of Boston and restructured the government of Massachusetts, and granted aid to the citizens of Boston. The General Assembly also established a Committee of Correspondence to improve its communications with other colonies, and the committee appointed Dyer, Roger Sherman, and Silas Deane to represent Connecticut at the First Continental Congress in Philadelphia. Fearing that a military conflict would erupt between the colonies and Britain, the General Assembly instructed the colony's militia to begin training and directed towns to stockpile military supplies.

Patriots in Connecticut also took measures designed to silence any Loyalist opposition within the colony. While Trumbull thought that individuals should not be persecuted for their political beliefs, he made little effort to protect Tories from harassment by radical Patriots within the colony. And as Tories continued to show allegiance to the British government, Trumbull came to view their actions as impeding the Patriot cause. Upon Trumbull's recommendation, the General Assembly approved legislation that monitored Loyalist behavior throughout Connecticut. This silenced most Connecticut Tories throughout the Revolutionary War. Others who feared harassment escaped to New York City or departed the North American colonies for England, New Brunswick, and Nova Scotia.

Connecticut, which as a charter colony had no royal governor or other royal officials beyond a few customs agents, severed all relations with Britain soon after the outbreak of fighting at Lexington and Concord in April 1775. Trumbull did briefly appeal to General Thomas Gage in Boston to reach some sort of truce with the Patriot forces after the opening battle, but Gage was in no mood to seek an accommodation and had no authority to do so. And when the inhabitants of Connecticut heard news of the battle, more than 3,000 men marched north to join the American forces stationed at Cambridge. While some colonies were initially reluctant to support the war effort, Connecticut proved unwavering in its efforts to aid the American cause.

Following the outbreak of war, Connecticut played an important role in supplying General George Washington's forces. When the Continental Army wintered at Valley Forge in 1777–1778, the troops received provisions on an irregular basis. Lacking adequate food and clothing, Washington's soldiers suffered from illness and hunger. Fearing that disease would decimate his army, Washington wrote to various state governors to send supplies to Valley Forge. Upon learning of Washington's pleas, Trumbull assigned Colonel Henry Champion to collect supplies for the American troops. Throughout the winter and spring of 1778, Champion and his agents overcame hazardous roads and poor weather conditions to bring aid to Washington's forces.

Connecticut also contributed gunpowder to the war effort. During the first two years of the war, the American states imported nearly 90 percent of their gunpowder from Europe. Connecticut's General Assembly lessened this dependence upon foreign gunpowder by establishing powder mills in Hartford, Salisbury, Glastonbury, Windham, New Haven, and Stratford. Although the insufficient supplies of saltpeter and sulfur limited the production of these mills, the state continued to supply gunpowder to American forces during the war. And Connecticut maintained this effort while repelling British raids at Horseneck (Greenwich), Danbury, New London, and Groton until nearly the end of the war.

Finally, Connecticut supplied men to the American cause. Sizable numbers of Connecticut soldiers and officers participated in most battles in the northern, middle, and Chesapeake regions throughout the war, from the capture of Ticonderoga in May 1775 to Yorktown. The state's contribution of military, political, and cultural leaders was just as impressive. Heading the list were Trumbull, one of the nation's most effective wartime executives, and his sons Joseph, the first commissary general of the Continental Army, and John, the foremost artist of Revolutionary battles and political drama after the war. In Congress, Sherman and Samuel Huntington played key roles into the late 1780s. Deane's checkered career as a congressional agent and diplomat in France was controversial but undeniably important. And in a class by himself was General Benedict Arnold, a genuine hero of the war for three years, a troubled leader for another two seasons, and then America's great traitor who ended his American career by attacking his own state at New London and Groton, where he presided, evidently unknowingly, over one of the last British massacres of American forces at Fort Griswold.

Following the conclusion of peace between the United States and Great Britain in 1783, Connecticut strongly favored a more centralized system of government for the newly established republic. At the Philadelphia convention in 1787, Sherman played a key role in leading the smaller states to secure parity with the larger states in the U.S. Senate. On 9 January 1788, Connecticut became the fifth state to ratify the U.S. Constitution.

Kevin M. Brady

See also

Arnold, Benedict; Congress, Second Continental and Confederation; Continental Army; Correspondence, Committees of; Danbury, Connecticut, Raid on; Deane, Silas; Dyer, Eliphalet; Fort Griswold, Connecticut, Attack on; Huntington, Samuel; New London, Connecticut, Raid on; Putnam, Israel; Sherman, Roger; Sons of Liberty; Trumbull, John; Trumbull, Jonathan; Trumbull, Joseph

References

Buel, Richard, Jr. *Dear Liberty: Connecticut's Mobilization for the Revolutionary War.* Middletown, CT: Wesleyan University Press, 1980.

Bushman, Richard L. *From Puritan to Yankee: Character and the Social Order in Connecticut, 1690–1765.* Cambridge: Harvard University Press, 1967.

Purcell, Richard J. *Connecticut in Transition, 1775–1818.* Washington, DC: American Historical Association, 1918.

Roth, David M. *Connecticut: A Bicentennial History.* New York: Norton, 1979.

Zeichner, Oscar. *Connecticut's Years of Controversy, 1750–1776.* Hamden, CT: Archon, 1970.

Connecticut Farms, New Jersey

See Springfield and Connecticut Farms, New Jersey, Raids on

Connolly, John (1750?–1813)

John Connolly, a Loyalist soldier and frontiersman, sought without success to establish British control over the upper Ohio Valley.

Born about 1750 at Wright's Ferry, York County, Pennsylvania, Connolly enlisted in the British Army at an early age and served in Martinique in 1762. He participated in two North American campaigns against the Indians from 1762 to 1764 and then spent a period of time traveling among the Native Americans. When Virginia's governor, John Murray, Lord Dunmore, granted land in the Kentucky area to veterans and thereby began Lord Dunmore's War with the Shawnees in 1774, Connolly served as a captain and then major with the Virginia militia.

By the summer of 1775, Connolly was in Pittsburgh. Upon receiving news of the Battle of Bunker Hill, he wrote to Dunmore for instructions and was advised to try to induce the Mingo Indians to join the British cause. Connolly also provided intelligence to militia officers on the long Virginia frontier and gave Dunmore's assurance of a land title and 300 acres of land to all who took up arms in support of the British.

Connolly next traveled to Boston to present his plan for establishing control over the West to General Thomas Gage. Connolly asked to be commissioned major commandant of such troops as he could raise on the frontier and planned to collect enough ordnance to destroy Fort Dunmore (Fort Pitt) and Fort Fincastle if their rebel garrisons should resist. He also sought authorization to make presents to the Indians to get them to aid in the attacks. Gage was to furnish the necessary arms. Gage accepted Connolly's proposals.

Connolly then proceeded to Virginia and received a commission as lieutenant-colonel commandant from Dunmore on 5 November 1775. On his way back to the frontier, Connolly's plans collapsed when the Committee of Safety in Hagerstown, Maryland, jailed him on suspicion of being a Loyalist. The committee shipped Connolly to Philadelphia, where his now-destitute wife joined him in jail.

Connolly languished in jail for more than three years and only gained his parole after General John Sullivan's defeat of the Iroquois in 1779 led Congress to believe that the Indians were too badly beaten to threaten the frontier again. Congress passed a resolution to exchange Connolly for any American lieutenant colonel in British prisons, and on 4 July 1780 he received his freedom.

Still plotting to take over the West, Connolly next presented a plan to Sir Henry Clinton for attacking frontier outposts and taking Pittsburgh. In 1781, he joined the British Army under Lord Charles Cornwallis and moved southward. At Yorktown, however, he accidentally wandered into territory commanded by American troops. Arrested again, Connolly remained a prisoner in Philadelphia until March 1782, when he was permitted to travel to New York City. Soon thereafter he sailed for London. Connolly moved to Montreal in 1799 and died in poverty on 30 January 1813 after a long illness.

Caryn E. Neumann

See also

Murray, John, Lord Dunmore; Native Americans; Pennsylvania; Virginia

References

Burton, Clarence Monroe. "John Connolly: A Tory of the Revolution." *Proceedings of the American Antiquarian Society* 20 (1909): 70–105.

Utley, Robert M., and Wilcomb E. Washburn. *Indian Wars.* Boston: Houghton Mifflin, 1987.

Constitution, United States (1787)

Framed in contentious debates between May and September 1787, the U.S. Constitution was the next to last major political achievement of the American Revolution and, with the addition of the Bill of Rights in 1789–1791, it became the enduring formal foundation of the new American republic. The Constitution proved able, over time, to do two remarkable new things. First, it give the young nation a political base that proved both flexible enough to accommodate two centuries of enormous economic, geographic, and demographic growth and equally dramatic social, cultural, and technological change and powerful enough to survive a major civil war. Second, it provided the American Revolution, at its conclusion, with a textual focal point that no previous document, whether the Declaration of Independence, the Articles of Confederation, or the pioneering and often highly revered constitution of any particular state, could begin to equal.

John Adams, a Massachusetts delegate to the Continental Congress, was considered somewhat of an expert on republican government. Delegates from Virginia, North Carolina, and New Jersey consulted Adams in the process of drafting their constitutions, and he eventually published a pamphlet, *Thoughts on Government,* that set out his views on effective republican government. In 1780, he drafted the Constitution of the Commonwealth of Massachusetts, which is the world's oldest continuous constitution still in use today. (Library of Congress)

By 1786, many Revolutionary leaders thought that the new American nation, governed by a small unicameral Congress under the Articles of Confederation since 1777, was in crisis. Some of them believed that the Revolution itself was in danger. In theory, congressional requisitions on the states were law and so were the confederation's treaties. In practice, violations of several articles of the Treaty of Paris by a number of the states were being used by Britain to justify its refusal to evacuate a string of forts in the American Northwest, from which Britain still controlled the fur trade and influenced Native American tribes whose warfare with the western settlements had never really ceased. Pirate raids had nearly closed the Mediterranean Sea to American merchant ships. And Spain had closed the mouth of the Mississippi River, locking up the trade of the American West. But the Confederation Congress had no navy, only a few hundred unpaid troops, and insufficient funds even to buy a treaty with the pirates.

In every year since the conclusion of the peace, state payments of requisitions to Congress had been smaller than the operating costs of the tiny central government, and federal revenues had never been remotely equal to the interest charges on its debt. Domestic creditors had not been paid for years, Congress had suspended interest payments on its debt to France and Spain, and the nation was approaching an exhaustion of its credit with Dutch bankers. New Jersey had resolved that it would pay its requisitions only if the most recalcitrant states would ratify the impost amendment, granting Congress power to collect an independent duty on foreign imports. Yet every effort to amend the Articles of Confederation had been to no avail due to the requirement of unanimous consent, and Congress was itself unable to agree on new proposals for reform. Indeed, its failure to agree on an amendment granting Congress power over trade persuaded the Virginia General Assembly to propose a meeting of delegates at Annapolis, Maryland, in September 1786 to consider better ways to regulate the country's interstate and international commerce.

As those delegates assembled, it seemed obvious to some that the American union was not just ineffective but in danger of imminent collapse, with drastic consequences for the Revolution. The world had not succumbed to the new nation's Revolutionary doctrine of free trade. Instead, the peace had brought a serious depression, which many blamed on European regulations restricting American trade. Several states had individually attempted to retaliate against the Europeans, only to be checked by the conflicting regulations of their neighbors. Most had tried to ease the economic suffering of their own citizens with paper money, moratoriums on taxes, or laws preventing creditors from suing for the recovery of debts—legislation that opponents saw as deeply threatening to rights that they believed the Revolution had been undertaken to protect.

Popular commotions stemming from the economic troubles were becoming deeply troubling as well. In Massachusetts, these would culminate in Shays's Rebellion in the fall of 1786, shortly after rising interstate resentments had provoked some serious discussion of the dissolution of the union. Indeed, just as the delegates were gathering for the Annapolis Convention, the Confederation Congress saw its sharpest sectional collision of the postwar years. From Pennsylvania north, the states were eager to secure a commercial treaty with Spain. But Spain was willing to conclude a treaty only if the United States would agree to the closing of the Mississippi for a generation's time, a price that every southern delegation was ferociously determined not to pay. Not surprisingly, the dozen delegates who actually assembled at Annapolis—an unimpressive fragment of the respectable convention hoped for in the spring—agreed to recommend another extraordinary meeting to Congress and to their states, this one with the power to consider *all* the defects of the Articles of Confederation. Congress endorsed their recommendation of a general convention to consider ways to make the central government "adequate to the exigencies of the Union." Badly frightened by events in Massachusetts or believing that the dissolution of the union would entail a replication of the fractured state of Europe with its tyrannies and wars, every state except Rhode Island answered the call.

Assembling at the Pennsylvania State House (Independence Hall), the Constitutional Convention opened on 25 May 1787 and sat until 17 September. Fifty-five delegates participated in the work, though there were seldom more than forty in the room on any single day. The nation might have organized an equally impressive meeting from the ranks of leaders who did not attend, including John and Samuel Adams, Thomas Jefferson, John Jay, and Patrick Henry. Still, most states had followed the example of Virginia, which had led throughout the process, sending several of their best and most experienced leaders, usually with slight regard for factional considerations. George Washington was at the head of the Virginia delegation, signaling his own and the Old Dominion's serious commitment to the project. Of course, he was immediately selected to preside.

Once again, Virginia took the lead. James Madison, who had initiated the Annapolis Convention, had been thinking problems through to a degree that no one else had done, taking careful notes on ancient and modern confederacies, preparing the formal memorandum "Vices of the Political System of the United States," and urging fellow members of his delegation to arrive in Philadelphia in time to frame some introductory proposals. Virginia's seven delegates assembled daily while they waited for the full convention to obtain a quorum, agreeing on a set of resolutions that might serve as a preliminary basis for discussions. Speaking for the delegation as a whole, Governor Edmund Randolph introduced these resolutions on 29 May, as soon as the convention had agreed on its rules.

The meeting turned immediately to a consideration of the Randolph (or Virginia) Plan. Together with the adoption of a rigid, carefully respected rule of secrecy that freed the mem-

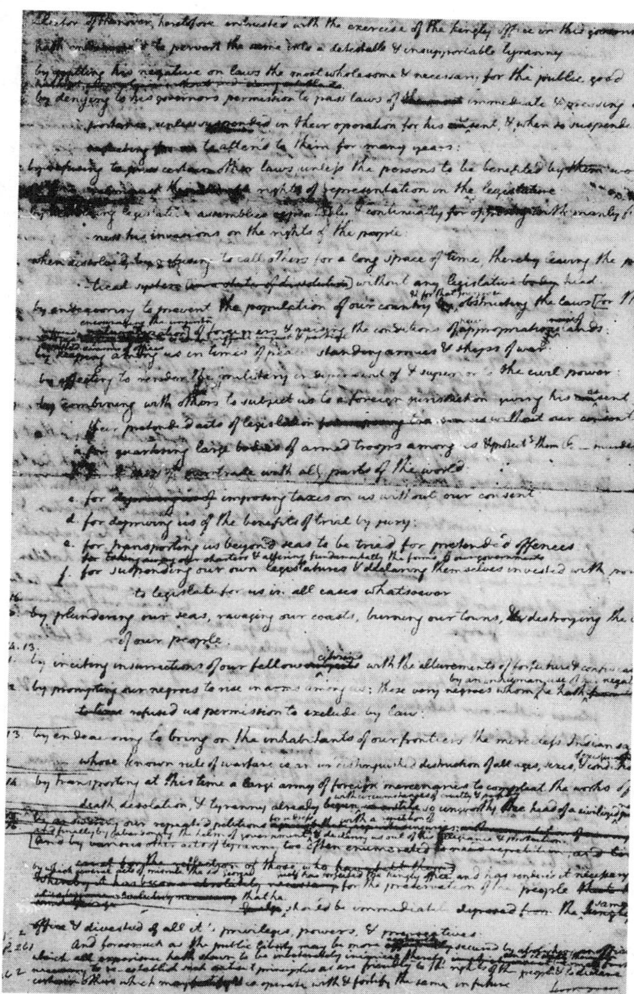

Thomas Jefferson's draft of the Virginia Constitution, circa 1776. (Library of Congress)

bers from external pressure and encouraged them to feel that they could change their stands if the deliberations changed their minds, this was a critical decision. The Virginia Resolutions, which were based primarily on Madison's ideas, did not propose to make the Articles of Confederation "adequate to the exigencies of the Union," as Congress had directed. Rather, they envisioned the complete replacement of the current central government with a republican regime of national extent. The present, single-chamber government would be reorganized in imitation of the complex constitutions of the states. Based directly on the people, it would have the right "to legislate in all cases to which the separate States are incompetent." To guarantee the central government's supremacy wherever common measures were required, the articles of union would be ratified by state conventions chosen by the people, and federal powers would include authority "to call forth the force of the Union against any member of the Union failing to fulfill its duty" or to veto state legislation inconsistent with the federal charter.

These proposals were, of course, more radical by far than many delegates expected. Still, Madison and his Virginia colleagues had correctly sensed, as other delegates trickled into town, that early sentiment was overwhelmingly opposed to patchwork, piecemeal efforts to amend the Articles of Confederation. Many thought that the convention might afford the last alternative to fragmentation of the union. Many feared, as Madison had put it in his preconvention letters, that America's republican experiment could not survive the dissolution of the union. Madison himself believed that popular commitment to the Revolution was already flagging as the ineffectuality of Congress reinforced the tendency in many states toward fluctuating, ill-considered legislation that reflected slight regard for either private rights or long-term public needs. He therefore warned the other delegates that they were not assembled merely to attend to the debility of Congress. Their ultimate objective, he insisted, must be nothing less than to "perpetuate the union and redeem the honor of the republican name."

This solemn sense of high responsibility and urgent, common purpose was essential to the meeting's great achievements, not least because most delegates were only partially prepared for such enormous change. Seizing the initiative for radical reform, Virginia's resolutions demonstrated an instinctive grasp of several broad, though hazy, understandings that would limit and direct the meeting's course. The delegates—leaders of a democratic revolution, including thirty veterans of the war—would not neglect the dangers posed by an unresponsive, distant federal power. Still, nearly all of them had come to think that an effective central government would need to have, at minimum, an independent source of revenue, authority to regulate the country's trade, and power to compel obedience to its legitimate commands. The fundamental issue, in the weeks ahead, was not the powers that might properly be placed in federal hands but whether the specific kinds of checks envisioned in these resolutions were sufficient to protect the people and the states.

Assisted by strong allies in the Pennsylvania delegation, the Virginians were prepared from the beginning to insist that powers of this sort could safely be entrusted to a well-constructed, fully representative republic. Indeed, the genius of their plan was that it offered a republican solution to the stubborn fear of concentrated central power. Overawed by the Virginia Plan, accepting many of its goals, and unprepared to offer comprehensive counterresolutions, dissenters were uncertain how to rebut its proponents in debate. They nonetheless insisted from the start that the convention was empowered only to reform the present federal system, not to overturn it. The framing of the Constitution thus became a complicated story of a fundamental conflict that occurred within the context of a common quest.

Between 30 May and 13 June, the delegates conducted a complete, initial run-through of the Virginia resolutions.

During these two weeks, with Madison and James Wilson of Pennsylvania at their head, a brilliant group of delegates from larger states developed a compelling case for radical reform. Distinguishing between a "national" government and one "merely federal," Wilson, Madison, Randolph, George Mason (Virginia), Gouverneur Morris (Pennsylvania), and others argued that the fatal weakness of the old confederation was its unavoidable dependence on the thirteen states for revenue and for a host of intermediary actions necessary to enforce its laws and treaties. Lacking independent means to carry its decisions into action, they explained, Congress had been baffled by the states even when its measures were supported by a huge majority and were undeniably within its proper sphere of authority. Grants of new responsibilities would only add new sources of frustration if the states retained the power to ignore or counteract the central government's decisions.

The inescapable necessity, these nationalists maintained, was to abandon the unworkable idea of a government over governments, a sovereignty over sovereigns, and give the central government the courts and other independent means to act directly on the individual members of society. Revolutionary principles required, however, that any government possessing the authority to reach the people's lives and pockets must represent its citizens immediately and fairly. Given the necessity for larger, more effective federal powers, the traditional equality between the states would have to be abandoned in order to preserve equality among the people and majority control. Both houses of the reconstructed Congress would have to be apportioned according to state populations.

Most of the nationalists' opponents, intellectually outclassed by men such as Madison and Wilson, squirmed without responding through the meeting's early days. But the Virginia Plan not only horrified the smaller states; it seemed to other members to depart too far from the essential spirit of a federal system or to call for more participation by the people than the people were equipped to make in national affairs. And as the skeleton of the Virginia Resolutions put on flesh, the confrontation that had loomed from the beginning could no longer be contained. New Jersey's delegates demanded a decision on apportioning the Congress, insisting on 9 June that proportional representation would destroy the smaller states and place the whole confederation at the mercy of a coalition of its largest members: Massachusetts, Pennsylvania, and Virginia. The division that would dominate proceedings for the next five weeks had burst into the open. It would prove the clearest, most dramatic, most persistent argument of the convention—the single conflict over which the gathering repeatedly approached collapse.

The first two weeks of the convention saw some striking nationalist successes. Like Madison, most delegates had come to Philadelphia as worried by conditions in the states as by the problems of the union. Although they genuinely shared the people's fierce resistance to hereditary privilege and power, nearly all were also powerfully determined not to reproduce the errors that they believed had been committed in the constitutions of the states. Here, again, the resolutions of 29 May successfully defined the boundaries of disagreement. Sound republics, they suggested, must incorporate two legislative houses: one directly elected by the people, the other chosen in a manner that would shield its members from the whims of the majority and thus assure continuing concern for the rights of the minority and long-term public needs. The legislature should be counterbalanced by a forceful, separate executive, and the judiciary should be independent of them both. Through almost four months of sometimes bitter quarrels, there was never any serious dispute about these fundamental principles of governmental structure. The Virginia Resolutions offered only a preliminary sketch of an improved republic. They did not specifically define which powers were beyond the competence of individual states. They did not decide if the executive should be a council or a single man. They did, however, both elicit and direct a general search for principles and structural devices that could guarantee a place for governmental energy and wisdom as well as for responsiveness to popular demands.

The plan survived its first examination fundamentally intact, its sketchy outline filling rapidly as the debates suggested and improved upon the broad agreements that were present from the start. Wilson, Madison, and other advocates of thoroughgoing change made it clear that what they wanted was to build a wise and energetic central government upon a broadly popular foundation, blending a responsibility to the majority with multiple securities against an overbearing, popularly elected lower house. Impressed by their analysis of the debilities of the existing system, the convention speedily agreed to substitute a complex and authoritative central government for the present feeble and unicameral regime. Sharing their dissatisfaction with the constitutions of several of the states, delegates worked from the beginning to establish genuinely independent, fully countervailing branches of government.

Madison and Wilson mostly had their way. On 31 May, with only two states voting no, the delegates overwhelmingly approved the popular election of the lower house (the House of Representatives). They easily decided on a three-year term for representatives and seven years for the executive and members of the upper house (the Senate). Insisting that the surest way to guarantee a safe but firm executive was to confer responsibility on one accountable individual, Wilson led a winning struggle for a single chief executive, though he could not prevent the fearful delegates from ruling that this magistrate could only serve a single term and was to be elected by the legislature, not the people. On 11 June, two days after the New Jersey delegates insisted on the critical decision, the convention voted seven states to three, with Maryland

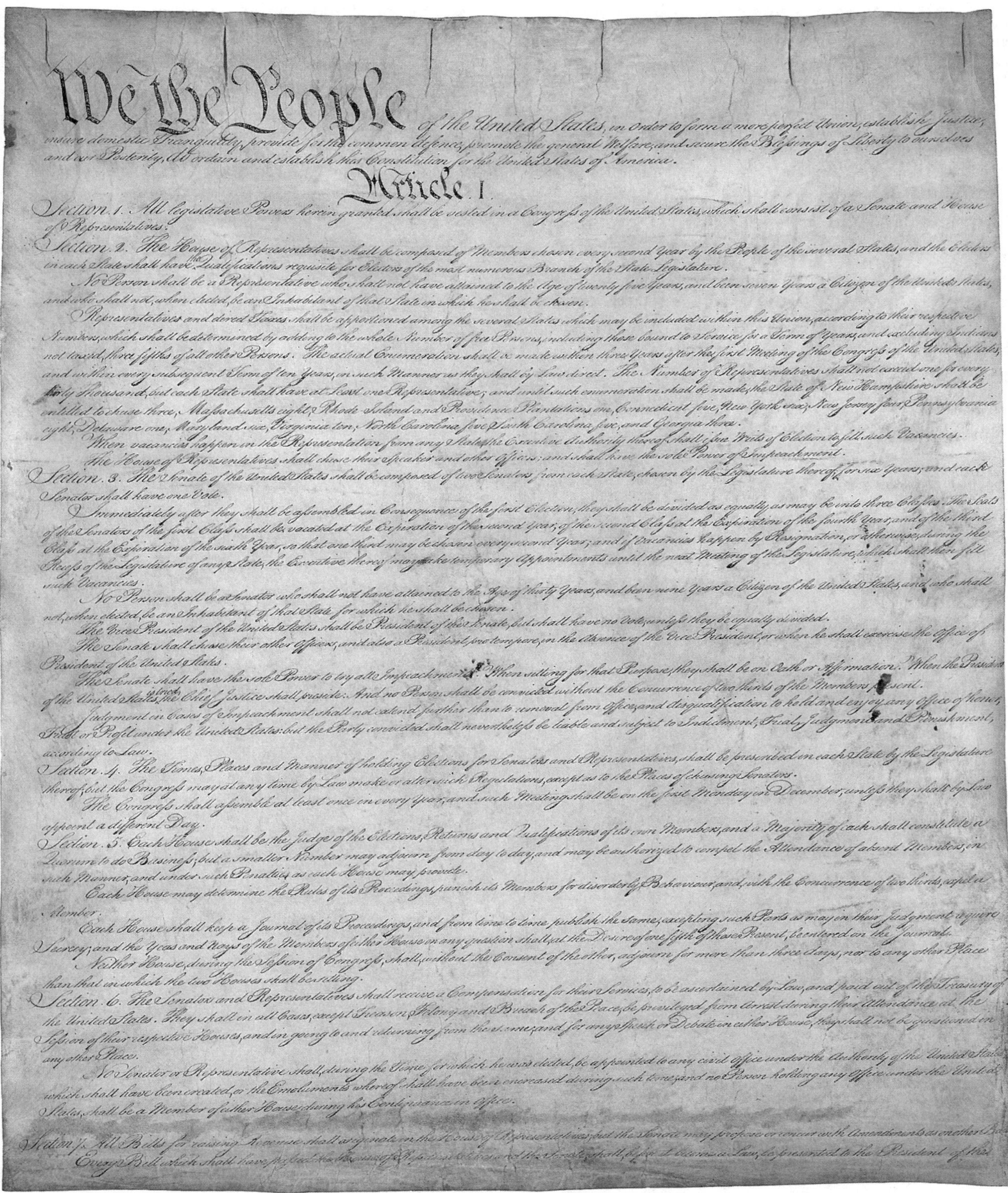

We the People of the United States, in Order to form a more perfect Union, establish Justice, insure domestic Tranquility, provide for the common defence, promote the general Welfare, and secure the Blessings of Liberty to ourselves and our Posterity, do ordain and establish this Constitution for the United States of America.

Article. I.

Section. 1. All legislative Powers herein granted shall be vested in a Congress of the United States, which shall consist of a Senate and House of Representatives.

Section. 2. The House of Representatives shall be composed of Members chosen every second Year by the People of the several States, and the Electors in each State shall have the Qualifications requisite for Electors of the most numerous Branch of the State Legislature.

No Person shall be a Representative who shall not have attained to the Age of twenty five Years, and been seven Years a Citizen of the United States, and who shall not, when elected, be an Inhabitant of that State in which he shall be chosen.

Representatives and direct Taxes shall be apportioned among the several States which may be included within this Union, according to their respective Numbers, which shall be determined by adding to the whole Number of free Persons, including those bound to Service for a Term of Years, and excluding Indians not taxed, three fifths of all other Persons. The actual Enumeration shall be made within three Years after the first Meeting of the Congress of the United States, and within every subsequent Term of ten Years, in such Manner as they shall by Law direct. The Number of Representatives shall not exceed one for every thirty Thousand, but each State shall have at Least one Representative; and until such enumeration shall be made, the State of New Hampshire shall be entitled to chuse three, Massachusetts eight, Rhode Island and Providence Plantations one, Connecticut five, New York six, New Jersey four, Pennsylvania eight, Delaware one, Maryland six, Virginia ten, North Carolina five, South Carolina five, and Georgia three.

When vacancies happen in the Representation from any State, the Executive Authority thereof shall issue Writs of Election to fill such Vacancies.

The House of Representatives shall chuse their Speaker and other Officers; and shall have the sole Power of Impeachment.

Section. 3. The Senate of the United States shall be composed of two Senators from each State, chosen by the Legislature thereof for six Years; and each Senator shall have one Vote.

Immediately after they shall be assembled in Consequence of the first Election, they shall be divided as equally as may be into three Classes. The Seats of the Senators of the first Class shall be vacated at the Expiration of the second Year, of the second Class at the Expiration of the fourth Year, and of the third Class at the Expiration of the sixth Year, so that one third may be chosen every second Year; and if Vacancies happen by Resignation, or otherwise, during the Recess of the Legislature of any State, the Executive thereof may make temporary Appointments until the next Meeting of the Legislature, which shall then fill such Vacancies.

No Person shall be a Senator who shall not have attained to the Age of thirty Years, and been nine Years a Citizen of the United States, and who shall not, when elected, be an Inhabitant of that State for which he shall be chosen.

The Vice President of the United States shall be President of the Senate, but shall have no Vote, unless they be equally divided.

The Senate shall chuse their other Officers, and also a President pro tempore, in the Absence of the Vice President, or when he shall exercise the Office of President of the United States.

The Senate shall have the sole Power to try all Impeachments. When sitting for that Purpose, they shall be on Oath or Affirmation. When the President of the United States is tried, the Chief Justice shall preside: And no Person shall be convicted without the Concurrence of two thirds of the Members present.

Judgment in Cases of Impeachment shall not extend further than to removal from Office, and disqualification to hold and enjoy any Office of honor, Trust or Profit under the United States: but the Party convicted shall nevertheless be liable and subject to Indictment, Trial, Judgment and Punishment, according to Law.

Section. 4. The Times, Places and Manner of holding Elections for Senators and Representatives, shall be prescribed in each State by the Legislature thereof; but the Congress may at any time by Law make or alter such Regulations, except as to the Places of chusing Senators.

The Congress shall assemble at least once in every Year, and such Meeting shall be on the first Monday in December, unless they shall by Law appoint a different Day.

Section. 5. Each House shall be the Judge of the Elections, Returns and Qualifications of its own Members, and a Majority of each shall constitute a Quorum to do Business; but a smaller Number may adjourn from day to day, and may be authorized to compel the Attendance of absent Members, in such Manner, and under such Penalties as each House may provide.

Each House may determine the Rules of its Proceedings, punish its Members for disorderly Behaviour, and, with the Concurrence of two thirds, expel a Member.

Each House shall keep a Journal of its Proceedings, and from time to time publish the same, excepting such Parts as may in their Judgment require Secrecy; and the Yeas and Nays of the Members of either House on any question shall, at the Desire of one fifth of those Present, be entered on the Journal.

Neither House, during the Session of Congress, shall, without the Consent of the other, adjourn for more than three days, nor to any other Place than that in which the two Houses shall be sitting.

Section. 6. The Senators and Representatives shall receive a Compensation for their Services, to be ascertained by Law, and paid out of the Treasury of the United States. They shall in all Cases, except Treason, Felony and Breach of the Peace, be privileged from Arrest during their Attendance at the Session of their respective Houses, and in going to and returning from the same; and for any Speech or Debate in either House, they shall not be questioned in any other Place.

No Senator or Representative shall, during the Time for which he was elected, be appointed to any civil Office under the Authority of the United States, which shall have been created, or the Emoluments whereof shall have been encreased during such time; and no Person holding any Office under the United States, shall be a Member of either House during his Continuance in Office.

Section. 7. All Bills for raising Revenue shall originate in the House of Representatives; but the Senate may propose or concur with Amendments as on other Bills.

Every Bill which shall have passed the House of Representatives and the Senate, shall, before it become a Law, be presented to the President of the

First page of the Constitution of the United States. The document was drafted by delegates from twelve states, meeting in Philadelphia between May and September 1787. (National Archives and Records Administration)

divided and New Hampshire not yet present, for proportional representation in the lower house. Only tiny Delaware and antinational New York, where Alexander Hamilton was overruled by Robert Yates and John Lansing, sided with New Jersey on the question.

Nevertheless, the democratic nationalists by no means carried every critical decision. The fierce resistance of the smaller states grew more and more imposing as it coalesced with opposition based on different concerns. Only three delegates were rigidly committed to a "merely federal" system, but Yates and Lansing could control New York, while Luther Martin often managed to divide the Maryland contingent. For each obstructionist, moreover, there were several others who participated deeply in the general fear of popular misrule, which reinforced a reluctance to surrender local powers to a popular majority in Congress. Although the delegations from Connecticut and South Carolina were especially inclined to be distrustful of a scheme that would erect a stronger central government on greater popular involvement, almost every delegation was composed of men who differed widely in their judgments of the people's competence as well as in their willingness to shift additional responsibilities into federal hands. As the smaller states found partial allies among convention delegates, it seemed unlikely that a national republic could secure approval both from a majority of states and from the representatives of a majority of the people. Even optimistic nationalists resigned themselves to a campaign that promised to extend throughout the summer.

Confronted with so many overlapping fears, the nationalists were handed one significant defeat. On 7 June, over loud objections from Madison and Wilson, majorities in every delegation, even Pennsylvania's and Virginia's, voted for election of the Senate by the legislatures of the states. Nearly everyone agreed that the Virginia Plan's provision for election of the Senate by the lower house might give that branch an overweening influence, while few were willing to entrust election of the Senate to the people, as Wilson recommended. Doubting that the people were equipped to make a fit selection or insisting that a Senate chosen in that way would prove unable to defend minorities against majority demands, many members saw election by state legislatures simply as a lesser evil. Many others, though, were forcefully impressed by the insistence of John Dickinson (Delaware) and Roger Sherman (Connecticut) that selection by state legislatures could collect the sense of states as states, assure a federal harmony, and offer firm securities against potential federal usurpations.

Committed nationalists were deeply disappointed. Fearing that election of the Senate by the states would build into the system just the flaw that was destroying the confederation, they also rightly sensed that the insistence on a federal role for states as states would reinforce demands for an equality between them. And, indeed, on that same day, the overwhelming vote for proportional representation in the lower house was followed by a very close decision on the Senate when Sherman's motion for equality was narrowly rejected, 6 to 5: Connecticut, New York, New Jersey, Delaware, and Maryland voted aye; Massachusetts, Pennsylvania, Virginia, North Carolina, South Carolina, and Georgia voted nay. Two days later the convention finished its initial run through the preliminary resolutions, but the opposition to domination by the large states had become so serious that the delegates immediately adjourned in order to permit opponents to prepare alternatives to the Virginia Plan.

William Paterson's New Jersey Resolutions, introduced on 15 June, were thrown together quickly by the coalition that had voted for an equal Senate days before. This coalition was united only by its opposition to the Virginia Plan, and its proposals did not represent the real desires of any of its framers. As Dickinson told Madison in private conversation, many members from the smaller states were willing to support a vigorous, bicameral regime but would sooner submit to a foreign power than be deprived of an equal vote in both houses. Paterson's proposals were, for them, essentially a strategy for forcing some concessions. Under the New Jersey Plan, the general government still would have had the power to impose a stamp tax, postal duties, and an impost; compel compliance with its requisitions; and regulate the country's interstate and foreign commerce. Federal laws would have overridden local legislation. There would have been a separate executive and federal courts. But every state would have had an equal vote in a single-chamber Congress.

The delegates debated the Virginia and New Jersey plans on Saturday, 16 June. Paterson and Lansing argued that the Virginia Resolutions could never win acceptance by the states. Wilson argued that the gathering was free to recommend whatever changes it considered proper and should not consent to an enlargement of the powers of a single legislative chamber that would not derive directly from the people. Randolph said again that the convention had to choose between a power to coerce the states, which would not work, and power to command the people, for which a body such as the current Congress was unfit.

Hamilton monopolized the floor on Monday, 18 June, to suggest that even the Virginia Plan might leave excessive powers with the states and that full security against the instability inherent in a democratic system might require a closer imitation of the British constitution than anyone was willing to support. Madison concluded the discussion Tuesday morning in his longest speech up to that date, listing several ways in which a merely federal reform would fail to overcome specific problems and appealing to the smaller states to recognize that no state had more to lose if the convention proved unable to agree. After Madison had spoken, the convention voted seven states to three, with Maryland again divided, to

Independence Hall in Philadelphia, where the Declaration of Independence and the U.S. Constitution were deliberated and signed. (National Archives and Records Administration)

adhere to the Virginia Resolutions. It had taken less than three full days to reconfirm the general agreement that a purely federal reform, however thorough, could not satisfy the union's needs.

Little else, however, was decided by this vote. As soon as the convention turned again to the Virginia Resolutions, Lansing moved again to vest the legislative powers in a single house. His motion brought a 6–4–1 division that would hold on several important questions in the days to come: Massachusetts, Pennsylvania, and the four states south of the Potomac were united against Connecticut, New York, New Jersey, and Delaware, with Maryland divided. Indeed, it soon became apparent that the conflict over representation overshadowed every other disagreement. Though Madison and Hamilton insisted that the small states need not fear a coalition of the large because the vital differences within the union were between the North and South, William Samuel Johnson of Connecticut replied that a general government was being framed for states as well as people and that even Mason had admitted that the states should have some means to guarantee their rights and place within the system. By the end of June, when the convention voted 6–4–1 again for proportional representation in the lower house, the meeting was approaching dissolution, and Connecticut again proposed the compromise that Sherman had suggested weeks before: proportional representation in the lower house but equal votes in the Senate. Wilson, Madison, and Rufus King (Massachusetts) continued to object. On 2 July, nevertheless, a motion for an equal Senate failed only on an even division: Connecticut, New York, New Jersey, Delaware, and Maryland aye; Massachusetts, Pennsylvania, Virginia, North Carolina, and South Carolina nay; and Georgia now divided. With the meeting at a deadlock and the large-state coalition showing obvious internal stress, the delegates agreed on the appointment of a grand committee to resolve the impasse.

To Madison and Wilson, the result was not a compromise at all but a surrender to the smaller states, and one that seriously marred the symmetry of the evolving system. For two more weeks, they pleaded with the smaller states to give up their demand for a concession plainly incompatible with democratic principles and larger federal powers. It was increasingly apparent, nonetheless, that several influential members from the larger states were less and less inclined toward a continued confrontation. Not only did they realize that the convention's work would surely be rejected if the smaller states walked out, but some of them conceded that a Senate representing states as states might help maintain a federal equilibrium while standing at a proper distance from the lower house and the people. Genuine consolidationists were every bit as rare in the convention as were members who were totally opposed to the replacement of the Articles of Confederation.

Sniffing the prevailing breeze, Yates and Lansing withdrew from the convention on 11 July, depriving New York of its vote. (Hamilton had left some days before and would return, as a nonvoting member, only to be present at the finish.) Three days later, Wilson, Madison, and others offered last appeals for an alternative that would have minimized disparities between the states without conceding equal votes. But on 16 July, the members voted 5–4–1 for the committee's compromise proposal: Connecticut, New Jersey, Delaware, Maryland, North Carolina aye; Pennsylvania, Virginia, South Carolina, Georgia nay; and Massachusetts now divided.

The decision of 16 July, as Randolph quickly noted, was not as narrow as the margin might suggest. New York, New Hampshire, and Rhode Island were unrepresented at the time. All would probably have favored equal representation in at least one house. In addition, several moderates from Georgia, Pennsylvania, and Virginia sympathized with those in Massachusetts, Maryland, and North Carolina who had voted for the Connecticut Plan. The large states held a caucus in the aftermath of the decision. Wilson, Madison, and others still preferred to try to face the small states down, but they could not secure a general agreement. All of the larger states returned to the convention, and the smaller ones were satisfied from that point forward that opponents of the compromise would not attempt to countermand it.

As Randolph also observed, the ruling of 16 July required rethinking every previous decision, as all of them had been affected by the supposition that proportional representation would prevail in both legislative houses. Nevertheless, the Great (or Connecticut) Compromise assured that the convention would succeed. Both the large states and the small, the North together with the South (for all the southern delegations had voted with the large-state coalition), could now anticipate control of one house of Congress. With every section's vital interests guaranteed, every delegate felt freer to address the national ills that none of them denied. Almost all the delegates had made it clear by now that they intended to define a middle ground between the ineffectuality of the confederation and excessive concentration of authority in central hands.

With the ruling that the upper house would represent the states, whose legislatures would select its members, the delegates had satisfied demands for more protection for states' rights and had reconfirmed a mode of indirect election that promised to secure the Senate's independence from the lower house without provoking popular suspicions. Thus, the members needed only ten more days to reach agreement on the basic features of the Constitution. This is not to say that the completion of the work proved quick or easy. Several complicated passages remained, and more than one debate became quite heated. Yet none of the remaining difficulties blocked the members' progress as completely as the conflict over representation had done.

Among the remaining difficulties, the most perplexing centered on the powers and selection of a chief executive. Having each secured control of one house of the Congress, neither coalition wanted to permit the other to control this branch. Moreover, nearly all the delegates were dedicated to a complex, balanced government yet reasoned from a heritage in which the influence and ambitions of executives had always been identified as constant dangers to a balanced system. Thus, although election by the legislature seemed most likely to secure the ablest man, it also seemed to threaten an improper link between the branches. Selection by the people would assure the branches' independence and permit the reelection of a solid choice, yet many at the meeting doubted that the people could possess the information needed for a sound selection. Eventually, another grand committee would be needed to consider these discussions and concoct a curious agreement that the nation's chief executive would be selected for a four-year term by electors chosen in such manner as the local legislatures should direct (or by the national lower house, from leading candidates, if no one had a majority in the Electoral College). This cumbersome procedure (the Electoral College) was deliberately contrived to balance the demands of the larger and smaller states. In addition, opponents of election by the people and opponents of election by the states could each find solace in a mode of indirect election that might start with either while securing a certain independence of them both. But the delegates were not yet ready to embrace this compromise and made a temporary decision—which satisfied few members—that the president would be elected by the legislature for a single term.

More threatening, though less perplexing, were certain differences that now arose between the North and South. On 24 July, the members eagerly agreed to adjourn until Monday, 6 August, for a Committee of Detail to put all its resolutions into order. While Washington went fishing and visited the old encampment at Valley Forge, this committee—Randolph, Wilson, John Rutledge (South Carolina), Nathaniel Gorham (Massachusetts), and Oliver Ellsworth (Connecticut)—took responsibility for much more than a careful ordering of the decisions reached in the convention to that point. Besides providing more elaborate descriptions of executive and judicial powers, they recommended that agreement by a two-thirds vote of the Congress should be necessary for the admission of new states or the passage of commercial regulations. They inserted prohibitions of a tax on exports or on interference with the slave trade, which C. C. Pinckney (South Carolina) had demanded as conditions for his state's agreement to the whole document. Most significantly of all, they offered an enumeration of the powers of the central government, a matter that the full convention had repeatedly postponed, and introduced a range of prohibitions on the sort of state legislation that Madison had hoped to counter by a federal veto on state laws.

All of August was consumed in close consideration of the work of this committee, most of it on two related issues that divided delegates in very different ways. Assisted by their broad agreement on the nation's needs and by their general alarm about majority abuses, the members reached agreement relatively quickly on the prohibitions on the states and most of the enumerated powers of the Congress. But Madison, Wilson, and Morris had objected from the start to a provision in the Connecticut Compromise that gave the House of Representatives exclusive power over revenues, though several of their colleagues in the larger states considered this a critical condition for the grant of equal suffrage in the Senate. Moreover, the Committee of Detail had given in completely to the South's demands for prohibitions of a tax on exports and any interference with the slave trade as well as the requirement of a two-thirds vote in Congress for passage of commercial regulations. Opposition mounted day by day to all of these concessions.

On 8 August, the smaller middle states joined nationalists in Pennsylvania and Virginia to strike the clause giving the House of Representatives exclusive control of money bills. Mason, Randolph, and Hugh Williamson (North Carolina) denounced a vote that would permit involvement in taxation by a body that would not directly represent the people, warning that this might compel them to retract their unenthusiastic willingness to go along with state equality in the Senate. Caleb Strong of Massachusetts moved that money bills might be amended by the Senate but would have to originate in the House of Representatives. Many delegations, though, were thoroughly confused by the variety of questions that had come to be encompassed in the issue, and the meeting narrowly decided to postpone Strong's motion.

Meanwhile, compromisers in New England's delegations had been struggling to secure the vital interests of their section without provoking secession by the South. Seconded by Morris, Rufus King had blasted the report of the Committee of Detail as so unreasonably biased in favor of the South that Northerners would justifiably reject it. For the purpose of determining the size of state delegations in the House of Representatives, King and Morris pointed out, the Southerners had been given the right to count three-fifths of their slaves, and it was little consolation that the three-fifths rule would also be applied for purposes of direct taxation, which might never be employed. Hating slavery in any case, King and Morris were infuriated by the prohibitions of congressional interference with new importations and by the ban on export taxes. The Constitution, they protested, would commit the North to defend the South against this great internal danger of slave rebellions, but the South would still be free not only to increase the evil through new importations of slaves but also to shield the products of slave labor from taxation. In addition, the requirement that two-thirds of Congress would be necessary to impose commercial regulations would impede the very national actions in the area of trade that were among the most important reasons that the shipping states, with their depressed economies, favored constitutional reform.

Complicated, often heated arguments concerning these provisions dominated the convention through the second half of August. Though Madison and Wilson joined with King and Morris to condemn the ban on export taxes, protesting that it would deny the government an easy source of revenue and an important weapon in its efforts to compel the Europeans to relax their navigation laws, the planting states were virtually unanimous in their insistence on this prohibition. Georgia and the Carolinas, though opposed by the Virginians as well as by the antislavery members from the North, were equally insistent on prohibiting congressional restrictions on the slave trade, making this an absolute condition of their states' approval of a plan. On 21 August, the compromisers from Connecticut and Massachusetts voted with the Southerners to reaffirm the prohibition of a tax on exports, seven states to four, but Sherman, Gerry, Ellsworth, Gorham, and their colleagues made it clear that they expected their conciliatory efforts to be met in kind. On 22 August, Morris moved referral of the slave trade, export taxes, and commercial regulation to another grand committee, where these subjects might provide materials for a "bargain" between the North and the South. Several Southerners approved, and the motion carried.

The August compromise between the North and South, between Massachusetts and South Carolina, was second in importance only to the bargain of 16 July to the completion of the Constitution. On 24 August, the grand committee recommended prohibition of legislative interference with the slave trade until the year 1800 and reaffirmation of the ban on export taxes but deletion of the clause requiring two-thirds of Congress for the passage of commercial regulations. On 25 August, Pinckney moved extension of protection of the slave trade until 1808, Gorham seconded the motion, and the prohibition carried seven states to four. Several Southerners continued to oppose control of trade by a majority in Congress, where they expected to be outvoted in both houses for a time, but despite their fierce resistance, South Carolina abided by its bargain. A motion to reinstitute the two-thirds rule failed 4–7 with only Maryland, Virginia, North Carolina, and Georgia voting in favor of the measure. On 31 August, the convention voted to refer all postponed questions to another grand committee, which untangled the convention's last remaining snarls, most notably the long-debated question of executive selection (the Electoral College). By 8 September, the convention was ready to entrust a finished plan to the Committee of

Style. There, with help from Hamilton, Johnson, Madison, and King, Morris imparted final polish to the phrasing.

On 10 September, several important members made final pleas for a reconsideration of certain features that had increasingly alarmed them. Randolph reminded the body that he had introduced "a set of republican propositions" (the Virginia Plan) on 29 May but that his resolutions had been so disfigured in the course of the deliberations that he might be forced to vote against the finished plan. Sharing Randolph's dread of hazy wording and majority control of commerce, together with his fear that an objectionable Senate might combine with a powerful president to overbear the people's representatives in the House of Representatives, Mason argued on 12 September that the convention also ought to add a bill of rights. Elbridge Gerry readily agreed.

Responding partly to these fears, the members did consent to substitute two-thirds of Congress for the three-fourths previously required to override a presidential veto. But with Sherman pointing out that nothing in the Constitution would repeal state declarations or infringe the liberties that they protected, the states unanimously declined to add a bill of rights. Mason also failed to win insertion of a clause requiring two-thirds of Congress for the passage of commercial regulations until 1808 (by which date, he may have hoped, the planting states would get substantial reinforcements from the West).

On 17 September, Benjamin Franklin, who was eighty-one years old and so enfeebled that Wilson read his speeches for him, intervened once more, as he had done at several anxious moments, to plead with everyone who still retained objections to "doubt a little of his own infallibility" and join in signing the finished plan. Hamilton appealed for unanimity as well, observing that "no man's ideas were more remote from the plan than his own were known to be" but that he could not hesitate "between anarchy and confusion on one side and the chance of good . . . on the other." No one, to be sure, had gotten everything he wanted in the course of the convention. No one, four months earlier, had entered the convention able to conceive the sort of Constitution that the members' compromises and collective wisdom had created. No one fully understood as yet—not even Hamilton or Madison—that the collective reasoning of the convention, together with the clashing interests of its delegations, had resulted in a system that would prove not only "adequate to the exigencies of union" but capable of serving as a new foundation for significant revision of the theory of representative democracy. Of the forty-two delegates still present on 17 September, however, all but Randolph, Mason, and Gerry felt able to sign. Most of them could now agree with Franklin's closing observation that the emblem on the chair in which the greatest hero of the Revolution had presided over their deliberations was, indeed, a rising, not a setting, sun.

Lance Banning

See also

Articles of Confederation; Constitutions, State; Dickinson, John; Hamilton, Alexander; Madison, James; Mason, George; Morris, Gouverneur; Randolph, Edmund Jennings; Sherman, Roger; Wilson, James

References

Banning, Lance. *The Sacred Fire of Liberty: James Madison and the Founding of the Federal Republic.* Ithaca, NY: Cornell University Press, 1995.

Bowen, Catherine Drinker. *Miracle at Philadelphia: The Story of the Constitutional Convention.* Boston: Little, Brown, 1966.

Collier, Christopher, and James Lincoln Collier. *Decision in Philadelphia: The Constitutional Convention of 1787.* New York: Ballantine, 1986.

Farrand, Max, ed. *The Records of the Federal Convention of 1787.* 4 vols. New Haven, CT: Yale University Press, 1937.

Hutson, James, ed. *Supplement to Max Farrand's The Records of the Federal Convention of 1787.* New Haven, CT: Yale University Press, 1987.

Jensen, Merrill. *The Making of the American Constitution.* Princeton, NJ: Princeton University Press, 1964.

McDonald, Forrest. *Novus Ordo Seclorum: The Intellectual Origins of the Constitution.* Lawrence: University Press of Kansas, 1985.

Rakove, Jack N. *Original Meanings: Politics and Ideas in the Making of the Constitution.* New York: Knopf, 1996.

Rossiter, Clinton. *1787: The Grand Convention.* New York: Macmillan, 1966.

Smith, David G. *The Convention and the Constitution: The Political Ideas of the Founding Fathers.* New York: St. Martin's, 1965.

Warren, Charles. *The Making of the Constitution.* Boston: Little, Brown, 1937.

Wood, Gordon. *The Creation of the American Republic, 1776–1787.* Chapel Hill: University of North Carolina Press, 1969.

Constitution, United States, Ratification of

On 21 February 1787 the Confederation Congress recommended that the states appoint delegates to a Constitutional Convention to revise the Articles of Confederation by giving additional powers to Congress to meet the needs of the country. Twelve of the thirteen state legislatures appointed delegates; only Rhode Island refused. It was generally assumed that any amendments to the Articles proposed by the convention would be subject to the ratification procedure contained in the Articles of Confederation, which called for the approval of Congress followed by unanimous ratification by the state legislatures. The difficulty—perhaps impossibility—of achieving this kind of approval was readily apparent. Periodically since February 1781, Congress had proposed amendments to the Articles, but none had obtained the unanimous approval of the state legislatures. The proposals of the convention stood a chance of being adopted only if a new ratification procedure could be devised.

George Washington presides at the signing of the U.S. Constitution on 17 September 1787. (Library of Congress)

The practical political problems of using the Articles' procedure for ratification were readily apparent. Rhode Island had not sent a delegation and was not expected to ratify any meaningful changes emanating from the convention. It was also widely assumed that New York would oppose any significant strengthening of Congress at the expense of the states. Thus, the ratification procedure of the Articles gave each state—including these two recalcitrant states—a veto power over any amendments proposed by the convention. The state legislatures, viewed collectively, were expected to be reluctant to give up any of their substantial powers to Congress. There appeared to be little likelihood that unanimity could be achieved.

As an alternative to state legislatures, it was suggested by some that each state elect special conventions to consider any amendments to the Articles. In the eleven states that had bicameral legislatures, the proposed amendments would need to run the legislative gauntlet twice to obtain a state's approval, but only once if state conventions were used. In addition, state conventions could concentrate solely on the one issue of ratification, not the myriad of things faced by state legislatures. Legislatures also usually had elaborate political coalitions at loggerheads with each other. Special single-purpose, limited-term conventions would probably not be fettered by such ingrained party politics. Conventions, not having any permanent power themselves, would be less reluctant to give Congress additional powers to the detriment of state legislatures. Conventions would meet, consider the amendments, and then adjourn never to meet again. The best people could be elected to state conventions—people who were serving in Congress or in state or local government or who were averse to serving in any political office. Finally, property qualifications for voters and residential qualifications for office holding could be reduced or abandoned completely in state conventions, making them at least theoretically more broadly representative of the people.

A handful of individuals such as James Madison of Virginia believed that ratification by state legislatures was a flaw in the Articles that should not be repeated because it called into question which entity was superior, the government under the Articles or the states that had ratified the Articles. Madison and a small number of like-minded Continentalists felt that a completely new form of government with unquestioned authority should be proposed by the Constitutional Convention and that the new form of government should be "ratified by the authority of the people, and not merely by that of the [state] Legislatures."

Madison also believed that the new government proposed by the Constitutional Convention had to be ratified or rejected in its entirety. Piecemeal ratification would be unacceptable, because not all the states would adopt the same provisions. Writing to his close friend Edmund Randolph on 8 April 1787, Madison said that "Particular States may view the different articles as conditions of each other, and would only ratify them as such. Others might ratify them as independent propositions. The consequence would be that the ratification of both would go for nothing." Years later, Madison reflected that if the individual parts of the Constitution had been voted on separately, many would have been rejected. Only as a whole, as a bundle of compromises, were the American people likely to have adopted the Constitution.

The general public expectation about the proposals anticipated from the Constitutional Convention dramatically differed from earlier proposals to amend the Articles of Confederation. Previously there was skepticism that Congress in proposing amendments simply wanted to strengthen its own power. Now, in late 1786 and early 1787, many people believed that the United States was in a period of crisis. Proposals had been printed in newspapers calling for the division of the country into three or four separate confederacies. Congressmen even privately considered where the boundary lines would be drawn between the new confederacies. Others talked about establishing a monarchy. Rumors circulated that Nathaniel Gorham, the president of Congress, had sounded out Prince William Henry, King George III's youngest son, about assuming a new throne in America. A sense of urgency permeated the country. George Washington wrote to Secretary for Foreign Affairs John Jay on 1 August 1786: "What Astonishing changes a few years are capable of producing. I am told that even respectable characters speak of a monarchical form of government without horror. From thinking proceeds speaking, thence to acting is often but a single step." The Philadelphia *American Museum,* a newly established monthly magazine, warned that "many, very many wish to see an emperor at the head of our nation. And unless the states very soon give to Congress the necessary powers to regulate trade and to form a system of finance for the support of national credit, such an event may take place suddenly. It may not be at the distance of one short year."

Threatened with this crisis, Americans were advised to accept whatever the Constitutional Convention proposed. The alternatives were spelled out in the *Pennsylvania Gazette* on 30 May 1787, which stated that under the Articles there would be "anarchy, poverty, infamy and SLAVERY"; under the new government there would be "peace, safety, liberty and glory." The *Pennsylvania Herald,* on 20 June 1787, commented on the uniqueness of what was happening in Philadelphia. "Whatever measures may be recommended by the Federal Convention, whether an addition to the old constitution, or the adoption of a new one, it will, in effect, be a revolution in government, accomplished by reasoning and deliberation; an event that has never occurred since the formation of society." On 30 June 1787, a *Massachusetts Centinel* correspondent predicted ominously: "unless an energetick, permanent continental government is speedily established, our liberties will be set afloat in the confusion that will inevitably ensue. At present we . . . are every day tottering on the brink of civil dissention. . . . It would be better to embrace almost any expedient rather than to remain where we are." Similar opinions filled the country's newspapers. Antifederalists would later decry this propaganda, but Federalists saw the newspaper campaign differently. David Humphreys in New Haven, Connecticut, wrote to Washington on 28 September 1787, shortly after the Constitutional Convention had adjourned. "Indeed the well affected have not been wanting in efforts to prepare the minds of the citizens for the favorable reception of whatever might be the result of your Proceedings. . . . Judicious & well-timed publications have great efficacy in ripening the judgment of men." Henry Knox, the Confederation's secretary at war, wrote to the Marquis de Lafayette on 24 October 1787 that "the Minds of the people at large were fully prepared for a change without any particular specification." The *Federal Herald* of 31 March 1788, late in the ratification process, reported that the editors of the *Northern Centinel* in Lansingburgh, New York, had admitted that they had "conceived it a duty incumbent on them to prepare the minds of their readers" for whatever the Constitutional Convention proposed. Thus even before the Constitution was published, Federalists were engaged in the battle to ratify the new form of government. As opposed to the previous suspicions of Congress's attempts to grasp more power, now there was a general, widespread predilection, at least at the outset, to accept whatever came from the convention.

In keeping with Madison's and others' ideas about the ratification process, the Virginia Plan submitted to the Convention on 29 May provided that the convention's recommendations should first be approved by Congress and then submitted by the state legislatures to specially elected state ratifying conventions. Some delegates opposed this idea and wanted to abide by the Articles' procedure. In addition, on 5 June, James Wilson of Pennsylvania proposed that a plurality of the states be sufficient to adopt the convention's recommendations. This was the first mention of abandoning the unanimity provision of the Articles, and no opposition was immediately voiced. Twelve weeks later the convention reconsidered the issue. Different delegates variously proposed that seven, eight, nine, or all thirteen states be required to ratify the new Constitution. Others argued that whatever the number of states required to ratify, the ratifying states must contain a majority of the country's population. Gouverneur Morris of Pennsylvania suggested that a smaller number of states be required for ratification if the ratifying states were contiguous and a larger number if the states were dispersed.

The U.S. Constitution is signed at the Constitutional Convention of 1787 in Philadelphia. (Library of Congress)

At this point John Dickinson of Delaware asked whether Congress's assent should be required for ratification (as specified in the Articles of Confederation) and whether the nonratifying states could be deserted. The convention decided that Congress should not be required to commit suicide by approving the new Constitution and that Congress should not control the fate of the Constitution. Once nine state conventions had ratified, the Constitution would take effect among the ratifying states. These were important decisions. Had the convention decided otherwise, it is uncertain that the Constitution would have been ratified.

As the Constitutional Convention ended, it approved two resolutions and a letter addressed to the president of Congress that was to be signed by Washington, the convention's president. The first resolution called for the convention to present the Constitution to Congress, which should transmit it to the states, but did not require that Congress approve it. The state legislatures would then call specially elected conventions that would give "their Assent and Ratification" to the Constitution and then notify Congress. The second resolution suggested that after nine states had ratified the Constitution, Congress should provide for the holding of the first federal elections.

The convention's cover letter to Congress was a masterstroke. It was the equivalent of Congress's letter sent to the states in 1777 with the proposed Articles of Confederation. Having Washington sign the letter for the convention was the equivalent of a public endorsement of the Constitution by the former commander in chief. The letter indicated that America's friends had long desired that the central government have the power to tax; make war, peace, and treaties; and regulate commerce—and have the corresponding executive and judicial authority to enforce these powers. Because the impropriety of granting such extensive powers to a single-house Congress was self-evident, the convention was forced to devise "a different organization." Drawing upon the social compact theory, the letter said that just like people, when states enter into a society they must give up certain rights to protect the balance of their rights. It was difficult to draw the line between the power of the central government and that of the states. But in all the convention's deliberations, the paramount importance of the Union was also primary. Impressed with the importance of Union, each state delegation was "less rigid on points of inferior magnitude." The Constitution was "the result of a spirit of amity, and of that mutual deference and concession which the peculiarity of our political situation rendered indispensable." It was unlikely that the Constitution would "meet the full and entire approbation" of any state. Had the interests of one state alone been consulted, "the consequences might have been particularly disagreeable or injurious to others." The Constitution was liable to "as few exceptions as could reasonably have been expected." The convention delegates hoped and believed that the Constitution would "promote the lasting welfare of that country so dear to us all, and secure her freedom and happiness." This letter was printed with the Constitution all over the country, and the words subscribed by Washington were quoted frequently in the public debate over ratification. Although Washington himself stayed out of the public debate over the Constitution, his letter to Congress reminded Americans where the former commander in chief stood on ratification.

Congress received and read the Constitution on 20 September 1787. Critics of the Constitution—soon to be called Antifederalists—wanted it submitted to the states with the acknowledgment that the convention had violated the congressional resolution of 21 February that called the convention for the purpose of revising the Articles of Confederation. Instead, the convention had proposed a completely new document. Opponents also wanted to point out that the delegates had violated their instructions from the legislatures that appointed them. Antifederalists also wanted to acknowledge that the convention had violated the Articles in proposing a new procedure—an unconstitutional procedure—for ratification. Supporters of the Constitution—called Federalists—wanted the Constitution sent to the states with the approbation of Congress.

On 27 September, Virginia delegate Richard Henry Lee moved that a bill of rights and other amendments be added to the Constitution. Federalists easily defeated Lee's motion. Clearly, Antifederalists could not prevent Congress, which met in secret behind closed doors, from endorsing the Constitution. Federalists, however, wanted to propagate the illusion that the Constitution was warmly supported by Congress. Consequently, a compromise was reached: Congress would transmit the Constitution to the states with neither approbation nor disapprobation, and all reference to Lee's amendments and the debate over approbation would be deleted from the journals. Federalists—great politicians that they were—adroitly worded the transmittal to say that Congress "*unanimously*" resolved that the Constitution be sent to the state legislatures, which should submit it to conventions elected by the people "in conformity to the resolves" of the Philadelphia Convention. Congressman James Madison explained all of this to Washington, who responded with his typical shrewd sense of public relations on 10 October 1787: "I am better pleased that the proceedings of the Convention is handed from Congress by a unanimous vote (feeble as it is) than if it had appeared under stronger marks of approbation without it.—This apparent unanimity will have its effect.—Not every one has opportunities to peep behind the curtain; and as the multitude often judge from externals, the appearance of unanimity in that body, on this occasion, will be of great importance."

Except for certain pockets of opposition, the initial public response to the Constitution was warm. Town and county meetings passed resolutions of support, and petitions circulated calling for state legislatures to speedily call ratifying conventions. Antifederalists, however, soon seized the initiative with critical newspaper essays in Philadelphia and New York City. Through the informal system by which printers in the eighteenth century exchanged their newspapers and reprinted each other's material, Antifederalists were able to disseminate their articles opposing the Constitution throughout the country. Federalists quickly realized that they had to respond, and they countered with their own massive newspaper campaign. Since the overwhelming majority of the country's ninety-five newspapers supported the Constitution, Federalists were able to inundate the press while limiting their opponents to only about ten newspapers nationwide.

The debate over the Constitution was conducted by gifted and well-practiced polemicists who for a quarter century had intensely debated the nature of government and how best to preserve the liberties of the people and the sovereignty of the individual states. This was not a purely theoretical debate. Americans had fought a costly and bloody war over these issues; they had formed a federal government and thirteen state governments, and many of them now believed that those governments were failing and endangering the principles of their Revolution.

Most Americans accepted the basic form of the Constitution, although everyone, even the most ardent Federalists, objected to some parts. But most people agreed that the Confederation government needed to be strengthened and that it would be dangerous to entrust significant additional powers to the single-house Confederation Congress without also creating executive and judicial branches of government. Therefore, in the eyes of Federalists, the issue was whether to ratify this Constitution in toto or to reject it. Antifederalists believed that the Constitution needed revisions to protect the states from being overwhelmed and to protect the civil liberties of the people. Some Antifederalists believed that these amendments had to be adopted before the Constitution was ratified; others, ultimately, were willing to ratify in anticipation of amendments to be made by the new government.

Alexander Hamilton, in the first of eighty-five newspaper essays known as the Federalist Papers, suggested that it was left for Americans to "decide the important question, whether societies of men are really capable or not, of establishing good government from reflection and choice, or whether they are forever destined to depend, for their political constitutions, on accident and force." Madison, in the fifty-first essay, said that "in framing a government which is to be administered by men over men, the great difficulty lies in this: You must first enable the government to controul the governed; and in the next place, oblige it to controul itself." Through an elaborate system of checks and balances, Federalists argued that the new federal government would be able to control itself. Antifederalists agreed with Federalists that the new government would be able to control the people, but they did not believe that it would be able to control those in power.

Antifederalists believed that the Constitution would create a national government that would annihilate the state governments and end in either monarchy or aristocracy. The Constitution was, in their judgment, a counterrevolution that would overthrow the principles of the Declaration of Independence. They maintained that the Constitutional Convention had violated the Articles of Confederation, the instructions to the delegates from the state legislatures, and the resolution of Congress of 21 February 1787 that called the convention. The president and the Senate, especially working together, were too powerful. The Senate had legislative, executive, and judicial powers, thus violating the commonly accepted theory that there ought to be a complete separation of powers among the different branches of government. A privy council, rather than the Senate, should advise the president on matters of appointments and on treaties. The House of Representatives was too small and could not adequately represent all segments of American society. Even so, it was the most democratic branch, but it had no role in treaty making or in the appointment process. Its impeachment power would rarely or never be exercised, and when it was, the Senate would seldom convict in trials of impeachment. Terms of office were too long, and Congress's power to regulate federal elections was dangerous. Congress also had other dangerous powers, some of which were undefined (the necessary and proper clause and the general welfare clause). Patrick Henry warned his fellow Virginians: "there are sufficient guards placed [in the Constitution] against sedition and licentiousness: For when power is given to this Government to suppress these, or, for any other purpose, the language it assumes is clear, express, and unequivocal, but when this Constitution speaks of privileges, there is an ambiguity, a fatal ambiguity;—an ambiguity which is very astonishing." Consequently, Antifederalists wanted the reestablishment of Article II of the Articles of Confederation, which provided that each state retained all of the powers that were not *expressly* delegated to Congress. Antifederalists also feared that federal officeholders would multiply under the Constitution and that taxes would escalate. These taxes, levied by Congress and collected by federal officials, were virtually unlimited and would encroach upon crucial sources of state revenue.

Jury trials in civil cases were not provided for, and in criminal cases the jury need not be from the local area. The jurisdiction of the federal courts seemed unbounded and a danger to the state courts. The federal court, through its unreviewable power of judicial review, was likely to construe the Constitution so as to enlarge federal power at the expense of the states. The appellate jurisdiction of the federal judiciary over both law and facts favored the wealthy and endangered the authority of juries in criminal cases.

Some Antifederalists also charged that various provisions of the Constitution recognized, condoned, protected, and even encouraged slavery. Amendments to the Constitution would be difficult to obtain after the new government was established, and therefore they should be proposed by the state ratifying conventions and should be considered in a second constitutional convention. Perhaps the most serious Antifederalist objection was that the Constitution lacked a bill of rights. This omission was especially dangerous, because the Constitution provided that it, as well as treaties and laws made pursuant to it, would become the supreme law of the land no matter what state judges said or what was in state laws, constitutions, or bills of rights.

Federalists responded that the Constitution would create a confederated republic with powers divided among legislative, executive, and judicial branches that would check each other. The Constitution, they believed, would preserve the fruits of the Revolution and was in essence a peaceful revolution in favor of government that would protect the nation from chaos and from the terrible and predictable consequences of failed revolutions. Federalists argued that the Constitution was unambiguous and that the new government would have only delegated powers; therefore, a bill of rights was unnecessary and might even be dangerous, because every right not listed would be presumed to be given away, and powers might be implied that were not given. The unanimity of the Constitutional Convention demonstrated that the Constitution was an accommodation among many states and many competing interests. The great men of the country—led by Washington and Benjamin Franklin—favored the Constitution, while opponents were labeled as self-interested state officeholders, demagogues, desperate debtors, Shaysites, Tories, and worse.

Federalists believed that the Constitution would secure economic liberties and encourage economic growth and prosperity. If the Constitution was ratified, money would be secure, capital would become available again, commerce would revive, the economy would flourish, public creditors would be paid, land values would rise, paper money would be abolished, government expenses would decrease, taxes on imports would finance the government, immigrants would flood into America, and the prestige of the United States would rise. Once the new government was functioning, defects in the Constitution could be corrected through the system's own process of amendment initiated by either Congress or the state legislatures if Congress was recalcitrant. Above all, Federalists opposed a second constitutional convention to propose amendments. They saw what such a convention could do and did not want another convention to gut their newly wrought Constitution.

The Constitution was considered in thirteen separate state debates, first over the issue of whether to call state conventions, then over the elections of delegates to those conventions, and finally within the conventions themselves. The first state to consider the Constitution was Pennsylvania. Two-thirds of its convention were Federalists. They allowed the convention Antifederalists to debate the Constitution by paragraphs, but when the *Pennsylvania Herald* began publishing the Antifederalist speeches in detail, Federalists became alarmed. Pressure was applied to the publisher, the editor of the *Herald* was fired, and publication of the debates ceased. Nevertheless, Federalists canceled their subscriptions, and the *Herald* was forced out of business. The minority of the Pennsylvania Convention, against the custom of the time, was not allowed to enter its objections in the convention journals; a bill of rights proposed by Antifederalists was similarly kept out of the journals. The convention ratified the Constitution by a vote of 46–23. Antifederalists had lost the first major battle in the state conventions, but Federalists had created the impression that they needed obnoxious tactics to obtain ratification.

Five days before the Pennsylvania Convention voted, Delaware's convention quickly assembled and with only a few hours of debate ratified the Constitution unanimously. New Jersey and Georgia likewise ratified unanimously with little debate in their conventions. Connecticut's newspapers published no locally written Antifederalist pieces, and its convention with little difficulty ratified the Constitution on 9 January 1788 by a three-to-one majority. Whenever Antifederalists in these first five state conventions proposed amendments to the Constitution, they were always voted down by Federalists who argued that the Constitution had to be either rejected or adopted without amendments. This situation was about to change dramatically in Massachusetts, the sixth state to hold a convention.

On 3 January 1788, ten of Boston's twelve delegates to the Massachusetts Convention held a dinner caucus. Governor John Hancock was ill with the gout and thus did not attend. But Samuel Adams did attend, and the old revolutionary broke his long public silence on the Constitution. Adams declared that he opposed the Constitution and intended to vote against it in the convention. Federalist leaders arranged for a meeting of Boston's tradesmen—Adams's base of political support—who strongly favored the Constitution in the belief that it would restore economic prosperity. About 400 tradesmen assembled and expressed their strong support for the Constitution and warned the Boston delegates that a vote against the Constitution would be "contrary to the best interests, the strongest feelings, and warmest wishes of the Tradesmen of the town of Boston."

When the convention assembled, Hancock was elected president. As usual, however, during difficult political times, the governor's gout made it impossible for him to attend. After three weeks of debate, Federalists realized that if a vote was taken, the Constitution would be defeated, albeit by a slim majority.

In an effort to win over a few votes to tip the balance in their favor, Federalist leaders decided to propose recommendatory amendments to the Constitution. Convention delegates would unconditionally ratify the Constitution, but they would also recommend that the state's future representatives and senators in the U.S. Congress support certain amendments to the Constitution. To ensure a warm reception for this plan, Federalist leaders asked Hancock, their longtime political opponent, to present the amendments to the convention as his own. In exchange, Federalists promised not to run a candidate opposite Hancock in the spring gubernatorial elections. Furthermore, Hancock was promised support for the vice presidency of the United States. And, if Virginia did not ratify the Constitution, thus making Washington ineligible, Hancock would be the obvious choice for the first president of the United States.

The bait worked. Hancock's gout improved enough for him to be carried into the convention on a litter to present "his" proposal. Adams, the consummate politician, who had been silent throughout the debates but now saw that ratification was inevitable, jumped on the bandwagon. On 6 February 1788, the convention voted 187–168 to ratify the Constitution. Key Antifederalist delegates acquiesced graciously and vowed to support and to encourage their constituents to support the Constitution.

The immediate response from Federalists nationwide was relief. Madison wrote to Washington: "the amendments are a blemish, but are in the least offensive form." Antifederalists such as Henry, in a speech in the Virginia Convention, argued that Massachusetts had "put the cart before the horse." After seeing the Massachusetts amendments, Thomas Jefferson, then serving as U.S. minister to France, changed his mind about the best procedure to follow in ratifying the Constitution. Writing to Edward Carrington, a fellow Virginian, on 27 May 1788, Jefferson said: "my first wish was that 9 states would adopt it in order to ensure what was good in it, & that the others might, by holding off, produce the necessary amendments. But the plan of Massachusetts is far preferable, and will I hope be followed by those who are yet to decide." Jefferson's wish came true, as six of the remaining seven states used the Massachusetts technique of ratifying the Constitution unconditionally while proposing recommendatory amendments. Without this form of ratification, the Constitution never would have been adopted. This, indeed, was the turning point in the struggle to ratify the Constitution.

After six straight victories, however, Federalists ran into greater difficulties during February and March 1788. False reports of North Carolina's ratification were exposed throughout the northern states. New York's legislature then just barely called a ratifying convention to meet in mid-June 1788. After meeting for only ten days, the New Hampshire Convention, instead of following its neighbor's example of ratifying with recommendatory amendments, voted on 22 February to recess until mid-June. New Hampshire Federalists could count on only 48 votes out of the 108 delegates in attendance. Many delegates had been instructed to vote against the Constitution, and it was estimated that as many as 30 such delegates now personally supported it. The recess would allow these delegates to go back home and get their instructions rescinded. Finally, on 24 March, Rhode Island freemen voting in their towns in a statewide referendum overwhelmingly defeated the Constitution 2,708–237. Even if the Providence and Newport Federalists had not boycotted the referendum, the Constitution would have been rejected by a three-to-one margin.

The events of these eight weeks had a sobering effect on Federalists. The seemingly triumphant march toward ratification was no longer inevitable. Men such as Washington and Madison feared what might happen if the conventions of Virginia and New York met in June without the required nine states already having ratified the Constitution. These two important states might deal the death blow to the new Constitution. Federalists could not afford another defeat or adjournment in Maryland and South Carolina—the next two states to sit in convention. Consequently, the Federalist majorities in both of these state conventions steamrolled the Constitution through by votes of 63–11 and 149–73, respectively. When the second session of New Hampshire's convention reconvened, it took but four days for Federalists to ratify the Constitution on 21 June, with recommendatory amendments, by a vote of 57–47. This was the crucial ninth state. The Constitution was ratified.

Even with nine states assenting to the Constitution, the Union would have difficulty surviving without the large and powerful states of Virginia and New York. The refusal of these two states to ratify the Constitution would have divided the new union into three small entities—New England, the Middle States, and the extreme South. The importance of Virginia and New York was realized by everyone, and both Federalists and Antifederalists exerted total efforts in these states.

In Virginia, George Mason and Henry led the Antifederalists. Henry suggested in a speech in the Virginia Convention on 7 June 1788 that if the Constitution were "wisely constructed, let us receive it. But shall its adoption by eight States induce us to receive it, if it be replete with the most dangerous defects?" Federalists, Henry asserted, "urge that subsequent amendments are safer than previous amendments, and that they will answer the same ends. At present we have our liberties and privileges in our own hands. Let us not relinquish them. Let us not adopt this system till we see them secured. There is some small possibility, that should we follow the conduct of Massachusetts, amendments might be obtained. There is small possibility of amending any Government; but shall we abandon our most inestimable rights, and rest their security on a mere possibility?" Without substantial amendments, Henry asserted on 9 June, the Constitution would "destroy the State Governments, and swallow the liberties of the people."

Madison and Governor Randolph, who had declined to sign the Constitution in 1787 but now supported it, led Federalists in responding to these arguments. The governor maintained that the Confederation was "too defective to deserve correction. Let us take farewell of it, with reverential respect, as an old benefactor. It is gone, whether this House says so, or not." The Constitution alone could save the Union. Madison and Randolph prevailed as a small majority voted 89–79 on 25 June 1788 to ratify the Constitution with a list of forty amendments—half protecting rights and half proposing structural changes to the Constitution.

In New York, despite the brilliance of the Federalist Papers, two-thirds of the delegates elected to the state convention opposed the Constitution without prior amendments. Federalist delegates led by Jay and Hamilton postponed the final vote on the Constitution until word arrived from the New Hampshire and Virginia conventions. But even after New Hampshire's ratification, New York's Antifederalists held firm. Only when word arrived on 2 July that Virginia had also ratified did New York Antifederalists change their attitude toward ratifying the Constitution. Antifederalist leaders realized that without New York's support in Congress, amendments would never be submitted to the states, and New York would remain out of the Union with Rhode Island. Being out of the Union, New York City would no longer be the federal capital. A compromise was negotiated. With the consent of the great Antifederalist leader Governor George Clinton, enough Antifederalists would either vote for ratification or absent themselves from the convention so that the Constitution would be adopted "in complete confidence" that an extensive list of recommendatory amendments would be adopted after the new government went into effect. In return, Federalists would unanimously endorse a circular letter to the other states and to Congress calling for a second constitutional convention to consider amendments to the Constitution. With this prearranged deal, New York ratified the Constitution on 26 July 1788 by a vote of 30–27, with twelve Antifederalists voting for ratification and eight delegates (seven of them Antifederalists) absent. According to Antifederalists, it was their goal to "improve the plan proposed: to strengthen and secure its democratic features; to add checks and guards to it; to secure equal liberty by proper Stipulations to prevent any undue exercise of power; and to establish beyond the power of faction to alter, a genuine federal republic. To effect this great and desirable object . . . the doors of accommodation [must be] constantly open." It was time for "men in all the states who wish to establish a free, equal, and efficient government to the exclusion of anarchy, corruption, faction, and oppression . . . to unite in their exertions in making the best of the Constitution now established." Judge Zephaniah Platt of Dutchess County, writing to a friend two days after New York's ratification, explained the Antifederalists' dilemma. He voted for unconditional ratification "not from a conviction that the Constitution was a good one or that the liberties of men were well secured. No—I voted for it as a choice of evils in our own present situation."

With the Constitution ratified by eleven states, the Confederation Congress passed an ordinance on 13 September 1788 that provided for the first federal elections. On 4 March 1789, the new government would commence. A bill of rights, but no substantive amendments, was adopted by Congress on 25 September 1789 and was sent to the states for ratification. The two remaining states—North Carolina and Rhode Island—ratified the Constitution in November 1789 and May 1790, respectively.

It had taken a long, hard-fought struggle to ratify the Constitution. Amazingly, this revolution in favor of government was accomplished peacefully, through a political process marked by compromise and conciliation. Federalists had adopted their Constitution, but Antifederalists had forced the adoption of a bill of rights and had made a decisive contribution to the Constitution. In the words of Jefferson, there had been "opposition enough to do good, & not enough to do harm."

John P. Kaminski

See also

Constitution, United States

References

Benton, Wilbourne E., ed. *1787: Drafting the U.S. Constitution.* 2 vols. College Station: Texas A&M University Press, 1986.

Conley, Patrick T., and John P. Kaminski, eds. *The Constitution and the States: The Role of the Original Thirteen in the Framing and Adoption of the Federal Constitution.* Madison, WI: Madison House, 1988.

Cornell, Saul. *The Other Founders: Anti-Federalism and the Dissenting Tradition in America, 1788–1828.* Chapel Hill: University of North Carolina Press, 1999.

Gillespie, Michael Allen, and Michael Lienesch, eds. *Ratifying the Constitution.* Lawrence: University Press of Kansas, 1989.

Jensen, Merrill, John P. Kaminski, et al., eds. *The Documentary History of the Ratification of the Constitution.* 18 vols. to date. Madison: Wisconsin State Historical Society, 1970–.

Kaminski, John P., and Richard Leffler, eds. *Creating the Constitution.* Acton, MA: Copley, 1999.

———. *Federalists and Antifederalists: The Debate over the Ratification of the Constitution.* Madison, WI: Madison House, 1998.

Main, Jackson Turner. *The Antifederalists: Critics of the Constitution, 1781–1788.* Chapel Hill: University of North Carolina Press, 1961.

Rakove, Jack N. *Original Meanings: Politics and Ideas in the Making of the Constitution.* New York: Knopf, 1997.

Rutland, Robert Allen. *The Ordeal of the Constitution: The Antifederalists and the Ratification Struggle of 1787–1788.* Norman: University of Oklahoma Press, 1966.

Storing, Herbert J., ed. *The Complete Anti-Federalists.* 7 vols. Chicago: University of Chicago Press, 1981.

Wilentz, Sean. *Major Problems in the Early Republic, 1787–1848.* Lexington, MA: Heath, 1992.

Constitutions, State (1776–1790)

During the Revolutionary War, the colonies that became the original thirteen states each underwent its own transition to independence. Even though these states worked together through the Continental Congress and were connected to that body and more loosely to each other by the Articles of Confederation, each drafted and enacted its own separate constitution. While often overshadowed historically by the U.S. Constitution and its drafting and ratification process, these state constitutions were crucial to securing independence. As a practical matter, each state formally agreed to its independence from Britain before America had any national frame of government, and each state established the basis of its own government. State constitutions had a significant ideological impact as well by enshrining certain rights and principles as supreme law. The process of state constitution making established the precedent that constitutions were compacts between the people and their government. Finally, the experience of making state constitutions gave Americans a model for creating and ratifying the U.S. Constitution in 1787–1788.

The first state constitutions and establishment of independent governments. At their founding, most English colonies were organized under either a corporate or a proprietary charter. These charters took various forms but had the common effect of serving as the official authorization, under the auspices of the British Crown, for the colonies to form their own colonial governments. During more than a century, however, most British charter colonies, including eight of the thirteen that rebelled in 1776, became royal colonies. Seven of these eight royal colonies functioned under royal commissions issued to their governors, which specified the essential parts of their government: a royal governor appointed by the British monarch; an appointed governor's council, which often played both legislative and judicial roles; and a legislative assembly, such as the Virginia House of Burgesses, elected by all those men who, under the colony's laws, were entitled to vote.

The royal commissions, which provided these colonies with their model of government, presented a problem once the Revolutionary War began. Because the commissions gave the colonial governments their authority, the war seemed to nullify the legal status of the commissions, in fact if not in law. The royal governors either left the colonies or were removed from office, along with many Loyalist council members. Political leaders in the rebelling royal colonies argued over who had the authority to govern and on what basis. Despite their doubts, however, with the colonies at war there was a pressing need for each of them to have a functioning government.

Six other rebelling colonies confronted different legal challenges. The three proprietary colonies—Maryland, Delaware, and Pennsylvania—faced a difficulty similar to that of the royal colonies, because even when they had a venerable proprietary charter, such as William Penn's Charter of Liberties (1701), they no longer had a proprietary family to supply an executive and a council. Of the three rebelling charter colonies, Massachusetts was governed under a royal charter, rather than a royal commission, that its inhabitants regarded as just as sacred as the truly corporate charters of Connecticut and Rhode Island. Yet Massachusetts, too, faced the question of how to supply a valid executive and council and concluded that it needed a new frame of government. Only Connecticut and Rhode Island, which chose all their officeholders under their corporate charters, did not need or make new constitutions in 1776.

In 1775 and early 1776, most of the rebelling colonies were governed either by their remaining assemblies or by special provincial congresses or committees of safety that were called for the purposes of organizing for the war and appointing delegates to and communicating with the Second Continental Congress in Philadelphia. In the vacuum left by the departed representatives of British authority, colonial congresses and committees began to assume the powers of government. These quasi-formal organizations served as transitional governments in the early part of the Revolution.

Faced with uncertainty about their legal status, several of the rebelling colonies now began to take measures to establish legitimate wartime governments. After the war began but before independence was declared, many colonial leaders wanted to find a working solution that would provide for effective government but not go so far as to imply full independence. In late 1775, the delegations of several colonies, including Massachusetts, New Hampshire, South Carolina, and Virginia, formally asked the Continental Congress for advice or instructions concerning the form and legitimacy of their governments. In November the Congress, not wanting to become too involved in several of the colonies' political difficulties, recommended calling representatives of the people to establish whatever form of government would, in their judgment, "best produce the happiness of the People." In early 1776, four colonies responded by enacting constitutions.

In these same months several colonial leaders also turned for advice to delegate John Adams of Massachusetts, who was regarded as something of an expert on republican government. Between November 1775 and March 1776, congressmen from Virginia, North Carolina, and New Jersey sought Adams's counsel. He responded with letters setting out his view of an effective republican constitution and then, in April 1776, with a brief pamphlet, *Thoughts on Government.* Adams, unlike Congress, committed himself to specific principles of government, although not to a specific plan. He strongly favored a two-house legislature and a strong executive. The extent of his influence is unclear, but the earliest constitutions of Virginia and New Jersey, enacted just before the Declaration of Independence, and of North Carolina, completed in December 1776, were generally compatible with his advice, as were the 1776 constitutions of Delaware and Maryland and the 1777 constitution of New York.

New Hampshire enacted the first written constitution by an English colony without the approval of the mother country. After receiving Congress's encouragement to form a new government in November 1775, the colony held elections for a provincial congress, with delegates from each town, to draft a new constitution. On 5 January 1776, the provincial congress ratified Revolutionary America's first constitution. It provided only for the basic operation of government without specifying the substantive political and legal rights that would be found in later state constitutions. The colony would be governed by a two-chamber legislature. The lower house, which the provincial congress subsequently declared itself to be, was to be elected by the people. This House of Representatives would in turn choose the fourteen members of the upper chamber, called the Council. The 1776 New Hampshire constitution was intended as a provisional document; it was only to remain in effect until the conflict with Britain was resolved.

Between March and early July 1776, three other colonies followed suit: South Carolina enacted a constitution on 26 March, Virginia's provincial congress passed a Bill of Rights on 12 June and ratified a constitution on 29 June, and New Jersey's provincial congress ratified a constitution on 2 July. South Carolina's constitution, like New Hampshire's, only provided the basics for establishing a government and was intended to last only as long as the war with Britain. Neither document was meant to declare independence. Virginia's constitution, however, was intended for independence, which the colony's delegates were supporting in Congress at that very moment, and New Jersey approved its constitution on the same day, 2 July 1776, that Congress voted to break with Britain.

When the Continental Congress took up the question of full independence from Britain in the spring of 1776, its discussions were intimately related to concerns about the nature and form of the colonies' Revolutionary governments. Delegates who favored independence argued that the colonies needed to create new governments that would abolish British authority. On 10 May 1776, Congress "recommended to the respective assemblies and conventions of the United Colonies, where no government sufficient to the exigencies of their affairs have been hitherto established, to adopt such government as shall, in the opinion of the representatives of the people, best conduce to the happiness and safety of their constituents in particular, and America in general."

On 15 May 1776, at the urging of Adams, Congress added a preamble to the resolution stating that "it is necessary that the exercise of every kind of authority under the [British] crown should be totally suppressed, and all the powers of the government exerted, under the people of the colonies, for the preservation of internal peace, virtue, and good order, as well as for the defence of their lives, liberties, and properties." The May 1776 resolution and preamble formed a de facto declaration of independence. A few weeks after the 15 May preamble, Congress appointed the committee that drafted the Declaration of Independence, which the full Congress approved on 4 July 1776. The decision to encourage the colonies to establish new governments and the decision to declare independence were intimately related.

The new states, as instructed by Congress, took steps to comply. In addition to the four colonies that had enacted new constitutions before the Declaration of Independence, six more states passed new constitutions in 1776 and 1777: Delaware (21 September 1776), Pennsylvania (28 September 1776), Maryland (8 November 1776), North Carolina (18 December 1776), Georgia (5 February 1777), and New York (20 April 1777). In 1778, South Carolina ratified a new state constitution to remove from its 1776 document the references to its provisional nature and its colonial status. Massachusetts's constitutional convention debated an elaborate document that Adams drafted in 1779, finally passed a revised version in early 1780, and submitted it to the people for approval. New Hampshire, however, did not revise its "temporary" 1776 constitution until 1784. Neither Connecticut nor Rhode Island enacted a new constitution during the Revolutionary era but instead passed laws to keep their colonial charters in effect as the frameworks for their new states. Yet in one way or another, all thirteen new states took the step of setting forth or ratifying written constitutional principles for the republican governments of independent states.

The new state constitutions drawn up in 1776–1777 were similar to New Hampshire's in that they focused generally on providing for the basic operation of government and the administration of justice. They typically provided for a two-chambered legislature, with executive powers vested in a governor or a council. They also set forth rules for apportioning representatives in the legislature, property qualifications for voting and holding office, and other mechanics of government. And the state constitutions—particularly those enacted after the Declaration of Independence—increasingly began to include provisions reflecting the philosophical principles of the Revolution: governments should derive authority from the consent of the people; governments should be republican in nature, with representatives chosen by the people; and citizens should have certain inalienable rights to liberty and property.

Within this general pattern, however, there were two important variations. First, nearly all of the earliest constitutions, reflecting the colonists' harsh experience with the British Crown, provided for weak governors and councils and powerful lower legislative houses. The first state to give its governor a suspensive veto, which could only be overridden by a two-thirds vote of the legislature, was New York in April 1777. In 1778 South Carolina strengthened its governor in its revised constitution, and in 1780 Massachusetts gave its governor a suspensive veto (although Adams had favored an absolute veto). Thereafter, most states strengthened their executive branch when amending or replacing their early constitutions.

Second, Pennsylvania, Georgia, and Vermont (the last not recognized as a state until 1791) combined weak executives with single-house legislatures and, in the case of Pennsylvania and Vermont, radically democratic voting rights. These ultrademocratic states also modified their constitutions toward the end of the Revolutionary era, just as America's nationalists (Federalists) were triumphing over the Antifederal advocates of small, local government. By the 1790s, all of America's state constitutions were structurally much alike, although they varied considerably in their requirements for voting, holding office, and allowing or forbidding slavery—all crucial ingredients in determining the changing character of America's democratic republics.

Securing the rights of the people. While most of the first American constitutions were pragmatic measures, intended primarily to establish the basic structure of government in the absence of English authority, in the years after the Declaration of Independence new state constitutions focused increasingly on providing substantive protection for both individual and collective rights. As the constitutions came to be viewed less as emergency wartime measures and more as permanent charters of government, they tended to include more substance and more principle. Provisions regarding republican government, popular sovereignty, separation of powers, and individual rights became common.

Most of the state constitutions included a clause guaranteeing that the state would have a republican form of government. What we now call "republicanism" was a collection of political ideas, several of which were long established in the British colonies, that rose to particular prominence in the ideology of the Revolutionary era. Ideas characterized as republican include government by elected representatives, the protection of individual rights, the fostering of public virtue, and governing to promote the common good. While the founders emphasized the classical heritage of republicanism, it was more recently traceable to early-eighteenth-century British opposition or Whig politicians and polemicists. While the exact meaning of republican government could vary from state to state, the guarantees of republican government in the state constitutions established representative government for the common good as the model form of American government and calmed popular fears of a return to monarchy or tyranny.

The early state constitutions, both in their substance and in certain of the procedures for enacting them, differed from our understandings of democracy today, but they were generally consistent with the highest ideals of republican government in the eighteenth century. Voting qualifications for choosing the constitutional conventions as well as for selecting the governments under the new constitutions varied from state to state but were generally limited to white males with certain amounts of property. Additional qualifications were often required for holding political office. Seats in the upper house or executive council were often filled by the legislature rather than by popular election. Some states included religious tests for office holding. Despite these features, however, the governments established under these constitutions were quite democratic for their time, and every state constitution embodied the principle that the government was ultimately based on the consent of the governed.

Most of the first state constitutions were not ratified by the people but were simply passed by the state legislature, almost as a normal act of lawmaking. Immediately after independence, however, beginning with Pennsylvania, states began selecting special conventions to create their constitutions. In 1779–1780 Massachusetts, after earlier failing to secure a new constitution through the usual procedures, combined the special constitutional convention with another innovation: it submitted a document created by its special convention to the people for ratification. The Massachusetts Constitution of 1780, although narrowly ratified amid some discontent, stood the test of time, and the method of its creation and approval was followed by nearly all states thereafter and in a modified form by the federal convention and ratification procedure in 1787–1788.

The state constitutions also protected individual rights. In addition to the colonial charters, another important foundation for Americans' understanding of government during the Revolutionary War era was the English constitutional tradition. The English government had for centuries acted on a set of constitutional principles, written not in one document but in many documents of varying age and character, that prevented both the king and Parliament from interfering with the basic rights of its subjects. Many Americans justified their revolution as a revolt against a British government that violated the British constitutional principles by trampling on the colonists' constitutional rights as English subjects. Declaring independence was a legitimate means to preserve their longstanding constitutional liberties.

Many of the new states, beginning with Virginia in June 1776, included in their constitutions a "Declaration of Rights" or similar section that listed certain rights and liberties to be enjoyed by all citizens under that government. Both Pennsylvania and Massachusetts began their constitutions with prominent declarations of rights. The most commonly invoked individual rights were the famous trinity, "life, liberty, and property," which had been articulated by the philosopher John Locke as fundamental to constitutional government. Other commonly listed rights were freedom of speech and of religion, the right to bear arms, protections against unreasonable searches and seizures and self-incrimination, and the right to a trial by jury. In fact, each of the rights that were later listed in the federal Bill of Rights added to the U.S. Constitution in 1791 was previously enacted in one or more state constitutions. State declarations or bills of rights were often intended more as statements of values than as specific legal measures, but they quickly established certain individual rights as founding principles for the new American states and soon became fundamental to state law.

Given the limited reach of Congress's power under the Articles of Confederation, the state constitutions provided Americans with the only protection of their individual rights before the U.S. Constitution and Bill of Rights were ratified in 1788 and 1791, respectively. But in fact, as the U.S. Constitution originally secured individual rights only against actions of the federal government, nearly all guarantees of individual rights remained with the states and their constitutions until the Fourteenth Amendment of 1868 began to protect certain liberties from abuse by the states, a protection that was not broadly applied by the federal courts for several more decades. Most of the interaction between individual Americans and their governments occurred at the state level from the Revolution until the twentieth century.

The Revolutionary state constitutions as models for American government. In addition to their vital importance in providing for wartime government, securing independence, and establishing individual rights, the state constitutions of the Revolutionary era served another important function: they set precedents for the federal constitutional convention of 1787 and its subsequent ratification. Adams, undoubtedly thinking of the Massachusetts Constitution of 1780, which he had drafted, believed that the basic structure of the U.S. Constitution was that of certain of the existing state constitutions "writ large." And indeed, his document, the first state constitution to strictly divide and label executive, legislative, and judicial powers in the text itself, is the most obvious forerunner to the federal compact. Moreover, many of the delegates to the federal convention, which Adams could not attend, had directly participated in the creation of their states' constitutions.

The state precedents of 1776 to 1780 that influenced later constitution makers were both in the substance of the documents and in the procedures for enacting them. Substantively, the state constitutions provided the Framers in Philadelphia with a set of ideas that had already been considered and debated for their worthiness as basic and supreme law. These ideas set the precedents for guaranteeing republican government; for bicameral legislatures of upper and lower houses, often chosen in different ways; for establishing the separation of powers; for guaranteeing fundamental individual rights; and for many other provisions that appear in both the U.S. Constitution and in nearly all subsequent state constitutions.

Procedurally, the manner of creating and securing a constitution perfected in Massachusetts in 1779–1780 set the precedents that foundational documents must be prepared by a specially elected convention, not by a sitting legislature, and must be ratified by the entire people. In addition, various early state constitutions contained procedures for either amending existing constitutions or replacing them with entirely new constitutions, thus further securing the ultimate control over government by the people. Finally, America's early state constitutions set an internationally observed precedent for securing every society's core political principles by preserving them in written form. It seems appropriate that the world's oldest written constitution still in effect—with many amendments—is the Massachusetts Constitution of 1780 and that the only first-world nation that still lacks a single, concise written constitution is Great Britain.

Matthew J. Festa

See also

Adams, John; Articles of Confederation; Congress, Second Continental and Confederation; Connecticut; Constitution, United States; Delaware; Georgia; Maryland; Mason, George; Massachusetts; New Hampshire; New Jersey; New York, Province and State; North Carolina; Pennsylvania; Rhode Island; South Carolina; Vermont; Virginia

References

Adams, Willi Paul. *The First American Constitutions: Republican Ideology and the Making of the State Constitutions in the Revolutionary Era.* 1980. Expanded ed., Lanham, MD: Rowman and Littlefield, 2001.

Kruman, Marc W. *Between Authority and Liberty: State Constitution Making in Revolutionary America.* Chapel Hill: University of North Carolina Press, 1997.

Lutz, Donald S. *Popular Consent and Popular Control: Whig Political Theory in the Early Constitutions.* Baton Rouge: Louisiana State University Press, 1980.

Main, Jackson Turner. *The Sovereign States, 1775–1783.* New York: New Viewpoints, 1973.

Peters, Ronald M., Jr. *The Massachusetts Constitution of 1780: A Social Compact.* Amherst: University of Massachusetts Press, 1978.

Rutland, Robert A. *The Birth of the Bill of Rights, 1776–1791.* Boston: Northeastern University Press, 1983.

Selsam, J. Paul. *The Pennsylvania Constitution of 1776: A Study in Revolutionary Democracy.* 1936. Reprint, New York: Octagon, 1971.

Wood, Gordon S. *The Creation of the American Republic, 1776–1787.* Chapel Hill: University of North Carolina Press, 1969.

Continental Army

The history of the raising, training, and operational deployment of the Continental Army is an important aspect of the American Revolution. Over the course of the war, around 230,000 men served within the ranks of the new American armed force known as the Continental Army. While it suffered defeats at the hands of the British, it was never completely destroyed and was able to inflict defeats in its turn. The army was able to muster each year, which enabled it to carry the war to the British and further the cause of independence. Without the ability of the Continental Army to wage war, the American Revolution would certainly have been lost.

The history of the Continental Army is best told in chronological order, because the army was raised from nothing and grew in proficiency and skill over the course of the war, mostly through battlefield experience. The ability of American commanders and politicians to create an armed force that was widely considered a professional one, given the financial and political constraints that impeded its progress, is impressive. The Continental Army's greatest strength was the experience of professional soldiers who had served in the British provincial forces, the British regular army, and the Prussian and French armies.

1775. The development of the Continental Army began in the thirteen colonies in late 1774 and early 1775, mainly in New England. As the threat of war with Britain grew, local leaders emphasized the need to make the militia more reliable. Many old men and men of dubious loyalty were replaced by younger and more committed individuals. Men who had seen service in the French and Indian War were often given command of units. Training and drilling were intensified. The development of a new type of militia unit was also undertaken; these units were expected to be called upon at quick notice, and these troops agreed to serve for a longer period than normal service contract required. These units became known as minutemen.

Members of the Massachusetts Provincial Congress met in April 1775 to discuss the future military organization of the colony and the New England region. They decided to form new regiments of professional soldiers to provide protection against British aggression. These regiments would be distinct

General George Washington taking command of the Continental Army at Cambridge, Massachusetts, on 3 July 1775, two weeks after the Battle of Bunker Hill. The creation of the Continental Army was authorized by the Second Continental Congress, on whose behalf the troops pledged to fight rather than on behalf of individual states. Soldiers normally enlisted for the duration of the war instead of for a fixed term, as was common to the militia. (National Archives and Records Administration)

from militia troops; like militia volunteers, regiment troops would be recruited but, like minutemen, would serve for longer periods and could be deployed outside the colony. The original idea was based upon the concept of provincial forces, which the British had raised in previous conflicts to fight alongside their regular troops. (The British also followed this practice during the American Revolution, raising Loyalist units known as the Provincial Corps. Many of the men who served also had seen service in the British Army or in the provincial forces during the French and Indian War.)

The British, hearing of this plan, initially attempted to preempt American efforts to arm themselves by marching on Lexington and Concord to seize weapons and leaders. They were met en route to their objectives by militia and minutemen, and the engagements ended with a British withdrawal to Boston. There they remained for a few months, surrounded by a hostile population. The Massachusetts Provincial Congress met again and pushed for the creation of a New England Army to be accelerated. The army was to number 30,000 men; Massachusetts would provide 13,000 men, and the other New England colonies would provide the rest. The regiments were organized to number about 600 men each, and provision was also made for an artillery regiment.

Even with the framework of the army decided, there was considerable confusion throughout April, May, and June about the organization of troops and number of men enlisting. Since the original enlistment period lasted until the end of the calendar year, many of the first militiamen and minutemen to muster were initially unwilling to commit themselves.

By June, Massachusetts had raised twenty-six regiments of infantry, while Rhode Island, Connecticut, and New Hampshire had each raised three. A number of the non-Massachusetts regiments had not yet arrived when the Battle of Bunker Hill occurred on 17 June. Organizational difficulties were rampant; most of the troops who had assembled around Boston were short of arms and ammunition, since all they had available were stocks from the militias and any matériel that had been captured from British forces. Many were armed with older models of the British Brown Bess musket. Local merchants began seeking trade with the Spanish and French for arms as soon as the army began raising troops, but delays were unavoidable.

The organization of the army outside Boston was also chaotic at first. As units arrived, they were deployed according to the needs of the day. The command structure, though initially well organized, disintegrated as senior officers bickered over seniority and command positions. Bunker Hill clearly demonstrated the need for better organization. Even though American troops successfully fended off several British attacks, their supplies ran out, their withdrawal was disorganized, and a concerted British attack could have completely destroyed the American forces in Charlestown. Senior American commanders recognized the army's shortcomings and waited for advice from the Continental Congress.

New York, meanwhile, had taken similar steps in organizing its own defense in response to an order from the Continental Congress after reports circulated that the British were planning to strike. At first, militias were reorganized and trained more frequently. Then a decision was made by the New York legislature to raise a force of 3,000 men that would serve in regiments similar to the units of the New England Army, with a term of enlistment expiring at the end of the year. The process of raising these troops was as slow as it had been in New England, and to fill the gaps a Connecticut regiment was sent to Fort Ticonderoga to safeguard against any British moves.

The Continental Army truly began in June 1775, when the Continental Congress voted to raise ten companies of riflemen. The riflemen were to be recruited from Virginia, Pennsylvania, and Maryland and sent to Boston to serve as light infantry. The Continental Congress also accepted responsibility for control of the New England Army and the forces in New York and ordered the other New England colonies to shift their men to Boston as quickly as possible.

On 15 June, the Continental Congress voted to appoint George Washington the commander in chief of the new Continental Army. On 20 June he received orders to proceed to Boston and take command. He was given authority to make strategic and tactical decisions, with the advice of the Council of War. Following this appointment, Congress spent the next few days appointing other senior positions within the new army. There were to be four major generals: Artemas Ward of the New England Army; Charles Lee of Virginia, a former British Army regular officer; Philip Schuyler, a French and Indian War veteran who received command of the New York area of operations; and Israel Putnam, another veteran of the French and Indian War. Eight brigadiers were also appointed, among them Nathanael Greene and Benedict Arnold, who both rose to prominence during the war for different reasons. The selection process was based on the number of men that each colony provided, with final appointment decided by the colonial delegates. This process created resentment among men who were serving in the militias who felt that they should be first in line for appointments. Other positions created at this stage included the adjutant, commissary, quartermaster, and paymaster generals. Congress also decided during this session to issue paper money to pay for the maintenance of the army.

Washington arrived in Boston in early July 1775 to take command. He recognized the need to organize the troops in the area and divided his command into three divisions and six brigades. Adjutant General Horatio Gates, a former British Army officer, arrived with Washington. Gates set out to handle all administrative matters for the army, including assessing the actual returns of all the regiments stationed in the area. The internal organization of the army was based on British Army structures, details of which were supplied by the many officers who had served with or in the British Army. Washington, for example, drew upon his experience in stressing the need for a proper medical corps for the army as well as proper sanitation and diet for men and officers. Following the British practice, each regiment had its own surgeon and staff, and Congress decided to supplement this with a centralized system of hospitals and medical supplies.

By October, Washington had successfully established discipline and order within the army. The forces arrayed against the British in Boston numbered just over 22,000 men. Some problems remained to be resolved regarding the organization of various regiments, mostly concerned with numbers of men and officers. The New England Army, with Washington in command, became the Continental Army's main army. The majority of American forces outside Boston performed garrison duties through the rest of the year.

Schuyler and his troops in New York were the main units to see action during the second half of 1775. Troops were raised by New York over the summer, while the 1st, 4th, and 5th Connecticut Regiments provided protection in the region. Schuyler commanded what was initially known as the New York Department and later the Northern Department and the Northern Army. On 31 August, Schuyler's troops launched an invasion against British forces stationed at St. John's, Montreal, and Quebec. A second group left Boston in September, and the two American forces met up outside Quebec on 1 December. Since the enlistment contracts of all the men were to expire on 31 December, it was imperative to launch an attack. The Americans did so and were disastrously repulsed. However, it was a significant achievement that the Americans had been able to invade and capture St. John's and Montreal, taking British forces there very much by surprise.

The first months in the development of the Continental Army were very successful overall. All of the established regiments nearly reached full strength, and the appointment of senior officers was, for the most part, smooth. Congress assumed command of the New England Army with little fuss, and cohesion improved over the course of the year. The

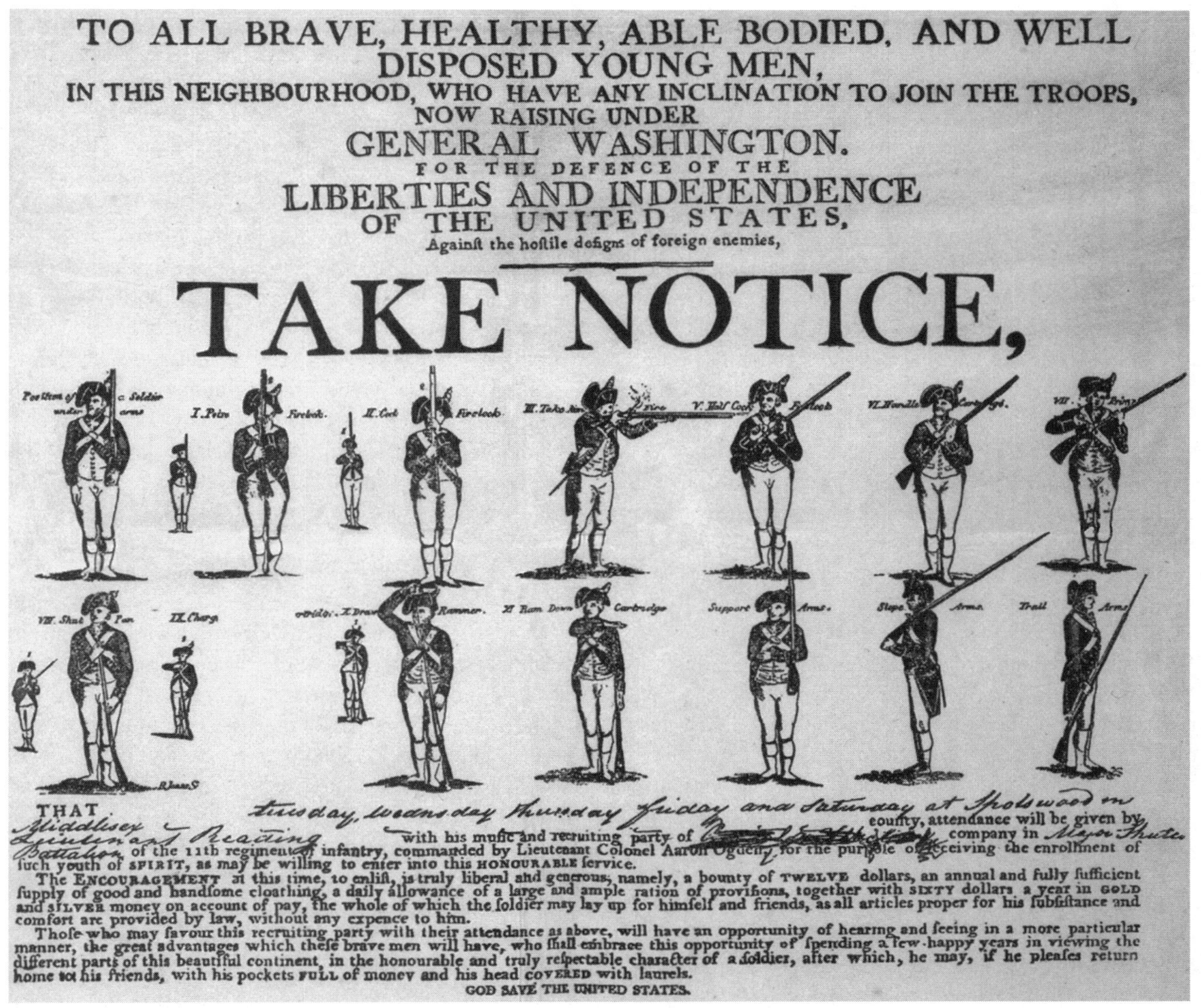

Recruitment broadside for the Continental Army appeals "To all brave, healthy able bodied and well disposed young men." In addition to incentives such as a bounty, some recruits were promised a parcel of land to be granted them after the war. (Library of Congress)

biggest headache that occurred happened at the end of the year, when all enlistment contracts expired. However, firm foundations had been laid to rebuild the forces in 1776.

1776. The campaigns of 1776 were the main testing ground for the organization and outlook of the Continental Army. Washington and his staff created a new, more streamlined infantry regiment in late 1775. It was to number around 728 men, divided into eight companies. The major change to the organization of this regiment was that it was not based on its standard British counterpart. Washington and his staff felt that there was a need for better command and control within the new regiment, and as a result the ratio of officers and noncommissioned officers (NCOs) to men was larger than in any other army. The regiment would deploy in two ranks, not three (the British Army also generally followed this practice in North America). The number of regiments was fixed as well; the main army outside Boston was to consist of twenty-six infantry regiments, one rifle regiment, and one regiment of artillery. The Northern Department, under Schuyler's command, had nine infantry regiments attached to it. One small reform, which was attempted but failed, was to disperse men from all the colonies among all the regiments. This idea did not find favor with many men and officers, so regiments remained organized by colony; regiments were numbered and included colony names as well.

The end of enlistment contracts left Washington and his officers fearful that they would not be able to muster the regiments to full strength in the spring. Their fears were somewhat justified; regiments were not at full strength, but more men did arrive to fill the ranks. On 17 March, the British withdrew from Boston and sailed for Halifax. Schuyler's forces remained in Canada through the first months of 1776, but their numbers were depleted by disease and expired contracts.

During the same period, many of the mid-Atlantic and southern colonies began to raise troops, following the same process as the New England colonies. The militia troops were organized first, and then the need for Continental troops for service elsewhere would be addressed. Congress also established two other armies, known as the Middle Department and the Southern Department. By the time Washington moved his main army from Boston to New York, all of the colonies had raised Continental regiments, and some were on their way to fight in New York. Some of the southern Continental regiments took part in the repulse of the British attack on Charleston, South Carolina, in June. The original plan of thirty-five regiments was augmented by raising regiments in the southern and mid-Atlantic regions. As with the northern regiments, the term of enlistment was set at one year.

The Continental Army's performance in battle in 1776 left much to be desired, with defeats in Canada, where troops were forced back to Fort Ticonderoga, and more notably in New York, at the battles of Long Island and White Plains, and at the defense of Fort Washington. The Continentals were grouped with various militia units during this period to augment their low numbers. Washington had been successful in a lightning campaign at Trenton and Princeton at the end of the year, obliging him and his generals, with input from Congress, to attempt to implement further reforms that their poor performance had rendered necessary.

1777. There were significant changes made in late 1776 that affected the army in 1777. The first was a change to the term of enlistment, which was set to last for the duration of the war rather than just for one year. Washington and his officers recognized that the army needed to match its British counterpart in training and experience in order to perform as a professional force. The militia system alone was not considered an adequate means by which to wage war; militiamen were considered part-time soldiers. This difference would create a strained relationship between the two forces for the remainder of the war and still forms part of the historical debate today. The plan was for men to remain in the ranks or officer corps and pass along their knowledge and experience of battle to new recruits. Linear tactics necessitated such a commitment, since it required professionalism, discipline, and expertise in drill. Later in the year, Congress amended this plan for a new term of service to be fixed at three years rather than for the duration of the war.

The proposed establishment of the army was also greatly expanded, to reach eighty-eight regiments. Each colony was required to raise a certain number of regiments according to its population. Thus, the largest burden fell on the largest colonies, such as Massachusetts and Virginia. This provision was also changed later in the year, increasing the number of proposed regiments to more than one hundred. This turned out to be far too many, and the establishment was revised again before the end of 1777. In March, Congress agreed to the raising of 3,000 light dragoons to serve with the army.

The Articles of War, which concerned discipline and military law, were also expanded, drawing upon the previously established British articles. Washington emphasized the need for stricter discipline and clearer definition of issues regarding desertions and courts-martial. Washington and his staff also set out to create a better supply system for the army. The French and, to a lesser extent, the Spanish provided aid, at first covertly, in the form of muskets, artillery, ammunition, and powder. By 1777, many Continental regiments were able to drill with the French musket model 1763, considered to be superior to the British Brown Bess. The French also supplied more than 200 artillery pieces to the army, and these were deployed to replace older captured British ordnance and locally produced iron guns.

The Clothier General's Department was created in December 1776 to purchase, store, and ship uniforms to the army. All officers recognized that uniforms were essential to instill discipline and order in American regiments, but the realities of the war meant that the Continental Army was perpetually short of uniforms. French observers noted the absence or shabbiness of American uniforms when they arrived in 1780, but this was after a concerted effort had been ongoing to outfit the army with basic navy blue uniforms. The British Army also began to experience similar problems as the war went on. The Continental Army was reorganized at the higher levels; brigades (four to five regiments) and divisions (two brigades) were structured to offer field commanders better flexibility in maneuvering. Brigades were to be organized permanently and operate as needed; this development further strengthened the main army and increased its ability to wage war. Anticipating the need to establish additional brigades and divisions, Washington, with Congress's approval, created more major and brigadier general positions.

Training improved considerably during the winter of 1777–1778, but the Continentals still had much to learn. Their performance on campaign was a mixed bag for the army; troops in the Northern Department fought well against General John Burgoyne, but the Continentals represented only a third of the men assembled. The rest were militia from New England and New York. The main army fought in the Philadelphia Campaign. Troops showed some ability to move across ground, such as at Germantown, but the army was still defeated by the British, who were more adept at battlefield maneuver. The main improvement was that unlike previous campaigns, most of the survivors of the 1777 campaigns were still with their respective regiments when they went into winter quarters. Extensive drilling and training were still required, and the winter of 1777–1778 was a critical period in the development of the Continental Army.

The anticipated expansion of the army in late 1776 and early 1777 did not occur. During the first half of 1777 it was apparent that the numbers were too large. Congress recognized this fact and called a halt to expansion, knowing that the regiments in the field needed reinforcements.

1778–1783. The period following the 1777 campaigns constituted the most important developmental phase for the army. After the defeats of the main army in Pennsylvania, a few generals and members of Congress wished to replace Washington as commander in chief. Despite such sentiments, the majority opinion was that Washington should stay, which he did.

The previous years' expansion and consequent failure to supply the men and officers of the new regiments prompted Washington, his staff, and Congress to reorganize the infantry once again, this time to more realistic levels. Such changes were also motivated by financial considerations; establishment of new infantry regiments would cost less than their 1776 predecessors. The new infantry regiment had more in common with its British equivalent; the number of men was set at around 550, with only 29 officers. Regiments were to consist of eight line companies and one company of light infantry. The actual number of regiments established also decreased, to eighty in 1779. The reorganization of the infantry did not actually begin until a lull in the fighting in 1778; it continued throughout 1779.

During the winter of 1777–1778 the Continental Army underwent still further significant reforms, one of which was to have an immediate effect on its performance in the 1778 campaign. This was the incorporation of training, drills, and tactical plans implemented by foreign officers. A series of foreign contingents, mostly from the French army, arrived over the course of 1777 and 1778. Some of the officers in the early years were not the best, which strained relations between the Americans and the French. This changed with the arrival of a contingent under the Marquis de Lafayette and the Baron de Kalb, both of whom went on to serve with distinction with the Continental Army. These advisors provided the American high command with a wealth of excellent advice regarding engineering and the building of fortifications, the most visible product of which was the construction of a series of forts along the Hudson River Valley. French officers also provided knowledge and expertise and were allowed to create special units, called legions, that combined mounted and infantry forces in one formation. These units were small but very efficient fighting forces and were extensively deployed in several major campaigns.

The Continentals also attracted officers from other European countries, the most famous of whom was a Prussian captain named Baron Friedrich von Stueben. Steuben had served with distinction in the army of Frederick the Great and had held several training positions in the Prussian army. He was released from Prussian service after the Seven Years' War and so was free to make his way, with the help of Benjamin Franklin, to the main army camp at Valley Forge in February 1778.

Steuben inspected the Continental Army and began to create a new training regime and standard drill manual for American troops. Previous to this, the Continentals had used a variety of drill manuals that were for the most part based on British drill manuals, particularly the 1764 edition. Washington and his staff also examined other manuals—developed by Henry Bouquet, a British colonel—that focused on fighting in forests, but usually the army followed standard linear tactics and drilling techniques. Steuben decided to create a new drill, based on the excellent existing Prussian drill but with amendments tailored to American soldiers unused to the iron discipline of the Prussian army. Marching was increased from sixty to seventy-five paces per minute. Steuben also emphasized the need for better bayonet training to counter the opponents' very effective use of this weapon and took note of tactical developments occurring within the French army. Overall, he stressed that the use of columns for marching and the ability to shift into line formation quickly were paramount. Unlike many Prussian officers, he recognized the success and abilities of light troops and considered them important to the Continental Army as well.

Steuben created a demonstration company in March 1779 to show his plans to Washington and his staff, who were delighted with the results. The model company was broken up, other officers were trained in the new tactics, and the units of the Continental Army stationed at Valley Forge were trained in the new drilling techniques within two months. Officers and NCOs were then sent to other Continental units elsewhere in the thirteen colonies to drill other formations. The training had an immediately recognizable effect, with the Continentals able to deploy and deliver more effective fire during the main engagement of 1778, the Battle of Monmouth.

The apparent success of the Americans at Monmouth (despite the fact that the battle was a draw) convinced the Continental Army Board to approve Steuben's drill with only minor changes. In early 1779 Congress agreed, and Steuben's drill manual was officially adopted and printed for the army. It was named the *Regulations for the Order and Discipline of the Troops of the United States, Part I,* and was unofficially known as the blue book. Steuben became a major general in the Continental Army and later served as the inspector general, with responsibility for training throughout the army. He eventually became Washington's chief of staff and held that post until the end of the war.

The Battle of Monmouth was the last major battle to take place in the North. For the remainder of the war, the focus of the fighting shifted to the Southern Department of the thirteen colonies. In 1780 Congress decided to lower the official quota of the Continental Army to under 30,000 men, but recruitment numbers still did not rise to officially authorized levels. Men continued to leave the service as their contracts ended. The main army remained stationed opposite New York for most of 1779 and 1780, and units were sent south in response to the British invasion of 1780. The lull in fighting in the North coincided with some significant problems for the Continental Army.

The United States was flooded with paper money, and the economy was on the verge of collapse. The soldiers continued to be issued their pay, but it was steadily being devalued by the economic climate. As the situation worsened, many regiments were paid late or not at all. This fact was not lost on European officers, who commented that French or Prussian troops would have mutinied long before.

In early 1781, Congress approved a further reorganization of the army that did provoke a mutiny. The number of authorized infantry regiments was cut to forty-nine, and certain colonies were required to disband units, often filled with men who had suffered from chronic shortages of supplies, uniforms, and pay. For many, this was the last straw. In January, elements of the Pennsylvania regiments had already mutinied. Congress dealt with the problem swiftly, sending representatives to address the mutineers' grievances. A similar problem erupted a few days later among the New Jersey regiments. This mutiny, however, was put down by the army alone; two ringleaders were shot. It was clear, though, that the army needed the distraction of a major campaign.

Even with breakdowns in discipline, the Continental Army of 1781 was a formidable war machine. Its units were well drilled, with a large cadre of experienced officers and men. The war in the South was not proceeding very well for the thirteen colonies, but the Continental units sent to fight had performed well. The movement of General Charles Cornwallis to Virginia gave Washington and his French allies the campaign they sought, enabling them to use their respective armies, which were ultimately successful in defeating British forces at Yorktown. Following the end of the Yorktown Campaign, Congress called for additional reductions in the size of the army, spurred by the great expense of maintaining such a large force in the field. As the threat of a major British attack diminished, the Continentals were further reduced.

The Continentals had been born from very humble foundations, but by the end of the war they could match their British counterparts in battle. Two reforms were critical in enabling the Continentals to reach this level of proficiency. The first was the extension of enlistment contracts from one to three years. The second was the infusion of foreign officers and their plans for developing drill, tactics, and organization into the Continental Army's officer corps. These developments changed the Continental Army from a ragtag collection of rebels into a professional fighting force.

Daniel Patrick Marston

See also

Arnold, Benedict; Boston, Siege of; British Army; Bunker Hill, Battle of; Canada, Operations in; Congress, Second Continental and Confederation; Fort Ticonderoga, New York; French Army; Gates, Horatio; Greene, Nathanael; Kalb, Johann, Baron de; Lafayette, Marquis de; Lee, Charles; Lexington and Concord; Loyalist Units; Musket; Mutiny, Continental Army; New England Army; New York, Operations in; Philadelphia Campaign; Putnam, Israel; Rifle; Schuyler, Philip; Southern Campaigns; Steuben, Friedrich von; Valley Forge, Pennsylvania; Ward, Artemas; Washington, George; Yorktown Campaign

References

Berg, Frederick Anderson. *Encyclopedia of Continental Army Units: Battalions, Regiments, and Independent Corps.* Harrisburg, PA: Stackpole, 1972.

Bolton, Charles K. *The Private Soldier under Washington.* New York: Scribner, 1902.

Conway, Stephen. *The War of American Independence, 1775–1783.* London: Arnold, 1995.

Hatch, Louis C. *The Administration of the American Revolutionary Army.* New York: Longmans and Green, 1904.

Higginbotham, Don. *The War of American Independence: Military Attitudes, Policies, and Practice, 1763–1789.* New York: Macmillan, 1971.

Martin, J. *Private Yankee Doodle Dandee: Being a Narrative of Some of the Adventures, Dangers and Sufferings of a Revolutionary Soldier.* New York: New York Times, 1968.

Peterson, Harold L. *The Book of the Continental Soldier: Being a Complete Account of the Uniforms, Weapons, and Equipment with Which He Lived and Fought.* Harrisburg, PA: Stackpole, 1968.

Royster, C. *A Revolutionary People at War: The Continental Army and the American Character.* Chapel Hill: University of North Carolina Press, 1979.

Steuben, Frederick William Baron von. *Baron von Steuben's Revolutionary War Drill Manual.* New York: Dover, 1985.

Weigley, R. *Towards an American Army.* New York: Columbia University Press, 1962.

Wilbur, C. Keith. *The Picture Book of the Continental Soldier.* Harrisburg, PA: Stackpole, 1976.

Wright, Robert K. *The Continental Army.* Washington, DC: Center for Military History, United States Army, 1989.

Continental Association (1774–1776)

The Continental Association was a plan of nonimportation, nonconsumption, and nonexportation passed on 20 October 1774 by the First Continental Congress. The association listed nine unfair acts passed by Parliament since 1763 and called for their repeal. Until relief was accomplished, the First Continental Congress pledged to put economic and political pressure on the British government by endorsing an immediate

WHEREAS we the Subſcribers have broke the Aſſociation of the late Continental Congreſs, by unloading a Part of the Cargo from on board the Ship Beulah; we do declare that we are ſorry for the Offence we gave the Publick thereby, and that we will for the future ſtrictly adhere to the ſaid Aſſociation, and to the further Orders of the Continental Congreſs, the Provincial Congreſs of the Colony of New-York, and the General Committee of Aſſociation for the City and County of New-York, ſaving to Robert Murray (who is one of the People called QUAKERS) his religious Principles. Dated at New-York, the 9th of June, 1775.

Robert Murray,
John Murray.

Public apology to the Continental Congress by two merchants for ignoring the nonimportation policy of the Continental Association, 9 June 1775. (Library of Congress)

colonial boycott of all imports and, if necessary, of all exports beginning the following year. The association mandated that counties and towns enforce nonimportation by organizing local committees of inspection, each responsible for ensuring full compliance with the boycott, and called upon Americans to alter their lifestyles in support of the "common cause" by developing domestic manufacturing and avoiding gambling and expensive entertainment. While the association reflected little new in colonial modes of resistance—several schemes of nonimportation had been attempted in the decade since the Stamp Act—it was the first official act of resistance by the Continental Congress. A moderate position, the boycott committed America to resisting Parliament through frugality and self-sacrifice, but not through the use of arms. Yet it was still confrontational, challenging Americans to make decisions about their own allegiance and the importance of union. Another significant consequence of the Continental Association was its organization of congressionally mandated committees of inspection, which, once Britain lost effective power, helped facilitate the legitimacy of new local governments and of a new national government.

The plan for an economic boycott that became the Continental Association grew out of the colonial reaction to Britain's passage of the Coercive Acts. Anger over the closing of the port of Boston, the radical alteration of Massachusetts's charter, and the Quebec Act's legalization of French civil law throughout the interior of North America north of the Ohio River led to a call for a continental congress. Once the First Continental Congress convened in Philadelphia on 5 September 1774, one of its chief tasks was to draft a formal list of America's grievances and decide upon an appropriate and effective way to get Britain to change its unfriendly posture toward the mainland colonies. In the preamble to the Continental Association, a document designed to achieve both ends, Congress listed its complaints with British administrations dating back to 1763. The grievances fell into three categories: Parliament's attempts to tax the colonies without their consent, the denial of their right to a trial by jury in certain circumstances, and the harsh punishment of Massachusetts.

Although the mainland colonies quickly decided that they should resist perceived British tyranny with one voice, the specific mode of that redress was still to be determined. Most agreed that some form of economic pressure should be attempted, as it had been used to encourage the repeal of the Stamp Act in 1765 and the Townshend Acts in 1769–1770. Still, despite a consensus for nonimportation, it would be the details—especially the question of when to halt exports and how to ensure popular compliance—that mattered most to delegates trying to best represent their colonies. For Massachusetts, the sooner an embargo on all goods could be set up the better. Massachusetts pushed for an immediate halt to both imports and exports until the Coercive Acts were repealed. Other colonies, however, saw their interests endangered in cutting off exports right away. Those colonies tied to staple products—especially Maryland, Virginia, and South Carolina—had a much more difficult time with exports than imports. Less diversified and commercial than the North, plantations in the South that exported only tobacco, rice, and indigo were severely threatened by an immediate freeze.

One month before the First Continental Congress convened in Philadelphia, Virginia held a convention to draft its colony's response to the Coercive Acts. On 6 August, the delegates passed an agreement, known as the Virginia Association, that called for all imports to cease after 1 November 1774 and all tobacco exports to be frozen after 10 August 1775. This document served as a blueprint for the Continental Association. It also reflected Virginia's unwillingness to abandon its current crop of tobacco. As much as Virginians sympathized with Boston and saw themselves as threatened by the Coercive Acts, the demands of a staple economy meant that Virginia planters could not fully commit to losing their year's income.

Part of the reason that Virginians felt they could not immediately halt tobacco exports was the degree of their indebtedness, which had grown rapidly throughout the mid-eighteenth century. Recent changes in the commercial tobacco system, including the introduction of Scottish agents, or "factors," on site in tidewater Virginia, made goods more readily accessible to planters. More liberal lines of credit, the wider availability of luxury items, and a growing desire to consume those goods meant that planters found themselves in a deepening spiral of personal debt. In the context of the imperial crisis, then, attempts to cut import goods off at the source were seen as doubly beneficial to those planters who realized that they were becoming increasingly dependent on British merchants. Not only could Virginia's elites show their support for resisting parliamentary tyranny, they could also use nonimportation as an opportunity to reduce their levels of debt and attempt to reassert their economic independence from the British commercial system.

The attention paid to frugality, industry, and strict economy in both the Virginia Association and the Continental Association reflects this attempt to do more than put political pressure on Britain. Both documents offered alternatives to reliance on Britain, including plans to promote diversified agriculture and manufactures in America, and a moratorium on those activities that demanded some of the most ostentatious goods, including the practice of buying expensive attire and giving mourning gifts at funerals. As a statement of union, however, the encouragement of virtue in the Continental Association revealed more than just a reflection of Virginia's desire to lessen its economic dependence. Alongside the promotion of manufactures, the eighth article of the Continental Association also invoked the still-palpable "Puritan ethic" by discouraging "every species of Extravagance and Dissipation," including horse racing, gambling, and the theater.

But the domestic plan for promoting economic nationalism and patriotic virtue did not mean an endorsement of nonexportation. While Massachusetts clamored for a complete economic embargo, southern staple economies saw this as a last resort. The fragility governing any collective action as a union meant that Congress would have to delay the deadline on nonexportation. The Continental Association proclaimed that 1 December 1774 would be the last date for any imports from Britain and for certain goods (slaves, molasses, coffee, and Madeira wine) imported from the British West Indies and other locations included as legitimate exporters to North America under Britain's Navigation Acts. If this nonconsumption did not achieve the repeal of grievances listed in the preamble, however, the Continental Association's fourth article stipulated that as of 10 September 1775, no commodities could be exported from the North American continent, with one exception. South Carolina's particular unease with the halting of exports forced Congress into a compromise. Since nonexportation would curtail the sale of both rice and indigo, South Carolina's economy stood little chance of surviving, so the association stipulated that rice could still be exported after 10 September 1775 to Europe. A direct violation of Britain's century-old Navigation Acts that allowed America to trade only with Britain and her empire, this provision demonstrated the lengths to which Congress believed it needed to go to ensure that its boycott secured a redress of grievances.

With the dates agreed upon, the other sticking point was enforcement. The difficulty in ensuring compliance had undermined previous American nonimportation and nonconsumption boycotts, especially the Townshend Acts boycott of 1769–1770. In Virginia, the planter elite wrongly thought that their example alone would make that boycott successful. Merchants in New York and Pennsylvania had also undermined previous attempts to restrict the importation of goods by moving their cargoes around and skirting detection. In the Continental Association, Congress learned from previous mistakes by explicitly determining the punishment for those who violated the embargo. Here again, Congress walked a fine line. Trying to resist Parliament with economic and political force yet maintain a still tentative union, Congress did not want to create internal enemies, namely those merchants who would most feel the boycott's bite. Therefore, Congress instituted a grace period for merchants, three months after the 1 December 1774 deadline, whereby importers had a choice about what would happen to their contraband goods. Any goods entering between December and February could either be returned, stored under the supervision of the local committee of inspection, or sold at auction, the profits of which would go to the relief of Boston. Even past the February grace period, imports would not be confiscated but simply sent back to their origin without harm. These mild measures were meant to retain the loyalty and participation of urban merchants and also to avoid infuriating British merchants who had traditionally been America's best lobbyists in Parliament. By not antagonizing merchants, Congress hoped it would limit the lengths to which importers would go to circumvent the Continental Association.

But the most important aspect of the Continental Association was article eleven, which created committees of inspection in every city, town, and county "whose Business it shall be attentively to observe the conduct of all persons touching this Association." Since the boycott ranged over the entire spectrum of the economy, this vague mandate made the local committees powerful entities. In some communities, committees of correspondence that had been organized before Congress met simply took on this new role of policing the association. Other locales followed the association by creating committees of inspection to work alongside the older correspondence committees. In all, article eleven assured that many more people would be mobilized in the burgeoning Revolutionary movement. The committees of inspection were often very large bodies, consisting of dozens of members. In some colonies, participation on local Continental

Association committees averaged one hundred members—numbers that would continue to grow throughout 1775. The several thousand people who served on the association's committees of inspection wedded more people to Congress, forcing people up and down the continent to make important decisions about their allegiance.

The scope of the Continental Association, however, served to create more than just organizations charged with prohibiting British goods. The assigned duties were enormous. Local committees were to supervise all local aspects of the boycott, promote diversification and alternative forms of manufacture, and encourage virtue and frugality. In short, they were to become a functional, if extralegal, form of local government. Because the association's committees energetically policed the boycott, with all that it entailed, an effective new form of local government made the process of replacing Britain's collapsing civil authority in 1775–1776 much easier to undertake. Due largely to article eleven, America did not fall into chaos when hundreds of localities first acquired home rule. Moreover, the committees of inspection existed only because of the Continental Congress; therefore, the authority and loyalty of the new local governments was tied to the new national authority. By creating these local governments, Congress inextricably attached them to itself, thus further legitimizing both the new American union and Congress as rightful sovereign over the colonies.

Robert G. Parkinson

See also

British Parliament; Coercive Acts; Congress, First Continental; Correspondence, Committees of; Navigation Acts; Nonimportation Agreements; Quebec Act; Stamp Act; Townshend Acts

References

Ammerman, David. *In the Common Cause: American Response to the Coercive Acts of 1774.* New York: Norton, 1975.

Breen, T. H. "Narratives of Commercial Life: Consumption, Ideology, and Community on the Eve of the American Revolution." *William and Mary Quarterly,* 3rd ser., 50 (1993): 471–501.

Carson, Cary, Ronald Hoffman, and Peter Albert, eds. *Of Consuming Interests: The Style of Life in the Eighteenth Century.* Charlottesville: University of Virginia Press, 1994.

Marston, Jerrilyn Greene. *King and Congress: The Transfer of Political Legitimacy, 1774–1776.* Princeton, NJ: Princeton University Press, 1987.

Morgan, Edmund S. "The Puritan Ethic and the American Revolution." *William and Mary Quarterly,* 3rd ser., 24 (1967): 3–43.

Ragsdale, Bruce A. *A Planter's Republic: The Search for Economic Independence in Revolutionary Virginia.* Madison, WI: Madison House, 1996.

Rakove, Jack. *The Beginnings of National Politics: An Interpretive History of the Continental Congress.* New York: Knopf, 1979.

Ryerson, Richard A. *The Revolution Is Now Begun: The Radical Committees of Philadelphia, 1765–1776.* Philadelphia: University of Pennsylvania Press, 1978.

Schlesinger, Arthur M. *The Colonial Merchants and the American Revolution, 1763–1776.* New York: Atheneum, 1968.

Continental Congress

See Congress, First Continental; Congress, Second Continental and Confederation

---

Continental Navy

Naval operations were immensely important to the outcome of the Revolutionary War. In 1775 the Royal Navy was the world's largest navy, and as recently as the Seven Years' War (1756–1763) it had defeated both the French and Spanish navies. Until 1778 and the official entry of France into the war on the American side, British naval superiority was unchallenged, for in 1775 the Americans possessed no navy at all.

Both sides in the struggle recognized the importance of control of the seas. With it, the British could transport troops and military supplies to North America. Given the appalling state of land transportation in the colonies, it was an immense advantage to the British to be able to move troops and equipment by water along the Atlantic coast and extract them should that prove necessary. Conversely, the Americans hoped to inhibit the British in such operations and to conduct a war against British commerce through privateering. Both sides sought to control the continent's great interior lakes and rivers. General George Washington, commander in chief of the Continental Army, recognized the need for a naval force early in the war, when he secured schooners in Massachusetts and sent them out to capture British supply vessels during the siege of Boston.

Although American Revolutionary leaders were divided about the wisdom of expending scarce resources to equip and dispatch ships against the British, four separate and distinct American navies took to the seas during the war. These were Washington's navy, the eleven state navies that engaged in coast and river defense, a large number of privateers, and, finally, the Continental Navy. During the war, the Americans also experimented with new types of weapons, such as the submarine (inventor Robert Bushnell's *Turtle* was the world's first) and naval mines.

Warships of the period were rated according to the number of guns they were designed to carry, but because they were essentially floating artillery platforms, warships often carried more guns than their official rate. Smaller antipersonnel guns did not count in the rate.

First rates were the largest ships, those of one hundred guns or more. The most powerful warships were known as ships of

The Continental flag is raised for the first time in American waters aboard the 16-gun brig *Lexington* in 1776. Operating out of French ports, the *Lexington,* together with the *Reprisal* and the *Dolphin,* took at least eighteen enemy vessels in European waters before itself being captured on its return journey to America. (National Archives and Records Administration)

the line, built to stand in the battle line. The workhorse ship of the line at the time of the Revolutionary War was the third-rate 74-gun vessel. Tactics of the day called for opposing fleets to sail in line-ahead formation and blast away at one another at near pistol range.

The United States built only one ship of the line during the war, the 74-gun *America* (projected to carry thirty 18-pounders, thirty-two 12-pounders, and fourteen 9-pounders). It was one of three ships of the line authorized by Congress in November 1776; the others were never built. Constructed at Portsmouth, New Hampshire, the *America* was offered to France in September 1782 to replace the *Magnifique,* a French ship of the line wrecked in American waters, and was officially transferred to France in June 1783.

In all, fifty-three ships served in the Continental Navy during the war. The largest were frigates. Designed for independent service, frigates served as the eyes of the fleet and conducted commerce raiding, the principal task of the Continental Navy during the war. Such ships carried from several dozen to forty or more guns.

Cannon were denominated by the weight of the shot they threw. Thus, a 12-pounder cannon fired a ball weighing 12 pounds. Virtually all cannon of this period were muzzle-loading smoothbores. The largest cannon in common service in the Continental Navy were 12-pounders. The large frigate *L'Indien,* built in Amsterdam, mounted twenty-eight 36-pounders in addition to twelve 12-pounders, but it was the exception.

Bronze was favored over iron for cannon manufacture (it was more forgiving than the more brittle iron) but was far more expensive than iron, and for this reason iron guns won out and predominated at the time of the American Revolutionary War. Iron was heavier than bronze, but this was not as much a factor at sea as on land.

Cannon were mounted on stout wooden carriages with four small wheels, known as trucks. The carriages were secured to the ship by stout rope known as breeching. The guns were trained laterally by tackle and iron handspikes. They were elevated by means of wooden wedges, known as quoins. Almost all the guns were carried in broadsides, although a few guns might be mounted at the bow and stern. Smaller man-killers, known as swivel guns, were mounted on the rails of the smaller vessels. Firing up to a half-pound shot, swivel guns were used to repel boarders or assist in clearing an enemy deck in battle. Swivel guns were not included in the official armament rating.

Captains tended to crowd guns on board, and their ships often carried more guns than their official rates. Ordnance and equipment for the ships were often in short supply, and as a result ships often went to sea with decidedly different batteries of guns from those that were intended.

Few ships were actually sunk in battle. Wooden warships could absorb tremendous punishment, and those that were captured were almost always incorporated into the victor's navy. Most ships lost at sea fell victim to fire or magazine explosions. Those captured were usually taken by boarding or surrendered as a consequence of personnel losses. Indeed, in battles at sea each side sought to disable the other vessel to the point that it would be possible to rake it at will. Raking involved placing one's own ship perpendicular to that of an enemy (known as crossing the "t"). This enabled one to fire all of one side of the broadside guns the length of the enemy ship, while the latter could reply only with a few bow or stern guns. Cannonballs racing down the length of the ship could exact frightful damage, but most personnel casualties aboard ship were the result of flying wooden splinters.

The most common projectile was a solid cast iron ball known as shot. Explosive shell was little used at sea, except for mortars aboard special vessels for shore bombardment, but shot was often heated, and hot shot might actually set a wooden vessel on fire. Warships also carried special disabling shot employed to attack spars and rigging. These were known as bar or chain shot (two half shot connected by a bar, or two shot with a chain secured to each). For close-range fire against boats and personnel, crews employed grapeshot or canister. Grapeshot consisted of a number of balls, usually nine, clustered around a spindle and held in place by a cloth bag wrapped with twine, the whole resembling a bunch of grapes. It would break apart on firing. Canister or case shot consisted of a great many musket balls or scrap iron held in a metal case that also broke apart. Its effect was much like that of a shotgun.

Ships' armories carried a bewildering assortment of different personal weapons. For boarding or repelling an attack, the crew might wield pistols, muskets, blunderbusses, cutlasses, swords, knives, and boarding pikes and axes.

Conditions of service were difficult for the seamen. They were forced to live in cramped conditions and subsist for the most part on inadequate rations. Sailors serving aboard American warships were, however, volunteers. The pay was poor, but all members of the crew could hope, if they were successful in battle, to share in the distribution of prize money. Discipline was harsh, with corporal punishment meted out for a large assortment of infractions, but conditions were far better than those for British sailors, most of whom were pressed (forcibly recruited). Discipline was brutal. Medical services of the day were quite primitive, and serious wounds usually resulted in amputation and death. During battle, surgeons, if aboard ship, set up in the cockpit below decks.

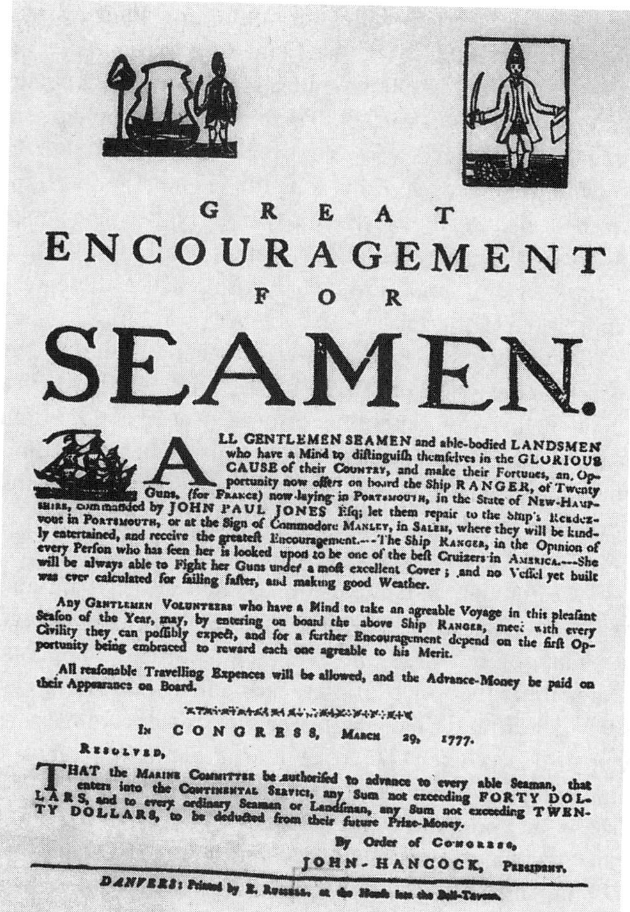

Continental Navy recruiting poster issued in 1777. Young men are encouraged to serve aboard the 18-gun sloop *Ranger* under Captain John Paul Jones. With this vessel Jones raided the port of Whitehaven on the northwest coast of England and captured the warship *Drake* in 1778. (Naval Historical Center)

There was little standard in uniforms. Officers might wear a blue coat with red facings and cuffs, red waistcoat, blue breeches, and white stockings as well as a cocked hat. Midshipmen might wear a white waistcoat, breeches, and stockings and a blue coat with white collar tabs and cuffs. Seamen wore loose-fitting trousers that were wide-bottomed and went to the knee, a shirt or vest, and perhaps a waistcoat with a kerchief around the neck and a broad brimmed hat, often of straw. The marine uniform consisted of a green jacket with red collar, lapels, cuffs, and turnbacks; buff waistcoats and breeches; and a hat with cockade.

On 13 October 1775, acting on a Rhode Island proposal, Congress authorized the outfitting of two vessels "of ten carriage guns . . . for a cruise of three months" against British supply ships and appointed a Naval Committee of three members—Silas Deane, Christopher Gadsden, and John Langdon—to supervise the work. On 30 October, Congress approved the outfitting of another four vessels and added another four men to the Naval Committee: John Adams, Joseph Hewes, Stephen Hopkins, and Richard Henry Lee. On 2 November, the Naval Committee voted $100,000 to obtain and equip vessels of war. On 10 November, Congress authorized the formation of a corps of two battalions of marines to provide shipboard security and antipersonnel musket fire from the fighting tops of the ships during battle. Meanwhile, Adams drew up the rules and regulations for the Continental Navy. Largely a simplification of British practice, these were approved by Congress on 28 November.

Continental Navy administration changed during the course of the war. From December 1775 to December 1779 a permanent Marine Committee of thirteen members, one from each colony, controlled naval matters. Then a Board of Admiralty was set up, composed of two members of Congress and three private citizens. Finally, after 1781, Robert Morris, who was concurrently director of finance, handled naval matters.

The first eight warships of the navy were all merchant conversions. The largest of these were the ships *Alfred* and *Columbus.* The *Alfred* was the first ship of the Continental Navy to fly the American flag. Lieutenant John Paul Jones raised the Grand Union flag on the *Alfred* on its commissioning on 3 December 1775. (The little schooner *Hannah* of 78 tons with four 4-pounders was reputedly the first armed vessel to sail under the Continental flag.) The *Alfred* was a former merchantman of 440 tons and mounted twenty-four 9-pounders. The *Columbus* mounted eighteen 9-pounders and ten 6-pounders. The remaining six vessels were the brigs *Andrew Doria* (fourteen 4-pounders) and *Cabot* (fourteen 6-pounders); the sloops *Providence* (twelve 4-pounders), *Hornet* (eight or ten 4-pounders), *Wasp* (eight 2-pounders), and *Fly* (six 9-pounders).

On 13 December 1775, on the motion of the Rhode Island delegation, Congress approved the construction of thirteen frigates (five of 32 guns, five of 28 guns, and three of 24 guns). Allocation of construction was assigned on the basis of political considerations rather than the actual ability to produce the ships. All were to be built by March 1776 and were intended as commerce raiders. The largest guns they carried were 12-pounders. The construction schedule was unrealistic, and only the *Hancock,* the *Boston,* the *Raleigh,* and the *Randolph* were able to get to sea in 1777. Ships constructed for the Continental Navy tended to be long and narrow, large for their classes, and fast.

Probably the finest ship in the Continental Navy was the frigate *Alliance.* Of 900 tons and commissioned in 1778, it was rated at thirty-six guns but actually mounted forty: twenty-eight 12-pounders and twelve 9-pounders. It had a crew of 300 men. The *Alliance* became the flagship of Jones's small squadron in European waters. Perhaps the most famous ship in the Continental Navy was Jones's *Bonhomme Richard.* This former East Indiaman, given or loaned to the United States by France, was 900 tons and rated at forty guns but mounted forty-two: six 18-pounders, twenty-eight 12-pounders, and eight 9-pounders.

On 22 December 1775 Congress appointed the first eighteen officers of the Continental Navy. The senior officer was Commodore Esek Hopkins, commander of the fleet. Below him were Captains Dudley Saltonstall, Abraham Whipple, Nicholas Biddle, and the commodore's son, John Burroughs Hopkins. Jones was the top ranking of five first lieutenants.

In early January 1776, Congress ordered Commodore Hopkins to take his squadron to sea. His orders called on him to destroy an enemy flotilla in Chesapeake Bay organized by the royalist governor of Virginia, John Murray, Lord Dunmore, then clear the North Carolina coast before returning to accomplish the same off Rhode Island. On 17 February Hopkins set sail with the eight ships acquired in November 1775. On the evening of 19 February, the *Hornet* and *Fly* lost contact with the other ships in the squadron and went their separate way. Taking advantage of a discretionary clause in his orders, Hopkins then ordered the squadron to sail to the Bahamas.

On 3–4 March, in the only successful large American fleet operation of the war, Hopkins landed 300 seamen and marines on New Providence Island and captured Nassau, securing there seventy-three cannon and mortars, munitions, and other military supplies. On 17 March the squadron departed on the return voyage. On 4 April, in the first engagement between the Continental Navy and the Royal Navy, one of Hopkins's ships, the *Columbus* under Whipple, captured the British schooner *Hawk* (6 guns). Shortly after midnight on 6 April the American squadron fell in with the British sloop of war *Glasgow* (20 guns). The Americans mismanaged the engagement and took only the *Glasgow*'s tender. In the engagement, the Americans lost ten men killed and fourteen wounded, while British losses were only one killed and three wounded. On 7 April, in an hour-long battle off the Virginia Capes, Captain John Barry's Continental brig *Lexington* captured the British sloop *Edward* (6 guns).

Most of the Continental Navy's engagements were single-ship actions, and for the first two years of the war the British were able to move by sea at will. In March 1776 the British evacuated Boston, which the Continental militias had blockaded from the land. In July 1776 Admiral Lord Richard Howe's fleet landed 32,000 British troops on Staten Island to begin the New York Campaign.

British naval weaknesses, including numerous ships in poor repair, were not apparent to the Americans as long as Britain was fighting the Continental Navy, but the formal entrance of France into the war on the side of the colonies in 1778, Spain in 1779, and the Dutch a year later transformed a largely localized struggle into a world war with the North

American theater only a secondary one for the Royal Navy, which lacked the resources to be successful everywhere. Only a combination of intra-allied disagreements, inept allied commanders, and effective actions by outnumbered British forces saved Britain from total disaster.

The entry of France into the war greatly aided the meager efforts of the Continental Navy, for it provided bases and some additional ships. Meanwhile, some American captains, notably Jones and Lambert Wickes, carried the war to British home waters and attacked British merchant shipping over a wide area. Such actions forced the British to introduce convoys and shift naval assets. The energetic Jones also won the most spectacular engagement of the war, the sanguinary contest between his frigate *Bonhomme Richard* and the British frigate *Serapis* on 3 September 1779. This action made Jones the first American naval hero. Yet, for the most part, the Continental Navy accomplished little—certainly nothing of a decisive nature—during the war.

In 1778 the British shifted their military operations to the American South, taking Savannah and then Charleston. Notwithstanding these successes on land, the naval war was about to turn with the arrival in North America of Admiral François de Grasse and twenty-eight ships of the line. In the inconclusive Second Battle of the Chesapeake of 5 September 1781, he held off a British fleet under Admiral Thomas Graves, making possible the Continental Army and French army victory on land at Yorktown that led to the fall of Lord North's government in London and Britain's decision to seek peace.

Meanwhile, the Continental Navy, poorly administered and supported and indifferently led, dwindled steadily in size as the war progressed. Only two of its ships, the frigates *Alliance* and *Hague,* were in service at war's end. The Continental Navy had played only a very limited role in the war. Despite its failings, it captured or sank almost 200 British vessels, carried dispatches to and from Europe, transported funds to help finance the Revolutionary cause, forced the British to divert naval assets for the protection of commerce, and helped to provoke the Anglo-French diplomatic confrontation that brought France into the war. It also provided a training ground for many men, including Barry, Thomas Truxtun, Richard Dale, and Joshua Barney, who would serve as officers in a new national navy created after the war.

The last naval action of the war took place on 10 March 1783 off the Atlantic coast of Florida when Captain Barry's frigate *Alliance* engaged the British frigate *Sybil* (32 guns). Although the *Sybil* was heavily damaged, Barry was forced to break off the battle with the arrival of two other British warships.

All the ships of the Continental Navy were sold at the end of hostilities. The *Alliance* was the last, sold in 1785. Captains such as Jones (who had hoped to be the first American admiral) who wished to pursue their profession were obliged to do so abroad in the French or Russian navies. The U.S. Navy was not officially established until 1794.

Spencer C. Tucker

See also

Adams, John; Bahamas; Barry, John; Biddle, Nicholas; *Bonhomme Richard* vs. *Serapis;* Bushnell, David; Chesapeake, Second Battle of the; Conyngham, Gustavus; Deane, Silas; Gadsden, Christopher; Hopkins, Esek; Hopkins, John B.; Hopkins, Stephen; Howe, Richard; Jones, John Paul; Langdon, John; Lee, Richard Henry; Manley, John; Marines, Continental; Morris, Robert; Murray, John, Lord Dunmore; Naval Operations, American vs. British; Nicholas, Samuel; Privateering; Prizes and Prize Money; Rathbun, John Peck; Royal Navy; Saltonstall, Dudley; Washington's Navy; Whipple, Abraham; Wickes, Lambert; Yorktown Campaign

References

Bowen-Hassell, E. Gordon, Dennis M. Conrad, and Mark L. Hayes, eds. *Sea Raiders of the American Revolution: The Continental Navy in European Waters.* Washington: Naval Historical Center, 2003.

Chapelle, Howard I. *The History of the American Sailing Navy: The Ships and Their Development.* New York: Norton, 1949.

Coggins, Jack. *Ships and Seamen of the American Revolution.* 1969. Reprint, Mineola, NY: Dover, 2002.

Gardiner, Robert, ed. *Navies and the American Revolution, 1775–1783.* London: Chatham, 1996.

Mahan, Alfred Thayer. *The Major Operations of the Navies in the War of American Independence.* Boston: Little, Brown, 1913.

Miller, Nathan. *Broadsides: The Age of Fighting Sail, 1775–1815.* London: Wiley, 2001.

———. *Sea of Glory: The Continental Navy Fights for Independence, 1775–1783.* New York: David McKay, 1974.

Silverstone, Paul H. *The Sailing Navy, 1775–1854.* Annapolis, MD: Naval Institute Press, 2001.

Smith, Charles R. *Marines in the Revolution: A History of the Continental Marines in the American Revolution, 1775–1783.* Washington, DC: History and Marines Division, U.S. Marine Corps, 1975.

Tucker, Spencer C. *Arming the Fleet: U.S. Naval Ordnance in the Muzzle-Loading Era.* Annapolis, MD: Naval Institute Press, 1989.

Convention Army

The Convention Army is the term given to General John Burgoyne's defeated army following the signing of the Convention of Saratoga and its subsequent internment by Congress over the next five years.

On 16 October 1777, Burgoyne and General Horatio Gates agreed to a cessation of hostilities between their two armies, facing each other beside the Hudson River at Saratoga, New York. The original terms proposed by Burgoyne—that his troops would return to Europe and never again bear arms against the forces of Congress—had been rejected by Gates, who had demanded that Burgoyne's army surrender and

Convention Army encampment at Charlottesville, Virginia. By the terms of surrender agreed to at Saratoga in 1777, General John Burgoyne's troops were to be paroled on the condition that they promised not to fight again in North America during the war. Wary that upon release the British would disavow their pledge, Congress violated the agreement and interned the prisoners for the rest of the war. (Library of Congress)

become prisoners of war. But the growing rumors of another British force coming up the Hudson from New York made Gates change his mind, and within hours he had agreed to Burgoyne's proposal almost verbatim.

The result was the Convention of Saratoga, which neither constituted a formal surrender nor made Burgoyne's men prisoners of war. Some 465 Canadians and a number of American Loyalists were allowed by the convention to return at once to Canada, while the 3,360 British and 2,431 German troops laid down their arms preparatory to being marched to a port from where they would be transported back to Europe. Together with some 300 British and German women and many children, the troops were marched 200 miles east to Cambridge and Boston, where they arrived on 6 November. The enlisted men, with three officers per regiment, were housed in rough barracks on Prospect Hill and Winter Hill, while the remaining officers were quartered in private houses. Massachusetts, however, could not cope with more than 6,000 unexpected guests, and shortages of accommodations, firewood, and food soon led Burgoyne (who had to spend £20,000 of his own money to supply his army) to write to Gates: "the public faith is broke."

From a present-day perspective, Gates's acceptance of the convention may seem bizarre, since the return of the troops to Britain would merely release others to come to America and fight in their place. It must be remembered, however, that such agreements were common in eighteenth-century European warfare and were therefore familiar to both Gates (who had served in the British Army before moving to America) and Burgoyne. In addition, the logistical requirements of sending substitute forces to North America and the effect of these demands upon the British war effort should not be underestimated. Nevertheless, the Continental Congress—including several members who understood why Gates had agreed to such terms—was not happy and immediately sought ways to delay the departure of the Convention Army in the vessels that had already begun gathering outside Boston Harbor by Christmas.

A special committee began seeking technicalities on which to suspend Congress's performance of the convention. The first opportunity for delay arose with the laborious process of recording the details of every soldier—essential to identifying anyone who might return in breach of the convention. Another came from a discrepancy between the number of cartridge boxes (645) handed over and the much greater number of soldiers (in fact, the missing boxes had been purloined by Gates's men). Then, an attempt by Sir William Howe to have the men shipped back to Britain and Europe from a British-held American port—New York City or Newport, Rhode Island—was deemed to be evidence of a plan to ignore the convention and add the soldiers to his own army. Burgoyne's outburst to Gates about inadequate provisions for the prisoners offered a further chance to "expose" British intentions to invalidate the convention, and on 3 January 1778 Congress demanded a "distinct and explicit" ratification by the king, reasoning that this would never be given as it would implicitly recognize American independence. When against expectation the royal ratification arrived later that year, Congress then demanded that a witness cross the Atlantic to authenticate the king's signature.

Eventually the burden of supporting the Convention Army became too great for Massachusetts. Congress voted to move the troops south in September 1778, and a Virginia representative offered to allow barracks to be built on his estate near Charlottesville. The troops, guarded by 600 militiamen, were not moved until November and spent twelve weeks marching the 600 miles on starvation rations. The timing was deliberate as was the route (passing through the German communities of Pennsylvania), both designed to encourage desertion among the Brunswickers. When the troops arrived, they found their accommodation half-built and had to complete the work themselves; suitable housing for the officers was so scarce that many were forced to live miles away. Nevertheless, the Convention Army became a self-supporting community (Thomas Jefferson was a frequent visitor and often attended plays put on by the troops). And despite the misgivings of some Virginians, most welcomed the army's skilled labor and its contribution to the local economy.

During the summer of 1780 there were rumors that Lord Charles Cornwallis was planning to march north from the Carolinas to rescue the Convention Army. Similar intentions by General Sir Henry Clinton at New York gained credibility when a high-ranking member of the Convention Army on parole, General William Phillips, was sent immediately after his official exchange to take charge of British forces raiding into Virginia. Late in 1780 the British prisoners in the Convention Army were moved to Maryland, where they encountered considerable hostility. The German prisoners followed in February 1781. The reality of the threat from Cornwallis was realized in June 1781, when the raid of his cavalry officer, Banastre Tarleton, on Charlottesville had as one of its objectives the location and release of any remaining Convention Army prisoners (although by then they had all been sent north). From then on, the treatment of the Convention Army deteriorated, as the individual states became less willing to house it. After 1781, the prisoners were divided between Virginia, Maryland, Pennsylvania, Connecticut, and Massachusetts, and it is almost impossible to trace what happened to many of the troops in the last two years of the war.

So deep was American distrust of the Convention Army that even the senior officers were held captive for long periods—an event almost unheard of in Europe. Burgoyne and two of his staff were allowed to return to England in April 1778, although only after he had settled all of the Convention Army's outstanding accounts; Burgoyne was not formally paroled until 1781. Phillips and General Friedrich Riedesel were released to New York City only in November 1779, and neither was officially exchanged until the following year. Many junior officers, British and German, were also paroled at the end of 1779, as were 149 Brunswick servants and 113 noncommissioned officers, these last two groups paroled in anticipation of an exchange of enlisted men that never took place. Of the several thousand enlisted men held prisoner, 655 Britons and 160 Germans had "escaped" by the time of Burgoyne's departure for England. Some deserted to the Continental Army (despite Washington's opposition to the enlistment of enemy prisoners), others disappeared into local communities, and still others attempted to regain their own lines and rejoin the fight. One, Sergeant Roger Lamb of the 9th Foot, joined another British unit and became one of the few British enlisted men to describe his military service in America. While the British had some incentive to escape, the Brunswickers did not, as they were still being paid under the terms of their hiring (and at higher rates than they would have received serving their own duke). In December 1781, there were still 1,053 Germans interned, although a figure for December 1779 gives only 906. In April 1783, Congress finally agreed to release the surviving members of the Convention Army, who by then numbered less than 2,500 men. They had endured the longest internment of any troops on either side throughout the war.

While American historians generally agree that the behavior of Congress toward the Convention of Saratoga was far from honorable, some have attempted to justify it by pointing to Howe's intention (revealed in a letter found in the Clinton papers in the 1930s) to exchange the British Convention Army troops for American prisoners captured in 1776, with only the Germans returning to Europe as agreed. In fact, however, such an exchange was allowed by Article III of the Convention of Saratoga, and Howe also considered it justified by Washington's apparent failure to honor a previous prisoner exchange.

Brendan D. Morrissey

See also

Boston, Massachusetts; Burgoyne, John; Gates, Horatio; Phillips, William; Prisoners of War; Riedesel, Friedrich Adolph, Baron von; Saratoga Campaign

References

Brown, Marvin, trans. *Baroness von Riedesel and the American Revolution: Journal and Correspondence of a Tour of Duty, 1776–1783.* Chapel Hill: University of North Carolina, 1965.

Dabney, William. *After Saratoga: The Story of the Convention Army.* Albuquerque: University of New Mexico Press, 1954.

Lamb, Roger. *An Original and Authentic Journal of Occurrences during the Late American War from Its Commencement to the Year 1783.* Dublin, Ireland: Wilkinson and Courtney, 1809.

Stone, William, trans. *Memoirs, Letters and Journals of Major General Riedesel.* New York: New York Times and Arno, 1969.

Conway, Thomas (1735–?1800)

Thomas Conway, an Irish-born French soldier, joined the Continental Army in 1777, and became embroiled in the so-called Conway Cabal, a supposed attempt to supplant George Washington with General Horatio Gates as commander in chief. Taken to France at an early age, Conway joined the French army in 1749 and quickly developed a reputation as a talented leader of infantry. He served in Germany in the 1760s and was a colonel by 1772.

At the beginning of the Revolution, Conway volunteered his services to Silas Deane, an American commissioner in Paris, and was accepted because he had a reputation for instilling discipline in untrained soldiers. In April 1777 Conway sailed from Bordeaux and on 13 May, not long after his arrival in America, was commissioned a brigadier general by Congress. He fought in the battles of Brandywine (11 September) and Germantown (4 October) and was distinctly unimpressed by Washington's military leadership. Upset by what he believed to be avoidable military disasters, Conway began to express criticisms of his commander in chief in private correspondence, especially with Gates, whom he probably met in January 1778. Word probably got back to Washington that Conway was disparaging him. In late 1777, when Congress began to discuss Conway's promotion to major general, Washington strenuously opposed the idea. Although Conway offered to resign from the army, Congress rejected his suggestion, instead promoting him to major general on 14 December and appointing him inspector general of the army.

Meanwhile, the notorious Conway Cabal had supposedly been discovered by Washington and his friends and nipped in the bud before it matured. According to Washington's supporters, Lieutenant Colonel James Wilkinson, one of Gates's aides, had become slightly inebriated and told an aide to General William Alexander about a letter Conway had sent to Gates. It was reputed to have said, among other things, "Heaven has been determined to save your country; or a weak general and bad councillors would have ruined it." Alexander told Washington, who frigidly informed Conway that his supposedly nefarious correspondence had been exposed. Washington also wrote to Gates, directing his letter through Congress, to let all the "conspirators" know that he was on to them. The objects of Washington's wrath—Conway, Gates, Thomas Mifflin, and the congressmen who had promoted Conway—were upset that the commander believed they were conspiring against him but never gave any hint in any of their correspondence that they were scheming to supplant him. As Washington poured out his scorn upon them, they responded ineptly, only confirming among those who were suspicious of a cabal that their fears were warranted.

In January 1778 Conway journeyed to Washington's headquarters at Valley Forge to assume his duties as inspector general and was given a frosty reception by the commander and his circle of officers. Hence, Conway was only too glad to receive word that Congress had, on 22 January, voted in favor of an expedition against Canada and that on 23 January he had been appointed second in command under his countryman, the Marquis de Lafayette. His hopes were dashed, however, when Lafayette, an admirer of Washington, refused to accept Conway, who was forced to join the expedition as a subordinate officer in the ranks. On 2 March, Congress abandoned the entire plan, voting to rescind the operation. Conway then proceeded with congressional orders to Albany, New York, where he put himself under the command of Major General Alexander McDougall. Dissatisfied with his situation, Conway wrote a letter full of complaints to Congress on 22 April in which he offered to resign his commission. To his horror, Congress accepted his resignation with alacrity, for his standing among the legislators had eroded seriously since the previous December. Conway hastened to York, Pennsylvania, where Congress was meeting and sought to clarify the meaning of his letter. When he failed in his attempt to be reinstated in the army, he asked that Congress provide him with a letter of recommendation, such as all officers received when they left the service. That request was also denied. Complaining to Gates that a cabal consisting of Samuel Adams and Richard Henry Lee was responsible for his humiliation, he asked Gates to allow him to serve as a volunteer. His wish was not fulfilled.

Resentments against Conway remained high among Washington's friends and supporters and were exacerbated by their belief that Conway continued to be critical of the commander in chief. On 4 July 1778, General John Cadwalader, a great admirer of Washington, challenged Conway to a duel. In the exchange, Conway was severely wounded in the mouth and neck and believed that he was dying. Rising above personal feeling and the ill treatment he had received, he wrote Washington a letter of apology on 23 July, declaring his "sincere grief for having done, written, or said any thing disagreeable to your Excellency."

Despite all expectations, however, Conway recovered from his wound. Unemployed and in disgrace, he was compelled before the end of 1778 to leave America for France. In 1779 he served in the French army in Flanders and two years later commanded a regiment at Pondicherry in India. He was promoted to *maréchal-de-camp* (brigadier) in 1784 and three years later was appointed governor of French possessions in India. In December 1787, he was made a commander of the Order of St. Louis. As governor, however, he quarreled with local rulers and perhaps weakened French authority in India. In 1792 he commanded a royalist army in the south of France. Compelled to flee from France with his wife, who was a daughter of Maréchal Baron de Copley, he died in exile.

Paul David Nelson

See also

Adams, Samuel; Alexander, William; Brandywine, Battle of; Cadwalader, John; Conway Cabal; Deane, Silas; Gates, Horatio; Germantown, Battle of; Lafayette, Marquis de; Lee, Richard Henry; McDougall, Alexander; Mifflin, Thomas; Valley Forge, Pennsylvania; Wilkinson, James

References

Ferling, John E. *The First of Men: A Life of George Washington.* Knoxville: University of Tennessee Press, 1988.

Knollenberg, Bernhard. *Washington and the Revolution, a Reappraisal: Gates, Conway, and the Continental Congress.* New York: Macmillan, 1941.

Nelson, Paul David. *General Horatio Gates: A Biography.* Baton Rouge: Louisiana State University, 1976.

Rossman, Kenneth R. "Conway and the Conway Cabal." *South Atlantic Quarterly* 41 (1942): 32–38.

———. *Thomas Mifflin and the Politics of the American Revolution.* Chapel Hill: University of North Carolina Press, 1952.

Conway Cabal (1777–1778)

The Conway Cabal was an alleged attempt by Major General Horatio Gates and his supporters, both in the Continental Army and in Congress, to replace General George Washington as commander in chief during the winter of 1777–1778. The word "cabal," from the French, connotes an underhanded plot by a group of intriguers to put something over on an unsuspecting victim or victims. This sinister-sounding word was chosen by supporters of Washington to underscore what they saw as the deviousness of the plotters against their hero. In October 1777, Brigadier General Thomas Conway, a French officer in American service, wrote Gates a letter (now lost) in which he criticized Washington as a military leader and expressed a wish to serve under Gates. Word of the letter finally filtered through to Washington, who on 9 November 1777 wrote Conway a frosty note: "Sir: A Letter which I received last Night, contained the following paragraph. In a letter from Genl. Conway to Genl. Gates he says: 'Heaven has been determined to save your country; or a weak general and bad councellors would have ruined it.' I am Sir Yr. Hble. Servt." Three weeks later Gates, learning of this correspondence from General Thomas Mifflin, became aware that he was suspected of plotting against Washington.

Thus emerged the so-called Conway Cabal, which Washington and his supporters believed to be directed against Washington. The cabal came to light at a time when tensions were high between Congress and the Continental Army, as certain Whiggish legislators expressed fear that the army was not showing due subordination to civilian authority. The officers at Valley Forge, however, were in no mood to accept censure, real or imagined, from congressmen who seemed incapable of managing the war and providing them with necessary pay and provisions. They had just suffered a summer of defeats at the hands of General William Howe, the loss of Philadelphia, and now cold and hunger. In this situation, Washington and his supporters seized upon scraps of evidence that really proved nothing, filled in the missing links with conjecture, and decided that there was a conspiracy afoot. Many historians have been prone to accept Washington's views on the matter, believing that inconsistencies could be explained by the conspirators' own circumspection once they had been exposed.

The scheme to replace Washington supposedly was engineered by a group of army officers, including Gates, Mifflin, and Conway, and congressmen John Adams, Samuel Adams, Richard Henry Lee, and James Lovell. The physician Benjamin Rush was also believed to be involved. Gates himself supposedly played no active part in the conspiracy; in fact, he was considered to be little more than a willing tool of the more astute plotters. These men, and others who were sometimes mentioned, were said to have realized that Washington was still in good standing with most congressmen, despite his military reverses and his Fabian policy of retreating before a powerful enemy. Therefore, they would have to use subterfuge to compel Washington to resign. They would need to deceive Congress into voting for anti-Washington measures by touting them as good for the war effort. First, Congress must be deceived into reorganizing the Board of War and appointing Gates the new chairman so that the board could be used as an instrument by the plotters. The reorganization was accomplished on 27 November 1777. Second, the board would propose army reforms and a plan to invade Canada, the command of which would be given to the Marquis de Lafayette, a young French officer, to lure him into their clutches. Once Washington was confronted with this fait accompli, he would have to bow to the will of Gates, the new chairman of the Board of War, or resign. If Washington acquiesced to any of the board's schemes, that body would have gained control of the war effort. If he resigned, Gates would take his place and hopefully prove to be a more competent commander in chief.

The intricacy and unreality of these supposed plans make their existence suspect. To believe that the conspirators could work together in harmony in the chaotic times of the winter of 1777–1778 shows little recognition of the difficulties they would face. To believe that sensible congressmen, most of them devoted to Washington, could be duped so easily defies common sense. Also, the correspondence of the supposed conspirators should show some evidence that the convoluted scheme was afoot, which it does not. Finally, Gates's actions as chairman of the Board of War do not point to an organized plan to embarrass Washington. Washington's own statements about the proof of the cabal must not be taken at face value. Giving due weight to his difficulties at Valley Forge, he could have been distorting the evidence, perhaps even deliberately, to bolster his political position with antimilitary congressmen. At the very least, his pronouncements should be measured against the words of other participants with other perspectives.

It is true that Washington's performance as a general was being discussed by some congressmen in late 1777.

Civil-military tensions were high at that time, and the commander in chief's performance was criticized by some small-government members, but only in private conversations. Henry Laurens, for instance, reported such gossip to his son. All the comments, though critical of Washington, showed no desire to replace him, and no such proposal was ever presented on the floor of Congress. In fact, congressmen seemed inclined not to criticize Washington publicly, believing that he was crucial to the war effort. Nor were their criticisms out of place, for Congress was, after all, a deliberative body that must work for the common good. Some Whiggish congressmen, it is true, were a little disturbed by the adulation of Washington expressed by army officers. Against these tendencies, Congress felt that it must assert its civilian authority or risk an overbalance of power to the military. Rush, medical director of the Middle Department, was also particularly critical of Washington in his private correspondence. Clearly he would have welcomed a movement to replace Washington, but there is no evidence that Rush had any confederates.

Gates's correspondence, and that of his supposed co-conspirators, shows no evidence of any desire to supplant Washington. Unaware of Washington's suspicions, Gates replied to Conway's much-discussed letter on 3 December and clearly stated his sympathy for Washington's difficult situation. When Gates received Mifflin's letter a day later, he responded by wondering who was tattling about confidential correspondence but showed no concern about being "exposed" as a conspirator. He initiated an exchange of letters with Washington on 8 December, and while Gates was unapologetic in his comments, he certainly showed no desire to try to backpedal from a conspiratorial position. Washington, in response, was scathing and sarcastic, and Gates realized by 9 February that Washington, whether for political or other reasons, was not rational on the subject.

On 19 February, Gates wrote to Washington solemnly disavowing any part in any scheme against the commander in chief. Gates also talked to Laurens, admitting to him that Conway had been too critical of Washington. On 24 February, Washington wrote to Gates that the matter would henceforth be buried in silence and oblivion. But on 28 February, Washington wrote to John Fitzgerald that Gates had involved himself in absurd contradictions in his letters. In a letter to Patrick Henry on the same day, Washington declared that a conspiracy existed against him, although he could not mark its precise extent. He did, however, specifically implicate Gates, Mifflin, and Conway, asserting that he had absolute proof of their complicity. He never made these proofs a part of the public record. In fact, Washington had involved himself in absurd contradictions in his inflammatory letter to Henry. As for Gates's correspondence with Washington, it contained "no contradictions, 'absurd' or otherwise."

While this war of words was going on, Congress was supposedly playing its part in the conspiracy by enacting measures to embarrass Washington. The reorganization of the Board of War was supposedly the first step, although in actual fact the Congress was merely responding to a widely perceived need for reforms. Washington himself was an advocate of reforming the board but would not have made Gates its chairman. Also, Congress's promotion of Conway to major general on 14 December 1777 and his appointment to the office of inspector of the army were seen as calculated insults to Washington. Again, the facts indicate otherwise. Congress promoted Conway because the members believed that he deserved the new rank and did so before they were aware of Washington's hostility toward him. Also, Congress appointed Gates, Mifflin, and Timothy Pickering on 10 January 1778 to a committee of conference to meet with Washington at Valley Forge to discuss military problems. Gates demurred from this service, and Congress excused all three from the duty because Washington was so hostile by this time.

Believers in the cabal were also convinced that Gates and the Board of War planned an invasion of Canada in early 1778, with the ostensible purpose of luring Lafayette away from Washington and embarrassing the commander in chief. Again, the facts indicate otherwise. When Gates had served in the Northern Department the previous year, he had become convinced that a winter campaign against Canada would bring good results. Congress and Washington were also interested. On 22 January, Congress voted to approve the invasion, while leaving the planning to the Board of War. The next day Congress appointed Lafayette to command the expedition and Conway to be his second in command because they both spoke French. Initially, Lafayette was enthusiastic about the new command, but after talking to Washington he angrily chastised the board for its supposed machinations against the commander in chief. After Lafayette had procrastinated for weeks in organizing the expedition, Congress finally realized that it was not feasible. On 2 March the invasion of Canada was canceled, supposedly by a chastened Congress that finally came to recognize the venture's true purpose.

Thereafter, the alleged Conway Cabal sputtered to an ignominious conclusion. By March, it was clear to Washington and his supporters that his position as commander in chief was secure, and everyone at headquarters relaxed a bit. Congressmen such as Jonathan Bayard Smith and Eliphalet Dyer asserted passionately in February and March that there was never the least intention in Congress to remove Washington. Hence, the small-government Whigs were thoroughly routed in their attempts to assert civilian authority. Conway, in a fit of disgust, submitted his resignation to Congress on 28 April, even though he did not intend to leave the army. To his surprise, his resignation was immediately accepted. He asked Gates in a number of letters to intervene in the matter but did not even receive a reply. On 4 July, offended at Conway's criticism of Washington, General John Cadwalader seriously wounded Conway in a duel. Believing himself near death, Conway wrote Washington a contrite letter of apology for having done, written, or said anything disagreeable to the commander in chief. Conway survived the wound, returned to France, and served there as an honorable and capable officer. Relations between Washington and Gates were permanently soured. The former remained convinced (or so he said) that he had been the victim of a plot. The latter believed, with some justification, that he had been used by Washington for political purposes. One point was clear, despite Washington's claim to the contrary: the evidence of a conspiracy was almost totally lacking.

Paul David Nelson

See also

Adams, John; Adams, Samuel; Cadwalader, John; Conway, Thomas; Dyer, Eliphalet; Gates, Horatio; Henry, Patrick; Lafayette, Marquis de; Laurens, Henry; Lee, Richard Henry; Lovell, James; Mifflin, Thomas; Pickering, Timothy; Rush, Benjamin; Valley Forge, Pennsylvania; War, Board of; Washington, George

References

Flexner, James T. *George Washington.* 4 vols. Boston: Little, Brown, 1965–1972.

Higginbotham, Don. *The War of American Independence: Military Attitudes, Policies, and Practice, 1763–1789.* New York: Macmillan, 1971.

Knollenberg, Bernhard. *Washington and the Revolution, a Reappraisal: Gates, Conway, and the Continental Congress.* New York: Macmillan, 1941.

Nelson, Paul David. *General Horatio Gates: A Biography.* Baton Rouge: Louisiana State University Press, 1976.

———. *William Alexander, Lord Stirling.* University: University of Alabama Press, 1987.

Rossie, Jonathan Gregory. *The Politics of Command in the American Revolution.* Syracuse, NY: Syracuse University Press, 1975.

Rossman, Kenneth R. *Thomas Mifflin and the Politics of the American Revolution.* Chapel Hill: University of North Carolina Press, 1952.

Sparks, Jared, ed. *Correspondence of the American Revolution.* 4 vols. Boston: Little, Brown, 1853.

Conyngham, Gustavus (1747–1819)

Born into a family of landed gentry in County Donegal, Ireland, in 1747, Gustavus Conyngham, who was to become one of America's earliest and most successful privateers, left home early to begin a life at sea. After an apprenticeship in the West Indies, he moved to Philadelphia to work for a shipping company begun by his older brother, Redmond. Conyngham progressed through the ranks of the mercantile service until he captained his own vessel, the brig *Charming Peggy,* by 1775.

At the outbreak of the Revolutionary War, the Continental Congress employed Conyngham to smuggle gunpowder from the Netherlands, and he sailed to Europe in September 1775. He found himself stranded, however, when British authorities learned of his cargo and demanded that the Dutch government seize his vessel. Tipped off by the Dutch, Conyngham offloaded his cargo before the British consul arrived, but the British insisted upon placing a guard aboard the *Charming Peggy.* Conyngham's crew overpowered the guard once the ship cleared the harbor, but the wind subsided and Conyngham, now clearly a criminal, quickly sold his ship to effect his escape.

Gustavus Conyngham fought as a privateer before receiving a commission in the Continental Navy in 1777. He captured more than fifty vessels during his cruise in the waters around Britain before he was eventually captured. (Naval Historical Society)

Unemployed, Conyngham languished in Dunkirk, France, for nearly a year until American commissioner William Hodge granted him a commission as captain in the new Continental Navy in March 1777, placing him in command of the privateer *Surprise.* The young captain immediately triggered a diplomatic crisis when he seized the British ships *Prince of Orange* and *Joseph,* the former a mail packet laden with correspondence for Europe and the latter a rich prize loaded with wine and fruit. The British, outraged over the brazen assaults by an American privateer outfitted and operating out of a French port, demanded through their ambassador, Lord Stormont, that the French return the prizes and arrest the "Dunkirk Pirate." The French, not yet at war with Britain, assented to the British demands and sent two armed sloops to prevent the *Surprise* from leaving port. The authorities arrested Conyngham, confiscated his American commission, and released his prizes. The British wanted Conyngham turned over to face trial for piracy, but the French contented themselves with imprisoning him in the local jail.

Hodge procured Conyngham's release after a month's confinement and gave him command of the privateer *Revenge* in July 1777, charging him to "retaliate in every manner in our power—Burn, Sink, and Destroy the Enemy." Upon leaving Dunkirk, Conyngham and his mostly French crew terrorized British shipping for the next two months, seizing ships in the North, Baltic, and Irish seas before docking in Ireland (under a fake Irish registry) to resupply. As a direct result of this first major American privateering expedition, British shipping insurance increased dramatically, trade declined as ships refused to leave port, and the British Admiralty faced severe political pressure to eliminate the American menace. The Admiralty organized convoys protected by warships to ease commercial concerns and withdrew ships from the North American squadron to protect English waters.

By the end of 1777, the Royal Navy had reassigned no fewer than twenty-eight warships to home waters to destroy the *Revenge* and capture Conyngham. But he continued to elude British warships to raid along the east coast of Scotland before sailing for the Bay of Biscay and ending this cruise at the Spanish port of Cap Ferrol. Although the British were aware of his presence, Conyngham next sailed into the western Mediterranean Sea, seizing more than twenty British ships between Gibraltar and Malta. While not a formal ally of the American cause, Spain sided with France in opposing Britain and opened its ports to American privateers. Conyngham found the Spanish readily willing to adjudicate his prizes and resupply his ship. Although the Spanish were not ardent supporters of the American Revolution, they were perfectly willing to see Britain weakened in a war with its colonies.

Along with a popular sympathy for the American cause, Conyngham's growing celebrity ensured that the Spanish gave the *Revenge* a welcome reception. In Cadiz, the British complained that Spanish authorities awarded the *Revenge* first preference in fitting out while keeping British ships waiting. The only major problem that Conyngham reported to Hodge was unruly crewmen. Comprised of several nationalities, Conyngham's crew sailed less for a Revolutionary cause than for material reward. When prize money was overdue, Conyngham spent more time dealing with unhappy sailors than with British warships. The issue came to a head when the *Revenge* seized a Swedish vessel, the *Henrica Sofia,* on 31 May 1778. Because Sweden was a neutral power, her ships were off limits to American privateers, but Conyngham's crew, unwilling to part with a potentially rich prize, insisted on taking the *Henrica Sofia* into a Spanish port, with or without its captain's permission. To avoid a mutiny, Conyngham permitted a prize crew to sail the Swedish vessel into port.

Acquiescing to his crew's demands had an unexpected consequence. British diplomats in Madrid railed against the wanton seizure of neutral ships, and Spanish authorities were unwilling to go to war with Britain for a few American privateers. By August 1778, Spanish authorities closed their nation's ports to Conyngham to preserve the peace with Britain, and Conyngham lost his base of operations. Denied supply bases and pursued by a growing British naval force, he departed for the Caribbean in September 1778. For the next six months, the *Revenge* prowled the West Indies, taking numerous prizes, including two British privateers plaguing French shipping near St. Eustatius. In early 1779, Conyngham received orders to sail for America with a load of supplies sent from France. He arrived in Philadelphia in February of that year, having taken a total of sixty British vessels (thirty-three destroyed and twenty-seven prizes) since leaving Dunkirk eighteen months earlier.

Unable to challenge the Royal Navy's dominance along the American coast, the Continental Navy had no use for the *Revenge* and put it up for sale. Conyngham found investors in Philadelphia willing to purchase the ship with him and engage in privateering as a commercial venture, and he prepared to return to sea armed with a letter of marque issued by the Continental Congress. Conyngham's luck, however, now deserted him. Only weeks into its second cruise, the *Revenge* ran into HMS *Gallatea* off New York City. Caught between shallow water and the superior firepower of the British warship, Conyngham surrendered the *Revenge,* and the British rejoiced that they had finally caught the Dunkirk Pirate. Instead of confining Conyngham aboard one of their infamous prison hulks, they shipped their captive off to England, jailing him first in Falmouth and later in Mill Prison in Plymouth.

Facing death for piracy, Conyngham twice attempted escape, until on his third try in November 1779 he managed to dig out of Mill Prison, contact sympathetic allies, and flee back to his starting point in Dunkirk. He immediately returned to his previous career as a naval officer, serving under John Paul Jones aboard the raider *Alliance* (Jones's new ship, which replaced the *Bonhomme Richard* after its famous fight with HMS *Serapis*), bound for the Bay of Biscay and Spanish waters, in December 1779. Thanks to increasing vigilance on the part of British merchantmen, however, the *Alliance* captured few prizes on its cruise, and Conyngham decided to return to the United States to exercise his naval commission and captain a ship of his own. In March 1780, Conyngham sailed for America aboard the prize *Experiment,* but again his luck ran out. British warships overtook the *Experiment* off the coast of Massachusetts, and Conyngham found himself back in Mill Prison. This time all of his escape attempts failed, and Conyngham spent the last year of the war securely in his cell.

Unable to escape, Conyngham now faced the real possibility of the hangman's noose. European nations considered privateering a legitimate form of warfare when it was practiced between established governments. The legal question regarding Conyngham and other privateers was whether America's rebel government constituted a legitimate government or whether its sailors were, however unwilling, still British subjects. The British considered the rebel Americans to be British subjects, and that made Conyngham a pirate and not a privateer. The British used the same justification for refusing to exchange privateers captured during the war. Given these convictions, it is not clear why the British did not try Conyngham for piracy; perhaps the recent exploits of Jones and other privateers had overshadowed the early triumphs of the Dunkirk Pirate. In the end, the British declined to prosecute Conyngham for piracy, and he remained in his cell until he was exchanged for some captured British officers. Conyngham returned to Philadelphia with the intent of recruiting another privateer crew, but with the war winding down he found few investors and little desire by the Continental Congress to aggravate the British while peace talks were under way.

After the war, Conyngham returned to the merchant service, operating mostly between Philadelphia and the West Indies. But the stagnant postwar American economy limited his ability to earn a living, and he sought to return to the navy. The U.S. government, however, denied that Conyngham had a right to claim an officer's rank. Despite his years of celebrated service to the Continental Congress, Conyngham did not possess any documentation that he had received the formal rank of captain in the old Continental Navy, as the French had seized his commission when they arrested him in 1777. Despite affidavits from Hodge and others, the government continued to reject not only Conyngham's requests for employment but also his requests for the pension granted to retired officers of the Continental Army and Navy. (Several decades after his death, Conyngham's commission turned up in the archives of the French Admiralty.) Unable to obtain relief from the government, he worked at various jobs, on both land and sea, until he retired. But Conyngham's days as a warrior were not quite over. In 1812, as a local official in Philadelphia, he helped to organize the defense of the city when war with Britain broke out again. He died in Philadelphia on 27 November 1819.

Steven J. Ramold

See also

Continental Navy; Jones, John Paul; Privateering; Prizes and Prize Money

References

Bowen-Hassell, E. Gordon, Dennis M. Conrad, and Mark L. Hayes, eds. *Sea Raiders of the American Revolution: The Continental Navy in European Waters.* Washington, DC: Naval Historical Center, 2003.

Coleman, Eleanor S. *Captain Gustavus Conyngham, U.S.N.: Pirate or Privateer, 1747–1819.* Washington, DC: University Press of America, 1982.

Neeser, Robert W. *Letters and Papers Relating to the Cruises of Gustavus Conyngham, a Captain in the Continental Navy.* Port Washington, NY: Kennikat, 1970.

Cooch's Bridge, Delaware, Action at (3 September 1777)

The only significant battle fought in the state of Delaware, the engagement at Cooch's Bridge is also known as the Battle at Iron Hill. In mid-August 1777, upon learning that General William Howe's army, which had sailed south from New York, was headed for Chesapeake Bay, General George Washington moved his forces south through Pennsylvania to meet them. Howe's objective was the capture of the American capital at Philadelphia, and he hoped to force a decisive encounter with Washington's army.

The British landed at Head of Elk, Maryland, and moved east into Delaware. To block Howe's route to Wilmington, Delaware, and on to Philadelphia, Washington sought out a low rise on which to place a portion of his army. The engagement at Cooch's Bridge was more of a delaying action than a general battle, with few troops taking part in the action. It has been said that this was the first battle of the American Revolution in which the American flag was used (the design of stars and stripes having been approved by Congress in June).

On the morning of 3 September, the American General William Maxwell deployed about 700 troops on Iron Hill, about 4 miles south of the main American army. By 9:00 A.M., the British vanguard began to skirmish with Maxwell's forces. Light infantry detachments and jaegers pushed the Americans back several times through the woods. Maxwell eventually broke off the engagement and fell back to the main army. Washington then pulled back into Pennsylvania to make a stronger stand there. The armies would meet eight days later in the Battle of Brandywine.

American losses at Cooch's Bridge were between twenty and forty, with the British losing two killed and twenty wounded. Today a monument marks the site, about 2 miles south of Newark, Delaware.

Robert M. Dunkerly

See also

Brandywine, Battle of; Maxwell, William

References

Boatner, Mark. *Encyclopedia of the American Revolution.* Mechanicsburg, PA: Stackpole, 1994.

Murfin, James. *National Park Service Guide.* Washington, DC: National Park Service, 1974.

Copley, John Singleton (1738–1815)

John Singleton Copley, the greatest American portrait artist of the eighteenth century, was born in or near Boston on 3 July 1738 to Irish immigrant parents. His father died when

Copley was young, and his mother ran a tobacco shop on Long Wharf. Copley's stepfather was the engraver and limner Peter Pelham. Copley learned his trade from Pelham and the painter John Smibert and was later influenced by Joseph Blackburn and by the Rococo style, especially *portrait d'apparat,* in which the subject is portrayed with objects used in everyday life.

Copley's earliest paintings date from his teens, but in 1765, at the age of twenty-seven, he painted a portrait that was to be the turning point in his career. Copley sent this portrait, of his half brother Henry Pelham, titled *Boy with a Squirrel* to London to be shown at the Society of Artists' 1766 exhibition. It was soon highly acclaimed by the British artist Sir Joshua Reynolds and the American artist Benjamin West. This portrait was the first American painting to be exhibited abroad and the first of any importance that was not the result of a commission. The exhibition of and praise for Copley's painting marked the beginning of his real success as an artist. He now promoted an artist-client working relationship in Boston and included in his work the added provision of a suitable frame for the patron's portrait. As word of his realistic renditions spread, his portrait studio was always busy, and the result was fame and financial success. In 1767, he wrote to his friend, the ship captain R. G. Bruce, that he was making 300 guineas a year.

One of Copley's most famous and often-reproduced paintings is his *Portrait of Paul Revere* (circa 1768–1770). This informal painting exemplifies Copley's early, simple, and forthright style, so indicative of his painting while in America. Revere is depicted in plain surroundings while working at his profession of silversmithing, well before he became a hero of the American Revolution. Copley portrays Revere making direct eye contact with the viewer while holding a teapot. In this same period, Copley painted much of Boston's commercial and political elite and executed superb portraits of several Patriot leaders, notably Samuel Adams and John Hancock.

On 16 November 1769, at the age of thirty-one, Copley married Susannah Clark, the daughter of Richard Clark, a wealthy Boston tea merchant and future Loyalist, who would become one of the tea agents involved in the Boston Tea Party. By 1772, the Copleys were an established family atop Beacon Hill. In 1774, however, Copley's practice was threatened by the political events that divided his patrons and soon escalated toward war. The number of his patrons began to decline as clients found less time to sit for portraits due to the deteriorating political and economic environment. On 10 June 1774, Copley left America to try his talent in England. He began his trip with a short study in Italy, but in 1775 he settled in London and set up his studio. Later the same year, his Loyalist family joined him.

In England, Copley's style changed dramatically, becoming more sophisticated, decorous, and fashion conscious. He achieved an uncanny ability to portray fabric and textile detail. In 1779, he was elected to the Royal Academy as a full member. Although he continued painting portraits, he made the transition to history painting, which was regarded as the highest genre of painting in England at the time. His first history painting was *Brook Watson and the Shark* (1778). Copley utilized the compelling formula of multifigure composition and heroic subject matter, which would be so well exemplified in his most famous history painting, *The Death of Major Pierson* (1783). Another important Copley history painting, *The Death of Chatham* (1780), portrays William Pitt, the Elder. Copley's exhibitions of his history paintings won him outstanding acclaim and rivaled the Royal Academy's own exhibitions.

Although Copley's style became more sophisticated, the compelling realism of his Boston portraits was lost, and his British work gradually lost popularity. By 1811, both Copley's success and his health began to decline. His mental and physical vitality deteriorated, and he died on 9 September 1815. His son, John, who became Baron Lyndhurst and Lord Chancellor of England, settled his father's debts.

Kathleen Hitt

See also

Adams, Samuel; Art; Boston, Massachusetts; Boston Tea Party; Hancock, John; Pitt, William, the Elder; Revere, Paul

References

Feld, Stuart. *American Portraits by John Singleton Copley.* New York: Hirschl and Adler Galleries, 1976.

Flexner, James Thomas. *America's Old Masters: First Artists of the New World.* 1939. Reprint, New York: Dover, 1967.

———. *John Singleton Copley.* New York: Fordham University Press, 1993.

Rebora, Carrie. *John Singleton Copley in America.* New York: Metropolitan Museum of Art, 1995.

Corbin, Margaret Cochran (1751–?1800)

Margaret Corbin, a precursor of "Molly Pitcher," was the first woman to receive a U.S. pension as a disabled soldier for taking the place of her deceased husband at his cannon during the action at Fort Washington (16 November 1776). Born in Pennsylvania, Margaret married John Corbin in 1772. When John enlisted as an assistant to a gunner, Margaret accompanied him. While washing, cooking, and cleaning for her husband, Margaret likely observed his drills and learned how to operate a cannon. John Corbin's artillery unit received orders to reinforce the garrison at Fort Washington, and he was on Forest Hill with a small complement of artillerymen when British and Hessian troops attacked. John assisted a gunner until the gunner was killed. At this point John took charge of the cannon, and Margaret assisted him. Some time later, John was also killed.

Taking no time to grieve, Margaret continued swabbing, loading, and firing the cannon by herself until she was wounded by three grapeshot that tore her left shoulder, mangled her chest, and lacerated her jaw. The injuries would cost Corbin the use of her left arm while leaving her physically incapacitated and in considerable discomfort for the remainder of her life. Other soldiers moved Corbin to the rear, where she received first aid. The British made her a prisoner on the field and then moved all the prisoners to New York City, 10 miles away.

It is not clear how Corbin left British custody; presumably she joined the other wounded Patriots in receiving parole and probably joined the group ferried across the river to Fort Lee. By June 1779, Corbin had found her way back to Pennsylvania. Facing hard times, she petitioned the state for assistance. The Supreme Executive Council, recognizing Corbin's bravery, directed that she be given thirty dollars, but the money proved insufficient to meet her needs. Pennsylvania requested that Congress lend aid as well. On 6 July 1779, Congress voted to give Corbin a pension of half the pay of a soldier for the rest of her life and one complete set of clothes or its cash equivalent. Shortly thereafter, Corbin enrolled in the Pennsylvania division of the Invalid Regiment and remained part of it until it was disbanded in April 1783. This regiment had been designed by Congress to be a retreat for those who suffered in the service as well as a recruiting corps and military school. Corbin probably remained in or near Philadelphia until late 1781, when the Invalid Regiment officially became part of the garrison at West Point. "Captain Molly" spent the remainder of her life in the West Point area, with the leaders of the military academy freely providing her with hospital supplies and commissary stores out of sympathy for her impoverished and disabled state.

Caryn E. Neumann

See also

Fort Lee, New Jersey; Fort Washington, New York, Fall of; Molly Pitcher, Legend of; West Point, New York

References

DePauw, Linda Grant. *Battle Cries and Lullabies: Women and War from Prehistory to the Present.* Norman: University of Oklahoma Press, 1998.

Hall, Edward Hagaman. *Margaret Corbin: Heroine of the Battle of Fort Washington, 16 November 1776.* New York: American Scenic and Historic Preservation Society, 1932.

Teipe, Emily J. "Will the Real Molly Pitcher Please Stand Up?" *Prologue: Quarterly of the National Archives Records Administration* 31(2) (1999): 118–126.

Cornstalk (1720?–1777)

The Shawnee Chief Cornstalk played a prominent military and diplomatic role in Anglo-Indian relations on the Virginia and Pennsylvania frontiers prior to and during the early years of the American Revolutionary War. He is best known for leading his tribe at the Battle of Point Pleasant in Lord Dunmore's War in 1774. His murder in 1777, while he was trying to keep the peace on the frontier, increased hostilities between Shawnees and Patriot settlers in Pennsylvania.

Cornstalk was born around 1720 and went by his Shawnee name of Keigh-tugh-qua. Like most Shawnee Indians, he allied himself with the French during the French and Indian (Seven Years') War. In that conflict he led several raids into western Virginia, where white settlements had recently encroached on Shawnee lands. During Pontiac's Rebellion, Colonel Henry Bouquet captured Cornstalk and several other Shawnees and used them to secure a peace.

In the following decade, Cornstalk sought to limit hostilities with the British. In 1774, when some Mingos and Shawnees sought retribution for the murder of eleven Mingo Indians at the hands of British colonists, Cornstalk intervened and tried to protect British traders from retaliation. But when frontier warfare escalated and militiamen from Pennsylvania and Virginia razed seven Mingo villages, an outraged Cornstalk led a force of 1,000 Shawnee warriors to drive the British off of Indian lands. On 10 October 1774, at the Battle of Point Pleasant near the confluence of the Kanawha and Ohio Rivers, the British drove Cornstalk and his warriors back across the Ohio River and onto Shawnee lands. When the British surrounded Shawnee villages on the Pickaway Plains, Lord Dunmore, British governor of Virginia, forced the Shawnees to surrender.

When the American Revolution broke out, many Shawnees saw it as an opportunity to drive American settlers off of their lands. Cornstalk disagreed and tried to keep the Shawnees neutral. Urged on and armed by the British, many Shawnees raided frontier settlements. Cornstalk remained optimistic that peace could be maintained and tried to assure American leaders that most Shawnees remained neutral.

On 6 October 1777, when two Shawnees who had professed friendship for the Americans were detained at Fort Randolph, Cornstalk and his son went to the fort to clear up the confusion. They too were taken hostage. On 10 November, in apparent retaliation for the death of an American soldier at the hands of Shawnee warriors, members of the militia broke into the fort and murdered Cornstalk and the other hostages. The murder of Cornstalk outraged Virginia's Governor Patrick Henry, who offered a reward for the apprehension of those responsible for his death. The attack also destroyed the voices of neutrality among the Shawnees, and in 1778 the tribe attacked Revolutionary outposts and white settlers in Kentucky and elsewhere.

Andrew K. Frank

See also

Kentucky; Murray, John, Lord Dunmore; Native Americans; Northwest Territory; Pontiac's Rebellion; Virginia

References

Calloway, Colin G. *The American Revolution in Indian Country: Crisis and Diversity in Native American Communities.* Cambridge: Cambridge University Press, 1995.

———. "'We Have Always Been the Frontier': The American Revolution in Shawnee Country." *American Indian Quarterly* 16 (Winter 1992): 39–52.

Cornwallis, Charles (1738–1805)

Charles Cornwallis, 1st Marquis and 2nd Earl Cornwallis, was a general and imperial statesman who influenced history on three continents. His surrender at Yorktown marked the end of major hostilities during the American Revolution. As governor-general and commander in chief in India, he effected long-lasting changes in British rule there. As lord-lieutenant and commander in chief in Ireland, he laid the groundwork for that country's legislative union with Britain.

Born in Suffolk, Cornwallis grew up at the estate of Culford and attended Eton for one or two years. He chose a military career, gaining a commission in the 1st or Grenadier Guards in December 1756, just before his eighteenth birthday. He attended the military academy at Turin for a few months. Then the long-anticipated dispute between Britain and France broke out, and the young man learned that his regiment had been ordered to the continent to join an Anglo-German army assembling under the command of Prince Ferdinand of Brunswick. Cornwallis joined Ferdinand without royal permission but obtained an appointment as aide-de-camp to the Marquis of Granby in August 1758. A year later Cornwallis became a captain in the 85th Foot, and in May 1761 he became lieutenant-colonel of the 12th Foot. He served as regimental commander at Kirch Donkern and Grebenstein in 1762 but returned to England in the summer of that year when he learned that his father had died. In November he assumed his seat in the House of Lords as the 2nd Earl Cornwallis.

As the new head of the family, it was Cornwallis's duty to provide suitable employment for his younger brothers and suitable marriages for his sisters. He also secured his own marriage in 1768 to Jemima Tullekin Jones, the daughter of Colonel James Jones of the 3rd Regiment of Foot Guards. Together they had one son, Charles, and one daughter, Mary.

Politically, Cornwallis's career took form around this time. He voted with the Rockinghamites to repeal the Stamp Act and to outlaw general warrants. In 1766 he voted against the Rockinghamites in opposing the Declaratory Act. In 1770 he was made a privy councilor, and in 1771 he became constable of the Tower of London.

His military career also advanced. In 1766 he became colonel of the 33rd Foot. After the American Revolution broke out, he was promoted to major-general (1775) and then lieutenant-general (January 1776). Ironically, the new military rank would clash with the political principles he had so recently evinced.

General Charles Cornwallis served throughout the Revolutionary War, including the expedition to Charleston in 1776, the campaigns in New York and Pennsylvania, and most notably the operations in the South, in which theater he commanded all British forces in 1780–1781. Notwithstanding his surrender at Yorktown, he ended his military career as governor-general of India. (National Archives and Records Administration)

For the next six years the British Army in America would receive most of Cornwallis's attention. He volunteered his services when the American colonies rebelled. It was a generous offer, since as a major-general in December 1775 he would be subordinate to Major-General Sir William Howe and Lieutenant-General Sir Henry Clinton in America or to Major-General Sir Guy Carleton in Canada. Cornwallis was to sail for the Cape Fear River to join Clinton for the purpose of giving support to Loyalists in North Carolina. By the time Cornwallis's storm-tossed ship arrived in May 1776, the entire object of the joint expedition had been nullified, since the Loyalists had risen prematurely, been defeated, and had scattered to the backcountry.

Clinton now consulted with Commodore Sir Peter Parker, the commander of the British fleet that had brought Cornwallis to America, and the two decided to attack Charleston, South Carolina. The decision conformed to a suggestion made by the commander in chief, Howe. The excursion was poorly planned and poorly executed. In such an inauspicious manner did Cornwallis's service under Clinton begin in America.

The British Army and Royal Navy now sailed for New York, where they joined Howe and his brother, the naval commander Admiral Richard Howe. By August the Howe brothers commanded between them the largest force that Britain had ever sent overseas. There now ensued actions at Long Island, Brooklyn, and Manhattan. Cornwallis commanded the reserve and Clinton the van, under General Howe's command. Instead of allowing his officers to press their moral advantage by carrying the Brooklyn lines, Howe decided to settle down for a siege. By dawn, the Americans had escaped to Manhattan. Cornwallis's second campaign in America had failed to bring a decisive victory.

Cornwallis crossed with the British Army to Manhattan and then to White Plains, but General George Washington eluded capture. Howe now sent Cornwallis in pursuit of Washington, who had crossed to New Jersey. This gave Cornwallis his first chance to act independently. Washington's forces fled desperately, and Cornwallis's forces pursued in like fashion. On 1 December when Cornwallis reached New Brunswick after marching his men 20 miles over very bad roads, he found the Americans gone and the only bridge over the Raritan destroyed. Here historians disagree, some saying that the British were too exhausted to offer further pursuit that night by fording the Raritan, others saying that had Cornwallis pushed a bit harder he could have captured the Americans en masse. The order from Howe to stop the pursuit at New Brunswick was not so binding that it had to be obeyed if there was a chance to capture the Americans under Washington. Howe joined Cornwallis on 6 December, and thereafter the same pursuit continued with the Americans always just escaping capture. The British arrived in Princeton at four o'clock in the afternoon, barely an hour behind the departure of Washington's rear guard. Again, at Trenton, Howe's forces arrived just as the last of the American army pushed off for the Pennsylvania shore in the only available boats.

Yet another example of dynamic energy alternating with strange lethargy followed, when Howe sent Cornwallis to confront Washington after the latter's defeat of the Hessians at Trenton. Cornwallis rode 50 miles from New York to Princeton, rounded up the British forces, and left for Trenton before dawn on 2 January 1777. Heavy rains had made the road a quagmire, and it took the British all day to travel the 10 miles to Trenton. Cornwallis decided that his troops were too exhausted to try a frontal assault across a swollen stream in the darkness. By dawn, Washington had made his famous escape by leaving a few soldiers behind to keep the campfires burning.

British troops under Lord Charles Cornwallis surrender at Yorktown on 19 October 1781. (Library of Congress)

Cornwallis was with Howe during the taking of Philadelphia and before that at the Battle of Brandywine. Cornwallis's other actions more nearly resembled skirmishes. Winter put an end to further major military endeavors, and Cornwallis requested and obtained leave to return home. He spent roughly the first three months of 1778 attending to personal affairs—wife, family, estate. In April he sailed back to America and reached Philadelphia just in time to take part in his last major battle in North America, the Battle of Monmouth. By that time Howe had resigned, Clinton was in overall command, and Cornwallis was second in command. Clinton had received the cabinet's orders to evacuate Philadelphia, and it was the ensuing maneuvers while en route back to New York that brought on the battle at Monmouth Court House. The American commander of the van, General Charles Lee, came into contact with the British rear under Clinton and Cornwallis. Lee's retreat brought him back into the body of the main American force under Washington. Clinton tested the

American left but suffered heavy losses. He then ordered Cornwallis to assault the American right with some of the best British units. Those units were exposed to an enfilading fire from the American artillery under General Henry Knox on Comb's Hill on the British left. Cornwallis suffered heavy losses, and his force was broken.

Monmouth Court House was a standoff, although Cornwallis may have viewed it as a Clinton-led defeat. Now the British retreated to sit out the ensuing winter in New York. Such inactivity did not suit Cornwallis. It may have been word of his wife's illness that made him decide to apply for leave to go home and resign his commission. Clinton granted him leave to return home, where Cornwallis arrived in December. After informing Clinton's cousin, the 2nd Duke of Newcastle, of Clinton's need for more troops and then seeing the king to resign his position as second in command in America, Cornwallis hastened to Suffolk to see his ailing wife. Her death in February 1779 quite overturned his feelings and emotions. He no longer wished to remain with all that he had loved, for it reminded him of his beloved wife. He decided to return to the army in America and arrived in July. He was about to enter upon the most active part of his career in America.

Because the ministry had not granted Clinton the reinforcements he had requested, he turned in his resignation. He had to remain in America, however, until he knew whether his request to resign had been accepted. Still, Lord George Germain agreed to a thrust to the south to besiege Charleston. Weather delayed the embarkation of the troops. They finally put to sea on 26 December and encountered more foul weather. Still uncertain who would be in command, Clinton and Cornwallis collaborated on plans for the siege of Charleston. On 19 March 1780, the long-awaited letter from Germain arrived, refusing Clinton's resignation of command. Now Cornwallis asked not to be consulted. Relations between Clinton and his chief subordinate grew very strained.

Clinton dispatched Cornwallis on a separate command. In cooperation with Admiral Marriot Arbuthnot, Cornwallis sealed the door by which the Americans might have escaped across the Cooper River from the coming siege of Charleston, which fell to the British on 12 May. Clinton returned to New York in early July, leaving Cornwallis in command in the South. Clinton's orders were for Cornwallis to maintain order in Georgia and East and West Florida, to pacify South and North Carolina, and then to take Virginia. It was for Cornwallis an opportunity for independent command, but he never had enough troops for the tasks.

Cornwallis's first major engagement after the fall of Charleston would be at Camden in the late summer of 1780. There, on 16 August, in less than an hour, Cornwallis shattered the only American army in the South. Although Major General Johann de Kalb stood his ground and fell, General Horatio Gates fled as fast as his horse would carry him.

Unfortunately for Cornwallis, his ability to pacify South and North Carolina would depend less on the quality of his own troops than on the mettle and resolve of the Tory militia. They had risen prematurely in 1776 and been defeated at Moore's Creek Bridge. Now they were often reluctant participants. The rebel militia might also have been content to sit out the war, save for the disastrous consequences of the proclamation issued by Clinton before he went back north that any released prisoner who would not take an oath of allegiance to the British and support the British actively would be treated as a rebel. In the South, the war between adherents of Britain and her opponents resembled a civil war. Cornwallis realized this but was not ruthless in his treatment of rebels.

Cornwallis decided to move north. His goal was Hillsborough, North Carolina. However, he was ill-served by Loyalist militia and their leaders, such as George Hanger at Charlotte and Patrick Ferguson at Kings Mountain. Cornwallis, who fell ill, decided to go to Winnsboro, South Carolina, for the winter of 1780–1781. There he suffered badly from lack of supplies, wagons, horses, and intelligence.

In January 1781 Cornwallis decided to pursue General Nathanael Greene into North Carolina. His reasoning was that he could not hold South Carolina until he controlled North Carolina, and the latter required defeating Greene's army. Cornwallis was harmed by Lieutenant-Colonel Banastre Tarleton's impetuous attack at Cowpens and the consequent loss of between 700 and 800 men, most of them cavalry and light infantry essential for gathering intelligence. On 18 January, the day after Cowpens, Cornwallis only had about 700 men until joined by Tarleton's survivors and by a force under Major-General Alexander Leslie, which brought the total to about 2,400 men. Cornwallis could now follow in pursuit of Daniel Morgan, hoping to catch him before Morgan could join Greene. Cornwallis was slowed by poor intelligence, by having to haul the British guns and baggage, and by the winter rains that had made the roads a muddy quagmire and had swollen the rivers and streams. At Ramseur's Mill, he tried to improve his speed by making a huge conflagration of his baggage and equipment, including most of his wagons. The British left Ramseur's Mill on 28 January marching toward the Catawba River, which had risen very high, but chose to use one of the fords rather than wait for the waters to fall. While the British went to Hillsborough, then the capital of North Carolina, to raise the British standard and invite the Loyalists to join them (they were largely unsuccessful), Greene made his way to Salisbury and then to Guilford Courthouse, which he had previously chosen for a future battle site. By the time Greene took up his stand there, he had received numerous reinforcements and had between 4,000 and 5,000 men. Since Cornwallis only had about 2,000 in his force, Greene outnumbered Cornwallis by more than two to one.

The British suffered severe losses from the beginning of the battle on 15 March. They had to cross a small stream and climb uphill for a quarter of a mile while under fire from riflemen and two 6-pounders. At last the British came into conflict with the third American line, during which they sustained their heaviest losses. An especially hot fight ensued between the second battalion of Guards and the Marylanders. When Cornwallis found the Guards in danger of being overrun, he ordered Lieutenant John MacLeod to load his two 3-pounders with grapeshot and fire into the struggling mass of men. The resulting carnage served its purpose, for the British held the field but could not pursue the retreating enemy. Cornwallis had sustained 532 casualties, more than 25 percent of his total force. The British had not eaten for twenty-four hours, had marched 12 miles, and had fought a fierce battle for two hours. To the 93 lying dead were added perhaps 50 wounded who died during the night.

Cornwallis now headed for Wilmington, North Carolina. The sixty-four worst wounded had to stay behind. By 6 April, eighteen had died and the rest became Greene's prisoners. Some of the wounded with Cornwallis died en route, including Lieutenant-Colonel James Webster of the 33rd Foot. The British arrived in Wilmington on 7 April. When they left on 25 April it was with 1,435 rank and file present and fit for duty. Cornwallis favored joining General William Phillips, whom Clinton had sent with 5,000 troops to the Chesapeake area. Cornwallis, however, waited to hear whether Lieutenant-Colonel Francis Rawdon in Charleston would need him. When he heard of Rawdon's defeat of Greene at Hobkirk's Hill, Cornwallis turned northward toward Virginia and crossed the Roanoke River on 13 May. He joined Phillips's army in Petersburg a week later but found that Phillips himself had died of fever and that Benedict Arnold had taken command of his forces. When more reinforcements arrived, the British had about 5,000 present and fit for duty.

Cornwallis read Clinton's orders to Phillips and was disconcerted to find that they were not for a grand offensive but instead for taking and holding a naval base and conducting raids. The Hessian whom Phillips had left in command at Portsmouth wrote that it was an undesirable location. Cornwallis wrote to Clinton that Yorktown was preferable because it offered better protection to ships and could be more easily fortified. Cornwallis also pleaded with Clinton for permission to launch an offensive in Virginia. While awaiting Clinton's reply, Cornwallis dislodged the Marquis de Lafayette from Richmond and carried out raids to destroy American magazines and stores. He then proceeded to Williamsburg to learn Clinton's orders, which reached him there on 26 June.

Clinton would not allow a major campaign. He knew that Germain favored Cornwallis's active campaign over his own sedentary campaign in New York. Clinton's orders to Cornwallis became less and less specific and increasingly contradictory. He told Cornwallis to take a defensive station and then send to him specified military units to reinforce him in New York. (He was aware of the meeting between Washington and the comte de Rochambeau at Wethersfield, Connecticut, and thought that it presaged an attack on him.) Cornwallis repeated to Clinton his arguments for an active campaign in Virginia but said that he would follow Clinton's orders. Cornwallis had inspected Yorktown and Gloucester and found them unsuitable. After he saw Portsmouth he could better estimate how many men would be needed to defend it or some other post. He had ordered the transports at Portsmouth to prepare to receive part of his army. After crossing the James River to Cobham, he received the first in a series of confusing and contradictory orders from Clinton. Cornwallis was to send a new force to Philadelphia for a raid, after which the force would join Clinton in New York. In accordance with these orders, Cornwallis had actually embarked the Queen's Rangers on their transport for Philadelphia when a new message from Clinton arrived on 20 July countermanding all that had been done: Cornwallis was to keep all the troops and hold Old Point Comfort to secure Hampton Roads. Cornwallis ordered an engineer to survey Old Point Comfort and then on 21 July received a second letter of the same date as the previous day's letter ordering him to take a naval station and allowing him to keep all the troops he had but then saying that he should decide how many troops he needed and send the remainder to Clinton. Cornwallis decided to evacuate Portsmouth and to fortify Yorktown and Gloucester, keeping all his army for the extensive labor necessary.

Without assistance, Cornwallis was almost certainly doomed when a Franco-American army under Rochambeau and Washington besieged Yorktown while the French fleets under the comte de Grasse and the comte de Barras arrived to bottle up the British, outnumbering Thomas Graves and Samuel Hood by thirty-six to nineteen ships of the line. Cornwallis had one chance: to fight his way out against Lafayette and the Marquis de St. Simon at Williamsburg before Washington and Rochambeau arrived. Cornwallis planned his attack but abandoned it when a letter from Clinton arrived on 14 September promising relief and also a fleet from Admiral Robert Digby. Cornwallis hurried to complete his works, consisting of an outer and inner line of fortifications. The inner works consisted of ten redoubts, of which the ninth and tenth were the most important during the siege. Cornwallis thought that he had six weeks' provisions. His biggest guns were 18-pounders. The Franco-American force outnumbered him by two or three to one, and it had siege guns.

Cornwallis needed to hold the outer fortifications for as long as possible, which would mean more casualties. Then, on 29 September, he received a letter from Clinton promising a joint army and a naval relief expedition that he hoped could leave New York by 5 October. Accordingly,

Cornwallis decided to retire within his inner works. The Franco-American forces occupied his outer works and turned them into offensive lines. Their 24-pounder siege guns began their bombardment. On 10 October Cornwallis received Clinton's note now suggesting that the promised relief could leave New York by 12 October. On the night of 14 October, Cornwallis lost the ninth and tenth redoubts. He was low on food and ammunition and could no longer show his guns. He tried to escape to Gloucester but needed three shifts of boats. The first shift had arrived and the second group had already been loaded when a violent storm blew up during the early morning of 17 October. By the time the storm moderated, it was too late for the planned operation against the combined forces of General George Weedon and the Marquis de Choisy at Gloucester. The first group of British troops returned to Yorktown in the morning of 17 October.

At about 10:00 A.M. Cornwallis sent a drummer out to sound for a parley. The commissioners of both sides met the next day to work out the terms of capitulation. Washington granted Cornwallis an honorable surrender. On the afternoon of 19 October the British marched out to ground their arms. Cornwallis gave the usual promise not to talk or act against the Americans until he had been exchanged. Clinton and Graves, who had left New York on 19 October, arrived outside the Capes on 28 October.

As a prisoner on parole, until exchanged by the Peace of Paris in 1783, Cornwallis avoided attendance at the House of Lords and any conversations regarding the war. He resigned his office of Constable of the Tower, as he had been appointed to this political office by the ministry that he had helped to defeat. (He was later reinstated in the constableship as a military office.)

Cornwallis refused military command in India unless he would also have supreme civil command. In 1786 the Pitt government finally met his terms, and Cornwallis accepted the joint posts of governor-general of India and commander in chief, which he held until 1793. He brought about various civil and legal reforms, called the Cornwallis Code or the "permanent settlement," that showed his belief that the British were superior to native Indians. He waged a successful, albeit expensive, military campaign against Tipu Sultan that ended in 1792 with a significant annexation of Mysore land by the British and payment of an indemnity by Tipu. The British government awarded Cornwallis with a marquisate (he became the 1st Marquis Cornwallis). He left India in 1793 and reached England in February 1794.

In 1795 Cornwallis became master-general of the ordnance, responsible for artillery, engineers, and munitions supplies. Rebellion in Ireland in 1798 offered new scope for his services there with the same supreme authority in both civil and military affairs that he had wielded in India. As commander in chief he suppressed the last remnants of rebellion and thwarted a French invasion. As lord-lieutenant he negotiated the Act of Union with Britain. Since the new Irish parliament would have fewer seats than the old one, he had to use his power of patronage to compensate some members for giving up their seats. Cornwallis steadily pressed, though in vain, for Catholic emancipation (the ability of Roman Catholics to hold office). In his work he was ably assisted by Robert Stewart, Viscount Castlereagh. Neither could achieve Catholic emancipation, and both resigned after passage of the Act of Union in 1801.

Cornwallis might have expected honorable retirement, but instead he was sent in 1801 to negotiate with Napoleon the Peace of Amiens. Restless, in 1805 Cornwallis accepted an assignment to India again. He died soon after his arrival at Gazipore on 5 October.

Mary B. Wickwire

See also

Arnold, Benedict; Barras, Jacques Melchoir, Comte de; Brandywine, Battle of; Camden Campaign; Carleton, Guy; Charleston, South Carolina, Expedition against (1776); Charleston, South Carolina, Expedition against (1780); Clinton, Henry; Cowpens, Battle of; Declaratory Act; Ferguson, Patrick; Gates, Horatio; Germain, Lord George; Gloucester Point, Virginia, Action at; Grasse, François-Joseph-Paul, Comte de; Graves, Thomas; Greene, Nathanael; Guilford Courthouse, Battle of; Hanger, George; Hobkirk's Hill, Battle of; Hood, Samuel; Howe, Richard; Howe, William; Kalb, Johann, Baron de; Kings Mountain, Battle of; Knox, Henry; Lafayette, Marquis de; Lee, Charles; Leslie, Alexander; Loyalists; Monmouth, Battle of; Moore's Creek Bridge, North Carolina, Action at; Morgan, Daniel; New Jersey, Operations in; New York, Operations in; Phillips, William; Pitt, William, the Younger; Ramseur's Mill, North Carolina, Action at; Rawdon, Francis; Siege Warfare; Southern Campaigns; Tarleton, Banastre; Trenton, Battle of; Vimeur, Jean-Baptiste, Comte de Rochambeau; Weedon, George; Yorktown, Virginia, Siege of; Yorktown Campaign

References

Anderson, Troyer Steele. *The Command of the Howe Brothers during the American Revolution.* New York: Oxford University Press, 1936.

Billias, George A., ed. *George Washington's Generals and Opponents: Their Exploits and Leadership.* Reprint. New York: Da Capo, 1994.

Cornwallis, Charles. *An Answer to That Part of the Narrative of Lieutenant General Sir Henry Clinton, K.B., Which Relates to the Conduct of Lieutenant General Earl Cornwallis during the Campaign in North America in the Year 1781.* London: J. Debrett, 1783.

———. *Correspondence of Charles, 1st Marquis Cornwallis.* Edited with notes by Charles Ross. London: John Murray, 1859.

Curtis, Edward P. *The Organization of the British Army in the American Revolution.* New Haven, CT: Yale University Press, 1926.

Gruber, Ira D. *The Howe Brothers and the American Revolution.* New York: Norton, 1972.

Mackesy, Piers. *The War for America, 1775–1783.* 1965. Reprint, Lincoln: University of Nebraska Press, 1993.

Peckham, Howard H. *The War for Independence: A Military History.* Chicago: University of Chicago Press, 1958.

Smith, Paul H. *Loyalists and Redcoats: A Study in British Revolutionary Policy.* Chapel Hill: University of North Carolina Press, 1964.

Wickwire, Franklin, and Mary Wickwire. *Cornwallis: The American Adventure.* Boston: Houghton Mifflin, 1970.

———. *Cornwallis: The Imperial Years.* Chapel Hill: University of North Carolina Press, 1980.

Willcox, William B. *Portrait of a General: Sir Henry Clinton in the War of Independence.* New York: Knopf, 1964.

Correspondence, Committees of (1772–1776)

The committee of correspondence was an innovative and characteristic institution in the coming of the American Revolution. This new creation, both at the local and provincial levels, played a central role in turning dozens of uncoordinated Revolutionary efforts in cities, towns, and individual colonial legislatures into a unified movement in just two years (November 1772–October 1774) and then helped lead the drive to independence in another twenty months. Understanding this achievement requires careful attention to the changing meanings of the term "committees of correspondence."

At the local level, primarily in America's port cities, committees that formed to oppose British taxation and legislation, usually by directing nonimportation or nonconsumption movements, would often designate a few of their number to correspond with committees that were engaged in similar activities in other cities. This happened during both the Stamp Act crisis (1765–1766) and the extended resistance to the Townshend duties (1768–1770). In the latter event, these correspondents played a crucial role in trying to coordinate the nonimportation movement among the major cities, but eventually they and their whole committees failed.

At the provincial level, several colonial assemblies, including some of the most conservative, had created standing committees of correspondence well before the beginning of the imperial crisis. Their main function was to write to the legislature's agent in London, directing him to lobby British officials concerning issues of importance to the lawmakers, and to receive the agent's reports. On one occasion, in Massachusetts in 1768, a standing legislative committee of correspondence wrote not to its agent but to other colonial legislatures to state its grounds for opposing British policy. This circular letter, and the defiance both of the Massachusetts Assembly in refusing to rescind it under orders from the British government and of the South Carolina Assembly in voting over the governor's objection to receive it, became deservedly famous among America's Patriots.

None of these committees, however, were Revolutionary committees of correspondence, because none took it as their goal to create, by correspondence, an alliance of many local communities, whether cities, towns, or whole colonies, into an enduring opposition to British policy. The first committee to attempt this was the Boston Committee of Correspondence, formed in November 1772 at the urging of Samuel Adams. Alarmed by the British government's recent decision to remove the right of paying the salaries of Massachusetts's governor and superior court judges from the legislature, and instead to pay them directly out of Crown revenues, Adams wanted an institution that would raise the sensitivity of Massachusetts's towns to the whole pattern of growing British power in the province. Over the next fourteen months, up until the Boston Tea Party, this committee, by sending out carefully crafted letters, receiving replies, and sending out fresh responses, persuaded nearly sixty Massachusetts towns, and even a few Connecticut towns, to create their own committees of correspondence and endorse Boston's view that Britain was engaged in a vast conspiracy to undermine American liberties.

This had two results. First, when Britain passed its Coercive Acts in the spring of 1774, the Massachusetts countryside was already substantially radicalized and ready to create a provincial government that was not based on British authority. Second, as soon as Britain closed the port of Boston as punishment for the Boston Tea Party, the town's Committee of Correspondence and its neighboring committees were ready to propose the formation of similar committees in communities extending hundreds of miles down the Atlantic seaboard. By June, in response to the closing of the port of Boston, every major seaport had chosen its committee, and by July many inland towns and rural counties had created their own committees. These bodies stood ready to endorse two moves: the calling of an intercolonial congress to determine the best means to meet the crisis, and the initiation of a more tightly coordinated nonimportation movement in all of Britain's North American colonies.

Each of these objectives was strongly supported by a second kind of committee of correspondence. In March 1773, Virginia's House of Burgesses became alarmed over reports that a royal commission of inquiry into the burning of the revenue cutter *Gaspée* in Rhode Island in 1772 had the authority to send suspected perpetrators to England for trial. In response, it formed a new committee of correspondence devoted explicitly to communicating with other North American colonies over any challenges to the traditional rights of Americans by the British government. This committee's first act was to write to the legislatures of twelve other British North American colonies, asking that they, too, form fresh committees of correspondence devoted exclusively to the imperial crisis. The new legislative committees, like Massachusetts's local committees, were designed to meet on short notice in any season, even when their legislatures were not in session. The assemblies of Massachusetts, Rhode Island, and Connecticut immediately agreed to appoint their committees. Seven other colonies followed suit within the next year. Of the thirteen colonies that rebelled in 1776, only North Carolina and Pennsylvania declined to create this new institution.

Britain's Coercive Acts—by punishing an entire community of thousands for the destructive behavior of certain unidentified persons (the Boston Port Act), by providing that both civil and military officers accused of criminal activity in the course of exercising their authority could be transferred to England for trail (the Administration of Justice Act), and by unilaterally altering a seventeenth-century provincial charter (the Massachusetts Government Act)—raised fears in every colony that the British Parliament believed there were no limits on its powers in America. This was just the catalyst the growing committee movement needed. By July, well over one hundred communities, urban and rural, had their own committees of correspondence, and nearly every legislature's committee of correspondence was calling for an intercolonial congress, whether its full assembly was able to meet or was prevented from doing so by its royal governor.

When delegates chosen by either legal assemblies or extralegal provincial congresses in a total of twelve colonies met as the First Continental Congress in Philadelphia in September 1774, they quickly recognized the value of the new committees in achieving their goals. Their first objective was to generate a declaration of grievances that all the colonists would endorse along with a set of addresses to audiences—principally King George III and the people of Britain—that, they hoped, would help them secure a redress of those grievances. Their second objective was to ensure that their message would be listened to by making it difficult to ignore. Their method was a coordinated nonimportation and nonexportation boycott that would not merely cripple but utterly suspend Anglo-American trade until their demands were met.

To achieve both objectives, but especially the second, Congress incorporated committees into its Continental Association of October 1774, labeling these bodies committees of observation, inspection, and correspondence in recognition of the three things they wanted each committee to do: *observe* both the political speech and the commercial behavior of all persons in their city, town, or county; *inspect* every ship and boat, every wharf and shed, and every wagon or cart, no matter how small, to ensure that no prohibited goods moved into or out of the colonies; and *correspond* with any persons, other committees, and Revolutionary provincial officials or congresses about any concerns they had about the exact performance of the Continental Association and the maintenance of patriotic commitment in their communities.

This broad mandate gave the new committees great power, and many colonists, not only Loyalists, had reason at one point or another to resent these thousands of new local rulers. A Virginia dramatist, Robert Munford, even wrote a play satirizing the heavy-handed work of the local committees. But America's committees of observation, inspection, and correspondence made the Continental Association a nearly airtight embargo and helped to prepare the colonists for the greater discipline they would need and the greater sacrifices they would have to make once open warfare began at Lexington and Concord.

Both legislative committees of correspondence and local committees of observation, inspection, and correspondence remained vital Revolutionary institutions until independence. Thereafter, new challenges were met by new local officials and institutions appointed by new state governments operating under new constitutions. And America's trading patterns and laws fundamentally changed as the nation's ports opened wide to new trading partners.

Finally, committees of correspondence, both before and after the First Continental Congress, not only dominated Revolutionary commercial regulation and political mobilization in America but also played the central role in recruiting a new Revolutionary leadership. Even before the creation of Congress, committees of correspondence, beginning in Boston in 1772, extended south to Charleston and in several colonies more than 100 miles inland by July 1774. This process probably brought more than 1,000 men into formal public life for the first time. The new committees extended the leadership far beyond the Sons of Liberty and similar informal groups that had dominated America's Revolutionary movement from 1765 to 1770, when that movement was largely confined to America's port cities.

In the fall of 1774, Congress's new Continental Association further increased the new leadership to more than 7,000 men. Not all, of course, would remain as leaders, either in America's emerging new state governments or in the Continental Army and Navy and the state militias after 1776. But a large proportion of the top leadership in every colony or state, from 1774 to 1781, first rose to power through committee service. In this vital sense, America's committees of correspondence were not merely characteristic of the coming of the American Revolution but absolutely central to the achievement of American independence in 1776.

Richard Alan Ryerson

See also

Adams, Samuel; Boston, Massachusetts; Boston Port Act; Boycotts; Coercive Acts; Congress, First Continental; Continental Association; *Gaspée* Incident; Massachusetts; New York City; Nonimportation Agreements; Philadelphia; Sons of Liberty; Thomson, Charles; Virginia

References

Ammerman, David. *In the Common Cause: American Response to the Coercive Acts of 1774.* New York: Norton, 1975.

Brown, Richard D. *Revolutionary Politics in Massachusetts: The Boston Committee of Correspondence and the Towns,*

1772–1774. Cambridge: Harvard University Press, 1970.
Countryman, Edward. *A People in Revolution: The American Revolution and Political Society in New York, 1760–1776.* Baltimore, MD: Johns Hopkins University Press, 1981.
Greene, Jack P., ed. *Colonies to Nation, 1763–1789: A Documentary History of the American Revolution.* New York: Norton, 1975.
Nash, Gary B. *The Urban Crucible: Social Change, Political Consciousness and the Origins of the American Revolution.* Cambridge: Harvard University Press, 1979.
Ryerson, Richard Alan. *The Revolution Is Now Begun: The Radical Committees of Philadelphia, 1765–1776.* Philadelphia: University of Pennsylvania Press, 1978.
Weir, Robert M. *"A Most Important Epoch": The Coming of the Revolution in South Carolina.* Columbia: University of South Carolina Press, 1970.

Cowan's Ford, North Carolina, Action at (1 February 1781)

Following the devastating defeat of a part of his army under Colonel Banastre Tarleton at Cowpens, South Carolina, on 17 January 1781, General Charles Cornwallis rapidly moved his main force into North Carolina to cut off and trap the victorious General Daniel Morgan's smaller American army. Cornwallis went so far as to burn his wagons to lighten his load, a drastic measure in enemy territory. At Cowan's Ford on the Catawba River, north of Charlotte, American General William Richardson Davie prepared to ambush Cornwallis's advancing forces with about 300 men. Davie had to split his command to guard the two eastern fords. The river crossing was an ideal place for an ambush: it was 500 yards across, and the British troops would be caught negotiating the swift current over the rocky ford. An army was most vulnerable at a river crossing.

On 1 February 1781, British troops approached the ford from the west and began to cross. The ford split in midstream, with one branch going straight and a second route veering southeast at a forty-five-degree angle. A local guide had taken the British to the ford but broke away when the crossing began. The British soon came under fire from the opposite shore. Not only were they caught in the open in a narrow river crossing, but they had to contend with swift current that played havoc with the frightened horses and men. Not knowing of the split in the ford, the British pushed ahead into the less shallow part, unintentionally bypassing the easier section that broke off to one side.

Generals Charles O'Hara and Alexander Leslie, however, soon rallied their men, but Cornwallis himself suffered the loss of his own horse in the action. Troops from the Brigade of Guards forced their way across as Davie attempted to rally his men to oppose them. A charismatic militia leader, Davie fell in the action, causing his men to lose heart and fall back. Although they had delayed Cornwallis, the American troops felt the loss of Davie keenly.

The Americans lost just three killed, including Davie. British losses were thirty-one killed and thirty-five wounded. Cornwallis continued north to pursue the American army before it reached the safety of the Dan River in Virginia. Despite grueling marches and the shedding of their baggage, however, the British eventually lost the Race to the Dan, due to many rearguard actions across the North Carolina piedmont. The battle also illustrates the type of irregular warfare that the British regulars were not used to waging.

Robert M. Dunkerly

See also

Cornwallis, Charles; Davie, William Richardson; Leslie, Alexander; O'Hara, Charles; Southern Campaigns

References

Barefoot, Daniel. *Touring North Carolina's Revolutionary War Sites.* Winston Salem, NC: John F. Blair, 1998.
Boatner, Mark. *Encyclopedia of the American Revolution.* Mechanicsburg, PA: Stackpole, 1994.
———. *Landmarks of the American Revolution.* Mechanicsburg, PA: Stackpole, 1973.

Cowpens, Battle of (17 January 1781)

The British came close to restoring full royal government in South Carolina in mid-1780. After capturing Charleston (then known as Charles Town) in May and defeating another American army at Camden in August, they were militarily close to success. Politically, however, a proclamation of 3 June 1780 requiring all men to join the Loyalist militia or be considered outlaws was a major strategic error. Patriots had given their word that they would not participate further in the rebellion with the understanding that they would not have to take up arms in support of the king. Coupled with depredations by Loyalist militia and brigands, the proclamation helped ignite a backcountry insurgency. Brutal attempts at suppressing the Patriots, particularly in Georgia and the Carolina backcountry, only made things worse. When Major Patrick Ferguson made threats against the Overmountain settlements, the result was the disaster at Kings Mountain that cost the British most of their provincial (Loyalist) light troops.

As 1780 drew to a close, General Nathanael Greene made it clear that South Carolina was not completely pacified by moving the Southern Continental Army across the border in two divisions. Greene stationed his main force on the Pee Dee River near Cheraws. Brigadier General Daniel Morgan's Flying Army marched westward to "spirit up the people." When Morgan took a position along South Carolina's Pacolet River,

The Battle of Cowpens. Lieutenant-Colonel Banastre Tarleton, in pursuit of Daniel Morgan's detachment through South Carolina, stumbled upon the Americans and suffered a shattering defeat. Morgan's superb double envelopment left hundreds of Tarleton's men killed and wounded and more than 800 taken prisoner. (National Archives and Records Administration)

he posed a clear threat to the British outpost at Ninety-Six. The threat became explicit when Lieutenant Colonel William Washington's dragoons destroyed a Loyalist force at Hammond's Store on 29 December 1780.

General Charles Cornwallis responded by dispatching Lieutenant-Colonel Banastre Tarleton and a strong force to protect Ninety-Six and then drive Morgan from South Carolina. After learning that Ninety-Six was safe, Tarleton moved against Morgan with his British Legion, the 7th Regiment of Foot, the 71st Regiment (Fraser's Highlanders), and a detachment of Royal Artillery. As he maneuvered against Morgan, at least one company of local Loyalists under Captain Alexander Chesney came along to serve as guides. Tarleton's force, some 1,250 men, started its pursuit with four days' provisions and marched rapidly toward Morgan's campsite.

Morgan had his own supply problems. After despoiling Chesney's plantation, the Americans stripped the area around their Grindal Shoals base camp of available food and forage. Morgan was so short of food that he sent Colonel Andrew Pickens's South Carolina militia brigade east to forage liberally from Union County Tories while blocking a major approach route leading to the Flying Army. When Morgan learned that Tarleton was advancing, he began a withdrawal.

Morgan ordered all militia to assemble at Cowpens, a well-known road crossing where both sides had camped during past campaigns. The road junction provided access to Broad River fords that the Americans could use as supply, reinforcement, or escape routes as the situation dictated. On the first night of the withdrawal, 15 January, Morgan camped at Burr's Mill on Thicketty Creek. Tarleton's forced marches paid off as he backtracked during the night, making a surprise river crossing at an unguarded ford. So rapid was this march that the Americans evacuated Burr's Mill, leaving food still hanging over their cook fires.

Morgan reached Cowpens during the afternoon of 16 January 1781, reconnoitered the field with local militia commanders, and waited for the situation to develop. American reinforcements from the Spartanburg district and from North Carolina were coming in from many directions. Even with troop strength rising, however, Morgan needed to evaluate the militia turnout and morale against the speed of the British advance.

Tarleton halted at Burr's Mill, feeding his men with the American food and then resting them for a few hours late on 16 January. The five-day pursuit had exhausted the British, leaving the men with few basic food supplies because the

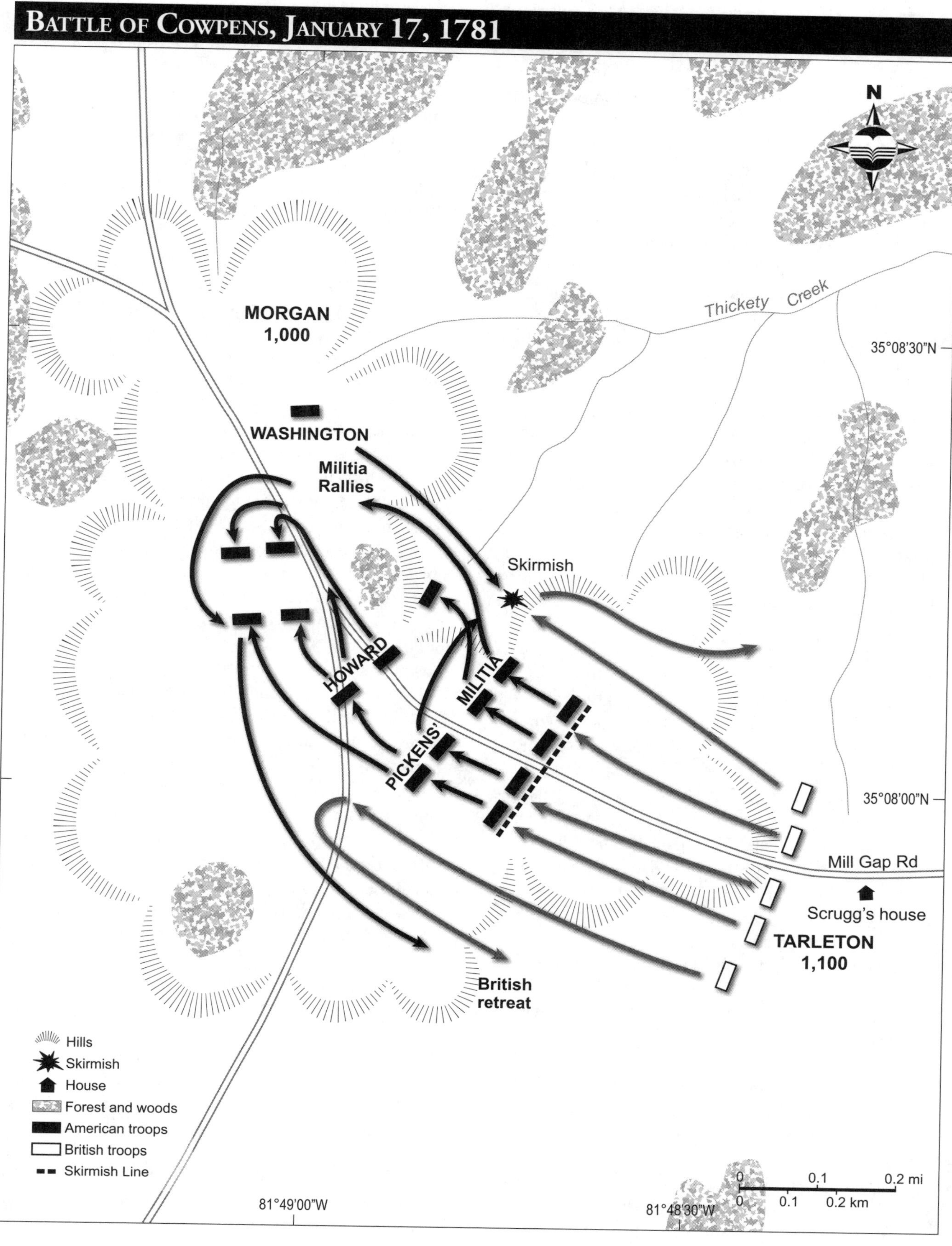

Battle of Cowpens, January 17, 1781
N
MORGAN
1,000
Thickety Creek
35°08'30"N
WASHINGTON
Militia
Rallies
Skirmish
HOWARD
MILITIA
PICKENS'
35°08'00"N
Mill Gap Rd
Scrugg's house
TARLETON
1,100
British
retreat
Hills
Skirmish
House
Forest and woods
American troops
British troops
Skirmish Line
81°49'00"W
81°48'30"W
0
0.1
0.2 mi
0
0.1
0.2 km

rapid marching did not allow replenishment until they seized Morgan's overnight camp. During the night, while the British rested, at least 900 militiamen joined Morgan. So did Virginia State Troops, who reported more marching toward Cowpens (one company arrived just as the battle began, another at noon). Sometime during the night, Morgan made the decision to fight at Cowpens and changed his disposition from a battle that might be forced on him to one that he wanted.

Tarleton had his men up before 2:00 A.M., when he sent off his advanced scouting party. The remainder followed an hour later. There was little difficulty following the route to Cowpens because the wet road had been torn up by the American horses and wagons the day before. The British reached the battlefield at about daybreak after a forced march of 12 miles. Morgan, reinforced to about 2,000 men, was already deploying his troops.

The battle can best be visualized as an attack northward up the Green River Road. On the southern end, there was a boggy area bordered by obstructions to the west and a low ridge line to the north and east. Morgan placed more than 300 North Carolina, South Carolina, and Georgia riflemen on the rising ground as skirmishers. About 150 yards behind the skirmishers, Pickens commanded a battle line of about 1,000 militiamen from Spartanburg, Union, and Laurens counties. These men were on the reverse slope of a slightly higher ridge that hid many from British scouts.

A third line farther down the slope was composed of Delaware, Maryland, and Virginia Continentals; Virginia State Troops; and militia. This line was 150 yards behind the South Carolina militia, close enough to support them and arranged to allow a militia withdrawal without disrupting their ranks. This was a very risky formation because it left gaps in the line that would have to be closed up just as the British came onto the American position. This main line was commanded by Maryland Lieutenant Colonel John Eager Howard, a superb combat officer. Finally, Continental dragoons and militia cavalry under Lieutenant Colonel William Washington served as a mobile reserve waiting "to charge them should occasion offer."

Tarleton faced a dilemma because his informants told him that reinforcements were heading to Morgan. With no way of knowing whether the force blocking Green River Road was a rear guard covering a river crossing or Morgan's advanced skirmish line prepared to initiate a major battle, Tarleton had to make his decision rapidly; any successful delaying action would allow Morgan's escape if it slowed Tarleton's advance. Tarleton's men were also low on food and had to be resupplied if they were to continue their pursuit.

The frontline skirmishers forced Tarleton to deploy a portion of his infantry east of Green River Road; then British dragoons attempted a reconnaissance by fire but were driven back. The British Light and Legion Infantry advanced about one hundred yards, driving the skirmishers back beyond the boggy ground and allowing the 7th Regiment space for deployment west of the road. When the ground frontage proved too narrow to allow the 71st Regiment room on the same line, the Scots were placed as a reserve. Tarleton ordered dragoon troops onto each flank, and then the entire line went forward at a trot.

The skirmishers moved back to the flanks when pressured and kept firing at long range. When the British closed within forty yards of the militia line, Pickens's South Carolinians fired at least five battalion volleys. These volleys were mostly close-range rifle fire aimed at the British, silhouetted against a lightening skyline. According to one British officer, two-thirds of the officers and nearly half the men were hit; some may have shammed wounds because they were former Continentals planning to rejoin their old regiments. Despite their losses, the British fired and charged with bayonets, routing the militia.

From this point, three separate lines of advance occurred. The British infantry re-formed and moved within twenty yards of the Continentals, engaging them in a firefight while British dragoons advanced on both flanks. On the American left, the 17th Light Dragoons rode through flank skirmishers and scattered re-forming militia. The British and Loyalist cavalry, disrupted by their attack, were driven away by Washington's cavalry, which outnumbered the British as much as four to one.

On the American right, British Legion dragoons and the 71st advanced, outflanking the main American line. They first drove through North Carolina skirmishers, who delayed the British for about three minutes. The right flank clash was short-lived but was at close range and exceptionally vicious, as evidenced by the bayonet, sword, and trampling wounds suffered by North Carolinians from Surry, Wilkes, and Burke counties. The Loyalist dragoons continued their ride beyond the American right as the Highlanders ran into a firing position outside the American battle line.

Washington, just returned to his support position, was re-forming when the British Legion dragoons broke through the right-flank skirmishers. The American cavalry charged through the Legion's dragoons and then turned and charged back, inflicting as many as 90 percent casualties. As Washington completed his return back through the opposing cavalry, he turned his men to deal with another crisis.

While the dragoons made their flank attacks, the infantry lines fought it out at very close range. Based on American casualty distributions, the British ranks were much reduced and presented a narrow front that did not extend across the entire field. The shortage of men left some American companies free to fire without being hit in return. The Delaware Company, stationed west of Green River Road, received the brunt of the 7th Regiment's fire, suffering perhaps 25 percent casualties in the short firefight. Virginia militia in and east of the road suffered several casualties, including one company commander. The Americans gave a good account of themselves, while the British reported American resistance as obstinate.

The 71st, after dispersing the North Carolina flankers, formed a firing line beyond the American right flank. When Howard, the American third-line commander, saw that his line would be outflanked by the advancing Highlanders, he ordered his far-right company, the Virginia Continentals, to turn and oppose the 71st. The maneuver failed because the Scots fired a volley into the American infantry just as they were changing their orientation. The 71st then charged forward. The Americans withdrew sequentially in good order, with each unit firing a parting volley and the men reloading as they marched to the rear.

Morgan and Howard met behind the retreating men and evaluated the situation. Morgan rode ahead to mark a point where the line should stop, re-form, turn, and fire. One hundred yards upfield, the Americans halted, faced about, and fired a series of rapid volleys, so shocking the Scots that many retreated. The American infantry charged into the Highlanders with bayonets just as Washington's cavalry rode onto their flank. The Scots broke and ran, pursued by American infantry and dragoons who swept across the battlefield shouting "Buford's Play," a reference to Tarleton's slaughter of Virginia infantry at Waxhaws.

The British artillery was galling the American counterattack. Howard called on a Captain Anderson to take the guns. Other officers, hearing the order, began racing toward the cannon as well. One gun was taken by an officer who used his spontoon to pole-vault ahead of his comrades onto the barrel. Noting that the gunner was about to fire, he adroitly used the spontoon to spear the artilleryman before the gun could be fired. Sharp hand-to-hand fighting around the guns left all the artillerymen dead or wounded.

Tarleton tried to get his reserve dragoons to counterattack and rescue the cannon, but the horsemen fled the field. As fighting around the cannon continued, some forty or fifty British dragoons made an effort to save the guns. This attack was driven off by Washington. The culminating episode was a celebrated "duel between Washington and Tarleton" that achieved great notoriety but probably did not actually involve Tarleton. Two officer participants, one Scottish and one American, did not state that Tarleton was involved. Washington did participate in some sort of personal engagement, and his horse was shot down. Given another horse, Washington led his dragoons 30 miles after the fleeing British but took the wrong road at a critical junction. The pursuing dragoons and their supporting infantry captured more than twenty British supply wagons, a traveling forge, and numerous prisoners.

The battle lasted less than an hour. The British artillery and virtually all their infantry were killed or captured; most British dragoons escaped. Total British casualties were over 800. American losses were approximately 25 killed and 125 wounded. The disparity reflects the brutal nature of backcountry warfare; when one side got the upper hand, they literally pushed their advantage to the hilt as the losers fled for their lives.

The Battle of Cowpens was the finest tactical American effort of the war. Morgan achieved success by blending Continentals and militia, infantry and cavalry, into a combined force capable of surmounting their fear of Tarleton and destroying his detachment. Morgan cleverly used the topography to enhance his weapons and deny the British accurate information about his dispositions. By deploying his men on the reverse slope, he placed the British at a disadvantage because they usually fired high, and men shooting downhill are even more likely to fire over their targets. The low American casualties reflect this high shooting. The third battle line was also slightly lower than the British and, except for Robert Kirkwood's Delaware Company, suffered few casualties. The unique initial placement of the third line that allowed the militia escape routes was innovative and risky but covered by Morgan's most disciplined men, all of whom were armed with bayonets.

While Morgan knew his men and their capabilities, he was still lucky. The militia knew their duty and carried it out almost to perfection. The unplanned right-flank resistance by North Carolina militia bought key time. The rapid movements of the American cavalry achieved mass at three key points in succession. Most importantly, the steady performance of the Continentals and the Virginia militia kept the British infantry engaged in a firefight they could not win, while the South Carolina militia re-formed and Washington maneuvered. The presence of perhaps fifty former Continental soldiers in Tarleton's ranks who would drop out of the fighting was another factor.

The battle profoundly affected the Revolutionary War's last phases and ultimately led to the British surrender at Yorktown. Attempting to recapture the prisoners taken by Morgan, Cornwallis burned his wagon train and pursued Morgan and Greene across North Carolina. The Race to the Dan wore out the British, who were forced to operate in a country largely swept clean of supplies by the Americans retreating before them. Cornwallis won a Pyrrhic victory at Guilford Courthouse on 15 March 1781, then marched to the coast and on to Virginia, where he surrendered to a combined Franco-American army at Yorktown on 19 October 1781.

After Guilford Courthouse, Greene returned his army to South Carolina. Although he did not win any battles himself, he defeated British forces in a "war of posts" during the summer of 1781. Greene's partisan supporters, especially those led by Pickens and Francis Marion, drove the British to the coast by October 1781, effectively ending British domination of the South Carolina interior.

Lawrence E. Babits

See also
Blackstock's, South Carolina, Action at; Camden Campaign; Charleston, South Carolina, Expedition against (1780); Cornwallis, Charles; Ferguson, Patrick; Fort Ninety-Six, South Carolina, Sieges of; Greene, Nathanael; Guilford Courthouse, Battle of; Hammond's Store, South Carolina, Action at; Howard, John Eager; Kings Mountain, Battle of; Loyalist Units; Morgan, Daniel; Southern Campaigns; Tarleton, Banastre; Washington, William; Waxhaws, South Carolina, Action at; Yorktown, Virginia, Siege of

References

Babits, Lawrence E. *A Devil of a Whipping: The Battle of Cowpens.* Chapel Hill: University of North Carolina Press, 1998.

Bass, Robert D. *The Green Dragoon: The Lives of Banastre Tarleton and Mary Robinson.* 1957. Reprint, Orangeburg, SC: Sandlapper, 2003.

Buchanan, John. *The Road to Guilford Courthouse: The American Revolution in the Carolinas.* New York: Wiley, 1997.

Fleming, Thomas J. *Cowpens "Downright Fighting": The Story of Cowpens.* Washington, DC: National Park Service, 1988.

Graham, James. *The Life of General Daniel Morgan.* 1856. Reprint, Bloomingburg, NY: Zebroski Historical Services, 1993.

Haller, Stephen E. *William Washington: Cavalryman of the Revolution.* Bowie, MD: Heritage Books, 2001.

Higginbotham, Don. *Revolutionary Rifleman.* Chapel Hill: University of North Carolina Press, 1961.

Moncure, John. *The Cowpens Staff Ride and Battlefield Tour.* Fort Leavenworth, KS: Combat Studies Institute, 1966.

Tarleton, Banastre. *History of the Campaigns of 1780 and 1781, in the Southern Provinces of North America.* 1787. Reprint, New York: New York Times, 1968.

Craik, James (1730–1814)

James Craik, son of a member of Parliament, was chief physician and surgeon of the Continental Army during the Revolutionary War. Craik was born near Dumfries, Scotland, and received his medical training at the University of Edinburgh. As a surgeon with the British Army, he went to the West Indies in 1750. The following year he immigrated to Virginia, and in 1754 he served as surgeon in the Virginia Provincial Regiment under Colonel Joshua Fry. It was then that Craik's lifelong friendship with George Washington, then Fry's lieutenant-colonel, began.

During the French and Indian War, Craik served under General Edward Braddock and from 1755 to 1758 as chief medical officer under Washington, then commander of Virginia's provincial forces. In 1758, Craik set up a medical practice in Port Tobacco, Maryland. In 1760 he married Marianne Ewell.

James Craik, a Continental Army doctor, was for many years George Washington's personal physician and was at the bedside of the dying general in 1799. (National Library of Medicine)

One of their nine children, George Washington Craik, later served as his namesake's personal secretary. In 1770, Washington persuaded Craik to join him in surveying lands that the Crown planned to apportion to himself, Craik, and others who had provided critical service in the French and Indian War.

As tensions escalated between the colonies and Britain, Craik supported independence. In 1777, Washington asked Craik to join the Continental Army's hospital department. Craik accepted, becoming assistant director general for "three dollars and six rations per day and two horses and traveling expenses." He served in the Middle Department, which extended from the Hudson River to the Potomac, and eventually rose to the army's second medical position, chief physician and surgeon.

In the fall of 1777, Craik discovered intelligence regarding the Conway Cabal, an alleged plot to replace Washington as commander in chief of the Continental Army with General Horatio Gates. Conveying the information to Washington, Craik warned: "Notwithstanding your unwearied diligence, . . . yet you are not wanting in secret enemies." Craik continued to serve in the army and was at Yorktown in October 1781 to witness Cornwallis's surrender. Following the war, Washington urged Craik to relocate closer to Mount Vernon. He agreed, moving near Alexandria, Virginia, where he served as physician to Washington, his family, and many of his slaves.

On the morning of 14 December 1799, Craik was called to Mount Vernon. Washington had contracted a throat infection and had already been bled. Craik repeated the treatment, and as the general's condition worsened, Craik attempted blistering and administered emetics and other treatments then considered medically advanced. Increasingly weak, Washington stated, "Doctor, I die hard, but I am not afraid to go," and expired not long after, with Craik by his side. Washington bequeathed to Craik his tambour secretary and desk chair. Craik was mustered out of the army in 1800 and spent the remainder of his life at his Virginia estate.

Rachel Scharfman

See also

Continental Army; Conway Cabal; Gates, Horatio; Washington, George

References

Blanton, Wyndham B. *Medicine in Virginia in the Eighteenth Century.* Richmond, VA: Garnett and Massie, 1931.

Pilcher, James Evelyn. *The Surgeon-Generals of the Army of the U.S.A.* Carlisle, PA: Association of Military Surgeons, 1905.

Toner, J. M. *The Medical Men of the Revolution.* Philadelphia: Collins, 1876.

Twohig, Dorothy, ed. *The Papers of George Washington: Retirement Series,* Vol. 4, *April–December, 1799.* Charlottesville: University of Virginia Press, 1999.

Crawford, William (1732–1782)

William Crawford was a farmer, surveyor, and military officer. He fought in the French and Indian War, Pontiac's Rebellion, Lord Dunmore's War, and the American Revolution, gaining vast experience in frontier warfare. It was during the last stage of the Revolution that he was captured by Indians, tortured, and burned at the stake. His death was witnessed by his friend Dr. John Knight and retold along the frontier and to the east, thereby furthering the fear of Indian attacks.

Crawford, born in Orange County, Virginia (in what later became Berkeley County, now in West Virginia), became a surveyor and farmer and surveyed land west of the Appalachian Mountains. During this time, he became acquainted with his contemporary, George Washington. When war between the French and British broke out, Crawford marched with General Edward Braddock on his ill-fated attempt to capture Fort Duquesne in 1755. Crawford led a detachment of men during the retreat from Braddock's disaster and gained recognition for his military skills. For the next three years, Crawford helped protect the frontiers of Pennsylvania and Virginia. By leading a group of scouts in the West, he gained valuable experience in frontier warfare against the Indians. In 1758, Crawford was part of the forces under Major-General John Forbes who were finally able to gain control of the forks of the Ohio for the British and replace Fort Duquesne with Fort Pitt. Crawford, then a captain, continued his military service for three more years. The experience he gained as a frontier fighter and scout was called upon again in 1763. Pontiac's Rebellion required Crawford and other British soldiers to end the Indian uprising along the Great Lakes.

After the French and Indian War, Crawford moved to the Youghiogheny River, a wilderness area south of Fort Pitt that he had become familiar with in his surveying duties. The area was disputed between Pennsylvania and Virginia, both claiming to hold jurisdiction. Crawford held several judicial offices for Pennsylvania and then for Virginia, including justice of the peace in Pennsylvania and justice of the Court of Quarter Sessions for Augusta County, Virginia. And he continued farming and surveying, even acting as a land agent for Washington.

In October of 1774, Crawford was commissioned a major by the colony of Virginia and fought against Indians on the frontier in Lord Dunmore's War. He led 500 men in an attack against the Shawnees at the Battle of Point Pleasant, Virginia (now West Virginia). Later that month, Crawford led a raid that destroyed two Mingo villages along the Scioto River. He participated in the preliminary treaty at Pickaway Plains and the Treaty of Camp Charlotte. His experience in frontier fighting provided for repeated success in battle.

In May 1775, western Pennsylvanians held a meeting at Pittsburgh to develop a committee of defense. Crawford was elected to this committee, whose duty was to protect the frontier against encroachments by Britain and its Indian allies. When war with Britain broke out, Crawford offered his services to Pennsylvania and its Committee of Safety, but the offer was declined because of his involvement in Lord Dunmore's War and Virginia's militia. Arthur St. Clair, an associate on the Pennsylvania bench, had criticized Crawford's role as inconsistent with Pennsylvania's peace policy.

Crawford then volunteered his services to Virginia, which authorized him to raise a regiment. This he did easily because of his reputation and prestige, becoming lieutenant colonel of the 5th Virginia Regiment. In October 1776, Crawford received a commission (backdated to 14 August) as colonel of the 7th Virginia Regiment. Crawford's troops fought in most of the major battles in the North. He and his men fought at Long Island and later crossed the icy Delaware with Washington to take part in the vital victories at Trenton and Princeton. Crawford was nearly captured at Brandywine and performed admirably at Germantown. He was recognized by Washington for his military and scouting abilities and was sent to the Western Department to lead Continental and militia troops under Brigadier General Edward Hand.

In the fall of 1777, Virginia sent Crawford to raise men to protect the frontier. His extensive experience in fighting the Indians made him the ideal candidate to boost militia enrollment. This militia force, the 13th Virginia, was raised to protect the frontier as required and to fight in the East if it was not needed in the West. The 13th Virginia was based at Fort Pitt (Pittsburgh). Crawford also often commanded Fort Crawford, built about 16 miles north of Pittsburgh. George Rogers Clark, who had fought alongside Crawford in Lord Dunmore's War, invited him to join his western campaign, but Crawford had to decline.

In 1778 the Americans planned an attack against the British at Detroit, which was believed to be the source of many Indian attacks against frontier settlers. That fall, Crawford and his troops helped to establish Fort Laurens and Fort McIntosh on the way to Detroit. The forts, however, were not well manned and fell quickly into disarray. By the end of the next year, the mission was abandoned, as were the forts, resulting in an increase in Indian attacks on frontier settlements. In response, Crawford, under the command of Colonel Daniel Brodhead, led attacks against the Indians of the area. Although these punitive attacks usually settled the frontier for a while, Crawford and others recognized that the origins of the attacks were in Detroit and Sandusky. In order to eliminate the Indian threat, the American forces would have to launch an attack on those sites. Crawford made an appeal in person to Congress in 1780 for more equipment and ammunition for the expedition, which did result in a small shipment to Fort Pitt. But Congress could not provide enough ammunition for such an ambitious venture, even though men were anxious to go. In 1781, Crawford resigned and returned home to his farm on the Youghiogheny River, in present-day Pennsylvania.

In May 1782, however, Crawford was again asked to lead troops against the Indians of the Ohio Country. He could not turn down the request; even in his retirement he had been an outspoken advocate of an attack on either Detroit or Sandusky as a means to quiet Indian attacks on the frontier. Crawford soon arrived at Mingo Bottom with his son John, nephew William Crawford, and son-in-law William Harrison.

As was customary, the militia elected their officers and chose Crawford as the leader of the entire expedition. His second in command, whom he defeated by only a slim margin, was the popular Colonel David Williamson. Williamson had been the leader of the attack on the Christian Indians at Gnadenhutten in Ohio in March 1782 that killed nearly 100 peaceful Delawares. As the militia moved north through the Ohio Country, the Indian scouts took notice and were well aware of their actions.

The Battle of Sandusky commenced on 4 June 1782, on the upper Sandusky River (in present-day Wyandot County, Ohio). The force against the Americans was made up of Captain Pipe's Delawares, Half-King's Wyandots, and British regulars under the direction of Captain William Caldwell. The American militia was able to gain ground, including a clump of pine trees called Battle Island, leaving the Indians and British in the surrounding prairie grasses. The battle continued the next day, but Crawford did not press his attack, and the British and Indians were eventually reinforced by Shawnee and Lake Indians. This uneven balance forced the Americans to retreat on the evening of 5 June. The militia was plagued by the harassment of British and Indians in their rear as they moved southward. On the afternoon of 6 June, at Olentangy Creek, the Americans decided to make another stand. In the Battle of Olentangy, however, the British and Indians routed the Americans, and several of their number, including Crawford, became separated from the main force. Williamson led one segment to safety. Crawford is said to have been looking for his son, nephew, and son-in-law and his aide-de-camp when he and Dr. John Knight were captured by Delaware Indians on the afternoon of 7 June 1782.

Crawford, who was familiar with many of the Indians, was brought to Half-King's town. Here, he met with Simon Girty, an agent for the British who lived among the Delawares. Crawford was acquainted with Girty, possibly from his frontier adventures, but they had also fought together in Lord Dunmore's War. It is thought that Crawford asked Girty to save his life, and some reports even say that Crawford offered Girty money, but their exact conversation is unknown.

Crawford was taken on 11 June to Old Town, where he was met by Captain Pipe and Wingenund of the Delaware tribe and was united with other prisoners who had been captured. Ultimately, all of these prisoners were killed before the Indians dealt with Crawford and Knight. On the east bank of the Tymochtee Creek, a fire was built outside the Delaware village. Crawford and Knight were stripped naked and beaten. Crawford's hands were then tied, and he was attached to a pole. It became apparent that he would be burned at the stake, and he questioned Girty, who acknowledged Crawford's fate. As the torture commenced, gunpowder was shot into his body, his ears were cut off, and then hot hickory poles taken from a burning fire were poked at his body. Crawford begged Girty to shoot him, but this was impossible; if Girty had tried to do so, he would have suffered the same fate as Crawford. Crawford then prayed to God to have mercy on him and collapsed, only to be scalped and covered with coals and ashes. He was stood up and again poked with fiery poles, this time seemingly unaffected by the torture. His ordeal lasted about two hours before he died and was covered with more coals. Crawford had been singled out for torture because he was the "Big Captain" of the attacking forces and in retaliation for the murder of the Christian Indians at Gnadenhutten, even though this was actually carried out by Williamson.

Crawford's death was reported by Knight, who had escaped while being transported to a Shawnee village, where the same torment probably awaited him. Knight's vivid account terrified Americans living on the frontier and even affected those living on the coast. Crawford's death, occurring after the Americans had won their war for independence and nearly all fighting had ceased along the Atlantic seaboard, highlighted the unstable environment on the frontier that would continue in the decades following the American Revolution.

Sarah E. Miller

See also

Brodhead Expedition; Crawford Expedition; Fort Laurens, Ohio; Fort McIntosh, Pennsylvania; Girty, Simon; Gnadenhutten Massacre; Northwest Territory; Sandusky, Ohio, Actions at

References

Anderson, James H. "Col. William Crawford." *Ohio History* 6 (1896): 1–34.

Butterfield, C. W. *Crawford's Campaign against Sandusky in 1782.* Cincinnati: Robert Clark, 1873.

———. *History of the Girtys.* Reprint. Columbus, OH: Long's College Book Company, 1950.

———, ed. *The Washington-Crawford Letters: Being the Correspondence between George Washington and William Crawford from 1767 to 1781 Concerning Western Lands.* Cincinnati: Robert Clarke, 1877.

English, William Hayden. *Conquest of the Country Northwest of the River Ohio, 1778–1783, and Life of Gen. George Rogers Clark.* Vol. I. Indianapolis, IN: Bowen-Merrill, 1896.

Knepper, George W. *Ohio and Its People.* Kent, OH: Kent State University Press, 1987.

Pieper, Thomas I., and James B. Gidney. *Fort Laurens, 1778–1779: The Revolutionary War in Ohio.* Kent, OH: Kent State University Press, 1976.

Crawford Expedition (June 1782)

This major American military expedition into the Ohio Country in June 1782 evolved into a series of engagements with the British and Indians and led to the torture and death of the American commander, Colonel William Crawford.

The conclusive character of the British surrender at Yorktown in October 1781 often obscures the military operations between belligerents that continued into 1782, especially in the South and the West. Particularly obscure are the battles fought beyond the Appalachian Mountains where American, British, and Native American forces engaged in furious guerrilla warfare that tolerated no neutrals. The chief American stronghold was Pittsburgh, which served as a base for expeditions into Ohio. The British base at Detroit provided political and military resources to interdict any American forays into the region. The region's powerful native tribes, such as the Shawnees, Delawares, and Wyandots, had allied with the British to oppose further American settlement on their lands. A final challenge for the Americans was the nature of the terrain, a vast wilderness that served as both a sanctuary for the Indians and an obstacle for any American military expedition.

During early 1782, many American frontiersmen conducted unauthorized raids into Ohio to destroy the sanctuaries from which the British and Indians had attacked settlements in Pennsylvania and western Virginia. One raid in March 1782 encountered the Christian Indian settlement at Gnadenhutten, where the American raiders massacred about 140 native Delaware men, women, and children. This atrocity infuriated the Ohio tribes, who sought retaliation at the earliest opportunity.

That opportunity came in June when Colonel William Crawford, a Continental officer from Virginia who had a long acquaintance with George Washington, organized an American expedition into Ohio. Crawford secured authorization from Congress to raid the Wyandot settlement at Upper Sandusky, which was believed to be a stronghold of native power. He then mobilized 485 mounted volunteers, including many men with prior experience in the Continental Army. During the rendezvous at Mingo Bottom on the Ohio River, Crawford organized his force into companies by distributing men from the same community into different units in order to reduce the effects upon any one community should the force suffer casualties.

Crawford's expedition was no secret to the Indians, who immediately rallied about 200 Wyandot and Delaware warriors to the defense of their homes. During this emergency they were supported by a Loyalist unit of approximately 100 men commanded by Captain William Caldwell of Butler's Rangers, who were then stationed at Detroit. Caldwell's force was augmented by several veteran members from the British Indian Department, including Simon Girty, Alexander McKee, and Mathew Elliot, all notorious in the eyes of Americans for instigating Indian raids.

Crawford led an uneventful march through the Ohio wilderness, but his army was constantly monitored by Indian scouts. The Americans passed through a vast plain, described as an ocean of grass as high as the saddle, to reach Upper Sandusky, located west of the Sandusky River, on 4 June 1782. They found the major Wyandot town abandoned, and the ominous quiet prompted Crawford to send out a small scouting party led by Major John Rose. Crawford had in fact stumbled into a beehive of villages situated in the shape of a horseshoe into which the Americans moved deeper.

Shortly around noon Rose's men were ambushed about 3 miles away from Crawford's main force by a small Indian party. Crawford ordered his small army forward to meet this attack and drove off the Indians, who retreated a short distance away while Caldwell and his rangers moved up to support them. At about two o'clock Caldwell arrived, the British and Indians counterattacked Crawford's force, and the fighting escalated, filling the landscape with smoke as men strug-

Delaware Indians burn William Crawford, an officer in the Continental Army, at the stake on 11 June 1782, in revenge for Crawford's punitive expeditions against Indian villages in the Ohio Valley. (Library of Congress)

gled to see their opponents through the tall grass. By four o'clock Crawford established a defensive position in a copse of woods, which provided cover. There was then a pause in the battle while the Indians set fires around the American perimeter to provide illumination so that they could continue sniping into the dusk.

The next day, 5 June, Butler's Rangers and the Delaware and Wyandot Indians resumed their attack on Crawford's position and were soon joined by reinforcements of 140 Shawnees and additional rangers with two small cannon; these troops moved to surround the Americans. By this time Crawford's army was low on ammunition and in desperate need of water. The officers debated whether to attack or look for an escape route. During the afternoon, Girty carried a white flag toward the American lines and called for surrender, which was refused. That night, Crawford decided to extract his force from the envelopment through an unguarded trail. Unfortunately, some of his men had fallen asleep in the tall grass, did not hear of the retreat, and were left behind. As the Americans withdrew, they had to fight through Indians who blocked their escape. The scene was chaotic as both parties delivered heavy fire, and Captain Caldwell was wounded in both legs by a single shot. Most of the Americans managed to escape back down the trail they had used two days before and returned to Mingo Bottom by 13 June. During two days of fighting, Crawford's force had suffered an undetermined number killed and wounded; the British lost five killed and eleven wounded, including Caldwell.

Meanwhile, Crawford, his nephew William, and several other soldiers became separated from the main force and were pursued for almost 20 miles. On 6 June, Crawford and his men attempted a final stand near Olentangy Creek. They were surrounded, captured by the Delaware, and marched 33 miles back to Upper Sandusky, where they arrived on 11 June. Because of the massacre at Gnadenhutten, the Indians sought retribution and decided to execute the prisoners. A few captives managed to escape, including Dr. John Knight, a surgeon on the expedition who later recorded Crawford's fate. The Delawares singled out Crawford for a prolonged torture ceremony during which he was beaten and scalped and his ears were cut off; he was finally roasted to death at the stake.

Crawford's gruesome death provided a justification for many Americans to intensify their pressure on Ohio's Indian tribes during a bitter conflict that witnessed acts of barbarism on both sides. But Crawford's defeat also delayed American pressure on the native tribes, and American settlers would not move deeply into the Ohio Country until the federal government established control of the area in the 1790s.

Steven J. Rauch

See also

Crawford, William; Girty, Simon; Gnadenhutten Massacre; Native Americans; Northwest Territory; Sandusky, Ohio, Actions at

References

Brown, Parker B. "The Battle of Sandusky: June 4–6, 1782." *Western Pennsylvania Historical Magazine* 65 (April 1982): 115–151.

———. "Reconstructing Crawford's Army of 1782." *Western Pennsylvania Historical Magazine* 65 (1982): 17–36.

———. "The Search for the Colonel William Crawford Burn Site: An Investigative Report." *Western Pennsylvania Historical Magazine* 68 (1985): 43–66.

Calloway, Colin G. *The American Revolution in Indian Country: Crisis and Diversity in Native American Communities.* Cambridge: Cambridge University Press, 1995.

J. Hector St. John Crèvecoeur. A writer, naturalist, and social analyst, his descriptions of America gained an international readership during the late eighteenth century. His work strongly influenced outside perceptions of the New World. (Hayward Circer, ed., *Dictionary of American Portraits,* 1967)

Crèvecoeur, J. Hector St. John de (1735–1813)

J. Herbert St. John de Crèvecoeur, whose celebrated *Letters from an American Farmer* (1782) provided insightful commentary on conditions in pre-Revolutionary America, was born Michel-Guillaume de Crèvecoeur in Caen, Normandy. His parents, Guillaume-Augustin de Crèvecoeur and Marie-Anne Therese Blouet, were members of the French nobility. In 1750, Crèvecoeur graduated from the Jesuit College Royal de Bourbon in Caen with distinction in literature and languages.

During the French and Indian War, Crèvecoeur served in the French army and was wounded during the British siege of Quebec. Following the defeat of French forces in North America, he changed his name to J. Hector St. John Crèvecoeur and began to speak and write in English. He first earned his living in America by serving as a trader, explorer, and surveyor on the frontier. But in 1765, he became a naturalized citizen of the province of New York. Four years later, he married Mehitable Tippett and purchased 120 acres in Orange County, New York. The marriage produced three children, and Crèvecoeur emerged as a leading scientific agriculturalist in his community.

Crèvecoeur's idyllic agrarian life was disrupted by the American Revolution. As a pacifist, he attempted to stay neutral in the growing conflict between the colonies and Britain, but Orange County was the site of considerable civil unrest, and Crèvecoeur was fined and imprisoned for failing to support the Patriot cause. In 1779, he embarked with his six-year-old son upon a journey to France to establish his children's inheritance claims. Accused of being a spy, Crèvecoeur was arrested by the British. This experience altered his Anglophile sentiments. Crèvecoeur and his son finally reached France in August 1781.

While Crèvecoeur was in France, the London firm Davis and Davis published his *Letters from an American Farmer.* In a series of essays blending fact and fiction, Crèvecoeur attempted to answer the question "What is an American?" In response to this query, the author stated that the soil of America offered Europeans the opportunity for regeneration in a place where "individuals of all nations are melted into a new one." The book became an international best-seller, earning Crèvecoeur a reputation as an authority on America.

In 1783 Crèvecoeur returned to America as French consul to New York, New Jersey, and Connecticut, only to discover that his wife had died and his estate had been burned during the war. But Crèvecoeur pursued his efforts to establish commercial relations between France and the new American nation and became a frequent correspondent with George

Washington, James Madison, Thomas Jefferson, and other prominent Americans.

Due to failing health in 1790, Crèvecoeur returned to France, where he was able to survive the turmoil of the French Revolution. He died on 12 November 1813 from natural causes at Garcelles, near Paris. Crèvecoeur's *Letters from an American Farmer* is still considered an essential source for understanding pre-Revolutionary America and is still widely read, especially in American colleges and universities.

Ron Briley

See also

Literature; New York, Province and State; Public Opinion, American

References

Allen, Gay Wilson, and Roger Asselineau. *St. John de Crevecoeur: The Life of an American Farmer.* New York: Viking, 1987.

Moore, Dennis, ed. *More Letters from an American Farmer.* Athens: University of Georgia Press, 1995.

Philbrick, Thomas. *St. John de Crevecoeur.* Detroit: Gale, 1970.

Crooked Billet, Pennsylvania, Action at (1 May 1778)

This devastating British raid on an American militia post in Bucks County led to charges of British atrocities as well as official inquiries into the effectiveness of American militia patrols. During the British occupation of Philadelphia in 1777–1778, the British frequently sent out foraging parties, raids to capture rebel leaders, and escorts to protect farmers who wanted to bring their produce to sell to the British in the city. Militia units from Chester and Bucks counties were assigned to harass these parties and raids while the Continental Army spent the winter at Valley Forge.

During April 1778, the British concentrated on raiding north and northwest of Philadelphia. One American militia unit in that region, under the command of Brigadier General John Lacey, was stationed in Bucks County at the Crooked Billet Tavern, about 15 miles north of Philadelphia. This weak militia force from Bucks and Cumberland counties sat astride Old York Road, the main route from Bucks County into Philadelphia. Lacey's command suffered from poor intelligence, minimal training, lax discipline, and questionable motivation; was under strength due to Pennsylvania's lukewarm commitment to stationing militia east of the Schuylkill River; and was certainly not adequate for covering the wide region under its responsibility.

By 1 May 1778, Lacey's force, which had started out at 450 men, had been reduced to fewer than 60 by enlistment expirations. Some of the troops had arrived in camp just the previous evening and had never experienced combat. That morning Lacey's force found itself confronted by Lieutenant-Colonel Sir Robert Abercromby's force of 400 light infantry and a detachment of 17th Dragoons in his front, with another 300 under the command of Major John Graves Simcoe in his rear. Lacey withdrew his force into a wooded area, where he was able to hold off the attack until he could take his men on a brilliantly executed 2-mile fighting withdrawal. Unfortunately, the hasty retreat caused him to abandon all of his unit's baggage, which included fourteen wagons filled with rum, whiskey, and other essentials. Losses in the battle were 26 killed and 8 to 10 wounded for the Americans, and 9 wounded for the British. The defeat effectively took the Pennsylvania militia out of the war for the remainder of the spring.

Some accounts of the action suggested that the British committed atrocities against wounded and surrendered militiamen. Many of the dead Americans were found burned beyond recognition in a field of buckwheat straw. Most of those claiming atrocity merely assumed that these men had been thrown into the fire alive. Only the deposition of Philadelphian William Stayner asserted that some British Light Infantry boasted to him that they had bayoneted Lacey's soldiers after their surrender and then threw the living wounded into the fire. Other British soldiers, however, told Warminster Township resident Thomas Craven that the Americans had been burned to death when their ammunition set the dry buckwheat fields afire.

In the wake of this catastrophe, the area north of Philadelphia was brought under direct Continental Army command, with Brigadier General William Maxwell recalled from New Jersey to investigate the reasons for the debacle and institute reforms. Lacey was removed from command and replaced by General James Potter.

Joseph J. Casino

See also

Maxwell, William; Simcoe, John Graves; Valley Forge, Pennsylvania

References

Baurmeister, Carl Leopold. *Revolution in America: Confidential Letters and Journals, 1776–1784, of Adjutant General Major Baurmeister of the Hessian Forces.* Translated by Bernard A. Uhlendorf. New Brunswick, NJ: Rutgers University Press, 1957.

Bodle, Wayne. *The Valley Forge Winter: Civilians and Soldiers in War.* University Park, PA: Penn State University Press, 2002.

Montrésor, Captain John. "Journal of Captain John Montrésor, July 1, 1777, to July 1, 1778." Edited by G. D. Scull. *Pennsylvania Magazine of History and Biography* 5 (1881): 393–417; 6 (1882): 34–57, 189–206, 284–299.

Simcoe, Lieutenant Colonel John Graves. *A Journal of the Operations of the Queen's Rangers.* 1844. Reprint, New York: New York Times, 1968.

Crown Point, New York

Located on the west shore of Lake Champlain, about 10 miles north of Fort Ticonderoga, Crown Point was a strategic site in early American history. Dutch and English traders established trading posts there, and in 1731 the French constructed Fort St. Frédéric at the site. Colonial and British expeditions failed to capture the fort in 1755 and 1756, but General Jeffrey Amherst succeeded in 1759. As the French had blown up Fort St. Frédéric, Amherst started constructing a large new post, named Fort Amherst, a few hundred yards away. This installation, never entirely completed, was partially destroyed by fire in 1773, but the British continued to occupy it with a small garrison.

On 12 May 1775, Seth Warner and 100 Green Mountain Boys seized Crown Point from the British. Warner captured 9 soldiers, 10 women and children, and some cannon. In the following summer and winter, General Philip Schuyler used Crown Point as a staging area to organize and supply America's invasion of Canada. On 24 August 1775, General Richard Montgomery sailed northward from there with an army of 1,200 men toward the Richelieu River. By June 1776, Montgomery was dead, the invasion had collapsed, and the American army was in full retreat. General Guy Carleton threatened to capture both Crown Point and Ticonderoga. That summer, American and British forces on Lake Champlain began constructing fleets to vie for control of Lake Champlain. General Horatio Gates, American commander at Ticonderoga, declared Crown Point indefensible in July and abandoned it. His decision was criticized by many of his compatriots, but he stoutly refused to change his mind.

In the Battle of Valcour Island (11–12 October 1776), the American fleet under General Benedict Arnold was soundly defeated, and Carleton swept triumphantly southward to capture Crown Point on 14 October. He occupied the post until 3 November, then withdrew his forces to Canada. British troops under General John Burgoyne captured Crown Point again in June 1777 as he marched toward Saratoga. After Burgoyne's defeat and capture in October, Carleton withdrew British troops from Crown Point and retreated northward once more. In October 1778, Colonel Christopher Carleton was given command of an expedition on Lake Champlain against Americans living along its shores, with orders to destroy their provisions, supplies, boats, sawmills, and gristmills and to take prisoners. On 24 October, he sailed southward from Île-aux-Noix. Three days later he posted the warship *Maria* off Crown Point to discourage rebel traffic on the lake. Americans under Captain Ebenezer Allen operated there, even capturing the stray deserter, but Carleton had no difficulty in raiding on the lake with impunity. He withdrew to Île-aux-Noix on 12 November, taking plunder and 39 prisoners with him. For the remainder of the war, Crown Point slumbered as a quiet backwater.

Paul David Nelson

See also

Amherst, Jeffrey; Arnold, Benedict; Burgoyne, John; Canada, Operations in; Carleton, Christopher; Carleton, Guy; Fort Ticonderoga, New York; Gates, Horatio; Green Mountain Boys; Lake Champlain, Operations on; Montgomery, Richard; Saratoga Campaign; Schuyler, Philip; Valcour Island, Battle of; Warner, Seth

References

Bird, Harrison. *Attack on Quebec: The American Invasion of Canada, 1775.* New York: Oxford University Press, 1968.

Nelson, Paul David. *General Horatio Gates: A Biography.* Baton Rouge: Louisiana State University Press, 1976.

Stanley, George. *Canada Invaded, 1775–1776.* Toronto: Canadian War Museum, 1973.

Cruger, John Harris (1738–1807)

The Loyalist officer John Harris Cruger played a major role in Britain's southern campaign during the American Revolutionary War, leading forces in key engagements at Savannah and Augusta, Georgia, and at Ninety-Six and Eutaw Springs, South Carolina.

Born into a prominent New York family, Cruger married into the powerful De Lancey family and carved out a career for himself in local politics. Having succeeded his father as a member of New York City's governing council, he served as mayor in the 1760s and was the city's chamberlain at the commencement of the Anglo-American conflict. During the war itself, Cruger commanded one of the Loyalist battalions raised by his father-in-law, Oliver De Lancey, the acknowledged leader of New York's large Loyalist population.

In 1778, Cruger traveled south with the expedition led by Lieutenant-Colonel Archibald Campbell and participated in the capture of Savannah, Georgia, on 29 December. The following year Cruger was stationed at Fort Sunbury, Georgia, until he and his battalion were ordered to take part in the defense of Savannah against the allied French and American siege. In the disastrous assault on the city on 9 October 1779, Cruger's battalion successfully held its ground against an attack mounted by General Isaac Huger. Cruger was captured by the Americans at Belfast, Georgia, in June 1780 but was quickly exchanged for John McIntosh. In mid-August Cruger succeeded Nisbet Balfour as commander of the Loyalist stronghold at Ninety-Six, South Carolina, and led the relief column from there that helped lift the American siege of Augusta in September 1780.

In successfully defending Ninety-Six against a long American siege the following spring (22 May–19 June 1781), Cruger further distinguished himself. To repel the Americans, he had to marshal not only his Loyalist troops but a considerable number of civilians and a noncombatant force of black slaves. Also, although he was well furnished with provisions, he only had limited artillery power at his disposal. But Cruger prevailed and was commended for his conduct and gallantry by Sir Henry Clinton. Soon thereafter Cruger joined the main British Army in South Carolina and participated in the major battle at Eutaw Springs on 8 September 1781. He then proceeded with the army to Charleston, which the British were able to hold against the surrounding American forces until the end of 1782. After the war Cruger immigrated to England and died in London in 1807.

Keith Mason

See also

Augusta, Georgia, Operations at; Campbell, Archibald; De Lancey, Oliver; Eutaw Springs, Battle of; Fort Ninety-Six, South Carolina, Sieges of; Huger, Isaac; Savannah, Georgia, Allied Operations against

References

Lawrence, Alexander A. *Storm over Savannah: The Story of the Count d'Estaing and the Siege of the Town.* 1951. Reprint, Savannah, GA: Tara, 1979.

Lumpkin, Henry. *From Savannah to Yorktown: The American Revolution in the South.* New York: Paragon, 1981.

Ward, Christopher. *War of the Revolution.* 2 vols. New York: Macmillan, 1952.

Pierre-André de Suffren was a French captain who fought valiantly in Indian waters during the American Revolution. (Leonard de Selva/Corbis)

Cuddalore, Battle of (20 June 1783)

The Battle of Cuddalore was the last of five extraordinary engagements fought between squadrons commanded by British Admiral Edward Hughes and French Admiral Pierre de Suffren in the Indian Ocean in 1782–1783. Every action revealed Suffren's tactical superiority.

Following the encounter between Suffren and Hughes off the Indian coast near Trincomalee on 3 September 1782, there were no further naval operations during the winter due to the monsoon and hurricane season. As Hughes did not have access to Trincomalee, he left Madras on 17 October and by December was anchored at Bombay with a reinforcement of five ships of the line that had arrived from home ports. Suffren, meanwhile, lay at Trincomalee, but lack of supplies led him to establish his winter anchorage on the western end of Sumatra, in the Dutch East Indies, where he arrived, via Cuddalore, on 2 November, having lost the *Bizarre* (64 guns) as the result of an accident. On 20 December he weighed anchor again for the Coromandel coast and eventually reached Trincomalee on 23 February 1783. On 10 March he was reinforced by two 74-gun and one 64-gun ships, newly arrived from European waters, together with 2,500 troops, which were sent on to Cuddalore.

On 10 April Hughes, who now had eighteen line of battle ships to Suffren's fifteen, passed Trincomalee on his course from Bombay to Madras. This naval advantage, combined with the death of Hyder Ali, the Mysorean leader then at war with Britain, and the consequent weakening of the French position in India, encouraged the British to open operations against Cuddalore by land and sea. Troops therefore marched from Madras and camped south of Cuddalore near the beach, where they were supplied by ships offshore and covered from interference by sea by Hughes's fleet, then cruising to the south.

By the beginning of June the British had completely surrounded the city. On learning this, Suffren left Trincomalee and sighted Hughes's ships anchored off Porto Novo, just south of Cuddalore. Contrary winds made it difficult for Suffren to approach, and meanwhile Hughes weighed anchor and attempted to gain the weather gauge, which proved impossible due to shifting winds. In so doing he left the city unprotected, enabling Suffren to anchor off Cuddalore and disembark 1,200 troops to bolster the besieged town. He weighed anchor again on 18 June in order to confront Hughes.

Action commenced on 20 June. In all probability Suffren knew that he could not achieve a substantial victory, but by inflicting damage on his opponent he probably hoped that Hughes would be obliged to withdraw from the waters around Cuddalore to make repairs. Indeed, if Hughes could be prized from his position, the besieged city would be open to support from the sea or, if necessary, could be evacuated. Hughes steered northward, forming line on a port tack. Suffren followed suit, and the two fleets were parallel with, yet distant from, one another before the French finally bore down and came within point-blank range. Fighting lasted from about

4:00 until 7:00 P.M., and though no serious damage was inflicted to the ships' rigging on either side, the hulls suffered badly, and losses were heavy: 99 British killed and 434 wounded; 102 French killed and 386 wounded.

On the following morning Suffren anchored 25 miles north of Cuddalore, and though Hughes sighted him there on 22 June, several British ships had been severely damaged, 1,200 men were afflicted with scurvy, and water supplies were very low. Hughes consequently made for Madras, which he reached on 25 June. Suffren had arrived back off Cuddalore two days earlier. His reappearance and Hughes's absence jeopardized British military operations, for without the presence of friendly warships off the city, the supply ships had to flee on Suffren's approach.

Thus, the French had triumphed, for they had run off the British naval component of the siege and could now assist the garrison, Hughes having left the waters off Cuddalore even before the battle. Nevertheless, this was to be the last major naval action of the war and had occurred, in fact, five months after the contending parties had signed preliminary peace terms. Official notice arrived on 29 June, when a British frigate reached Cuddalore with news of the conclusion of peace.

Gregory Fremont-Barnes

See also

Hughes, Edward; India, Operations in; Negapatam, Battle of; Porto Praya, Battle of; Providien, Battle of; Sadras, Battle of; Suffren, Pierre-André de; Trincomalee, Battle of

References

Cavaliero, Roderick. *Admiral Satan: The Life and Campaigns of Suffren.* London: Tauris, 1994.

Clowes, William Laird. *The Royal Navy: A History from the Earliest Times to 1900.* 7 vols. London: Chatham, 1996.

Gardiner, Robert, ed. *Navies and the American Revolution, 1775–1783.* London: Chatham, 1996.

Morrissey, Brendan. *The American Revolution: The Global Struggle for National Independence.* San Diego, CA: Thunder Bay, 2001.

Currency, American

The most important financial innovation by Americans prior to independence involved the creation of paper currency backed solely by the fiat of provincial governments. Following the efforts of several colonies, over many decades, to issue paper money in an economy that was always short of circulating hard currency, at least three states commenced new issues of paper currency by May 1775 to strengthen their resistance movements, much as they had done during previous wartime emergencies.

Once delegates to the Second Continental Congress agreed to field a conventional military force, they too faced the daunting task of paying for it. Encouraged by Gouverneur Morris, Congress passed a currency bill on 22 June 1775 that issued $2 million in bills of credit. Congress apportioned the issue to the several states, first on the basis of wealth and then, when that proved incalculable, according to their estimated populations. Congress's initial goal was to retire the issue by collecting the currency as taxes rather than redeem it with specie, but less than 5 percent of Continental currency was ever collected through taxation. Continental currency would ultimately pay for nearly one-fourth of the cost of fighting the Revolutionary War, but not without severe inflationary consequences.

By the end of 1775, the issue of Continental currency had grown to a total of $6 million, a considerable sum given that the total money supply of the colonies at the beginning of 1775 was only $12 million. The market value of the currency immediately dropped due to the lack of a specie base and Congress's unwillingness to exercise self-restraint with new issues. By 1779 total emissions held a face value of $226.2 million but an estimated specie value of $45.5 million. The exact value of Continental currency, however, is nearly impossible to determine at any point.

In addition to Continental currency, state government paper issues totaled $210 million at face value and roughly $6 million in specie. Typically state governments devalued their currency to market value before implementing tax measures to retire their currency. The aggressiveness taken to redeem or retire the currency, however, varied from state to state.

The political and social repercussions of these substantial issues of paper currency are difficult to fully assess, but there is little question that rapid inflation damaged the war effort and contributed to political unrest. Soldiers, initially paid in Continental currency, were understandably shocked to see its purchasing power erode so quickly. Farmers refused to sell supplies to the Continental Army for paper currency, preferring instead to take specie, sometimes from the British Army, or to wait for higher prices.

Nationalists lost little time in trying to overcome the inevitable inflationary spiral of Continental currency. Many states passed legal tender laws to support their own ailing currencies. When these failed to increase demand for their paper, state governments implemented price controls to cap the inflationary spiral. From late 1776 to the summer of 1777, local committees set foodstuff prices, transportation rates, and even wages. Violators and speculators were fined, imprisoned, banished, or worse. In December 1776, the New England states agreed to a uniform schedule of prices and wage rates. Congress urged the middle and southern states to adopt a similar uniform code, but it was rejected. Another move for a uniform code gained momentum in early 1778. When Massachusetts rejected any further attempt at price controls, Congress called for their repeal everywhere. A few localities, however, continued them into 1780.

The American colonies began circulating their own currency prior to their independence. States issued their own, with Continental dollars coming a few months later. The issuances were initially unregulated, which caused a loss of market value and extreme inflation. (Library of Congress)

Farmers and merchants responded to price controls by hoarding their own supplies or refusing to sell goods at below-market prices. Taken together, inflation and price controls, combined with increased military demand, caused shortages in important goods. Soldiers suffered the most, best illustrated by George Washington's winter encampments at Valley Forge and Morristown. Hungry and unable to purchase needed supplies for themselves or their troops, Continental officers resorted to confiscation, which only alienated more potential suppliers.

In January 1780, the Continental currency was worth approximately one-fortieth of face value and worsened to at least a 100 to 1 exchange rate to specie by the end of the year. As a result, Congress deliberately devalued the "old tenor" dollars to one-fortieth of par and issued "new tenor" dollars to be exchanged for the old at a ratio of 1 to 20. The new tenor bills were to be redeemed in specie by 1786 and accrued 5 percent interest per year, a condition Congress proved unable to meet. Congress reserved 40 percent of the new issue for itself and distributed the remaining 60 percent among the states. The new tenor bills soon dropped to the value of their predecessors and then hovered at a low of 15–20 percent of par. But despite depreciation, the new tenor issue probably gave Congress and the states upwards of $6 million in specie purchasing power.

By the end of 1781 all Continental currency stagnated at a near worthless specie exchange rate of 100 to 1. Reaching such a negligible level, Continental currency began passing out of circulation. Had anyone tried to use these bills after 1781, it is estimated that they would have been worth no more than 500 to 1 in specie. State paper suffered a similar demise as states ceased trying to support their currencies and even repealed their legal tender laws. States accepted their own paper currency for tax payments, but only at the depreciated market value, which in Georgia and Virginia had slumped to a low of 1,000 to 1 in specie. Wartime paper currency was completely withdrawn from circulation by the end of 1783.

But the old currency was not destroyed. Speculators gambled that the national government or state governments would do something to redeem their currency. Their gamble paid off in September 1787, when the Philadelphia Convention announced its plan for a new government under the United States Constitution. All official debt instruments immediately began rising in value. As part of Alexander Hamilton's funding program in 1790, the new Congress redeemed the circulating old tenor monies at 100 to 1 and the new tenor monies at par.

Cary Roberts

See also
Congress, Second Continental and Confederation; Morris, Gouverneur; Morris, Robert

References

Ferguson, E. James. *The Power of the Purse: A History of American Public Finance, 1776–1790.* Chapel Hill: University of North Carolina Press, 1961.
Nettles, Curtis P. *The Emergence of a National Economy: 1775–1815.* New York: Holt, Rinehart and Winston, 1962.
Perkins, Edwin J. *American Public Finance and Financial Services, 1700–1815.* Columbus: Ohio State University Press, 1994.
Rothbard, Murray. *Conceived in Liberty.* Auburn, AL: Mises Institute, 1999.

Currency Act of 1764

Eighteenth-century Great Britain's economic policies were guided by mercantilism, a system of political economy that sought to direct the greater share of the economic output of a commercial empire, and particularly its hard currency, to its metropolitan center. But this system could create cumbersome monetary arrangements in overseas colonies. Britain's North American colonies lacked any standard, sound currency suited to their needs and had to use several awkward mediums of exchange. Import-export merchants used bookkeeping to record and balance trades in several currencies, but this did not meet the demands of the growing colonial economies. Other mediums of exchange included foreign and locally minted coins, but neither could be counted upon for ready acceptance. The colonists also used bills of credit, bonds, and large amounts of paper currency issued by various agencies, including several colonial governments. But with all these devices, the lack of a uniform currency usable in both Britain and the colonies hampered the ability of the colonists to conduct business and made it more difficult for British merchants to be paid for the goods delivered in America.

The Currency Act of 1764 was enacted by Parliament under the ministry of George Grenville, at the insistence of Britain's Board of Trade and its president, the Earl of Hillsborough, as a compromise between the positions of several interest groups, including merchants in the colonies and in Britain. The act specifically applied to Britain's American colonies south of New England, but it continued the basic policies of the Currency Act of 1751, designed solely for New England, as well as earlier laws. The 1751 act had permitted the issuance of paper money as legal tender for public debts but not private ones. The 1764 act prohibited both uses of paper.

Britain's effort to deal with America's currency problems seemed promising but ultimately failed. The colonists initially welcomed the law, but within a year there was strong support on both sides of the Atlantic for its repeal. This was due to the shrinking money supply in the colonies and to the fact that British merchants were finding that remittances were difficult to collect and sales hard to make when the colonists lacked an effective medium of exchange and were reduced to bartering.

The Currency Act was to be enforced in the colonies by the unpopular vice-admiralty courts, which had jurisdiction over a number of matters affecting shipping and the commerce it carried. But the passage of the Revenue Act of 1764 (the Sugar Act) overshadowed the Currency Act, passed just two weeks later. And when news of the Currency Act arrived in the colonies, it was accompanied not only by the Revenue Act but by news of the proposed Stamp Act, which occupied most colonists' attention for the next two years.

After the Stamp Act's repeal, however, Patriot organizations in several colonies sent news and information about the difficult currency situation to other colonies, and their legislatures pressed British officials to change the statute. The colonists never were able to gain the repeal of the Currency Act of 1764, and their attempts to subvert it met with limited success. Parliament did agree to make some modifications to the law in the Currency Act of 1770, but the Currency Act of 1764 remained an irritant and eventually became one of the grievances that the colonies held against Britain when the imperial crisis entered its final stages in 1774.

Andrew J. Waskey

See also
Currency, American; Grenville, George; Hill, Wills; Trade, Board of

References

Ernst, Joseph Albert. *Money and Politics in America, 1755–1775: A Study in the Currency Act of 1764 and the Political Economy of Revolution.* Chapel Hill: University of North Carolina Press, 1973.
Green, Jack P., with Richard M. Jellison. "The Currency Act of 1764 in Metropolitan-Colonial Relations, 1764–76." Pp. 429–463 in *Negotiated Authorities: Essays in Colonial Political and Constitutional History.* Edited by Jack P. Green. Charlottesville: University of Virginia Press, 1994.

Currytown, New York, Action at (9 July 1781)

In the action at Currytown, New York, a raiding party of Loyalists and Native Americans attacked the town, located near Canajoharie, killing some of the settlers and taking others as prisoners. Following the attack, a Patriot scouting party was able to track the raiding party to Sharon Springs Swamp, where a larger Patriot force attacked the raiding party. Mixed Loyalist–Native American raids in this part of the Mohawk Valley occurred during most of the war in an effort to drive the settlers away and deprive the Patriots of food supplies from the valley.

At about noon on 9 July 1781, a force of several hundred Loyalists and Native Americans surprised the settlers of Currytown when many of the inhabitants were in the fields working their crops. Realizing they were under attack, many of the settlers fled to their local fort or into the woods to hide. Unfortunately, not all were able to escape, and several settlers were captured or killed.

The first indication of the raid to those outside the settlement was columns of smoke rising from the village. The smoke was spotted by the troops at Fort Rensselaer, and the militia in the surrounding area was called out and collected. Captain Robert McKean led a militia party to Currytown and arrived at the village in time to help put out the fires and save some of the buildings.

A Patriot scouting party had been sent out before the raid. After the smoke was spotted from Fort Rensselaer, a messenger was sent after the scouting party to inform it of the raid. The scouts searched in the direction of Currytown, found the trail of the retreating raiders, and followed it to their camp in Sharon Springs Swamp. The scouting party relayed the location of the camp to Colonel Marinus Willett, who was commanding the local Patriot forces. Using this information, Willett gathered all available local militia and set out after the raiding party. The Patriots caught up with the raiding party at Sharon Springs Swamp and attacked them there.

Dallace W. Unger Jr.

See also

Loyalists; Native Americans; Sharon Springs Swamp, New York, Action at; Willett, Marinus

References

Boatner, Mark. *Encyclopedia of the American Revolution.* Mechanicsburg, PA: Stackpole, 1994.

Mays, Terry M. *Historical Dictionary of the American Revolution.* Historical Dictionaries of War, Revolution, and Civil Unrest Series, no. 7. Lanham, MD: Scarecrow, 1999.

Stone, William L. *Life of Joseph Brant-Thayendanegea: Including the Border Wars of the American Revolution, and Sketches of the Indian Campaigns of Generals Harmar, St. Clair, and Wayne, and Other Matters Connected with the Indian Relations of the United States and Great Britain, from the Peace of 1783 to the Indian Peace of 1795.* Vol. 2. 1838. Reprint, New York: Kraus, 1969.

Customs Commissioners, Board of

The Board of Customs Commissioners was established by the Townshend Acts as a part of the Customs Service reorganization in North America, with its headquarters in Boston. This body, as well as the other legislation detailed in the acts, drew the ire of the colonials, who indicated their displeasure through the dissemination of letters and pamphlets such as John Dickinson's *Letters from a Farmer in Pennsylvania.* Violence also erupted, leading to the event known as the Boston Massacre.

Operations in the colonial theater of the European wars of the previous fifty years eliminated potential dangers from Indians, the French, and the Spanish. The colonials believed that the end of hostilities on the American frontier would now result in greater economic and political freedoms for the colonies. However, Parliament now adhered to Sir William Blackstone's doctrine of virtual representation whereby all British subjects were deemed represented in Parliament, regardless of actual colonial participation. Such action by London only reinforced American determination to rely on the traditional rights of British citizens as reflected by the Magna Carta.

Prior to Charles Townshend becoming prime minister, the colonies had an ally at court in William Pitt (the Elder). Pitt believed that the colonials were entitled to all the rights of other English subjects, no matter which side of the Atlantic was their home. His appreciation for the application of English laws made him popular with the colonials, but when he became ill, Townshend, as chancellor of the Exchequer, was given the responsibility of regulating colonial finances. Whether Townshend did not recognize the subtleties of Pitt's application of English law to the colonies or simply didn't care is not clear. What is significant is that Townshend's conduct and application of the law to the colonies only further exacerbated tensions and gave the colonial radicals additional reasons to pursue independence.

The imposition of the Townshend Acts allegedly to procure funds for the operation of the empire angered the colonists. The Crown charged that its successes through the Treaty of Paris (1763), purportedly in defense of the colonies, had resulted in the existing financial and economic problems. Therefore, greater assistance was required from the members of the British Empire.

At the urging of their namesake, the Townshend Acts were passed by Parliament in 1767. While they taxed many items necessary to colonial life—glass, lead, paint, and tea—the

British political cartoon, circa 1774, titled "A new method of macarony making, as practised at Boston," showing colonists tarring and feathering a customs officer. (Library of Congress)

most onerous provision of the acts was the creation of the Board of Custom Commissioners. Its purpose was to curb and prevent smuggling, piracy, and exorbitant insurance claims for cargo on vessels marooned or beached intentionally. Up to the time of the board's creation, colonial customs had yielded approximately £2,000 in income at a cost of £9,000 for enforcement. Under the board, Britain's customs revenue grew to £30,000, compared to £13,000 in operating expenses. To enforce its new customs laws, the High Court of Admiralty would be represented in the colonies by vice-admiralty courts. Since admiralty courts were not of common-law derivation, juries were not required. The colonials saw this as a clear violation of rights granted them at Runnymede in 1215 and a method through which to control colonial government.

In December 1767, John Dickinson, a Philadelphia attorney, reacted to the Crown's actions. He did not mention the alleged legal specifics violated by the British Parliament but was one of the more forceful advocates of opposition to Parliament's actions. He wrote a dozen essays that denied London's right to tax the colonies but also charged the British government with corruption for the purpose of enslaving the colonies. His actions helped inspire resistance from organizations such as the Sons of Liberty. Dickinson's writings were disseminated throughout the colonies and served to incite an American population already on the verge of rebellion. He and other opponents of the Crown were especially concerned with the enforcement of British law toward the colonies under the new admiralty courts.

Prior to the Townshend Acts, colonial interests could easily frustrate Britain's enforcement of the Navigation Act of 1696 by influencing the conduct of both customs commissioners and the admiralty courts. But after the creation of the new Board of Customs and the reform of the vice-admiralty courts, the uncertainty regarding legal authority caused concern for the colonial merchants, who soon became apprised of the changing legal atmosphere. Since the admiralty courts were not common-law courts, neither provincial legislatures nor juries hindered them. The Board of Custom Commissioners also had the power to issue search warrants and writs of assistance (the First Continental Congress spoke against this intrusion of personal freedom), possessed greater and ill-defined search powers, and oversaw the operation of coastal search vehicles, all of which would be financed by customs revenues.

Arthur Steinberg

See also

Blackstone, Sir William; Boston, Massachusetts; Dickinson, John; *Liberty* Incident; Nonimportation Agreements; Pitt, William, the Elder; Townshend, Charles; Townshend Acts

References

Barrow, Thomas C. *Trade and Empire: The British Customs Service in Colonial America, 1660–1775.* Cambridge: Harvard University Press, 1967.

Dickerson, Oliver M. *The Navigation Acts and the American Revolution.* 1951. Reprint, New York: A. S. Barnes, 1963.

Ubbelhode, Carl, *The Vice-Admiralty Courts and the American Revolution.* Chapel Hill: University of North Carolina Press, 1960.

D

Dalling, John (1731?–1798)

John Dalling, a British Army officer and the governor of Jamaica, launched two unsuccessful offensives against Spanish Central America in 1779 and 1780.

Dalling was born in Suffolk, England, and entered the army as a young man. He attained the rank of captain by early 1753, was promoted to major in the 28th Regiment in February 1757, and came to America later that year. He took part in the 1758 capture of the French fortress at Louisbourg and in the decisive victory at Quebec in 1759, where he was wounded. In 1760 he received a promotion to lieutenant colonel of the 43rd Regiment, which he joined in Jamaica, and led the unit in the siege of Havana that same year. After the end of the Seven Years' War in 1763, he remained in Jamaica, serving with different regiments.

In 1767, Dalling was appointed lieutenant-governor of Jamaica and then served as acting governor from 1772 to 1774. He received a promotion to full colonel in January 1776 and the following year was promoted to major-general and became Jamaica's official governor. As governor, however, he was not particularly successful and quarreled frequently with the Jamaica Assembly. Jamaica's legislators blocked his efforts to withdraw troops from rural posts and resisted his plan to raise two regiments of free blacks to defend the island during an invasion scare in 1779. Dalling responded by angrily comparing the assembly to the American Congress.

Dalling had preferred a military command to the governorship and was soon devising plans to strike at Spanish possessions in Central America if Spain entered the war in support of France against Britain. His first expedition, an attack on Honduras in October 1779, captured Fort Omoa, but the Spanish recaptured it the following month. Dalling then undertook a more ambitious attempt to conquer Nicaragua and advance to the Pacific. This expedition set off in February 1780 but again ended in failure; the surviving troops were withdrawn in November. Although he was supported in these offensives by Lord George Germain, Dalling's expeditions into America's interior caused him to neglect the defense of West Florida. This resulted in the surrender of Pensacola to the Spanish in May 1781.

The Jamaica Assembly also disapproved of Dalling's military adventures, believing that he had placed the island's security in jeopardy by sending away troops needed for the island's defense against possible French or Spanish attack. The legislators demanded that the British government remove him, and in November 1781 he was replaced by Archibald Campbell.

Dalling returned to England, where he received a promotion to lieutenant-general in 1782 and was made a baronet in 1783. The next year he went to India to assume the command at Madras, which he held until 1786. He became a full general in 1796 and died two years later.

Jim Piecuch

See also

British West Indies; Jamaica; Nicaragua, Operations against; Omoa, Honduras, Capture of; West Indies

Reference

O'Shaughnessy, Andrew Jackson. *An Empire Divided: The American Revolution and the British Caribbean.* Philadelphia: University of Pennsylvania Press, 2000.

Dana, Francis (1743–1811)

The lawyer and public official Francis Dana served the Revolutionary government as a congressman and as a diplomat in France and Russia. His disappointing experience at the Russian court contributed to the support for isolationist policies in early American foreign affairs.

Although deeply sympathetic to American complaints against British rule, Dana initially hoped for reconciliation between Great Britain and its colonies. In 1774 he was elected to the Massachusetts House of Representatives but never served. Instead, he embarked on a secret trip to London, armed with letters of introduction from members of the Sons of Liberty, in an attempt to gauge official attitudes toward the possibility of relaxing some of Britain's colonial policies. He spent more than a year in England meeting with friends of the colonial cause but returned to America in April 1776 convinced that reconciliation could not be achieved.

Once Dana became a firm believer in the cause for independence, he committed himself to it wholeheartedly. Massachusetts again elected him to serve in its state legislature as well as in Congress. Though he had no military training or experience, he was selected to serve on Congress's Board of War. In 1778, he visited General George Washington at Valley Forge to discuss the Continental Army's command structure. Factions in Congress were unhappy with Washington and the course of the war and wanted more tactical control over the army. Dana negotiated a compromise between Congress and Washington, which resulted in a reorganization that was in line with Washington's needs. Dana was also part of the committee appointed by Congress to respond to the Carlisle Peace Commission, sent to America in 1778 by Lord North. George Johnstone, the most imprudent and naive of the three active commissioners, hoped that his long friendship with Dana would encourage negotiations, but Dana did not accommodate him. The commission's peace proposals did not recognize full independence, and Congress soon severed all communication with the commissioners.

Dana, meanwhile, quickly grew tired of the sectional politics and debates in Congress and returned to Massachusetts in 1778, where he was again elected to the state legislature. In 1779, although he had no prior diplomatic experience, he was nominated by John Adams to serve as official secretary to Adams's new mission to negotiate peace with Britain. Dana accompanied Adams on the voyage across the Atlantic and then over land through Spain and France. As they proceeded, Adams and Dana discussed their fear that America was in danger of becoming a French protectorate and shared their views of the proper direction of American foreign policy. They were concerned about the lack of activity or even attention in Congress in regard to foreign matters. The committee in charge of foreign affairs rarely met, so authorization for any action came slowly. Dana and Adams also disagreed with Congress's emphasis on political alliances, instead recognizing that the future of the United States lay in negotiating effective commercial relations with foreign nations. Adams developed such a deep trust in Dana that when he traveled to Holland to secure loans for America, he left Dana in charge of all his public business in Paris.

Francis Dana. Secretary to John Adams and American representative to the Court of St. Petersburg for two years, he was unsuccessful in persuading Russia to support the Patriot cause. Dana also signed the Articles of Confederation. (Library of Congress)

On 19 December 1780, Congress appointed Dana to serve as America's first envoy to Russia. Several neutral European nations, under Russian leadership, had formed an alliance called the League of Armed Neutrality to protect neutral maritime shipping against the Royal Navy. Congress hoped that Dana could secure recognition for the United States from the league and bring about a quicker end to the war. Before Dana left for Russia, he consulted with both Adams and the French foreign minister, the comte de Vergennes, on how to approach the Russian court of Catherine the Great. They agreed that Dana should travel as a private citizen and first determine the Russian court's openness to receiving an

American official before trying to present his credentials. Adams arranged for his own son, John Quincy Adams, to accompany Dana and serve as his secretary. The two left Holland for Russia on 7 July 1781.

Dana and the young Adams arrived in St. Petersburg on 27 August 1781. As he had no official status, Dana had to rely on intermediaries to learn or do anything. His orders from Robert R. Livingston, Congress's new secretary of foreign affairs, subordinated Dana to the French minister to Russia, the Marquis de Verac. According to Dana, Verac was even less knowledgeable of foreign affairs and the current Russian court than Dana himself. His one contact at court, Count Panin, had fallen out of the tsarina's favor and was no longer an asset. Dana spent two years in Russia but achieved little. After the military defeat of General Charles Cornwallis at Yorktown in October 1781 and then Holland's recognition of American independence in April 1782, Dana's stock in Russia rose, but not enough to convince Catherine to recognize either him or America. Dana's unofficial status, the opposition of the influential British minister to Russia, and the diplomatic custom of offering cash gifts to important persons at court all prevented Dana from obtaining an official audience with Catherine, much less a favorable position with the League of Armed Neutrality, and Dana left Russia in August 1783.

Although Dana did not achieve diplomatic victories while in Europe, his experience there would have a lasting impact on American foreign policy. Dana was convinced that America's interests in foreign affairs, particularly in Europe, should be commercial only. His reports spoke of the "entangling alliances" of Europe that America should avoid. Congress officially affirmed Dana's isolationist views in a formal resolution passed while Dana was on his voyage back to the United States, and America's aversion to political alliances would persist in the administrations of Washington and Adams in the 1790s.

Upon his return to America, Dana declined any further foreign service and, in May 1784, agreed to return to Congress as a delegate from Massachusetts. Less than a year later, however, he resigned his seat to return to his private law practice. In 1785, Massachusetts's Governor John Hancock appointed Dana to the Massachusetts Supreme Judicial Court, where he would serve until he retired in 1806. Dana also attended the state's constitutional convention in 1788, where he argued in favor of Massachusetts ratifying the new federal Constitution. He remained in Massachusetts until his death in 1811.

Michael C. Miller

See also

Adams, John; Carlisle Peace Commission; Catherine II, Empress of Russia; Continental Army; Diplomacy, American; League of Armed Neutrality

References

Cresson, W. P. *Francis Dana: A Puritan Diplomat at the Court of Catherine the Great.* New York: Dial, 1930.

Dana, Elizabeth Ellery. *The Dana Family in America.* Cambridge, MA: Wright and Potter, 1956.

Madariaga, Isabel de. *Britain, Russia, and the Armed Neutrality of 1780: Sir James Harris's Mission to St. Petersburg during the American Revolution.* New Haven, CT: Yale University Press, 1962.

Wharton, Francis, ed. *The Revolutionary Diplomatic Correspondence of the United States.* 6 vols. Washington, DC: U.S. Government Printing Office, 1889.

Danbury, Connecticut, Raid on (25–28 April 1777)

In late April 1777, Major-General William Tryon conducted a destructive raid against Danbury, Connecticut, then fought his way back to the safety of British warships on the coast. In the spring of 1777, General William Howe at New York formulated his plan of operations for the upcoming campaign, part of which was to destroy American supplies, particularly gunpowder and cannon, at the outset. On 20 April, he gave Tryon command of an expedition against Danbury, where a large magazine of Patriot military stores was located. Assisted by Sir William Erskine and Brigadier-General James Agnew, Tryon embarked 1,800 troops in transports on 21 April and a day later sailed eastward on Long Island Sound under escort of two frigates. On 25 April, Tryon landed on the eastern side of the Saugatuck River and marched by way of Redding Ridge through the night and the following day toward Danbury. Reaching the town in the late afternoon, he swept aside a force of 150 Continental soldiers, then put his men to destroying thousands of barrels of beef, pork, flour, and rum as well as clothing and tents. The troops also burned the houses of prominent rebels.

On 27 April, Tryon began his return march to the coast by way of Ridgefield. Soon he received word that American militia forces under Generals Benedict Arnold, David Wooster, and Gold Silliman were gathering to contest his passage. About 5 miles from Danbury, Wooster attacked Tryon's rear guard with 200 men but was killed. His men retreated. At Ridgefield, Arnold and Silliman, with 500 militia, established a barricade across Tryon's route. In midafternoon, as Tryon approached the American position, he gave tactical command to Erskine. Throwing out flanking parties, Erskine routed the rebels and very nearly captured Arnold. A mile beyond Ridgefield, Tryon encamped his exhausted soldiers for the night. On the morning of 28 April he recommenced his march.

As he proceeded, Tryon was beset on all sides by the angry inhabitants of Connecticut, who fired from houses and from behind stone walls and fences. Bypassing two rebel roadblocks, he finally reached Compo Hill and saw British ships awaiting him about 5 miles away. He also saw Arnold's militiamen arrayed for battle, ready to oppose his use of a bridge across the Saugatuck River. But a Loyalist guide led Erskine around the American position to the landing place. There the British broke an American attack with a bayonet charge, and Tryon was able to embark his men without further difficulties. By 1 May, Tryon was back in New York, having suffered 171 casualties. The Americans had lost 95 men. The British considered the raid a success, but it did little more than inconvenience the Americans, who had removed all gunpowder and cannon before Tryon arrived.

Paul David Nelson

See also

Arnold, Benedict; Tryon, William

References

Lossing, Benson J. *The Pictorial Field Book of the Revolution.* 1951. Reprint, Rutland, VT: Tuttle, 1972.

Nelson, Paul David. *William Tryon and the Course of Empire: A Life in British Imperial Service.* Chapel Hill: University of North Carolina Press, 1990.

Ward, Christopher. *War of the Revolution.* 2 vols. New York: Macmillan, 1952.

Dartmouth, William, 2nd Earl of

See Legge, William, 2nd Earl of Dartmouth

Davidson, William Lee (1746–1781)

William Lee Davidson, a Continental officer and brigadier general of North Carolina militia, was born in Lancaster County, Pennsylvania, the son of Scots-Irish immigrants. In 1750 the family moved to Rowan (now Iredel) County, North Carolina. Educated in Charlotte, North Carolina, Davidson saw his first military action in Governor William Tryon's campaign against the Cherokee Nation in 1767. Commissioned a captain in the Rowan County militia in 1772, Davidson, a staunch American Patriot, became a member of the Rowan County Committee of Public Safety in 1774 and later took part in the Snow Campaign against Carolina Loyalists in December 1775.

Commissioned a major in the 4th North Carolina Regiment of the Continental Line, Davidson saw service in the Cape Fear region in May 1776 and later joined General George Washington's army in Pennsylvania. Promoted to lieutenant colonel for his brave service at the Battle of Germantown in October 1777, he returned to North Carolina on recruiting duty for the state's depleted regiments in April 1778. Following further active service in New Jersey, he accompanied the North Carolina Continentals on their march south to join General Benjamin Lincoln's garrison in Charleston in 1780. Davidson had been granted a furlough to visit his family and, unable to rejoin his regiment, escaped Lincoln's surrender in May. Although Davidson was a regular Continental officer, he then placed himself under the local militia commander in western North Carolina, General Griffith Rutherford. Seriously wounded at Coulson's Mill in July 1780, Davidson, a popular local figure, was appointed brigadier general of militia in the Salisbury District on 31 August 1780.

In an attempt to delay General Lord Charles Cornwallis's pursuit of General Daniel Morgan following Morgan's defeat of Colonel Banastre Tarleton's forces at Cowpens in January 1781, General Nathanael Greene ordered Davidson to oppose Cornwallis's crossing of the Catawba River. Dividing his forces to cover both Beatty's and McCowan's fords, Davidson commanded a mounted reserve force to the rear. Cornwallis sent a diversionary force to Beatty's Ford on the night of 31 January 1781 while attempting a major crossing at McCowan's Ford. Alerted by picket fire, Davidson led his mounted force to McCowan's Ford where, while attempting to rally his forces, he was mortally wounded in the chest. His militia fled the field, and Cornwallis marched on to occupy Charlotte. An effective officer and partisan leader, Davidson was remembered by his fellow North Carolina Presbyterians in 1835 when they named Davidson College in his honor. Many of his personal effects are still on display in the college library.

Rory T. Cornish

See also

Cherokees, Operations against; Cornwallis, Charles; Cowpens, Battle of; Germantown, Battle of; Greene, Nathanael; Lincoln, Benjamin; Morgan, Daniel; Rutherford, Griffith; Tarleton, Banastre; Tryon, William

References

Davidson, Chalmers. *The Life and Times of General Lee Davidson.* Davidson, NC: Davidson College Press, 1951.

Rankin, Hugh F. *The North Carolina Continentals.* Chapel Hill: University of North Carolina Press, 1971.

Davie, William Richardson (1756–1820)

A legendary military leader during the Revolution, William Richardson Davie would become an advocate of reforming the Articles of Confederation, a delegate to the Constitutional Convention, a governor of North Carolina, a diplomat, and a lawyer of great importance to the life of the early republic.

Born in County Cumberland, England, the son of Archibald and Mary Richardson Davie, William Davie was of Scottish descent. With his family, he immigrated to the Waxhaw settlement in South Carolina before pursuing his education in Charlotte, North Carolina, and at the College of New Jersey, where he earned his degree in 1776. After graduation, he proceeded to study law in Salisbury, North Carolina.

With the onset of the Revolution, Davie also joined the military effort and was quickly promoted in rank. As an officer, he served in many and varied capacities, including a stint as a cavalry officer, and was wounded at Stono, near Charleston, South Carolina. After a brief convalescence, he recruited and organized his own troops and assumed a major role in stopping the advance of General Charles Cornwallis at Charlotte Court House in September 1780. Davie was promoted to the rank of commissary general under the command of General Nathanael Greene, and in this role as a staff officer and key advisor Davie helped shape the military strategy that brought the Americans to triumph over the British Army in the South. By the end of the conflict, he was an acknowledged war hero and one of the most respected persons in North Carolina.

After the war, Davie resumed his legal career for several years but soon returned to public life. In 1786 he was elected to the North Carolina House of Commons, the state's lower house, where he would serve for twenty-two years. Chosen by the state to serve as a delegate to the Constitutional Convention, he advocated the need for a government that was "partly federal, partly national" while affirming the need to protect the status of individual states. He believed that states were the proper repositories of sovereignty in the federal system, and for this reason, he is most accurately characterized as a mild Federalist.

In the first North Carolina ratification convention, Davie was one of the strongest advocates for the adoption of the proposed U.S. Constitution. When the initial ratification effort failed, Davie began to organize and prepare for a second convention. At the second North Carolina ratification convention in November 1789, the Constitution was approved. Elected governor of North Carolina in 1798, the Federalist Davie successfully worked with the state legislature, even though that body was dominated by Jeffersonians. Amid rising tensions with France, President John Adams appointed Davie as a brigadier general in the army in 1799. In this capacity, he traveled to France in 1800 and helped negotiate the Convention of Mortefontaine, which calmed America's difficult relationship with France. Returning to North Carolina, he essentially retired from public life, except for an unsuccessful bid for the U.S. House of Representatives in 1803. Davie died on his estate in South Carolina in 1820.

H. Lee Cheek

See also

Adams, John; Charlotte, North Carolina, Action at; Constitution, United States; Constitution, United States, Ratification of; Greene, Nathanael; Stono Ferry, South Carolina, Action at

Reference

Bradford, M. E. "William Richardson Davie." Pp. 172–174 in *Founding Fathers: Brief Lives of the Framers of the United States Constitution,* 2nd ed. Lawrence: University Press of Kansas, 1994.

Dayton, Elias (1737–1807)

Militia captain, soldier in the Continental Army, and public official, Elias Dayton was a prominent citizen of Elizabeth Town, New Jersey. Trained as an artisan, he served as lieutenant and then captain in the Jersey Blues, a colonial militia unit in the French and Indian War (1754–1763). He was present at the signing of the peace treaty with Chief Pontiac outside Detroit in 1764.

Dayton served as a member of the local committee of thirty-one appointed in December 1774 to enforce the measures of the First Continental Congress. In January 1776 he became colonel of the 3rd Battalion, New Jersey Line, in the Continental Army. That same month, he led the capture of the *Blue Mountain Valley,* a British merchant ship that ran aground off Sandy Hook, New Jersey. This coup prompted the Continental Congress to authorize privateering to encourage the seizure of enemy vessels.

Stationed at Albany, New York, in May 1776, Dayton's unit built Fort Dayton and Fort Schuyler and defeated Indian raids at Johnstown and German Flats. On 21 May 1776, General Philip Schuyler dispatched Dayton with 300 men to arrest Loyalist leader Sir John Johnson at Johnson Hall. By the time Dayton arrived, Johnson had fled to Canada. Returning to Morristown, New Jersey, in March 1777, Dayton's unit saw action at Bound Brook, Staten Island, and Brandywine and defended New Jersey from British raids in 1779. In 1779, Dayton also accompanied General John Sullivan on his western expedition. Dayton's regiment participated in the action at Springfield on 23 June 1780, successfully keeping British troops from reaching Morristown. In the reorganization that followed a mutiny by New Jersey troops in January 1781, he was made colonel of the 2nd New Jersey Regiment. The regiment, together with a second regiment from Rhode Island, served under his command at the siege of Yorktown in the fall of 1781. While leading his troops, Dayton had three horses shot dead from under him—at Springfield, Germantown, and Crosswick's Bridge. Upon Washington's recommendation, Dayton was made a brigadier general in January 1783 and served until his unit's discharge in November of the same year.

After the war, Dayton was a member of Congress (1787–1788), a New Jersey assemblyman (1791–1792 and 1794–1796), and mayor of Elizabeth Town (1796–1797 and 1801). In 1799, the State of New Jersey promoted Dayton to major general of its second militia division. Dayton had married Hannah Rolfe in

1757. Their eight children included Jonathan (1760–1824), a delegate from New Jersey to the Constitutional Convention. Dayton died in Elizabeth Town on 22 October 1807.

Jason Mazzone

See also

Bound Brook, New Jersey, Action at; Brandywine, Battle of; Elizabeth Town, New Jersey, Raids on; Fort Dayton, New York; Germantown, Battle of; Johnson, Sir John; Morristown, New Jersey, Continental Army Winter Quarters; New Jersey, Operations in; Privateering; Schuyler, Philip; Springfield and Connecticut Farms, New Jersey, Raids on; Staten Island, New York, Actions at; Sullivan, John; Sullivan Expedition; Yorktown, Virginia, Siege of

References

Bill, Alfred Hoyt. *New Jersey and the Revolutionary War.* New Brunswick, NJ: Rutgers University Press, 1992.

Di Ionno, Mark. *A Guide to New Jersey's Revolutionary War Trail for Families and History Buffs.* New Brunswick, NJ: Rutgers University Press, 2000.

Wright, William C., ed. *New Jersey in the American Revolution.* Trenton: New Jersey Historical Commission, 1973–1976.

Silas Deane. The first American diplomat sent to France during the American Revolution, he became one of the most vilified men of the Revolutionary era after being accused of mismanaging American funds for his own profit through his connection with the dummy company Rodrigue, Hortalez et Cie. He was recalled from Paris after France joined the war in 1778. (Library of Congress)

Deane, Silas (1737–1789)

In 1776, after two terms in the Continental Congress, the Connecticut merchant and lawyer Silas Deane traveled to France to purchase arms and trade goods for the United States. He served as a joint American commissioner to France from December 1776 until March 1778, helping negotiate commercial and military treaties with the French government. In 1778 Congress recalled him to Philadelphia in order to investigate charges that he had misappropriated public funds. Although Deane was not formally charged with wrongdoing, the investigation and the intrigue surrounding it destroyed his diplomatic career. He soon returned to Europe, eventually settling in London. When letters in which he urged reconciliation with Britain were published in the Loyalist press, his contemporaries assumed that he had entered the service of the British government. Deane died amid mysterious circumstances, possibly by suicide or murder. Cupidity and contentiousness marred his diplomatic career. His friendship with the American doctor and British double agent Edward Bancroft led Deane to be accused of espionage, but he was probably guilty of little more than opportunism and poor judgment.

Born into a Connecticut family of modest means, Deane graduated from Yale, became a lawyer, and added the "e" to the end of his surname. Two canny marriages catapulted him to affluence and political power. He was elected to the Connecticut General Assembly in 1768 and served several terms. By the mid-1770s he was actively protesting British policies, contributing to the relief of Boston after the closure of its port, and acting as secretary of the Connecticut Committee of Correspondence. He was also a member of the Susquehannah Company, a group of Connecticut merchants who laid claim to the Wyoming Valley in northeastern Pennsylvania and sponsored settlement efforts there.

Deane represented Connecticut during 1774–1775 in the First and Second Continental Congresses. Already a firm advocate of independence, he focused his energies on commercial development. He served on committees to arm Continental troops and provision the Continental Navy. He also appropriated Connecticut funds for the Ticonderoga expedition, earning him the nickname "Ticonderoga." He clashed with his fellow Connecticut delegate Roger Sherman, however, and as a result was not reappointed to Congress in October 1775.

Frustrated in his political career, Deane sought other government appointments and soon secured a brace of diplomatic commissions to France. On 19 February 1776, the Secret Committee of Congress, created to obtain munitions and military supplies from abroad, contracted with him at a 5 percent commission to purchase goods for the Indian trade. The Committee of Secret Correspondence, the Continental Congress's embryonic diplomatic service, commissioned him in March 1776 to sound out French intentions with respect to American independence, contact American agents and American sympathizers in Europe, and purchase 100 pieces of artillery and uniforms for 25,000 troops.

Setting off immediately, Deane traveled to France by way of Spain, arriving in Paris in early July 1776. For the next five months he was the only congressional agent in France. He spoke no French and posed as a merchant traveling on private business in a halfhearted attempt to deceive British spies. Though anxious about his reception, Deane succeeded in obtaining a private interview with the French foreign minister, the comte de Vergennes, who hinted that outmoded French weaponry might be made available to the rebellious colonies. Vergennes put Deane in touch with Pierre-Augustin Caron de Beaumarchais, a playwright who had previously handled delicate diplomatic missions for the French court.

Beaumarchais and Deane soon created a dummy company, Rodrigue, Hortalez et Cie, to disguise the sale of French arms to Congress. The French government lent the company money with which to purchase obsolete weapons from French arsenals; the company then sold these weapons to Congress on credit. By March 1777, Beaumarchais and Deane had chartered nine merchantmen to carry French arms to North America. Many of them reached New York (via Portsmouth, New Hampshire) in time to assist American troops in defeating General John Burgoyne's army at Saratoga in October 1777.

Deane, however, soon found it difficult to repay Rodrigue, Hortalez et Cie for the arms he had purchased on credit. According to his contract with the firm, Congress was supposed to repay Rodrigue, Hortalez et Cie by shipping tobacco and other goods to France as soon as vessels could be obtained. But as the months went by, no tobacco arrived, and Congress did not reply to the company's numerous letters. Arthur Lee, who joined Deane as an American agent in Paris at the end of 1776, had persuaded Congress that the company's arms shipments were meant to be gifts of the French government and that Deane and Beaumarchais planned to appropriate any payments for themselves. Although Lee's explanation of the arms shipments clearly contradicted Deane's contract with Beaumarchais, Congress found it convenient and did not pay the company. Vergennes eventually excused Congress from paying for the arms shipments.

Although Deane's efforts to obtain French arms for Congress were successful, he blundered in other aspects of his mission. He obtained few goods for the Indian trade, and he badgered Vergennes and other French officials to recognize American independence before official word of the Declaration of Independence arrived in France in November 1776. When French military men besieged Deane with pleas for commissions in the Continental Army, he hired many of them without congressional authorization. Two of Deane's choices, Johann de Kalb and the Marquis de Lafayette, turned out well, but others proved unpopular or embarrassing. Deane also recruited a pyromaniac, James Aitken, to set fire to British naval stores at Portsmouth, an absurd scheme that angered Vergennes.

Deane's worst blunder, however, was his involvement in a shady stockjobbing scheme with the American-born London physician Edward Bancroft. From his base in Paris, Deane passed secret information to Bancroft, who used it to manipulate the London stock and insurance markets. In order to maximize his profits, Bancroft also arranged to sell the information he received from Deane to the British government. Deane was probably unaware that Bancroft was a spy; Bancroft duped Benjamin Franklin as well. Lee later accused Deane of having cleared a profit of £60,000 from stockjobbing, but Deane claimed that he merely broke even.

In the autumn of 1776, Congress, intent on obtaining French military and financial assistance, appointed three commissioners to negotiate with the French government. In December, Lee and Franklin joined Deane in Paris, and a new phase of Deane's diplomatic mission began. He soon clashed with Lee, who had long distrusted him. Deane cooperated better with Franklin but continued to bully the French government in a manner that Franklin considered impolitic. In one episode, which took place in the summer of 1777, Deane's secretary, William Carmichael, countermanded the orders for an American naval captain, Gustavus Conyngham, to return home directly and instead authorized him to resume attacking British merchant ships. Conyngham had already been imprisoned for compromising French neutrality by using Dunkirk as a base for military cruises. It is not clear whether Deane connived in Carmichael's plot, but his impatience for French recognition of the United States often embarrassed or angered his French associates.

Between December 1777 and February 1778, Deane, Franklin, and Lee negotiated two treaties with Vergennes' deputy, Conrad-Alexandre Gérard. The Treaty of Amity and Commerce provided for commercial reciprocity and French recognition of the independent United States, while the Treaty of Alliance secured France's entrance into the American Revolutionary War and forbade either France or the United States from making a separate peace with Britain. Even before these negotiations opened, however, Congress had grown increasingly dissatisfied with reports of Deane's activities in Paris. In September 1777 Congress repudiated Deane's unauthorized military commissions to French soldiers and in November 1777 recalled him to the United States.

Congress's recall of Deane was controversial in Paris. It alienated Vergennes, who interpreted it as a preemptive strike against the Franco-American Alliance. It also sparked a squabble between Lee, who was Deane's harshest critic, and Franklin, who penned an approving letter to Congress on Deane's behalf. When Deane reached America in July 1778, accompanied by Gérard, who had been designated the first French minister to the United States, he stepped into an even muddier political arena. New England and Virginia radicals, led by Samuel Adams and Richard Henry Lee, Arthur Lee's brother, united in criticizing Deane's conduct, while more commercially minded moderates, such as James Duane and Robert Morris, defended him.

In September 1778 Congress began to investigate charges that Deane had misappropriated public funds. It also considered whether dissension among the American commissioners in France had harmed the conduct of public business. The inquiry dragged on for months without proving any substantial wrongdoing. Gérard, who perceived the Adams-Lee party as hostile to the French alliance, took Deane's side. In December, Deane injured his own cause by publishing the ferocious *Address . . . to the Free and Virtuous Citizens of America,* in which he charged Arthur Lee with opposing the French alliance, corresponding with prominent Britons, and elevating his own family at the expense of the public good. Deane's indictment of Lee touched off a press war that raged for months.

In August 1779 Congress finally discharged Deane, at the same time declining to settle his accounts from his diplomatic mission. Deeply embittered, Deane was obliged to return to France to set his affairs in order and recoup his fortune. In the summer of 1780 he reestablished himself in Passy, where he sought to break into the Franco-American trade and secure contracts to outfit French and Spanish naval vessels. Both ventures failed, as did his land speculations in the Old Northwest.

During Deane's second sojourn in France, rumors circulated that he had ceased to support the American cause. Vocal and opinionated, Deane alienated many Americans with his repeated complaints about Congress's treatment of him and with his insistence that European regard for the United States was declining. In 1781, some of Deane's letters, supposedly intercepted in transit, were published in the New York Loyalist press. Many Patriots concluded that Deane had become a British publicist; Franklin, once supportive of Deane, broke off contact with him. Deane denied having sold out to the British, but he acknowledged having written the bitter sentiments expressed in the published letters. This alone was enough to alienate many of his former allies.

In 1781 Deane, impoverished and friendless, moved from Paris to Ghent; in 1783 he settled in London. There he received visits from Benedict Arnold. Arnold's advances embarrassed Deane by confirming popular suspicions that he, like Arnold, was a traitor. A more welcome visitor was Bancroft, who offered Deane financial and medical assistance. Deane continued to dabble in grandiose commercial schemes, such as the construction of a canal from Lake Champlain to the St. Lawrence River. Congress tarried in settling Deane's accounts. As early as 1784, Deane complained that he feared they would never be settled; in June 1789 he appealed unsuccessfully to President George Washington and to John Jay to intercede with Congress on his behalf. The Board of Treasury did not complete its report about the debts of the old Congress until 14 August 1789, and Deane, who died in England five weeks later, probably never learned about it.

In the summer of 1789 Deane decided to return to the United States. He died suddenly aboard ship, just off the British coast at Deal, Kent, on 23 September 1789. Deane's death has been variously attributed to stroke, tuberculosis, suicide, or murder. Bancroft, who was an expert in exotic poisons, has often been implicated in Deane's death. The true cause, like the precise reasons for his passage from American diplomat to British sympathizer, may never be determined.

Darcy R. Fryer

See also

Adams, Samuel; Arnold, Benedict; Bancroft, Edward; Beaumarchais, Pierre-Augustin Caron de; Carmichael, William; Conyngham, Gustavus; Diplomacy, American; Franklin, Benjamin; Gravier, Charles, Comte de Vergennes; Jay, John; Kalb, Johann, Baron de; Lafayette, Marquis de; Lee, Arthur; Rodrigue, Hortalez et Cie; Secret Committee of the Continental Congress

References

Boyd, Julian P. "Silas Deane: Death by a Kindly Teacher of Treason?" *William and Mary Quarterly* 16 (1959): 165–187, 319–342, 515–549.

Dull, Jonathan. *A Diplomatic History of the American Revolution.* New Haven, CT: Yale University Press, 1985.

Goldstein, Kalman. "Silas Deane's Preparation for Rascality." *The Historian* 43 (1980): 75–97.

James, Coy Hilton. *Silas Deane, Patriot or Traitor?* East Lansing: Michigan State University Press, 1975.

Potts, Louis W. "Deane, Silas." *American National Biography* 6 (1999): 296–298.

Declaration of the Causes and Necessity of Taking Up Arms (6 July 1775)

Congress issued its Declaration of the Causes and Necessity of Taking Up Arms in early July 1775. Written by John Dickinson of Pennsylvania and Thomas Jefferson of Virginia, principally for an American audience, the declaration was designed to be read by George Washington to the newly formed Continental Army gathering in Cambridge, Massachusetts. In the aftermath of the Battle of Bunker Hill, Congress intended the declaration to show that the American colonies had been unduly attacked and to build support for the colonies by explaining the reasons they had justifiably responded with force.

One of several statements made by Congress in the summer of 1775, including addresses to the people of Ireland, Canada, Jamaica, and Great Britain, the declaration was prepared by a five-member committee nominated on 23 June. The following day the committee delivered to Congress an ardent draft composed by John Rutledge of South Carolina. After some debate, Congress postponed further consideration of the draft until 26 June, when Dickinson and Jefferson were added to the committee.

Jefferson, who had first entered Congress only two days earlier, set aside the Rutledge copy and wrote his own draft. Congress, however, also found Jefferson's submission too extreme in its language, and the more moderate Dickinson reworked it during the next two weeks. Moderating some of Jefferson's rhetoric yet retaining his core ideas, Dickinson strengthened the overall document. Jefferson's distinctive voice, especially his theory of empire, can still be seen in the finished text. Reminiscent of arguments found in Jefferson's pamphlet *A Summary View of the Rights of British America* (1774), the final declaration explained that settlers had come to America at their own expense in money and blood, in the process settling the "distant and inhospitable wilds of America, then filled with numerous and warlike barbarians." The prosperous societies they founded, Dickinson and Jefferson argued, had even saved the British Empire in the Seven Years' War. But Parliament's "pernicious project" to enslave their "devoted colonies" destroyed this once healthy relationship.

Patriotic ardor and shock at the outbreak of hostilities governed this document, even from Dickinson's cooler pen. After listing familiar grievances, centering on unjust taxes and the denial of basic English rights, Jefferson and Dickinson turned to immediate events from April to June 1775. Commenting on the occupation of Boston by British troops, they wrote: "By this perfidy wives are separated from their husbands, children from their parents, the aged and the sick from their relations and friends, who wish to attend and comfort them; and those who have been used to live in plenty and even elegance, are reduced to deplorable distress." British troops had "butchered our countrymen" and had "wantonly burnt Charlestown," while General Thomas Gage was "exerting his utmost power to spread destruction and devastation around him." In the final draft, Dickinson reported breaking news that purported to prove Britain's unnatural and uncivilized prosecution of hostilities had larger objectives than Boston. "We have received certain intelligence that General Carleton, the Governor of Canada, is instigating the People of that Province and the Indians to fall upon us; and we have but too much reason to apprehend, that Schemes have been formed to excite domestic Enemies against us." Further evidence of the plot unfolding before them, Britain's excitement of proxy fighters, including Indian tribes and the vague term of "domestic enemies"—which could mean anything from Tory sympathizers to emancipated slaves—was the final justification needed to prove that America's self-defense was justified and right.

"Our cause is just. Our union is perfect. Our internal Resources are great, and if necessary, foreign Assistance is undoubtedly attainable." These strong words reflect the Continental Congress's angry mood in July 1775. Yet despite this defiant statement declaring America's resolution to resist force with force, any movement toward national independence was distant. Leaving open the possibility for reconciliation, the conclusion reflects Dickinson's discomfort with the strident earlier drafts: "Lest this Declaration should disquiet the Minds of our Friends and Fellow-Subjects in any part of the Empire, we assure them that we mean not to dissolve that Union which has so long and so happily subsisted between us, and we sincerely wish to see restored." Dickinson went on to reassure wary colonists: "We have not raised Armies with ambitious Designs of separating from Great Britain."

At this early stage of the war, Dickinson was not the only delegate concerned with how Congress appeared in the view of the wider world. Although no copy of the Rutledge draft has survived, it must have been much too extreme. The purpose of the Declaration of the Causes and Necessity of Taking Up Arms was for Washington to read it to the assembling army, and since he had left Philadelphia on 23 June, any delay would have prevented him from receiving it in time for it to be his first statement to the troops. Had Rutledge's copy been sufficient, it could have been rushed to Washington en route. Instead, it took more than two weeks to get the tone just right, and Washington had arrived in Cambridge before Congress agreed to the Jefferson-Dickinson iteration on 6 July. Dickinson's cooler draft, especially his leaving the door open for reconciliation, was more acceptable to a shocked but still mostly loyal public. Once the declaration did arrive in Massachusetts, the president of Harvard read it to the troops on 10 July, to loud shouts and, according to one newspaper report, acclamations for the soldiers, who were promised that "their names, unsullied, would be transmitted to the latest catalogue of fame."

Robert G. Parkinson

See also

Boston, Massachusetts; Bunker Hill, Battle of; Carleton, Guy; Congress, Second Continental and Confederation; Dickinson, John; Gage, Thomas; Jefferson, Thomas; Rutledge, John

References

Boyd, Julian P. "The Disputed Authorship of the Declaration on the Causes and Necessity of Taking Up Arms, 1775." *Pennsylvania Magazine of History and Biography* 74 (1950): 51–73.

———, ed. *The Papers of Thomas Jefferson.* Vol. 1. Princeton, NJ: Princeton University Press, 1950.

Marston, Jerrilyn Greene. *King and Congress: The Transfer of Political Legitimacy, 1774–1776.* Princeton, NJ: Princeton University Press, 1987.

Rakove, Jack. *The Beginnings of National Politics: An Interpretive History of the Continental Congress.* New York: Knopf, 1979.

Declaration of Independence

On 4 July 1776, the Continental Congress endorsed and agreed to publish the Declaration of Independence. This defining document of the American Revolution was the first

The presentation of the draft Declaration of Independence to Congress by the committee: John Adams, Robert Livingston, Roger Sherman, Thomas Jefferson, and Benjamin Franklin. (National Archives and Records Administration)

public announcement that the thirteen British North American colonies had declared themselves totally free from British authority and regarded themselves as constituting a new nation, the United States of America. The core of the Declaration, coming after an introductory statement that included a brief set of constitutional principles that would guide the new nation, was a detailed public justification for this revolutionary action.

Given the nationalistic consequences of the American Revolution for the United States, it is easy to believe that the Declaration of Independence was the culmination of a long movement by colonial Americans to achieve full national independence and self-determination. Yet prior to 1774, the colonists had rarely considered the idea of independence, and even after fighting began in 1775, few openly advocated it before Thomas Paine compellingly declared "'tis time to part" in *Common Sense*, published in January 1776. Indeed, many colonial delegates to the Continental Congress remained open to the possibility of a full reconciliation with Great Britain in the fall of 1775. British officials, by contrast, voiced concerns about the possibility of American independence throughout much of the eighteenth century. By the 1760s, these concerns intensified as several Britons came to portray independence not only as the natural result of American population and economic growth but also as a budding American aspiration that required preemptive, corrective policies by Great Britain.

To check colonial aspirations for autonomy and to gain revenue, the British government made several attempts to restrict the rights and power of its North American colonies in the 1760s. Royal supervision of the colonial assemblies tightened, and in 1763 the Crown issued the Royal Proclamation Line, which barred the colonists from settlement and trade in the area west of the Appalachain Mountains. Parliament enacted new taxes upon the American colonies in its Stamp Act (1765) and Townshend Acts (1767); in its 1766 Declaratory Act it declared the colonies subordinate to the laws and authority of the king and Parliament "in all cases whatsoever." The American colonies vigorously rejected and resisted these new restrictive policies, sometimes violently, and justified many of their actions with customary British arguments that taxation without representation was tyranny. In the mid-1760s, James Otis and a few other colonials saw colonial representation in Parliament, not independence, as the best means of solving the conflict over Parliament's authority to tax the American colonies.

By the early 1770s, few American or British leaders openly advocated the extension of parliamentary representation. Parliament, however, still asserted its authority to govern the

American colonies. In the winter and spring of 1774, it enacted the five Coercive (or Intolerable) Acts as a punitive response to the Boston Tea Party of December 1773. Again, the American colonies coordinated a unified resistance to Parliament's claimed authority over them, but even aggressive British enforcement of these acts did not prompt clear commitments by Americans for independence. Rather, colonial delegates to the First Continental Congress agreed to a broad commercial resistance against efforts to subordinate the American colonies. Most important for the subsequent development of the Declaration of Independence, this Congress commissioned, and on 14 October 1774 endorsed, a Declaration of Rights, which asserted that the delegates had convened "to obtain such establishment, as that their religion, laws, and liberties may not be subverted." This declaration firmly rejected Parliament's authority to tax the colonies without their consent and demanded the repeal of a list of acts by Parliament that violated American rights to life, liberty, and property as well as, among others, the right to representation in their colonial assemblies and the right to assemble peacefully.

The path to independence in 1776 became clearer, although still not inevitable, once British troops fought with Americans at Lexington and Concord, Massachusetts, in April 1775. Colonial delegates to the Second Continental Congress met in May 1775, and by mid-June they agreed to establish the Continental Army to defend the colonies. In its Declaration of the Causes and Necessity of Taking Up Arms, Congress declared in July 1775 that it had no "ambitious designs of separating from Great Britain, and establishing independent states." The declaration concluded: "With an humble confidence in the mercies of the supreme and impartial Judge and Ruler of the Universe, we most devoutly implore His divine goodness to protect us happily through this great conflict, to dispose our adversaries to reconciliation on reasonable terms, and thereby to relieve the Empire from the calamities of civil war."

In August 1775, King George III proclaimed in his Privy Council that the American colonies were in open rebellion, effectively withdrawing his protection from them. British troops could now be deployed in any American town and against any American colonials considered to be in rebellion, and Britain began raising additional troops to secure the submission of the colonies. In December 1775 the king signed an act of Parliament prohibiting all trade with the American colonies until their rebellion ended. By April 1776, the Second Continental Congress responded with legislation that defiantly opened American ports to the world, authorized the seizure of British goods, and banned the importation of slaves—in effect, declaring the colonies independent of the authority of both the British king and Parliament. In May 1776, Congress called upon the colonies to establish new governments that would "best conduce to the happiness and safety of their constituents in particular, and America in general." Congress also learned that more than 10,000 British-hired German mercenaries had been sent to the rebellious American colonies and called for the active suppression of royal authority to preserve the "internal peace, virtue, and good order, as well as for the defense of their lives, liberties, and properties, against the hostile invasions and cruel depredations of their enemies."

Various provisional assemblies also made commitments to colonial independence. On 12 April, North Carolina authorized its congressional delegates to vote for independence; other delegates received similar instructions that permitted them to do so as well. On 15 May 1776, the Virginia Assembly more decisively instructed its congressional delegates to propose a formal declaration of independence, the formation of foreign alliances, and the creation of a formal plan for an American confederation.

Given its own explicit rejection of Parliament's authority over the colonies in its 1774 Declaration of Rights and its rejection of all royal authority in the American colonies in May 1776, and given its hopes for foreign (i.e., French) assistance in resisting Britain's army and navy, Congress was coming to recognize the necessity of a public declaration of national independence. On 7 June 1776, Virginia delegate Richard Henry Lee, acting in accord with his state's 15 May instructions, proposed that Congress resolve "that these United Colonies are, and of right ought to be, free and independent states, that they are absolved from all allegiance to the British Crown, and that all political connection between them and the state of Great Britain is, and ought to be, totally dissolved." A final vote on Lee's proposal was delayed for more than three weeks (until 2 July 1776), but Congress promptly appointed a five-member committee to draft a public declaration announcing American independence to the American people and the world. This committee consisted of Thomas Jefferson of Virginia, John Adams of Massachusetts, Benjamin Franklin of Pennsylvania, Robert R. Livingston of New York, and Roger Sherman of Connecticut.

Jefferson chaired this committee, and its members concurred that he should take the lead in writing a draft of the Declaration. Jefferson was a young and relatively junior member of the Virginia delegation, having entered Congress only in 1775, but he was the celebrated author of the pamphlet *A Summary View of the Rights of British America* (1774), in which he argued on behalf of American rights and freedoms despite the "many unwarrantable encroachments and usurpations" by Parliament "upon those rights which God and the laws have given equally and independently to all." He was also known for his contributions to the most important congressional pronouncement since his arrival in Philadelphia, Congress's Declaration of the Causes and Necessity of Taking Up Arms.

Jefferson worked on the draft of the Declaration of Independence from 11 June until 28 June 1776. Few records of his efforts during this period exist, but according to his own recollection, his assigned task was "not to find new principles, or new arguments, never before thought of, not merely to say things which had never been said before, but to place before mankind the common sense of the subject; in terms so plain and firm as to command their assent, and to justify ourselves in the independent stand we are compelled to take." In short, "it was intended to be an expression of the American mind." To complete a working draft, Jefferson drew upon his previous writings, including his recent drafts for Virginia's state constitution. He was also influenced by the recently published Virginia Declaration of Rights, written by George Mason, and by the political works of Aristotle, Cicero, Algernon Sidney, and especially John Locke, among other writers. At Jefferson's invitation, fellow committee members Adams and Franklin reviewed and edited his work. According to the count of one historian, there were at least forty-seven editing changes made to Jefferson's first copy of the Declaration.

On 28 June 1776, the five-member committee submitted the draft of the Declaration of Independence to Congress for debate. The document bore the title "A Declaration by the Representatives of the United States Of America in General Congress Assembled." Congress debated the committee's work for three days, making substantive and stylistic changes that Jefferson at the time thought partially distorted his original work. Congress agreed to delete paragraphs that denounced the British people for their support of the Crown's violations of American rights, and it dropped the unnecessarily specific ethnic reference to the "Scotch & foreign mercenaries" hired by the Crown. In hindsight, the most significant change was the deletion of a paragraph written by Jefferson that identified the cruel injustice of human slavery and blamed its initiation and perpetration on the American people and on the slave trade supported by the British king.

On 2 July 1776, Congress approved the substance of Lee's 7 June motion by resolving that "these United Colonies are, and of right ought to be, Free and Independent States." The vote was unanimous except for New York, which temporarily abstained because its delegates lacked the necessary instructions. On 4 July, Congress approved its edited version of the Declaration of Independence. Less than a week later the New York Convention approved the Declaration, and on 19 July, after the 4 July text had been published and widely circulated, Congress resolved to have the Declaration engrossed on parchment with the title "The Unanimous Declaration of the Thirteen United States of America." It additionally agreed to permit every member of Congress at the time to sign the document, which most did over the next few months.

The Declaration of Independence was circulated in several ways. Printed copies of the initial document approved on 4 July 1776, signed only by President of Congress John Hancock and Congress's Secretary Charles Thomson, were sent to the provisional state assemblies, conventions, and committees of safety from New Hampshire to Georgia and to the commanding officers of the Continental troops. General George Washington, commander of the Continental Army, ordered it to be read to his troops in New York as a demonstration that "the peace and safety of this Country depends (under God) solely on the success of our arms." Copies of the now familiar 19 July version of the Declaration, with the signatures of fifty-six members of the Continental Congress added in August and later, were printed and circulated in January 1777.

The text of the Declaration of Independence has several distinct parts. It opens with the statement that the decision of the several colonies to dissolve the connection to an existing political order and become a new nation required a public declaration of "the causes which impel them to the separation." The Declaration continues with its most philosophical and famous statement: "We hold these truths to be self-evident, that all men are created equal, that they are endowed by their Creator with certain unalienable Rights, that among these are Life, Liberty and the pursuit of Happiness." The document subsequently contends that governmental authority is only legitimate when it aims to secure these rights and when it is based upon the consent of the governed. When a government neglects its proper purpose and when it acts without popular consent, it is a people's right and their duty "to throw off such Government, and to provide new Guards for their future security."

Like Congress's 1774 Declaration of Rights, the body of the Declaration of Independence provides a long list of British "abuses and usurpations" upon the American people. But whereas in 1774 these charges were made against Parliament, or against Britain generally, the 1776 Declaration levels a much longer list of accusations directly at George III and states that these "repeated injuries and usurpations" had as their "direct object the establishment of an absolute Tyranny over these States." As a result, the Declaration concludes that "these United Colonies are, and of Right ought to be Free and Independent States; that they are Absolved from all Allegiance to the British Crown, and that all political connection between them and the State of Great Britain, is and ought to be totally dissolved."

As a statement of constitutional belief, the Declaration gives voice to five general principles. The first principle is derived from the Declaration's foundational characterization of the physical world and of human nature in terms of their prior and shared Divine cause. The world is portrayed as the possession of God (or "Nature's God"), and the distinct human qualities of being "created equal" and "endowed" with individual rights that include "Life, Liberty, and the Pursuit of Happiness" are "unalienable" human endowments because they were given first by the "Creator," not by any particular government.

The second general principle, following from the first, is the Declaration's universalism. Although clearly intended as a statement with specific nationalistic significance for the United States, the Declaration boldly speaks out about human rights and the legitimacy of government in terms that extend across particular borders, peoples, and times.

The Declaration's third principle is its clear endorsement of forms of government dependent upon and open to public participation. Indeed, the Continental Congress commissioned and published the Declaration to be a public appeal to the American people and the world. The document, in addition, includes direct references to the "rights of Representation" and "the consent of the governed," thereby confirming the necessity of establishing and maintaining an elected, representative, and accountable form of government.

The fourth principle also concerns the form of government endorsed by the Declaration. Although less explicit than its unmistakable advocacy of popular forms of government, the Declaration declares the creation of both the "United States of America" and new "Independent States." It thus concisely articulates the dual nature and working tension of what subsequently came to be known as Federalism.

The fifth general principle defines the legitimate purposes of governments that are guided by "the consent of the governed." These governments, according to the Declaration, are to secure the human rights of "Life, Liberty and the pursuit of Happiness"; to pursue "the public good"; to maintain "the Administration of Justice"; and to protect the people from the "dangers of invasion from without, and convulsions within." When, however, a government fails in these basic purposes and "becomes destructive of" its proper ends, the Declaration recognizes "the Right of the People to alter or to abolish" their government "and to institute new Government."

Publication of the Declaration of Independence had immediate effects upon its intended domestic and international audiences. Domestically, it first was employed to rally and to give common direction to the efforts of the Continental Army as well as the Revolutionary leaders and armed militia already organized within each state. The Declaration also affected the whole American public, although in varied ways and to varying degrees. In many localities, the Declaration was published and read in public ceremonies, a practice widely ritualized by the 1790s into annual local Fourth of July celebrations of the birth of the United States. By contrast, for American Loyalists in 1776, the publication of the Declaration signaled that their lives likely would be disrupted, threatened, and possibly terminated by a disastrous civil war.

Internationally, the Declaration found other receptive audiences, and it was translated into several languages between 1776 and 1790. In Great Britain, the Declaration must have seemed anticlimactic to some because it confirmed what had long been suspected: namely, that the Americans aspired to independence and that the retention and submission of these rebellious colonies would be costly. To other European powers, such as France and the Netherlands, the Declaration of Independence and the Continental Congress's companion commitment to formulate a plan for an American confederation gave credibility to American agents seeking formal recognition of and financial and military support for the new United States.

Charles A. Kromkowski

See also

Adams, John; British Parliament; Congress, First Continental; Congress, Second Continental and Confederation; Franklin, Benjamin; George III, King of England; Jefferson, Thomas; Lee, Richard Henry; Paine, Thomas; Proclamation of 1763; Stamp Act; Townshend Acts

References

Becker, Carl L. *The Declaration of Independence: A Study in the History of Political Ideas.* New York: Knopf, 1942.

Friedenwald, Herbert. *The Declaration of Independence: An Interpretation and an Analysis.* New York: Macmillan, 1904.

Gewalt, Gerard W. "Drafting the Declaration." Pp. 1–15 in *The Declaration of Independence: Origins and Impact.* Edited by Scott Douglas Gerber. Washington, DC: CQ Press, 2002.

Kromkowski, Charles A. "The Declaration of Independence, Congress, and Presidents of the United States." Pp. 118–141 in *The Declaration of Independence: Origins and Impact.* Edited by Scott Douglas Gerber. Washington, DC: CQ Press, 2002.

———. *Recreating the American Republic: Rules of Apportionment, Constitutional Change, and American Political Development, 1700–1870.* Cambridge: Cambridge University Press, 2002.

Maier, Pauline. *American Scripture: Making the Declaration of Independence.* New York: Knopf, 1997.

Waldstreicher, David. *In the Midst of Perpetual Fetes: The Making of American Nationalism, 1776–1820.* Chapel Hill: University of North Carolina Press, 1997.

Declaration of Independence Signers

On 4 July 1776, the Second Continental Congress adopted the Declaration of Independence by a vote of 12 to 0, with New York abstaining. Immediately following the vote, Congress ordered that the Declaration be printed and distributed to all public officials, the Continental Army, and newspapers. John Hancock of Massachusetts, the president of Congress, and Charles Thomson, the secretary of Congress, signed the document with the changes from the final debate marked in it and sent it to a local printer. The original draft that went from Congress to the printer has never been found, but at least six other handwritten copies, five made by Jefferson and one made by John Adams, have survived. Sixteen of the original broadsides printed immediately after the vote have also been found.

A celebraton of the signing of the Declaration of Independence in Philadelphia, Pennsylvania in 1776. (North Wind Picture Archives)

On 8 July 1776, the Declaration was read to the American people for the first time in the yard of the Pennsylvania State House (Independence Hall). The Declaration was also read in public meetings in other major American towns, including Boston, Newport, New York City, Williamsburg, Charleston, and Savannah. On 9 July 1776, General George Washington ordered the Declaration read to every brigade in the Continental Army. At 6:00 P.M. on the evening of the same day, he mounted his horse and took his post with his men as they heard the Declaration read for the first time. He later reported to Congress that listening to the Declaration of Independence had a good effect on both his officers and his regular troops.

One week after the first public reading of the Declaration, the delegates from New York declared their support for independence. Four days later, on 19 July 1776, Congress ordered that the Declaration be written on parchment and made ready for all the delegates to sign. Congress also ordered that the title of the document be changed from "A Declaration by the Representatives of the United States of America in General Congress Assembled" to "The Unanimous Declaration of the Thirteen United States of America." The newly renamed document was finally ready for signing in Philadelphia on 2 August 1776. Delegate William Ellery of Rhode Island came to the front of the assembly and stood next to Thomson. Ellery said that he wanted to see each man's face as he signed his own death warrant. Hancock signed first in a large and bold hand. "There!" he said. "John Bull can read my name without his spectacles, and may he double his reward of £500 for my head. *That* is my defiance!" Hancock reminded his fellow delegates that if they wished to remain in Congress, they must all sign. "We must be unanimous," he said. "There must be no pulling different ways. We must all hang together." Benjamin Franklin lightened the mood by saying, "Yes! We must all hang together, or most assuredly we shall hang separately!" Benjamin Harrison of Virginia added that at least a big man such as himself would die quickly, while other smaller fellows would be swaying in the breeze for hours.

While fifty-six men eventually attached their names to the Declaration of Independence, probably only fifty took part in the signing ceremony on 2 August. A few delegates, such as Maryland's Charles Carroll of Carrollton, had not been present for the important votes on 2 and 4 July but signed in August. A few other delegates who had been present on those two days, such as General Oliver Wolcott of Connecticut and Colonel Thomas McKean of Delaware, were now away fighting with the Continental Army. Richard Henry Lee and George Wythe of Virginia, Elbridge Gerry of Massachusetts, and Matthew Thornton of New Hampshire were absent and so signed later. And John Jay of New York resigned from Congress so that he would not have to sign. Yet newly elected delegates who were not members of Congress in July, such as Benjamin Rush of Pennsylvania, signed because they were members in August.

The fifty delegates who were present in August signed in six columns arranged from right to left. After Hancock had signed, the delegations signed in the standard voting pattern from north to south, with New Hampshire listed first and Georgia listed last. Since signing the Declaration was a dangerous act, the names of the men were kept secret for several months. It was only after Washington's victories at Trenton and Princeton that Congress felt safe enough to reveal the names, and on 18 January 1777, it authorized a printing of the Declaration with the names of all the signers attached.

Of the fifty-six men who signed the Declaration, fourteen came from New England, twenty-one came from the middle colonies, and another twenty-one came from the South. Pennsylvania, with nine signers, had the largest group, while Rhode Island, with two, had the smallest. Most of the men were American-born and all were of British, and mostly English, descent. The eight signers who were not natives of the colonies had all been born in the British Isles. While a very few considered themselves Deists, most were Protestants. Only one, Carroll, was a Catholic. They were generally well educated by the standards of their day. About one-half had attended colleges in the colonies or in England, and most of the remainder were carefully educated at home or in local academies, but a few were totally self-taught. Most of the signers were prosperous men. Several had inherited their fortunes, but many others had amassed their wealth totally on their own. More than half of the signers were trained as lawyers, although many of them no longer practiced law. Other signers' trades ran the gamut from wealthy merchants and planters to ministers, doctors, craftsmen, and farmers.

While virtually all the signers were political, economic, and social leaders of their respective colonial societies, these fifty-six men risked losing everything, including their lives, by signing the Declaration of Independence. One-third of the signers served as militia officers, and a few of them saw actual combat at some point during the Revolutionary War. While none of the signers died directly at the hands of the British, they were all targeted for arrest. The British captured four of them and held them in prison for several months. The homes of nearly one-third of the signers were damaged or completely destroyed by the British Army or Loyalist forces. Many of their families, especially in New York and in the southern states, were scattered during the war. Still others loaned money or sold their own property to help finance the war. With few exceptions, most of the signers of the Declaration of Independence, like many officers and common soldiers in the Continental Army, found themselves to be much poorer men at the end of the American Revolution than they had been at the beginning. Yet despite the hardships the signers endured, most of them went on to serve in the governments of their home states and in the government of the United States created under the Constitution.

A table of the fifty-six signers, listed in alphabetical order by state and then by last name, appears below. For the order in which they signed in their state groupings, see the text of the Declaration of Independence in volume 5.

Connecticut	Samuel Huntington Roger Sherman William Williams Oliver Wolcott
Delaware	Thomas McKean George Read Caesar Rodney
Georgia	Button Gwinnett Lyman Hall George Walton
Maryland	Charles Carroll Samuel Chase William Paca Thomas Stone
Massachusetts	John Adams Samuel Adams Elbridge Gerry John Hancock Robert Treat Paine
New Hampshire	Josiah Bartlett Matthew Thornton William Whipple
New Jersey	Abraham Clark John Hart Francis Hopkinson Richard Stockton John Witherspoon
New York	William Floyd Francis Lewis Philip Livingston Lewis Morris
North Carolina	Joseph Hewes William Hooper John Penn
Pennsylvania	George Clymer Benjamin Franklin Robert Morris John Morton George Ross Benjamin Rush James Smith George Taylor James Wilson

Rhode Island	William Ellery Stephen Hopkins
South Carolina	Thomas Heyward Jr. Thomas Lynch Jr. Arthur Middleton Edward Rutledge
Virginia	Carter Braxton Benjamin Harrison Thomas Jefferson Francis Lightfoot Lee Richard Henry Lee Thomas Nelson Jr. George Wythe

Mary Stockwell

See also
Declaration of Independence

References

Bakeless, John, and Katherine Bakeless. *Signers of the Declaration of Independence.* Boston: Houghton Mifflin, 1969.

Cooke, Donald E. *Fathers of America's Freedom: The Story of the Signers of the Declaration of Independence.* Maplewood, NJ: Hammond, 1969.

Ferris, Robert G. *Signers of the Declaration: Historic Places Commemorating the Signing of the Declaration of Independence.* Revised ed. Washington, DC: United States Department of the Interior National Park Service, 1975.

Fradin, Dennis Brindell. *The Signers: The 56 Stories behind the Declaration of Independence.* New York: Walker, 2002.

Declaratory Act (18 March 1766)

With the end of the French and Indian War in 1763, Great Britain implemented a new policy of governance in its North American colonies. The intent was to make the colonies a more malleable and productive component of the British mercantile system. To accomplish this, the colonies would have to adhere more closely to customs regulations and forgo some of the independence they had enjoyed for more than a century, especially in regard to taxation. One of the strongest statements of this new imperial policy was the Declaratory Act of 1766, which asserted Parliament's complete authority over the colonies "in all cases whatsoever." When Americans realized the constitutional implications of the Declaratory Act, the legislation became an important obstacle to reconciliation between Britain and the thirteen American colonies.

The immediate precursor of the Declaratory Act was the Stamp Act of 1765, which aroused such violent opposition throughout the colonies that it was never implemented. Parliament repealed that act to prevent harming the commerce of the empire, but as part of the necessary compromise in Parliament for repeal, some of America's friends in the House of Commons agreed to join imperial hard-liners in passing the Declaratory Act on the very same day that the Stamp Act was repealed. Parliament thus temporarily sidestepped the constitutional dilemma by yielding on an unpopular statute to regain law and order in the colonies while asserting its constitutional authority to enact any measure it desired.

The preamble to the Declaratory Act, often overlooked by historians, stated that various colonies had illegally claimed "the sole and exclusive right of imposing duties and taxes upon his Majesty's subjects" and had in their assemblies "passed certain votes, resolutions, and orders, derogatory to the legislative authority of parliament, and inconsistent with the dependency of the said colonies . . . upon the crown of Great Britain." The body of the act declared that the colonies "have been, are, and of right ought to be, subordinate unto, and dependent upon the imperial crown and parliament of Great Britain" and that the Parliament "had, hath, and of right ought to have, full power and authority to make laws and statutes of sufficient force and validity to bind the colonies and people of America, subjects of the crown of Great Britain, in all cases whatsoever." Consequently, all colonial resolutions, votes, orders, and proceedings that questioned this imperial authority were declared to be "utterly null and void." The act brushed aside colonial arguments that Parliament could enact external legislation regulating trade but could not constitutionally enact internal taxes aimed at raising revenue.

As they rejoiced over the repeal of the Stamp Act, Americans at first paid little attention to the Declaratory Act. It seemed more important that an actual infringement on colonial constitutional rights was repealed than that a general theoretical authority was being enunciated. Many Americans thought that by repealing the Stamp Tax, Parliament was acknowledging in practice the validity of the American position that parliamentary taxation of the colonies was unconstitutional. The Declaratory Act was merely a face-saving maneuver. Fifty years later in a letter dated 1 January 1816 to Jedidiah Morse, John Adams reminisced about the American reception of the act. "The stamp act was repealed. Universal rejoicings had run like wildfire through the continent. But Chatham's declaratory act of the sovereignty of parliament hung like a cloud over the whole American continent. Thinking men and discerning eyes saw it, and amid all the popular rejoicings dreaded its ominous appearance. The public opinion thought it a brutum fulmen, a mere device to preserve the nominal dignity of Great Britain without any intention of ever bringing it forward into action."

Americans, however, soon began to appreciate the full significance of the Declaratory Act when in 1767 Parliament enacted the Townshend duties on selected imports into the colonies from Britain. This new tax package was the first legislation to follow the intention announced in the Declaratory Act. Other parliamentary measures in the years following fur-

British political cartoon showing a funeral procession on the banks of the Thames for the Stamp Act. While colonists rejoiced at the repeal of the Stamp Act, Parliament declared its sovereignty over the colonies in the Declaratory Act, enacted the same day as the repeal of the Stamp Act in 1766. (Library of Congress)

ther alienated the colonists, who came to realize that the Declaratory Act gave the imperial government carte blanche to do whatever it wished in administering the colonies. As long as the Declaratory Act stayed on the books, reconciliation was impossible.

Some politicians, more so in Great Britain than in America, believed that Americans objected more to the implementation of the right announced in the Declaratory Act than to the mere statement of principle. Charles James Fox asserted this opinion in the House of Commons in May 1775. In the same month William Pitt (the Elder), celebrated as one of America's greatest friends, proposed a conciliatory measure in the House of Lords that would, in effect, reword the Declaratory Act to recognize a limitation on parliamentary authority in America according to the objective of its legislation. Parliament, however, did not enact the bill.

Eventually, the Declaratory Act became an insuperable obstacle to reconciliation. Benjamin Franklin in February 1775 wrote that reconciliation with Britain was possible only if Parliament repealed the Declaratory Act, all acts levying taxes on American colonies, all acts repealing American colonial charters or constitutions, and all acts restricting the growth of American manufactures.

The Second Continental Congress, in its Declaration on the Causes and Necessities of Taking Up Arms (6 July 1775), asserted that there was no need to "enumerate our injuries in detail" because the Declaratory Act alone summarized Parliament's autocratic desire to rule over America. "By one statute it is declared, that parliament can 'of right make laws to bind us in all cases whatsoever.' What is to defend us against so enormous, so unlimited a power? Not a single man of those who assume it, is chosen by us; or is subject to our controul or influence; but, on the contrary, they are all of them exempt from the operation of such laws, and an American revenue, if not diverted from the ostensible purposes for which it is raised, would actually lighten their own misery in proportion as they increase ours." Congress declared that Americans wanted to live peacefully within the British Empire but "that our attachment to no nation upon earth should supplant our attachment to liberty." Rather, Americans would fight any nation "in defence of the freedom that is our birthright." Members of Congress from all of the colonies were of "one mind resolved to dye Free-men, rather than to live Slaves."

American writers used the Declaratory Act to justify their actions in declaring and then in defending their independence. Thomas Paine, in the opening paragraph of the first essay of *The American Crisis* (19 December 1776), encouraged Americans to stand up and fight for their liberties. "Tyranny, like hell," he wrote, "is not easily conquered; yet we have this consolation with us, that the harder the conflict, the more glorious the triumph. What we obtain too cheap, we esteem too lightly: it is dearness only that gives every thing its value. Heaven knows how to set a proper price upon its goods; and it would be strange indeed, if so celestial an article as FREEDOM should not be highly rated. Britain, with an army to enforce her tyranny, has declared that she has a right (not only to TAX) but 'to BIND us in ALL CASES WHATSOEVER,' and if being bound in that manner, is not slavery, then is there not such a thing as slavery upon earth. Even the expression is impious; for so unlimited a power can belong only to GOD." Paine asserted that the Declaration of Independence was a defensive act to protect American rights, not an offensive declaration of war.

Four months later, in his "Crisis" essay dated 19 April 1777, the second anniversary of the battles of Lexington and Concord, Paine again criticized the Declaratory Act as "the loftiest stretch of arbitrary power that ever one set of men, or one country claimed over another." The various taxes passed by Parliament, he argued, were merely the method that the British chose to implement their arbitrary policy. After the Americans had rejected all of Britain's taxes, the ministry resorted "to arms, as a means to establish both the right and the practice" of giving Parliament total authority. The ministry's real long-term goal, Paine believed, was the seizure of all American private property, which it would sell to pay the huge debt incurred in fighting the French and Indian War.

In 1778 the British ministry gave instructions to its peace commissioners (the Carlisle Peace Commission) that allowed them to back away from the Declaratory Act. But it was too late. By this time Americans had been fighting for their independence for nearly two years, and there was no turning back. The former colonies would no longer be satisfied with their old inferior status. Paine's analogy to Newtonian scientific logic in *Common Sense* (January 1776) had worked its magic in America. "Small islands, not capable of protecting themselves, are the proper objects for kingdoms to take under their care; but there is something very absurd in supposing a continent to be perpetually governed by an island. In no instance hath nature made the satellite larger than its primary planet, and as England and America, with respect to each other, reverses the common order of nature, it is evident they belong to different systems; England to Europe, America to itself."

When in 1777 Congress proposed a constitution providing for a perpetual union among the states and a new confederation government, the federal relationship was spelled out clearly. Article II of the Articles of Confederation provided that each state would retain its sovereignty and independence. Congress was to have only those powers that were "expressly delegated" to it by the Articles.

Four years after the end of the war, however, an American debate over the principles in Britain's Declaratory Act resurfaced. Antifederalists denounced the "necessary and proper" clause (the last clause of Article I, section 8) of the newly proposed Constitution of 1787 as a reincarnation of the despised British statute. According to the Constitution's critics, this indefinite clause would allow Congress to bind Americans and their states in all cases whatsoever. Federalists, however, maintained that the Constitution only delegated powers over general matters that the states were incompetent to handle. Although the Constitution was ratified, lingering doubts about the extent of Congress's power led Antifederalists to demand an explicit statement that Congress had only enumerated powers.

The Tenth Amendment to the Constitution (the last amendment in the Bill of Rights, passed by Congress in 1789 and ratified by the states in 1791) provided this clear statement, thereby setting a general guideline for the new American federal relationship. "The powers not delegated to the United States by the Constitution, nor prohibited by it to the States, are reserved to the States respectively, or to the people." Congress enjoyed many more powers under the Constitution than it had under the Articles of Confederation, but it would not have the total constitutional and political authority claimed by Parliament in the Declaratory Act.

John P. Kaminski

See also

Articles of Confederation; Carlisle Peace Commission; Congress, Second Continental and Confederation; Constitution, United States; Declaration of the Causes and Necessity of Taking Up Arms; Paine, Thomas; Stamp Act; Townshend Acts

References

Derry, John. *English Politics and the American Revolution.* London: Dent, 1976.

Donoughue, Bernard. *British Politics and the American Revolution: The Path to War, 1773–75.* London: Macmillan, 1964.

Jensen, Merrill. *The Founding of a Nation: A History of the American Revolution, 1763–1776.* 1968. Reprint, New York: Hackett, 2004.

Jensen, Merrill, John P. Kaminski, et al., eds. *The Documentary History of the Ratification of the Constitution.* 18 vols. to date. Madison: Wisconsin State Historical Society, 1970–.

Morgan, Edmund S., and Helen M. Morgan. *The Stamp Act Crisis: Prologue to Revolution.* 1953. Reprint, New York: Collier, 1963.

Reid, John Phillip. *Constitutional History of the American Revolution.* Abridged ed. Madison: University of Wisconsin Press, 1995.

Thomas, P. D. G. *British Politics and the Stamp Act Crisis: The First Phase of the American Revolution.* Oxford, UK: Clarendon, 1975.

———. *The Townshend Duties Crisis: The Second Phase of the American Revolution, 1767–1773.* Oxford, UK: Clarendon, 1987.

De Lancey, Oliver (1718–1785)

Born on his family's Long Island estate in 1718, Oliver De Lancey was the younger brother of James De Lancey, leader of the Anglican and Tory political faction in New York colonial politics and acting governor from 1753 until his death in 1780. As the longtime enemies of the Livingston and Schuyler families, the De Lanceys had cultivated close relations with both royal governors and influential figures in Great Britain. During the Seven Years' War, Oliver made a fortune provisioning British troops while also serving as the brigadier-general of the southern New York militia and leading them in an attack on Fort Ticonderoga in 1759. As a member of the governor's council, he made a brief alliance with the Sons of Liberty during the Stamp Act crisis in 1765, but quickly abandoned them over the issue of nonimportation.

Thereafter, De Lancey consistently sided with the British government, arguing that Boston should repay the costs of the tea destroyed at the Boston Tea Party and supporting Massachusetts's military governor, General Thomas Gage, whose wife was a De Lancey relative. As a Loyalist, De Lancey was removed by New York's Revolutionary government from his political and military positions in June 1776 and barely escaped arrest by the Committee against Conspiracy. He fled to the floating headquarters of New York's royal governor, William Tryon, where he waited for the arrival of the British Army and Royal Navy. When they arrived, the British commander, General William Howe, commissioned De Lancey to raise Loyalist regiments on Long Island and gave him extraordinary powers to enforce loyalty oaths among local property owners.

Along with his son-in-law John Harris, De Lancey raised and equipped 1,500 volunteers, organized into three battalions as the De Lancey Brigade. The brigade was present on Jamaica Heights during the Battle of Long Island and remained the primary coastal defense of Long Island throughout the British occupation of New York City. Its troops also performed as military police in New York City and brokered supplies from the Loyalist inhabitants for British forces. In 1778, two of De Lancey's three battalions went south to join the British Army, which was then besieging Savannah, and took heavy casualties, but De Lancey stayed behind with his third battalion to protect Loyalists on Long Island.

De Lancey, whose sons held regular commissions in the British Army, was particularly despised by New York's revolutionaries and suffered the sack of his Manhatten estate, Bloomingdale, in a clandestine raid in November 1777 and its confiscation under the Act of Attainder of October 1779. As traditional enemies of the Patriot Livingstons, Morrises, and Schuylers, there was no chance that the family could remain in New York after a British defeat. De Lancey and his family were evacuated with the British from Long Island in 1783, and he retired to Great Britain, where he died in 1785.

Margaret Sankey

See also

Associated Loyalists; Howe, William; Long Island, New York, Raids on; Loyalists; New York, Province and State; Savannah, Georgia, British Capture of; Tryon, William

References

Bonomi, Patricia. *A Factious People: Politics and Society in Colonial New York.* New York: Columbia University Press, 1971.

Fingerhut, Eugene R. "De Lancey, Oliver." Pp. 372–374 in *American National Biography,* vol. 6. Edited by John A. Garraty and Mark C. Carnes. New York: Oxford University Press, 1999.

Ketchum, Richard M. *Divided Loyalties: How the American Revolution Came to New York.* New York: Holt, 2002.

Sabine, William H. W. *Murder, 1776, and Washington's Policy of Silence.* New York: Theodore Gaus' Sons, 1973.

Delaware

First settled in the 1630s by Swedish and Dutch colonists, Delaware came under English rule in 1660. Delaware and Pennsylvania were governed as one colony by members of the Penn family or their designated lieutenants from the 1680s until 1776, but after 1701 they had separate legislatures. Many political leaders served as legislators, governors, or judges in both colonies, however, both before American independence and, as in the cases of John Dickinson and Thomas McKean, in the early national period as well. As with the other middle colonies, Delaware contained a wide variety of ethnic and religious groups by the time of the Revolution.

With a 1770 population of about 33,000, Delaware was, after Georgia, the least populous of the thirteen colonies that would rebel against Britain. The colony's location at the mouth of the Delaware River tied much of its economy to shipping, but it also produced abundant grain crops as well as fruit, cattle, and lumber. Numerous gristmills used the power of the Brandywine River just below the Pennsylvania border. The colonial capital was New Castle, but nearby Wilmington was both the colony's and the state's largest town. Other important towns included Dover, which later became the state capital, and Lewes in the heavily agricultural southern part of the state. Delaware stood at an important transportation crossroads: the Philadelphia Wagon Road ran through the northern part of the colony, and the Delaware River tied its economy to the coastal trade with several colonies.

Although a small state, Delaware proved of critical importance during the heated debate in Congress over independence in June and July 1776. Two of Delaware's delegation were split on the issue: McKean favored independence, while George Reed opposed it. The colony's third representative,

Thomas McKean served as a Delaware representative to the Continental Congress and later was chief justice of the Supreme Court of Pennsylvania. He remained prominent in both states for many years. (Library of Congress)

Caesar Rodney, was at home battling cancer. Each colony voted on each issue as one state, and Delaware's deadlock prevented Congress from the unanimous vote it needed on such a momentous issue. Informed of the deadlock, the ailing Rodney mounted his horse and rode 40 miles to swing Delaware into line for independence. With this vote, Delaware also gained full autonomy from Pennsylvania and drafted a new constitution later in 1776.

The war briefly came through Delaware during the 1777 Philadelphia Campaign. General William Howe's British army came up Chesapeake Bay to land at Head of Elk, Maryland, and marched through the northwest corner of Delaware on its way to Philadelphia. A brief skirmish at Cooch's Bridge, south of Newark, was the state's only Revolutionary War battle. The armies then moved north to fight at Brandywine. The Delaware River itself, however, remained strategically important since it provided access to Philadelphia. After the American capital fell to the British in late September 1777, the British fleet moved its base of operations from Chesapeake Bay to the Delaware River to supply Howe's army and stayed on the river until the British evacuated Philadelphia in June 1778.

Delaware contributed approximately 2,400 Continental soldiers and more than 1,000 militia to the war effort. The state also took pride in the Delaware Regiment, one of the best units of the Continental Army, that fought in nearly every major engagement of the war. The Delaware Regiment became famous for its tenacity at the battles of Long Island, Camden, Cowpens, and Guilford Courthouse.

After the Revolution, two of Delaware's opposing congressmen, McKean and Reed, helped write another state constitution. And following the Constitutional Convention in Philadelphia, Delaware was the first state to ratify the U.S. Constitution, earning it the nickname it employs to this day, "the first state."

Robert M. Dunkerly

See also

Constitution, United States, Ratification of; Cooch's Bridge, Delaware, Action at; McKean, Thomas; Rodney, Caesar

References

Commager, Henry, and Richard Morris, eds. *Spirit of 76.* New York: Da Capo, 1995.

Greene, Jack. *Pursuits of Happiness: The Social Development of the Early Modern British Colonies and the Formation of American Culture.* Chapel Hill: University of North Carolina Press, 1988.

Malone, Dumas. *The Story of the Declaration of Independence.* New York: Oxford University Press, 1975.

Murfin, James. *National Park Service Guide.* Washington, DC: National Park Service, 1974.

Taylor, Dale. *Everyday Life in Colonial America.* Cincinnati, OH: Writer's Digest Books, 1997.

Demerara and Essequibo, Dutch Guiana, Seizure of (1781, 1782)

These two Dutch settlements, on the Demerara and Essequibo Rivers in Guiana (now Guyana), South America, east of Venezuela, were seized by the British in February 1781 and then seized from the British by the French in 1782.

In the late 1500s and early 1600s the Dutch began settling on the Demerara and Essequibo Rivers, where they grew cotton and sugar. During the American Revolutionary War many Dutchmen, both in the Americas and in Europe, secretly supported the Americans. The British discovered this support and were determined to end it. In August 1780, the Dutch protested the British seizure of an American privateer anchored at their colony on the Caribbean island of St. Martin. The British replied that the Dutch had been supporting the American Patriots. On 20 December 1780, in part to prevent the Netherlands from joining the League of Armed Neutrality, Britain declared war on the Dutch. With the declaration of war, the British moved to seize several Dutch colonies in the West Indies and South America: St. Eustatius, St. Martin, Saba, Demerara, and Essequibo.

On 27 February 1781, six British privateers sailed up the Demerara River, seized fifteen Dutch ships anchored there, and threatened to attack Dutch settlements along the Demerara River and other rivers in Guiana. But the British governor of Barbados had just sent a demand that the Dutch colony surrender to the British. The Dutch opted to surrender to, and get protection against the privateers from, the governor of Barbados.

In 1782, a French force led by the Marquis de Lusignan captured Demerara and Essequibo from the British. The French returned the colonies to the Dutch, their allies, just after the war in 1784, but over the next thirty years the colonies would move back and forth between Dutch and British control until 1815, when Britain finally secured them. In the nineteenth century they became part of British Guiana and in the twentieth century were included in the independent nation of Guyana.

Dallace W. Unger Jr.

See also

British West Indies; French West Indies; League of Armed Neutrality; Netherlands; St. Eustatius, Operations against; West Indies

References

Burns, Sir Alan. *History of the British West Indies.* 2nd ed. London: Allen and Unwin, 1965.

O'Shaughnessy, Andrew Jackson. *An Empire Divided: The American Revolution and the British Caribbean.* Philadelphia: University of Pennsylvania Press, 2000.

Portrait of John Dickinson, Revolutionary leader, holding his *Letters from a Pennsylvania Farmer,* circa 1770. (Library of Congress)

Dickinson, John (1732–1808)

The Pennsylvania lawyer, politician, and statesman John Dickinson was one of the foremost political pamphleteers and orators of the American Revolutionary era. The work for which he is most often remembered, his series of newspaper articles later published collectively as *Letters from a Farmer in Pennsylvania* (1768), circulated widely throughout the colonies and met with immediate approval. But while the letters were popular, Dickinson was not afraid to take unpopular political stands. The most unpopular was his decision to oppose independence in the final debate in Congress because he still believed, as late as the summer of 1776, that reconciliation with Britain was the best course of action. Once Congress had declared independence, however, Dickinson supported the Revolution. After the war he became a strong supporter of the U.S. Constitution, writing the important "Fabius Letters" and playing a prominent part in the political life of the early American republic.

Dickinson was born on 8 November 1732 in Talbot County, Maryland, to moderately wealthy parents, Samuel and Mary Cadwalader Dickinson. When he was eight years old he moved with his family to Kent County, Delaware, where his father had accepted a judgeship, and settled at the plantation known as Popular Hall. Dickinson's early education was at the hands of his parents and then, with his older brother and neighbors' sons, by private tutors, including an Irishman named James Orr. At age eighteen Dickinson began reading law, first in Philadelphia with John Moland, a leading colonial lawyer, and then in London at the Middle Temple. Perhaps it was in this period that Dickinson acquired his lifelong interest in English legal and constitutional history, an interest that deeply influenced his political thought. Returning to America in 1757, he soon settled in Philadelphia where, being admitted to the bar, he opened his own legal office.

Having attained a measure of financial security, Dickinson turned to politics. In 1759 he was elected to the legislature for the Lower Counties (i.e., Delaware), in which he served from 1760 to 1762 as a member and as Speaker. In 1762 he was elected to the neighboring Pennsylvania Assembly. In 1764, he opposed the effort of Benjamin Franklin and Joseph Galloway to persuade the British Crown to nullify the proprietary charter of the Penn family and appoint a royal governor in Pennsylvania. Dickinson wanted the charter maintained. He thought that this was the safest course of action for Pennsylvania because he feared a changed atmosphere in London whereby the colonies risked losing the freedom they had hitherto enjoyed. It was during these eventful years that Dickinson became deeply interested in working out a better relationship between the colonies and the mother country.

In 1765, Dickinson published *The Late Regulations Respecting the British Colonies on the Continent of America Considered, in a Letter from a Gentleman in Philadelphia to His Friend in London* (1765). He argued, largely on pragmatic grounds, that the proposed changes in taxation contained in the Sugar Act of 1764 would be just as injurious to British commercial interests as they would be to the colonists forced to pay the increased taxes. In the midst of colonial opposition to the Stamp Act of 1765, Dickinson was appointed to represent Pennsylvania in the Stamp Act Congress held at New York. His reputation as an orator and writer must already have been well established by that time, for he was asked to draft the Congress's Declaration of Rights and Grievances, which he did. The following year he published a minor Revolutionary pamphlet, *An Address to the Committee of Correspondence in Barbados* (1766).

It was the twelve *Letters from a Farmer in Pennsylvania,* first published serially in the *Pennsylvania Chronicle* from December 1767 to February 1768, however, that gained Dickinson intercolonial and then international fame. In the letters, Dickinson provided an extended and measured attack on the Townshend duties. Modern scholars have rightly noted the rhetorical dimension of Dickinson's case, calling attention to its opening paragraph: "I am a Farmer, settled, after a variety of fortunes, near the banks of the river Delaware, in the province of Pennsylvania. . . . My farm is small; my servants are few, and good; I have a little money at interest; I wish for no more; my employment in my own affairs is easy; and with a contented grateful mind, undisturbed by worldly hopes or fears, relating to myself, I am completing the number of days allotted to me by divine goodness."

More persuasive to his contemporaries, however, was the political learning to which Dickinson's traditionally bucolic style was attached. He wrote in his second paragraph: "Being generally master of my time, I spend a good deal of it in a library, which I think the most valuable part of my small estate. . . . I have acquired, I believe, a greater knowledge in history, and the laws and constitution of my country, than is generally attained by men of my class." As this passage hints, Dickinson's political thought was not based on abstract natural rights but rather on rights historically particularized. He maintained that as British citizens, the American colonists had the right to be taxed only with their own consent. This was a position he found defended in David Hume's popular six-volume *History of England* (1754–1762), a work to which Dickinson frequently referred, as he did to Hume's four-volume *Essays and Treatises on Several Subjects* (1753).

Each of Dickinson's "Farmer" letters was immediately reprinted in other Pennsylvania papers, such as the *Pennsylvania Journal* and the *Pennsylvania Gazette,* and then reprinted, time and again, by newspapers throughout the British North American colonies. By March 1768, the individual letters had been collected together and published in Philadelphia as *Letters from a Farmer in Pennsylvania, to the Inhabitants of the British Colonies.* New editions soon followed. Colonial imprints survive from Philadelphia, New York, Boston, and Williamsburg; overseas editions appeared in London, Dublin, Paris, and Amsterdam. Circulating widely, the *Letters from a Farmer in Pennsylvania* set much of the agenda for colonial political debate in the late 1760s and early 1770s and established Dickinson's reputation, in America as well as in Britain, as the "Penman of the American Revolution."

Dickinson's authority was formidable in the years following the publication of the letters. He was recognized with an honorary doctorate from the College of New Jersey (now Princeton University) and was feted at public gatherings. His features were captured in a wax mold by London's "Promethean modeller," Patience Wright, and circulated in an engraving by Paul Revere. In 1770, Dickinson married Mary Norris, a devout Quaker heiress whose father, Isaac Norris, had been for many years the leader of Pennsylvania's Assembly. Thereafter much of Dickinson's domestic time was spent at Fairhill, the Norris estate.

As tensions mounted within the British Empire, Dickinson supported colonial rights and played a major role in organizing the Revolutionary movement in Philadelphia, but he also continued to hope, speak, and write for reconciliation. He did so as a member of the Pennsylvania Assembly, by short pieces for the newspapers, and as a delegate to the First Continental Congress in October 1774, where he helped draft various documents, including the "Address to the People of Quebec" and the "Address to the King." In the Second Continental Congress in July 1775, he helped prepare the so-called Olive Branch Petition to King George III and apparently wrote the final draft of the Declaration of the Causes and Necessity of Taking Up Arms. Even after the armed conflict at Lexington and Concord, however, Dickinson strove to bring the colonies back from the brink of rebellion. That stance lost him favor with many congressional delegates from New England, most notably John Adams, whose private letters (including one letter captured and published by the British) contain some unflattering references to Dickinson.

Dickinson's decision to speak against independence during the final floor debate on 1 July 1776 was not surprising; his stand was consistent with all he had written. Even in the final installment of his celebrated letters, he recommended to his fellow colonists, "You have nothing to do, but to conduct your affairs peaceably—prudently—firmly—jointly. By these means you will support the character of freemen, without losing that of faithful subjects—a good character in any government—one of the best under a British government." But Dickinson's consistent position began to look increasingly moderate against the growing radical spirit of the times.

Why Dickinson worked so long for reconciliation, even against a decidedly quickening tide, is not clear. It may have been that his experience with sectional interests in the colonies, coupled with his close reading of Hume, alerted him to the factional strife likely to result should the colonies become free and independent states. The Quaker faith of his wife, and his own early exposure to Quaker teachings, must also have played a role. Yet Dickinson came, slowly, to reconcile himself to the likelihood of military confrontation with Britain. He accepted a commission as colonel of the First Battalion of Associators in the City and Liberties of Philadelphia, an office that saw him directly involved with the city's earliest military maneuvers.

In 1779, Dickinson was elected to Congress as a representative from Delaware. In 1781 he was elected president (i.e., governor) of Delaware. The following year he was elected president of the Supreme Executive Council of Pennsylvania, although not without opposition from a radical element that had long suspected Dickinson of not being sufficiently committed to the Revolution as they saw it. In 1783 he helped to found a college in Carlisle, Pennsylvania, that was named, in his honor, Dickinson College.

In 1787, Dickinson was one of Delaware's delegates to the Constitutional Convention in Philadelphia. There, he continued to steer a pragmatic political course, explaining: "Experience must be our only guide. Reason may mislead us. It was not Reason that discovered the singular and admirable mechanism of the British Constitution. It was not Reason that discovered or even could have discovered the odd and in the eye of those who are governed by reason, the absurd mode of trial by jury. Accidents probably produced these discoveries, and experience has given sanction to them." Dickinson's nine "Fabius Letters," first published in the *Delaware Gazette,* helped to secure the Constitution's early ratification, especially in Delaware and Pennsylvania.

In 1801 Dickinson gathered together some of his major writings, which were published as *The Political Writings of John Dickinson, Esq., Late President of the State of Delaware and of the Commonwealth of Pennsylvania.* In his remaining years he was often in ill health. He died on 14 February 1808 and was buried at the Quaker burial ground in Wilmington, Delaware.

Mark G. Spencer

See also

Congress, First Continental; Congress, Second Continental and Confederation; Constitution, United States; Declaration of Independence; Franklin, Benjamin; Hume, David; Philadelphia; Stamp Act

References

Bradford, M. E. "A Better Guide than Reason: The Politics of John Dickinson." *Modern Age* 21 (1971): 39–49.

Colbourn, Trevor H. "John Dickinson, Historical Revolutionary." *Pennsylvania Magazine of History and Biography* 83 (1959): 271–292.

Flower, Milton E. *John Dickinson: Conservative Revolutionary.* Charlottesville: University of Virginia Press, 1983.

Ford, Paul Leicester, ed. *The Writings of John Dickinson,* Vol. 2, *Political Writings, 1764–1774.* Philadelphia: Historical Society of Pennsylvania, 1895.

Fredman, Lionel E. *John Dickinson, American Revolutionary Statesman.* Charlotteville, NY: SamHar, 1974.

Jacobson, David L. *John Dickinson and the Revolution in Pennsylvania, 1764–1776.* Berkeley: University of California, 1965.

Kaestle, Carl F. "The Public Reaction to John Dickinson's Farmer's Letters." *Proceedings of the American Antiquarian Society* 78 (1968): 323–359.

McDonald, Forrest, ed. "John Dickinson's Letters from a Farmer in Pennsylvania." Pp. 3–85 in *Empire and Nation.* Indianapolis: Liberty Fund, 1999.

Scull, Florence D. *John Dickinson Sounds the Alarm.* Philadelphia: Auerbach, 1972.

Stillé, Charles J. *The Writings of John Dickinson,* Vol. 1, *The Life and Times of John Dickinson, 1732–1808.* Philadelphia: Historical Society of Pennsylvania, 1891.

Tyler, Moses Coit. *The Literary History of the American Revolution, 1763–1783.* 2 vols. New York: Putnam, 1897.

Dickinson, Philemon (1739–1809)

Philemon Dickinson was a militia commander in New Jersey who offered crucial support to the Continental Army through most of the American Revolutionary War and later served as a statesman. He joined the New Jersey militia in 1775, was appointed colonel of a battalion, and by the end of the year was a brigadier general. Throughout the war he commanded militia units and proved to be very good at handling these sometimes unreliable forces. He excelled at reconnaissance, raiding, and harassing the British. His most successful raid was in January 1777 at Somerset Courthouse, New Jersey. Later that year he was promoted to major general and spent 1778 and 1779 harassing British troops in New Jersey and around New York City. After the war he was active in New Jersey politics, served in the Confederation Congress, and sat in the U.S. Senate.

Dickinson was born in 1739 in Maryland but grew up in Delaware. His father owned several estates in both states that young Dickinson managed before the Revolutionary War. He attended the College of Philadelphia, graduating in 1759, and then read law with his older brother, the celebrated Revolutionary pamphleteer John Dickinson. Philemon Dickinson was also a cousin of the prominent Philadelphian (and later Pennsylvania militia commander) John Cadwalader and married Cadwalader's sister Mary in 1767. After Mary's death, Dickinson married another of Cadwalader's sisters, Rebecca.

By 1775, Dickinson was living on his own estate near Trenton, New Jersey. In July, when New Jersey raised several battalions of militiamen, he was appointed colonel of one of them, the Hunterdon County Battalion. In October 1775, he was promoted to brigadier general for the province of New Jersey, and in 1776 he was elected to New Jersey's Provincial Congress.

Most of Dickinson's military career was spent leading militia troops, most often on raids or reconnaissance missions. During 1776 and 1777 he raided and harassed British foraging parties. His most spectacular success was on 20 January 1777 at Somerset Courthouse, New Jersey. There he led a force of 450 militiamen against a foraging party of 400

British regulars. Dickinson's men forced the British to withdraw, leaving behind forty supply wagons and one hundred horses. Dickinson resigned his commission on 15 February 1777, but on 6 June 1777 he returned to service with a promotion to major general and was made commander in chief of the New Jersey militia.

In November 1777, Dickinson led his troops as part of a raid on Staten Island, and in 1778 he took part in the campaign leading up to the Battle of Monmouth (28 June). Prior to the battle, his troops provided reconnaissance reports to General George Washington as the British advanced from Philadelphia. This timely intelligence kept Washington informed of where the British were moving and allowed him to react to their movements. Dickinson's men also destroyed bridges and roads in front of the advancing British force to slow them down prior to the battle. His troops, however, were not engaged in any significant fighting during the battle.

From December 1778 until November 1779, Dickinson was responsible for keeping open the communications line between the Delaware River and the Continental Army's headquarters at Newburgh on the Hudson River. He returned to a combat command in 1780, serving under General Nathanael Greene, and helped to defend against the British raid on Springfield, New Jersey. Dickinson also helped put down the mutiny by units of the New Jersey Continental Line in January 1781.

In 1782, Delaware elected Dickinson, who owned land in that state, to represent it in Congress. But by 1783, Dickinson was turning his full attention to New Jersey politics and served on the New Jersey Council as vice president from 1783 to 1784. Even during the war itself, Dickinson had run for governor in 1778, 1779, and 1780 but had lost each election to William Livingston. In 1785, Dickinson was chosen to serve on the commission charged with selecting a new site for the national capital, and in 1788 he ran for the U.S. Senate under the new Constitution but was defeated by William Paterson. When Paterson became governor of New Jersey, however, Dickinson was chosen to finish out Paterson's term from 1790 to 1793. Dickinson died in 1809.

Dallace W. Unger Jr.

See also

Cadwalader, John; Dickinson, John; Livingston, William; Militia, Patriot and Loyalist; Monmouth, Battle of; Somerset Courthouse, New Jersey, Actions at; Springfield and Connecticut Farms, New Jersey, Raids on; Staten Island, New York, Actions at

References

Blanco, Richard L., ed. *The American Revolution, 1775–1783: An Encyclopedia.* New York: Garland, 1993.

Boatner, Mark. *Encyclopedia of the American Revolution.* Mechanicsburg, PA: Stackpole, 1994.

Mays, Terry M. *Historical Dictionary of the American Revolution.* Historical Dictionaries of War, Revolution, and Civil Unrest Series, no. 7. Lanham, MD: Scarecrow, 1999.

Purcell, L. Edward. *Who Was Who in the American Revolution.* New York: Facts On File, 1993.

Diplomacy, American

The diplomacy of the new American nation had its roots in the relationship of the British North American colonies to the government in London. And from these beginnings, throughout the Revolutionary War, and into the postwar period, that diplomacy can best be described as making the best—often with great skill and surprisingly good results—out of inherently difficult situations. From its colonial origins to America's entry onto the world stage as an independent nation, the direction of American foreign policy was heavily influenced by the whims of more powerful states.

The Seven Years' War (1756–1763) was waged for nothing less than control of North America. The British decision to end the French presence on that continent held far-reaching consequences for the colonies. First, Britain had to secure control of its new territories. To do this, the government decided to garrison soldiers in the colonies and tax them to support the troops. Britain's military victory also forced the French to search out American political and commercial interests in the hopes of retaining some influence in North America. Etienne-François de Stainville, Duc de Choiseul, the French foreign minister under Louis XV, sent secret agents to America before the ink had dried on the Treaty of Paris (1763). These agents tried to cultivate a relationship with Benjamin Franklin but were spurned. The French representatives reported to Choiseul that a rebellion in America was inevitable, but not in the near future. Choiseul accepted these opinions without hesitation and bided his time.

British Prime Minister George Grenville's first mistake, in the eyes of the colonists, was his support of the Revenue Act of 1764, popularly known as the Sugar Act. This statute was designed to regulate trade in the colonies and to garner revenue from molasses. The act was a revision of the 1733 Molasses Act, but Grenville planned to vigorously enforce the 1764 version. Customs officials had never had much luck plying their trade in the colonies, and smuggling was rampant. According to Grenville, the Sugar Act would collect a moderate sum from the colonies (£78,000) to be used for the maintenance of the 7,000 soldiers stationed in America.

The Sugar Act and American opposition to it first began shaping the goals of a nascent diplomatic corps. American diplomacy for the next eleven years was a constant plea by Americans to have their rights (as they saw them) recognized and upheld by the king's ministers, then by Parliament, and finally by King George III himself. The first American diplomats were the colonial agents employed by various colonial legislatures to entreat with the British government. These agents had long represented individual assemblies in dealing with British authority. Most of the agents were not colonials but

The American commissioners (*from left to right,* John Jay, John Adams, Benjamin Franklin, and Henry Laurens) with Britain's David Hartley (*far right*) at the signing of the Treaty of Paris in 1783. (Library of Congress)

rather native Englishmen who had been enlisted by the colonies to represent them. The most famous colonial agent, however, and the father of the American diplomatic corps, was the Boston-born Philadelphian Benjamin Franklin. Other agents included Joseph Sherwood, Edward Montague, Jared Ingersoll, Charles Garth, and Richard Jackson. Jackson was, at various times and often simultaneously, not only a colonial agent for Massachusetts, Pennsylvania, and Connecticut but also a member of Parliament and secretary to Britain's chancellor of the Exchequer. These men sought to further their colonies' interests with both the government and the merchant class. In the 1760s, however, their role gradually changed from that of representatives of one or more colonies to spokespersons for the larger American cause. The event that began this change was the threatened passage of the Stamp Act.

When Grenville presented his Revenue Act of 1764 to Parliament, he added that it might be necessary to pass a Stamp Act to secure a revenue sufficient to meet the expense of governing and protecting America. He realized, however, that the colonies had never experienced a Parliament-imposed stamp duty and so postponed its enactment by one year. In the meantime, he waited to hear from the colonial agents concerning suitable alternatives to his proposal. In February 1765, just as Grenville was ready to present his stamp duty to Parliament, he met with Franklin, Ingersoll, Jackson, and Garth to discuss colonial reaction to the new measure. The colonial agents repeated the central argument they had been reciting for a year: the colonies preferred to tax themselves, and a stamp act would subvert representative government. Grenville ignored their arguments; he was determined to see his proposal through Parliament.

The Stamp Act was greeted with outbursts of resentment and hostility from Maine to Georgia, and Boston became a hotbed of radical activity and saw the worst violence during the riots following the act's passage. The Grenville ministry fell in July 1765 and was replaced by the ministry of Charles Watson-Wentworth, the Marquis of Rockingham. Rockingham planned to use the colonial agents to soothe any problems between Parliament and the colonies. Working with the London merchant community and the colonial agents, the Rockingham ministry quickly devised a repeal of the Stamp Act on economic grounds.

In the decade between the Stamp Act crisis and the outbreak of hostilities between America and Britain, the colonial agents increasingly found themselves in one of two camps as they repeatedly faced the question of imperial taxation. One side grew increasingly cool to their instructions from the colonial assemblies. By the time of Lexington and Concord, these agents, including Jackson and Edmund Burke, could not reconcile the colonial demands for legislative rights with the constitution of the British Empire. They could not come to terms with ideas that offended them as advocates of empire and as British subjects. Most agents of native English birth were in this camp.

Conversely, agents who had been raised in America, notably Franklin and Arthur Lee of Virginia, recognized the dilemma and supported the assemblies. The imperial crises of 1767 and 1773 only served to further the gulf between agents sympathetic to the American cause and those who grew exasperated with the colonies' outbursts. The colonies lost a key ally when they protested against the Townshend duties in 1767. The London merchant community withdrew its support for colonial protests because it grew tired of continual colonial threats of nonimportation and nonexportation. British merchants and colonial agents also soured on the shift in arguments from the colonies and saw the contest as no longer about being about taxation but rather about sovereignty. Agents such as Burke and Garth could not countenance such a challenge to the British constitution. While the British-born agents found themselves in a quandary, the colonial assemblies pondered their utility. New reasoning dictated that only American-bred agents could faithfully represent colonial interests. By the time of the passage of the Tea Act (1773), Franklin was the only agent who maintained any credibility among colonial assemblies. In the aftermath of the Boston Tea Party and the Coercive Acts (1774), the two camps finally set out clear boundaries concerning what the colonies could and could not do, and the agents sympathetic to the new colonial attitude began to see themselves as representatives of all the colonies.

The colonial response to the Coercive Acts was to convene an intercolonial meeting, the First Continental Congress, in Philadelphia in September 1774. Congress fell back on economic coercion, the mainstay of colonial protests. It prepared a petition, addressed to the king, stating its grievances, as by this time America did not even deign to address Parliament. Congress then instructed Franklin and Lee to present the petition to George III. This petition marks the first time that a unified American front, approximating a central government, gave orders to its agents abroad that they represent its interests to what was, in effect, already a foreign government.

As many Americans expected, however, George III did not respond to the petition but forwarded it to Parliament without even listening to arguments on its behalf. Even then Britain's secretary for America, Lord Dartmouth, attempted to negotiate a deal with Franklin. By early 1775, however, the American constitutional position had advanced too far to accept anything less than substantial autonomy within the empire. If the British could not accept this, a bid for full independence was inevitable—though it would take most American statesmen another year to see this. Yet even stalwart defenders of American liberties such as Burke and Lord Chatham (William Pitt the Elder) could not bring themselves to condone any action that might completely sever the ties between the colonies and England.

When the Continental Congress reconvened in May 1775, the recent outbreak of armed conflict had sharply reduced any hope for reconciliation, but the delegates made one last attempt. Despite the violence at Lexington, Concord, and Bunker Hill, there were those in Congress who still hoped for rapprochement with Great Britain. Congress addressed its last petition (the Olive Branch Petition of July 1775) to the king, and, making no mention of Parliament, asked George III to remove all obstacles to reconciliation. The petition never made it past the ministry's American department, and in August 1775 George III proclaimed the colonies in a state of rebellion.

While George III and his first minister, Lord North, were preparing to quell the rebellion, the French foreign minister, Charles Gravier, the comte de Vergennes, acting on the advice of the French ambassador to Britain, sent a secret agent to treat with the Continental Congress. Julien-Alexandre Achard de Bonvouloir's mission to America was a milestone in American diplomacy. Bonvouloir, working with Congress's Committee of Secret Correspondence, laid the groundwork that would provide the Continental Army with supplies and eventually an ally. As Bonvouloir was preparing to depart for America, a dramatist and entrepreneur offered his services to Vergennes. The minister put Caron de Beaumarchais (later the author of *The Marriage of Figaro*) on the French secret service payroll and ordered him to London, where he was to report on British attitudes toward the rebellion. Beaumarchais quickly fell in with Lee, and together the two, along with Bonvouloir, would play an important role in establishing the Franco-American Alliance.

In order for an alliance to develop, however, Americans had to respond to French efforts. In the summer of 1775, Congress was initially hesitant to explore alliance possibilities with European nations, even though Franklin, now a member of Congress, had urged his colleagues to do this since his return in the spring. Once the king declared the colonies in open rebellion, Congress acted to gauge world opinion of its activities. On 19 November 1775, Congress established a Committee of Secret Correspondence "for the sole purpose of corresponding with our friends in Great Britain, Ireland, and other parts of the world." This committee, consisting of Franklin, Benjamin Harrison, Thomas Jefferson, John Dickinson, and John Jay, would (with several changes in membership) control American foreign affairs until 1781.

To accomplish its task the committee immediately began meeting with the newly arrived Bonvouloir and instructed Lee in London to gather information on the attitudes of several foreign powers concerning the rebellion. Bonvouloir's amicable personality and forthright assurance that France would aid the rebellion prodded Congress to enlist Silas Deane, already in France, to purchase uniforms, arms, and artillery pieces from the French government. The secret negotiations came to fruition in spring 1776 when, against the advice of his finance minister, Louis XVI agreed to aid the colonists. Louis arranged for a grant of 1 million livres to the Americans under the auspices of the fictitious trading company Rodrigue, Hortalez et Cie. Louis also arranged for his Spanish counterpart, Charles III, to donate a similar amount to the American cause. Another gesture, less surreptitious than the trading company, was the opening of French ports to ships flying American flags.

It quickly became apparent to many Patriots that having France and Spain take a more active role in the war would be of great importance to the Americans. John Adams undertook the study of forming alliances with European powers during the summer of 1776. But Adams's Model Treaty, soon accepted by Congress, offered little to potential allies in its attempt to buck the balance of power theory that had long ruled European diplomacy. The Model Treaty was irrelevant by the time Congress adopted it because of the dire circumstances surrounding the military conduct of the war. General George Washington was retreating from New York, and his army dwindled daily. Congress had to abandon any bargaining power in an attempt to save the Revolution. Thus, when Franklin sailed for France in October 1776, he carried with him the power to offer American assistance to help France reconquer its lost West Indian islands.

Joined by Deane and Lee, Franklin met with Vergennes in December 1776. The French foreign minister rejected Franklin's offer of treaties of amity and commerce but reassured the

Benjamin Franklin at the court of Louis XVI. Franklin was a principal member of the commission sent to France to gain support after the United States declared independence from Britain. He is credited with securing war loans, official recognition, and, ultimately, a French declaration of war against the British. (National Archives and Records Administration)

American commissioners of French friendship with a gift of 2 million livres. The commissioners tried again in February 1777, offering a pledge not to make a separate peace with Britain if France joined in an alliance. Vergennes delayed any decision on this new offer because of military uncertainty. His mind did not appear to have changed until July, when two articles appeared in the *Affaires de l'Angleterre et de l'Amerique,* an official journal of the French government. The authors argued that war between France and Britain was inevitable, and the French would be better served with the Americans as friends.

Only in December 1777, however, shortly after hearing the news of General John Burgoyne's surrender at Saratoga, did Vergennes finally accept the American offer of an alliance. The victory gave Vergennes evidence to present to Louis XVI that the Americans could defeat the British. The Americans drafted a treaty of amity and commerce, and the French composed a treaty of alliance. The main stipulation of the latter was that neither France nor America would make a separate peace with Britain; therefore, the war would continue until America was independent. French and American negotiators signed both treaties in February 1778, and one month after Congress approved the treaties, in June 1778, France and Britain went to war, transforming the Revolutionary conflict into a world war.

After the formal alliance was solidified, Congress's Committee of Foreign Affairs (the successor to the Committee of Secret Correspondence) attempted to gain France's full support in forever reducing British power on the American continent. In tandem, they again invited Spain to join the alliance (the Spanish Foreign Minister Jose Monino y Redondo, Count de Floridablanca, had hesitated in the spring of 1778) by offering to help Spain regain Florida from Britain. The Spanish delayed still. Floridablanca had long been suspicious of American designs on Spanish claims west of the Appalachian Mountains, and he did not want to help America become independent only to have it inspire rebellion in, or seize outright, Spanish territory. But after the French failure to end the war quickly, Vergennes realized the critical importance of Spain to the French war effort. He pledged to support Spain's land claims east of the Mississippi and in 1779 concluded the Convention of Aranjuez, which stated that France and Spain would continue the war until Spain had regained Gibraltar from Britain. The convention also stated that France could not make peace until America had won its independence—this was the closest Spain came to an alliance with America.

Frustrated over its failure to conclude an alliance with Spain, the Committee of Foreign Affairs looked to the war's end by appointing a slate of diplomatic representatives.

Franklin and Jay were named ministers plenipotentiary to France and Spain, respectively. Adams was given the assignment of chief negotiator of a peace treaty with Britain, much to Vergennes' disgust. Adams, who had served briefly in commission with Franklin and Lee in 1778–1779, returned to Paris in 1780 and quickly earned Vergennes' animosity. Vergennes instructed the new French minister to the United States, the Chevalier de la Luzerne, to press Congress for Adams's recall. Congress partly acquiesced to the French demands. Instead of recalling Adams, Congress, in June 1781, created a commission of five members (Adams, Jay, Franklin, Jefferson, and Henry Laurens) to settle the peace. To streamline the handling of foreign affairs, Congress also created the position of secretary of foreign affairs and named Robert R. Livingston the first secretary. Congress then instructed the commissioners to conduct no negotiations without French advice.

Laurens was soon captured by the British en route to Europe, and Jefferson withdrew from the commission due to his wife's illness. Adams (who spent all of 1781 and much of 1782 negotiating a commercial treaty and a loan with the Dutch), Jay (who spent nearly as much time on his largely futile mission to Spain), and Franklin, though different in temperament yet were determined to claim all they could for America. They also possessed the fortitude to disregard Congress's instructions and pursue an independent peace with Great Britain.

The British surrender at Yorktown in October 1781 did not immediately end the war, but it spurred a change of government in England. Lord North resigned on 20 March 1782 and was replaced as first minister by Rockingham. George III, however, could not abide Rockingham, so the Earl of Shelburne, secretary of state for the Southern Department, served as an intermediary between the two. The lack of support in Parliament for the continuation of the war forced the new government to negotiate with the Americans, and Shelburne sent Richard Oswald to treat with his old acquaintance, Franklin.

Oswald found a convivial partner in Franklin, but the negotiations stalled because Shelburne had not empowered Oswald to deal with Franklin and his fellow commissioners as representatives of an independent nation. Shelburne still referred to the Americans as colonists and also hesitated to accede to Franklin's demand for the cession of Canada. The comte de Vergennes now opened clandestine contacts with the British, and the commissioners feared that they might lose their French ally. Franklin and Jay (who had arrived from Madrid during the summer) quickly adopted a more flexible attitude toward their official status vis-à-vis the British, which allowed Oswald's new official commission in September 1782 to empower him to treat with "the Commissioners appointed by the Colonys, under the title of Thirteen United States."

Adams, the head of the American commission, traveled from Holland to Paris in October, and the three commissioners—Adams, Franklin, and Jay—concluded the preliminary articles of peace on 30 November 1782. The first article recognized America's independence. The Americans did not receive Canada but did secure their claim to all land north of the thirty-first parallel, up to the Canadian border and the Great Lakes, from the Atlantic Ocean to the Mississippi River. American fishing rights off the coast of Newfoundland were to be respected, and British creditors were allowed to collect their debts. The treaty also stated that Congress would recommend to the states that confiscated Loyalist property be returned. Even though the Americans' separate negotiation with Britain violated the congressional instructions of 1781 that Adams and Jay had found so offensive, it did not breach the Franco-American Alliance because the preliminary treaty was not to take effect until France and Great Britain had negotiated their own peace, which they did in early 1783. The preliminary articles of November were further delayed by resistance in Britain but were finally approved and signed, without substantial change, as the definitive Treaty of Paris on 3 September 1783.

From 1783 to 1788 the conduct of foreign affairs was inextricably tied to the question of the strength of America's Confederation government. Article VI of the Articles of Confederation forbade any state from making treaties with foreign powers; that power, along with the sole right to conduct foreign affairs, was reserved for Congress through Article IX. The Confederation government, however, could make little headway in concluding commercial treaties with European nations, including Great Britain, and had difficulty in paying the interest on its foreign debts. This international weakness, combined with Congress's inability to secure strong state support for its basic operations, united many people in favor of a stronger central government.

Secretary of Foreign Affairs Livingston tried to broaden the scope of his office, but he never succeeded in gaining the exclusive right to initiate diplomacy. Congress always loomed large over Livingston's conduct, and the fact that both Congress and Livingston could receive ambassadors and deal with diplomats muddled America's already weak international position. Livingston left the government in June 1782, and Congress dallied in naming a replacement. A host of names, from Philip Schuyler to Lee and Jefferson, were put forward as Livingston's successor. Elbridge Gerry broke the impasse when he nominated Jay, who was appointed in late 1784. Jay was a compromise choice between more nationalist leaders and their more localist opponents, who continued to support the weak Confederation.

Jay would serve as secretary for the remainder of the Confederation period, and his most pressing problems were gargantuan in nature. He had to present America to the world as a viable entity, just as most European courts were wagering when the republican experiment would fail. The lead detractor was Great Britain, which proved to be a thorn in Jay's side for his entire term.

During the initial peace negotiations in 1782, Shelburne had realized the importance of commercial reciprocity between the two nations and granted free access of American goods and ships to British ports. In short, America was to have all the benefits that the colonies possessed under the old Navigation Acts system. Unresolved British resentments against America and criticism of current American behavior, however, eventually led to the cancellation of this agreement. Leading the way was the Earl of Sheffield, who argued that by restricting Americans from the British Empire, England could regain the West Indian trade that had been dominated by colonial shipping. A series of British orders-in-council in the mid-1780s reduced America to just another nation outside of the British Empire's protected orbit of trade.

In addition to thwarting American attempts to gain most favored nation status, the British, citing the failure of Congress to force its citizens to repay their British creditors and to force the states to restore Loyalist property, violated the peace treaty by refusing to evacuate their military posts in the Northwest. Britain's decision to remain in the Northwest, however, was made even before the final peace treaty was ratified. The Miami and Wabash Indians of the Ohio Country benefited greatly from the continued British presence at Detroit and other forts as they harassed Americans for another ten years, until General Anthony Wayne's victory at the Battle of Fallen Timbers in 1794.

A more internally divisive problem for Jay was America's relationship with Spain. Charles III's government had not recognized the United States even after the conclusion of peace by all the belligerent powers in 1783. More devastating, however, was Spain's decision in 1784 to close the Mississippi River to free navigation by American ships. Incensed frontier farmers clamored for the government to alleviate this draconian measure. The Spanish envoy to the United States, Diego de Gardoqui (who was not an official minister, so as to not confer any legitimacy to the new nation), exploited sectional tensions in America to benefit Spain. He went so far as to enlist the aid of the Revolutionary War veteran General James Wilkinson to foment rebellion in Kentucky. Negotiating with Jay, Gardoqui did agree to a treaty of commerce and alliance, in which Spain promised to recognize the United States in return for America relinquishing its claims to the free navigation of the Mississippi River for a period of twenty to thirty years. In 1786, Jay signed the treaty, but Congress never ratified it.

America's principal Revolutionary War ally, France, did not provide any succor to the infant nation after the conclusion of peace, but neither was it a source of grief. Jefferson replaced Franklin as America's minister plenipotentiary to Versailles in 1785 and brought with him the utopian goal of converting Europe to the American view of an open, liberal international economic order. Any efforts to this end, however, faltered due to the leaking ship of state that was France's ancien régime. Between his courting of French society and his accumulation of French books and artistic objects, Jefferson did manage to warn his country about the danger that the Barbary states posed to American commerce in the Mediterranean. And he would heed his own warnings when, in his presidency, he declared a virtual war against the Barbary pirates.

Many of the faults of American diplomacy during and after the Revolutionary War, however, can be traced to the inefficacy of Congress and its manner of dealing with foreign affairs. It often failed to give strong support to its diplomats, particularly Franklin, Adams, and Jay, whose major triumphs—the Franco-American Alliance (1778), the Dutch-American Treaty of Amity and Commerce (1782), the preliminary settlement with Britain (1782), and the definitive Treaty of Paris (1783)—were largely their own unaided achievements. And when delegates convened in Philadelphia in May 1787 to discuss a new frame of government, foreign affairs was, again, not a prominent matter in their minds. The nation's internal flaws demanded attention first; any external problems would have to be addressed later, as a matter of course.

Ryan Staude

See also

Achard de Bonvouloir, Julien-Alexandre; Adams, John; Beaumarchais, Pierre-Augustin Caron de; Carmichael, William; Dana, Francis; Diplomacy, British; Diplomacy, French; Franklin, Benjamin; Gravier, Charles, Comte de Vergennes; Jay, John; Jefferson, Thomas; League of Armed Neutrality; Lee, Arthur; Northwest Territory; Oswald, Richard; Paris, Treaty of (1763); Paris, Treaty of (1783); Spain

References

Dull, Jonathan R. *A Diplomatic History of the American Revolution.* New Haven, CT: Yale University Press, 1985.

———. *The French Navy and the American Revolution: A Study of Arms and Diplomacy, 1774–1787.* Princeton, NJ: Princeton University Press, 1975.

Hoffman, Ronald, and Peter J. Albert, eds. *Peace and the Peacemakers: The Treaty of 1783.* Charlottesville: University of Virginia Press, 1986.

Hutson, James. *John Adams and the Diplomacy of the American Revolution.* Lexington: University Press of Kentucky, 1980.

Kammen, Michael G. *A Rope of Sand: The Colonial Agents, British Politics and the American Revolution.* Ithaca, NY: Cornell University Press, 1968.

Kaplan, Lawrence S. *Colonies into Nation: American Diplomacy, 1763–1801.* New York: Macmillan, 1972.

Madariaga, Isabel de. *Britain, Russia, and the Armed Neutrality of 1780: Sir James Harris's Mission to St. Petersburg during the American Revolution.* New Haven, CT: Yale University Press, 1962.

Middlekauf, Robert. *The Glorious Cause: The American Revolution, 1763–1789.* 1981. Reprint, Oxford: Oxford University Press, 2005.

Morgan, Edmund S. *Benjamin Franklin.* New Haven, CT: Yale University Press, 2002.
Morris, Richard B. *The Peacemakers: The Great Powers and American Independence.* New York: Harper and Row, 1965.
Stinchecombe, William C. *The American Revolution and the French Alliance.* Syracuse, NY: Syracuse University Press, 1969.
Stourzh, Gerald. *Benjamin Franklin and American Foreign Policy.* 2nd ed. Chicago: University of Chicago Press, 1969.

Diplomacy, British

British diplomacy was unable either to prevent American independence or keep France and Spain from waging war with Britain, but it was able to limit the long-term damage from the conflict.

When hostilities began between the colonists and the British in the spring of 1775, the main diplomatic goal of Lord North's government was to ensure that Great Britain's traditional European enemies, France and Spain, did not use the insurrection as an opportunity to weaken British power and prestige. To this end, the government tried to effect a quick end to the conflict. It also sought to prevent neutral countries from engaging in trade with the rebellious colonies through diplomatic pressure and the use of an extensive naval blockade.

The British government was soon aware that the American Congress had sent delegations to several major European states in an effort to purchase weapons and ammunition and to establish commercial relations. When the playwright and spy Pierre-Augustin Caron de Beaumarchais established the bogus trading firm of Rodrigue, Hortalez et Cie to secretly funnel French aid to the Americans, the British quickly learned of the venture's true purpose. In addition, Edward Bancroft, who acted as the unofficial secretary to the American commissioners in France, was actually a British spy who kept London well informed of American diplomatic maneuvers. And the British were able to secure an agreement from the French in 1776 that allowed ships of the Royal Navy to search French merchant ships for contraband goods on the high seas but not in French ports, including in its colonial possessions.

Although they were fully aware of French support for the Americans, the British deliberately sought to avoid provocations that might prompt France to officially enter the war on the side of the Americans. Consequently, they made only minor objections to covert French aid to the rebels. Because of the importance of seaborne trade and commerce to their empire, however, the one area in which the British did press the French was in the use of French ports by American privateers and naval vessels. The two nations had a treaty dating back to 1713 under which each agreed not to accept into its ports the privateers or prizes of states that were engaged in combat with the other nation, nor could ships be built or fitted out in their ports for action against the other nation. In 1777, the British ambassador to France, Lord Stormont, presented proof that American privateers were using French ports, and the French foreign minister, the comte de Vergennes, was forced to expel American vessels from ports in France. Stormont indicated that France might receive an ultimatum on the issue if the practice continued, and Vergennes responded by dispatching orders to stop the clandestine shipments of arms and ammunition to America. He even temporarily canceled the leaves of French officers and soldiers who had volunteered to fight on the side of the Americans. Nonetheless, these moves were temporary. Following the American victory at Saratoga, France was prepared to enter the war openly.

Recognizing immediately the potential international impact of Saratoga, the North government attempted reconciliation with the colonies and used private channels to contact the American commissioners in France. British agents met with Benjamin Franklin and Silas Deane on several occasions in December 1777 and January 1778, but neither commissioner was willing to commit to direct negotiations. Meanwhile, the mere possibility of an accommodation between Great Britain and America led the French to accelerate the establishment of a formal alliance with the Americans.

Again, the British were well aware of French intentions and even obtained knowledge of the contents of the two treaties between France and America before their completion and signing in early February 1778. In that same month, the North government tried one last attempt at neutralizing the new alliance by securing parliamentary approval for new terms of accommodation with America, and in April it sent the Carlisle Peace Commission to negotiate with Congress. Soon after the commissioners reached America, however, their efforts collapsed completely, leaving the British no option but to accept American independence, which they were far from ready to do, or to continue the conflict. The government also continued its effort to avoid bringing France into open war, but when Versailles publicly announced the treaties on 13 March 1778, the British were forced to recall their ambassador, and the French soon reciprocated. The French then recognized the American commissioners in Paris as the diplomatic representatives of the United States.

Although both nations were at the brink of war, each wanted the other to attack first. The French had a defensive treaty with Austria and hoped that a British attack would either draw the Austrians into the conflict as an ally or at least cause them to remain neutral, which would allow France to remain neutral in a likely war between Austria and Prussia. Meanwhile, Great Britain also had a defensive treaty with the Netherlands and hoped that a French attack would bring the Dutch into the war on the side of the British. The character of the actual onset of hostilities between the British and French

Political cartoon shows Britain, represented as a large dog, muzzled and chained, being attacked by several men, representing the countries of the League of Armed Neutrality and the allies: a Swede, a Dane, a Frenchman with an umbrella, a Spaniard with a cane, a Dutchman (holding the dog by the tail), an American (at far right with a single feather in his hat), and one woman (Catherine the Great of Russia holding a caduceus and a sword). In the background, a woman, labeled "Queen of the Sea," stripped to the waist, wearing a crown, and hanging by her wrists from a gallows, is being whipped by John Paul Jones. (Library of Congress)

navies at Ushant on 13 June 1778 was ambiguous enough to allow each nation to claim to be the victim of the other's aggression. As a result, both Austria and the Netherlands remained neutral (although the Dutch would later be drawn into the war). Over the next two years, the British presented three formal calls on the Dutch to respect their treaty obligations, but the Dutch government maintained that since the war started in America, they were not obliged to provide military assistance to the British. On 17 April 1780, the British formally declared that the Dutch had violated their treaty obligations, annulled the treaties between the two states, and rescinded any privileges the Netherlands enjoyed under treaty with Great Britain.

With France in the war, the British foreign ministry's attention turned to efforts to keep Spain from entering the fray. At the heart of Anglo-Spanish discussions was the status of Gibraltar. The Spanish offered to enter the war on the side of the British if London was willing to relinquish the strategically important fortress. The Royal Navy assured the government that it could defeat the combined navies of Spain and France, and the Spanish offer was rejected. In response, the Spanish agreed in April 1779 to enter the war on the side of France when they were given assurances that they would be allowed to take Gibraltar; they declared war on Britain in June. A decisive British naval victory at the Battle of Cape St. Vincent off the coast of Portugal in January 1780 heavily damaged the Spanish navy and almost forced Spain out of the war, but the overstretched British were unable to follow up on their victory.

The British government was also anxious to keep other neutral powers from entering the conflict. Of the major European powers, only its traditional ally, Portugal, was firmly on the British side. Frederick the Great of Prussia maintained official neutrality but tacitly supported the Franco-American Alliance. The British were more persuasive with other European monarchs who were afraid of the precedent that a successful rebellion might set and were able to secure the neutrality of Austria and the Grand Duchy of Tuscany. The North government dispatched James Harris, generally regarded as the foremost British diplomat at the time, to Russia to try to establish an alliance with St. Petersburg. Harris was unable to secure a formal alliance but wrote to London that he had gained Russian neutrality on terms favorable to Great Britain.

From 1778 onward, the main European strategy of the British was to intercept the supplies going to America and to stop American trade with the major European states. Consequently, its principal diplomatic imperative was to convince other nations not to trade with the Americans. This led to constant disputes with the Netherlands, which was America's main neutral trading partner. British policy also exacerbated tensions with the Baltic nations, which were major suppliers of naval stores to the French. In response to pressure on this trade by the Royal Navy, Catherine II of Russia proposed the creation of a League of Armed Neutrality on 28 February 1780. This stunned Harris and the British government, who had counted on tacit Russian support in the war. Sweden and Denmark soon joined the league, and in order to prevent the Dutch from joining, which might force them into a war with all of the league members, the British declared war on the Netherlands on 20 December 1780.

During the course of the war, one successful area of British diplomacy concerned relations with several Native American tribes of North America. Initially, the British sought to keep the Native American peoples neutral since London believed that the war would be short. As the conflict wore on, however, the British began to seek support from the frontier tribes. In 1777, British promises of protection from American expansion and bribes in the form of trade goods and weapons convinced four of the six tribes of the Iroquois Confederacy to join the British. For the next several years, the Iroquois launched raids against American settlements in New York and Pennsylvania and tied up a number of American troops. In 1779, however, a campaign by the American General John Sullivan devastated the Iroquois and greatly reduced their ability to threaten the frontier.

In the aftermath of General Charles Cornwallis's surrender at Yorktown in October 1781 and following the loss of West Florida to the Spanish and the Caribbean colonies of Tobago, St. Christopher, and St. Eustatius to the French, Parliament decided on 27 February 1782 to end its support for the war in America. In response, North resigned on 20 March and was replaced by the Marquis of Rockingham. Divisions within the government constrained British diplomatic efforts in the final years of the Revolution. Yet as 1782 wore on, the British were resurgent in their global war. At the Battle of the Saintes on 17 April, the Royal Navy routed a French fleet and captured its admiral, the comte de Grasse. Concurrently, a crisis between Russia and the Ottoman Empire removed much of the pressure on Great Britain as several European nations reexamined their allegiances and alliances.

Now serving in the new Rockingham government, North's old nemesis, Charles James Fox, saw these developments as an opportunity to detach the Americans from their alliance with the French by negotiating a separate peace and then continuing the war against the European states. The war-weary Parliament, however, repudiated Fox on 30 June 1782, and the next day Rockingham died. He was replaced by the Earl of Shelburne, who decided to use the threat of a separate peace with America as a means to gain concessions from the French. Shelburne even dispatched the captured de Grasse back to France to carry his terms and as a gesture of goodwill. This led Vergennes to dispatch Joseph-Mathias Gérard de Rayneval to Great Britain to start serious peace negotiations in September 1782. Shelburne and Rayneval met at Boswood, the prime minister's country estate. Shelburne also tried to negotiate directly with the Americans and authorized General Guy Carleton in New York to enter into talks with George Washington, but the American general refused, and the Continental Congress adamantly insisted that all negotiations be conducted through its commissioners in Europe.

While Congress had instructed the American commissioners to heed the advice of Vergennes, the Americans quickly realized that they could negotiate a better deal themselves with the British and that the French had their own interests to pursue—interests that did not always coincide with those of the Americans. The American commissioners and the British negotiator Richard Oswald concluded a preliminary treaty in November 1782, which Vergennes was forced to accept. The four final peace treaties, between Britain on the one side and America, France, Spain, and the Netherlands on the other, were all concluded in September 1783. In the end, the British were able to secure a much more favorable peace than might have been expected, as mistrust between the allies and growing internal financial pressures in France prompted Vergennes to capitulate to most British demands. Although America was granted independence, the Ohio Valley, and fishing rights off Newfoundland, Great Britain retained Canada, and the Americans agreed to honor debts from the prewar era and provide indemnities for Loyalists who lost property. Spain regained Florida and Minorca, which it had lost in the Seven Years' War, but it did not gain Gibraltar. France and the Netherlands gained virtually nothing but the relief of being at peace.

Tom Lansford

See also

Adams, John; Cape St. Vincent, Battle of; Catherine II, Empress of Russia; Congress, Second Continental and Confederation; Cornwallis, Charles; Diplomacy, American; Diplomacy, French; Florida, East and West; France; Franco-American Alliance; Franklin, Benjamin; Grasse, François-Joseph-Paul, Comte de; Gravier, Charles, Comte de Vergennes; Jay, John; Louis XVI, King of France; Murray, David, Lord Stormont; Netherlands; North, Lord Frederick; Oswald, Richard; Petty-Fitzmaurice, William, 2nd Earl of Shelburne; Privateering; Saintes, Battle of the; Spain; Ushant, First and Second Battles of; Washington, George; Watson-Wentworth, Charles, 2nd Marquis of Rockingham

References

Bemis, Samuel F. *The Diplomacy of the American Revolution.* 1935. Reprint, Bloomington: Indiana University Press, 1957.

Donoughue, Bernard. *British Politics and the American Revolution: The Path to War, 1773–75.* London: Macmillan, 1964.

Dull, Jonathan R. *A Diplomatic History of the American Revolution.* New Haven, CT: Yale University Press, 1985.

Hoffman, Ronald, and Peter J. Albert, eds. *Diplomacy and Revolution: The Franco-American Alliance of 1778.* Charlottesville: University of Virginia Press, 1981.

Horsman, Reginald. *The Diplomacy of the New Republic, 1776–1815.* Arlington Heights, IL: Harlan Davidson, 1985.

Jensen, Merrill. *The New Nation: A History of the United States during the Confederation, 1781–1789.* 1950. Reprint, New York: Knopf, 1965.

Norris, John. *Shelburne and Reform.* London: Macmillan, 1963.

Scott, H. M. *British Foreign Policy in the Age of the American Revolution.* New York: Oxford University Press, 1990.

Van Alstyne, Richard. *Empire and Independence: The International History of the American Revolution.* New York: Quadrangle, 1965.

Varg, Paul. *Foreign Policies of the Founding Fathers.* East Lansing: Michigan State University, 1963.

Diplomacy, French

From an American standpoint, French diplomacy in the American Revolutionary War seems a simple progression from limited aid to full involvement in the war to shared victory over the British. From the standpoint of the French royal government, however, the American Revolution soon ceased to be a triumph to be celebrated. Instead, it became a disaster to be explained. France had expected to weaken Great Britain by depriving it of its monopoly of American trade, yet soon after war's end Britain had regained a near monopoly of that trade. Within five years Britain also had ended its diplomatic isolation and regained its prestige, signing alliances with Prussia and the Netherlands. King Louis XVI of France, however, was unable for financial reasons to do anything to prevent the loss of his own alliance with the Dutch; indeed, now effectively bankrupt, he had to beg unsuccessfully for help from an assembly of French notables. Soon royal government itself would collapse. How had the French court come to make so terrible a mistake?

The traditional explanation of France's involvement in the American Revolution is that it wished to take revenge for the loss of Canada to Britain in the Seven Years' War (known in America as the French and Indian War). There are difficulties with this explanation, however. The chief agent of the French involvement was Charles Gravier, the comte de Vergennes, who was the French secretary of state for foreign affairs. Vergennes' background was not in the diplomacy of Western Europe but rather of Central, Northern, and Eastern Europe; he had been the French representative in Constantinople during the last war and after the war served in Stockholm. The three undersecretaries who served him—Conrad-Alexandre Gérard, Joseph-Mathias Gérard de Rayneval, and Pierre-Michel Hennin—were all experts on Poland. During the American Revolution, Vergennes showed no interest in regaining Canada, and during the peace negotiations his main concern

French troops, under the command of Jean-Baptiste Vimeur, the comte de Rochambeau, disembark at Newport, Rhode Island. (Library of Congress)

about the Ohio-Mississippi Valley region was in making sure that a consideration of its fate not delay the conclusion of a final treaty. Even before peace was concluded, he sought British cooperation in dealing with Eastern Europe; in 1786 he was condemned by the French public for making a disadvantageous commercial treaty with Britain. What accounts for his leading France into a war in a region of little interest to him?

A persuasive answer was suggested nearly a century ago by the great diplomatic historian Albert Sorel. During Vergennes' years in Constantinople and Stockholm, he had been France's official diplomatic representative as well as an agent of a secret diplomatic organization controlled by King Louis XV (the grandfather and predecessor of King Louis XVI) but working outside of normal channels without the knowledge of French foreign ministers. This organization was called Le Secret du Roi (the King's Secret). When Louis XVI succeeded his grandfather in 1774, he learned of the organization and had it disbanded but did not overly concern himself with the fact that Vergennes, whom he named his foreign minister, had been a member, not realizing that Vergennes' diplomatic philosophy was that of the King's Secret. Vergennes was not alone. Hennin had been a leading agent of the King's Secret, and the Gérard brothers had shared in its work. Louis XVI, wishing peace, had selected Vergennes because of his reputation for moderation; instead Vergennes led France into a disastrous war to further the objectives of the secret organization. Truly, as Sorel pointed out, the choice of Vergennes as foreign minister was the triumph of the King's Secret.

Louis XV had founded the secret organization in the mid-1740s in order to work for the election of a Frenchman as king of Poland when the throne (which was elective) next became vacant. For both diplomatic and family reasons this had to be kept secret, as the existing Polish king was a French ally (and the father of Louis' daughter-in-law). Naturally, he wanted a member of his own family to follow him. Soon, however, the organization took on a larger purpose. France's chief rival in Poland was Russia, whose power was growing. Although the King's Secret eventually was given other tasks (such as mapping potential landing sites in England in the late 1760s for a future invasion), its main purpose became that of blocking Russian expansionism against France's friends in Eastern, Northern, and Central Europe, such as Poland, Sweden, and the Ottoman Empire (which included not only Turkey but most of the Balkans as well).

Vergennes spent virtually his entire diplomatic career worrying about the Russians, a worry that became particularly acute after 1772 when Russia joined with Austria and Prussia in annexing large sections of Poland. Britain, which earlier had helped a Russian fleet on its way to fight the Turks in the Mediterranean, did nothing to help Poland. Moreover, when it appeared that Sweden would be Russia's next victim, the British rejected French offers of friendship and even prevented France from mobilizing a fleet on Sweden's behalf. Vergennes, in Stockholm at the time, witnessed the cooperation between the Russians and the British. If participation in the American rebellion was France's revenge on Britain, it was due more to this insult than to the loss of Canada. It was a sign of Lord North's overconfidence that having humiliated France in the Swedish crisis, he now turned toward another project: the Tea Act. He little realized the dangers of American rebellion and the potential usefulness of French cooperation in suppressing it; instead, he soon saw the French government doing all it could to help the rebels.

Vergennes seems to have been a kindly man who preferred peace to war. He probably was motivated less by a desire for revenge than by desperation. In 1774 Russia capped its gains in Poland by taking substantial territory from the Ottoman Empire. France seemingly had lost all its influence in Eastern Europe, and this posed a threat to its long-term security. France had a brief window of opportunity, though. The Russians were exhausted from their long war with the Turks and with the Polish underground. For the time being, they would pose little danger. If Britain could be weakened, Russia would lose a valuable support. Perhaps a weakened Britain might even listen to France the next time it offered better relations. As Vergennes later wrote to Louis XVI, the greatest period of French security was the 1720s, when France and Britain had been allies.

The moment of decision was the spring of 1776, and Vergennes was ready. The previous year he had sent an informal representative, a young man named Julien-Alexandre Achard de Bonvouloir, to Philadelphia to assure the American rebels that France had no designs on Canada, to wish the Americans well, and to say that France would welcome American ships in its ports. In December 1775, Bonvouloir met secretly with Benjamin Franklin and three other members of a congressional committee. This Committee of Secret Correspondence requested information about France's dispositions, two military engineers, and the right to trade American provisions in French ports for guns and military supplies. Bonvouloir's visit stimulated Congress to send a commercial agent, Silas Deane, to France in March 1776.

In the same month the results of Bonvouloir's mission provoked a debate in Louis XVI's Council of State between Vergennes and Controller General (Finance Minister) Anne-Robert-Jacques Turgot on whether to comply with the American requests. Turgot warned his colleagues that involvement in the American conflict would bring great dangers and no lasting benefits, but they did not listen. Vergennes triumphed, largely because he realized the king's aversion to war and portrayed compliance as the course of prudence: France could prolong the American rebellion while it saw to its own defenses. Moreover, the royal government could avoid direct involvement by subsidizing a trading company, Rodrigue, Hortalez et Cie, to trade French guns and military supplies for American tobacco. The company was headed by the playwright Pierre-Augustin Caron de Beaumarchais, whom Vergennes had used in 1775 to pay off a blackmailer who had been an agent of the King's Secret when it was mapping landing sites in England.

Neither the naval rearmament nor the secret arms aid, however, could be kept secret from the British; rather than making France safer, they made war more likely. It should be noted that Vergennes' closest ally in the Council of State was the brilliant French Naval Minister Antoine-Raymond-Gualbert-Gabriel de Sartine. During the reign of Louis XV, Sartine had been the chief royal administrator of Paris and a key member of the King's Secret. He was also an old friend and patron of Beaumarchais. In early 1778, with naval rearmament virtually complete, Vergennes convinced Louis XVI that France needed to assist the United States openly and officially. Vergennes was greatly aided in this effort by the three-member American diplomatic mission in France. In the fall of 1776, Congress had ordered Franklin and Arthur Lee to join Deane in Paris to work for a commercial treaty with their secret ally. Led by Franklin, the American commissioners pretended that they were conducting serious negotiations with Great Britain, thereby helping to frighten the French king into a formal commitment to the United States. They then agreed to sign both a commercial treaty and a treaty of military alliance. These were concluded on 6 February 1778.

France's subsequent wartime diplomacy was driven in large part by the needs of the predominantly naval conflict, but the program of the King's Secret also continued to affect French diplomacy. The central premise of the King's Secret was that France needed an active policy in Eastern, Northern, and Central Europe to protect France's friends—Poland, Sweden, and the Ottoman Empire—in order to maintain long-term French security. The partition of Poland was not only the work of Russia but also of Prussia and Austria. Prussia was a Russian ally, and France reluctantly had fought Prussia during the Seven Years' War. By 1778, however, Prussia had become for a time a defender, like France, of the territorial status quo.

Austria, however, was another matter. France was allied with Austria, but mostly to prevent it from allying with Britain. Some members of the King's Secret, such as the publicist Jean-Louis Favier, were violently anti-Austrian, and their opinion would have a great impact on the diplomacy of the French Revolution. Vergennes, more moderate, was a consistent opponent of Austrian expansion but was careful not to withdraw from the alliance. In 1778, Austria went to war with Prussia because of Austrian designs on Bavaria. France remained neutral in spite of Austrian appeals for support, as Austria was providing no help to France against Britain. The nearly bloodless War of the Bavarian Succession ended with a peace treaty blocking Austrian expansion. Eventually Austria and Russia would offer their mediation of the war in America, but neither Britain nor France (nor indeed the United States) was interested in their help.

Meanwhile, in mid-1778 France became an open belligerent in the American war. When France's attempt to end the war in a single campaign failed, it was forced to purchase the entrance of Spain and its navy into the war by agreeing to fight until Spain acquired Gibraltar from Britain. France now had to balance the often conflicting desires of Spain and the United States. Spain, for example, wanted French naval help in Europe, while American diplomats such as John Adams wanted France to send substantial naval forces to American waters. Moreover, the United States needed substantial French financial aid; Franklin performed a great service in convincing the French that such aid was necessary but had less success in convincing Congress that France had financial problems of its own. And France soon became fearful that both Spain and the United States would make such unreasonable demands of Britain that it would be impossible to make peace. Using his diplomatic representatives in Philadelphia, Vergennes convinced Congress in 1781 to establish a peace commission to be ready when negotiations started and to order it to consult with the French government. By now France had yet another demanding ally. At the end of 1780, Britain declared war on the Netherlands to prevent it from joining the League of Armed Neutrality, which Tsarina Catherine II of Russia had founded to protect neutral shipping rights in the Baltic and North seas from the British navy.

French secretary of state for foreign affairs, Charles Gravier (the comte de Vergennes), British minister Alleyne Fitzherbert, and Spanish minister Conde de Aranda sign the preliminary articles of peace at Versailles on 20 January 1783. (Library of Congress)

This league served French interests because France imported naval matériel from the Baltic. Russia, however, continued to exert pressure on France's friends in Eastern Europe, particularly the Ottoman Empire. In 1782 Russia, hoping to profit from French and British involvement in the American war, threatened war with the Ottomans over the control of the Crimean Peninsula. Fear of a general war in Eastern Europe, and particularly of a disastrous defeat of the Turks, was of enormous importance in leading France to make peace as quickly as possible. The Earl of Shelburne, the British prime minister, made great use of Vergennes' fears while negotiating a peace with France. He even suggested to Gérard de Rayneval, whom Vergennes sent to England on three occasions in 1782 during the peace discussions, that he shared Vergennes' fears about Russia and was anxious to help once peace was concluded. Shelburne was also able to play off the United States against France, giving the Americans generous terms so that they would make a separate peace agreement. When the Americans reached a preliminary agreement with Britain in November 1782, France was forced to abandon all hopes of direct gains for itself. Only by convincing Spain to accept Minorca and Florida instead of Gibraltar was Vergennes able to win the general peace agreement that a financially and militarily exhausted France desperately needed.

The conclusion of a peace treaty with Britain brought France little respite from its problems in Eastern Europe. Shelburne lost his position as prime minister soon thereafter, and for the next five years Britain showed little interest in helping to counter Russian expansion. The general war that Vergennes feared was averted only because the Ottoman Empire, unable to find support for war, was forced to make substantial territorial concessions, including the cession of the Crimean Peninsula to Russia. For the next few years Vergennes was able to protect the European status quo against the expansionist designs of Austria and Russia (who became allies in 1781). Soon after Vergennes' death in February 1787, however, a series of disasters struck French diplomacy: government bankruptcy; the defeat of France's friends, the Patriot Party, by an invading Prussian army in the Netherlands; a war of Austria and Russia against the Ottoman Empire (during which France was as helpless as during the Russo-Turkish War twenty years earlier); revolution in France; the invasion of France by Prussia and Austria (while the Russians crushed Poland); and finally the execution of King Louis XVI and Queen Marie Antoinette.

Not all of this can be blamed on the French involvement in the American Revolution, of course, but Vergennes inadvertently did enormous harm to the monarchy he loved by not realizing that the greatest dangers it faced were internal rather than external. Russia and Austria were lesser threats than were the monarchy's debts, its inefficient tax system, and its inability to separate itself from the so-called feudal privileges of the aristocracy. This is not to deny that France, like all European states, existed in an international system without effective laws, a world in which war and invasion were constant threats. The members of the King's Secret at least realized that France needed to concern itself with protecting its friends in Northern, Central, and Eastern Europe if it was to remain secure. As would later occur in the 1920s and 1930s, France tried to construct a barrier to protect not only itself but the weak states of Eastern Europe; in both cases France lacked the strength to compensate for the weakness of those it hoped to protect. Vergennes' desire to maintain both peace and the diplomatic status quo on the European continent was heroic and doomed. His intervention in the American Revolution was a preventive move, designed to weaken Russia by weakening Russia's supporter, Britain. Like many other preventive wars, it helped bring about the disasters it hoped to prevent.

Jonathan R. Dull

See also

Adams, John; Beaumarchais, Pierre-Augustin Caron de; Catherine II, Empress of Russia; Deane, Silas; Franco-American Alliance; Franklin, Benjamin; French Navy; Gravier, Charles, Comte de Vergennes; Jay, John; Spain

References

Dull, Jonathan R. *A Diplomatic History of the American Revolution.* New Haven, CT: Yale University Press, 1985.

———. *The French Navy and the American Revolution: A Study of Arms and Diplomacy, 1774–1787.* Princeton, NJ: Princeton University Press, 1975.

———. *The French Navy and the Seven Years' War.* Lincoln, NE, and London: University of Nebraska Press, 2005.

Hardman, John, and Munro Price, eds. *Louis XVI and the Comte de Vergennes: Correspondence, 1774–1787.* Oxford, UK: Voltaire Foundation, 1998.

Hoffman, Ronald, and Peter J. Albert, eds. *Diplomacy and Revolution: The Franco-American Alliance of 1778.* Charlottesville: University of Virginia Press, 1981.

———. *Peace and the Peacemakers: The Treaty of 1783.* Charlottesville: University of Virginia Press, 1986.

Hudson, Ruth. *The Minister from France: Conrad-Alexandre Gérard, 1729–1790.* Euclid, OH: Lutz, 1994.

Ozanam, Didier, and Michel Antoine, eds. *Correspondance secrète du Comte du Broglie avec Louis XV (1756–1774).* 2 vols. Paris: C. Klincksieck, 1956–1961.

Roberts, Michael. "Great Britain and the Swedish Revolution, 1772–73." *Historical Journal* 7 (1964): 1–46.

Scott, H. M. *The Emergence of the Eastern Powers, 1756–1775.* Cambridge: Cambridge University Press, 2001.

Sorel, Albert. *Essais d'histoire et de critique.* 4th ed. Paris: Plon-Nourrit et Cie, 1913.

Diseases

Warfare and disease have always come hand in hand, and the American Revolutionary War was no exception. Diseases that particularly afflicted soldiers during the war appear to have included dysentery, smallpox, typhus, typhoid fever, respiratory infections, scurvy, scabies, yellow fever, and malaria.

In the campaigns of 1775–1776, the most serious problem was smallpox. Smallpox bears a good portion of the blame for the disasters that befell the Continental Army in its ill-fated invasion of Canada at the start of the war. Farther south, at the same time, smallpox also erupted among the runaway slaves who responded to British promises of freedom in Virginia. Here the disease killed hundreds of members of the Ethiopian Regiment that served under Virginia's royal governor, Lord Dunmore. European-born soldiers of the British Army were more likely to have acquired immunity to smallpox than native-born Americans, but George Washington's decision to inoculate the Continental Army in 1777–1778 effectively put both armies on an equal immunological footing as far as smallpox was concerned.

Dysentery, a painful intestinal ailment marked by diarrhea and bloody stools, plagued both armies wherever they went. The most famous and fateful episode of dysentery in the war occurred in August 1780, before the Battle of Camden in South Carolina. For nearly two weeks prior to the battle, an exhausted and underprovisioned army of Americans under General Horatio Gates had inched its way southward to confront the British. Along the way, the troops relied on raw corn and green peaches to quell their incessant hunger. On the night of 15 August, Gates decided to press forward against the enemy. Beforehand, he ordered his officers to replace the men's standard ration of rum with a gill of molasses, consumed alongside a meal of bread, undercooked beef, and cornmeal mush. The result was explosive diarrhea so irrepressible that the men "were breaking the ranks all night" as they moved into the darkness to confront the enemy. In the battle that ensued the next day, Gate's weakened army of 3,000 relinquished the field to a British army two-thirds its size.

Although malaria afflicted both armies in their northern and southern campaigns, this disease probably took its greatest toll on "unseasoned" British forces in the South. Eighteenth-century nomenclature for malaria was varied and vague. The most identifiable appellations were "intermitting fever" and "fever and ague," both referring to the alternating fever and chills that characterized the infection. But writers at the time often referred to malaria simply as fever, lumping it together with many other diseases and making it hard to identify for historians. Nevertheless, it can often be distinguished by its symptoms and distinctively seasonal nature.

Carried by anopheles mosquitoes, malaria confers a modicum of immunity to those repeatedly exposed to it. It is therefore likely that the American reliance on local militia units in the South was beneficial to the Patriot cause, at least as far as malaria was concerned. After their victory at Charleston in May 1780, British troops under General Charles Cornwallis marched inland to "pacify" the interior. By July, according to Robert Jackson, "the intermitting fever began to shew itself." In fact, malaria probably contributed to the diminished size of the army with which Cornwallis defeated Gates's diarrhea-plagued men at Camden.

Malaria affected Patriot forces as well, but with so many "seasoned" local men in the field, the Americans may have had an immunological edge. In fact, the militiamen's resistance to malaria may well have counterbalanced their vulnerability to smallpox in the southern campaign. Health returned with the end of mosquito season. But the next summer, as the war reached its climax on the swampy shores of the tidewater region of Virginia, malaria appeared once again. At Yorktown, the victims included both British soldiers and American regulars, many of whom were newly arrived from New York.

Yet another problem during the war was a conglomeration of illnesses known by such names as "camp fever," "jail fever," and "putrid fever." These appellations often referred to typhus, but it is important to bear in mind that at the time of the Revolution, typhus (borne by lice) had not been distinguished from typhoid (in most instances a food-borne disease spread by fecal contamination). Thus either of these infections may have occurred, and conditions appear to have been suitable for both, as lice and poor sanitation were a fact of life during the war. The American soldier John Greenwood described his comrades in 1776 as "fellows as lousy, itchy, and nasty as hogs."

Less serious but equally annoying for troops during the Revolution was scabies, usually called "the itch" in the eighteenth century. Scabies results from infestation by the microscopic mite *Sarcoptes scabei,* which burrows beneath the skin and elicits an intensely itchy allergic reaction in its victims. It is likely that both armies endured this extremely unpleasant plague during the war, for it is highly contagious and thrives in crowded conditions. The Americans complained of scabies throughout the hostilities, although a particularly severe outbreak occurred at Valley Forge during the winter of 1777–1778. Here desperate doctors and soldiers utilized cures that ranged from ointments of sulfur in hog's lard to mercury salves and the consumption of copious quantities of rum.

Nowhere was disease more prevalent than aboard the prison ships that the British used to house American prisoners of war. An inmate on the notorious *Jersey,* anchored in Long Island's Wallabout Bay, described the ship in 1781 as an "abode of suffering, despair and death." The ship "contained pestilence sufficient to desolate a world," including "dysentery, small-pox, and yellow fever." Although yellow fever, another mosquito-borne illness, plagued soldiers throughout the war, it appears to have been particularly common aboard British prison ships. In September 1780, a doctor treating captured Americans onboard vessels in Charleston Harbor described an epidemic that was almost certainly yellow fever. Its victims were marked by "a yellow suffusion, petechied over the breast and trunk," and other characteristic symptoms.

Although we lack sound statistics, it is likely that the American Revolutionary War fit a pattern found in many other military conflicts in which more men lost their lives to disease than to wounds incurred on the battlefield.

Elizabeth A. Fenn

See also

British Army; Cochran, John; Continental Army; Continental Navy; Craik, James; French Army; French Navy; Prisoners of War; Royal Navy; Rush, Benjamin; Shippen, William

References

Cash, Philip. *Medical Men at the Siege of Boston.* Philadelphia: American Philosophical Society, 1973.

Cochran, John. "The Medical Department of the Revolutionary War." *Magazine of American History* 12 (1994): 241–260.

Duncan, Louis C. *Medical Men in the American Revolution, 1775–1783.* Carlisle Barracks, PA: Medical Field Service School, 1931.

Gibbes, Robert Wilson, ed. *Documentary History of the American Revolution.* 1853–1855. Reprint, New York: Arno, 1971.

Greenwood, John. *The Revolutionary Services of John Greenwood of Boston and New York, 1775–1783.* New York: De Vinne, 1922.

Hawkins, Christopher. *The Adventures of Christopher Hawkins.* 1864. Reprint, New York: Arno, 1968.

Jackson, Robert. *A Treatise on the Fevers of Jamaica, with Some Observations on the Intermitting Fever of America.* Philadelphia: Campbell, 1795.

Pancake, John S. *This Destructive War: The British Campaign for the Carolinas, 1780–1782.* University: University of Alabama Press, 1985.

Reis, Oscar. *Medicine and the American Revolution: How Diseases and Their Treatments Affected the Colonial Army.* 1998. Reprint, New York: McFarland, 2005.

Saffron, Morris H. *Surgeon to Washington: Dr. John Cochran, 1730–1807.* New York: Columbia University Press, 1977.

Dogger Bank, Battle of (5 August 1781)

The Battle of Dogger Bank, an Anglo-Dutch action fought in the North Sea, was characterized by impressive bravery and stubbornness on both sides. In August 1781 Vice-Admiral Hyde Parker, formerly Admiral George Rodney's second in command in the West Indies, was proceeding through the Baltic on his return journey to Britain. He had with him a large merchant fleet protected by seven sail. On 5 August he sighted a Dutch squadron, also of seven vessels with its own convoy, to the southwest, near Dogger Bank. As the courses of the rival squadrons were bound to bring them into contact, Parker directed the merchant vessels to make for England, on a westerly course. Meanwhile, he would engage the Dutch with his squadron. The Dutch commander, Rear Admiral Arnold Zoutman, chose not to detach his merchant ships, instead forming a protective line with his warships to shield them from the British.

Parker's force was of mixed quality: all but two of his vessels were of different rates, and most were antiquated and in poor condition. Those of Parker's squadron in particularly poor condition had had their heavier guns replaced with lighter ones, thus reducing the force of their respective broadsides. His two 74-gun ships were, however, recently built, as was the *Dolphin* (44 guns). Parker's squadron consisted of the *Princess Amelia* (80 guns), the *Berwick* (74 guns), the *Fortitude* (74 guns), the *Buffalo* (60 guns), the *Preston* (50 guns), the *Bienfaisant* (64 guns), and the *Dolphin* that, although a frigate, fought in the line. The British also had four smaller frigates and one cutter plus seven other vessels protecting the convoy. Zoutman's ships included one 74-gun, two 68-gun, three 54-gun, and one 40-gun. He also had five frigates and one cutter plus four other vessels accompanying his convoy. The Dutch ships were probably in scarcely better condition than the British.

The sea was calm, with a northeast breeze. The Dutch stood to leeward, on the port tack, moving southeast by east, waiting for the British to approach. Parker signaled a general chase and was probably more than usually anxious to engage the Dutch, for he had suffered strong criticism from both the Admiralty and from Rodney over his supposed hesitation to attack the French-held islands in the West Indies during the time he had been in temporary command there. At 6:10 A.M. he hoisted the signal for line abreast, and within a short time all his vessels were moving quickly; at 6:45 there was only one cable's length between them. Just before 8:00 Parker issued the signal for battle.

The Dutch held their fire until they sighted the signal flying over the *Fortitude,* thus allowing Parker to maneuver slightly windward of the Dutch without interference and to position himself well within musket range. Almost certainly by accident Parker neglected to position his flagship opposite Zoutman's, such that the two opposing lines—each of seven ships—ought to have engaged their opposite numbers. Instead, one of Parker's rear ships overlapped and thus for a while had no target. This left two of his ships to fight three of Zoutman's. This problem was rectified when at 8:00 Parker altered the signal to "close action." The fighting raged fiercely until 11:35, by which time the two lead vessels on both sides were considerably leeward of their compatriots. When the battle ended, both sides had sustained serious damage. They remained close to one another for some time before the Dutch made sail for Texel, toward the safety of which their convoy had already headed during the course of the battle. Parker's squadron was too heavily damaged to pursue.

Both sides had shown great tenacity, but in spite of this there was no decisive result. The convoys reached their respective destinations, and only one Dutch warship was lost when it sank the following day. With such determination on both sides and with the rival lines so close together, heavy casualties were inevitable. Parker lost 104 killed and 339 wounded. Zoutman lost 142 killed and 403 wounded. Evidence after the battle confirmed that both squadrons had directed their fire against their enemy's hulls, and at least two of Parker's ships were shot through below the water line. The Battle of Dogger Bank demonstrated that no matter how hard-fought a naval action, if numbers and quality were about equal and neither side had the advantage of superior maneuver, a costly stalemate would almost certainly result.

Gregory Fremont-Barnes

The naval action off Dogger Bank, 5 August 1781, between a British squadron under Vice-Admiral Hyde Parker and a Dutch squadron led by Rear-Admiral Arnold Zoutman. After more than three hours of intense fighting, the rival forces separated with no result, apart from heavy casualties on both sides. (Naval Historical Society)

See also

Netherlands; Parker, Hyde; Rodney, George

References

Clowes, William Laird. *The Royal Navy: A History from the Earliest Times to 1900.* 7 vols. London: Chatham, 1996.

Gardiner, Robert, ed. *Navies and the American Revolution, 1775–1783.* London: Chatham, 1996.

Ireland, Bernard. *Naval Warfare in the Age of Sail.* London: Collins, 2000.

James, William. *The British Navy in Adversity: A Study of the War of American Independence.* 1926. Reprint, New York: Russell and Russell, 1970.

Syrett, David. *The Royal Navy in European Waters during the American Revolutionary War.* Columbia: University of South Carolina Press, 1998.

Tilley, J. A. *The Royal Navy in the American Revolution.* Columbia: University of South Carolina Press, 1987.

Dominica, First Battle of (17 April 1780)

The First Battle of Dominica was the most significant of the three inconclusive naval engagements fought in the West Indies between British forces under Admiral Sir George Rodney, commander of the Leeward Islands station, and French forces under Admiral Luc-Urbain de Bouexic, the comte de Guichen, in the spring of 1780.

Not long after Guichen took command of the French fleet in the West Indies, he settled plans with the Marquis de Bouillé, governor of Martinique, to launch attacks on some of Britain's Caribbean possessions. To this end, Bouillé supplied 3,000 men, who embarked aboard Guichen's fleet on 13 April. The fleet's first task, however, was to escort a convoy bound for Santo Domingo. On learning of Guichen's sailing, Rodney, with twenty ships of the line, one 50-gun ship, and five frigates, decided to seek him out, and on 16 August he discovered the French to leeward of Martinique and making a course for the channel that separates it from Dominica. Rodney chased his opponent to the northwest, and at 5:00 P.M. he discovered that Guichen commanded a force of twenty-three line of battle ships, including one 50-gun ship and a few frigates, although none of these were three-deckers (90 guns or more).

As the sun set, Rodney formed his ships in line of battle on the starboard tack. He carefully remained to windward of the French and ordered his frigates to watch his opponent closely. Rodney realized that Guichen's movements revealed a desire to avoid a fight; Rodney, on the other hand, was keen for action.

At sunrise on 17 August, Rodney observed the French four to five leagues to the west, sailing on a port tack and forming line of battle. With the wind blowing east, the French would be moving south-southeast. Rodney ordered his ships to maintain a distance of two cables between one another and to continue their bearing to the north and west. At 7:00 A.M. he reduced the length to one cable so as not to be overextended. The two lines of ships passed each other on opposite tacks, almost parallel, bringing Rodney's better-formed line abreast of the French rear, against which he sought to bring the most pressure to bear. At 8:00 A.M. he issued a signal to concentrate on that part of the French line and half an hour later ordered his vessels to form line abreast. Then, with his own ship, he bore down against the French.

As Rodney's intentions were now obvious, Guichen ordered his force to wear together on the starboard tack, converting his rear into his van, with the new rear now overstretched and seeking to catch up with the rest of the line. Rodney immediately hauled to the wind, on the port tack, engaging what now became, owing to his new maneuver, the French rear. He also increased the intervals between his ships to two cable lengths. The two fleets were therefore again sailing on parallel courses, in opposite directions, both sides having reversed their order. Rodney's line was, however, more compact than his adversary's, which stretched about 12 miles compared to Rodney's of about 5 miles long.

Both fleets maintained opposite parallel courses, with Guichen proceeding north by west and Rodney south by east until the respective flagships—the *Sandwich* (90 guns) and the *Couronne* (80 guns)—came abreast of one another. At 10:10 Rodney issued a signal to wear together, thus forming line of battle on the same tack as the French. Not satisfied with the slow manner in which his order was being carried out, Rodney repeated it, emphasized by his specifically signaling the *Sterling Castle* which, as the rearmost vessel, was meant to commence the maneuver. By 10:30 the fleet had finally come about, but as the ships remained apart by two cables, Rodney ordered the line to tighten. At 11:00 he signaled the fleet to prepare for battle, followed shortly thereafter by instructions to alter course to port, in the direction of the French.

At 11:50 came the signal for the fleet to bear down and for each ship to take its respective station immediately opposite its counterpart in the French line. A few minutes later came the signal to engage, underlined a short time after that by Rodney's command that his ships were to do so at close quarters, following the example set by the flagship. It was natural for Rodney to expect that the lead vessel, the *Sterling Castle,* whose course and conduct would be emulated by the ships that followed it, would steer a course for the French ship closest to hand. However, the captain of that ship, Robert Carkett, apparently misunderstood Rodney's signal, interpreting it as an instruction to engage the ship at the head of the French line and not the vessel that happened to be parallel with him at the point when the fleet bore away. As such, Rodney's lead vessel took a radical course in order to confront the head of Guichen's line and in so doing tacitly encouraged a number of other ships in the van to follow it.

Just after 1:00 one of the leading British ships began to exchange fire at long range, but the engagement did not become serious until somewhat later, when the *Sandwich* became closely engaged with the *Actionnaire* (64 guns), the second ship astern of the *Couronne.* The *Sandwich*'s superior weight of fire quickly forced out of the line both the *Actionnaire* and the next ship behind, the *Intrépide* (74 guns), which arrived to eliminate the gap thus created. At approximately 2:30 the *Sandwich,* for reasons that are not clear, was positioned leeward of the French line, with the *Couronne* on its weather bow. Rodney therefore signaled for the *Yarmouth* (64 guns), which was to windward, and the *Cornwall* (74 guns) to close the distance with the French.

Guichen interpreted these maneuvers as a deliberate attempt by Rodney to cut the French line. This was probably not the intention of the British admiral, who had yet to break the orthodox rules of eighteenth-century line of battle tactics. In all likelihood Rodney's plan was to direct his entire force against Guichen's rear and center rather than piercing his line. Nevertheless, the French admiral suspected otherwise and ordered his vessels to wear together. Under normal circumstances this maneuver would have shifted the fleet slightly to leeward, but as all of his ships had sustained varying degrees of damage and many were in fact disabled, the execution required more space than usual. This and the need to re-form the line along the new position brought the fleet even farther to leeward, and as it bore away the action closed.

Casualties were heavy on both sides: Rodney lost 120 killed and 354 wounded; Guichen lost 222 killed and 537 wounded. These figures reflect the respective tactics employed by each side, with the British favoring attacks against their adversaries' hulls and the French preferring to aim at their opponents' rigging. Rodney undertook repairs at sea and, by maintaining a position between Guichen and Martinique, was able to deny that key island as a refuge to the French admiral, who instead put in at Guadeloupe. Rodney reconnoitered there close to shore before assuming a new station off Fort Royal, Martinique.

Gregory Fremont-Barnes

See also

British West Indies; Dominica, Second Battle of; French West Indies; Guichen, Luc-Urbain du Bouexic, Comte de; Parker, Hyde; Rodney, George; West Indies

References

Breen, Kenneth. "George Bridges, Lord Rodney." Pp. 225–246 in *Precursors of Nelson: British Admirals of the Eighteenth Century,* ed. Peter Le Fevre and Richard Harding. London: Chatham, 2000.

Clowes, William Laird. *The Royal Navy: A History from the Earliest Times to 1900.* Vol. 3 of 7. London: Chatham, 1996.

Gardiner, Robert, ed. *Navies and the American Revolution, 1775–1783.* London: Chatham, 1996.
James, William. *The British Navy in Adversity: A Study of the War of American Independence.* 1926. Reprint, New York: Russell and Russell, 1970.
———. *The Naval History of Great Britain: During the French Revolutionary and Napoleonic Wars.* 4 vols. Mechanicsburg, PA: Stackpole, 2003.
Lloyd, Christopher. "Sir George Rodney: Lucky Admiral." Pp. 327–353 in *George Washington's Generals and Opponents: Their Exploits and Leadership.* Edited by George Athan Billias. 1964. Reprint, New York: Da Capo, 1994.
Spinney, David. *Rodney.* London: Allen and Unwin, 1969.
Tilley, J. A. *The Royal Navy in the American Revolution.* Columbia: University of South Carolina Press, 1987.

Dominica, Second Battle of (9 April 1782)

The Second Battle of Dominica was an Anglo-French naval engagement fought in the West Indies between Admiral François Joseph, the comte de Grasse, who was planning an attack on Jamaica, and Admiral Sir George Rodney, the new commander in chief of the Leeward Islands station.

Following the French capture of St. Kitts on 13 February 1782 by troops landed by de Grasse, Rear-Admiral Sir Samuel Hood weighed anchor and headed around the northern end of St. Kitts toward Antigua. He intended to return to Barbados, but on 25 February, while windward of Antigua, Rodney, having arrived from England the week before, joined him with twelve line of battle ships. Rodney sought to intercept de Grasse before he could reach Martinique, but the French admiral managed to get there on 26 February. As a result, Rodney sailed to St. Lucia so that Hood might refit his ships and to prepare his strategy for the defense of Jamaica, which was believed to be the allied objective in the next campaign. For the French, success very much hinged on the arrival of an enormous convoy. Rodney was aware that this convoy had left Brest bound for the West Indies in order to allow repairs to those ships damaged by a recent raid conducted by Rear-Admiral Richard Kempenfelt as well as those damaged by a bout of severe weather that followed in December.

Hood suggested to Rodney that he divide the fleet, then consisting of thirty-six ships of the line, in half, assigning one half the task of cruising in the channel north of Dominica while the other half stood guard over the approach from the south, between Martinique and St. Lucia. Rodney rejected this idea, however, and adopted a plan that divided his force into three parts. The division under Hood would take up a station to windward of the northern end of Martinique, extending north to a point not farther than the latitude of Dominica. The center and rear divisions would meanwhile stand off the central and southern parts of Martinique. Mutual communication was to be maintained by vessels positioned at points separating the three divisions. Although Hood attempted to extend his cruisers gradually northward, persuaded that he would detect the French in so doing, Rodney recalled those vessels.

The consequence of Rodney's dispositions was that the French convoy, accompanied by two ships of the line, avoided British detection and arrived safely at Martinique on 20 March. This increased the force under de Grasse to thirty-five line of battle ships, including two of fifty guns each, compared to Rodney's thirty-six ships of the line. A week later Rodney left for St. Lucia, anchored, and carefully monitored the opposing fleet at Fort Royal by employing a series of frigates, arrayed in a chain, that could quickly pass signals back to him.

De Grasse now faced the extremely difficult problem of having to ensure that the convoy arrived safely at Cap François, for the supply ships of which it was composed were vital to any attempt at the conquest of Jamaica. At the same time he had to protect a homeward-bound merchant fleet—a total of 150 unarmed vessels—with his 35 ships of the line against the 36 the British had on station. With a fair wind available to him, de Grasse planned to sail a course that kept him in close proximity to a series of friendly ports, thus providing refuge for the convoy if the need arose.

De Grasse sailed on 8 April. Around midday Rodney, quickly informed of the fact, put to sea in pursuit. The significance of Rear-Admiral Samuel Barrington's capture of St. Lucia in December 1778 now became apparent, since without British possession of that island, French movement could only have been reported to the more distant anchorage at Barbados, 100 miles away instead of 30. Rodney was thus able to respond more quickly than would otherwise have been the case. Even had he attempted to compensate for this disadvantage by patrolling the waters around Martinique, he would have had trouble obtaining water and other supplies, which now the nearby island of St. Lucia could offer.

The fact that de Grasse experienced the disadvantage of having his opponent watch him from such close quarters was not simply owing to Barrington's earlier achievement: blame may be placed on d'Estaing's shoulders for the lackluster manner in which he had attempted to take St. Lucia, giving priority instead to Tobago and St. Kitts. The fact that now de Grasse was encumbered by a huge convoy was not his fault, but much of his predicament now rested on the fact that he was soon to be chased by thirty-six ships of the line, when twenty-one of these might have been destroyed in detail only a matter of weeks before at the Battle of St. Kitts, quite apart from the opportunity lost to the French at the Battle of Martinique in April 1781.

At 2:30 P.M. on 8 April the French fleet was sighted by British patrols, and by 6:00 A.M. the following day both de

Grasse's fleet and convoy were clearly visible about 10 miles away, bearing northeast and extending from opposite the central part of Dominica toward Guadeloupe to the north. Rodney had covered a good distance in the course of the night, and by dawn he was off Dominica, leeward of the French rear, which remained sluggish under becalmed conditions. However, when the French van reached open waters in the channel separating Dominica and Guadeloupe, fresh winds arose, allowing individual ships to join de Grasse's fleet from time to time. Hood, on the other hand, with the British van, also took advantage of the favorable breeze and headed north with his eight ships, all arranged in order of battle.

To the northwest of Hood lay two French vessels, separated sufficiently from the main body that they risked being cut off. Undaunted, they bravely stood down and crossed the head of the British van, one so close to the lead vessel, the *Alfred* (74 guns), that its captain, William Bayne, had to bear up in order to avoid a collision and allow it to pass. At 6:40 Rodney ordered his ships to engage, but no sooner had he hoisted the signal than he hauled it down again, leaving Hood to withhold his fire until explicitly ordered to do so. As a result, the isolated French ship rejoined the main body without incident. At 8:30 French colors were seen aloft, and shortly thereafter their entire force tacked and steered south to come parallel with Hood.

De Grasse appreciated that he could not avoid fighting unless the convoy remained with his fleet. Thus, he detached two 50-gun ships to accompany these vessels to Guadeloupe, which they reached in safety later in the day. He then decided to head to windward, passing between Dominica and Guadeloupe and the small group of islands there known as Les Saintes. By adopting this course, he hoped not only to draw Rodney away from the convoy but also to leave behind his pursuers through his advantage in speed. He could rejoin the convoy and attempt to complete his task without having thus far sustained any damage. This plan was perfectly feasible, for French ships, being of superior design, sailed faster than their British counterparts, possibly including those British vessels whose speed had been markedly improved by the recent advance known as coppering.

No sooner did de Grasse begin to execute this plan, however, than he changed his mind, for in seeing Hood in a vulnerable position, exposed as he was with respect to the main body, de Grasse decided to engage him. The French admiral nevertheless committed only half of his force, believing that this would be sufficient to inflict enough damage on the British to deter Rodney from further pursuit. Responsibility for this maneuver fell to the second in command, the Marquis de Vaudreuil, who bore down from windward and engaged the rear of Hood's column. Then, advancing north, parallel with Hood's line, the French proceeded to tack in succession, coming full circle before forming again and repeating the attack, beginning with Hood's rearmost vessel.

In so doing the French brought fifteen ships against eight in a continuous elliptical loop—all possible owing to Hood's self-imposed slow progress, necessitated by his desire not to extend to too great a distance the gap separating him from Rodney's center and rear. Rodney's vessels in fact remained practically stationary due to becalmed conditions prevailing off the northwest coast of Dominica. As circumstances allowed the French the freedom to choose the distance at which the engagement would be fought, they did so at long range, for the British well outnumbered them in carronades—a weapon of heavy caliber but very short range. Thus the French preserved their hulls and rigging in a brief contest that lasted, according to Hood, from 9:48 until 10:25 A.M. A lull followed until 12:15, when firing resumed with greater intensity. During this time much of the British center reinforced Hood, though again the engagement remained at long range. This continued until 1:45 when the action ceased, and fifteen minutes later Rodney hauled down the signal for battle.

Broadsides had been issued at such extreme range that damage to the British ships was minimal, and none were obliged to detach themselves from the fleet in order to undertake repairs. Nevertheless, the *Royal Oak* (74 guns) was deprived of its main topmast, and two days later the *Warrior* (74 guns) lost its main topmast, probably weakened from fire. This damage did not, however, impede Rodney's pursuit, and to facilitate this he placed Hood's vessels in the rear, thus allowing them to repair and refit while still enabling them to offer support if necessary. Only one French ship, the *Caton* (64 guns), was sufficiently damaged to render it a liability in a chase, and this de Grasse detached to the safety of Guadeloupe. On the night of the action Rodney halted to carry out repairs, but he resumed the chase the following morning and would finally reengage his opponent a few days later at the Battle of the Saintes.

Gregory Fremont-Barnes

See also

Barrington, Samuel; British West Indies; Dominica, First Battle of; French West Indies; Grasse, François-Joseph-Paul, Comte de; Hood, Samuel; Jamaica; Martinique, Battle of; Rodney, George; Saintes, Battle of the; St. Kitts, Battle of; St. Lucia, Naval and Military Operations against; West Indies

References

Breen, Kenneth. "George Bridges, Lord Rodney." Pp. 225–246 in *Precursors of Nelson: British Admirals of the Eighteenth Century*, ed. Peter Le Fevre and Richard Harding. London: Chatham, 2000.

Clowes, William Laird. *The Royal Navy: A History from the Earliest Times to 1900*. Vol. 3 of 7. London: Chatham, 1996.

Gardiner, Robert, ed. *Navies and the American Revolution, 1775–1783*. London: Chatham, 1996.

James, William. *The British Navy in Adversity: A Study of the War of American Independence.* 1926. Reprint, New York: Russell and Russell, 1970.
———. *The Naval History of Great Britain: During the French Revolutionary and Napoleonic Wars.* 4 vols. Mechanicsburg, PA: Stackpole, 2003.
Lewis, Charles Lee. *Admiral de Grasse and American Independence.* 1945. Reprint, New York: Arno, 1980.
Lloyd, Christopher. "Sir George Rodney: Lucky Admiral." Pp. 327–353 in *George Washington's Generals and Opponents: Their Exploits and Leadership.* Edited by George Athan Billias. 1964. Reprint, New York: Da Capo, 1994.
Spinney, David. *Rodney.* London: Allen and Unwin, 1969.
Tilley, J. A. *The Royal Navy in the American Revolution.* Columbia: University of South Carolina Press, 1987.
Tornquist, Karl Gustaf. *The Naval Campaigns of Count de Grasse during the American Revolution, 1781–1783.* Philadelphia: Swedish Colonial Society, 1942.

Donop, Carl von (1740–1777)

A professional soldier from Hesse-Kassel, Count Carl von Donop was devoted to and enthusiastic about his duty, but in the end he fell victim to his own pride and rashness. By 1776 he had risen to the position of adjutant to the Landgraf of Hesse-Kassel. That year, he was given command of the grenadier battalion with the rank of colonel in a Hessian army hired by Britain to fight in America. He sailed in May 1776, arriving in New York on 13 August. In the Battle of Long Island, on 27 August, he capably commanded the Hessian grenadiers, plus a jaeger unit, under General Leopold Philip von Heister in the British center. During General William Howe's pursuit of American forces across New Jersey, Donop continued to perform well. In early December he was given command of Hessian outposts at Trenton, Bordentown, and Burlington under General James Grant.

By mid-December, Donop and Colonel Johann Rall at Trenton were worriedly informing Grant that the Americans under George Washington intended to attack their outposts, but Grant disparaged their concerns. On 21 December, Donop marched his grenadiers to Mount Holly after hearing rumors that the enemy was about to attack there. Five days later, Washington's troops defeated and captured Rall's forces at Trenton and killed Rall. Immediately Donop, with Grant's concurrence, withdrew all his troops to Princeton. When Howe and General Charles Cornwallis criticized this action, Donop bristled, insisting that he had to consolidate his isolated and exposed posts. In the campaign of 1777, Donop served at Bound Brook, Brandywine, and Germantown and at the capture of Philadelphia. Still smarting from Howe's and Cornwallis's taunts, he was openly critical of Howe's strategy. Desirous of proving the worth of his Hessian troops, he volunteered to attack Fort Mercer at Red Bank on the Delaware River to help open a supply route for the British Army in Philadelphia.

On 21 October, Donop ferried 1,800 Hessian troops across the Delaware River and marched to Haddonfield, New Jersey. The next day he reconnoitered Fort Mercer and its outer works and confidently decided that a direct assault against the fort would be successful. Although he did not possess siege guns or scaling ladders, he apparently assumed that these would be unnecessary. Also, he had not discovered that the American outer works were abandoned and that row galleys mounted with cannon supported the fort's defenses. All his preparations and plans evinced overconfidence and a lack of caution. He demanded that Colonel Christopher Greene, commander of the fort, surrender the post's 600 defenders and was promptly rejected. He then ordered his troops to storm the post, and the assault became a slaughter. In a forty-minute fight, 153 of his men were killed and more than 200 wounded. Donop's hip was shattered, and three days later he died. The total failure of this action meant that it was the end of November before Howe could finally open the Delaware River to British shipping.

Paul David Nelson

See also

Bound Brook, New Jersey, Action at; Brandywine, Battle of; Cornwallis, Charles; Fort Mercer, New Jersey, Assault on and Capture of; German Mercenaries; Germantown, Battle of; Grant, James; Greene, Christopher; Long Island, Battle of; Rall, Johann; Trenton, Battle of

References

Atwood, R. *The Hessians.* 1980. Reprint, Cambridge: Cambridge University Press, 2002.
Ketchum, Richard M. *The Winter Soldiers.* Garden City, NY: Doubleday, 1973.
Smith, Samuel S. *Fight for the Delaware, 1777.* Monmouth Beach, NJ: Philip Freneau, 1970.

Dorchester Heights, Massachusetts (4–5 March 1776)

Dorchester Heights lies just south of Boston. In 1776 it proved to be a decisive position for the American forces surrounding and blockading British troops stationed in the city. The American commander, General George Washington, recognized the strategic importance of Dorchester Heights. The British commander, Lieutenant-General Sir William Howe, failed to do so until it was too late.

During the winter of 1775–1776, the British forces were hemmed in on the Boston peninsula. The American forces commanded the countryside around Boston. The onset of

The British evacuate Boston on 17 March 1776, after George Washington and his troops bombarded William Howe's forces from Dorchester Heights. (Library of Congress)

winter discouraged major military actions, but Washington used the respite to devise a bold plan for the following spring. Believing that he lacked sufficient infantry forces to attack the British positions in Boston, he decided to use artillery instead.

The Americans had seized Fort Ticonderoga from the British in May 1775 in a daring raid by New England militia under the command of Ethan Allen and Benedict Arnold. In November 1775, Washington ordered that the heavy artillery from Fort Ticonderoga be moved to Boston so that he could use it to bombard the British positions, and he sent Colonel Henry Knox to retrieve and transport the cannon.

The transfer of the guns took place during midwinter 1775–1776. The distance from Ticonderoga to Cambridge was more than 300 miles. Knox and his men brought the cannon back over snow on sledges hauled by oxen; the train of artillery arrived in Cambridge in February 1776. Thanks to this arduous undertaking, the Americans were now in possession of proper siege artillery.

Howe and his staff were unaware of this new threat. Numerous artillery duels had occurred during the course of the winter, and Howe had launched various small-scale raids to keep the American forces off balance. On 13 February, Howe deployed a raiding party to destroy all the houses and any American positions on Dorchester Neck. Despite this maneuver, Howe never seemed to recognize the strategic potential of Dorchester Heights. Possibly he thought that the Heights were too far from Boston to be of use to the American artillery, not realizing that the Americans had acquired heavier pieces.

Washington's decision to occupy Dorchester Heights and install artillery was carried out overnight on 4–5 March. His orders to Massachusetts militia Brigadier John Thomas were as follows: "Brigadier General Thomas is to take command of 2100 men which are to be paraded at Dorchester at 6 o'clock this evening [4 March] with which to proceed to Dorchester Point and then throw up such works on the two commanding hills as he with the advice of the engineers shall think most proper for the defense of the ground and annoyance of the enemy and defend the same."

Washington also ordered artillery to fire from Lechmere Point at Cambridge to cover the noise created by the movement of troops and guns at Dorchester and ordered the building of positions on the Heights. Howe's batteries responded to the bombardment, and the resulting duel completely muffled any noise from the operation.

An American officer present on the Heights recorded the British reaction when, on the morning of 5 March, they became aware of the new American artillery. He stated in a report to Thomas: "about eight o'clock [on 4 March] we ascended the high hills, and by day light got two hills defensible. About sun rise, the enemy and others in Boston appeared numerous on the tops of houses and on the wharfs viewing us with astonishment, for our appearance was unexpected to them. . . . [T]he enemy turned their fire towards us on the hills, but they soon found it was to little effect."

Washington's plan anticipated that Howe would attack the Americans on Dorchester Heights, and he hoped that the British would launch a second costly assault as they had done the previous June at Bunker Hill (Breed's Hill). Washington's offensive plan for such a British attack was to reinforce the American defenses at Dorchester Heights and to launch an attack against Boston and the weakened British forces remaining in the city.

As soon as the positions were operational, the American artillery on Dorchester Heights opened fire upon Boston and British shipping in the harbor. Howe, as Washington had hoped, decided to organize a force to attack the Heights. An American officer witnessing events reported: "we discovered large bodies of troops embarking in boats with their artillery, which made a formidable appearance. . . . [W]e were now in a good posture of defense, and had two thousand men added to our number." An attack on the position would probably have been costly, but Howe had to change his plans when a storm blew up and forestalled the British attack. The reprieve allowed the Americans time to strengthen their defenses even further.

Because of Howe's delay, the American position soon became too strong for the British to dislodge by a direct assault without great loss of life. Howe had received orders that he could evacuate the city when he chose to sail for Halifax, Nova Scotia. He now decided to take the option of evacuating, as the continuing bombardment from Dorchester Heights was proving too costly. On 17 March, British troops withdrew from the city and soon sailed for Nova Scotia. Washington's bold strategy had paid off; the guns atop Dorchester Heights had proved to be the decisive factor in the successful siege of Boston.

Daniel Patrick Marston

See also

Allen, Ethan; Arnold, Benedict; Boston, Siege of; Bunker Hill, Battle of; Fort Ticonderoga, New York; Howe, William; Knox, Henry; Thomas, John

References

Black, Jeremy. *War for America: The Fight for Independence.* Stroud, UK: Alan Sutton, 1991.

Conway, Stephen. *The War of American Independence, 1775–1783.* London: Arnold, 1995.

Higginbotham, Don. *The War of American Independence: Military Attitudes, Policies, and Practice, 1763–1789.* New York: Macmillan, 1971.

Mackesy, Piers. *The War for America, 1775–1783.* 1965. Reprint, Lincoln: University of Nebraska Press, 1993.

Drayton, William Henry (1742–1779)

One of the most influential of South Carolina's low-country planters, William Henry Drayton served as the chief intellectual proponent of the province's independence during the final imperial crisis.

Drayton's grandfather, the Barbadian planter Thomas Drayton, was one of the first settlers in the Carolina colony. William's planter father, John Drayton, and his uncle, William Bull Jr., lieutenant governor of the colony, secured William's place in South Carolina society following his education in England. Like his relatives, the young Drayton sided with the Crown during the Stamp Act crisis and refused to participate in the nonimportation movements of the late 1760s. Once the controversy had subsided, however, and Drayton took an extended tour of England from 1770 to 1772, his opinion of the king's friends who dominated Parliament soured considerably. The time he spent in England made Drayton far more sympathetic to the colonial cause, to the point that he began thinking of himself as a Carolinian, not an Englishman.

Drayton's role in the American Revolution typifies the conservatism of South Carolina's low-country planter elite. Upon his return from England in 1772, he was appointed to the governor's council, and in 1774 he became a judge. When open conflict with Britain erupted in 1775, Drayton was instrumental in the creation of South Carolina's new government. But it was as a spokesman for the cause of traditional English rights during the imperial crisis that Drayton became best known.

During the crisis, Drayton published his most important pamphlet, *A Letter from a Freeman of South-Carolina,* and spoke on liberty before grand juries at Camden and Cheraw. In *A Letter from a Freeman,* he proposed an imperial arrangement that somewhat resembled Joseph Galloway's Plan of Union, whereby the colonies would be left to govern their local affairs under the auspices of a continental government charged with collecting taxes for the British Crown. Through his writings and speeches, Drayton insisted on the rule of law and the sanctity of English rights. His ideas helped galvanize the Patriot wing of Carolina society behind a movement that was more reactionary than revolutionary—a movement to restore lost rights rather than refashion a new society.

Drayton justified South Carolina's separation from Great Britain on numerous philosophical grounds, including the natural right of self-preservation. He rested his case on the foundation of English history and its legal tradition, and he linked the actions of South Carolinians with those of the authors of the Petition of Right of 1628 and the participants in the Glorious Revolution of 1688.

During the eventful year of 1775, Drayton continued to serve in the new Provincial Congress and on the Council of Safety. In November he was elected president of the Provincial Congress and supervised the creation of South Carolina's new constitution, the first in the rebelling colonies. Following independence, he was chosen in 1778 to be the state's first chief justice under the new government. In 1779 he was elected to the Continental Congress, where he was an outspoken critic of any further centralization of power and opposed the adoption of the Articles of Confederation. He died of typhus in Philadelphia before his term expired.

Cary Roberts

See also

Bull, William, Jr.; Congress, Second Continental and Confederation; Galloway, Joseph; South Carolina

References

Bradford, M. E. "No Master but the Law: The Legacy of William Henry Drayton." Pp. 111–136 in *A Better Guide than Reason: Federalists & Anti-Federalists.* With a new introduction by Russell Kirk. New Brunswick, CT: Transaction, 1994.

Krawczynski, Keith. *William Henry Drayton: South Carolina Revolutionary Patriot.* Baton Rouge: Louisiana State University Press, 2001.

Duane, James (1733–1797)

A dedicated member of the Continental Congress, the first mayor of New York City after independence, and a strong supporter of the U.S. Constitution, James Duane was one of New York's most influential and distinguished Revolutionary figures.

Born in New York City on 6 February 1733 to Anthony Duane, a merchant, and Althea Kettletas, young Duane chose to pursue a career in law and clerked for attorney James Alexander. Following his admission to the bar in 1754, Duane quickly established a lucrative legal practice and was especially successful in the years immediately preceding the Revolution. Connections forged by his marriage in 1759 to Mary Livingston, daughter of Robert Livingston Jr., helped advance Duane's legal career.

Duane also became heavily involved in land speculation on the New York frontier. Inheriting land in what later became Schenectady County from his father in 1747, Duane continued to acquire tracts in this area throughout his life. He soon developed his holdings by surveying the land and recruiting settlers to live there, starting in 1757. Beginning in the 1760s, Duane made an annual visit to the site, and in 1764 he successfully petitioned the New York government to incorporate approximately 40,000 acres in the area into a township known as Duanesburgh. Though at the time he owned less than half of this land, he continued to accumulate thousands of acres more, and by the end of his life he owned and rented virtually the entire township. Duanesburgh suffered during the Revolution but became a successful settlement after the war.

Duane also invested heavily in land in the Green Mountains that is now part of Vermont. The legal ownership of this contested area was a source of tension between New England and New York for decades. Although the British government

James Duane, a delegate from New York to the First and Second Continental Congresses. Serving on various committees dealing with Native American affairs, finance, and other matters, Duane was noteworthy for his strident opposition to independence, a stance that opened him to charges of disloyalty. With support from prominent proindependence colleagues, however, his reputation remained intact, and he served as mayor of New York City after the war. (National Archives and Records Administration)

acknowledged New York's claim to the region in 1764, settlers moving onto the land from New Hampshire, Massachusetts, and Connecticut complicated the situation considerably, and the validity of the New York proprietors' holdings became increasingly unclear. Duane himself was at the forefront of their efforts to retain control over this territory and became a recognized authority on New York's land and boundary disputes. Though attempts were made to resolve the conflict before and during the Revolution, it persisted well into the 1780s. New York finally lost this struggle, and Vermont was admitted to the union as a separate state in 1791. Despite his many years of hard work and frustration, Duane's substantial investments in this territory proved virtually worthless.

Although Duane thought that the Stamp Act was unconstitutional and approved of New York's nonimportation agreement to protest the Townshend Acts, he was conservative by nature and abhorred the social upheaval associated with radical resistance. In 1774 he was chosen as one of the moderate men on New York's Committee of Fifty-one and then was named a delegate to the First Continental Congress in September. Allied with the future Loyalist Joseph Galloway in that body, Duane and fellow delegates John Jay and Isaac Low found themselves in the minority as they confronted the growing radicalism of the other colonies. Though they signed the Continental Association, New York's delegates had misgivings about the proceedings. Through 1775 and early 1776, Duane remained cautious and, along with other moderates such as John Dickinson, was eager to negotiate a resolution to the crisis with Great Britain. He did not initially support the decision in May 1776 to urge the colonies to form new governments, and he was absent from Congress in late June and early July when the body debated and declared independence. Once the separation took place, however, Duane wholeheartedly supported the Patriot cause throughout the Revolution. While often reluctant to embrace change and more than willing to voice his opposition to radical measures during congressional debates, he also felt that once decisions were made in Congress he should publicly support them.

Duane served in Congress regularly from its beginnings through the end of 1783. As Congress took on the responsibilities of a national government supplying an army and financing a war, the efficient and hardworking Duane found himself sitting on many different committees, often as chairman. He was also made head of the new Treasury Board when it was formed in early 1776. Involved in problems of Indian diplomacy as well as finance, he attended conferences with the Iroquois, belonged to the standing Committee of Indian Affairs, and became New York's Indian commissioner in 1778. He helped draft the Articles of Confederation, including the ninth article that created a procedure for resolving land disputes between the states, but the disputes that most concerned Duane and other New Yorkers were ultimately resolved outside of this system.

Returning to New York City when the British evacuated at the end of the war, Duane became its first mayor in February 1784 and applied his considerable administrative skills to revitalizing the city and its institutions, such as Trinity Church and King's College, soon to be renamed Columbia College. During the 1780s Duane was also a state senator, stepping down in 1789 after seven years of service. Although he narrowly missed election to the Constitutional Convention in Philadelphia, he was a strong advocate of the new federal government and pushed for the Constitution's ratification at the state convention in Poughkeepsie. He spent the final five years of his long legal and political career as a federal judge before retiring from public life in 1794. Moving to upstate New York, he died there on 1 February 1797, just short of his sixty-fourth birthday.

Karen Northrop Barzilay

See also

Congress, First Continental; Congress, Second Continental and Confederation; New York, Province and State; New York City; Vermont

References

Alexander, Edward. *A Revolutionary Conservative: James Duane of New York.* New York: Columbia University Press, 1938.

Countryman, Edward. *A People in Revolution: The American Revolution and Political Society in New York, 1760–1790.* Baltimore, MD: Johns Hopkins University Press, 1981.

Matson, Cathy. "James Duane." Pp. 933–934 in *American National Biography,* Vol. 6. Edited by John A. Garraty and Mark C. Carnes. New York: Oxford University Press, 1999.

Duché, Jacob (1738–1798)

The Anglican priest Jacob Duché served as chaplain for the Continental Congress from 1774 to 1776. While he was sympathetic to the colonies' desire for some form of self-rule, he was opposed to war and American independence. When he finally opposed independence openly, he was labeled a traitor and forced into exile.

Duché, a Philadelphia native, was ordained in 1762 in London and named rector of St. Peter's Church in Philadelphia. Poor eyesight forced him to memorize his sermons, and he attracted large congregations with his powerful orations. Duché also turned his pen to criticism of British policies in the colonies. In 1772–1773, he published a series of letters in support of the colonies in the *Pennsylvania Packet* under the pseudonym (and acronym) "Tamoc Caspipina" (The Assistant Minister of Christ Church and St. Peter's in Philadelphia in North America).

When the First Continental Congress decided to open with a religious invocation, John Adams proposed that it be given by Duché, who was appointed chaplain on 6 September 1774. His prayers at Congress were as powerful as his sermons, and he was reappointed on 10 May 1775 and on 9 July 1776. But while he continued to believe that the colonies had legitimate complaints against British policies, as an Anglican priest he was officially an officer of the Crown, and he did not support independence. At first, he believed that the Declaration of Independence was a bargaining tool. When he realized that Congress really wanted independence for the colonies, he resigned as chaplain on 17 October 1776 but continued preaching at his church in Philadelphia.

In September 1777, Duché began offering prayers to the king, as was Anglican custom, despite a congressional resolution against the practice. His actions led to a brief jail term. After his release, he wrote a letter to General George Washington stating that he was opposed to the war and that the members of Congress were the lowest members of society. Washington turned the letter over to Congress, and Duché quickly went from beloved preacher to traitor. On 9 December 1777, he announced to his congregation that he was returning to London. As he was labeled a traitor, however,

Congress seized his properties and assets in Philadelphia, and his family was unable to secure passage to England until 1780.

Duché's skills as a preacher quickly secured him employment in England. The church forgave him for his pro-American activities, and he was named chaplain of the Asylum for Female Orphans at St. George's Fields. He was also invited to preach at area churches and published a number of his sermons. While his prominence grew in London, he still considered himself an American and longed to return to Philadelphia. In 1783 he wrote letters to Washington and to his friend Francis Hopkinson in which he admitted his mistake in sending the initial letter to Washington and hoped to obtain permission to return to the United States. Despite his efforts, he was unable to return until 1792. After his return, however, he secured a personal visit to Washington, who received him cordially. Duché died in 1798.

Michael C. Miller

See also

Congress, First Continental

References

Garrett, Clarke. "The Spiritual Odyssey of Jacob Duché." *Proceedings of the American Philosophical Society* 119 (1975): 143–155.

Hastings, George E. "Jacob Duché, First Chaplain of Congress." *South Atlantic Quarterly* 31 (1932): 386–400.

Willian Duer. American businessman and member of the Continental Congress, Duer set off the nation's first financial panic and spent seven years in debtors' prison. (Library of Congress)

Duer, William (1743–1799)

The congressman, Treasury Department official, military contractor, and aggressive speculator William Duer had a meteoric rise in American business and society before setting off the nation's first major financial panic and spending the latter part of his life in debtors' prison.

Born in Devonshire, England, on 18 March 1743, Duer attended Eton College before joining the army and traveling to India in 1764. He soon became secretary to Lord Clive, the governor-general of the East India Company, but shortly thereafter returned to England for his health. Duer next sailed to the West Indies to supervise properties that he had inherited from his father. He first visited North America in 1768, traveling to New York to find the contacts he needed to meet a contract he had obtained to supply equipment to the Royal Navy. He briefly settled at Fort Mills, where he erected the first saw and gristmills, and later constructed snuff and powder mills. Acting on the advice of Philip Schuyler, he also purchased a tract of timberland north of Saratoga. After returning to England to settle his affairs there, he moved permanently to the province of New York in 1773.

In New York, Duer soon became an ardent member of the Patriot Party. He declined an appointment as deputy adjutant general of the Continental Army in August 1775 out of concern for jeopardizing his family interests in the West Indies, but he served on the New York convention's executive Committee of Safety and its committee for detecting conspiracies. In 1777 he was elected to the Continental Congress, where he served from April until November 1778 and sat on the Board of War. In that role he strongly supported George Washington against the criticisms of the Conway Cabal. Following his congressional service, Duer supplied the French army and secured contracts for supplying American forces. He also served in several judicial posts in New York and eventually moved to Fishkill, where he erected the first cotton mill. Because of his education and his contacts and experience as a rising member of American society, he was tapped by Washington to gather intelligence, beginning in early 1777. In 1779 Duer married Catherine Alexander, the daughter of the wealthy American General William Alexander (often called Lord Stirling).

After the war for independence, Duer and his family moved to New York City and began living in style. He now began to reap the profits from his land speculations and other business dealings. In 1786 he accepted an appointment as secretary of Congress's Treasury Board and served for four years as a key Treasury official under both the Confederation and Federal governments. But he did not put aside his active land speculation. He organized the Scioto Company, which was connected with the Ohio Company, and invested in land in northern New England as well.

Duer seemed especially qualified for working with Alexander Hamilton on America's fiscal problems in the new federal government. In September 1789, working through family connections, Duer gained the position of assistant secretary of the Treasury Department. Secretary Hamilton trusted Duer and was not aware of his assistant's improper actions. But the wealthy Philadelphian William Bingham, an associate of Duer, understood the new possibilities of making a profit. He borrowed £60,000 in Amsterdam for use in speculation with the federal debt. As a government official, however, Duer was not allowed to speculate in federal securities and therefore resigned in early 1790.

Having served as the secretary of the Treasury Board under the Confederation, Duer also had knowledge that was beneficial to his relationship with another speculator, Alexander Macomb, and they agreed to work together for one year speculating in stocks and bonds. Duer began purchasing stock in the Bank of New York when rumors spread that the bank would become part of Hamilton's proposed Bank of the United States. Duer and Macomb foresaw huge profits as the bank stock rose; yet under their arrangement, if the two banks did not merge only Macomb would lose financially.

Many individuals lent Duer money to invest since he had the reputation of being an excellent financier. But as the nation's financial and economic situation took a downturn in 1792, investor anxiety grew. While Duer kept speculating in bank stocks, another group of speculators had an interest in seeing the price of stocks fall, and interest rates began to rise. This hurt Duer, whose attempts to obtain additional credit failed. On 22 March 1792, Duer's empire collapsed in New York City's first financial panic. The following day he was sent to debtors' prison along with Macomb. Numerous bank failures quickly followed.

The Antifederalists led by Thomas Jefferson, who opposed a national central bank, were ecstatic. The panic only confirmed Jefferson's concerns about the dangers to the new nation from fiscal centralization and from speculators, who calculated their losses at $5 million. Despite Hamilton's efforts to help him, Duer was never able to pay his debts and was only released from debtors' prison in early 1799 on account of poor health. He died about two months later, on 7 May 1799. Duer was buried in the family vault under the old church in St. Thomas, West Indies, but was later reinterred in Jamaica, Long Island, New York.

Duer's financial disaster had important results. Shortly after the crash, participants in the market in stocks decided to find a permanent home for their exchange and establish regulations for its proceedings. In May 1792, traders in the stock market met and signed the Buttonwood Agreement, whereby the parties agreed to make a permanent home for their exchange. This organization eventually led to the establishment of the New York Stock Exchange in the 1830s. And Hamilton, in his role as secretary of the Treasury, was able to control the panic and keep his critics from destroying his proposed Bank of the United States. He used federal funds to support the national market and allowed some flexibility in the payment of import duties at the federal customhouses, which did not require immediate payment in hard currency.

Arthur K. Steinberg

See also

Alexander, William; Congress, Second Continental and Confederation; Conway Cabal; Hamilton, Alexander; New York, Province and State; New York City; Schuyler, Philip; Washington, George

References

Bean, Jonathan J. "William Duer." Pp. 14–16 in *American National Biography.* Edited by John A. Garraty and Mark C. Carnes. New York: Oxford University Press, 1999.

Bruchey, Stuart W. *Enterprise: The Dynamic Economy of a Free People.* Cambridge: Harvard University Press, 1990.

East, Robert A. *Business Enterprise in the American Revolutionary War Era.* 1933. Reprint, New York: AMS Press, 1969.

Jones, Robert F. "Economic Opportunism and the Constitution in New York State: The Example of William Duer." *New York History* 68 (1987): 356–372.

———. *"The King of the Alley," William Duer: Politician, Entrepreneur, and Speculator, 1768–1799.* Philadelphia: American Philosophical Society, 1992.

Dulany, Daniel, Jr. (1722–1797)

The Stamp Act prompted the Maryland barrister and politician Daniel Dulany to write one of the earliest and most influential pamphlets opposing British taxation of the American colonies. As the Revolution reached a crisis, however, Dulany continued to support both Maryland's proprietor and British authority and finally sat out the Revolutionary War as a neutral with strong Loyalist sympathies.

Dulany, the son of the prominent Annapolis residents Rebecca Smith and Daniel Dulany Sr., was born in Maryland but received an English education at Eton and Clare College, Cambridge, before entering the Middle Temple to study law in 1742. Five years later he returned to Maryland, where he created a profitable law practice in Annapolis and acquired six lots in Frederick Town as well as substantial acreage in western Maryland. In 1749 he firmly established himself as a member of the Maryland elite by marrying Rebecca Tasker, daughter of a wealthy planter who was president of the Governor's Council.

In 1751 Dulany was first elected a delegate from Annapolis to the lower house of the Maryland General Assembly. The proprietor, Frederick Calvert, Lord Baltimore, appointed Dulany to the Council in 1757 and in 1761 named him provincial secretary, positions he held until the Revolution. In 1761 poor health compelled Dulany to travel to England to seek medical attention, but he used the visit to forge an even stronger bond with the proprietor and his London court. When he returned to Maryland in 1763, he closed his law practice and devoted his attention to politics and the management of the proprietor's landed estates.

The year 1765 was a challenging one for Dulany. He both opposed the passage of the Stamp Act by Parliament and denounced the local mob action that the act precipitated among Annapolis's Sons of Liberty. As a counter to violence, he encouraged the adoption of legal and orderly means of protest and justified orderly opposition to the new tax in *Considerations on the Propriety of Imposing Taxes in the British Colonies,* which he published anonymously in Annapolis in October. Considering the Stamp Act to be illegal, he rejected the British ministry's justification that the colonies were virtually represented in Parliament but cautioned that prudence and duty required submission to the law. The pamphlet immediately gained wide popularity in America, especially for its argument against virtual representation, but it also earned Dulany the reputation of a political mediator and was influential in the campaign in Parliament to repeal the Stamp Act in 1766.

Beginning in 1770, however, Dulany supported Maryland's proprietary governor, Robert Eden, in the fee proclamation controversy. In January 1773, he published "A Dialogue between Two Citizens" anonymously in the *Maryland Gazette.* A newspaper war ensued when Dulany, writing first as "Second Citizen" and later as "Antilon," defended himself against attacks by "First Citizen" (Charles Carroll of Carrollton), who denounced the proprietary government's fee proclamation as arbitrary and unconstitutional. Now viewed as an opponent of the popular will, Dulany refused to support Maryland's revolutionary convention government in the summer of 1775. By early 1776, still maintaining his loyalty to the proprietor and the British Crown, he moved his family from Annapolis to his country estate in Baltimore County.

Dulany professed neutrality during the Revolutionary War, but his family took sides: one son became a Patriot, the other an active Loyalist; one brother remained neutral in the colonies, the other immigrated to England as a Loyalist. By war's end, divided loyalties so fragmented the family that Dulany never achieved prominence in Maryland politics again, but he occasionally practiced law until his death in Baltimore in 1797.

Martha King

See also

Carroll, Charles

References

Hoffman, Ronald. *A Spirit of Dissension: Economics, Politics, and the Revolution in Maryland.* Baltimore, MD: Johns Hopkins University Press, 1973.

Land, Aubrey C. *The Dulanys of Maryland: A Biographical Study of Daniel Dulany, the Elder (1685–1753) and Daniel Dulany, the Younger (1722–1797).* Baltimore, MD: Johns Hopkins University Press, 1955.

Dumas, Charles-Guillaume-Frédéric (1721–1796)

A naturalized Dutchman of French parentage and Swiss birth, an ardent political liberal, and a strong supporter of American independence, Charles-Guillaume [William]-Frédéric Dumas served as America's secret agent and later chargé d'affaires in the Netherlands during the Revolutionary War.

Dumas met Benjamin Franklin when the latter visited the Netherlands early in 1775, and the two struck up a lively correspondence. In December 1775, Franklin, now back in Philadelphia and chairman of the Continental Congress's Committee of Secret Correspondence, asked Dumas to tend in secret to American interests at the Dutch court at The Hague as a paid agent. The committee instructed Dumas to determine whether any of the European powers would, first, recognize American independence and, second, join an alliance with the new nation.

Due to a delay in the transatlantic mail, Dumas' acceptance did not reach the committee until April 1776. He reported that France and Spain favored American independence because they believed it would weaken British power. Dumas notified Franklin that he had learned from private conversations with the French minister to the Netherlands that France also wished to pursue a treaty of alliance with America. France, he informed Franklin, feared that an Anglo-American reconciliation would enormously strengthen Britain vis-à-vis France. Armed with this intelligence, Franklin was sent to Paris by the Continental Congress to negotiate a treaty of alliance with France. After the Franco-American Alliance was signed in February 1778, Dumas officially presented the Treaty to The Hague on 10 April 1778.

For the next two years Dumas continued, in an unofficial but paid capacity, to represent American interests in the Netherlands. Upon the arrival of John Adams as the American representative in 1780, Dumas became Adams's secretary and translator. Dumas helped Adams, through a steady flow of information and regular advice, to secure recognition of American independence from the Netherlands (April 1782), negotiate a series of much-needed loans from Dutch bankers (the first in June 1782) that were widely credited with keeping America afloat for much of the decade, and conclude a Treaty of Amity and Commerce with the Netherlands (October 1782). After Adams returned to Paris in October 1782 to join Franklin and John Jay in negotiating the preliminary treaty with Britain that would ultimately end the Revolutionary War, Dumas became America's chargé d'affaires at The Hague, where he assisted Adams in concluding additional loans from Dutch bankers through the late 1780s. Thereafter he remained in The Hague without any further

American duties but lived to see Adams's son, John Quincy Adams, whom he had tutored in Latin in 1783, return to the city as American minister to the Netherlands in 1795.

Chris Tudda

See also

Adams, John; Diplomacy, American; Franco-American Alliance; Franklin, Benjamin; Netherlands; Secret Correspondence, Committee of; Treaty of Amity and Commerce with the Netherlands

References

Bemis, Samuel F. *The Diplomacy of the American Revolution.* 1935. Reprint, Bloomington: Indiana University Press, 1957.

Schulte Nordholt, Jan Willem. *The Dutch Republic and American Independence.* Translated by Herbert H. Rowen. Chapel Hill: University of North Carolina Press, 1982.

Sparks, Jared, ed. *The Diplomatic Correspondence of the American Revolution.* Washington, DC: John C. Rives, 1857.

Wharton, Francis, ed. *The Revolutionary Diplomatic Correspondence of the United States.* 6 vols. Washington, DC: U.S. Government Printing Office, 1889.

Dutch Republic

See Netherlands

Dyer, Eliphalet (1721–1807)

The distinguished Connecticut leader Eliphalet Dyer served in numerous political, diplomatic, and judicial posts in his home state throughout the Revolutionary era and spent several years in Congress. He was also deeply involved in the Susquehanna Company, which pitted Connecticut against Pennsylvania over claims to the Wyoming Valley.

Born to prominent residents of Windham, Connecticut, on 14 September 1721, Dyer received a classical education at Yale and went on to study law. Starting in the 1740s, Windham voters elected Dyer to all major local offices: town clerk, selectman, moderator, and deputy to the General Assembly. He also rose through the ranks of the colonial militia, seeing active duty during the French and Indian War as a lieutenant colonel. In 1762, Dyer became a member of the Council, the powerful upper house of Connecticut's government, serving there continuously for more than twenty years.

Dyer spent nearly three decades advancing the interests of the Susquehannah Company, a private venture dedicated to the sale and settlement of land in the Wyoming Valley, which lay within the borders claimed by Pennsylvania. Asserting that Connecticut's charter, which predated that of Pennsylvania, encompassed this territory, Dyer and other prominent Connecticut residents purchased it from the Iroquois Confederacy in 1754. In 1763 Dyer sailed for London, where he spent a year acting as the company's agent. The Proclamation of 1763 had prohibited settlement west of the Appalachian Mountains, and Dyer found the British government equally cool to the development of the Wyoming Valley, which, although east of the Appalachian watershed, was on the frontier with Indian country. But after the Treaty of Fort Stanwix opened parts of the West to settlement in 1768, the company established a permanent settlement in the Wyoming Valley and gained the official backing of the Connecticut government. The ensuing contest between Pennsylvania and Connecticut over the ownership of the Valley was finally resolved in Pennsylvania's favor under congressional authority in 1782, using procedures included in the Articles of Confederation. Dyer helped argue Connecticut's unsuccessful case.

Dyer's enthusiastic involvement in resisting British authority began with his opposition to the Stamp Act and his attendance at the Stamp Act Congress of 1765. Proudly wearing homespun, he strongly supported nonimportation in the late 1760s. Dyer was chosen to represent Connecticut at the Continental Congress, serving from 1774 through early 1776 and again in the late 1770s and early 1780s. Though an early advocate of separation from Britain, he was not a member of Congress when the Declaration of Independence was signed. He was a notoriously long-winded but able legislator.

In 1784, following a vote in Congress that was extremely unpopular with his constituents, Dyer lost his seat on the Council. But he served one last term as a deputy in the state legislature, where he was chosen Speaker of the House. As a delegate to Connecticut's convention to ratify the U.S. Constitution in 1788, Dyer expressed reservations about the document but ultimately voted for its adoption. A judge on Connecticut's Superior Court since 1766, he became chief justice in 1789 and retired in 1793. He continued as a justice of the peace in his hometown until 1798, when he finally withdrew from public service. He died on 13 May 1807.

Karen Northrop Barzilay

See also

Congress, First Continental; Congress, Second Continental and Confederation; Connecticut; Stamp Act Congress

References

Collier, Christopher. *Roger Sherman's Connecticut: Yankee Politics and the American Revolution.* Middletown, CT: Wesleyan University Press, 1971.

Willingham, William. *Connecticut Revolutionary: Eliphalet Dyer.* Hartford: American Revolution Bicentennial Commission of Connecticut, 1976.

Index

Page ranges for main entries appear in boldface type. Pages for documents also appear in boldface type and are followed by "Doc."